CASE STUDIES *in*

Counseling

and Psychotherapy

Edited by

ARTHUR BURTON, Ph.D.

1959 | PRENTICE-HALL, INC. *Englewood Cliffs, N.J.*

616.8914
B 974

PRENTICE-HALL PSYCHOLOGY SERIES
Paul E. Meehl, Editor

Library of Congress Catalog Card No.: 59-13585

Printed in the United States of America
11836

Preface

Conceptually, the editor of a book such as this is in an unenviable position. He may assume, for example, that psychotherapy is an operational process with predictive properties and that its methodology at any instant can be reinforced by appropriate theory. On the other hand, along with Szasz, he may say that psychotherapy is unique; that is, that there are only psychotherapies, and that to search for fundamental unifying features is tantamount to wishful thinking. On the one hand there is the security of specific doctrine and technique and, on the other, the anarchy of multiple operations and theories. Yet we have the obligation of communicating to the uninitiated just what it is that we do in psychotherapy.

Other questions compound the problem: What level of therapeutic operation shall we accept as psychotherapy at all? What goal and intensity of relationship can we distinguish in this way as constituting psychotherapy? And who administers psychotherapy? These questions are now so ancient as to be boring, but as yet there are few guides in the literature of psychotherapy.

In this work we have asked the reader to look first hand at what the mature and accepted psychotherapist does, without our imposing restrictions on what he does. But let us insist at the outset that the psychotherapist attempt to define the implicit theories and concepts behind his operations—so that the science in psychotherapy can at least match the art. In this way we may then begin to approach psychotherapy as a generality within the framework of science. Thus, this book contains techniques called psychoanalytic psychotherapy, counseling, hypnotherapy, psychotherapy based on learning theory, rational or intellectual approaches, and so on. But in every instance, the focus is not on the success or failure of the case, that is, on the outcome, but on the process—and on the concepts supporting the process.

In a formalized way, we confronted each psychotherapist with an

iii

Addendum in which basic questions regarding his psychotherapy were put. For example: How do you select the patients you treat? What cultural factors are involved in your treatment? Do you make a diagnosis before you begin? How do you conceptualize your role? What aspects of your theory of psychotherapy have you found particularly useful? How do you terminate therapy? We asked that the responses be related to the case discussion in question, and in this way we attempted to preserve the essence of the case study method and yet not be limited by it. As expected, this approach did not meet with unanimous acceptance. Several psychotherapists complained that such abstractions destroyed the uniqueness of the psychotherapeutic process. At any rate, we hope that, next to the actual psychotherapy of a case, the reader will find in this book a medium for his own explorations into the role of the psychotherapist.

We would like to add two editorial notes of interest: (1) Because so little is known of the excellent psychotherapy that is done outside of the United States, we called upon psychotherapists from several other countries to participate; (2) a perusal of the Table of Contents will reveal that the contributions are not confined to the psychotherapy of the neuroses, as is customarily the case. There are, in fact, a remarkable number of cases involving the treatment of schizophrenia—because of the increasing preoccupation of psychotherapists everywhere with schizophrenia, but principally because the psychotherapy of a chronic schizophrenic carries with it certain interpersonal commitments relevant to all psychotherapy only now becoming clear.

We have modified names, dates, places, and other identifiable material without doing violence to the structure of the reports themselves. Because of this, it would be difficult indeed to identify any of the people involved.

Although many people helped in its preparation, I am particularly grateful to Don D. Jackson, M.D., for his assistance in helping to plan the broad outline of the work; to Norman Elrod, Ph.D., for his help with European contributors; and to my wife, Edith Burton, to whom I am indebted in more ways than I can mention. Barbara Tabachnik and Audrey Curry were kind enough to assist with the many secretarial functions involved.

Arthur Burton

Contributors

Nathan W. Ackerman, M.D., Associate Clinical Professor of Psychiatry, Columbia University, New York City

Arthur Burton, Ph.D., Psychotherapist in Private Practice; Chief Psychologist, Agnew State Hospital, Agnew, California

Heinz Häfner, M.D., Ph.D., Professor, Psychiatric Clinic, University of Heidelberg, Heidelberg, Germany

Don D. Jackson, M.D., Chief of Psychiatry, Palo Alto Medical Clinic; Assistant Clinical Professor of Psychiatry, Stanford University School of Medicine, Palo Alto, California

Jolande Jacobi, Ph.D., Professional Psychotherapist; Member of the Board of Directors of the C. G. Jung-Institute, Zurich, Switzerland

Bruno Klopfer, Ph.D., Clinical Professor of Psychology, University of California, Los Angeles, California

Marcille H. Lakos, M.S., Clinical Psychologist in association with Nathan W. Ackerman, M.D., New York City

Madge K. Lewis, Ph.D., Staff Research Counselor, Counseling Center, University of Chicago, Chicago, Illinois

Thomas P. Malone, M.D., Ph.D., Private Practice in Psychiatry, Atlanta Psychiatric Clinic, Atlanta, Georgia

Ruth L. Munroe, Ph.D., Visiting Professor, Graduate Department of Psychology, College of the City of New York

James W. Parker, Ph.D., Chief, Clinical Psychology, Mental Hygiene Consultation Service, Fort Ord, California

Carl R. Rogers, Ph.D., Professor of Psychology, Department of Psychology and Psychiatry, University of Wisconsin, Madison, Wisconsin

Raoul Schindler, M.D., Chief, Department of Psychotherapy, Psychiatric-Neurological Clinic, University of Vienna, Vienna, Austria

Jerome M. Schneck, A.B., M.D., Clinical Associate Professor of Psychiatry, State University of New York, College of Medicine, New York City

v

John M. Shlien, Ph.D., Assistant Professor, Counseling Center, University of Chicago, Chicago, Illinois

Joseph C. Solomon, M.D., Associate Clinical Professor of Psychiatry, University of California Medical School, San Francisco, California

Thomas S. Szasz, M.D., Professor of Psychiatry, Upstate Medical Center, State University of New York, Syracuse, New York

M. L. von Franz, Ph.D., Staff Member, C. G. Jung-Institute, Zurich, Switzerland

Samuel Waldfogel, Ph.D., Psychologist, Judge Baker Guidance Center; Lecturer on Education, Harvard University, Cambridge, Massachusetts

John Warkentin, M.D., Ph.D., Private Practice of Psychiatry, Atlanta Psychiatric Clinic, Atlanta, Georgia

Carl A. Whitaker, M.D., Private Practice of Psychiatry, Atlanta Psychiatric Clinic, Atlanta, Georgia

Joseph Wolpe, M.D., Lecturer, Department of Psychiatry, University of Witwatersrand, Johannesburg, South Africa

Table of Contents

PART ONE— *Psychotherapy of the Child*

CHAPTER 1

Ego Defenses
in Child Therapy

—JOSEPH C. SOLOMON[1]

Introduction

One of the difficulties encountered in psychotherapeutic work with children is the lack of understanding on the part of the parents of the nature of the treatment process. The case that I am going to present in this chapter does not fall into this category. In fact, it was because of the enlightened attitude of the parents that the necessity for psychiatric treatment was discerned. Both the parents were in psychoanalysis during the therapy of the child. The mother had been in analysis for about two years with two different analysts, and the father began his analysis with another therapist shortly after I had begun with the child.

Although this case report will be devoted mainly to the discussion of the therapy with the child, it must be understood that the indirect therapy involving the appreciation and modification of the traumatic atmospheres which brought about the problem in the first place, must be considered an

---

[1] A.B., Syracuse U., 1924; M.D., Syracuse, '27; Interne, City Hosp., Welfare Island, N.Y., '28-'30; Resident in Pediatrics, Sea View Hospital, Staten Island, N.Y., '30; Postgraduate: Ped. and Child Behav., Clinique Médicale des Enfants Malades, Paris; Klinik Pirquet, Vienna, '31; Adj. Ped., City Hosp., N.Y., '31-'33; Asst. Psychiat., Kings Park State Hosp., N.Y., '35-'36; Fellow, Nat. Comm. Ment. Hyg., Baltimore, '36-'38; Assoc. Prof. Psychiat., U. of Maryland Med. Sch., '36-'39; Assoc. Chief, Dept. Psychiat., Mt. Zion Hosp., San Francisco, '39-'47; Consult., Mt. Zion, '47-'50; Asst. Clin, Prof. Psychiat., U. of Calif. Med. Schl., S.F., '46-'55; Assoc. Clin. Prof., '55— ; Major, M.C., A.U.S., '42-'46; Consult., U.S.A.F., U.S. Army, Vet. Admin.; Member, S.F. Psychoanal. Soc. and Inst.; Fellow, Amer. Psychiat. Assoc., Amer. Orthopsychiat. Assoc.

integral part of the therapeutic program. Even though I had occasion to confer with both analysts who were treating the parents, I still had regular interviews, about a month apart, with one or both parents during the entire treatment process. I saw the child for one hour a week. I would like to have seen him more frequently, but this was not feasible.

Let me give a running account of the case: One day I received a telephone call from a medical colleague with the request that I see his eight-year old boy who seemed to be having some emotional problems. I told him that I would like to schedule an appointment for him, or his wife, or both, to get some data on the problem and also to obtain some background information. When both parents appeared for the scheduled appointment, we entered into a serious discussion of the problem without any comment on the fact that we had met on several occasions in a social situation. As they entered my office, I recalled that when we had first met I had considered them both intelligent and charming people. The husband had appeared to be more stable in the social situation than the wife, but not remarkably so. During the interview, the wife (who will now be referred to as the mother) carried the brunt of the conversation. She did not make her statements with an air of certainty and glanced at her husband frequently for confirmation of her remarks. It was difficult to obtain a clear picture of the exact nature of the problem even though both parents seemed to want help very much.

The Presenting Problem

The chief complaint, as reported by the mother, was that Joel, the older of two children, was having speech difficulties. It was with some effort that I was able to get a good description of the type of speech disorder from which the child was suffering. It turned out that the child did not speak very much (especially in school) and, when he did, it was quite difficult to understand what he was saying. Furthermore, Joel often did not understand the spoken word. In addition, there was a serious reading problem. For the latter condition, he had been treated by a psychologist.

It was clear that the mother had been entertaining some thought that Joel was not very intelligent. This prompted me to ask for a detailed developmental history. Mother stated that he was born after a normal, easy delivery lasting five hours. It turned out that the obstetrician used low forceps. There was no cyanosis or convulsion at birth. From the start he was not a good eater. He had difficulty in nursing. He cried a great deal as a baby. Teething was a difficult time. He was an active baby and walked at one year. His bowel and bladder training were quite late. He became "housebroken" at the time he entered nursery school at the age of three.

His younger sister, Cynthia, was born when Joel was one year old.

Mother stated frankly that her second pregnancy was unwelcome. She knows that Joel did not receive her full attention with the birth of the second baby. However, he could not go unnoticed because of the marked temper outbursts which seemed to occur frequently. Up to the time of the first interview, the display of violent temper tantrums was a most disquieting phenomenon. The mother reported that when Joel was crossed he would become so noisy and violent that she feared he would hurt himself or someone else. He would lock himself up in his room and refuse to be comforted or pacified until he felt inclined to do so. An additional complaint was that he still sucked his thumb. He did this only in private during the day and when he went to bed at night. Although the mother did not mention it, I found out later that he was also a nail biter.

Mother considered Joel a conscientious pupil. He never complained of school. Actually he worked very hard at his school work, possibly to the extent of pushing himself beyond his abilities. In the private school he attended, much of the teaching was carried out by the project method, and Joel became involved with complicated projects. He also took part in athletics, for which he showed noteworthy capability.

I spent part of the hour talking to the mother about preparing Joel for his visits with me. Although this may be a very touchy problem in many cases, the mother did not think there would be a problem here. "He loves attention from adults," she said. Furthermore, he had already had some testing and remedial reading with a clinical psychologist. More significant was the fact that the mother had established a pattern of talking to a doctor about her own problems, so that for him to do likewise seemed to be a most natural course of events. This, indeed, proved to be true, at least on the surface.

From the foregoing description of my first interview with the parents, I am certain that the reader will not have drawn a clear picture of their personalities, the emotional atmosphere in the home, or the true nature of Joel's problems. I could run ahead of the story and condense some of the disclosures that turned up later, but I would rather report the case as it developed and let the data emerge chronologically through the narrative. The only facts that I can add at this point are that the father appeared to be an attractive professional gentleman, and the mother an intelligent but delicate china-doll. It was not known from the first interview that there was tension between the parents, but there was some evidence that differences existed as to the manner in which Joel had been or should be handled.

The Beginning of Treatment

The mother brought Joel the first time. On later occasions the father would bring him and mother would pick him up at the end of the hour.

On the first visit, after being introduced, he came into the examining room without a moment's hesitation. He did not even look back at his mother and seemed to know exactly what was expected of him. He accepted a seat and allowed himself to be engaged in a friendly conversation without much spontaneity, but with a ready answer for anything I cared to discuss. There was no noticeable speech difficulty except for an occasional word which he enunciated poorly.

In response to direct questioning, he told me which school he attended, the names of his teachers, and the things he did in school. I asked him to tell me about all the other teachers he had had in the past; then to list them in order of his preference. Although he was in the third grade, he listed a first grade teacher as having been the best teacher he ever had. This was significant, since children usually select their current teacher as their favorite. Other choices generally point to a current problem in the schoolroom situation. Significantly, his current teacher was a male; his favorite, however, was a female.

He also stated that he had many friends. He listed the names of four boys and placed them in order of preference. When he listed his school activities in order of preference, he gave as his first choice, "recess."

I then postulated the story of the sinking ship. Everybody in the world is on a ship; it is sinking and he can save only one person. He chose to save his father first; second, his friend Kenny; third, his mother; fourth, his friend Peter; fifth, his closest friend, Howard; and sixth, his sister. There were a few boys in his class he would not save at all. I called his attention, in a joking way, to the fact that he did not save me. He grinned and said he would save me.

I also asked him during this first hour if he could tell me the very first things he could remember. He said that his earliest memory was of when he was about two years old. He fell off a three-wheeler. "My daddy took me to a hospital," he said. Another early memory was, "My father gave me a piggy-bank." Without much encouragement he talked about other things like dreams and scary feelings.

He said he had a dream about a man in the basement. "He started throwing things at me." He was evasive about his own fears, but said that his sister was scared of "cave-ins," the Wizard of Oz, and witches. From the content of the interview and the seemingly open and friendly manner of his communication, I thought that therapy would proceed in an easy fashion. Subsequent interviews showed little difference in this friendly conversational interchange. He always presented a picture of apparent poise that was quite disarming. What I would like to bring out in this case report are the less obvious ego defenses which are sometimes completely obscured by a superficial social façade.

Because Joel had brought out a rather strong preference for his father during the first interview, I explored the possibility that this attachment may not have been pure, uncomplicated affection. This hypothesis could not be developed through direct conversation with the child because his ego would have been too threatened by the disapproval of his own super-ego and by the possible disapproval of the therapist. I used several approaches to help get at some of his inner thinking.

My favorite medium in past years has been the use of created play situations with a family of dolls.[2,3,4,5] I found that this child did not fall into the usual pattern of talking about the thoughts of the anonymous doll or representing himself in any manner that would give a ready clue to his inner self and to his reactions to the pertinent people in his environment. Instead, he would take off into wild fantasies that bore no relation to his life situation but which revealed, I felt, his true feelings, many of which were probably completely unconscious to him. Let me illustrate what I am trying to point out. Here is part of a typical session after two months of weekly interviews:

A Typical Session

I came to get Joel in the waiting room. He greeted me in the usual friendly fashion and preceded me as I ushered him into my office.

Q. How are you?
A. I'm fine.
Q. What would you like to do today?
A. Anything. What would you like to do?
Q. You decide. A doll story, drawing, or anything else?
A. Let's make up a story with the dolls.

I opened a drawer where I keep dolls and other play material and took out some of the dolls.[6] I presented four dolls and said, "This could be the father, this the mother, and these a boy and a girl." He took the play up from that point and hardly permitted me to say a word.

The boy wants to hold the girl. The mother said, "No!" The boy jumped on the mother. He was mad at her. [He carries out the action.] So the baby fell in the water. She tripped over a rock. The boy and his dog [adding a dog figure to the play] went after the baby. They saved her. Then they come home. The father wakes up. He was glad. He said,

2 J. C. Solomon, "Active Play Therapy," *Amer. J. Orthopsychiat.*, 8 (1938), 479-98.

3 J. C. Solomon, "Active Play Therapy. Further Experiences," *Amer. J. Orthopsychiat.*, 10 (1940), 763-81.

4 J. C. Solomon, "Therapeutic Use of Play," in *An Introduction to Projective Techniques*, eds. H. H. Anderson and G. L. Anderson (New York: Prentice-Hall, Inc., 1951), pp. 639-61.

5 J. C. Solomon, "Play Technique and the Integrative Process," *Amer. J. Orthopsychiat.*, 18 (1948), 402-11.

6 I find that with some children it is better not to leave too much play material in full view, because they are likely to become too distracted to maintain any continuity. This sacrifices to some extent observation of the kind of material a child chooses, but I think the gain in the other direction often counterbalances this disadvantage.

"Good!" Then they go to the police station to tell them what happened. They did this so the police would fix the place where people fall into the water. Everybody went home, but they forgot about the children, so the parents went to the police station to look for them. So they found the children playing. The policeman said, "Don't ever play jokes like that again." So they went home. In the meantime a fireman came along. He said there was a fire but it was really a joke played by the policeman. But there really was a little fire. [He put it out by spraying an imaginary hose.] So the fireman fights with the policeman. The fireman gives the policeman a knockout. So the policeman jumped up and knocked out the fireman. So the policeman ran away, but he tripped over the water thing and he went out to the sea.

I interrupted him at this point. "Am I in this story too?"

Yes, you work for the police station. So you ask where the policeman was. They said he was sick. But you get in a fight with the man there. The father came out and said, "What did you do with my son?" So you fight him and knock him down. So the son comes and you have a fight with him. [At this point all the dolls are fighting with each other.] You fall off the cliff. The fireman gets into the fight too. Somebody said, "You knocked Dr. Solomon off the cliff!" So the policeman and the fireman fight. The fireman gets knocked off the cliff. You weren't hurt very much, so you and the fireman fight some more. So the father comes back in and fights with you. So you go to the police station but he knocks you down. The grandfather comes along and then the son. So they get in a fight too. The grandfather hangs off the cliff. Then the policeman trips and falls off the cliff. You come out and say, "Where's everybody?" So you go down to the people, but you have to fly down with your arms out. The little boy saw the whole thing. He said, "This gives me an idea for a mystery story." He told his parents about it. They all have a conference, but they get into a fight. The policeman and you come in and fight. More people fall off the cliffs. The boy said, "What is happening?" So he wakes up and finds it is all a dream. He said that this sure was a good mystery story. Then he said, "I don't want to go to school, I want to fly." So he really flew. [The boy flew around the room.] But then he really woke up and went to school. That's the end of the story.

I asked him if he could tell me what he thought was the meaning of the story. He replied that policemen shouldn't play jokes like that. Then he went on telling some more fantastic things in the same general vein that he had been doing.

I tried again that same hour to set up a specific play situation, such as a mother and father talking together and the boy standing nearby. I asked what the boy was thinking about. This was a signal to take off again on another long episode of policemen, firemen, fighting, water, and more "mystery stories." When I asked him point blank at the end of the hour to tell me how things were at home, he replied, "Oh, fine!" and left cheerily with the remark, "See you next week."

We can see from this interview that the content of the material was replete with primitive, impulsive expression; he showed a great deal of aggression first toward mother, then toward baby sister, but most of all toward male figures. But let us examine more closely the types of defensive maneuvers he employed to cover up his basic impulses. Most noteworthy is the fact that he did not get trapped into talking about his problems by placing his conscious thoughts directly into the mouth of the substitute of himself. A few thoughts come to my mind in this connection. First, his problems are of such great intensity that he cannot face them even in the third person of a boy remotely resembling himself. Second, he is too clever to allow himself to be tricked into telling his secrets through such a device. Or, third, he is just not intelligent enough to be able to utilize the medium of play to aerate his personal problems. Another defensive maneuver he used was denying throughout the play that anyone was hurt. He reported the most violent fighting, yet no one was injured. If they were rendered *hors-de-combat,* it was only for a brief period and the figure would return to the game. This constant reversibility prevented the youngster from developing any anxiety in the game. In fact, he considered the whole thing "fun." The fighting failed to show any expression of anger on the part of the patient, even though he indicated that some of the characters might have been angry. Two other devices for removing the destructive quality of the play patterns were (a) to say it was only a trick that was being played, and (b) to say it was only a dream or a mystery story. These devices involve pushing into fantasy that which is too painful to be faced in reality terms. The discrepancy between the friendly feelings toward his father and aggressive hostility he showed toward male figures in the play is, of course, quite evident. In keeping with this is the discrepancy of attitude he showed in his treatment of the therapist doll and the friendly way he talked to me directly.

My goal early in the therapy of this case was to work toward a coordination of the symptom patterns presented by the child with the emotional interchanges that were taking place between both parents, between the child and each of his parents, and between him and his younger sister. This case report will be disappointing from the standpoint of any spectacular disclosures of reciprocal dynamisms between the child and the other members of his family, except for a type of contagion of defenses or resistances which were exhibited by the parents in their respective therapies and in the child in his therapeutic sessions with me. The case study should be looked upon as a study in ego defenses and in the methods I used to isolate the areas of conflict.

Defensive Function of the Ego

Let us digress for a moment to talk about the defensive function of the ego. From an early age the child is provided with the necessary equipment for preventing an overloading of his system with tension. These devices are operative in the direction of survival. They are to be considered as temporary expedients on the road to maturity. The main force is one of turning the attention away from the painful situation. At a conscious level the simple medium of denial exists in all persons, even the very young toddler. Suppression is the consequence of the operation of denial and evasion, and is still considered a conscious mechanism of ego defense. Stronger survival needs effect the removal from consciousness of all or portions of the painful situations through the mechanism of repression. Repression in some form furnishes the basis for all other defense mechanisms. This repression may effect the removal from the conscious perceptual system of the memories of the actual situations that caused the organism trouble, but there may be retained the emotions that accompanied the forgotten incidents. Conversely, there may be complete recollection of many incidents in the past with partial or complete repression of the emotions or affects that accompanied the experiences. The repression of visual imageries with retention of affect is typical of the hysterical syndrome; the repression of the emotion with retention of the imageries is typical of the obsessive-compulsive diagnostic category. Such was the case of Joel. My efforts were directed toward the recovery of some of his repressed emotions.

Before proceeding further with the case, I would like to speak of the elaboration of ego defenses that proceed from the initial denial or repression. *Sublimation* is the defensive manner which redirects the repressed energies into socially acceptable channels. *Reaction formation* is the shifting in an opposite direction from the direction of the original motivation. *Rationalization* is the device which gives spurious reasons or excuses instead of factual causations. *Libidinization* is making pleasurable that which may have been originally unpleasurable or painful. *Displacement* is the device whereby the affects from one situation are transferred to another. *Projection* is the mechanism which attributes to some outside source feelings which exist within the self. The reader is invited to locate these defense mechanisms in Joel's productions, which unfortunately must be presented in an abbreviated form. More subtle mechanisms such as *introjection* and *identification,* which are the incorporation and assimilation of traits of the parents, are also demonstrable in the case material.

Studying Ego Defenses Through Drawings

Although it was vital that I maintain a friendly channel of communication between Joel and myself, I felt that in order to help alleviate his problems I had to use every available means to break through his strong barrier of ego defenses. He responded avidly to the medium of drawing. I suggested the comic strip technique, which I have found very useful.[7]

_____
[7] *Amer. J. Orthopsychiat.,* 10, 763-81.

I knew that some of his difficulties involved the school situation and therefore I asked if he wanted to draw a school story. He obliged. I was surprised to observe how well he drew. His drawings were done very carefully. In contrast to the rapid-fire sequences that he used in his doll play, the drawings were drawn in abundant detail and with a minimum of action. He would draw quietly, did not mind my watching him, and was willing to report at any point what he was drawing. I usually allowed him to finish his drawings, then would ask him to describe each of the sequences. It would not be feasible to reproduce all his drawings, but let me describe the first drawing he made, the one about school:

First picture: The teacher reads a story. The boy is being bad. He is laughing. The boy has to sit down next to the teacher.
Second picture: The boy has a horse. The teacher doesn't know this. The teacher sends the boy to the principal because he was bad.
Third picture: He jumps on his horse and goes home. His mother said, "Why are you home so early?"
Fourth picture: Mother sends the boy back to school.
Fifth picture: He comes in to the principal's office with his horse. The principal told him he couldn't do that. He had to leave school.
Sixth picture: The teacher got all confused. So the principal said it was not the boy's fault. So he let him go back to school.

We can see that the drawing medium revealed the defensive attitude of this child. He softens both the aggressive attitude of the boy as well as that of the parental figures. It indicates that there is a good deal of contention, but there is still extreme reluctance to give expression to anything where somebody can be hurt.

One of his drawings early in his treatment (2½ months) was very interesting. I gave him free reign to draw anything he wanted. He drew a sequence (Figure 1) which depicted a big statue and some little people. This is the story as he told it:

> Some men went out for a little vacation. They searched for a big statue. Then they ran into a huge statue. The statue didn't like these people. The statue sent fire out of his mouth. There was also a mountain that shot fire out at the good guys. Then the motors in the statue made a big flood over the city. The statue got so flooded and the mountain so muddy that the statue fell. It then caught on fire. It opened up and all the bad guys got out. The good guys came over and arrested them. They looked inside to see how it was made, but they were not allowed to make such a statue because it was too dangerous.

This story again illustrates the fear of aggression. He is willing to follow the formula of "good triumphant over evil," yet he is intrigued with the mechanics of such great capacity for destruction. The bad guys inside the statue can be looked upon as his own introjected hostile impulses

FIGURE 1. *Free Drawing Early in Treatment: A Big Statue and Little People.*

which are capable of great destructive power. Of importance, too, is the frequent use of fire in his play and drawings. Although in some instances fire can be symbolic of sexual excitement, it appears more regularly in Joel's productions as a force of destruction. Water, which also has a destructive capacity, is used in his fantasies as a medium for putting out fires and thus has the quality of neutralizing aggression.

The next week Joel wanted to make another story drawing. This time I threw in a suggestion. "How about a story of an unhappy boy?" He said, "O.K." He chose as the name of his story, "The Man Is All Confused." (If I was not confused at the outset, I certainly was confused trying to follow the details of his story.) There were eight pictures. The action was not intelligible until he supplied the captions which he gave in essay form as follows:

> A lady wants a man to work for her. He doesn't want to, so they get into an argument. The man goes to work in his factory. He gets trees that are cut down and makes them into wood. He comes home from work all worried and confused on account of the argument he had yesterday with the lady. He comes home and gets into another argument. Finally he says, "OK, I'll work for you." He comes back into the factory and sees it is the same one, so he gets unconfused. He did not work any more. Then the lady tells him what happened to her. It was all on account of a forest fire that she started. The man missed so many days work that he lost his job. The lady lost her job, too. She worked in the same factory but the man never saw her.

I pursued the story a bit in order to elicit further associations in his thinking:

Q. What about the children?
A. They don't have any. They are not married.
Q. If they were?
A. Then daddy would have to work.
Q. Do married people sometimes argue?
A. My mommy and daddy have arguments. When they do, mommy calls us and we get out of bed to help daddy to stop getting mad at her.
Q. Is mommy always right?
A. No, sometimes daddy is.
Q. Then what do you do?
A. We just break it up.
Q. How?
A. We just jump on him. I say, "OK, I'll stop him." One time he said mommy started it but we didn't jump on mother. If she doesn't call us, we don't know there is an argument.

When he told about the arguments between his parents, he did not show any untoward emotion. In fact, it was slightly amusing, judging from his facial expression. I determined at this point to get more information from the parents and from their therapists about the nature of the atmosphere in the home. When I questioned the mother about arguments between her and her husband, she stated that at times there were words between them but she was certain that they did not take place in the presence of the children. In regard to the situation I described above, the mother laughingly stated that there was a bit of playful teasing between her and her husband in which she would call out in jest as the children were getting to bed—"Joel, come help me, daddy is beating me up!" She said the whole situation was a joke and nobody seemed upset about it.

For several weeks after this, the play patterns seemed to take on a fairly repetitious character. In fact, they began to be stereotyped. I had learned from previous experience that stereotypy in play patterns is often an indication that there is something wrong or traumatic taking place in the home situation. I thought that the tension between the parents may have been the major factor, so I again called the mother. I found out that she was in the hospital in neck-traction because of a whip-lash injury to her spine. Joel had not told me a word about it.

Repetition and Compulsion as a Defense

At this point, I should like to depart from the description of this case to speak of the defensive maneuver of repetitive or stereotyped actions. In a previous publication[8] I pointed out that if a child shows similar repetitive play configurations in his therapeutic sessions, one should suspect that there are new traumata operating in his life. Freud pointed out[9] in his early studies of the obsessive-compulsive phenomenon that the compulsive act is performed when the individual is caught between the polarities of irreconcilable opposite motives. The person does something definite to counteract the tension that ensues when he is beset by the feeling of uncertainty. It is a measure to gain active control of a situation that is otherwise out of control. The compulsion itself need have no relation to any goal-directed activity of its own, but merely serves to discharge energy that has no other outlet because of the conflicting motivations. The child who shows the repetitive play pattern seems to be holding back the clock. He repeats the familiar because he cannot move into new areas that seem too dangerous.

As long as we are on this subject, I would like to further touch upon the matter of compulsive actions and the closely related one of obsessive thoughts or ideas. Repetitive and stereotyped actions have been produced in experimental animals. Masserman[10] and Maier[11] have shown that by

---

[8] *Amer. J. Orthopsychiat.*, 10, 763-81.

[9] S. Freud, *Notes Upon a Case of Obsessive Neurosis*, Vol. III (London: Hogarth Press), 269.

[10] J. H. Masserman, *Principles of Dynamic Psychiatry* (Philadelphia: W. B. Saunders Company, 1946).

[11] N.R.F. Maier, *Frustration: The Study of Behavior Without a Goal* (New York: McGraw-Hill Book Company, Inc., 1949).

subjecting animals to confusing and insoluble stimuli that stereotyped, nonproductive actions of a repetitive nature are produced. In the human subject, the tenacious hold on fixed patterns of action, and later on to fixed ideas acts as a defensive maneuver in the service of the integrative function of the ego. We can say that repetitive patterns in the adult represent a continuation of the child's propensity for holding on to fixed play patterns as a stabilizing force in the face of ego disequilibrium. In libidinal terms, it is similar to such phenomena as thumb-sucking or the "security blanket" in which the individual sucks on ideas or motor patterns instead of the thumb or blanket. As such, it is similar to an addiction. In this connection, it will be recalled, Joel was a thumbsucker at the beginning of treatment.

During one of the mother's visits, she told me of other compulsive manifestations that Joel exhibited. When he was about four or five years old, he had the habit of repetitive hand washing. This did not last very long. Also, he made it a practice to take meticulous care of his toys. He would put them away neatly in orderly rows without being pressed to do so. These compulsive actions can be looked upon as magical gestures which are attempts to create a feeling of equilibrium in an otherwise turbulent atmosphere. In the young child this turmoil is essentially external. It does not take long, however, for it to become internalized, which it does in the obsessive-compulsive state. As to the hand washing itself, the symbolic reference to getting rid of dirt suggests that a strong indoctrination of an anti-feces attitude exists. There is no indication from the history that rigid bowel training prevailed, yet there is indication that the mother was quite doctrinaire about many other matters of personal conduct. Although they were not too evident at the time of beginning treatment, the ego traits of orderliness, cleanliness, and taciturnity lent credence to the theory that this child had been traumatized in the anal period, or the period of training and indoctrination. Apparently, Joel had made some attempts at ego integration by the formation of specific traits. These traits were showing some dissolution even before the beginning of therapy. This indicates that either the attitudes and handling of the home were improving, or that the decision to place the child in treatment had had some salutary effect towards primary mastery, thus rendering the secondary integrative processes less essential.

Before going further, I notice that I have bandied about some terms which may be unfamiliar to the student reader. *Primary integration, secondary integration, autonomous ego traits* and other similar terms are only useful if they convey some meaning. I feel obliged to become a bit didactic. Hartmann[12] developed Allport's[13] idea of functional ego auton-

---

12 H. Hartmann, "Comments on the Psychoanalytic Theory of the Ego," in *Psychoanalytic Study of the Child*, Vol. V (New York: International Univ. Press, 1950).

13 G. Allport, *The Nature of Personality* (New York: Addison-Wesley, 1950).

omy into the concept of the formation of primary and secondary forms of ego autonomies. The process of simple mastery of instinctual forces results in the formation of primary autonomous ego traits. Mastery in the face of pain or conflict requires the use of defensive forces or healing processes and, when accomplished, produces the secondary autonomous ego traits. Both of these forms of mastery are examples of the operation of the integrative function of the ego: the first is termed primary integration; the second, secondary integration. Let me clarify this a bit further.

The primary integrative process operates as the conflict-free neutralization of id impulse by the external object. Such stored memories of gratification or primary masteries constitute the primary autonomous portion of the ego. Secondary integration involves the processes of repair and defensive action in the establishment and maintenance of harmony in the face of discordant motivations. Stern[14] introduced the term *reparative mastery* for this aspect of the integrative function.

Let me illustrate the results of both types of integrative process by a clinical example. *A* and *B* are both seemingly generous individuals. *A*, however, seems more sincere in his generosity. He enjoys doing favors for people when he can. When he gives his time or material things, he does so out of regard for the recipient and not because he expects reciprocation. *B*, on the other hand, always does things for people, but in a different way. He makes it a point to constantly remind the recipient of all he has done for him. He feels uncomfortable, however, when anything is given to him, and would rather feel that nothing is being done for him. Nevertheless, he gives of himself to such a degree that his display of altruism is for him a way of life.

Of the two, *A* is obviously the healthy, well-adjusted person and *B* is the neurotic one. *A* seems to derive uncomplicated pleasure out of his generosity. He gives for the sake of giving, in proportion to the need of the recipient, his regard for the recipient, and his available resources. He reflects on the fact that others have given to him and that he is willing and ready to give to others. It represents a reflection of the stored memories of primary mastery.

B, on the other hand, has developed a trait of pseudo-generosity which represents a reparative mastery of emotional conflict. Such a case can show a variety of defense mechanisms and adaptations. Let us say that his motivation to be good to people stems from his childhood, when he was very good to his little brother. To go into the matter more deeply, we find that *B* really hated his little brother when the brother was a baby. He could not show his hatred because he would be punished. Furthermore, he would lose the affection of his mother because she loved the baby.

---

[14] M. Stern, "Anxiety, Trauma, and Shock," *Psychoanal. Quart.*, 20 (1951), 179-203.

As a result, *B* chose to be nice to his little brother. This could give him a feeling of importance, both because of the favor he obtained from his mother, and because it put him in the position of power over his brother. Furthermore, his taking care of his brother meant that his mother would not need to give the little one that much attention. All of these factors, and many others, which include libidinal and hostile impulses and defenses against anxiety, are condensed in a single motivating system. The other more basic motivation may be a masochistic attitude derived from an ambivalent mother, which had not only provoked the original aggressive attitude but had invited the suffering as an attempt to establish a symbiosis with the sadistic mother.[15]

It can be seen that the integrative process represents an establishment of harmony within the self. In the child this internal harmony is contingent upon the establishment of external harmony. The external harmony represents a balance between the libidinal forces in the child and the libidinal forces of the mother. This primal harmony is the precursor of the harmony within the self and forms the basis for the establishment of the harmonious relations with the father, siblings, and persons outside the home. Secondary integration or reparative mastery is the process whereby internal (or external) harmony is established by the energy invested in the ego. Both the primary and secondary integrative processes are motivated by the same basic survival or homeostatic principles.

I hope it does not complicate the subject further if I add a few more ideas and terms on the subject of secondary ego integration. The concept, as described in the previous paragraphs, represents in some measure the way in which Hartmann originally described the process. The well established ego traits set up motivations of their own which can become useful or are at least in some sort of harmony with the organism. Such traits are said to be ego syntonic. On the other hand, the integrative process can operate to establish homeostasis but can produce some sort of manifestation which will, in itself, be uncomfortable to the organism. I will be more descriptive in a moment, but first let me offer a couple of new terms. The term *para-integration* seems to be a good one for the secondary ego autonomies which are ego syntonic and which include all the character disorders, eccentricities, foibles and peculiarities of people. In Joel's case, compliance, defiance, orderliness, and taciturnity can be considered para-integrations. *Mal-integration* is the term which I would like to offer for some phenomena which are manifestations of the secondary integrative function but which produce conditions which are sources of discomfort

[15] For more detailed appreciation of this subject, the reader is referred to the "Table of Ego Organization" which appears in my book, *A Synthesis of Human Behavior, An Integration of Thought Processes and Ego Growth* (New York: Grune and Stratton, 1954).

or conflict in themselves. In the case of Joel, such mal-integrative phenomena will be shown in compulsive actions, in nail-biting and in stuttering. The dynamic factors that operated will be brought out in the case material.

The therapeutic goal that I employed with Joel was to try to incorporate as many forces as possible under the category of primary mastery. By bringing to light some of his feelings about individuals, I was hoping to help him handle his own reactions. Noteworthy in this regard, is Joel's duality of compliance and defiance, and of submission and rebellion. Throughout his early interviews, the need to comply and the covert wish to defy seemed quite apparent. His ability to integrate these motivations, and especially to find his relative position with each of his parents, put a great deal of strain upon the integrative forces of his ego.

The Therapy Continues

Let us now return to the therapeutic sessions with Joel. In the next couple of interviews he drew pictures of buildings catching fire, and airplanes dropping bombs which set buildings on fire. He spoke about "destroying the enemy" but gave no indication of people being hurt or killed. The destruction was limited mostly to objects rather than to persons. Then came a story acted out in some degree with the dolls. The title was, "Everybody's Happy but One Is Mad." The cast of characters were Father, Mother, Boy, and Girl.

> They were all talking. The boy wants to go out but it's raining. Mother said, "No!" The boy gets mad. All the other people were just talking. The boy is too big a boy to get mad. He is eleven. On a different day it was sunny. He went out to find kids to play with. He went from one door to another and found different friends were too sick to play because they went out to play on the rainy day. So he went home and told his mother that he was glad he didn't go out to play on the rainy day. He said he will always believe his mother again.

The foregoing sequence clearly reveals the boy's motivation to express his aggression against his mother, yet at the same time he is motivated to propitiate her and to justify her discipline. Information regarding the parents revealed, in fact, that the mother was obliged to perform the disciplinary functions in the home, whereas the father was highly permissive. This threw him into confusion on the compliance-defiance theme. Joel made up another story. He called it, "The Lady and the Man That Always Fuss."

> They were married four days ago. The man said, "Why don't we have some children?" The lady said she would have them but she really didn't want to. She was afraid she would get him mad. So she said she

would go to Chicago for a month; but she really didn't want to. She went away because she didn't want children. He caught up with her. She said, 'I just don't want children." The man was mad because he wanted to have been with his children and with their friends. He got *so* mad at her that he didn't want to be married to her any more. So he got divorced. He got a new wife. She was a nurse. [He may have gotten this idea from the nurse doll which was available.] She wanted children. So they went out and got 12 children. [I pressed for a few details.] It turned out that these children weren't real people. They were just motors. [I guess the 12 children were a little difficult to take.] So the real wife comes and fights with the nurse. So he takes her back. Another man comes along and says that the nurse is his wife. So everybody starts fighting with everybody else. [All available dolls were then put into the play. The play included boys knocking over police, everybody getting thrown into a well, etc.] The boy did it. He went home and told his mother about the fight. She gets mad and fights with the boy. The people get out of the well and the fight starts over again. After some more action he knocks the mother down the well, but he dives in after her and brings her home. Then they live happily ever after.

After the story was completed, I asked him if he could tell me what the story meant. He replied rather irrelevantly, "He should know how to swim and he should learn how not to fight people so that this should not have happened." At this point I noticed his badly bitten finger nails. I called this to his attention. He said that he bit his nails all the time. I said that if he really understood why he bit his nails he could get over it. He turned to me. "Do you know?" I replied, "Yes, I think I do." "So tell me," he continued, "I want to get over it." He seemed anxious for me to offer some explanation for it. This I did. I did not record exactly what I said, but in essence it was as follows:

"When people are angry they feel like hurting somebody. Just like an animal who wants to bite with his teeth and claw with his nails. But just like the stories you have been telling about the boy who wants to hurt people, he also tries very hard not to hurt anyone. So he feels like doing both. What he does then, instead of biting and clawing at people, is to bite at his own claws, which are his fingernails. So he gets rid of his mad feelings and still doesn't hurt anybody except himself." He replied, "I understand." Shortly thereafter I had occasion to see the therapists of both parents. They both told me how Joel had gone home after this hour and expounded on the meaning of nail biting.

Let me interject a few further comments on the subject of nail biting. From the foregoing material, there was no reason for me to have pointed out the oral sadistic (biting) aspects of his aggressive feelings. From experience with other cases, however, I felt free to discuss the subject of nail biting as I did. As I pointed out in a previous publication,[16] individ-

---

[16] J. C. Solomon, "Nail Biting and the Integrative Process," *Int. J. Psychoanal.*, 36 (1955), 393-95.

uals who are strongly motivated aggressively, and who are also strongly
motivated to deny aggressions, are fit candidates for the symptom of nail
biting. By biting at the nails, a closed circuit is formed satisfying several
needs in a single integrated act. The act of nail biting, then, can of itself
serve as an autonomous agency for self-containment in the face of any
anxiety.

An interview with the mother shortly after this interview with Joel
brought out some interesting data. Quite spontaneously the mother reported that Joel was much more relaxed and that he was improving in his
reading. She told about her hospitalization for the whip-lash injury to her
neck (she was still wearing a Thomas collar). She reported that Joel
seemed to be very angry lately. "When I was in the hospital he did not
speak to me for three days. Also, he got into trouble with some kids at
school, but I'm certain that he was not the aggressor." Apparently, she
felt that Joel's role at school was that of an "angel child." The mother told
about his having discussed the subject of nail biting. She quoted him as
saying, "Sometimes when you are mad, you bite your nails instead of biting
other people." She then reported for the first time that Joel had bitten
his own arm for years every time he was angry. This was a part of his
temper tantrums. More recently his tantrums had not contained this element. Mother also reported that at the time of his biting he also bit his
mother's arm, especially when she tried to restrain him.

I inquired about the early details of his life. Mother was very vague.
All she seemed to remember was that he had trouble with teething. He
cried a great deal. Mother admitted that she had been very tense during
his babyhood. "My mind would go blank when play or temper would
get out of hand." She claimed that the whole household was tense at that
time. It was when her husband started his practice. She claimed that she
found comfort in her child, had tried to nurse him but was not able to. A
second baby, Cynthia, was born one year after Joel's birth. This baby
was nursed for three months. The second baby had "colic" and had to be
held a great deal. When she was four months old, she was placed in Joel's
room. The mother said that Joel relaxed after that. When asked to explain
this further, she said, "He stopped howling over going to bed." It was
one month later, however, that he started to have his temper tantrums.

Mother also reported that he now likes to be read to, whereas formerly
he could never follow a story. The teacher reported that he is more "with
it." He now talks to other children. In nursery school he had been quite
mute, or incomprehensible when he spoke. She asked me whether Joel
had reported a fantasy that he discussed with his father. The fantasy was
that of three little men to whom he speaks. He tells one of them to do
something about having a sunny day. I told the mother that Joel never
reported this fantasy.

For the next few sessions there were more stories about fires and fights, but nothing particularly different was revealed. Then came a period when he became interested in using my wire recorder. This instrument is sometimes useful in therapy because by hearing his own voice it affords the child an opportunity for the establishment of self-differentiation, a way-station toward the formation of his own identity. He told a long story into the microphone about a boy who was always teased. On one occasion he became very excited as he told one of his stories and his voice had a noticeable stutter. I even pointed it out to him on the play-back.

We went through the same routine that we did on the nail biting issue. "Do you know why boys stutter?" "No, do you?" "I think I do." "Well, tell me." I said that sometimes people stutter when they want to say angry things and polite things at the same time. He shook his head knowingly. He then told the story of "The Angry Boy" on the wire recorder. During the recording, I encouraged him a bit by saying that the boy did not sound very angry. His response was to raise his voice in mock anger into the microphone. The following is the transcription of "The Angry Boy" story:

Well, this is going to be an angry boy, very, very angry, and he wanted to say many things, but he couldn't say it because his mother wouldn't let him, and he was so upset, he said angry things and he didn't care if he was yelled at or anything; so this is the story about the angry boy, and the angry boy was 8, no, the angry boy was 9, 9, 9, and he was very angry. OK. This is the story now.

One day the angry boy was having a terrific time playing soldier with his friends and one time his mother had to go shopping and his mother called him and he said, "No, I want to stay here and play with Joe" and one boy said, "go on," then he got mad and angry and then he went. He wished he could have got real mad at that boy, so he kept it secret and didn't tell his mother, and he thought he said it, and he closed his mouth real fast, so he went and didn't think if he should do it or not because he didn't want to get yelled at because he didn't want to be more upset; so when he got home his friends came to ring the door bell and they said, "Can the angry boy play out?" Then they all laughed and then he heard and then he got more and more upset. [At this point I encouraged him to show how angry he really was.]

Then the angry boy got so mad he went downstairs, pushed his mother away and he threw mud in their faces and got them all dirty, and then locked the door, pushed them off the steps and they slipped and they got so mad they had a big fight. Well, he went downstairs and he was so angry but he didn't hit them really and he said to his mother—then he pushed his mother and said, "Go away, mother." Then he said, "Why are you calling me an angry boy?" And they said, "ha, ha, ha, you know why? Because you didn't go to the store with your mother." "Yes I did, now get *out* of here before I wrap a mud pie in your face." He got real, real mad and the children laughed and laughed, then the boy got real *real* mad. And his mother said, "Stop that now; you know those boys are your friends." "Then why do they call me the angry boy? And get out of here mommy." Then he said, "Get out of here, mommy, go." Then he locked all the doors and his mother tried to get in some way, but he was just lucky enough she didn't have a key and the little boy did and the little boy was so upset he broke glasses, messed up his room and after that he went away, he snuck out of the house, he packed up and he snuck out of the house. Then his mother knew she shouldn't have been so *mean* to him. Then his mother said she didn't *mean* to yell at him but the mother had to yell at him to obey and said, "Come back here, you angry boy! COME BACK HERE!" And then his name, because they didn't name him yet, so everyone called him the angry boy and he didn't like to be called the angry boy. And he was getting so upset he wished he could've "blewd" up the house so the angry boy said, "Do you want to make up?" And they said, "Heck no, we want to laugh more." So that made him more upset so he snuck out and there was a little store down aways where there were lots of rocks where you would always fall down. They had dynamite down there so they could blow up the rocks when it looks like it was going to fall; so he snuck down there and took it, then he ran up and he lit a match which he never did. Then he blew up the house, and he ran away, and he didn't know what he was doing. He ran away and was caught by the police, and he got so angry he blew up and blew up more things and the policeman. It is his mother's fault because his father was very, very nice to him and anything that would happen to him like that, his father would get mad at the man and would really get mad and his mother was upset because his father died in the army when he got shot; his mother was upset and it was really all the children's fault. When they found out it was their own fault, everything was OK again for the angry boy.

When he went to bed then the children came in and he said, "Do you want to play?" And they said, "No, we're too upset" and then the angry boy laughed. Well . . . well, the angry boy wanted to make up again when he blew up the house. Those little boys were very nice, but then they would be nice. Well, uh, see the angry boy was very unhappy, then they were bad. When the angry boy would know it, for a long, long, long time until he was a grown up, he was called the angry boy. Then when he was a grown up, people called him the angry boy. And he got so, so, so mad! And he didn't know what to do so what he should have done was . . . well, the angry boy, when he was a grown up, he was very mad and he never saw the other boys, because he wanted to, then he would get real mad at them and then they had to . . . One time the angry boy . . . The children called the angry boy that they're grown up and then they were going to say they were sorry and before they knew it, the grown up angry boy he started a big fight. He won and then this made him more excited. Then the next day they came and he got more excited. Then they told him that they were sorry. So then they lived happy ever after, but they had some arguments and when they said they were going to live happy ever after, then he thought they would and sometimes they had some arguments, but they still lived happy ever after, and then . . . The big boy got hurt very badly and then he had to stay in the hospital for a week and then he made up and said they were all sorry and then he lived ever after happy.

For the next few weeks he was content to hear the recording of "The Angry Boy" and then add a few minor embellishments. At about this time the mother asked to see me about school plans. It seemed that the private school which Joel and his sister were attending might not reopen next year for either financial or administrative reasons. Mother had been worried about public school because he did not talk much. On a recent school visit, however, she was informed by the teacher that he was now active, assertive, and sometimes quite aggressive. "Thank goodness; he was such a mouse," she said. Mother again brought up the marked contrast with his former behavior. He had stopped speaking shortly after the birth of his sister. Later he did speak around the house, but was especially quiet around grown-ups.

Mother again brought up his temper tantrums, which he now no longer has. He gets angry, but realistically so. He upbraided his mother for not having the kind of cookies he likes, but he was over it in an instant. She reported that Joel had told his father about a few disturbing dreams he had had. It was something about a boy putting his penis into something and somebody telling him that he might get hurt. The patient never reported this dream to me, nor had he up to this point referred to any part of his anatomy.

Two other points of interest are worth mentioning. At this period of therapy there was a large earthquake. That night Joel crawled into bed with his father. It was interesting that he chose his father rather than mother. This may be easily explainable on the basis of the fact that the father was in actuality more protective, but there was probably other factors that would only lead us into the field of speculation.[17]

The mother reminded me of a bit of advice that I had given her at the outset of therapy. I had told her to take Joel on her lap when no one was around and "play baby." She was to say, in effect, "When you were a baby, this was how I held you." She was to remind him of how he looked, how he ate, and so forth, all in an atmosphere of friendly acceptance. She reported that when she did this with him, he "ate it up." She admitted, however, that she did not get around to doing it very often.

At the next interview with the boy, he asked for the wire recorder. I told him that it was out being repaired. (This was true.) I asked him if he wanted to see the transcription of his "Angry Boy" story. I started to read it to him, then asked him to read it. This turned out to be a great therapeutic crisis. He read a few words, then guessed at the others. He seemed a bit tense. I then put the paper away and said that I would let him read it when his reading improved. He said he would practice all week.

Let me digress for a few moments to explain why I said what I did to Joel. I knew that he had been having trouble with his reading and I wanted in some way to bring this into the treatment situation. My motive in

---

[17] For many years I have advised parents that if a child is frightened during the night, that the parent of the same sex should comfort him. There are many good psychodynamic reasons for this. To enter this discussion would be beyond the scope of this chapter.

saying that he could read it when he was able to was to exercise some leverage in this direction, particularly to uncover his defenses against reading.
I was reminded of the time I used to read the funnies to my own children.
When the older boy was about five or six years old, I read all the comic
strips for him except one. The one exception was "Dick Tracy." I told
him that this was mostly for older boys; that, after he learned to read,
he could read it himself. This acted as a stimulus for him to learn what
the characters were saying. It worked fine for him, but let us return to
Joel.

The rest of that hour I had difficulty interesting him in making up a
story or engaging in any form of play. He chose to draw a picture story
but could not think of any subject he would like to draw. I offered suggestions. Angry boy? Teasing boy? Quiet boy? Noisy boy? Scared boy?
He chose the noisy boy. It was to be a story about a boy who wouldn't read
because he didn't want to make noise. After he completed the drawing,
he said the title was, "The Boy Who Talks Too Much and Doesn't Listen."

After this hour I received a frantic phone call from the father. He reported that Joel was in a panic. He did not want to come back any more
because he knew that he would not be able to read what I expected him
to. I told the father that Joel had not understood me and that I would
call him on the phone and speak to him personally. This I did. He showed
not a trace of anxiety on the phone and was just as pleasant and cheerful
as he had ever been. I told him that I understood that he was a little
worried about the reading that I had planned for him. Before he had a
chance to affirm or deny his feelings, I reassured him that I would not
ask him to read until he wanted to by himself. The father called me back
the next day to report that Joel was no longer panicky but that he was
furious at him. "You got me in trouble with Dr. Solomon!"

At the next hour he came into the office in his usual friendly manner.
He made no mention of the reading incident. He chose to draw a picture
story. The story itself appeared quite disorganized. The first picture was
a hotel where a boy lived. The next picture was a house not far from the
hotel. The third picture depicted a boy making a dummy ("a stuffed
person"). The next, the nearby house on fire.

> Then the dummy gets burned up. Then he gets mad at his brother. They
> had a terrible argument, first with words, then with fists. Mother stopped
> the fight. [There were no more pictures but he continued the narrative.]
> Then they went on teasing each other. Then they got along with each
> other. On and on.

Although the history clearly indicated that there was every reason in
the world to believe that he harbored great resentment toward his younger
sister, he managed to repress, or at least suppress, any overt indication of
hostility in that direction. It was more face-saving for him to fight with

one of his peers or even an imaginary brother than to fight a younger sister. Inasmuch as he did not have a brother, it gave him the chance to preserve his anonymity and still abreact some of his feelings. I continued to see Joel week after week. He still seemed anxious to come and was superficially friendly and cooperative. He talked, made up stories with the dolls, and drew picture stories. He showed a particular desire to improve his drawing technique. Content at times revealed no serious conflict.

> The story [Figure 2] is that of a boy who was living in a city. He wanted to see his friend Tom. His father asks him if he wants to go to the woods. He was mad but he went. The family went to the woods. When he came back he saw Tom. He was happy.

Other stories again continued to show buildings on fire. I asked him once if he had ever seen a real fire. He reported two memories. When he was four or five he saw a real fire, but it was mostly smoke. He said there was a man in front who would not let them squirt the water. At least that is what he thought his father had said. The other memory was that of seeing a building that had had a big fire, but he did not see the fire. Some of his stories had a great deal of action with people getting involved in all sorts of dangerous situations but managing to escape. He also included ferocious beasts like lions which fought people, but they too made friends and got along. One story involving terrible giants began to be a bit frightening, so he defended himself from any catastrophe by saying that it was only a dream and the boy woke up to find it was not true. However, as time went on, he allowed some people to get hurt. In one atomic bomb story, eight people were killed, twenty were injured, and ten houses were knocked down. Then he decided to make a hydrogen bomb. "It was so worse it could blow up 28 homes."

I continued my efforts to coordinate what was happening in therapy with me with what was going on in the home. Mother continued to complain that regardless of what Joel did, father did not interfere, nor did he back her when she took a firm hand. Through her own analysis and that of her husband's, she concluded that the father was indulgent with Joel because of his identification with the boy and because of his desire to protect him from "bossy women." In conference with the therapists of both parents, I learned that the mother continually complained of the father's leniency with Joel. The father was showing resistance to facing his own problems. In the words of his therapist, "He freezes with fear."

An interesting side-light came to my attention in a conference with one of the physicians who had seen the mother for her whip-lash injury. She was treated by an orthopedist and a neurologist. The neurologist, who is also psychoanalytically oriented, described the mother as being rather dependent upon her husband. Actually, there was a kind of symbiosis in which the father took over the role of the physician, prescribing medica-

tions, etc., and the mother readily fell into the role of being child-patient to her husband. When the father was told that he was not to play the role of doctor to his wife, the situation changed. It was after this that the mother settled down to serious psychoanalytic work.

In the meantime, Joel continued his stories. In the doll games he also had buildings catch fire and burn to the ground. Sometimes people (unidentified) would burn to death, but usually everyone was safe. He seemed to engage more and more in the game of squirting water on the blazing buildings. He said he had a toy at home which squirted real water. Although I felt that there was some symbolic reference to urination as a mode of expression, I made no interpretation along these lines at that time. I kept in mind, however, the ego manifestations of masculine urination, namely power and ambition. I used the ego manifestations in the following sequence. It was a story about buildings, a big building and a little building:

There was somebody on each building throwing bombs. It was a contest. The one on the smallest building won the contest. This one had the biggest explosion. Part of the bomb exploded on the big building, but nobody was hurt. It was only a contest. [I interrupted to ask which was the father building, the mother building and the boy building.] He pointed to the smallest building. He said that this one had the best bomb. I said, "Just like little boys have strong voices." He laughed. He said he had a loud voice. I invited him to let me hear it. "Now?" he asked. He picked up a doll [nurse] and in a fairly loud voice yelled, "Work!" Then he took off on a game in which everybody was either yelling or being yelled at, "Work! Work!"

Around this time I again noticed his finger nails. They were grown in. He said, "I forgot all about my nails." I then asked him if he remembered what we had said about nail biting. He said he did not remember. I reminded him about the angry and not-angry feelings. He said, "Oh, yes," and went on to make up a story with the dolls. The game consisted of all sorts of fighting, first between boys and later between adults. I was not able to discern any specific reaction to a doll which represented me. I was particularly eager to work through with the patient any evidences of a transference reaction. The "Dr. Solomon" doll figured in much of the play, but did not seem to be either spared or singled out for attack. At times he referred to "the doctor" but this could also have been his father who was a physician. Other reality features which entered into his spontaneous play patterns included earthquakes, which had not only been a part of his actual experiences, but which had also been a general subject of conversation for months after the actual events.

In order to explore further some of Joel's thinking, I tried structuring some of his story material. I drew what I thought looked like an adult male, an adult female, a male child, and a female child in stick drawing, as the first picture of a comic strip. I then told him to continue the story with plenty of action. Instead of reacting to the figures as a family, he took the adult figures to be a "big boy and girl directing traffic on a school day." The story continued with the little boy and girl not obeying the traffic boy and girl and both getting hit by a car. An ambulance comes and takes them to the hospital. The teacher says, "Always mind the traffic boy and girl; it is dangerous. You might get runned over." Later, the boy and girl are out of the hospital; they say to the traffic boy and girl they are sorry for what they did. I asked about actual traffic accidents. He told about a boy on his block, age three, who was hit by a car. For the next few weeks there were stories of either serene family scenes or those involving a good deal of destruction—one to a big water pipe—but they always came to a happy conclusion.

At this point in therapy the school term ended. I made it clear to Joel that I wanted to continue to see him. I had asked him on a previous occasion how many more times he wanted to come. He replied that he wanted to come until he was nine years old. This was still several months away. I felt that there was still a great deal of thought material that had not been brought into our sessions. Notably absent from his productions thus far had been any reference to sexual matters. Masturbation, which the mother had mentioned to me, had never been openly discussed by the patient. It seems that he was more resistant about sexual matters in the therapy situation than he was at home. At one of the most recent interviews I tried to elicit some discussion regarding sexual differences. The subject came up in connection with mention about a baby. I asked if it was a girl baby or boy baby. From this point questioning led to how we could tell the difference between a boy baby and a girl baby. He said the face was different, the hair was different, the clothes were different. Without clothes? He professed ignorance. Then I drew two faces exactly alike and asked which was the boy. He chose one of the faces. Then I drew in an undifferentiated body. He still clung to his choice. When I put long hair on the one he selected as the boy, he changed his choice. After much hedging, I finally pointed to the genital area. Oh, yes, he knew the difference. Also, he knew the difference between little girls and ladies. He showed no evidence of anxiety other than his extreme evasiveness in discussing these matters. Nevertheless, there is reason to think from some of his productions (e.g. the broken pipe and the dream he reported to his father) that he is working through some phases of his castration anxiety.

At one of the sessions during his school vacation, I told him that I was going to be away for a few weeks. He did not show any overt emotional reaction of either pleasure or displeasure. It was a bland, "O.K." When I returned, I called his mother to arrange to continue his therapy. I gave her the time I wanted to see Joel. She was pleased, but asked that he be seen another day as he had some place to go on the usual morning of our appointment.

When we resumed our sessions, after the three-week interval, Joel seemed friendly. In the examining room he said he would either draw a picture story or play with the puppets. Because I was particularly anxious to get a sounding on what had been going on, I suggested a puppet story. I even suggested that I would supply the action and he could supply the words. He agreed. I put a mother and father doll together.

> Q. What are they saying?
> A. The father said he had to go see his boy in the hospital. The father goes to the hospital and visits his son who is sick in bed.

I then depicted the mother coming in. Joel started a narrative of the mother saying that there had been a boy at the house who turned in a false alarm for a fire. He was ready to take off on one of his usual stories. I stopped the game to interject an interpretation that he wanted it to appear that the other boy was the bad one. At this point I made the game very specific. I put the parent dolls facing the boy doll.

> Q. If there were a real fire and the boy could only save one person, which one would he save?
> A. He would want to save his father, but he would really save his sister. I guess he would save his father, then his mother, then his sister.
> Q. What makes him so angry at his mother?
> A. He and his mother are always having trouble.
> Q. What kind of trouble?
> A. The mother told the boy not to eat cookies in the study when he watches television. But he did. The mother came in and she was mad. The boy said the sister did it. He didn't want his mother to be mad at him. So the mother sent the sister to her room. [I supplied this action.] The sister got confused. She figured it out that the brother got her into trouble. So she went to her brother's room. They got into an argument. The mother came in saying, "What are you arguing about?" The boy said the sister got the crumbs in the room. But the sister said "No." Then the mother knew the boy did it. So she spanked the boy. The boy was mad.

At this point I had the father walk in on the scene. I showed the father in a protective role to the boy. He took the boy's side. Joel was fascinated but said nothing. Then I said, "The father was away all day at the office and didn't know how naughty the boy had been." I also put words in the mother's mouth suggesting that if he knew how naughty the boy had been then he wouldn't be so lovely-dovey. At this point Joel grinned.

I thought I might have stirred up some anxiety or resentment toward myself for having brought this issue to such a climax. To relieve any such tensions, I supplied a scene of the therapeutic situation. I said, "So the boy has problems. He went to a doctor." Joel said, "If the boy told his father about himself he would be awfully mad at him."

Q. How does the boy feel about the doctor knowing his secrets?
A. He doesn't mind.
Q. If the boy really minded, he could do something.
A. He could have a fight. [I put them in a fighting position.] It isn't really a fight because he is not mad. The doctor was worried how he could straighten out the whole family. So the doctor decided to give the boy presents, so he would be happy and like everybody. But he really had presents like that. It was a truck. So the boy decided that he wouldn't make crumbs, and if he did he would clean them up. Then he wouldn't have any more problems. He wouldn't have fights with his mother. And the father wouldn't have to be mad at the mother. And everybody would get along. The doctor was sorry he gave the boy the present. I interjected, "I don't think so at all." But the boy wasn't poor. He had a truck. I suggested he could give it to some poor children and this pleased him. He closed with "Gee, that was a long story!"

Termination of Therapy

A few days after this interview, I received a telephone call from the father. He said that he wanted to see me. I gave him an appointment for the day prior to Joel's next appointment. He gave me no inkling whatever as to the reason for this sudden request. I saw the father at the appointed time. He asked me to express my opinion as to how Joel was getting along. I told him that I thought he had been working out some of his difficulties and alluded to part of the content of the last hour. He said he knew all about the story because Joel had recited every last detail about it at home.

Although I did not say this to the father, it is a good therapeutic sign when a child is able to discuss with his parents, without disturbing emotion, some of the subject matter of the therapeutic sessions. I might add that it should be spontaneous and without coercion. If he does it out of fear of the therapist it is an entirely different matter.

Let us proceed with the last interview with the father. He wondered whether I saw anything terribly wrong with Joel. He said that he got along so well at home, and in the group, that he saw no further need for treatment. Actually Joel was now a leader with the children on the block. He told of an older boy, age 14, who had taken an interest in his son, and had been teaching him how to throw a football, etc. He had taken Joel along on his paper route. This necessitated getting up at four o'clock in the morning. Father thinks that the boy's only problem is his reading. He is getting a tutor. Father said that Joel had been tutored a bit at the beginning of summer and had responded quite favorably by reading avidly for her.

The father blamed the private school for Joel's reading problem. He referred to the school as an "insane asylum." The first grade teacher was marvelous but the second grade was terrible. There was a bunch of wild kids in the class and they were handled poorly by a teacher who claimed to know "group psychotherapy" of children. It was a holy mess. Joel, who the father claimed had always been respectful of authority, was confused by the unruly behavior of the other children. The third grade teacher had a bad time because the class was so out of hand that she could not get them back in line. This was when Joel was subdued and non-communicative. He could not learn in that atmosphere. Father discussed future school plans. He decided to send him to a new public school under construction in their neighborhood. He asked for advice as to what to do in the semester prior to his transfer and suggested getting a tutor to help with his difficult subjects.

I asked the father quite directly about the current atmosphere at home. Things were much better. The mother had constantly complained that he "never backed me up." He decided that it boiled down to one incident when the mother wanted Joel to take a nap "because she was sleepy" and wanted the home to be quiet. Father said he felt that this was unreasonable and said so. In general, however, they were getting along nicely in the last few months.

It became quite obvious during the hour that the father was anxious to terminate treatment. "Do you think Joel is going to require psychotherapy indefinitely?" he asked. I told him that I did not want to see Joel indefinitely, but I reminded him of some of the problems that he had originally presented. I mentioned thumbsucking, nail biting, his compulsive traits, and his temper outbursts. Father said these were all gone now. I asked specifically how he was getting along with his sister. "They fight some," he said. "Joel teases her. They have their fights. But she worships him and is constantly imitating him."

Inasmuch as the family was going on vacation in two weeks, I suggested that I would discuss termination with Joel at the next two sessions. Perhaps, if things went well during the trip, he would not want to return for further therapy.

At the next session, Joel said he wanted to make up a puppet story. The story consisted of everybody in a circle, dancing. Then there was a contest. There was a little fighting but nobody was hurt. I introduced the boy doll and later the thespian doll. They all joined in having a lot of fun swinging from a long rope. It was a lot of fun but it was dangerous. I discussed with him the number of times more he wanted to come to see me. At first he said he wasn't sure. When I reminded him that at one time he said he wanted to come until he was nine, he said, "I'll be nine pretty soon." I suggested he could come again next week, then decide for sure after his vacation.

Father called a few days later to cancel the last appointment. He said that Joel wanted to quit but was ashamed to tell me so.

Although I am certain that the father was consciously sincere in his evaluation that Joel was doing well, there may have been other factors that influenced his desire to terminate therapy. Realistically, it must have been a big strain on the family budget to pay for his own and his wife's psychoanalysis; hence, to be relieved of the expense of Joel's therapy was a projection of the intense resistances he displayed in his own analysis, thus bolstering the tenacity of the child's defenses.

The main purpose in presenting this case report is not only to illustrate the actual operation of the psychotherapy of a child, but to illustrate some features of ego defense mechanisms. Although I did not spell it out each time it appeared in the therapeutic sessions, the reader must have sensed the tug-of-war that existed between the therapist and the inner thought processes of the patient. I say "inner thought processes" rather than "unconscious fantasies" because it is difficult to say that they are all unconscious. I am sure that there were many things that Joel consciously withheld from revealing in his spontaneous play productions. That unconscious repression also operated cannot be gainsaid. The mechanism of denial, then, by conscious suppression or unconscious repression, served to turn the individual away from facing painful affects. Other defense mechanisms which are derivative of the motivation for denial or evasion shown in this case are displacement, reaction formation and sublimation. Projection and introjection mechanisms can also be detected in the careful study of the case material.

The case further illustrates that in direct therapy the therapist must address himself to the ego rather than to the id. This is the portion of the self which mediates the primary instinctive drives in terms of the internalized forbidding commands (the internalized or introjected parent figures) and the demands of reality. Of course, reality for the child of this age is still plastic. Changed parental attitudes and handling help to modify the former threatening internal images. Had Joel not been placed in therapy, there may have occurred a secondary integration of his ego, incorporating his instinctive needs with his defense mechanisms into single autonomous functioning units which would have created lasting pathological character traits. Through the therapeutic relationship and the improved attitude within the home, there was afforded an opportunity for relieving the ego of making such secondary healings necessary. In the course of therapy the repressed affects were brought to the surface, together with the other ingredients that entered into the para-integrative and mal-integrative phenomena. In this manner the conflicting forces were brought to the surface where they could be mastered through the primary integrative process. Primary integration, being the original way needs are gratified, acts as a medium for ego mastery in a conflict-free atmosphere.

Addendum

1. *Optimally, what criteria do you use for accepting or rejecting patients for psychotherapy?*

Optimally, the criterion for placing a child in therapy is the determination that many of the existing difficulties spring from events that have anteceded the current life situation. When there are current difficulties in the home, as there usually are, some program for treatment or understanding of the forces that are operative in the parents must be undertaken.

2. *Do you make a diagnosis before psychotherapy begins?*

Only a tentative diagnosis of the existence of an emotional problem. A diagnosis of mental deficiency sometimes closes doors to treatment when there may be modifiable emotional factors that could render the child more effectual. In the case report there were many features which indicated that the child was feeble-minded, but other aspects of the case indicated the precursors of the obsessive-compulsive syndrome.

3. *Do you attempt to persuade the patient or significant relative to change his (the patient's) environment?*

The only environmental change discussed with the parent was the proposed change of school. In no sense did I find it necessary or advisable to "persuade" any change in the environment other than the appreciation of their own motives.

4. *How did you conceptualize the therapist's role in this case?*

Although the material suggests that I was merely a catalyst for some of the child's reactions, there were clear indications of my role as a parent. In part, I played the role of a real parent and, in part, the transference parent. He projected much of his super-ego on to the therapist, both in his desire to appease and to avoid disapproval.

5. *What aspects of your theory of psychotherapy were particularly apparent or useful in the case presented here?*

The child must be able to maintain some of his defenses when disorganization of the child or the therapeutic situation is threatened. Although I paid considerable attention to the content, I was always mindful of the operation of the therapeutic relationship.

6. *Do you feel that this case developed significant insight? If not, can improvement be maintained?*

Yes.

7. *What aspects of your own cultural orientation facilitated or impeded the treatment of your case?*

[Not Answered]

8. *If we consider that a continuum exists from superficial to deep psychotherapy, where would you place your own case?*

Although it appears that the therapeutic process was directed mainly towards a break-through of ego defenses in an atmosphere of emotional support, deeper layers of instinctual conflict were certainly touched.

9. *What did you think about the outcome of this case and what criteria did you use for evaluating such outcome?*

There seemed to be greater degrees of ego integration shown in his outside relations than appeared from the content of his sessions. In fact, the localizing of his psychopathology to the therapeutic sessions could be considered as a salutary outcome of treatment.

10. *How do you terminate psychotherapy?*

There are various ways of terminating therapy with a child. Often the first move comes from the child himself. If all seems to be going well at home, at school, and in the therapeutic relationship, it may be well to ask the child how many more times he would like to come. He may say 200 times and next time say 10 and finally quit.

CHAPTER 2

Emotional Crisis in a Child

—SAMUEL WALDFOGEL[1]

Introduction

The case presentation that follows represents a departure from conventional psychotherapy with children. The therapeutic principles employed were developed during the course of a clinical investigation into the causes and treatment of school phobia under the auspices of the Judge Baker Guidance Center.[2] One of the primary aims of the study was to develop more effective and economical techniques for dealing with this problem, which at times can be particularly troublesome for both clinicians and teachers.

School phobia refers to the reluctance to go to school because of acute fear associated with it. Usually this dread is accompanied by somatic symptoms with the gastro-intestinal tract being most commonly affected. The somatic complaints come to be used as an auxiliary device to justify

---

[1] B.S., Wayne U., 1938; M.A., U. of Mich., '39; Ph.D., U. of Mich., '46; Dept. Psychol., Wayne U., '41-'47; Res. Assoc., Dept. Psychiat., Harvard Med. School, '47-'52; '54— ; Lect., Dept. Psychol., Boston U., '48-'50; Head Psychol., Mass. Gen. Hosp., '49-'52; Lect., School Soc. Work, Simmons Coll., '50-'57; Dir. Res., Judge Baker Guid. Cent., '52-'57; Res. Consult., James Jackson Putnam Children's Cent., '53— ; Res. Consult., Boston Children's Serv. Assoc., '53— ; Res. Assoc., Dept. Psychiat., Children's Hosp., Boston, '56— ; Lect. in Educ., Harvard U., '57— . Member: Amer. Psychol. Assoc., Mass. Psychol. Assoc., Amer. Assoc. Advancement of Science, Sigma Xi; Assoc., Amer. Orthopsychiat. Assoc.
[2] This investigation has received the partial support of the U. S. Public Health Service through Mental Health Grants MH-661 and M-826.

the child's remaining at home and often vanish once he is assured that he will not have to attend school. The characteristic picture is of a child nauseated or complaining of abdominal pain at breakfast and desperately resisting all attempts at reassurance, reasoning, or coercion to get him to school. In its milder forms school phobia may be only a transient symptom; but where it becomes established, it can be one of the most disabling disorders of childhood, lasting even for years.

In the initial phase of the study the cases were all seen at the Judge Baker Guidance Center, having been referred there by the schools. Since a research team had been organized for the express purpose of studying these cases, they were being referred earlier in the course of the disturbance than is often the case. Even more important, it was possible to begin treatment without the customary delay that results from a long waiting list. It was soon noted that there appeared to be a distinct relationship between prompt therapeutic action and remission of the acute symptom, which suggested that delay in starting treatment increased the likelihood of the disturbance becoming chronic.[3]

It was also observed that the acute symptom appeared to be associated with widely varying degrees of personality disturbance, ranging from those cases where it appeared as a developmental crisis against a background of relatively successful personal adjustment and stable family relations to those in which a high degree of emotional pathology was evident.[4] The more severely disturbed children were more likely to be found among those cases where the first acute outbreak occurred beyond the fourth or fifth grade. In most of these cases, interestingly enough, forebodings of the problem had been present from the earliest school years. No attention, however, had been given to these indications, and the problem had remained relatively quiescent until it erupted in a particularly virulent form.

On the basis of the above observations it was decided to proceed with an exploratory preventive program based in the schools. The aims of the program were: (1) to identify cases of school phobia at their earliest manifestation; (2) to differentiate them on the basis of the severity of the underlying personality disturbance; (3) to develop methods of "emergency" treatment within the school for those cases where the problem appeared to be a focal one; and (4) to refer those cases where the symptoms appeared to represent a more widespread and serious personality disturbance to the clinic for more intensive treatment. It was hoped that, aside from effecting significant economies in therapeutic time, a program of this kind could prevent chronic phobias from developing.

---

[3] S. Waldfogel, P. B. Hahn, and E. Landy, "School Phobia: Causes and Management," *School Counselor*, 3 (1955), 19-25.

[4] S. Waldfogel, J. C. Coolidge, and P. B. Hahn, "The Development, Meaning, and Management of School Phobia," *Amer. J. Orthopsychiat.*, 27 (1957), 754-80.

The cooperation of the public schools of certain suburbs of Boston was secured for carrying out the program. The elementary school principals were instructed in identifying the early signs of school phobia, and they were encouraged to refer promptly any children manifesting these signs. Upon referral, the child was seen as quickly as possible by a member of the Judge Baker Research Unit who evaluated the problem and determined the course of action to be taken. The case that follows is an example of an acute crisis in a child whose ego seemed fundamentally sound. The therapist's role and the rationale of his therapeutic approach are described in detail.

Dynamics of School Phobia

Before discussing the case itself, a brief description of the psychodynamics of school phobia will be presented in order to help clarify the rationale of treatment.[5] Like all phobias, the symptom in school phobia represents a displacement of anxiety. When the anxiety is traced to its source it is invariably found to originate in the child's fear of being separated from his mother. The child's anxiety about separation is an outgrowth of the mother's own anxiety on this score. With her this stems not from a primary wish to abandon the child, but rather from her concern that she does not have the capacity for adequate mothering. She defends herself against these fears through over-compensatory devices that increase the child's dependency upon her so that he comes to expect her to be immediately available in the service of his needs, especially in emotionally stressful situations. A vicious circle is soon established with the child becoming more demanding and the mother more resentful of her subservience to these outrageous demands and yet unable to assert herself without overwhelming guilt. Aggressive feelings for both the parent and child come to assume cataclysmic proportions, but they defend themselves against these feelings by undoing and reaction formation. That school phobia has its genesis in this underlying hostile-dependent relationship was first observed by Adelaide Johnson and her co-workers, who further noted that any crisis which threatens the precarious security of relationship between mother and child propels them even closer toward one another for safety.[6]

The crisis may be precipitated by factors either within or outside the school. It may result from the stress of having to attend school for the

---

[5] The dynamic formulation presented here is based on our own work and on the observations of others who have studied this problem. The statements may appear somewhat arbitrary, but no attempt will be made here to document them. A more complete statement can be found in the previously cited article by Waldfogel, Coolidge, and Hahn.

[6] A. M. Johnson, E. I. Falstein, S. A. Szurek, and M. Svendsen, "School Phobia," *Amer. J. Orthopsychiat.* 11 (1941).

first time or from being confronted by new demands in the school situation. A new teacher, an embarrassing episode, the expression of hostility by either classmates or teacher—any of these may trigger the phobic reaction. Often the precipitant is external to the school. In such instances it usually has its origin in some disturbance of the family equilibrium. This might include an illness or death of a family member, a crisis in the relationship between the parents, or increasing tension among the siblings.

The resulting anxiety and hostility become too great for the child to manage. Under these circumstances he will attempt to re-establish the condition of infantile dependency upon his mother, who because of her own anxiety unwittingly supports it. By clinging to his mother the child protects himself both from the dangers of external reality and the mounting threat of his own hostile fantasies. As the regressive situation continues and becomes intensified, the phobia becomes increasingly severe. Our experience indicated that if the regressive state persists without alleviation, it will tend to become fixated and refractory to any kind of intervention. On the other hand, prompt intervention can relieve the acute symptom and prevent the child's ego from becoming chronically incapacitated, thereby freeing it for further growth and development. It was for this reason that in our treatment great emphasis was placed, not only on early intervention, but also on the necessity for keeping the child in school or returning him as soon as possible. In addition we focused on those areas of conflict which our dynamic conceptualization pointed to as being most crucial.

Randy: Summary of First Interview

Randy, who was in the second grade, was referred for study in the fourth month of the school year because he had been crying in class and had experienced occasional attacks of nausea. In the classroom he would become upset whenever the work seemed too difficult, but his most severe anxiety occurred in relation to art work. Despite his acute discomfort, Randy's mother had insisted on his continuing in school, although she was becoming increasingly concerned about the severity of his physical symptoms and growing more uncertain of the wisest way to handle the situation.

I first observed Randy in his classroom, where he was busily engaged in doing arithmetic when I arrived. There were no obvious signs of anxiety at this time and, in fact, the only things that might have distinguished him from the other children were his somewhat smaller stature and a certain air of solemnity. This was most evident in his eyes which, while bright and alert, conveyed a feeling of sadness. Despite his slight build he did not appear either childish or effeminate. On the contrary, in both his dress and carriage (in which he seemed almost consciously striving for an effect) he gave the impression of genuine boyishness.

The informal atmosphere of the class made it easy for me to engage Randy in a conversation about his work without making him too conspicuous. His mother and teacher had told him that he would be having a visitor, and he was not surprised to see me. As we chatted, I informed him that I had already spoken with his teacher about his difficulties in school, but also wanted an opportunity to talk alone with him. I suggested that we go to another room where we would not be disturbed. He came unhesitatingly, but it was obvious that he was apprehensive in the presence of this strange adult who had appeared so suddenly in his life.[7] Once we were alone, I could explain more fully my purpose in coming to see him. I told him that I had heard about the troubles he'd been having in school lately and that I wished to help him just as I had helped other boys and girls with similar problems.[8] I asked him about his art work, and he explained that it was not drawing or painting that particularly bothered him, but having to cut things out of paper. (This was a distinction that the teacher had not observed.) He added somewhat shamefully that it was only when he used the scissors that he became afraid and felt like crying. I expressed sympathy for these feelings and asked if he had ever had them before. He then informed me that he used to cry sometimes in kindergarten and that the other children called him "cry baby." I said I knew that there were times that boys, even when they grew bigger, felt like crying and suggested that maybe when he was in kindergarten there were times when he would rather have been home with mother.[9] He agreed at once that this was the case, which led me to suggest that perhaps some of these wishes still persisted. His affirmation of this suggestion was a little more tentative, but I pursued this lead a bit further and wondered if at times he feared that something might happen while he was away from mother. After a pause he responded with several rapid and somewhat jumbled associations. One thing he mentioned was that he liked to hurry home from school and became frightened if for any reason he had to stay

---

[7] It came as a real surprise to us to see how readily the children were able to accept our presence and establish a therapeutic relationship. We had expected that, since the school was already endowed with phobic properties, they might be suspicious, apprehensive, and even terrified of us. Instead, almost without exception, they turned to us for support in their attempts at counter-phobic mastery.

[8] This explanation is given to relieve the child of his sense of being strangely unique and to reassure him that he can be helped to overcome his problem.

[9] My intention here was to let him know that I could understand and accept his crying. However, I tried to go beyond this by suggesting the wish that lay behind the overt expression of affect. It was fortunate that the first mention of this subject dealt with an earlier period of his life, which made it easier for him to admit his regressive wish to be near mother. This paved the way for the explanation of his current feelings that followed.

beyond the regular time. He spoke also of the time he fell on the ice while he was going home but fortunately didn't fall through. Finally, he described the field he had to cross to reach home. There was quicksand in one corner of the field and, unless one was especially careful to walk in the right places, it was possible to sink in.[10]

Following these disclosures by Randy, I remarked that it seemed there were many things that frightened him when he was away from home. I told him again that I could understand that this made him feel small and like crying, and I added that I imagined at times like these he wished he might have mother along to take care of him. At this he averted his eyes and remained silent. I assured him I knew it wasn't easy to talk about feeling this way because I was sure he wanted to feel like a big boy who could take care of himself. I continued that even big boys needed help sometimes, and that I wanted to help him. I then told him that I would like to come back again to talk some more about the things that frightened him. We agreed that I should come back the following week, and at this point I returned with him to his classroom.[11]

Summary of Second Interview

When I returned the following week, Randy's teacher informed me that he had been expecting me and was eagerly looking forward to my arrival. When we were alone together, he told me at once that his mother, with whom I had arranged an appointment for that afternoon, was making

---

[10] By this series of associations Randy corroborates the dynamic formulation that the central anxiety in school phobia is separation from the mother. He tells us quite unmistakably of his yearning for the safety of his mother's presence and the real danger of being engulfed or annihilated when he is away from her. Our experience has shown that such anxieties are commonly *conscious* with children who have school phobia. Knowing this, the therapist can focus directly on this area. It is important to note that, up to this point in the interview, no interpretations have been made; there has been only an exploration of feelings. By using this technique the therapist can proceed as rapidly as the child will permit. While Randy certainly did not find this discussion easy, he was not overwhelmed by anxiety. On the contrary, he seemed to be getting some relief through airing his troubled feelings. The pace of the interview may seem a rapid one to some, but we have been impressed over and over again how readily these children appear able to discuss their feelings with the therapist. In point of fact, it has been our distinct impression that less resistance is encountered in the school than in the clinic, where the therapist's role is more explicitly that of a "mental doctor" and may thus be perceived as more threatening.

[11] The total time of the interview was actually about twenty-five minutes. Interviews seldom lasted more than a half-hour. To have continued them much longer would have meant keeping the child away from his class for too long a period. The therapist was also guided by the amount of anxiety that the material seemed to be evoking. In this instance Randy was showing both by his silence and by his fidgeting that we were beginning to invade painful, emotional regions, and to have pushed further might have precipitated feelings that he could no longer manage effectively. Since these children use phobic defenses, it is important for the therapist to avoid becoming a part of their phobic system.

plans to see me.[12] Randy seemed pleased rather than threatened that mother should be seeing me to discuss his problems. I assured him that whatever he and I talked about was strictly between the two of us. He demonstrated his trust in me by promptly telling me that the teacher had put his name on the board for talking and added, "She always gets so mad." I said that it must be very frightening when the teacher gets mad, and he agreed, emphatically. I then asked him if his mother ever got mad at him. To this he replied, "When I am bad." I asked when this was, and he replied that it was bad to fight with his brothers. He went on to explain that his brothers liked to hit him and to take away his money. He would call to his mother for help, but often she was angry with all of them. I wondered if his brothers sometimes called him a "cry baby."[13] He admitted shamefully that they did, and was reminded by this of how in kindergarten the other children called him "cry baby." He became tearful as he talked about this. I asked if he could remember why he cried in kindergarten, and he answered that he had been afraid to go to school. When I asked why this was, he replied it was because "They had taken his tonsils out that year." Then, after a brief pause, he spontaneously began with great intensity to describe his hospital experience approximately as follows:

"They fooled me," he began. "The nurse said I was going to watch TV. They had four men to do it. They put the ether on me; I think there must have been six men all in white. I don't even know where the tonsils are. They never should have fooled me like that." He then inquired about the location of the tonsils. I asked him if he remembered that his throat hurt. He said that he did, and I indicated that this is where the tonsils were located. I then asked if he knew how the tonsils were removed. He said he supposed that they were washed out by the ether, but wasn't sure. I then suggested that sometimes he might wonder if the tonsils were cut out, but he found this idea too frightening to believe. He replied somewhat as follows: "It makes me sick to think of being cut, and I know that's not the way they take your tonsils out because *when they cut you, you die*. I saw this once on a TV program."[14]

I replied that I thought he might have been worrying about this possi-

---

[12] It was customary to see the mother before seeing the child. In this case, it would have meant a delay of almost two weeks. It was decided, therefore, to see the child first in the interest of prompt intervention and to get mother's version of the problem afterward.

[13] My intention here was to lead up to the parallel between his position at home and at school. It is apparent that he quickly sensed the similarity and developed the implications far more rapidly than I would have expected.

[14] This is a most interesting sequence of associations. In this fragment Randy lays bare for us some of his most anxious preoccupations. The dangerous rivalry with his brothers, his fear of helplessness, yearning for mother's protection, guilt about his "badness," and his fear of punishment by mutilation and death.

bility and added that one doesn't die from being cut by a doctor. Randy was listening very attentively as I continued. I explained about tonsillectomies in general, and I told him I felt he was worried that they were going to harm him in some way when they removed his tonsils, but that, although the doctor did indeed cut them out, this didn't really damage him in any way. Still trying to deny what he knew, he asked again if the doctor really cut them out. I assured him that this was really so, but that the tonsils were not needed and that such an operation leaves one just as good as ever. He said he had heard of operations and wanted to know what "stitches" were. I explained this to him and he seemed greatly relieved to have all this clarified.

Summary of First Interview with Mother

That same afternoon I saw Randy's mother for the first time. Mrs. G. was a warm and friendly person who obviously had a good deal of affection for her son. She expressed concern about Randy's fears and traced them back to the kindergarten, when he used to cry and crawl under the desk. His worst fears subsided after a few weeks, but she felt he was never really comfortable during that year. Things improved during the first grade, but the problem returned with a vengeance in the second grade. She was unable to trace the recurrence to any specific precipitating factor.[15] She reported that when he was very upset he cried and occasionally threw up. Recently he had been crying before going to school and didn't have much appetite in the morning.

Mrs. G. stated that Randy had been somewhat of a feeding problem all along and then confessed somewhat shamefacedly that even now she would feed him occasionally. "I guess I have babied him too much," she added, "but then, after all, he is the baby in the family." Her husband, she admitted, was annoyed at the way she babied him and then confided that she had really wanted a girl after having already had three boys. She felt that it had been hard to accept the fact that she had a fourth boy and (since this was going to be her last child) to give up the wish to have a girl. She was even able to recognize that at first she had in a way thought of Randy—who was more delicate than the others—as her little girl and had, perhaps, babied him more for that reason.[16]

While she was able to understand and sympathize with Randy's acute

---

[15] Usually one can find a precipitant. A possibility in this instance was that the teacher was expressing more open hostility than Randy could tolerate. Remember his comment "She always gets so mad."

[16] Although this is an unusual insight, it was consistent with the final impression of mother that she could be more objective about her relationship to her child than many of the mothers in this group. This had an important bearing on the decision to settle for limited therapeutic intervention in this case. More will be said later of the other factors that entered into this decision.

discomfort in the classroom, she felt it was important for him to attend school. In regard to his symptom she seemed to feel sorry for him rather than angry.[17] She did express anger, however, in regard to other behavior. The constant bickering and fighting among the boys annoyed her, and she felt particularly resentful that Randy would maneuver her into siding with him against the others. She would become especially annoyed with his constant demands upon her and felt that at times he could be quite tyrannical. She admitted that she felt trapped by her own need to indulge and protect him, and again she commented on how he seemed more frail and in need of her than the other boys.

As we discussed his physical condition, she related that, although he had never had any serious illness, he had frequent colds and sore throats which led finally to the decision to remove his tonsils. She remembered that this had been very upsetting to Randy, and was guilty but somewhat evasive about his preparation for the operation. The tonsillectomy had occurred about the same time as he had begun school, but she could not remember the exact sequence of events and had never connected it with the fears which he developed at about the same time. She mentioned also that the fear extended to the dentist and that he hated the doctor to give him needles.

I informed mother that these fears were probably interrelated, and that for the time being I would continue to see Randy in the school to help him deal with them. I explained that I would also want to see her again at some later date. In the meantime I encouraged her to keep Randy in school and to contact me if she had any questions about his behavior.[18]

Summary of Third Interview with Randy

A combination of circumstances, including a school holiday, made it impossible for me to see Randy again before three weeks had passed.[19] According to his teacher he had become much more comfortable in the classroom, although he would still get upset at times and even become tearful under pressure. The most dramatic change had occurred in connection with his art work: he no longer seemed to be terrified of cutting out things.

One of the first things Randy told me when we were alone was that his

---

[17] Other mothers—where the prognosis is generally less favorable—feel a sense of helpless rage toward the symptom but are so identified with the child's suffering that they encourage his staying home.

[18] In this limited type of intervention, therapy is child-centered. In contrast to conventional child guidance, no attempt is made to deal with the parent's own problems. If they are so severe as to interfere with therapeutic progress in the child, then obviously the present approach is inadequate.

[19] Ordinarily it would not seem advisable to wait this long during the beginning phase of the relationship, especially when such highly charged material was being produced.

maternal grandmother had died since I had last seen him. He apparently had been fond of her and she of him, so that he felt the loss directly. He asked many questions about death and its causes, which clearly indicated that he was concerned that it could happen to other members of his family or himself. He was trying hard to assure himself that people died only when they grew old. I agreed with him that this was generally so but that children sometimes worried that their parents might die and leave them before they were grown up and could take care of themselves.[20] He admitted that he had worried about this and then began almost at once about his tonsillectomy again. He still found it hard to believe that the tonsils could be cut out, and repeated that he had always thought that you would die if you were cut.[21] As he talked about this he held his hand down by his genitals. I told him that I appreciated how terrified he had been at the time of the operation and added that it must have seemed as though he would never see his parents again. His voice trembling, he replied with considerable vehemence that they shouldn't have fooled him. When I suggested that he might be angry with his parents he had to deny it, so I offered the interpretation that children usually think that they are being very wicked when they get angry with their mothers or fathers. I tried to relieve him of some of his guilt by helping him to understand that it was inevitable to feel this way at times and was not inconsistent with loving your parents.

I felt it important to explore Randy's feelings of guilt further, especially in regard to fears of retribution, and directly suggested that sometimes children are afraid that dreadful things might happen to them when they think they have been bad. He replied that his mother gets angry with him when he is bad, for example, when he doesn't eat or gets his clothes dirty. He doesn't like it when mother is mad, even though she does not spank him. I explained that all mothers get angry with their children at times, and the fact that his mother gets angry with him does not mean he has been so bad that she no longer loves him.

He listened attentively and then remained silent for awhile. Finally, when he began to talk, he referred again to the fights with his brothers.[22] He admitted now how angry he became with them, especially when they teased him by calling him a baby. He added that he used to be a cry baby but wasn't any longer. I told him I knew how much he wanted to grow up, but recognized how hard this could be at times. I assured him again that I

---

[20] It was felt important to focus on this not only because of his current anxiety but because it touched on the central concerns of separation, loss, and abandonment.

[21] The direct association between his grandmother's death and his own traumatic experience of abandonment and mutilation suggests that anxiety about her terminal illness may have been another factor in the development of acute symptoms at this particular time.

[22] Had the previous interpretation helped him to feel free to express his hostility toward his siblings more openly?

could understand his feeling of wanting to cry at times, but that this didn't make one a baby. We talked for a while about how hard it was to be the smallest one—the baby—but I pointed out that there were advantages and sometimes it was tempting to be mother's baby. He could agree with this and we could talk comfortably about the relative advantages of being big versus being little. On this note the interview was concluded.

Assessment Following Third Interview

In our study of school phobia, the decision of whether to treat a referred child briefly in the school or more intensively in the clinic was not made until after the initial therapeutic contacts. This decision was based on an evaluation of both the child and his mother (sometimes the father) and the extent to which their relationship appeared to be characterized by pathological elements. In Randy's case it was felt that continued treatment in the school on an intermittent basis would suffice. The factors that influenced this decision will now be considered in some detail.

Randy's apparent capacity to make use of this circumscribed therapeutic situation was an important consideration. In only a short time he had established a good working relationship, and demonstrated his ability to introduce and discuss highy relevant material without being overwhelmed by anxiety.[23] Moreover, a definite improvement in the symptomatic picture had accompanied the exploration of painful emotional material. Since there was no evidence of other incapacitating symptoms or any generalized impairment of ego functioning, it was felt that relieving the acute symptom could free him for further autonomous personality development. His own active struggle against his symptom was regarded as a favorable sign and was in marked contrast to some children with the same symptom who succumb to the temptations of the regressive dependent state and in the absence of external pressures often find it quite comfortable.

While it was true that Randy's phobia (like all school phobias) had its roots in the hostile interdependency between him and mother, the traumatic tonsillectomy undoubtedly was an important contributing influence. The prominence of this traumatic event, occurring just at the time that he was starting school, distinguished this case from others where traumatic influences are less important and the disturbance in the mother-child relationship may be much more exaggerated.

Finally, Randy's ability to tolerate the death of his grandmother without any exacerbation of the problem was regarded as an extremely favorable prognostic sign. The loss of a family member stirs up fears of death (either one's own or of someone close) in any child and is especially threatening where the child already has intense fears of death and loss. Since it was

---

[23] In this connection it is worth noting his ability to directly verbalize his feelings and fantasies. This was not only an additional advantage in brief therapy but also made the introduction of play material unnecessary.

his maternal grandmother that had died, it meant that his mother, too, had experienced the shock of loss. Under these circumstances, it would not have been at all surprising had the two of them clung to each other more fiercely. That this did not occur indicated that both mother and son were motivated and ready to continue along the path of greater autonomy and maturity.

With the mother it has already been noted that she had less investment in maintaining the symbiotic bond between her child and herself than is often the case. Because of this she was able to maintain pressure on Randy to attend school without being incapacitated either by his or her own anxiety at facing this daily ordeal. From the outset she had shown the ability to face some of her feelings and motives honestly, and it was regarded as particularly promising that she did not need to treat her hostile feelings toward Randy with blanket denial. Where the mother is able to admit and face some of her own anger toward her child, the child can usually face his own hostility with less guilt, thus reducing the need for displacing it to the symptom.

The Remaining Interviews

Randy was seen six more times during the remainder of the school year at gradually lengthening intervals. The initial interviews, which were characterized largely by the cathartic expression of feelings and their clarification, had succeeded in reducing his acute anxiety enough to permit him to attend school comfortably. The remaining interviews were intended to reinforce the feeling of mastery and secure his therapeutic gains by helping him to a better understanding of the relation between his fears and his underlying conflicts.

At the close of the third interview, Randy had introduced a basic problem, namely, the conflict around dependent wishes. This issue came up repeatedly during the sessions that followed. Even prior to this he had indicated that the task of gaining more independence—which was represented most directly and concretely by the school—was fraught with the terrifying threat of being alone and helpless. To escape this threat he longed desperately for the protection and comfort of the dependent, infantile state. However, he was deeply ashamed of these regressive wishes, which were largely unconscious, and tried hard to compensate for them. The strategy of treatment was, on the one hand, to reduce his guilt over his regressive wishes, and on the other, to support his own strong drive toward emotional growth.

One of the central issues that had to be faced was his ambivalence toward his mother. He liked being her "baby," and in fact boasted openly in the fourth interview that she intervened on his behalf when his brothers picked on him. At the same time he resented her domination of him and her need to infantilize him, which also carried with it the threat of emasculation. These feelings erupted with full force in the sixth interview when he recalled his tonsillectomy again. This came up in association with a friend who had recently had his appendix removed. As he repeated the horror of his experience, he held his hand by his genitals. At the same time he denounced his mother for having deceived and abandoned him much more vigorously than he had on the previous occasion. My goal was to persuade Randy that such feelings were natural under the circumstances, and that it didn't make him a bad boy to feel so angry toward his mother. I tried also to assure him that having such feelings would not produce a similar catastrophe.[24]

As he was relieved of some of his guilt over anger, he could express his resentment toward his brothers more openly.[25] In the seventh interview he confided that he became angriest with his brothers when, after provoking him to tears, they would then call him a "little girl." Prior to this he had stated only that they called him a cry baby. I explored with him some of his own concerns about the relation between crying like a baby and being like a girl, at the same time assuring him that all boys felt at times like crying without losing their masculinity. He seemed to be aware that his mother was disappointed that there were no girls in the family and sensed that he had been destined for that role. However, he stated with considerable feeling that it was far preferable to be a boy and that, in fact, a girl wouldn't have a chance in their family of all boys.[26] I tried to help him reconcile his masculine strivings with his regressive longings to be mother's baby, and assured him that these longings were felt by other boys too.

In the eighth interview Randy told me about a television program he had seen in which a midget sat on a woman's lap smoking a cigar. This had really tickled him and as he laughed about it he confided—half in jest —that when he grew up it might be nice to be like the midget, both child and adult at the same time. I shared his joke with him, and at the same

---

[24] This kind of magical thinking in relation to hostile fantasies is an important element in any phobia, and it is important to interpret it at some point.

[25] As far as could be ascertained from the material, the brothers were viewed as more threatening than the father, who emerged as a fairly benign figure, although somewhat remote. However, not enough information was obtained to determine to what extent his fear of his brothers may have been displaced from his father.

[26] Despite his rather obvious ambivalence on this score, it was felt that his basic masculine identity was established beyond doubt. As stated earlier, the impression he gave was distinctly one of boyishness. In addition, much of the time in interviews was spent in talking about heroes with whom he closely identified, the cowboys and ballplayers idolized by all boys.

I focused primarily on his reluctance to give up his passive-dependent relationship to mother on the assumption that this was the basic source of his conflict in the area of masculine identification. Unquestionably, the threat posed by his Oedipal fantasies was also a contributory factor. This would account for the prominence of castration material.

time we were able to relate this to other things he had told me that had expressed the same central conflict. It was felt that his ability to face this issue with humor, insight, and self-tolerance indicated that he was beginning to resolve it constructively.

The following interview came near the end of the school year and was devoted mainly to saying goodbye. Randy and I talked about his plans for the summer, a time he was looking forward to with much excitement. I reminded him that in the fall he would be starting another grade, but I expressed confidence that he would be able to get along without my help. At the same time I promised to visit him from time to time to see how he was getting along.[27] He was pleased at this arrangement and seemed to be facing the future with hope and confidence.

Further Contacts with Mother

It is of paramount importance to include the mother in the treatment of school phobia. It has already been stated that the problem of separation is generally as great for her as for the child. Furthermore, during the time of crisis, when the child's anxiety is heightened and he clings more to his mother, her impulse is to respond with increasing concern and protectiveness, thereby encouraging the child's dependence on her. As their distress mounts, mother and child gravitate more strongly toward each other, so that any attempt to separate them is apt to be met with resistance by both. It is important, therefore, for the therapist to be prepared to support not only the child's anxiety but his mother's as well and to recognize that the mother, despite her conscious attempts to help the child, will often unwittingly undermine the therapist's efforts by her oversolicitousness.

The intensity of the mother's need to perpetuate the neurotic relationship varies a great deal from one instance to another and, as has already been pointed out, this need was less compelling with Randy's mother than is often the case. With those mothers where the need is very strong, a long period of psychotherapy for both the mother and child is required.[28]

---

[27] This made "goodbye" less final. In general, it was our practice to make the separation process a gradual one in these cases because of the anxiety around loss and separation. There was the added consideration that the new school year usually brings new stresses with it, and it is helpful to provide some support to the child during this anxious period.

[28] The degree of the mother's own need to perpetuate the child's dependence upon her can be roughly gauged by her readiness to yield to the child's pressure to remain at home. Sometimes a mother, who has been successful in maintaining at least sporadic attendance, will succumb to the child's resistance once treatment is begun, relinquishing her responsibility to the therapist. It is important for the therapist to make it plain that he regards continued attendance as desirable and to encourage and support both the mother and child in their efforts to conform to the demands of the school. Of course, he must expect to become the target for their hostility as he takes an active stand in favor of greater independence and be prepared to work this through.

During the period that Randy was being seen, I had two additional interviews with his mother as well as several telephone conversations. I called her from time to time in order to check on his progress, and she was encouraged to phone me whenever any question arose regarding his behavior.[29]

The discussions centered on her current relations with Randy without getting very much into his case history and not at all into hers.[30] She was aware that during the recent school crisis she had begun to vacillate more in discipline, and out of guilt had begun to pamper Randy more. While she had been able to apply enough pressure to get him to school despite his resistance, she realized that she had herself begun to waver and had been tempted to yield to his protestations. She recognized this as part of her general tendency to infantilize him and freely expressed guilt over this.

Her need to submit to his demands, which sometimes became tyrannical, she saw as her most serious problem in relation to Randy. She was encouraged to express some of her hostility toward him and her guilt over these feelings, and it became easier for her to maintain a consistent stand on basic issues. We did not go into the deeper sources of her guilt, which stemmed from her disappointment at his not being born a girl, as this would have been inappropriate in such a brief contact.

As Randy's behavior gradually improved, she herself showed less concern about separation. In fact, the following year she found herself a part-time position which kept her out of the home a good deal. Randy did not appear perturbed by this, although the previous year it had made him anxious to have mother out of the house.

Work with the Teacher

A child with school phobia inevitably poses a threat to the teacher. The irrational character of his fear, unresponsive to ordinary kindness and reassurance, gives her a sense of helplessness. Since the child often projects his fear to her, and since often there is an increase in anxiety following pressure imposed by her, she is likely to perceive herself as partially responsible for his problem. Neither the feeling of helplessness nor of guilt is a comfortable one, and these feelings may in turn generate feelings of irritation toward the child, which she cannot always justify. Caught by these conflicting feelings, the teacher is apt to vacillate between being

---

[29] It is especially important in the beginning of treatment for the therapist to make himself available in this way in order to permit the mother to express her anxieties and to provide her with the necessary support for her own dependency.

[30] In intensive, long-term therapy one would expect to explore both areas thoroughly.

stern and lenient, unwittingly duplicating the mother's ambivalent relationship to the child. This exposes him to another adult, who not only
acts inconsistently, but often acts in one way when she patently feels
another—for example, being considerate when she feels annoyed. Because
of this, working with the teacher to help her better understand the nature
of the child's problem and to clarify her own feelings is an important part
of the total therapeutic effort.

In keeping with our regular practice, I discussed Randy's problem with
the teacher before he was first seen and then briefly on each subsequent
school visit. In the initial contact with the teacher the dynamics of school
phobia were explained simply and the teacher assured that the child's
problem was not primarily a result of anything that might have happened
in school. I could offer additional support through being in the position
to relieve her of the burden of dealing with the pathological aspects of
his behavior. As was often the case, this enabled her to examine her own
classroom behavior and to express bewilderment as well as misgivings
about some of the things she might have done wrong. Further reassurance
was given that feelings of exasperation and helplessness were quite natural
in this situation, and it was agreed that she and I would talk over problems
as they appeared and arrive jointly at stratagems for coping with them.
In subsequent meetings I was able to explain to her some of the underlying causes of his specific fears. Seen in this new light, they appeared
less ominous to her, and she found it easier to tolerate them with greater
equanimity. This resulted in her being more patient and less demanding
of him when blocking in performance or breakdown in controls occurred.
As her composure increased and as the symptomatic picture improved,
she found it possible to feel more genuine sympathy, to show more kindness, and to give encouragement when difficulties arose. Thus, the diminution of the reality threat in school coincided with Randy's increasing
feeling of inner security and helped to reinforce it.

Review of Progress

During the period in which I saw Randy, striking changes occurred
in his school adjustment. The resistance toward attending school disappeared and along with it the physical symptoms of distress. Virtually no
trace of his morbid fear of art work remained. In fact, on one of my visits
at about the middle of the year, I found him in charge of preparing the
class book—a poster-sized folio—that required much cutting, pasting, and
coloring. He still remained quite a perfectionist, however, and quite sensitive to failure and even implicit criticism, although the tendency toward
tears diminished considerably.

The improvement continued through the following year, during which

I visited him several times. His new teacher reported that only occasional signs of discomfort appeared and these only at the beginning of the semester. It was encouraging to note that as the semester wore on he was able to display a certain amount of fractious behavior that he had not previously permitted himself. This coincided with a diminution of infantile, demanding behavior at home. Coincident with this was some relaxation of his perfectionist standards. These gradual character changes following the removal of the acute symptom augured well for the future and suggested that a genuine therapeutic process had been set in motion.

Summary and Analysis of Therapeutic Techniques

The preceding case illustrates the successful use of limited intervention in school phobia. Similar results have been obtained in other cases, and a detailed evaluation of these findings will be presented elsewhere. It is felt that success in these cases resulted from the application of specific therapeutic principles that were evolved empirically, but were rooted in certain theoretical assumptions relative to both the dynamics of the disturbance and the process of therapy. By way of summary, those factors considered to be therapeutically effective will be identified and their significance discussed.

1. *Early detection and prompt intervention.* It can hardly be claimed that this principle is new. More to the point is the demonstration that it can be applied successfully in an acute condition to forestall the development of a chronic one. This parallels findings in other acute states, notably the war neuroses. Moreover, this preventive principle is consistent with both learning theory and psychodynamic theory. In fact, the practice of child guidance in general is based on the assumption that therapeutic intervention before the maladaptive pattern has become firmly established will result not only in economy in total treatment time but will enhance the possibility of success. It is unfortunate that all too often, even in the treatment of children, referral is delayed until the disturbance has become chronic. Experience has shown that with school phobia this may lead to a protracted period of incapacitation in relation to school even lasting for years. There can be little question that this may have disastrous consequences for the development of the total personality that endure throughout the individual's lifetime.

Even in the present instance there was evidence of an acute problem two years earlier when Randy was in the kindergarten. It would be reasonable to assume that, had competent help been available during this critical period, a recurrence might have been avoided and he could have been spared much suffering. Of course, it can be argued that the acute phase might have been self terminating in the second instance just as it was in the first and that he would have been no worse off for the experience. However, even had the second crisis not led to a fixation of the phobia, it seems a gratuitous assumption that repeated exposure to traumatic experiences is of no consequence to the development of personality.

2. *Therapeutic exploitation of the emotional crisis.* There is justification for hypothesizing that intervention during an acute emotional crisis can do more than merely counteract its traumatic impact. It seems theoretically sound to assume that the existence of an intensified emotional state may actually facilitate the therapeutic process. This point of view is certainly implicit, if not explicit, in the concept of the "corrective emotional experience" advanced by Alexander and French.[31] They emphasize that the basic therapy in virtually all forms of psychotherapy is the same—namely, the reactivation of repressed emotions that could not be handled in the past. It is the therapist's function to aid the patient in mastering these troublesome feelings under more favorable circumstances. This is often accomplished through the use of the transference relationship. However, due to the patient's resistance, evoking the emotional conflicts of the past is often a time-consuming process. An acute crisis, on the other hand, by its very nature recapitulates certain features of earlier emotional struggles and reinstates identical affects. This is a ready-made situation for the therapist which by proper intervention he can re-structure to the advantage of the patient.[32] This can be achieved, as was demonstrated in the present case, by the use of some of the classical maneuvers of psychotherapy summarized below:

(a) *Catharsis.* Simply by offering himself as an understanding and compassionate listener at a time of acute distress, the therapist is able to provide the child with relief from his troubled feelings when there is no one else to whom he can talk.

(b) *Clarification and interpretation of focal conflicts.* Through his understanding of the dynamics of the disturbance, the therapist is able to focus on basic conflicts in terms that are neither too remote from consciousness nor too threatening to the child. In school phobia the child's problems of dependency and hostility are the most salient. These can be clarified for him especially in relation to his fear of separation.

(c) *Relief of guilt.* By accepting the child's hostile fantasies, his shameful fears, and his regressive longings without disapproval, the thera-

---

[31] F. Alexander, T. M. French, and others, *Psychoanalytic Therapy* (New York: The Ronald Press, 1946), pp. 66 ff.

[32] Recent theoretical developments in the field of social psychiatry have called attention to the "crisis" as a focal point in the development of emotional pathology, and have emphasized the need for developing methods for their amelioration as part of a rational approach to the problem of community mental health. For an excellent statement on this subject, see E. Lindemann, "The Meaning of Crisis in Individual and Family Living," *Teacher's Coll. Rec.,* 57 (1956), 310-15.

pist can reduce the child's guilt over these feelings and free him from their pathological grip.

(*d*) *Ego support*. By presenting himself initially as a supportive figure in a dangerous situation, the therapist bolsters the child's faltering ego. He continues by encouraging the child's own strong desire to move on to greater maturity and autonomy. The actual experience of mastering the phobic situation is in itself an important ego building event in the life of the child.

3. *Utilization of the natural milieu for therapeutic purposes*. In dealing with school phobia, the therapist has a number of advantages by operating directly in the school environment. First of all, he can offer the kind of direct support to the child referred to above. Beyond that, he can provide support to the teacher and principal by relieving them of their bewilderment, sense of impotence, and guilt. By altering their feelings toward the child, he is able to work with them toward modifying whatever reality elements in the situation aggravate the child's fear. Often special adjustments need to be made—for example, reducing the pressure of work, allowing the child to attend only part of the day, or even in some cases shifting the child to another class.[33] The therapist who is on the spot is much better able to assess the situation as it develops and plan his strategy accordingly. The child is sensitive to shifts in the teacher's attitude and responsive to modifications in the school setting. The reduction of the external threat reinforces the therapist's efforts to deal with the feelings that threaten the child from within.

Implications for Preventive Mental Health

The preventive value of early case finding and focused intervention in school phobia has already been amply discussed. The evidence that prompt, effective action may prevent the onset of a chronic, incapacitating disturbance has implications that go beyond this particular disturbance. It is well known that other emotional disturbances often find their central expression in the school, appearing as behavior problems, learning problems, and the like. The school is the community agency most strategically located for discovering these problems early in their development. This gives it tremendous case finding potential which has as yet hardly been tapped. Moreover, by employing persons with suitable training to administer limited therapeutic help within its own confines, the school might prevent the necessity for more extended treatment at some later date.

One word of caution is in order. While the techniques that have been

---

[33] The latter is sometimes necessary when the teacher and child have become particularly threatening to one another and obviously the utmost delicacy in handling and the careful preparation of all individuals concerned are required in such cases.

described may appear simple, they depend for their proper execution on a person with a thorough knowledge of the dynamics of emotional disturbance, and one who is well trained in psychotherapy. He must have enough experience to know when the situation requires more help than he is able to offer, and on such occasions be prepared to make appropriate referral elsewhere. These operations cannot be performed by a neophyte; they require a person of clinical skill and professional maturity.

Addendum

1. *Optimally, what criteria do you use for accepting or rejecting patients for psychotherapy?*

   The therapeutic techniques described here were developed specifically for children manifesting the early signs of school phobia. Even in such cases brief intervention is indicated only when the pathology in the mother-child relationship is not too great. Criteria for making the decision have already been discussed. In brief, a case is considered suitable when the interdependence of mother and child is not so great that they respond to the threat of treatment by intensified efforts to re-establish the earlier, infantile condition. Prognosis is good when: (a) the mother has some degree of insight into her relationship with the child and seems motivated to modify it; (b) the child is similarly motivated to establish a greater degree of independence and is making active efforts at mastery of his fear; and (c) when they are both able to face and express some of their hostile feelings.

2. *Do you make a diagnosis before psychotherapy begins?*

   A diagnosis of school phobia is made on the basis of the symptomatic picture before treatment is begun. The decision to engage in either short term or long term treatment is deferred until after the initial therapeutic contacts.

3. *Do you attempt to persuade the patient or significant relative to change his (the patient's) environment?*

   Since the child's phobia is primarily a result of neurotic anxiety, there is ordinarily no necessity for modifying the environment to any great degree. "Environmental manipulation" is employed in the sense that the parents are encouraged to keep the child in school to discourage regression. Consultations with the child's teacher may lead to a modification of some of her attitudes and classroom practices. Only rarely is it necessary to transfer the child to another teacher.

4. *How did you conceptualize the therapist's role in this case?*

   The therapist's role is initially supportive. He comes as an ally to the child who finds himself in a desperate situation. Beyond that, the therapist provides an opportunity for the cathartic expression of fear, rage, and guilt. He helps the child to clarify some of his confused feelings and to understand his conflicting impulses, particularly in the area of his regressive wishes.

5. *What aspects of your theory of psychotherapy were particularly apparent or useful in the case presented here?*

Three basic principles of the psychotherapeutic theory advanced in this presentation were especially relevant: (a) psychotherapeutic intervention is apt to be more effective during the initial stages of the disturbance; (b) the presence of an acute emotional crisis enhances the corrective emotional experience; and (c) intervention directly in the setting in which the child is experiencing difficulty facilitates the therapeutic process.

6. *Do you feel that this case developed significant insight? If not, can improvement be maintained?*

It is felt that some insight was developed in regard to guilt around dependency and hostility. With the acceptance of these feelings by the therapist relief of guilt occurred, thus diminishing the need for neurotic defenses against them.

7. *What aspects of your own cultural orientation facilitated or impeded the treatment of your case?*

I am not sure what is intended by this question or if it applies here.

8. *If we consider that a continuum exists from superficial to deep psychotherapy, where would you place your own case?*

This case would be placed somewhere on the superficial side of the spectrum. The term *superficiality*, however, applies to the level of genetic reconstruction rather than to the depth or intensity of feelings.

9. *What did you think about the outcome of this case and what criteria did you use for evaluating such outcome?*

The outcome was regarded as very satisfactory. Criteria for evaluating this included both status of the symptom and the adjustment at home and school.

10. *How do you terminate psychotherapy?*

Therapy was terminated gradually. The interval between interviews was gradually increased, and arrangements were made for "check ups" the following year.

CHAPTER 3

The Treatment
of a Child and Family

—NATHAN W. ACKERMAN[1] *and* MARCILLE H. LAKOS[2]

Introduction

Principles of psychotherapy are secondary to a systematized understanding of human problems and defined forms of maladaptation and illness. The specific techniques of psychotherapy are derived, step by step, from an integrated theory of personality development, social interaction, and psychopathology. This theory provides us with a set of normative expectations with regard to the endo-psychic organization of personality, relations of individual, family, and wider society, and a corresponding set of standards for judging a range of deviations from the norm. The purpose of treatment is to correct what is deviant and wrong in a person's life adaptation and in his endo-psychic organization. The treatment process stands or falls according to the validity of this judgment as to what is wrong with a person at a given time and in a given social place.

Our purpose here is to describe the treatment of a disturbed child within the frame of a concomitant program of therapy for the child's

[1] A.B., Columbia U., 1929; M.D., Coll. of Physicians and Surgeons, Columbia U., '33; Interne, Montefiore Hosp., '33-'34; Resident, Neuropsychiatry, Menninger Clinic and Sanit., Topeka, Kans., '35-'36; Psychiat., Menninger Clinic, '35-'37; Psychiat. and Asst. Med. Director, Stony Lodge, Ossining, N. Y., '37-'38; Private practice, Psychiat. and Psychoanal., '38— ; Assoc. Clin. Prof. of Psychiat., Columbia U., '55— ; Diplomate, Amer. Bd. of Psychiat. and Neurol.; Pres., Assoc. for Psychoanal. Med., '57; Fellow, N. Y. Acad. of Med.; Member, Amer. Psychoanal. Assoc.

[2] B.S., U. of Ore., '47; M.S., U. of Ore., '49; Assoc. Member, Amer. Psychol. Assoc., '55— ; Member, N. Y. State Psychol. Assoc., '56— ; N. Y. State Clin. Psychol. Assoc., '57— .

family. The treatment of a disturbed child requires us to respect the child's individuality. But the concept of individuality in a child is often incorrectly understood. A child's "individuality" may be healthy or pathological. This distinction is an important one.

The concept of individuality in a child is frequently treated as if it meant everything in the child that is separate or different from his parents. Such an interpretation emphasizes the child's separateness, and even his opposition to parents, while seeming to ignore the principle that healthy separation in the child cannot go forward except in the matrix of healthy emotional union or identification with his parents. In other words, healthy individuality in a child represents a balance between two components: a component of togetherness with parents and family, and another component of autonomous development. Individuality in this sense absorbs within itself much of the social interactional content of family experience. It does not represent exclusively tendencies in the child which are different from or opposite to those of parents and family.

The unfolding of a child's personality is, in great part, the product of social process. The family is the basic group within which the child is socialized. The child takes into himself something of the mother and something of the father, but also develops something unique and different. The child's uniqueness is influenced, beyond hereditary factors, by differences between the parents and the child's perception of the emotional relations between them. This interaction and merging of mother and father epitomizes the emotional essence of the family as a group; it is the core of the psychological identity of the family.

A child's personality is the end result of a certain fluid balance between tendencies toward psychic union with the parents and separation from them. The secure development of autonomy in the child's personality is thus contingent upon secure identity of the child with parents. Healthy identity with the parents means healthy separation; pathological identity means pathological separation. In circular fashion, whatever is deviant in the process of separation further distorts the pattern of emotional identification with parents and family.

The emotional disturbance of a child cannot be evaluated or treated in a social vacuum. Whatever is deviant in the child's behavior needs to be viewed as a symptom of the social psychopathology of the family group. In this sense, the traditionally demarcated professional field of child psychiatry might justifiably be called, instead, family psychiatry. If the pathological trends in a child's personality are to be successfully treated, the pathological trends within his family group must also be treated concurrently. If the child is to be restored to a path of healthy autonomous development, he must be restored to a position of healthy emotional union with parents and family. The unit of diagnosis and therapy is the child and family as an integral phenomenon rather than the child as an isolated being.

In the field of child psychotherapy, it is often claimed that family therapy is carried out at the same time as the therapy of the child. This usually means treatment of the child and mother, sometimes by separate therapists, sometimes by the same therapist. In a strict sense, however, this is not family therapy. This is an atomistic approach to child and mother as separate individuals, and it does not constitute a true therapy of the family group. Ordinarily, such treatment does not encompass a systematized conceptualization of the child-mother pair as a functional expression of the psychological configuration of the family as a whole. In the setting of traditional child guidance practices, the disturbances of parental attitudes are mainly related to the parents' individual personality, but not to the totality of role relations within the family group.

It is within the framework of viewing the child and family together as the basic phenomenological unit that we try to evaluate a disturbed child. It is within this conceptual orientation that we now describe the treatment of a particular case.

The primary patient is a ten-year-old boy referred with a series of complaints: failure in school work, chronic reading difficulty, depression and withdrawal, fear of father, jealousy of sister, and fears of illness and injury.

The early clinical interviews occurred in the following sequence: interview with both parents, with the child alone, with both parents again, each parent individually; then, interviews of child with both parents together and with each parent separately.

Initial Interviews with Parents

In the first interview with the parents, the father assumed the initiative. The mother sat by with a stony, impassive face but obviously listening very intently. The father placed himself instantly in the dominant position with a tacit assumption of superiority to his wife. He was clearly worried. There was a note of panic in his voice but his outward demeanor was controlled and reasoned. His wife sat stiff, constrained, frozen, offering only an occasional comment if her husband made a direct inquiry of her. At this time, and for some months thereafter, two significant pieces of information were lacking: the father was in personal analysis; and the school had recommended psychiatric consultation for the child two years back, but the parents delayed action on this recommendation right up to the point where the marriage was about to crumble. It was at the very peak of the family crisis that the parents became urgently motivated to request psychiatric help for the boy.

Sharply in evidence in the first interview was the father's wrath toward the child. He confessed it candidly. He stated that he never liked him, was critical of his intellectual failure, but also revealed his intense personal torment and guilt over the child's rejection. Ostensibly, his son was a severe disappointment to him because he seemed so stupid. The father leaned over backward to take the blame upon himself. He carefully sidestepped any temptation to be openly accusatory to his wife. We learned later, however, that in his own mind the father associated the boy with his mother and chalked them both up as stupid. He seemed to treat the boy exclusively as belonging to his mother. The mother was aware of this and said nothing. But the air between them was thick with unexpressed tension. Being an intellectual perfectionist, the father could not abide even the appearance of stupidity in any member of his family. Mother and son acted dumb, but weren't. It was merely that the father expected them to be so.

In the second interview with parents, the mother thawed out of her frozen state sufficiently to show some intense emotion. She choked up and cried. Only with support and encouragement from the clinician could she express even a small part of her tormented feelings. She felt an enormous guilt for the failure of both her and her son in the father's eyes.

First Interview with the Child Patient

Hubert was slightly undersized for his age, but, what is more important, he acted like a much younger child. He appeared blank and withdrawn. He was dull, sluggish, extremely walled-off. His attitude was removed, taciturn, depressed. He was unspontaneous and uncommunicative. He engaged in play in a self-absorbed way, ignoring everyone about him. Using building blocks he constructed a garage which he called a fortress. He admitted on questioning that it would be extremely difficult to get inside the walls of this building. When asked how long it would take, he muttered under his breath, "At least two years." He seemed to be intensely barricaded. His behavior suggested deep preoccupation with inner fantasies of power and destruction. Later, he alluded in a low voice to the toy building as the place where his father worked. His father was the director of an engineering school.

Historical Background

The problems of this boy can hardly be understood except against the background of the disturbed relations of his parents and the twisted path of the development of his family. There was a religious difference between the parents; the father was Jewish, the mother Protestant. There was, beyond this, a further clash of cultural background which created a critical barrier between man and wife. This was especially complicated by the husband's extreme mistrust of the wife, a condition testified to by her husband's family.

Originally, this man and wife met at his place of work. She was a research assistant in the engineering school of which he was director. The courtship was a troubled one. It involved a long struggle with the man's parents to get them to accept the marriage. Throughout this struggle he was torn with conflict—trying, on the one hand, to placate his family, and, on the other, to win acceptance of the woman he wished to marry.

The opposition of his mother continued to be sharp and overt until a particular event occurred involving a bitter verbal battle between his older sister and mother. Out of her vindictiveness the sister declared vehemently that whether her mother liked it or not, her brother would be married. Promptly thereafter the mother collapsed, went to bed, but following this ceased to oppose the marriage.

The first phase of the marriage was tense and difficult. The new wife made an early but unsuccessful attempt to become pregnant. She felt she should have a child to please her husband. She was plagued with fears of sterility. Finally, she had a miscarriage which caused considerable anguish to her and her husband. Somewhat later she became pregnant with our patient, Hubert, but by this time her husband was inducted into the armed services. He left to go abroad with the military during her pregnancy. He arranged for his wife to live with his older sister. This arrangement was motivated strongly by his suspicion of his wife, his jealousy, and his fear that she might be unfaithful.

This jealousy is epitomized in one dramatic episode. On one occasion, the father, on returning home, secretly searched the mother's dresser drawer to be sure that her diaphragm was in its accustomed place. He was unable to find it, became infuriated, and charged his wife with infidelity. She was profoundly hurt and angry. All the time, the diaphragm was exactly where it should have been, but in his anxious haste the father had overlooked it. But the mother, as usual, and despite her humiliation, sided emotionally with her husband against herself. She felt, too, that a woman was not to be trusted. She shared with her husband an attitude of contempt and disparagement toward women. There were several critical episodes in her personal life in which she felt cruelly betrayed by women whom she had trusted as friends.

Hubert's birth took place while the father was abroad in military service. He was the first of four children. Prior to his birth, the mother dreamed idealistically of motherhood but was painfully disillusioned when the child finally arrived. She felt abandoned, utterly alone, and frightened and burdened by the responsibility of the child. She had little communication with the sister-in-law with whom she was then living. She felt tied to the baby but had virtually no other human contacts.

During the first phase of the child's life the mother was isolated and depressed. The child cried constantly. The mother used phenobarbital to quiet his crying and administered enemas to alleviate his cramps. He cried and screamed almost continuously up to the age of four months. She resented the baby's demands and felt estranged from him. She rarely held him in her arms or showed him any affection. His development was slow. It was two years before he spoke his first words. At 18 months he had difficulty with adenoids. He had distressed breathing and drooled at the mouth. Though depressed and deeply guilty, the mother kept her emotions to herself. This was the character of the mother's life situation until the father's return from the military.

Hubert was two years of age when the father returned. When the boy first saw his father, he screamed and refused to have anything to do with him. If he saw his father approaching his mother, he cried out in anguish. He seemed to go into acute panic when he saw his father in bed with his mother. Every member of the family was at this time severely troubled. The mother told the father little of how she felt. She was run down, exhausted, and did not look well. The father himself was morbidly unhappy. The parents felt estranged. The father showed little trust in the mother's affection for him. He escaped to his professional work. He came home late and saw little of his wife or the boy.

This situation continued until the mother became pregnant with the second child, a girl, toward whom Hubert later felt intense jealousy. During this period the boy continued his state of isolation; he did not play with other children. At the age of four or five Hubert became increasingly destructive. He showed no warmth to either parent, teased and struck his sister, and suffered criticism from both his parents. At five years he had a tonsillectomy, after which his mouth breathing and drooling diminished. The mother continued to be stern and cold toward him.

In kindergarten he was slow in learning and socially withdrawn. The teachers were puzzled because of his good intelligence. He daydreamed a good deal. The father, believing he was stupid, treated him harshly. During these years, Hubert had several minor accidents and developed an intense fear of bodily injury. The parents continually disagreed about the way to handle him.

The father tended to be indifferent to the child until his behavior became unbearable. He would then become abusive and insist, "That's enough." After an outburst of irritability, he would feel guilty and apologize to the boy. Otherwise, the father would simply ignore him. The mother resented this, and was critical of the father for not being more strict with the boy. The boy was consistently more difficult when the father was present. Later, two other children were born, making a total of four. The father enjoyed the younger children, and was especially fond of the second child, a girl. This tended, of course, to aggravate the patient's jealousy. These are the salient features of this boy's history.

At the time of referral a severe barrier existed between mother and child, also between father and mother, and father and child. The mother drew back sharply from the boy as if he were the worst part of herself. Both mother and boy felt they were to blame for the father's rejection of them; it was their own doing.

Progress of Therapy

It seemed evident that if we were to make progress with this case we would have to confront the family problem as well as the boy's. We would have to move in the direction of dissolving the emotional barrier first between mother and child, after that between the parents, and finally, do something to restore the father's acceptance of the boy. Regardless of the father's involvement in personal analysis, our orientation was to commit both parents to participation in the therapy of the child. The father was involved in his family role as parent to this child and as husband to his wife. The mother was involved as parent to the child and as wife to her husband. The therapy was therefore conducted at several levels: individual sessions with the child, sessions with child and mother, individual sessions with mother, group therapy in a mother's group, and, later, sessions with the child and father. Therapy was mainly conducted by the female therapist, under the supervision of the male psychiatrist. Periodic family conferences were held, in which both male and female clinicians took part.

One event colored the entire course of treatment and should be related first. After about nine months of therapy, the mother terminated her individual sessions. Therapy of the child was continued, but the mother withdrew. The reasons were not immediately clear. The mother had an outburst of anger at the therapist when she discovered in group therapy sessions for mothers that women could enjoy sex and even experience orgasm. She felt bitter that her husband had withheld this information from her all these years. Until now she believed that men had a corner on sex and that women submitted purely out of a sense of duty. She was hurt and angry at her husband, but blew up at her female therapist. This was the precipitating situation.

But there were other reasons. Both she and her husband were suspicious of the therapist and fearful of injurious personal exposure. Her husband supported her decision to quit individual therapy, partly because of his belief that she was too stupid and too fragile, partly because of a submerged fear that she might get out of hand and turn toward another man. His jealousy of his own son was clearly a factor. Though interrupting individual therapy, the mother wished to continue in group therapy. It was judged wise, however, to remove her from group therapy as well, since we would have then no control over her emotional response to the group experience. This she resented. For a relatively short period, we continued the isolated treatment of the child, partly because of our uncertainty as to how this situation would unfold.

With the passing of the summer months, however, the mother returned, confessed that she was in error, expressed resentment regarding her exclusion from group therapy and asked to be reinstated both in the group and individual treatment. She did this on her own, with the father reluctantly assenting.

A quick preview of the sequence of changes in therapy is helpful for purposes of orientation. There occurred first a melting of the emotional barrier between mother and child. A new level of joining and emotional intimacy was established in this family pair. Following this there was improvement both in the boy and the mother. This left the way open for a beginning change in the relations between the two parents. It was the improvement in the parents' sexual relationship and the father's increased receptivity to both mother and boy which ultimately induced him to request a more active participating role in the boy's therapy. He also asked to have individual sessions to guide him in his paternal attitudes. Ultimately, there was substantial improvement in the intimacy of family relations at all levels.

The direct therapy of the boy began slowly. Initially, he appeared both oppressed and depressed. He bowed his shoulders; his movements were laboriously slow. He scuffed his feet as he walked across the room. He rarely looked at the therapist. His eyes were glazed and dull. His face was mask-like. His thought processes seemed to be split off from the movement of his hands. He was extremely reticent; he knelt quietly in a corner of the room and played with blocks in a feeble, detached, lifeless way. From time to time he interrupted his play to simply sit and indulge his fantasies. He seemed to resent any attempt at conversation. The therapist, therefore, sat by quietly, saying extremely little.

This type of relationship persisted for four sessions with almost no verbal communication of any sort. There was only a slight show of interest when the therapist offered candy to the boy.

Beginning about the fourth session, his building activity became somewhat more organized and he showed increasing alertness to the therapist's presence. Now and then he cast sidelong glances at her and asked a few questions concerning the blocks. The therapist recognized his frightened and disguised appeal for her to take part in his game. She responded. He seemed pleased by this and proceeded then to test the therapist's reaction to his urge to destroy the building. When there was no sign of criticism, he proceeded to destroy the house, making a loud bang and relishing it.

In general his behavior continued to be cautious, fearful, suspicious, and walled-off. While believing himself to be stupid, he was nonetheless under compulsion to display his intellect to the therapist. This occurred mainly in the form of reciting to her fragmented pieces of information about current events. Gradually, as he felt safer in this relationship, safer both from criticism and from any compulsion to behave according to her dictates, he became more accessible. The therapist continued warm, friendly, but non-intrusive, waiting for cues from the boy as to the level at which he would accept her participation.

In the sixth session there came another change. He dropped his interest in blocks and proceeded to become interested in ball-playing. He confessed his total failure as an athlete. He said his fingers got in the way; he was awkward. But he seemed to appeal to the therapist to raise his confidence. She responded by joining him in a game of catch. At first his coordination was extremely poor. He was all hands and feet, but he was tenacious and the ball-playing continued. He improved rapidly. After a time, he jumped, and caught and threw the ball quite skillfully. His interest moved to other activities: finger painting, drawing (mostly of submarines), and depicting his own fantasies of outer space. He was ambitious to be the first man to visit Mars. He felt he might be happier there than on earth. The therapist was a full participant in all these activities. She talked only if the boy seemed to welcome it.

During this growing intimacy between boy and therapist, the boy slowly offered small confidences about his parents. This came without any pressure whatsoever. He was aware that his mother was coming to see the therapist once a week. He made clear how utterly alone he felt, how unable to communicate with anyone in the family. He felt incredibly inferior and dumb. He gradually became more assertive and complained of his parents' failure to understand him. He felt stripped of confidence as a result of the mother's alienation from him and also as the result of her guilty over-protection.

The mother, in response to her own conflict, tended to protect him from the father's criticism and tended to do the talking for him; in effect, she put words right into his mouth. She lived his life for him, treating him as a piece of herself rather than as a separate person. This was clearly the effect of her fright of the father's criticisms.

As the boy revealed himself increasingly to the therapist, he cautiously hinted that he would like his mother to join the session with him. He wanted to show her his drawings and display his new facility in ball-playing. But he was frightened. He wanted to ask her if she loved him, but he didn't dare. She would misunderstand and get bossy.

The mother was invited to be part of the boy's sessions. Initially, both boy and mother were extremely awkward with one another. Gradually, he drew her into games with him and hesitantly showed some of his feelings. The mother had previously felt completely rejected by the boy. She was shocked and elated to discover that she was so deeply important to him. When they sensed that each really needed the other, the relationship, at first wooden and blocked, warmed up. Finally, the boy, while caressing a toy animal, sat next to his mother, and took hold of her hand. The mother was touched to the core and could hardly hold back her tears. She seemed stilted, self-conscious, fumbling, and hardly knew what to do or say. Finally, in a labored, awkward manner she put her arm around her boy and they sat quietly together. They agreed later—it felt good! They walked out of the office arm in arm.

The patient responded to this reunion with his mother with an excited, buoyant mood. Their play together in therapeutic sessions became hectically animated. They reached a point where they experienced a climactic shared excitement in a playful fight with water guns. The boy doused the mother from head to foot; while at first self-conscious and scared, she came gradually to love it. Emotional communication became intense. They laughed and cried together.

Let us turn now to a consideration of what was happening in the meantime in individual sessions with the mother. Initially, she seemed frozen, guilt-ridden, defensive, and aloof. Her conversation was almost entirely on the surface. She surrounded herself with this protective wall as though to ward off expected attack. Nevertheless, she was earnest in her desire to help the child. She revealed quite unmistakably her feeling of lack of worth in her husband's eyes, and her tendency to agree with him that she was stupid. Yet, paradoxically, she rose to the challenge to try to prove her good intellect to the therapist, exactly as did the boy. She tried in every conceivable way to build up her sense of worth and importance, and to impress her husband and the surrounding community. Small successes meant nothing to her. The slightest disappointment confirmed her conviction of inferiority. Her whole demeanor seemed to radiate shame for herself and for her son. At first she showed little feeling. This gradually changed. She revealed her fear of admitting openly any closeness with the boy. She wanted to disconnect herself from the boy in her husband's mind.

At another level she discussed her husband's character, his severe suspiciousness, his jealousy, and his accusations of infidelity. Within the family there was no spontaneous joy. All issues were met with a heavy hand. There was little relaxation, no play, no humor. The emotional climate of the entire family group was heavy and depressive.

The therapist's role with the mother was one of sympathetic support and acceptance, providing abundant opportunity for the free expression of her conflicting emotions. The significant parts of her relations with the child and husband were discussed frankly with her. At times she was given direct advice concerning her conduct with the boy. She was encouraged to learn to listen to him as she herself was listened to.

A sharp change occurred when she learned in the mother's group that women had sexual orgasms. This was a real shock. She came to her individual session with anxious, pressured questions. Hitherto, she had carried out her obligation with her husband in a passive, frigid, immobile manner. This, to her, was the normal state of affairs in married life. As she talked, she became increasingly irate at the way she'd been cheated. She exploded at the therapist and quit. As has earlier been indicated, after a lapse of several months she began again where she had left off. The therapist responded earnestly to her urge to explore this sexual discovery. There was candid discussion of the sexual potentials of a woman. The mother was encouraged in the expectation of personal pleasure. Following a particularly tense session in which the mother discussed at length her experiences of treachery at the hands of women and confessed her fear of betrayal by the therapist, she began to show increasing interest in her sex life. She overcame her vindictive feeling toward her husband and participated more freely in sexual love with her husband. Her husband in turn reacted with considerable surprise, but also genuine appreciation. For the first time she had succeeded in winning from him overt, enthusiastic expressions of approval. This was a turning point in the relations between man and wife.

It also marked a change in her attitude toward the therapist. Following this improvement she became much more trusting. She confessed much more frankly her previous suspicions of the therapist, her fear of betrayal, her contempt for women, and her need to cut off her feeling in her dealings with them. About this time, she began to show intense feelings in the therapeutic sessions. She dropped her defensive barricade and literally poured out emotion.

Gradually, the mother's rigidity mellowed. She responded with increasing warmth to the boy; he, in turn, moved closer to her. The melting of the mutual mistrust between mother and son opened the way to a new level of emotional identity. Of particular importance in this newly discovered intimacy were the water fights in which Hubert directed a steady stream against his mother. It was quite striking to note in this connection the boy's increasing freedom in emotional communication with his mother. He dropped his mask. He no longer acted dumb. In place of his previous dull apathy, he now displayed some spark and real intelligence. He showed his most acute fear in connection with an open show of tears. He was convinced that it was weak and foolish of him to cry; but when mother and son cried together, his fear was eased.

As the intimacy between the mother and son unfolded, the boy talked increasingly about what was wrong with his relations with his father. He became guilty concerning this, however, and showed strong reluctance to belittling his father in his mother's eyes. The recognition of the boy's guilt over the temptation to use one parent against another induced the therapist to suggest sessions for the boy and father. While considering this plan, the boy entered a plateau. He seemed for a time to freeze and he was unable to make further progress.

The anticipation of joined sessions with his father induced again a compulsive urge to prove his worth through a display of superior factual knowledge about the world. It was as if the father could tolerate the boy only at this level of intellectual superiority. Ordinarily, conversation between father and son was sparse and impersonal. When it did occur, it took the form of a detached, intellectual discussion, which tended quickly to deteriorate into an irritable argument about who was right or who knew better.

By this time the boy had a clear picture of his father's rejection of him, his suspiciousness, and criticism of his stupidity. With increasing awareness of his father's preference of the other children, the boy's hate and fear of his father emerged quite sharply.

In the therapy sessions with the boy and father, the father was at first reserved and defensive. His intelligence, essential honesty, and desire to really understand came to the fore, however. He listened both to the boy and the therapist with some respect. Gradually, the boy overcame his fear sufficiently to express directly to his father for the first time his conflicting feelings. The father was deeply impressed. He tended partly to justify his attitudes and partly to confess his guilt for failing to understand the boy. He admitted to the boy that he lacked confidence in him, that he preferred the other children, that at times he was disdainful and indifferent. While making these confessions, the father seemed depressed.

For this reason the therapist had several sessions with the father alone. She gave emotional support to the father for his intellectual understanding and his earnest desire to help his son. At the same time, a number of the father's misconceptions of the boy were challenged and discussed freely. When issues arose that had to do with the relations between mother and father, the father showed much more animation. He was at first more interested in his wife than his son. His motivation to improve his marital relations was stronger than his urge to help the boy. In short, he was more preoccupied with his own needs than with his son's needs.

Discouraged in the beginning, he talked of the complete stalemate in his relations with his wife; he did not know which way to turn. After a time, however, he gave recognition to a distinct change for the better in the behavior of both boy and mother. He was impressed with the improvement in his wife's sexual response.

At about this time, a joint conference was arranged which included the man and wife, the male psychiatrist, and female therapist. The purpose of this was to survey progress and decide further steps in therapy. The father admitted a lessening of his hostile feelings toward the mother. They were now finding more satisfactions together, which gave him real hope. Both man and wife agreed that things had been rough but they now expressed a desire to make the marriage a lasting one. The wife remarked, "I've learned something. I feel now that you don't have to know exactly what is going on but if things work out it is satisfying enough." She meant by this that she had dropped her effort to prove her intellectual adequacy, had ceased to cut off the flow of her feeling, and felt more alive. Of particular importance in this interview was the more candid discussion of the difficulties that resulted from the husband's jealousy. The wife was able to "tell her husband off." She expressed more openly her resentment of the father's jealousy and his refusal to allow her to leave the house unattended.

A month later, there was a very distinct change in the attitude of the father. He was more positive, no longer depressed, and spoke enthusiastically of the change in his relations with his wife. She was warmer, he was less suspicious; they found real pleasure in one another's company. This enabled him now to show a genuine interest in the boy.

In the meantime, Hubert responded well to the therapeutic sessions with the father. He regarded the achievement of a new contact with his father as something outstanding. Following this, he showed substantial improvement in his work at school. He was a more spirited, interested student. He continued to be a slow learner but his achievement was distinctly on the upgrade. At the same time he was less hostile toward his sister.

When the mutual hostility and suspiciousness between father and son eased, there were further individual sessions with Hubert. He began now to talk increasingly of his sexual feelings. He confessed his masturbation but was troubled because he got little feeling from it. During one such session Hubert showed considerable agitation and anxiety; he fidgeted and wrung his hands. With encouragement he related his worries. He confessed to several episodes of exploratory sex play with his sister. His reaction after these experiences was one of intense guilt and disgust. He was given every opportunity to talk himself out in these matters and much relieved to discover that his sex urges were by no means unique. They did not make him a bad, perverted person.

This encouraged him to talk more and more of his body experiences. He began to value his body more. His appearance changed; he became neater, and paid more attention to his looks. He began also to learn more of the skills which were required of him in social relations, ballplaying, and dancing. Through dancing lessons, he acquired a girl friend.

One day he came to therapy quite depressed and far away. He seemed lonely, and said little. After a considerable period of tortured reticence, he admitted finally that he continued to be worried about his masturbation. He hated to "jerk off," felt very guilty about it, and was sure that it hurt his penis. He complained that it was actually painful. He imagined that the liquid would run dry if his glands were overworked, and that they would cease to function. He had the thought that the semen was infected with germs and was a real danger if allowed to stay on his pajamas.

Discussion of these conflicts and fears led to the realization that he wanted to hear the male psychiatrist's view of these problems. This was arranged for. The problem of his masturbation and associated fears was discussed with female therapist and male psychiatrist together. The discussion was lengthy. The core of this conflict emerged finally: the boy was intensely disappointed because the pleasure of seminal discharge was somehow impaired. In fact, at times, he did not realize that he was having an orgasm unless he looked directly at his penis. It was discovered that in masturbation, he was actually hurting his penis. He rubbed it harshly, angrily. Through various hints, it seemed probable that he was unconsciously equating his penis with his father. In the act of beating his penis, he was attacking his father—a symbolic act of vengeance. He seemed to disconnect himself from his penis, disowning it and treating it as if it belonged to his father. This disguised rage against the penis, the guilt, and fear of retaliation, took the pleasure out of the act. Interpretation of this conflict and further discussion of his anger and competitive battle with his father eased the patient's depression and worry.

This boy and family have been in therapy three years. It continues to the present time. The unity of the family has been preserved and enhanced. There is now no danger of a break-up of the marriage. The parents have a new bond. They enjoy one another. The relations of mother and son are vastly improved. The relations of father and son, though better, are still an area of tension. The boy himself is much happier and no longer withdrawn and depressed. He feels he has made great strides. He now feels accepted at school; he does better both academically and athletically.

ADDENDUM[3]

1. *Optimally, what criteria do you use for accepting or rejecting patients for psychotherapy?*

I use a series of criteria:

   (*a*) The diagnostic judgment of the problem appraised in clinical, developmental, dynamic, and causal terms. This includes appraisal of relations of individual and group, and adaptive failure in performance of specific life roles.
   (*b*) The sincerity of the patient's motivation for change.
   (c) The measure of accessibility of the disorder to psychotherapeutic influence, influenced partly by the character of the primary patient, partly by the patterns of relatedness of this individual to his family group or an equivalent group.

---

[3] By Nathan W. Ackerman, M.D.

(d) An estimate of the quality of empathy, communication, and potential identification between the particular patient and myself as therapist. This implies a prediction of the possible outcome of a particular pairing of patient and therapist. I consider this criterion most important; it is something above and beyond the estimate of the patient's personality and the characteristics of a particular therapeutic personality. It is a question of understanding different kinds of therapeutic marriage.

2. *Do you make a diagnosis before psychotherapy begins?*

My answer to this question is emphatically in the affirmative. I consider it of the utmost importance to achieve a clear diagnostic definition of the patient's disorder before making any final commitment about accepting a patient for treatment. This does not mean, however, that the diagnostic study is pursued in any routine or ritualized manner. It is not a question and answer interview. The clinical interview itself is a dynamic, open-ended process. Its flow is determined by the perception of significant cues as to foci of pathogenic conflict and anxiety. The early interview contact, while primarily diagnostic, is simultaneously oriented to the patient's therapeutic needs. Nevertheless, a final decision as to the acceptance of a particular patient for treatment rests on a clear picture of the nature of the patient's disorder. In order to apply therapy in a psychologically specific manner, one must know exactly what is wrong with the patient. The diagnostic study includes clinical psychiatric evaluation and, wherever other examinational procedures may be indicated, psychological studies, a home visit, a medical examination, and so forth.

3. *Do you attempt to persuade the patient or significant relative to change his (the patient's) environment?*

Under ordinary circumstances the answer to this question is in the negative. Both the diagnosis and the treatment of the patient encompass a careful survey of the patient's emotional integration into his environment, which means a dynamic diagnosis of the interrelations of individual personality and social role performance. In some instances a change of environment may be deemed to be a constructive influence. If so, however, this decision must be arrived at jointly by a working through of the relevant considerations between patient and therapist. A closely related problem is the clinical judgment as to whether a given patient is virtually trapped in a role position from which he cannot escape and which intensifies the disposition toward emotional illness. If, in evaluating the patient's environment and the potentials of role change in that environment, it is concluded that the patient cannot get well without a radical alteration of the patient's role position in his group environment, it is sometimes necessary to engage simultaneously in a therapy of the patient's environment. Of special importance is a concomitant therapy of disordered family relationships. If this is intelligently carried out, it may be possible to liberate the patient from a trapped role position to make possible further progress in therapy.

4. *How did you conceptualize the therapist's role in this case?*

The therapist's primary responsibility in this case was to deal with the conflicts of the child, and yet at the same time to draw into the center of the child's therapeutic experience those relevant members of the family with whom he was locked in conflict. In other words, the therapist had a primary therapeutic investment with the child, and beyond this extended the therapeutic responsibility to deal therapeutically with the pathogenic content of the child's relations with each of the parents as individuals, the parents as a couple, and the sibling pair.

5. *What aspects of your theory of psychotherapy were particularly apparent or useful in the case presented here?*

This is already alluded to in the above statement. In essence it is the principle that the psychotherapy of an emotionally disturbed child can be effectively executed only when one views the child as a part of the family. The child is an emerging individual, to be sure, but he is simultaneously a functioning psychological unit in a family group within which his relationship experience continues to influence the fate of his personal conflicts. Following these principles the treatment involved direct therapy of the child as an individual and, parallel with this, a therapy for the conflict patterns of the significant family pairs.

6. *Do you feel that this case developed significant insight? If not, can improvement be maintained?*

In this case the patient did succeed in integrating an effective understanding of his conflicts, those which he contained secretly within himself and those others which he shared with family members. However, I am not of the opinion that "insight" alone is the core of therapeutic progress. The larger emphasis lies in the emotional capacity through better understanding to open oneself emotionally to new experience, to accommodate to change, and, through this, to learn new possibilities in human relations and thereby achieve further development of personality. It is the conviction of success in discovering new and more satisfying levels of adaption that brings lasting improvement rather than "insight" alone.

7. *What aspects of your own cultural orientation facilitated or impeded the treatment of your case?*

In this particular instance the cultural orientation of the therapist was in many ways similar to the cultural orientation of the patient and his family. This experiential familiarity with the culture-bound experience of the patient is helpful in facilitating emotional communications and improves the efficiency of therapeutic activity.

8. *If we consider that a continuum exists from superficial to deep psychotherapy, where would you place your own case?*

In conventional terms, the treatment of this patient constitutes depth therapy. However, I do believe that there is some fallacy in drawing too sharp a distinction between superficial and depth levels of therapeutic contact with the patient. In my view, psychotherapy is not easily pigeonholed in these presumed terms of difference, as between superficial and deep psychotherapy. A really rigorous and skillful form of psychotherapy requires that the therapist accord equal respect to all levels of the patient's experience, surface and deep, in accordance with an understanding of the patient's needs and conflicts.

9. *What did you think about the outcome of this case and what criteria did you use for evaluating such outcome?*

The patient is still in therapy but the results so far have been exceedingly good. The outcome of therapy is judged in a variety of ways: by the diminution of anxiety, by the increased emotional flexibility of the patient's behavior, by the increased satisfaction of the patient in his activities in life, by his objective performance in various social roles, and by the change in quality of his relations with family, friends, and the wider community.

10. *How do you terminate psychotherapy?*

Decision as to termination of psychotherapy is reached jointly between the patient and therapist. It is not an arbitrary decision in any sense. There is no sharp end point. It is a flexible judgment arrived at in a shared way and is influenced by a number of overlapping considerations. These are the following: the disappearance or diminution of symptoms, the easing of pathogenic foci of conflict and anxiety, a shift of defenses against anxiety toward greater flexibility and health, positive growth of personality with an increased freedom of choice in life, and greater range of adaptability to social role requirements. Improvement at these various levels is tested in terms of the degree of competence the patient shows in his life roles, the change in the quality of his social relations, and the shift in values which joins the satisfaction of the patient's needs with the welfare of other persons. Of special importance is the evaluation of the improvement of the patient's relations with his own family.

PART TWO— *Psychotherapy of the Adult*

CHAPTER 4

Recollections of a Psychoanalytic Psychotherapy: The Case of "Prisoner 'K.'"

—THOMAS S. SZASZ[1]

Psychoanalysis is not, in my opinion, in a position to create a *Weltanschauung* of its own. It has no need to do so, for it is a branch of science, and can subscribe to the scientific *Weltanschauung*.

—S. Freud[2]

I have assumed . . . that psychoanalysis is not a specialized branch of medicine. I cannot see how it is possible to dispute this.

—S. Freud[3]

---

[1] A.B. with Honors in Physics, U. of Cincinnati, 1941; M.D., Coll. of Med., U. of Cincinnati, '44; Interne, Fourth Medical Serv. (Harvard), Boston City Hosp., '44-'45; Asst. Res. in Med., Cincinnati Gen. Hosp., '45-'46; Asst. Res. in Psychiat., U. of Chicago Clinics, '46-'47; Train. and Resear. Fellow, Chicago Inst. for Psychoanal., '48; Vol. Asst. Res. in Psychiat., U. of Chicago Clinics, '48 (six months); Vol. Fellow, Inst. for Juvenile Resear., '48 (six months); Resear. Asst., Chicago Inst. for Psychoanal., '49-'50; Cert., Chicago Inst. for Psychoanal., '50; Staff Member, Chicago Inst. for Psychoanalysis, '51-'56; Certif. in Psychiat., Amer. Bd. of Psychiat. and Neurol., '51; Lect., Elgin State Hosp., '52-'54; Lieut. to Commander, U.S.N.R., U. S. Naval Hosp., Bethesda, Md., '54-'56; Prof. of Psychiat., State U. of N. Y., Upstate Med. Cent., Syracuse, '56— ; Consult., V. A. Hosp., Syracuse '56— ; Syracuse Psychiat. Hosp. '56— ; Marcy State Hosp. '56— ; Member of the Editorial Bd. of *J. of Nervous and Mental Disease*. Fellow: Amer. Psychiat. Assoc.; Member: Amer. Psychoanal. Assoc., Internat. Psychoanal. Assoc., Chicago Psychoanal. Soc., Amer. Psychosomatic Soc., AAAS, AMA, N. Y. State Med. Soc., Amer. Assoc. of Univ. Professors.

[2] S. Freud, *New Introductory Lectures on Psycho-Analysis* (New York: W. W. Norton & Co., Inc., 1933), p. 248.

[3] S. Freud, "Postscript to a Discussion on Lay Analysis," in *Collected Papers*, Vol. V (London: Hogarth Press, 1950), 207.

On the Presentation of Psychoanalytic Treatment

Some Historical Considerations

To present the treatment process in the form of a complete account of the interaction of analyst and patient has been a keenly felt need ever since psychoanalysis became a distinct form of psychotherapeutic intervention. And yet no such account exists. Nor do I think it can be written. Freud[4] said this much and regretfully likened the task of describing the technique of psychoanalysis to that of chess. Relying on this analogy, he thought that the most that could be done was to describe a few typical opening and closing "games"—and that the remainder would have to be learned in the course of one's work. In accordance with this thesis, the psychoanalytic literature contains only technical "rules" pertaining to the beginning and end phases of treatment. These are generally formulated in terms of technical maneuvers, such as the use of the couch, free association, the frequency of interviews, and other methods used in the beginning phase, or in terms of ideal abstractions, such as resolution of the transference neurosis or the "new beginning" used at the end of the treatment. Rarely, if ever, are these notions illustrated by case material. What sort of psychoanalytic case material is there? In an overview of roughly a half-century of psychoanalysis, two types of material may be distinguished. First, there are excerpts of individual historical material, presented to document a particular thesis concerning the patient's "psychopathology," its origin, its cause, and its "meaning." Second, there are accounts in which excerpts from clinical material are used to illustrate certain "therapeutic interventions" which resulted in what was judged to be "improvement." Many psychoanalytic contributions contain both types of material. This differentiation has been offered for purposes of clarification, and specifically to call attention to the prevalent *aims* motivating these reports. Breuer and Freud's original case reports in *Studies on Hysteria*[5] offer a classic example of a work whose purpose was *both* to advance the thesis that historical events act as pathogenic agents and to show the efficacy of catharsis as a form of "therapy." Most of Freud's subsequent case histories are aimed primarily—sometimes solely (as in the Schreber case[6])—at presenting "psychopathology." Its medical counterpart,

---

[4] S. Freud, "Further Recommendations in the Technique of Psycho-Analysis: On Beginning the Treatment; The Question of the First Communication; The Dynamics of the Cure," in *Collected Papers*, Vol. II (London: Hogarth Press, 1948), 342-65.

[5] J. Breuer and S. Freud, *Studies on Hysteria* (New York: Basic Books, Inc., 1957).

[6] S. Freud, "Psycho-Analytic Notes upon an Autobiographical Account of a Case of Paranoia (Dementia Paranoides)," in *Collected Papers*, Vol. III (London: Hogarth Press, 1948), pp. 387-470.

if any, would be an autopsy report. Turning now to more recent psychoanalytic contributions, it can be said that these generally have the same sort of goal as that which governed Breuer and Freud's original work —namely, to present evidence of a particular "conflict" or "disorder" and to describe how a specific therapeutic intervention resulted in an amelioration of it. To my knowledge, there is only one report of an "entire psychoanalysis."[7] and it surely fails (in my opinion at least) to convey very much about the distinctive features of this form of psychotherapy. Instead, it, too, focused on exposing "psychopathology" and the nature of the "cure."

These considerations are mentioned to highlight the difference in emphasis which I propose to place in my presentation. I shall focus, in conformity with the general aims of this volume, on the nature of the *therapeutic relationship*. The material which I shall present is intended to convey a picture of the human relationship which existed between a particular patient and myself—how it began, developed, and ended. The fact that the patient had certain "troubles" which caused him to initiate his contact with me is, of course, a part of the social reality within which our relationship developed. This, together with his (and my) expectation that we would be able to minimize his "troubles" as a result of our interaction with each other, is taken as the general socio-psychological matrix within which we worked. Beyond this, however, I have found that considerations of "sickness" and "health" do not enhance clarity of thought in this area and I have made an effort in this exposition, much as I do in my practical work, to avoid slipping into clichés borrowed from the medical model of treatment.

Selection of Material and Method

It is well known that the publication of case material obtained in psychotherapeutic practice presents certain difficulties. Most important among these are the need to preserve the patient's anonymity and the need for discretion in the way of self-disclosure on the therapist's part. In attempting to organize a presentation of my own style of working with patients, I encountered some additional problems. First, the matter of anonymity posed a special problem because a relatively large proportion of my patients have been professional men and women, many of them physicians. This, of course, is true for the practice of many analysts nowadays. I mention it because it necessitated the exclusion of the majority of my patients from among those whose treatment, no matter how disguised, I wished to consider for presentation. The next problem, also a typical one for psychoanalysis, was that I kept no notes about my work with patients! In other

---

[7] C. Berg, *Deep Analysis, The Clinical Study of an Individual Case* (New York: W. W. Norton & Co., Inc., 1947).

words, I have no record that would bring to mind the specific sequential patterns so characteristic of the analytic process. I write an occasional note after an interview, and sometimes even during one, but these usually have more to do with my current interests than with any special therapeutic relevance of the event or thought.

In view of these circumstances, the account which follows is based very largely on my *recollections*. Moreover, in order further to insure the patient's anonymity, I have selected the therapy of a man who first came to see me nearly a decade ago. We saw each other for two and a half years and have had no contact since then. Accordingly, my memory is not exactly fresh concerning many of the details of this treatment. It is worth noting, also, that my style of working has changed somewhat during the intervening years. This, I think, is an unavoidable occurrence in the life of every therapist, reflecting as it does not only his own learning of his "trade" (if indeed such learning has occurred) but also changes in his personal life, meaning thereby both his external and internal object relationships. Against these difficulties which stand in the way of reproducing a relatively accurate account of this therapeutic relationship, there stand two factors which have helped to recapture it. First, I made and saved a few notes concerning various aspects of the patient's chief "symptoms" and their communicational meanings as these emerged in the course of the treatment. Secondly, I found that in the course of preparing this report, I was able to recall a large number of events.

From what I have said, it should be evident that the therapeutic experience which I shall describe is not offered as a typical—or *ideal*—sample of what "psychoanalysis" is, or ought to be. It is presented rather as an account of a particular instance or example of "psychoanalytic psychotherapy."[8] Various features of this patient's personality and some of the circumstances of the therapy have made for some differences between this treatment and what could be regarded as the *theoretical model of psychoanalysis*. I might add, however, that I consider the "ideal psychoanalytic model of treatment" as something analogous to the "ideal gas" of physics. That is to say, it is a theoretical model which helps us to conceptualize a process and thus serves as a *guide* in our daily work. The laws governing the behavior of "ideal gases" provide an abbreviated description of the

---

[8] The term "psychoanalysis," as I use it here, refers to a *category* of psychotherapy based on certain principles and utilizing specific methods. The patient whose treatment I shall describe fell into that group which nowadays is designated as the "borderline case." Since such patients do not develop "transference neuroses" (which is not to say that they do not develop "transferences"), their treatment, properly should not be designated as "psychoanalysis." It is principally for this reason that in referring to my relationship with my patient, I shall speak of it as "psychoanalytic psychotherapy." Inquiry into the similarities and differences between this form of treatment and psychoanalysis proper is, of course, not within the scope of this presentation.

behavior of vaporized substances under very special conditions. The fact that these special conditions cannot usually be reproduced does not deprive this model from a great measure of usefulness under conditions which only approximate those of an "ideal gas." Similarly, while we strive to approximate the model of the "ideal analysis" as far as the patient's condition and our own knowledge and ability permit, we realize that it is something of a rarity.

The nature of psychoanalysis as "treatment" lends itself more readily to a theoretical than to a clinical description and I have presented my views on this subject elsewhere.[9] To illustrate these principles by means of clinical material, it would be necessary—at the very least—to recapture the sequential evolution of an analytic relationship. As I have mentioned, I had never attempted to do this. And I doubt whether it could be done. Others, perhaps, may try it some day. There is considerable interest in this general subject at present and numerous "research projects" have been designed to record the analytic relationship in a form which will make it available to others for examination and study. It has become fashionable to sound-record psychiatric (and even so-called psychoanalytic) interviews and attempts are being made to both sound-record and film an entire "analysis." I think these devices, by means of which investigators seek to convert the privacy of the analytic relationship into "public data,"[10] miss the very problem which concerns us here and thereby distract attention from its eventual clarification.

Without entering into the complexities of this issue, I wish to make my point of view clear. I consider the analytic relationship to be a *private* matter between the two participating persons. This is what is meant by a two-person situation. No one else can enter into it or share it. It is similar, in this regard, to other significant human relationships, though in certain ways it is different from any of them. I would therefore compare the *analytic relationship* to the relationship with one's mother, father, brother, wife, friend, and so forth. None of these could be captured, so to speak, for public examination by, for instance, recording everything that went on between the participants. An even simpler, and therefore better, example of the privacy of this type of data is the relationship between a spectator and the Rembrandt masterpiece he is contemplating. His experience of *beauty* can in no way (that we know about) be recorded. It is a private matter between him and his object. There is, however, a relatively simple means by which we can gain access to this material, namely, by communicating with him. Accordingly, if we wish to learn about a human relation-

9 T. S. Szasz, "On the Theory of Psycho-Analytic Treatment," *Int. J. of Psycho-Anal.*, 38 (1957), 166-82; and "On the Experiences of the Analyst in the Psychoanalytic Situation," *J. of the Amer. Psychoanal. Assoc.*, 4 (1956), 197-223.

10 B. Russell, *Human Knowledge: Its Scope and Limits* (New York: Simon & Schuster, Inc., 1948).

ship, we must communicate with the participants in it.[11] When we ourselves are the participant in a relationship, we are in a position to disclose certain things about it to others. It seems to me that what we are not prepared to reveal, others will have a difficult time finding out. In other words, what analysts or other psychotherapists withhold concerning their activities with patients, cameras and sound-recorders may not succeed in uncovering. True, it may be possible to disclose with this technique some happenings not otherwise "admitted," but the alteration of the privacy of the two-person situation complicates our task to such an extent that there is reason for grave doubts about where this method will lead us.

The most accurate method of rendering human relationships "public" is, of course, that of the *novelist*. Indeed, we regard it as his distinctive task to portray *human relationships from the inside, as it were*. Clearly, it is easier, psychologically, to do this with hypothetical people than with real ones, particularly when the "real person" is oneself. Nevertheless, some biographies, and also a few autobiographies, do manage to convey the human drama which is their subject with amazing fidelity. Viewed in this light, recounting the story of an analysis *in toto* would call for the skills of a novelist and a book the length of a sizable novel. Moreover, if the widest possible coverage of this interpersonal relationship were desired, it would be necessary to obtain descriptions of the interaction from both participants: analyst and patient. Attempts of this sort, while not without difficulties, would offer more promise, in my opinion, than recordings or other attempts at pseudo-objectification of analysis. Short of such novelistic efforts, which require gigantic investments of interest and knowledge,[12] analysts can contribute to the task of making their work available to others by the publication of fragments of analyses and by descriptions of the essential features of their work. It is my hope that the following fragmentary account of my work with a patient will furnish a glimpse into what is otherwise a private, or two-person situation.

The Unfolding of the Therapeutic Relationship and of the Patient's History and Personal Identity in It

> Someone must have been telling lies about Joseph K., for without having done anything wrong he was arrested one fine morning.
>
> —Franz Kafka[13]

In searching for a pseudonym for my patient, it occurred to me to call

---

[11] For a more detailed exposition of my views concerning the need to distinguish between private and public data in psychology, and the role of psychoanalysis in bridging the gap between them, see T. S. Szasz, *Pain and Pleasure, A Study of Bodily Feelings* (New York: Basic Books, Inc., 1957).

[12] E. Jones, *The Life and Work of Sigmund Freud*, Vols. I-III (New York: Basic Books, Inc., 1953, 1955, 1957).

[13] F. Kafka, *The Trial* (New York: Alfred A. Knopf, Inc., 1948), p. 3.

him simply "K.," the designation which Franz Kafka used for his hero in *The Castle* and *The Trial*.[14] The theme of these novels revolves around Kafka's struggles with his introjected objects, mainly his parents. "K.," the protagonist, represents, without much doubt, the author himself. With great artistic skill, Kafka conveyed his feelings of being guilty of some wrong-doing, his pervasive sense of "being at fault," and of futility and impending doom. The similarity of his personal tribulations and feelings and my patient's occurred to me during the treatment and we discussed it on many occasions. It thus seems logical now to call my patient "K." and specifically to direct the reader's attention to the many significant similarities between the hero of *The Castle* and *The Trial* on the one hand, and my patient on the other. In Kafka's case we know,[15] too, how he had tried to heal himself, so to speak, through an unusual kind of love relationship, his adoption of fanatical Zionism as a "cause," and last but not least through his artistic creativity—and how all these had failed to do more than temporarily stave off his tragic demise. My efforts to interpose psychoanalytic influence in an attempt to alter and ameliorate my patient's similar drift toward tragedy and doom may be viewed in the light of this background. Yet, we cannot ascertain from the later developments of my patient how effective or ineffective my efforts were, for I have had no contact with him, nor any news about him, since our last meeting. It was not my intent, however, to relate an historical account of a patient and his subsequent life, and so I ask the reader to be satisfied with the material at my command.

Beginning of the Treatment

"K." was a man of mature years engaged in a complicated profession for which he had undergone prolonged training and preparation. His intelligence was superior, his appearance was pleasant, and his interest in helping himself through analysis, once he embarked upon it, was both earnest and persistent. He was unmarried and had practically no friends. Although he was veritably alone, he did not feel lonely. He was friendly, and had many superficial personal relationships, all of them harmonious. He held himself back, almost consciously, however, from any personal involvements. His main interest was his work. Much attention, of course, had to be paid to keeping himself uninvolved in various human relationships for which opportunities constantly arose. This feature of his personality, that is, his single-minded *defense against new object relationships,* became evident as he described himself during the first several interviews, and it was an important reason why he had not sought psychoanalytic help ear-

14 F. Kafka, *The Castle* (New York: Alfred A. Knopf, Inc., 1930); and footnote 13.
15 M. Brod, *Franz Kafka, A Biography* (New York: Schocken Books, 1947).

lier. For many years he had had conscious thoughts about seeking treatment, vaguely desired it, but never did anything about it. He was, of
course, painfully aware of his dangerous symptom: exhibitionism, but
sought to "control" it by himself. When questioned about his reluctance
to seek therapy earlier, he was puzzled and could give no explanation for
it. It was as if something—an invisible hand—had held him back, much as
he was held back from any and all human relationships which required a
measure of psychological commitment on his part.

It seemed to me that the manner in which he finally entered into the
therapeutic situation had something to do with the pattern sketched above.
This impression grew and gained support from various historical determinants as the story of his life unfolded.

The specific circumstances under which "K." began treatment follow. He
was arrested by the police for "indecent exposure." As soon as he came
before the judge for this offense, it was suggested to him that, if he were
to seek psychiatric help, charges would be held pending, and would perhaps be dismissed later. He seized upon this opportunity to seek psychotherapy. Nor was this particular outcome of his arrest surprising to him.
Rather, it was as if he had expected it. Accordingly, there existed the
possibility that his arrest was largely self-determined and had certain *pur-
posive aspects*. Among these, its meaning as a desperate, yet disguised,
cry for help seemed immediately apparent and relevant. This conjecture
was supported by the fact that the patient had had the impulse to exhibit
himself for many years, and had done so on rare occasions, but had never
been apprehended for it.

I might note, in this connection, that much of the therapy was concerned
with filling in all of the minute details of his exhibitionism, meaning
thereby its antecedents, his thoughts and affects at the time and thereafter,
the effects on others and himself, and so forth. This should not imply that
this was the main focus of our work, or that he was directed to concentrate his attention on this topic. Nor does it mean that this was done with a
"cathartic" aim, that is, that by verbalizing as much as possible about this
symptom and its probable determinants, he was to be "cured" of it. Instead
of these points of view, the one by which I was governed, and to which I
still adhere in my work, was that a full view of this area of his life, and of
many other areas, help both the patient and me to see what sort of person
he is. The unfolding of the "history" is therefore regarded as the process
by which the patient's "identity" comes into focus in "the open," where
both he and I can look at it. This, in turn, is done as a prerequisite for seeing how he has lived and how he continues to conduct himself. In the light
of this knowledge, and armed by it, the patient achieves a measure of
mastery and control over his previously unconscious object relationships.
He is then in a better position to decide *for himself* how he wants to alter
his own "identity," partly by altering his own internal objects ("working

through"), and partly by a more conscious, and if necessary cautious, selection of his external object relationships. This digression is offered here to explain why much of the material that follows is in the nature of socio-historical data about this patient. I shall intersperse comments concerning certain therapeutic activities on my part and observations relevant to the analytic situation proper. This mode of presentation obviously will not recreate the continuity of the original therapeutic process, nor is it intended to achieve that goal. It is hoped, rather, that it will recapture the continuity of a recollection which, after all, is the source of this account.

In the initial period of my acquaintance with "K.," he was mortified by shame because of his symptom. He also felt humiliated and "dirty." He went to some lengths to reassure me that his desire for "help" was genuine and not motivated solely by the legal compulsion to undertake it. There then began the self-disclosure which characterizes the early phases of most analyses: the endless details concerning parental behavior, homes, meals, schools attended, exploits and frustrations, and so forth. Other "symptoms" were mentioned. He was afraid of "homosexuality." Why was he not married? He had no interest in marriage and could not imagine himself with a wife and children. He had sexual interest in prostitutes. Occasionally he befriended these girls and then had a remote kind of personal and sexual relationship with them. The girls looked upon him as a friend and he did not pay them, although he knew that they had other partners who did.

He formerly had a speech impediment ("stuttering"). It had begun at about puberty, and it had been most pronounced when he spoke to his parents. I saw no sign of it. Nor had he any trouble in speaking to others at this time. Later, when I became an object of more importance and one with whom he had conflicts, this symptom reappeared in the therapeutic situation.

He had a fear of venereal disease, particularly syphilis, but he believed that he could control this fear. His main sexual activity was masturbation, which he regarded as "very infantile," words he used to mean that it was "bad." He regarded the urge to masturbate as "compulsive" because he could not stop it. Gradually, there emerged a picture of himself as a "growing kid."

His parents did not really take him seriously. They were ever "helpful," "interested," and "kind"—but this was their role in the real-life play in which they were acting. The parents acted the roles of "good," solicitous, mature "adults"; the patient's role was that of the failing son. He was an only child. Early in life he found his life-role in the family defined for him in the Kafkaesque style to which I referred earlier. Both parents were intelligent and highly educated. Their education, however, was a symbol and substitute for achievement in other areas. According to the patient's account, they were deeply unfulfilled. Their ambitions to do creative work were never achieved. They rationalized their failings with near-psychotic fictions: past illnesses which required physical care at the expense of intensive effort, social non-recognition, ill luck, and last but not least, their need to sacrifice themselves for their son's upbringing. In accordance with these parental needs, "K.'s" childhood development took a particular turn. He developed an inner sense of two separate identities, or perhaps, two trends toward separate roles. One role was complementary to his parents' —mostly his mother's—behavior toward him. This necessitated perseverance with good behavior and important adult achievements as goals toward which he should strive but never reach. Illustrative of this pattern is the following episode which occurred when the patient was in his thirties. Following his participation in an event which was socially regarded as an achievement, his mother inquired whether he was sorry that he had not pursued another activity which he had abandoned long ago. While his mother knew about his current achievement, she behaved as though she were totally unaware of it. And, in fact, there was good reason to assume that this was not an "act" in the sense of a deliberately contrived performance, but rather that it reflected the mother's thorough-going repression or denial of these events.

The other direction in which his feeling of self (or identity) developed was much less clear-cut. There was merely a very vague and uncertain feeling that the "self" described above, which was the dominant and consciously experienced one, was somehow not all that there was to him. This "inner self" was merely a minute fragment of his total personality, a fragment that was kept uncontaminated by his parents. It was formed on the basis of his identifications with others—a sensible cousin here, a friend's criticism of his mother there, and so forth—and could be regarded as a vestige of his "unmodified ego." There was, finally, an element of the well-known split of the ego into observing and experiencing portions (or aspects) which was reflected in these two "identities." The bad, guilty, Kafkaesque self was the experiencing and acting "K."; his "inner self," though mostly absent, was sometimes the observer, disassociated from the behavior it saw.

The first several months of the treatment led to the unfolding of the patient's picture of himself as a terribly disordered, "cursed" individual. Father used to say, sarcastically, that he was a carbon copy of his mother. What did this mean? It meant, chiefly, that the patient was terribly mentally disturbed, as the father (correctly) considered the mother to be. It also meant that father disapproved of him. Since the father was weak and helpless vis-à-vis his wife, he could express his dissatisfactions with her only by using his son as a substitute victim. And, of course, it meant many other things pertinent to the family homeostasis which was maintained by the particular ways in which father, mother, and "K." related to each other. The quintessence of this family's image of itself was that the mother had to think of herself as a supremely successful "mother" and "wife."

This was to be her solace for all her frustrations in life, which included the loss of her own mother (i.e., "K.'s" maternal grandmother) early in life and other terrible blows from which she never recovered. Indeed, her solution seemed to be, at least after her marriage, to make no *effort* to meet problems and come to grips with them. Instead, she would overcome all obstacles through make-believe maneuvers. In these tragi-comic substitute-masteries she was supported by her husband, and later by "K." Only after a considerable length of time in therapy were various pieces of this picture of "K.'s" mother illuminated by his recollections. Mother had innumerable personal peculiarities related to eating, family relationships, social events, and so forth. These were confined, for the most part, within her own household, and thus never led to social or psychiatric complications, so to speak. Yet they were evident enough, so much so that several of the patient's more distant relatives had stated unequivocally that she was "crazy." Many would refuse to visit in her house. Yet the patient had had to repress and deny these perceptions of his mother. The reasons that he had to repudiate this threatening "reality" and thereby falsify his own sense of himself and of everything about him were basically twofold. First, as long as he lived at home, in the role of a child dependent on his parents, he obviously could not admit to himself that his life was in the hands of such unreliable and, indeed, partly malevolent persons. Fairbairn[16] has aptly compared this problem of the child to the religious dichotomy of God and devil. It is safer for man (child) to believe that he himself is bad, or that he is possessed by the devil but with a benevolent God's care assured for his needs than to contemplate a world governed by the devil. The introjection of the parent's "badness" is a typical solution of this psychological dilemma. "K." had been exposed to precisely this type of trauma, one that probably is not at all uncommon and plays a particularly important part in personality developments with marked psychotic proclivities.[17] The second reason for the development of "K.'s" view of his parents, and of his whole world, may be said to have originated in the world-view which he had been *taught*. Inasmuch as it is the parents who generally *define* for the child what his environment (human and otherwise) is like, the latter's so-called "distortion of reality" may be considered to stem, partly, from the discrepancy between the grown child's (or "patient's") and the observer's respective "educations."

The World of Internal Objects

"K." related a number of striking incidents in connection with his relationship to his mother, of which I remember only a few. An outstanding

---

16 W. R. D. Fairbairn, *Psychoanalytic Studies of the Personality*. London: Tavistock Publications, Ltd., 1952, Part I, Chapter 3.

17 T. S. Szasz, "A Contribution to the Psychology of Schizophrenia," *A. M. A. Arch. of Neur. and Psychiat.*, 77 (1957), 420-36.

memory of his was of an occurrence when he was about 7 or 8 years old. Shortly after coming home from school one day, something occurred which made him feel very displeased with his mother and he angrily shouted, "I hate you." His mother's response to this was devastating. She acted as though she had literally collapsed, almost as though he had beaten her nearly to death. "K.'s" father had to "explain" later that "K." "really did not mean it" and that he loved her. He himself had to "apologize" and promise that he would never *say* such a thing again as long as he lived. The implication of all this was clear enough. Mother could not be challenged in her concept of herself as someone *always* good and lovable. And, of course, "K." received the impression that he had tremendous power over her, and others, and that he must be careful not to hurt anyone. He dated the beginning of the intense feelings that he was "peculiar," different from others, somehow unalterably "bad," from this event. His stuttering, too, began shortly afterwards and, as I mentioned, was most pronounced when he had to speak with his parents! A related event occurred some time later when his father was said to have suffered a coronary occlusion. However, he never again had any trouble referable to this illness. Indeed, from all that could be learned from the patient's recollections there was considerable doubt about whether this diagnosis was correct, or whether it formed a part of his parents' defensive operations against psychological inroads on them. In any case, from his early adolescence it was impressed upon "K." that he must be very careful in what he *said* and *did,* lest by his actions he hurt his parents. He was thus made to learn certain rules of conduct, based however on principles that were to some extent self-contradictory. These were, briefly, as follows: (1) His parents were all-loving, good, wise, and very powerful. He had to do what they wanted him to do, for they alone knew what was best for him. (2) His parents were also extremely weak and fragile, but this was not to be dwelled upon. Thus his mother could not stand criticism of any sort and his father might die of a heart attack at any time (if he misbehaved). Father also had no control over mother's "peculiarities," but instead of admitting his limitations in this regard, he acted as though there was nothing whatever in her behavior that he disliked. (3) He—"K."—was a little boy full of malicious destructiveness which had to be controlled and disguised by his parents', and his own, educational efforts. These efforts, of course, were destined to fail, but they must at least try their best to inhibit his proclivity toward "badness."

Although "K." had been vaguely aware of many things about the family situation in which he grew up, his adult life, prior to his coming into treatment, was conducted in such a way that he diverted himself from looking straight at these facts, historical as well as current. He regarded the psychotherapeutic situation as his first opportunity to pour out his soul. Yet, he did this with a measure of detachment. It was striking that he always avoided any open criticism of his parents. What he did was to present certain occurrences and then let either the "facts speak for themselves," or, as an alternative, he waited for the analyst to make some comment. It soon became apparent that he was *still* afraid to speak ill of his parents. When this assumption was communicated to him, he agreed. At this point, his speech became noticeably affected and he manifested an irregular stuttering for many months. Outside of his relationship with me, however, his speech remained unaffected.

His fear of hurting his parents was impressive. That he *wished* to hurt them, he knew, of course, but yet he did not do so. It is difficult to describe these psychological events in ordinary English, or any other language, since the logic of our everyday language does not permit the expression of *layerings* (or *"polyvalences"*) *of affects,* and of object relationships, as these actually occur in human relationships. Instead, we can express only a single, *monovalent affect* or relationship in one sentence, and must *follow it* (in temporal and spatial sequence) by another, and then by still another "layer" of the *same relationship.* We should at least be cognizant of this linguistic limitation which is responsible for a great difficulty in correctly describing certain human events. Thus, when we say that someone was conscious of something, we imply that he was *not also* unconscious of some other aspects of this *same thing.* Yet we know that combinations of such states are in fact the rule. Similarly, the concept of "denial" implies fairly total unawareness—yet denial and a certain *kind* of awareness tend to coexist. So much for this problem of the limitations of ordinary language for the scientific description of human affects and relationships.

"K.'s" fear of expressing disapproval of his parents manifested itself in numerous ways. His overt relationship to them was completely "harmonious." He never criticized them, never disagreed with them, and tried always to do what they requested. Yet he held himself aloof and tried to escape from them by placing geographical distance between himself and them. This maneuver was a substitute for any more overt attempt to separate himself from them. He felt, of course, that he could not openly do this, for his parents would regard it as an affront and a reproach indicating that they were not as good as they had thought they were. Then they would get sick and die, and he would be "responsible." Above all, he did not want to be "responsible."

"K." had had a long-standing fantasy which he related during our discussions of his relationship with his parents. It condensed and expressed his problem with them in a striking manner. He imagined himself driving his car, being forced off the street by a truck, and hitting and injuring (killing?) a child. His guilt, even in the fantasy, was intense. Yet, he would tell himself that it was not his fault! *He was forced into this situation.* Then he would tell himself that he could still *not blame* anyone else.

When I connected the fantasy with his relationship with his parents, a connection which he had never been able to make himself, he agreed enthusiastically that this was exactly the difficulty. He could not blame his parents for any wrongdoing. It would be terribly ungrateful to do so, after the way they had stood by him, no matter what he would do. The meaning of this fantasy is, I believe, self-explanatory in the light of what has been said. In this connection, "K." also related a persistent feeling, which he had had ever since his teens and which consisted of *a dread of doing some unalterable wrong*. What the "wrong" would be was vague; nor was it important to him. What was important was, as he put it, ". . . that the memory of the defection will always be there . . . you can never make it up." He was filled with a constant anticipation of being apprehended—for what he did not know. When he was, finally, arrested at least this sense of uncertainty—namely, *for what* he would be arrested—disappeared. The apprehension about being arrested for some wrongdoing persisted, however. Intimately connected with it was the feeling that he was "not guilty." Also there was the notion that he would not be able to convince anyone that he was innocent.

As his relationship with his parents became increasingly clear and explicit, he gradually freed himself of his fears of them. His inhibitions in relation to them also diminished. His own need for his parents, due partly to his continued dependence on them and partly to his essential "objectlessness," was deeply buried beneath his conviction that his parents needed him (which was also true).

*   *   *   *   *

Two important "external" events occurred during the first year of treatment, before—I might add—many of the ramified meanings and functions of his chief symptom, exhibitionism, could be elucidated.

The first was that the patient's probationary period expired. In connection with this topic he developed marked anxieties and extensive fantasies. Outstanding was the fear of the "record" of his misdeed. He felt that this would always hang over him like the sword of Damocles. He would never be able to get rid of this record. How could he ever get married now? How could he pursue his work, and carry on his usual activities? He thought that even if, with the help of treatment, he could rid himself of his exhibitionism, this would, in the end, do him no good. He would be doomed by his "record." Fantasies such as these led to comparisons between himself and Kafka's hero in *The Castle* and *The Trial*. And, in turn, it slowly became possible for him to see that the "record" that sentenced him to everlasting doom was a vision of his parents, as "bad objects," who continued to control him. Only after extensive working through of his relationship to his parents (as internal objects), did it become possible for him to approach the matter of the "record" realistically. It then developed that since his offense was never legally "confirmed," the record of his arrest had been destroyed. We have slipped ahead of our narrative, however. As the end of his probationary period approached, the question of what sort of contact I would have with the legal authorities arose. On the one hand, he wanted me to intercede on his behalf; on the other, he wished, as I believe *all* (adult) patients do, that I should have no contact with anyone in regard to him. He asked what I would do. I told him that my position was (and is) to have no contact with anyone but the patient with whom I work, and I indicated that I thought a stand of non-involvement could be maintained in his case, too. This turned out to be true. When the appointed time came for "K." to speak to the legal authorities again, he appeared on the scene armed with competent legal aid, and succeeded without trouble in having all charges against him dropped. He had, apparently, no difficulty convincing the authorities that he was in treatment with me, for I was never even contacted to confirm this fact.

These events proved—then and during subsequent months—to have been exceedingly important not only "realistically" (as they indeed were) but also in certain symbolic-communicative ways. What I have in mind is this. The "legal problem" had come up, now and again, during the initial months of the analysis. Both of us knew that at the end of the probationary period further legal action would be taken. It seemed likely, of course, that the charges against "K." would simply be dropped, thus ending the legal phase of this matter. But "K." could not convince himself that this was likely to happen. Accordingly, he felt quite outnumbered, so to speak, by the legal forces which he believed were pitted against him, and he sought for an ally in me. I pointed this out to him. We also discussed the possibility that he might engage an attorney if what he wanted was literally an "ally." He continued to speculate, however, about how my testimony on his behalf might be helpful to him. It was my impression at the time, and this became amply confirmed later, that had I consented to his wishes, this would have resulted in a catastrophic situation in the treatment. It probably would have led to the acting out of his exhibitionism and a breakdown of the treatment, since a repetition and re-enactment of the original pathogenic family situation would have been fostered in his relationship to me. For if I had consented to "help him out," and if I had written or spoken to the appropriate people as he wished me to do, telling them that "K." was in treatment with me and doing well, I certainly would have communicated to him the following adventitious messages as well. First, since I had tried to "help" him in this way, it must prove that he was indeed as bad and sinful as he had thought he was; without my help, there was no telling what would have happened. Second, he might have thought, and I believe correctly, that I, as a psychiatrist, was merely an extension of the law-enforcement agencies of society. What would I do in case he again exhibited himself? Would I report it to the police? Would

I continue to treat him? These questions, I might add, never actually arose. I am merely suggesting that they would have arisen had I assumed the "role" of (a) protecting him from the police and (b) protecting society (in collaboration with the police) from him. As it happened, I adhered to the role to which I like to adhere (unless, as rarely happens, I can convince myself that there are other relevant factors which justify a departure from it), namely, trying to help "K." by "analyzing" him. By this term I refer to the process of assisting the patient to acquire as clear a picture of himself and of his human relationships as is possible, thus enabling him *to decide for himself* how he wants to change. If this endeavor is successful, the patient usually finds it possible to implement his wishes effectively, for he is no longer constrained by conflicting goals arising from his unconscious relationships to internal objects.

The second important event, occurring during the first year, was that the treatment was to be interrupted for several weeks during my summer vacation. Prior to this time, the therapeutic work had been "going well" in the sense that "K." had been successful—and without undue anxiety on his part or upheavals in his actual life situation—in consistently enlarging his grasp over the historical and psychological determinants of his relationship with people. The connections between these object relationships and his chief symptoms became progressively clearer. It was during this period, which "K." felt had been so useful to him, that my vacation was to interrupt the therapy. He was, of course, unhappy about it. We discussed the fact that the vacation came in the middle of his treatment and that the interruption was an unpleasant prospect for him. Much of this discussion occurred several weeks before my departure from the city, when I first communicated my vacation plans to him. Then for weeks we went along much as before. On the day of our last meeting until after my vacation, "K." reported a dream. He had relatively few dreams, and dream-analysis occupied only a very small part of our previous work. The dream had occurred the night before this interview. It was a "nightmare," in which he felt horribly anxious, and awoke feeling as though he had been "through a wringer." The dream was simply this: "A crime had been committed . . ." He added that he did not know what the crime was, or who committed it.

Before reporting the dream, "K." began the hour by speaking about his exhibitionism. He reviewed how he had been feeling and concluded that he had felt quite free of any impulses in that direction. But, he added, he wondered whether he was, or could be, "really cured" of exhibitionism. Then he related the dream. Without going into unnecessary details, I will add only one more factor for consideration before commenting on the meaning of the dream. It is simply that it was quite clear to both "K." and me that the treatment was *not* far enough advanced, at this time, to have freed him sufficiently from this symptom. He felt its disappearance depended, in good measure, on the therapeutic relationship, and that it did not yet lie as within himself. I agreed with his appraisal of the situation. We proceeded to discuss this in the light of the following interpretation which I had placed on the dream.

It seemed to me that the dream occurred in response to a seriously threatening disturbance in the therapeutic situation. My departure promised to leave "K." alone, perhaps unable to cope with his "bad" internal objects and/or sexual impulses, which threatened him because of their ego-alien, socially-alien, and self-destructive potentialities. In the dream, and by reporting it to me, "K." had addressed me something as follows: "What will happen to me when you leave . . .? *This* . . . [crime (exhibitionism)] . . . is what might happen! Please do not leave." That this should have been communicated in *dream form*, rather than more directly, was due, I believe, to the fact that the patient's conscious ego, which was in many ways mature and very capable, could not fully endure the thought (1) that he might still be so vulnerable to his internal objects and unconscious impulses, and (2) that he was so dependent on me for help. Thus the dream was viewed as an *indirect communication*, both to himself and to me. To himself, "K." spoke of the danger facing him indirectly—"What crime? By whom?" To me, he spoke of his vulnerability, and hence of my responsibility. "What crime and by whom?" in this connection, may have meant the therapist and his leaving.

All this we discussed. He made no suggestion that I should stay, nor did I offer to change my plans. Clearly, there was a measure of risk either in leaving or in staying. This I did *not* discuss with "K." then, although I think I did, in retrospect, much later in the treatment. What I have in mind is that if I had acknowledged his plea for support and stayed, I would have corroborated his own fear of being unable to control himself. This was, and is, the danger in any therapeutic tendency (in analysis) toward assuming a so-called "protective" role. On the other hand, there was danger also in the course of action which I took. While it tended to convey to him, implicitly, not only that I "trusted" him, but more significantly that I thought he was "safe" enough until my return, it also exposed him to the danger of a recurrence of real-life (i.e., social and legal) difficulties. Let me emphasize that I do not believe the matter of "trusting" the patient was of primary importance here—although many therapists lay stress on it—because our relationship was not based on his having to please me by "behaving properly." Hence there was no issue of either trusting or not trusting him. Our relationship was in no way conditional upon his "good" behavior—except, of course, for the fact that he had to be available to come to my office. It was, therefore, understood that if he were to break any laws and end up in jail, which he had fantasied occasionally, then I could not treat him. It did not seem to me that there was need for me to implement this "condition" of the analysis with "threats" of my own. In fact, to have done so would have been quite foreign to my orientation to this problem. Last but not least, contemplating what effects such behavior on my part would have had on "K.," I could not help but feel that he would have interpreted it as an excessive, and wholly unnecessary, attempt on my part to control him. If he was hypersensitive about anything it was this, and perhaps he made me hypersensitive in turn to his own needs for maximum self-determination compatible with the needs of the task at hand. I might add, however, that it seems to me that most patients who are oriented to treatment by analysis desire to have their self-determination encroached on as little as possible as a result of treatment.

As it turned out, "K.'s" life during the interruption of the treatment was uneventful.

*   *   *   *   *

We continued to deal with the various historical determinants of his self-concept. On occasion he had "obsessive" thoughts, such as "What would happen if I did something *peculiar?*" "Peculiar" meant overt homosexual activity, exhibitionism, and, later, various other anti-social acts. His first thoughts turned to the fear of losing control over himself or his "impulses." By having such thoughts consciously he was also testing himself, showing himself that indeed he was *not* doing any of these things. But why should he? His mother, we learned, showed much interest in his sexual development and, later, in what she fantasied might be his sexual activities. This began with her compulsive attention to where he kept his hands during sleeping, a pattern which dated back as far as "K." could remember. In this case, as in other situations, "K.'s" mother claimed that she was acting on behalf of her son's best interests. He should keep his hands outside the covers, or else he will have the most terrible nightmares. As "K." neared puberty—or perhaps he only noticed it then—he became aware that his parents were exceedingly demonstrative with each other in his presence. They acted like newlyweds. This embarrassed him. In looking back during the analysis, "K." thought this fitted into the pattern of his parents' acting the role of the perfectly mated couple. They were ecstatically happy with each other, and were the perfect parents for him. Accordingly, as "K." became a teen-ager, they were anxious for him to be "maximally normal." Actually, as with themselves, this meant that he should *act* the role of social normality. This role, they were evidently *convinced,* was the proper cover-up for the terrible "abnormalities" that must lie hidden in the deeper recesses of his personality (as they felt was the case with them). "K.'s" parents, and particularly his mother, gave many overt expressions of this morbid preoccupation. She wanted to know if he had girl friends and passionately encouraged his "dating" activities. This lesson, so to speak, was deeply impressed upon "K." and he used to have many dates. He proved to his mother—and, of course, also to himself (the difference was a matter of viewpoint and emphasis)—that he was "normal." This dating-pattern played an important part in triggering off his occasional exhibitionistic acts. Later in his teens, his mother began to speak more openly of her fears that he would become a homosexual. Whenever she read of some sexual crime in the newspapers, she would muse about how terrible it would be (for her, that is!) if her beloved son, "K.," developed such proclivities. She thus treated sexual deviation as some mysterious plague which might be visited upon anyone at any time, but particularly as some divine punishment visited upon parents via the perverted behavior of their grown children. She could, indeed, never learn to regard "K." as a separate human being. She viewed him either as a part of herself, her "bad" self, or else she tended to confuse him with others, mainly her husband (who was still another part of her). She often made slips of the tongue and called "K." by the wrong name. She could never remember the names of any of his friends. These are merely samples of the innumerable recollections which "K." started to have once he was able to look at his mother (and father). He was thus forced to conclude that, at least in her relationship to him, her orientation was an essentially "psychotic" one.

She would say, for example, that if "K." were to become a homosexual, she would kill herself. "K.," of course, became increasingly angry, and somewhat depressed, as he began to realize that these reconstructions of his family life must eventuate in the loss of his parents. In fact, he now had to lose them *twice*. First, he had to lose them as the "good" parents that he imagined them to have been. Second, having revised his ideas about them, and himself, he had to lose them as the "real objects" that they were; for, as he now saw them, he was of course no longer interested in having very much to do with them. The mobilization of this real-life conflict, with which he had never dealt before (as it could not previously have assumed this shape), he attributed, correctly, to the therapy. And he was angry at me for it. Traces of his resentment over this never quite left him—or so it seemed to me. Perhaps this is the sort of phenomenon to which Freud referred when he spoke about the patient having to face, as a result of analysis, the realistic unhappiness of life.

Yet, it never seemed to me that he was really dissatisfied with this turn of events. It was evident, too, that he would have preferred that his symptoms could be removed somehow without the necessity of any changes in his ideas concerning, or behavior toward, any *actual persons*. Thus, he would have preferred to view his exhibitionism, and all sorts of bad impulses in himself, as his very private "badness," due solely to his "innate sins" (due perhaps to "genetics"), which somehow should be removed (as by a surgical operation). He thus desired, at least initially, to be "himself without his badness." The possibility that his "badness" was at once himself and not himself, in the sense of it having been *learned* by his ante-

cedent human relationships, made him feel uncomfortable. He was especially unhappy to assume that his parents affected him as I thought they
perhaps did. For, if they did, they might still do so, and this would neces-
sitate changing his relationship to them. This he still feared. It was in
this connection that once again we could discuss and "work through" his
fears that he might destroy them. His anxiety on this score was, in turn,
nurtured by his repressed rage. Each of these affects and orientations of
his was discussed with him only as he actually experienced them and
complained about them.

Although "K." was a man of mature years, he was peeved at me because
when he felt a need to separate himself from his parents he experienced
what he called a feeling of "disloyalty" toward them. This, among other
things, was a defense against his facing the trauma of separation. He was
torn between feeling "bad and dirty" but secure in his object-relationship
with his parents, on the one hand, and the possibility of acquiring an improved sense of self-esteem together with a measure of at least initial
loneliness and personal insecurity, on the other hand. I pointed this out to
him. His feeling of "disloyalty," however, expressed also his own peculiar
fear of the world, which he shared with his parents. The three of them had
developed a *Weltanschauung* similar to the narcissistic-paranoid orientation of some small nations. This may be paraphrased as follows: "We are a
small group of exceptional people, supremely *loyal* to one another, who are
surrounded and threatened by an alien, inferior, and destructive world."
This self-aggrandizing fiction, of course, is extremely effective as long as
it works. And it tends to work as long as the person directs his chief expectations toward members of the in-group and does not associate with
outsiders. This was still true for "K.," while he was in treatment, and this,
too, was a subject for our discussion. He really had no persons other than
his parents from whom he expected anything, except, that is, me. This
was the main reason, of course, why he listened to me and was in fact so
interested in being involved in "disloyalty" to his parents. In other words,
I offered him something which he could not get from his "own group," in
spite of all of their bragging about their own greatness. The more I could
prove my usefulness to him, the more convinced he became that he did
not need his parents, as he had previously believed.

In this connection we touch on the complex matter of his feelings of
"badness" and how it nevertheless guaranteed an exalted status for him,
at least in the world as he had pictured it. It was necessary, therefore, not
only for him to realize that perhaps he was not as "bad" as he thought he
was, but also that he needed to revise his opinions about the exceptional
and exalted nature of his parents, and indirectly also of himself. This
sounds like a logical contradiction, and in *logic* it would be a contradiction.
Yet, in *psychology* such antithetical beliefs, self-concepts, and affects are

not only non-contradictory, but are in fact common, if not invariable, occurrences.[18]

Thus, behind "K.'s" feelings of worthlessness and sinfulness, there lay an equally intense feeling of self-importance and sense of exceptionalness. In this, too, he showed a great similarity to Kafka's literary hero and, of course, to Kafka himself.

Exhibitionism as an Experience

Let us now return to "K.'s" chief symptom, exhibitionism, and see what we learned about it. Some time after the first few months of treatment, "K." would mention on occasion that he had thought about exhibiting himself. He felt he did not do it now because if he did he would have to tell me, and that would make him unbearably *ashamed*. Incidentally, this attitude also reveals why it seems to me that it is unnecessary for the therapist to take an aggressive stand against the patient's symptom of sexual deviation (as sometimes advocated).[19] Focusing on this particular case, it was obvious to the patient that this was a potentially self-destructive activity. In our relationship, it was taken for granted that we *both* knew this. My therapeutic orientation consisted of *trying to help him to help himself* in his own struggle with his symptom. If the therapist takes a more active stand against the symptom (with an analyzable patient), it seems to me that he encourages certain complications with which it may be extremely difficult to cope later on. Most important among these is the inference which the patient will draw, or which may even be stated explicitly by the therapist—namely, that the therapeutic relationship will be endangered, or will be discontinued, if the patient "disobeys" the therapist. This, I think, tends to make the patient even more phobic about his "impulses" than he already is, and makes facing his appropriate internal objects, and coming to terms with them, increasingly difficult and usually impossible. Symptom-cure may, of course, still be achieved, but it will probably rest on phobic avoidance mechanisms and on unconscious identifications with the therapist as an aggressive-benevolent "parent."[20]

The full details of the circumstances which led up to the exhibitionistic act for which he was arrested emerged only gradually. Much of what follows is a condensation of all that was learned about this symptom during the entire course of the treatment. No attempt will be made to reconstruct the sequence in which various meanings of the exhibitionism emerged since I do not have the records which would be required for

---

[18] T. S. Szasz, *Pain and Pleasure: A Study of Bodily Feelings* (New York: Basic Books, Inc., 1957), Chap. 9.

[19] L. C. Kolb and A. M. Johnson, "Etiology and Therapy of Overt Homosexuality," *Psychoanal. Quart.*, 24 (1955), 506-15.

[20] T. S. Szasz, "The Role of the Counterphobic Mechanism in Addiction," *J. Amer. Psychoan. Assoc.*, 6 (1958), 309-25.

this task. Yet I must note that a sequential portrayal of these events would be very helpful for understanding the therapeutic process.

Exhibitionism is, of course, intimately connected with masturbation. It is generally assumed in psychiatric texts that by exhibitionism it is meant that the patient exhibits his penis *and* that he masturbates at the same time. The further assumption is that the patient gains consciously pleasurable feelings from his "perverted" behavior. Yet, from all that I could learn from "K.," he never felt anything that he could describe as "sexual pleasure" (or any other pleasure) from exhibiting himself. Rather, his conscious experience was that he was under some sort of compulsion to act in this way, and following his overt exhibitionistic acts he would feel relieved of this need. Neither the need nor its satisfaction could, however, be referred to any bodily part. In this regard, as well as in many other of its features, the exhibitionistic behavior bore certain resemblances to patterns of counterphobic mastery, such as are evident in some sports, or in addictions.[21] In simple terms, the crux of the matter seems to be that the patient carries out some bit of behavior that is dangerous, or which is forbidden, and he gains some satisfaction from thus proving both his independence (from whomever it may be) and his success in facing and surviving a dangerous situation.

Most of "K.'s" exhibitionistic behavior was of the following sort. He would lie in bed in the morning and would *feign sleep* while a woman, usually a maid, would try to tidy up his room. He would then uncover himself and handle his penis. He never ejaculated or experienced sexual arousal or orgasm. The exhibitionistic behavior seemed to be rather a *gesture,* that is to say, a *communication* achieved not through the use of words but by means of a body part and its movement. Certain phases of the treatment were chiefly concerned with attempts to make the necessary and correct *translations* from this gestural idiom to the language of everyday English. What was he communicating and to whom by these "abortive" exhibitionistic movements in bed? "K." himself, of course, had never really tried to "understand" this behavior. He took it for granted that it existed and that it was terribly evil, but he tried to think as little as possible about it. He regarded it as a dreadful secret, perhaps like a contemporary American intellectual might regard his past affiliation with a subversive group. The dreaded "thing" was himself, or a part of himself, and yet he felt it was not. He feared, most of all, that "it" would be discovered. It was important to learn, in this connection, that his actual state of mind during exhibitionism was a peculiar one. He was not fully conscious in the sense of his own "normal" waking consciousness. He felt as if he were half-asleep, or sometimes he felt de-realized or depersonalized. In other words, he felt in part like an automaton which was exhibiting *its* penis, and all

---

[21] *Ibid.*

the while another part of him, completely devoid of feeling, was sitting somewhere outside watching what the automaton was doing. Needless to say, all this became clear to "K." only gradually, and only as he made his own exhibitionistic behavior an *object of observation and study.* He had never before done this, nor indeed had it even occurred to him that such a thing could be done.

By feigning sleep while exhibiting himself, he protected himself against the danger of being apprehended. If the cleaning woman did see him, she would think that he was asleep. Hence there would be no untoward consequences. He was further "insured," so to speak, by the uncertainty of whether or not he would be seen. Since he kept his eyes closed most of the time, he did not know if the woman looked in his direction. Actually, at the end of each of these episodes—which occurred quite infrequently, perhaps a few times a year—he never actually knew if he had been seen exhibiting himself or not. On rare occasions he had exhibited himself in a more direct manner, but always with considerable precautions against being apprehended. The episode that lead to his arrest was entirely at variance with his customary exhibitionism. Although the full details must be omitted, it can be stated that it was far more direct; so much so, in fact, that it was practically certain that the woman involved (whom he did not know personally) would summon others with the result that he would be apprehended. It was thus, in part, a gesture *to invite arrest.*

The circumstances which lead to his arrest were briefly these. "K." became involved with a marriageable young woman toward whom he felt his mother was pushing him. This, too, was a repetitive pattern. His mother would "find" girls for him—which he would let her do, although he inwardly objected to it—and he would "go out" with them but try to arrange things so that they would lose interest in him. And all the while he tried to conduct himself in such a way as to not "offend" anyone, especially his mother. It was unthinkable that he should refuse to go out with these girls. After all, he felt, his mother had proved to him that these were "nice girls" and good potential wives. What argument could he have against this? He literally became rooted to the "logic" of his mother's argument and ignored the "logic" of the total situation, and particularly his relationship to his mother. A situation now arose in which he believed his entanglement with a woman was getting out of hand. She was interested in him and for her own personal reasons was desperately eager to get married. This threw "K." into a panic. How was he to extricate himself? What could he tell his mother? What should he say to this woman? There seemed to be no way out—for he was confronted now with the one situation he was least able to handle, namely, to assert himself *openly,* verbally, vis-à-vis an important woman! The difficulty was, indeed, doubled, for he was confronted by *two women* who demanded that he do something which he felt he could not do. He felt powerless. Yet to pursue further the relationship with this woman seemed out of the question. He thought that it was certain to lead to marriage, and this was unthinkable. Just before his next date with her he exhibited himself in such a way that he was arrested. He immediately felt relieved from the mounting panic about being pushed into marriage. His arrest would *have* to be made known to his parents. This, of course, would mean that he would not be able to associate further with this woman. He could break with her, deliberately and definitely, once he convinced himself, by his arrest, that he was a "sexual pervert," a "dirty" and unworthy person. Thus he was not "refusing" her something that she wanted, but rather was "protecting" her. This turn of events also made it possible for "K." to promptly seek and begin analytic treatment, something which he had long desired. This, too, he felt he could undertake now without antagonizing, or implicitly criticizing, his parents.

Exhibitionism as a Communication

Certain communicative implications or meanings of his exhibitionism were brought to the fore in the very first interview. Having related that he had "exhibited himself" (I did not know *exactly* what he meant by this), and that he had been arrested, he added that *of course* he would now be *forced* to tell his parents about this. It was evident that at least one part of him—the part that felt "good" and "clean"—did not want to do this. In accordance with his conscious wishes he had kept everything concerning his sexual life a secret from his parents until this time. It did not seem to me that there was any obvious reason to communicate to them *now* anything which caused him to feel ashamed, any more than there had been before, and I told him so. He was taken aback by this. It did not seem *possible* to him *not* to tell them about this catastrophe. It is important to note that while "K." was generally able to entertain multiple possibilities and have rational doubts about various courses of action, in this instance only one course of action seemed open to him. And that was to tell his parents what happened. His feeling about breaking off with the woman whom his mother wanted him to marry was similarly single-minded. That is to say, it had not occurred to him that he might *still* marry her. This, of course, immediately suggested that the sexual act (and probably the arrest, as well) had been intended, in part, as a communication to his parents, particularly his mother. Ample evidence appeared later to support this assumption, and I shall present it shortly. Before doing so, however, I must note here that raising the question of the necessity for communicating with his parents, which I did in the first hour, proved to be quite a significant event. As it happened, he never again communicated anything he regarded as shameful to them, a behavior pattern in which he had engaged and for which he "hated himself." Calling his attention to this proved to be significant for two interrelated reasons. First, it made him aware that he did not wish to shame himself before them but that he felt this was expected of him. Second, it made him aware of an internal struggle between feelings of "badness" and unworthiness on the one hand, and a self-image of, and striving for, "goodness" and decency on the other hand. By not communicating with his parents, he felt later on, he saved himself another actual event that he would have listed on the debit side of his character.

Numerous facets of the communicative meanings of his exhibitionism were touched on in the course of the treatment. In a general way, the dominant meaning and determinant of this act was that *it was a covert sign of rebellion against—and self-assertion from—his parents.* He regarded himself as imprisoned and viewed his parents as omnipresent wardens. During his adult years, when he lived in cities at a distance from his parents, "K." still felt "imprisoned" by them. They were now his internal objects and manifested their presence by constantly reminding him, by means of self-accusations and feelings of shame and guilt, that they stood over him, as they had done before, and that they continued to condemn him. This was the single most dominant theme of "K.'s" self-experience. I commented on this earlier when I remarked on the similarities between "K.'s" dominant self-experience and object relationships on the one hand, and those of "Joseph K.," the hero of two of Kafka's novels, on the other. Hence, the sub-title of my presentation: *The Case of Prisoner "K."*

I have already commented on some of the reasons *why* "K." developed such an intense feeling of *being controlled* by his parents. Determinants of his efforts to establish self-control (to "rebel") in the specific ways he did were as follows:

1. His mother's monomaniacal preoccupation with his masturbation, that is, his touching his penis. In exhibiting himself he did *precisely* what his mother most stringently prohibited. Hence it had the special *symbolic value* of signifying his independence from her. In terms of its deepest unconscious meanings, this symptom (exhibitionism) further signified killing his mother (and father). And his strong fears and defenses against exhibiting himself derived, in part, from his wish to protect himself against committing this symbolic homicide.

2. A curious event occurred at about the age of eight, when he was actually asked to "exhibit himself," so to speak. What happened was this: While playing with a little girl, he was "accidentally" kicked in the genital area by her. He experienced considerable pain and the adults in charge feared that he was injured. A female relative and the little girl's mother insisted that he show them "where it hurt," and this meant showing them his penis. He was extremely embarrassed and ashamed, but finally ac-

ceded. He did not know why he gave in. Perhaps because they persuaded him, or because he was afraid that he was hurt, or perhaps for other reasons. There was, however, no significant physical injury. After this experience he developed a *secondary shame and embarrassment* over having been embarrassed. He was told "It was all right" to show his genitals, hence, he told himself, he should *not* have felt embarrassed. The memory of this event, and of these affects, was quite fresh; he had never ceased thinking about it. I might add that "K." suffered from nocturnal enuresis until shortly after this incident.

3. His mother's interest—and to a lesser extent his father's too—in his sexual life was revealed clearly in their anxious preoccupation concerning his "sexual normality." At some point well along in his treatment, he recollected the experience of his first ejaculation at about the age of nine or ten. He was masturbating, had an orgasm, and saw some milky fluid exuding from his penis. He felt scared and bewildered. He went into his parents' bedroom and told them that he was *awakened from a bad dream.* He thereupon told his father—and indirectly his mother, who was also present—that he "dreamed" that he was urinating, but that instead of urine "something else" came out. His father "understood" the message correctly, that is, as it was intended, and told the little boy that it was all right and that they would talk about it in the morning. "K." did not remember whether they had talked about it again. What seemed to me especially significant in this incident was, first, that "K." framed his communication to his parents in the *form of a dream,* and second, that it was a clear expression of the need to "confess" his "bad sexuality" to them. The latter was an important feature of his exhibitionism. In this form he communicated and confessed his "bad sexuality" to his parents who were hidden, so to speak, in the anonymous woman to whom he exhibited himself. The communication was addressed to "himself" as well, for his parents continued to reside within him as internal objects.

Telling his parents that he had a dream, when in fact he did not, is an important phenomenon in itself, but I cannot explore its various psychological implications here. Note, however, that by doing this, he accomplished at least two things. First, his communication about his sexual behavior was sufficiently *indirect* so as to assure himself that he could not be blamed for it. Second, he diluted his own sense of "badness" and guilt for what he felt was a reprehensible activity. Not only do others not blame us for what we do in our dreams, but we treat ourselves in a similar manner. This childhood dream-communication was re-enacted in all of its essential details in his habitual exhibitionism while simulating sleep. In his outward behavior, he created the impression that he was asleep; while in his inner experience, he felt depersonalized, that is to say, not "fully awake."

4. During his teens, "K.'s" mother told him how a man had once *exhib-*

ited himself to her in the subway. As he grew older, she also made a point of commenting on the accounts of "sex crimes" in the newspapers, adding that it would "kill her" if "K." ever did anything like that.

5. The exhibitionism was, in a sense, also a communication which originated in one part of himself and was directed to another. Its source was his feeling of doubt about his *sexual identity*. This is to say, was he "his mother" or "his father"? He wanted to be neither. Was he castrated? And so forth. *Seeing and touching his penis at least defined his sexual identity and role as clearly "masculine."* One of the meanings of the exhibitionism could thus be paraphrased as follows: "I am not a woman—I am *not crazy* like my mother."[22]

Termination of the Treatment

In this presentation I have drifted, perhaps unavoidably, far afield in the course of setting forth many of the things which "K." and I discovered in talking with each other. I have said little concerning his "transference neurosis," in the sense of the development of many of the conflicts with me which he had with his parents. The reason for this is partly that "K.'s" relationship to me never became nearly as intense as it did to his parents. A more "full blown" transference neurosis develops with some of my patients. In this case, however, since "K." felt so intensely threatened by being controlled, much of his relationship to me remained on the level of his *fears* of a repetition of this sort of a situation in treatment. He had similar fears concerning marriage. Accordingly, it seemed to me that "K." wished most of all to become less fearful of human entanglements. This could be shown to him, in innumerable forms, in his defenses against the "transference," or more correctly, against trusting me to the point of relinquishing his vigilance for fear that I would misuse my power over him. In view of his personal history and situation, however, it seemed that for "K." this point would constitute precisely the state in which he would not need, and would have no further interest in, psychoanalytic treatment. All this we discussed. As his relationship to me became less guarded, he talked frankly and forthrightly, and displayed a psychologically pene-

---

22 It is not within the scope of this essay to consider all the ramifications—psychological as well as sociological—of the phenomenon of sexual exhibitionism. In conformity with the main theme of this essay, I have presented only those features of this "symptom" which seemed to be relevant to this particular therapeutic process and which were actually utilized in it. Clearly, in addition to various factors in the life of the patient, the therapist's "understanding" of his particular case will also function as a selective determinant in establishing which features of the patient's behavior (in the widest sense of this word) will be brought to the fore. I think this principle is valid for every therapeutic situation. Hence, the accurate portrayal of psychotherapeutic principles and methods ought to tell us a great deal not only about the "psychopathology" of patients (as is commonly assumed), but also about the personality of the therapist, including his social (and ethical) orientations.

trating attitude toward me and himself. At the same time, he longed to be "free" of me and of the treatment. After everything was said and done, he felt, the "therapy," and his very relationship to me signified to him that he had had the problem of "exhibitionism," and it, in turn, signified his "bad" parental objects from whom he wanted increasingly to free himself. His relationship to his parents and others underwent considerable changes. He continued to maintain a superficially friendly contact with his parents, but in reality had almost no relationship with them. And he felt increasingly free of them. He was comfortable with the thought that he would know how to cope with anything which might arise—trying to master in his imagination, for example, how he would conduct himself if his father were to die first, or if his mother died first, and so forth. His sexual behavior also became more comfortable and less "driven." He lost interest in prostitutes and masturbated occasionally with satisfaction and without apparent conflict. Masturbation had meant, among other things, that he had a right to his body, including his penis, and could do as he wanted with it. It was another facet of the all-important matter of "Who controls him?"—is it his mother or father, the analyst (as "real" external or as internal objects)—or himself? Last, but not least, with the extensive "mapping out" of his exhibitionism—its origin and its various meanings, old as well as recent—and the working through of his relationship with his parents and me, his interest in exhibiting himself disappeared. What gratified him even more, however, was that he did not have a *fear* of its recurrence. I mention this specifically because before treatment he could imagine that he would not exhibit himself as a result of therapy, but he could *not imagine* that he would not contemplate and fear its recurrence.

It was at this point in our relationship that the treatment was terminated. This came about primarily in response to his own inclination to discontinue treatment. He felt that he had learned enough about himself and others; and while he felt no interest in a serious relationship with a woman, he could comfortably contemplate such an occurrence and thought that some years hence he might wish to be married. Last, but not least, *he felt free* and enjoyed this feeling immensely. He read more widely, he enjoyed his daily activities more fully, and he was astonished at his freedom from feelings of "sinfulness," "dirtiness," and "badness," which had always plagued him so much. He felt like a decent human being. The main thing which now constrained him was the treatment. We discussed in detail the connection he made between "receiving psychotherapy" and "being sick or sexually abnormal," as if the former state would prove to him the existence of the latter. He willingly scrutinized these, and similar connections, but the wish to discontinue treatment remained unaltered. There was, simply, nothing more that *he* wanted from the treatment, or from his relationship with me. Last but not least, he was putting to a test—or so I thought—whether or not I meant to *control* him, as did his parents before me. In other words, it seemed as though he wanted to see whether he was "really free" in relation to me, and he could prove this in no better way than by ascertaining my reaction to his wish to discontinue the treatment. We discussed this, and also the underlying assumption which continued to linger on, namely that I was a "bad" (persecuting and controlling) object, much like his parents were to him, and that my helpfulness was merely a façade. He could see the relevance of these constructions and could even acknowledge feeling a certain apprehension in relation to me, stemming from the above-mentioned sources. Yet, the fact remained that he felt that, at this time, he could gain more by stopping the treatment than by continuing it. He also felt that my interpretations of his wishes to stop were designed to make him continue. The situation with which I was confronted was simply as if he had said: "Actions speak louder than words." The subject-matter about which he spoke, in terms of this proverbial metaphor, pertained to his self-determination: Could he, or could he not, decide to stop the treatment? He had started it under duress. He was now asking whether he should continue under duress or whether he was free, at least in relation to me. All this we discussed. And we agreed to stop the treatment. It was clear to him that if in the future he wished to learn more about himself and his relationship to people, he could—and would have to—initiate further therapy on his own volition.

Finally, at about this time, an opportunity arose for "K." to engage in an activity closely related to his work which strongly appealed to him. To avail himself of this opportunity, he had to move to another part of the country. He welcomed this turn of events, not only for the "primary" benefits which they afforded, but equally as much for the opportunity to separate himself still further (geographically) from his parents, and from me—and lastly also from the scene of his arrest, which remained, at least while I still saw him, a place where he did not want to live for the remainder of his life. I concurred with "K." that this was an opportune time for us to part. We had now been seeing each other four times a week for thirty months.

Conclusions: Nosology and Psychotherapy

Traditional language always *seems* clear. There seems to be great clarity in such sentences as these: *Heat flows. Life left him. He is possessed of a devil. He has a disease. He has a neurosis.* But, for all their apparent clarity, they are surely all wrong. Their categories are wrong. All of them assert false substantives, when the discussion should be couched in terms of processes.

—G. Hardin[23]

---

[23] G. Hardin, "The Threat of Clarity," *Amer. J. of Psychiat.,* 114 (1957), 392-96. (Reprinted by permission of the American Psychiatric Association.)

Before concluding this account of my efforts to bring a psychoanalytic type of "influence" (a term which I prefer to that of "treatment") to bear on my patient, "K.," I would like to offer some brief comments on "K." as a person and on the treatment process which I described.

I have for some time now been firmly convinced that our contemporary systems of psychiatric nosology[24] are worthless insofar as our interest is to understand the patient, and our aim is to help him by means of psychoanalytic treatment. This does not negate the *usefulness* of a so-called "psychiatric diagnosis" for other purposes, for instance for determining whether or not legal action should be taken toward someone who has violated the law. These two tasks, however, have practically nothing in common. They are combined so often only because the *same persons* (i.e., psychiatrists) have assumed social roles in both therapeutic and legal situations. In accordance with this view, I do not believe that there is such a thing as "psychopathology" independent of a *social situation* in which it is anchored and from which it derives the *values* of "normal" and "pathological." Hence, I would not offer any "diagnosis" to identify the "mental illness" from which "K." could be said to have suffered. Obviously enough, according to present day psychiatric usage, his "illness" would be labelled a "sexual perversion," sometimes more elegantly called a "sexual deviation." Or he might have been simply "diagnosed" as an "exhibitionist." Clearly, none of these designations tells us anything whatsoever about "K." as a human being, what troubled him, and what he was trying to do about it.

In regard to "K.'s" chief "symptom," the exhibitionism, I came to the conclusion on the basis of what I was able to learn from him that there was very little that could be said to have been "sexual" about this behavior. I hasten to add that by "sexual" I refer to an *affect* which is experienced as *erotic feeling* or which can become so by becoming conscious. In this sense of the word "sexual," *exhibitionism proved to be, at least for "K.," a form of non-sexual behavior and communication implemented by means of the (male) genital organ.* The prevalent lay opinion as well as professional (i.e., medical and psychiatric) opinion which views this form of behavior as a "perversion," that is as a particular ("abnormal") form of *sexual experience* and *sexual gratification* stems from confusion in regard to what the experiencing person feels and what the observer of this behavior believes he feels. The manifest genitality of the behavior impresses the observer as a sign of sexual activity, and hence, *by inference,* as a sign of sexual experience (affect). This inference, while usually valid for many forms of sexual activity, is still an inference, and *not* an *equivalence.* "K.'s" exhibitionism was principally an expression of his struggle for "freedom" from

---

[24] T. S. Szasz, "The Problem of Psychiatric Nosology: A Contribution to a Situational Analysis of Psychiatric Operations," *Amer. J. of Psychiat.,* 114 (1957), 405-13.

his oppressive internal (and external) objects. He experienced his need to exhibit himself as a vague and unverbalized tension-state. It was definitely not a form of "sexual tension." The experiencing of sexual tension was an affective state, familiar to him, which he was prone to relieve by masturbation (without exhibitionism) and by sexual intercourse with prostitutes. Since my experience with "K.," several other cases have confirmed my impression that exhibitionism is a form of non-sexual behavior expressed by means of the genital organ. In none of these cases, however, did I know the patient as well as one knows a patient in analysis. In fact, I saw these other patients only for purposes of "diagnosis" during my period of service as a navy psychiatrist. None experienced erotic feelings during the act. And while all of them assumed—in conformity with the prevalent social view—that this was a "sexual deviation," when I asked them directly whether they felt that their exhibitionism was "sexual" they were all nonplussed. The act seemed to have been directed, in each case, toward one or another parent, and, in condensed form, expressed the patient's conflict with this oppressive object (his rebellion against the object, his statement of self-assertion from the object, and his submission to the object through guilt and/or apprehension). The communicative role and significance of this behavior was shown further, in "K.'s" case, by his speech impediment. So much for the psychology of "K.'s" exhibitionism.[25]

Although I indicated my wish to avoid using any of the misleading diagnostic labels currently fashionable, it might be useful to think of "K." as having a "schizoid personality" (or "schizophrenic core"). By this I simply mean that he might be more prone to have a schizophrenic type of "breakdown"—given the proper circumstances for it—than would someone else who had had the good fortune to have better internal objects less controlling, less ambivalent than he had. At the same time, "K.'s" relatively objectless living-pattern, both at the beginning and at the end of this treatment, is something that the word "schizoid" conveys quite well. In this, it stands in contrast to what may be considered as "more healthy" (at least for purposes of having a warm human relationship, though not necessarily for purposes of being a good "worker" or effective political or religious leader)—namely, the ability and proclivity for making lasting commitments to a few significant persons. I mention "K.'s" schizoid personality organization only because it had a bearing on the nature of the therapeutic relationship which evolved between us. It was characterized, as I noted before, by a certain "distance" between us. Instead of an extensive "transference neurosis," his predominant "transference" lay in the fact that in his relationship to me he manifested and experienced the same fears and reservations concerning "getting involved" (in an oppressive situation) as

---

[25] See in this connection M. Schmideberg, "Delinquent Acts of Perversions and Fetishes," *Int. J. of Psycho-Anal.*, 37 (1956), 422-24.

he did in relation to other people. This excessive self-protection derived from his deep conviction that behind various human façades there lurked, in everyone, the sort of person that his parents were to him. He feared re-exposing himself to "bad" (persecuting and controlling) objects. And, of course, we discussed—and I think he was able to see—that he also perceived me in this light. Much of the "analysis of the transference" revolved around this theme. Properly speaking, however, this sort of work should be labeled "analysis of the *defenses against* the transference."

While I believe that this method of therapy was appropriate, even inevitable in this particular situation, I want to emphasize that I think it is important to differentiate this from *other types of transference-analysis*.[26] In people whose schizoid disposition is slight, the analytic process tends to evolve in a somewhat different fashion. Briefly, following analysis of the defenses against the transference (against the fears of a power-dependent relationship, as with one's parents), there appear in the patient's relationship to the analyst, re-enactments of features of his earlier relationship to his parents. This second type of "transference" behavior, and its analysis, was by no means completely absent in my work with "K."; but it was fragmentary and tended to be limited to certain isolated occurrences. This was the reason why I stated at the beginning of this essay that I did not consider this case to be the story of a "typical" analysis. It illustrates, however, many of the things which I consider to be characteristic of the psychoanalytic treatment relationship and process.

Addendum

1. *Optimally, what criteria do you use for accepting or rejecting patients for psychotherapy?*

   I cannot answer this question in this form, since I believe that there are a very large (if not limitless) number of different psychotherapies. Different methods of selection would apply to each. (See in this connection my answer to question 11.) My answer, therefore, applies only to psychoanalysis, and in part perhaps only to a somewhat idealized version of it. My main criteria for *accepting* patients for analysis (the criteria for rejecting can be inferred from the degree to which the prospective patient fails to meet these criteria) are the following:

   (a) The patient should seek therapy because of some disturbance which he feels is his; he should not consult the therapist solely because he is driven to him, in one form or another (as is frequently the case) by others, and he must not request to be analyzed for the sake of others. Instead, he should desire and hope to achieve a *personal goal* of his own.

   (b) He should be at least of average intelligence, and should possess the interest and the ability to *look at himself* and at his relationships (past, present, and future) with people. He may not be able to do this for cultural, religious, and "psychopathological" reasons. These three categories

---

[26] See in this connection T. S. Szasz, "A Contribution to the Psychology of Schizophrenia," *op. cit.*

which overlap are used here mainly descriptively. Illustrative considerations are the following. Does the person value action or contemplation? Does he favor religious group-identity or scientific solitude? And finally, does he tend toward "psychotic" certainty or is he comfortable with "normal-neurotic" doubt?[27] I deliberately exaggerate and dichotomize certain psychological phenomena to make a point. The closer the patient approaches the first position in these paired characteristics, the less likely am I to accept him for psychoanalysis (or analytic psychotherapy).

(c) The patient should be as *free* as possible in his social and economic relationships. (According to this criterion, children are excluded—"by definition," so to speak—from being proper subjects for psychoanalysis. They may be excluded on other grounds as well.)

(d) Diagnostic considerations, in the sense of formal nosological entities, play virtually no part in my selection of patients for psychoanalytic psychotherapy. (See question 2 below.)

2. *Do you make a diagnosis before psychotherapy begins?*

I cannot answer this question without commenting on the word "diagnosis," which I consider to be seriously misleading if used in connection with psychotherapeutic considerations. In other words, if "diagnosis" refers to ascertaining the kind of "psychiatric disease"—such as hysteria, obsessive-compulsive neurosis, schizophrenia, and so forth—the patient "has"— then my answer would be that *I do not make a "diagnosis"* before beginning psychotherapy. If, however, "diagnosis" refers to gaining an impression of the sort of person the patient is, how he grew up, the nature of his personal relationships and his work, the degree of his freedom in the conduct of his life, and so on (see question 1)—then I would answer emphatically "Yes!" *I do make a "diagnosis."*[28]

3. *Do you attempt to persuade the patient or significant relative to change his (the patient's) environment?*

No. I refrain from such measures if I expect to conduct any kind of psychotherapy (including psychoanalysis) designed to help the patient to *learn* more about himself. The avoidance of this and other types of direct influence rests on the premise that if the patient learns more about himself and his human relationships he will be in a position to make his own decisions. If learning on the part of the patient is *not* considered to be the primary goal and function of the psychotherapy, then I would regard giving advice as appropriate.[29]

4. *How did you conceptualize the therapist's role in this case?*

My concept of the therapist's role in this case was that of a particular form of the "analytic role." By this I refer to a distinctive human rela-

---

[27] See in this connection T. S. Szasz, *Pain and Pleasure: A Study of Bodily Feelings,* Chap. 8.

[28] See in this connection, T. S. Szasz, "The Problem of Psychiatric Nosology: A Contribution to a Situational Analysis of Psychiatric Operations," *op. cit.,* and M. H. Hollender and T. S. Szasz, "Normality, Neurosis and Psychosis. Some Observations on the Concepts of Mental Health and Mental Illness," *J. of Nerv, and Ment. Dis.,* in press.

[29] T. S. Szasz, and M. H. Hollender: "A Contribution to the Philosophy of Medicine. The Basic Models of the Doctor-Patient Relationship," *A. M. A. Arch. of Inter. Med.,* 97 (1956), 585-92.

tionship (the analytic situation), and in it to the analyst's endeavor to assist his patient solely by means of interpretive communications. (See question 3 above.)

5. *What aspects of your theory of psychotherapy were particularly apparent or useful in the case presented here?*

I think my thesis that psychoanalytic psychotherapy is a form of *learning* for the patient is apparent in this case. Specifically, the patient learns what sort of a person he is, and how he became what he is. This occurs in and through the analytic relationship, and usually enables the patient to use this relationship (and others) to modify his internal object-world, and hence "himself." To assist in making such self-transformation possible is one of the distinctive functions, in my opinion, of the work of the analyst.[30]

6. *Do you feel that this case developed significant insight? If not, can improvement be maintained?*

For the sake of brevity, I want to say simply "Yes, I think this patient developed insight." (See question 5 above.) But to speak of "insight" without specifying "into what?" is to invite ambiguity.

7. *What aspects of your own cultural orientation facilitated or impeded the treatment of your case?*

I do not think that any particular orientation, beyond that implicit in psychoanalysis itself, played a significant part in the conduct of this treatment. Any method of psychotherapy which undertakes an inquiry into the patient's (and less explicitly into the therapist's) personal relationships, history, values, and so forth, rests on the premise that increased information and knowledge are positive values. This, in turn, rests on the further premise that the person is motivated by the hope of achieving mastery of his problems in relation to internal and external objects with the aid of increasingly complex psychological operations. The values implicit in psychoanalysis—at least as I see them—are thus in covert (sometimes direct) conflict with certain cultural and religious values; specifically, the two are in conflict whenever the latter explicitly declare that certain parts of "reality" must not be made the objects of skeptical inquiry (as some religious and political systems do). Such prohibitions recreate in adult life the various prohibitions which are generally imposed upon children in most civilized societies. In some families, there is a specific prohibition against scrutinizing the parents' activities. This was of particular importance in the case which I presented. Similar prohibitions in the therapeutic situation, particularly on curiosities and doubts concerning the therapist, would tend to recreate the patient's original (childhood) "pathogenic" environment in his adult life.

8. *If we consider that a continuum exists from superficial to deep psychotherapy, where would you place your own case?*

I do not find the words "superficial" and "deep" in connection with psychotherapy at all useful. It seems to me that these words are used only as value judgments of the therapy to which they are applied. Thus, "super-

---

[30] For a more detailed discussion of my views on this subject, see T. S. Szasz, "On the Theory of Psycho-Analytic Treatment," *op. cit.*, and "On the Experiences of the Analyst in the Psychoanalytic Situation. A Contribution to the Theory of Psychoanalytic Treatment," *op. cit.*

ficial" seems to mean "poor" (or make-shift) and "deep" means "good" or "very effective." The distinction rests on, and embodies, the medical model of psychotherapy with "superficial" standing in the same relationship to "deep" as, say, aspirin stands in relation to penicillin in the treatment of pneumonia. This model is misleading. Accordingly, I would not rate my case in these terms.

9. *What did you think about the outcome of this case and what criteria did you use for evaluating such outcome?*

I consider the outcome of this case as satisfactory. My criteria for evaluating the outcome of therapy are multiple and range from the simplest and most concrete (for example, symptom change) all the way to the most abstract and difficult to assess (for example, estimation of what the patient has "learned" about himself and significant others). In this case, there was of course an important change ("improvement") in the chief symptoms (exhibitionism and stuttering). In addition, there were extensive changes in the patient's internal object-world, and concomitantly, there occurred major changes in his relationship to significant external objects (mostly his parents). Last but not least, he appeared to have been able to successfully understand and master some aspects of his relationship to me.[31]

10. *How do you terminate psychotherapy?*

I generally adhere to two principles in regard to terminating psychotherapy. The first principle is that I allow the patient complete freedom to discontinue therapy whenever he wishes. The second principle is more general than the first and consists of making the termination of the therapy itself the object of analytic scrutiny. I thus try to make this a collaborative decision to be arrived at preferably only after extensive considerations of both the advantages and disadvantages that may result from continuing or stopping the treatment. Once I have accepted a patient for psychotherapy, I rarely, if ever, stop treatment as long as the patient wants to continue. If I think continuation is undesirable, I communicate this to the patient, stating my reasons for this recommendation. This has been an infrequent occurrence in my experience, but whenever it has occurred this procedure has proven to be satisfactory. The difficulties often mentioned by contemporary analysts in regard to "weaning" the patient away from analysis (or his allegedly "excessive dependence" upon the analyst) seems to me to stem directly from an unnecessarily authoritative feature of many analytic arrangements. I refer to the fact that it is understood, either overtly or sometimes by hidden innuendo, that the patient *must not* stop the analysis once he has started it without the express consent of the analyst, and preferably only at the latter's suggestion. Thus the patient is made to step from the relative freedom of his pre-analytic state, in which he was at least "free" to decide whether or not he wished to pursue analysis, into what must seem to him as an "analytic bondage." He often adapts to this by the well known maneuver of turning passivity into activity: "If I have to stay, I want to stay . . ." I think it is desirable that the patient should have at least as much freedom in regard to his therapeutic relationship as he had when he (and the therapist) chose to initiate it. If psychotherapy is at all successful, the patient will only be in a *better*

---

[31] See in this connection, T. S. Szasz, "On the Theory of Psycho-Analytic Treatment," *op. cit.*

position (than he had been before) to decide for himself with the assistance of the therapist how long therapy will be profitable to him. And lastly, in case of a serious difference of opinion between patient and therapist about whether or not to stop, it seems to me incompatible with the psychological structure and philosophy of psychoanalysis (and psychoanalytic psychotherapy) for the therapist to try to arrogate to himself the role of making such an important decision as this for his patient.

11. *Other*.

I wish to call attention to what I consider to be a matter of paramount importance in connection with considerations of *psychotherapy*. It is that the word "psychotherapy" denotes a global type of concept and an almost infinite variety of actual therapeutic operations. In this regard, it is comparable to words such as "medicine," "mathematics," or "democracy." If we should ask what these things are, our answers could not be sought in simple definitions, nor even in extensive descriptions and illustrations. Instead, meaningful answers to such questions can only be found by studying and becoming familiar with *entire scientific disciplines*. This is—and must be—as true for psychotherapy as it is for medicine, mathematics, or political history and sociology. The methods of psychotherapy range all the way from hypnosis, giving advice, and "brain-washing" to various highly "democratic" (or equalitarian) forms of patient-therapist collaboration; and even within these collaborative methods, huge differences between different forms of psychological influencing exist, depending upon both the theoretical-scientific grasp of the participants concerning psychological happenings and upon the types of influence which they bring to bear on each other. To think, in the face of these differences, that "psychotherapy" possesses some fundamental unifying features (other, that is, than its obvious difference from physical methods of intervention) is nothing short of indulging in wishful thinking. Its net result is the codification of "psychotherapy" as a naively simplified and concretized "method"—a conception which only hinders progress toward the appreciation of the specific features of individual techniques. I visualize the collection of essays assembled in this volume as a contribution to this important goal.

CHAPTER 5

A Case
of Writer's Cramp

—JOLANDE JACOBI[1]

Two considerations led me to choose this case out of many. The first is that the relatively short duration of the treatment—25 analytical sessions —allows a fairly well-rounded presentation; the second, that it touches upon a number of important facets of the psyche and raises many problems allowing different approaches and viewpoints. This kind of case is also, as far as I know, not very frequent in analytical practice and may engage the interest of the reader on this score.

The Anamnesis

Carl was a German, born in 1910 somewhere near the Lake of Constance. He was thirty-five years old, a Protestant, the younger son of parents who, after the father gave up his business as a butcher, owned a restaurant in a small place not far from Bern. The only other child was a brother, eight years older than Carl; he was a mechanic in another town, was married, had children, and had seemingly been well adjusted through-

---

[1] Professional psychotherapist; lecturer in different areas of psychology in various institutions; member of the Board of Directors of the C. G. Jung-Institute, Zürich; well-known writer; Ph.D. in Psychology, Univ. of Vienna; managing vice-president of Austrian Kulturbund (1928-'38); decorated with *"Ritterkreuz des österreichischen Verdienstordens"* for cultural and scientific work by Austrian Government. Since 1938, residing in Zürich. Further studies and personal analysis with Prof. C. G. Jung. English publications include: *The Psychology of C. G. Jung* (Yale, 1943); *Paracelsus, Selected Writings* (Bollingen, 1951); *Psychological Reflections* (Bollingen, 1953); *Complex, Archetype, Symbol* (Bollingen, 1958), and various articles.

out his life. For many years the two brothers had had virtually no contact with one another, for Carl was the mother's favorite from the beginning, and the rivalry between the brothers had separated them in their adolescence. The mother pampered Carl in his early childhood and later expected him to build up an outstanding character, to be morally perfect, industrious and exact in his work. She was a very narrow-minded woman, non-religious but puritanical, and full of prejudices. The father was not much interested in the boys. He was a simple and rather crude businessman, honest, but bad-tempered and aggressive. Carl was blond, with soft skin and pink cheeks; he was of a short, pyknic stature and was, in contrast to his father, very shy.

Carl completed his primary and, with difficulty, his secondary schooling and attended a private commercial school for one year. He then spent another as an apprentice in his father's butcher shop where he was a slow but willing worker. However, he was uninterested in the work and his attention constantly lapsed. When he reached the age of 20 he was appointed a clerk in the Butchers' Association in the town where his parents lived. This was his first real job, and he remained at it for five years though it was hard and demanding.

The first symptoms of his writer's cramp appeared at this time. During his school days his mother had instilled in him the conviction that one's level of morality, one's values and qualities as an individual, are irrefutably expressed in one's writing. Therefore, if one is to be socially accepted and appreciated as a person, one needs to have perfect penmanship of the kind prescribed in school. Unfortunately, there was, among the people working in the same room with him, a female secretary who had, in his opinion, more perfect and beautiful writing than he. In trying to emulate her he began to feel a cramp in his right forefinger some time during the third year of his work there. The duration of the cramp varied, but he did not pay much attention to it believing that it came from fatigue. He did not even give it any particular notice when, in his last year of service, it lasted for nearly a week and continued until Sunday. The cramp caused his finger to stiffen in the position in which he was holding the pen or pencil.

He was not accepted for military service because of a small heart defect; nor did he engage in sports. He did not remember having had any kind of illness beyond the usual colds. He was a rather passive, introverted type, apparently without much vitality, and the only object of any real endeavor was his professional work into which he put all his will for perfection; this was especially so in regard to his attempt to write clearly and beautifully. Thus he spent his time either in his office, where he sometimes worked two or three unpaid hours longer than required, and the rest at home or sitting in his father's restaurant watching people, but without conversing with them.

Abiding by the moral ideals of his mother, he did not dare go out with girls and his whole sexual development was delayed, consisting of fantasies and some masturbation. He had no conscious inclination toward homosexuality and denied having had any homosexual contact. However, his femininity was nonetheless obvious when I met him, expressing itself even in his outer appearance. More importantly it suggested a deep infantility, as if he were still at the beginning of puberty, when homosexual tendencies are not yet awakened and only the relationship to the mother is dynamically effective.

He was twenty-five years old when he first had intercourse having been seduced by a waitress in the restaurant. He recalls his relationship with her as physically satisfactory and sometimes passionate, but one which made him feel guilt and all kinds of anxiety, particularly over the possibility of pregnancy. Thus, after some months, he suddenly broke it off, decided to leave his parents, and then went to live near Bern. Six months later he left his job and took a position as a bookkeeper in an import-export firm in a town near the Swiss capital. There he was highly appreciated and found work which he liked. When he was thirty he met a woman in a restaurant, the only daughter in a family of farmers with large holdings. She tried successfully to win his affections and they began an intimate relationship which, after four months, led to marriage but which remained childless. Soon his feelings toward his wife began to cool, and a secret hostility arose between them which had, by the time of Carl's analysis, lasted many years.

Carl came to me for the first time on June 16, 1945. His writer's cramp had become worse and worse, and his boss, who was very fond of him and highly satisfied with his work, finally asked him to attempt psychotherapy to get rid of it. The boss chose me as he had heard about me from a mutual friend and trusted my approach. He even decided to pay half of the fees without telling Carl, who would not have been able to cover the expenses of analysis on his own salary, an offer which I accepted. It seemed that the boss found it of great importance for his firm, as well as for Carl himself, to try the utmost to get him on his feet again—a point to which I shall return.

During the first month Carl came to me twice a week, then more or less irregularly, excusing his absence with such comments as "too much work in the office." With all my admonitions, I could not convert him to any real degree of regularity, but when I saw that even with relatively sporadic sessions he made progress, I accepted his rhythm. In Jung's view too frequent sessions are—except in specially serious cases—not always advantageous, for the patient must have time to assimilate the material with which he was confronted in the analytic hour before being able to face more. By giving credit to the self-regulating capacity of the unconscious in this manner, sessions with the patient take on a less reluctant character and help the ego of the patient by giving way to important repressed contents, thereby allowing new insights.

Carl and the medical doctors had thought the writer's cramp to be a manifestation of a rheumatic disease, and Carl underwent mud baths, massages, and all kinds of hydrotherapy without results. The most recent diagnosis, that he had a kind of neuritis—the pains now reached from the fingers to the shoulder—brought new attempts at therapy by electrical waves, pills, and X-rays, but these too were fruitless. On the contrary, he had only to take a pen or a pencil in his hand, and immediately, even before writing, his forefinger withdrew and completely stiffened in a crooked position. No amount of will, nothing in the world, would relax it as long as he wished to write. It should be clear what a desperate state Carl was in and how terribly frightened that he would lose his job if psychotherapy, this latest attempt at healing, should also fail. For in reality he did not believe in it at all and tried it only as a last resort, and upon the insistence of his boss.

His life was absolutely monotonous, with his days spent in the office full of despair and fear and his nights spent at home where he talked little and was in bed by nine o'clock. He never went out either alone or with his wife. Thus, since he did not mention any dreams, there was not much unconscious or even conscious material for discussion. After having recorded the anamnesis, I began to search for the roots of his symptoms. I learned that the writer's cramp came up again some months after his marriage, at first from time to time, and then more regularly. For about a year now he had not been able to write except with a typewriter, and even this required great effort; thus it had been nearly impossible for him to comply with his duties as a bookkeeper, for which handwriting was necessary. When he had reached this state, it was no longer possible to hide it from his boss.

There could be little doubt that the cramp was deeply connected with his mother's ideal of performing everything perfectly and that his writing had become the object on which he projected all the demands of his mother and his own demands. The coincidence that the writer's cramp began at a time when he wanted to please a girl-secretary colleague, and that it re-occurred shortly after his disappointment in his marriage, also suggested a close bond between his disturbance and his relationship to the feminine in himself and to women in general. He was obviously frightened of both of these. As the active, penetrating finger, which stretches independently, the forefinger is a well-known phallic symbol, a symbol of procreative power. The fact that it was this finger that was afflicted supported my hypothesis that masculinity and activity presented a tremendous problem to him. Thus, the cramping and crooking of his finger, understood as a penis-substitute, seemed to express anxiety over and withdrawal from the feminine, an unwillingness to be in active, penetrating contact with it.

In his attempts to demonstrate his cramp to me we found that the larger the letters he had to write the greater the possibilities of avoiding a strong cramp. And I soon discovered that he had about the same chances if he wrote with a soft pencil instead of a hard pen or a pencil with a sharp point, these being the kinds of instruments to which he was almost compulsively attached. It was as though the smaller the writing (the smaller the space to which his personality reduced itself), the stronger and more painful the cramp became. His willful concentration on writing perfectly caused the letters of his words finally to shrink to full-stops. This observation clearly implied the way out—only enlarging the field of his consciousness would create a more dynamic outlet of the mind and a correspondingly larger and freer writing which would in turn dissolve the cramp.

The Paintings

At our third session, I had the idea of letting him try to make simple stripes on a paper with water colors and a brush which I had on hand. As I expected, with a brush he had no cramp at all. In the beginning we used this method only in the analytic sessions. Later I asked him to do it by himself at home, and examples of a series of the results may be seen in Figures 1, 2, and 3. I encouraged him to continue and soon he brought a picture, his first, in which hope and feeling had already begun to be expressed. In this picture (Figure 4) the ball-like form, in Jungian terms suggesting totality, surrounded by twelve red spots, expressive of feeling, has a green center; green in the symbolism of color stands for hope, growth, and nature. The ball, in the picture and outside of it, represents a kind of totality and expresses balance and peace. The two tulips (one dark, one light) of opposing psychic qualities reveal, since they are "containers," a feminine connotation, and represent, as do the two daisies, the number "two"—generally associated with qualities of the feminine. The whole picture speaks of Carl's readiness to offer all his feminine feelings to me. I made a point of expressing my pleasure and did not lay too much stress on interpreting them to him. This picture was followed by a sudden outburst of "inner fire," represented in a painting (Figure 5) by a pile of burning wood, its high flames portrayed in dark red colors.

By this time his depression seemed much less severe than before and Carl began to overcome his reluctance to paint which he had felt in his first attempts. On July 20th we also began to do writing exercises with a soft pen, and he succeeded in executing them without too strong cramps. But the letters needed to be very big and the writing dynamic in contrast with the precise writing of small numbers required in his bookkeeping.

My suggestion that Carl paint was a hunch, and I do not know whether a similar method has ever been used by other psychotherapists in the treatment of this kind of disturbance. As this was the first case of writer's cramp I had had to deal with, I was placed on my own. I had, however,

FIGURE 1. *Red Stripes.*

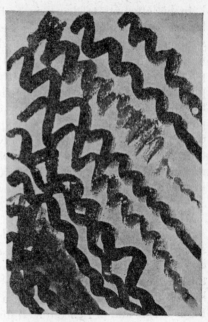

FIGURE 2. *Red Lines.*

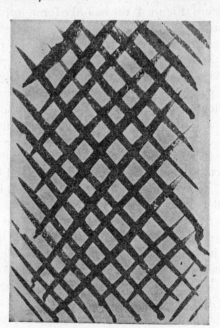

FIGURE 3. *Dark Blue Lines.*

FIGURE 4. *Tulips and a Ball.*   FIGURE 5. *Red Fire on Brown Wood.*

learned from C. G. Jung the great value of such drawings and paintings, no matter what sort of medium is used. Jung was, in fact, one of the first to introduce them as an essential instrument of psychodiagnosis and psychotherapy for both normal and emotionally disturbed adults. By such means the verbally inexpressible can often, be "portrayed," be made visible, allowing one to get a glimpse of the hidden landscape of the psyche. And what was produced at first spontaneously and without conscious reflection can, once meditated upon and delivered of its meaning by a thorough interpretation, reveal important material unknown to the patient who made the picture. Making it can remove the block and release vital energy, whether or not it is interpreted and understood. But if its meaning to the patient is made conscious, it will serve even further to enlarge his consciousness and nurture psychological development (having a healing effect). Products of this kind should, of course, never be compared or confused with "art," not even when they are produced by a real artist. Aesthetic and technical considerations must be put aside. What kinds of patients should be encouraged to express themselves by such means, and at which stages of the analytical process, is unpredictable. It is completely up to the fine touch of the analyst to decide upon the right persons and moments. This is also true of the problem: if, when, to whom, and how much the pictures should be interpreted. No two cases are identical.

When I started to let Carl paint, I had two aims in mind: first, to find an immediately effective way of ending his writer's cramp; second, to constellate some "movement" in his "dammed up" and blocked psychic energy, to promote its redistribution, to change his energy potential, and by this activate his whole psychic system. For I thought that on the one hand he would have to hold the brush in his hand differently, with less pressure of the finger than when using a pen or pencil; and on the other, I hoped that the use of colors would perhaps stimulate his fantasy, help him to express something of his repressed feelings on a constructive level and bring a release to his desperately thwarted and paralyzed psyche, of which his cramped forefinger was only a symptom. It was my hope that in painting, in which he had neither experience nor ability, he might become again like a child and be forced to give up his exasperating, never-ending efforts to concentrate his whole mind on a rigorous perfectionism. For spontaneously playing with colors—and I assured him that nothing more was wanted from him—would draw his mind into different, less rational channels.

The results of his endeavor were meager. He painted on the whole about twenty pictures, all of a most infantile, undifferentiated character. And, in the first place, this was certainly not because he was unskilled in painting, for we know from experience that it depends on the strength and vivacity of the inner image and the energy invested in its representation whether or not a patient is able to reproduce it in an impressive way. He did not put much work into the paintings and was devoid of the necessary patience both in their production and in attempts to reach a deeper understanding of them. In spite of this, the pictures brought about an astonishing modification of his cramp and exerted a visibly good effect on his whole being. Now, about six weeks after the beginning of the analytical sessions, the transference was well established and Carl seemed to have gained full trust in me.

On the 9th of August he brought me a picture of his hand (Figure 6), surrounded by the "blackness of death," as he described it. It was a lifeless, pale, boneless hand, as if it were made of wax. It was badly formed and more like a glove than a human hand. The thumb, usually expressing independence, looked as if it wished to resemble the other four fingers; the lack of activity and of the ability to handle things and situations was thus underscored. The nails, which protect the most tender part of the fingers, were missing; the hand could not serve as a weapon for attack or defense. Carl did not remember having bitten his nails when he was a child or having had any problems about them later, but this does not, of course, mean that he could not have repressed such memories out of guilt feelings to the extent of their total extinction.

The most striking and puzzling thing about this picture was, however, the fact that he painted the *left* hand in spite of having the cramp in the

FIGURE 6. *Bright Yellow Hand*
Surrounded by Blackness.

right forefinger. On this left hand the forefinger was not crooked and therefore it could be depicted without reference to his affliction. On my inquiry he could not give any reason for this and assured me that he had done it quite spontaneously by looking at his left hand from above and unreflectingly copying it as he painted with the right one. The reason could also have been the much deeper one of an unconscious displacement, since we know that "left" symbolizes the "dark, sinister, unconscious, the feminine side." It might almost have been a slip of the mind which revealed the source of his disturbance (the conflict hidden in the unconscious side of his psyche). He did not want to confront the "real" place of his trouble and demonstrated by his picture that somewhere in his depth he knew where it was located.

The dark clouds around the hand, clouds of depression, disclosed that something quite unconscious was involved, something which not only gave him pain and suffering but also some satisfaction. For the hand was lying in this dark frame as in a womb, in a state of embryonic being, permitted to remain passive and "contained" even though it could be put into the frame and pulled out, since the blackness did not completely enclose it.

Nevertheless, this painting had a marvelous effect on Carl. He talked more than he ever had in the previous sessions having been until now rather taciturn. He talked about his youth, his first love, and so forth, as if he were laboring to disperse the depression through the magic of words.

The very next day he brought a picture of a second hand (Figure 7), again the left hand, just as flat as the first one, and even paler, but some-

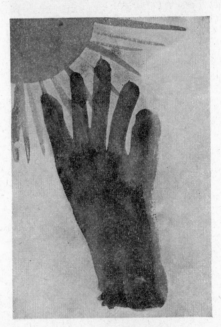

FIGURE 7. *Light Yellow Hand
and Pale Yellow Sun.*

what more masculine, and this time no longer "contained," but free and exposed to the clarity and warmth of the sun and natural vitality. In putting the paintings of the two hands side by side, there was no question, despite their similarity, of their difference, caused—as Carl himself explained—by the warm beams which allowed the hand in this picture to grow and "fortify itself." The sun, symbol of consciousness and of the male principle, was shining on the hand with long, powerful rays, and thus it was a most promising picture. Carl was full of optimism and hope.

These two pictures gave me the opportunity for a detailed discussion about his relationship to hands, to "handling" in all its aspects, to work, to activity in particular, and to his philosophy of life. This philosophy was very primitive, simple, without any individual cast, and directed only toward approval by the social environment. I found it better not to enter too deeply into the interpretation of the different aspects of the picture and kept my ideas about his choice of the left hand to myself, thus leaving him with the naïveté in which he had until now painted. Anyway, with his rather narrow mind he could not have understood all the connotations which his pictures revealed to me. And it was important to leave him, like a child, the pleasure of bringing me each of his pictures as a kind of "present" of which he seemed to be proud since I told him something about the meaning of flowers as gifts. By this time his cramp had improved sufficiently so that he could write one hour a day without it and the pains were reduced to his wrist and hand.

Because Carl was slow-minded, had little education and only a few interests, it was not easy to talk with him about deeper problems and scarcely possible to enter with him into an analysis of the unconscious. He pretended never to dream, and could not recollect any dream he had had earlier, and he had the greatest difficulty in bringing up associations and in taking the initiative in talking on any topic whatsoever. This was perhaps a symptom of resistance toward the analytical work, but it also corresponded with his constant fear of unmasking himself to the world and failing in some way; and also with his urge to focus his attention exclusively on his job (his writing). Consequently, I restricted myself to trying to help him apply some common sense to his narrow-minded, conventional opinions, full as they were of prejudices about people and the world. I gave him some books to read during our vacation period, popular biographies, descriptions of journeys to foreign countries, short stories, i.e., material to enlarge his field of knowledge somewhat. I recommended that he read a newspaper daily and report to me about the topics it contained, and we discussed the political and moral problems thus touched upon. Although he had no confessional convictions and no religious background at all, we also talked a little bit about the teachings of the Bible and the Ten Commandments. Slowly I succeeded in awakening his interest in and improving his understanding of his own situation and life in general.

The Dream

At the end of August I left on vacation, and when we began again in October Carl was full of expectancy about continuing his work with me. His finger-cramp was still in more or less the same state as when we parted— somewhat better than at the beginning of our sessions. However, by this time the ice seemed to have been broken and I felt that we had attained the threshold of a new phase of our work. When Carl entered my consulting room I observed that something important must have happened to him. His whole attitude was less passive and his face showed confidence. Proudly, like a child who has successfully accomplished a difficult task, he said: "I have a dream for you, a most exciting dream!" And he began at once to pour out a lot of intimate material about his sexual life.

Until now, whenever we touched his private domain, he slipped over it as quickly and superficially as possible, and I did not, of course, insist on it. He now revealed to me in a sudden afflux of sincerity his great secret: that for a long time he had been able to arrive at a real orgasm only when riding a horse. He told me that his passion for horses began soon after he broke off his relationship with the only woman he had had sexually before his marriage, and his horseback riding had continued for about five years. However, after his marriage he felt that his marital and financial situation would not allow such an expensive sport, and he engaged in it only two or three times a year. On those occasions he rode for one or two hours and was thereby brought to a full orgasm. Each time he had the feeling of great release and of awakening power, but also of guilt toward his wife and society in general. Accepting conventional opinions, he blamed himself for hidden "perversity," but, on the other hand, he secretly had to admit that only on a horse did he feel "whole." He needed the touch with the "animal" to feel that he was a man. "On a horse the rider is placed on his true foundation," he said to me.

The horse has always been considered a symbol of man's underlying instinctual basis, as the "maternal ground" which carries him and to which he is linked in a most subtle and sensitive relationship. In the history of symbolism the horse has often represented "the mother," an archetype of the maternal femininity, a vehicle on which men can rest, rely, and go forward. In riding a horse Carl felt sure of his masculinity; he felt as if he were mastering the animal nature within himself just as he was mastering the horse, and that at the same time his own sexual drive was fused with that of the horse in a feeling of voluptuous union.

His greatest wish was that his wife should allow him to have sexual intercourse with her in a similar position, from behind, as though he were riding on her back, like a rider on a horse. Such a position would give him—he thought—a feeling of superiority and security, for by not having to confront his wife's face, he could also avoid its probably negativistic and contemptuous expression of which he was so very much afraid. For even in the dark he dreaded her searching eyes which he felt directed toward him. But she sternly rejected his wishes and had never complied with any position but the generally accepted one of the woman's lying on her back with the man above her. And she also refused to make any helpful movement or caress during the intercourse. Under these circumstances Carl's interest in her diminished and, some months after his marriage, he discovered that he was impotent. Psychoanalysis would declare his castration-complex to be in full command. All his attempts to correct his condition by good will failed and he soon abandoned them.

She was, of course, hurt, and reproached him all the time for his lack of love and masculinity; and this behavior hardly made her sexually more desirable. They were both disappointed that under such circumstances they could not have a child, but in their negligence and passivity they never thought of consulting a doctor of any kind. She attributed all the blame to him and consequently he was deeply filled with feelings of inferiority. He described to me how he fell more and more into a hopeless depression for which his professional work was the only compensation. When finally his job, too, was in danger of being taken from him because of his incapacity to write, he felt that he had come to the brink. He confessed later that when he was sent to me by his boss, the only thing in his mind was committing suicide.

That he was able to tell me about his deepest "shame," as he called it, represented for him an immense relief. It was the first time in his life that he dared to talk about it to anybody in the world. I listened to his confession without many questions and comments; only when he seemed at a loss for words or too embarrassed did I speak some encouraging, empathetic words. It was clear to me that we had arrived at a highly decisive moment in our work and that everything depended on the subtlety with which I succeeded in dealing with it. The dream which he had had about the middle of October—the only one he had during his work with me—and that he brought to our first session after vacation, threw an even more piercing light on the relationship with his wife than anything he had reported until then. It had the following content:

> Two square rooms to which no door led, except for one in each of them going to a small balcony. The balcony represented the only possibility of communication between rooms, because the wall separating them was without a door. In one of these rooms was his wife, in the other Carl himself. These rooms were on the thirty-fifth floor of a skyscraper, which probably was not yet finished, for the balcony had no railing. Carl strongly wished to get into the room of his wife, but she seemed to have no intention of coming over into his. Several times he began to take the tremendous risk of crossing the balcony to reach his wife's room, and each time he shrunk back, not only because he was terrified by the lack of railings and the subsequent risk of his life, but also because he noticed that a great crowd of people was on the street below watching anxiously to see if he would succeed in his undertaking. After several vain attempts he finally gave up and awoke depressed and sweating.

Here is a diagram of the situation:

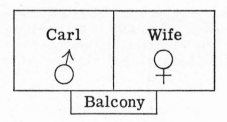

In interpreting this dream, I want to take it—in accordance with Jung's teachings—as a self-representation of the unconscious at a given moment which complements or compensates the contents of the conscious mind by revealing a situation of which the conscious mind has not been aware, or not enough aware. The recognition of this situation is highly important for the psychic balance of the dreamer. For in contrast to Freud's understanding of each dream as a way of "fulfillment" of repressed sexual wishes and drives, a "façade" behind which one has to search by "free association" for a "latent" meaning (*i.e.* the repressed sexual contents), Jung's view is that each dream expresses in a direct form, although often in a symbolic language which has to be deciphered, just what it has to communicate and add to the field of consciousness. Each word and image used by the dream must therefore be taken in its proper sense. However, there are two aspects from which most dreams can be looked upon: they can be interpreted on the "object-level," in which one has to take the contents of a dream as given parts of the dreamer's environment, and on the "subject-level," in which they are symbolical representations, personifications of the dreamer's inner psychic traits. On the object-level the ego of the dreamer (in the dreams the ego is always represented by the person of the dreamer himself) reveals the kind of relationship in which it is engaged with the outer world and with persons with whom he is in a vitally important contact—the parents, the wife, the analyst, the boss, etc. The subject-level, on the other hand, portrays the ego's way of relating itself to these same persons, but only as they are within himself; it shows what is being enacted on the inner stage of the psyche, the play or tragedy, the peaceful or warlike situation of its many different qualities. And thus the bond of relationship to the outer world mirrors or reflects the relationship of an ego to its inner world in a corresponding way.

In this sense Carl's dream points out the drastic kind of relationship he has to his wife (if we take the dream on the object-level), and at the same time it reveals his way of contacting his "inner" wife—(his own femininity) —with which he has to share his life (if we take the dream on the subject-level). Both ways of interpretation are necessary and valid in this case and both give an impressive picture of the dreadful situation in which Carl was caught.

A room may symbolize an enclosure, a protective home, or a receptacle and container for the ego; but here it has become a prison. Neither of the rooms had an entrance, and the fates of the two persons, the only occupants of the rooms, are to be bound together in an enslaving marriage with no chance of escape. The doorless wall which separates them shows, if we interpret it on the "object-level," the degree to which Carl has lost contact with his wife and, on the subject-level, the rigid obstacle within his own psyche, showing how far the ego is split off from the "other side," the unconscious inner femininity. Only a single possibility of mutual contact remains: to pass over the balcony. However, the balcony was unfinished, a small platform without a railing to protect him from the depth below. Reaching his wife thus presented the danger of falling from the height he wanted to maintain and of exposing himself to death.

The balcony is a part of the façade of the house, and if we take the house, as has often been done, as a symbol for the whole personality, or for a "great mother" figure, a balcony may well suggest the most exposed part of the house just as the female breasts are that of the body. Even though he was pampered by his mother, her breasts, too, were for him a place of very great danger; clinging to them was in a sense still his major problem, preventing him from growing into a natural masculine adulthood. This was the problem which had to be solved before any further step in the psychic development was possible. There was no way to avoid crossing the balcony, if he was to commit himself as a man communicating with the woman in all her implications. However, he seemed, unfortunately, not yet capable of taking such a step.

The dream makes it obvious that for Carl this meant a risk of life, as it would for anybody stuck in such an undeveloped and undifferentiated psychic state. Still, we know that no psychic change is ever possible without a total transformation of one's attitudes, and that in the healing of every neurosis the patient has to pass through a severe crisis before the treatment succeeds. For in Jung's view a successful analysis must transform the whole personality, not its basic structure but the patient's philosophy of life, his approach to his inner reality and to the outer world. Such a transformation entails something like an earthquake, in which everything that is not solid collapses and which requires a new way of life to be found.

One must consider the fact that the rooms and the balcony without railing were situated on the thirty-fifth floor, an unusual height that, curiously enough, coincided with the years of Carl's age. This coincidence, however, did not express a psychic equivalence, but rather a striking disparity between his drive to live at such a height of perfection and his infantile state of development. It is as though his ambition had made him begin climbing to this height and isolation at the time of his birth. This "height" was a symbol for the extremity to which his perfectionism had pushed him and in which he was desperately in danger and for the impossibility of his ever in reality living up to his ideals. There are no such skyscrapers in Switzerland, and he had only seen them in magazines. But the thirty-fifth floor of a skyscraper was an excellent image for the position into which he had maneuvered himself.

The outer appearance of the house, the façade with its balconies, can also be looked upon as a symbol for the *Persona* of the individual, a term chosen by Jung to designate those characteristics of the ego through which it meets its environment. The *Persona* is a bundle of qualities revealing how the ego would like to appear to others and be valued by them. It thus becomes the field in which vanity, the hunger for prestige, conventional lies, and all kinds of make-believe are expressed, and form a "mask" behind which, when it becomes too rigid, the genuine personality may be crushed and even extinguished. Carl was seriously threatened by this kind of danger, as are most persons who would like to appear "perfect." He had a strong prestige problem and felt that he should be more masculine—be able to perform his male duty toward his wife under the eyes of a huge, critical environment. He tried hard to live up to a *Persona* which would allow him to look down on the crowd which he felt was watching him critically from below. The gap between him and the natural people in the street, and the disparity between the anonymous collective traits in his own nature and the perfectionistic height of his ego (plus its split-off feminine side), was so enormous that bridging it over was obviously impossible. Only by "going down" could he have found a means of contact with the masses on the street. He felt their staring up at him as critical, but could just as well have merely expressed longing toward him, the wish to get in touch with his isolated ego. However, the distance could only be bridged by his descent. But how? Jumping down would have been fatal. No door led out or downward. There remained the possibility of breaking through the wall of his room. But with what? With his hands and his cramped finger?

The dream shows a most desperate situation and insoluble conflict, at least at that time and under the given circumstances. It could have been solved only if Carl were ready to risk his life in passing slowly and cautiously, in spite of his dread, along the balcony over to his wife. Once a union with her had been reached, the whole psychic state could change and perhaps a new way out would then reveal itself—a way of escaping the closed rooms and finding his way down to the ground floor—to a more realistic state. But I was not optimistic about Carl's readiness to take this risk; it went, at least for the level of his state at that moment, beyond his forces. I foresaw, therefore, that we might soon become stuck in our work because of his lack of courage and tenacity.

Carl was immediately aware of the importance of the dream, but of its meaning in only a very restricted sense. "Should I not avoid trying to reach my wife, if the attempt is so terribly dangerous?" was his first question. And his second: "Am I not right to be afraid to face all those who stare up at me from the street?" He could not remember ever having been in a situation resembling the one shown in the dream. Railings, balconies, doorless walls did not play any special role in his life and he did not have any recollection of ever having been afraid of being punished by "imprisonment." He never suffered dizziness from height or from a confrontation with his environment. It was impossible to link the dream back to childhood events, and a reductive interpretation threw only little light on its meaning. Thus it had to be understood as an impressive description, a thrilling and enlightening image of the dreamer's actual state and conflicts, even though this state may be rooted—as everything present is based on the past—in character traits resulting from traumatic experiences in earliest years.

In Jung's opinion neuroses can be healed just as well without digging up the whole infancy by making conscious and assimilating the "truth" with which the unconscious faces us at a given time (for example, in the images of a dream). I interpreted and explained the dream to Carl only in broad outlines, for it spoke—as I thought—for itself and because I did not want to risk destroying by too many words the deep emotional effect that I expected it would have on him. However, he was, at least with his intellect, not able to understand its full meaning and could comprehend it only in a limited way. He felt shaken as he recognized the risk involved in his attempt to contact his wife, but he did not realize what it meant to be confined on the thirty-fifth floor. He was not at all worried about his dangerously high "standpoint"; on the contrary, he considered it to be a kind of distinction and felt proud to have an apartment in a skyscraper. For thus he was far enough above the crowd and he felt it imperative to be separated properly from it. All his associations (questions) showed that he was not yet prepared to accept the fact that he had to put all his energy into finding a solution and getting out of his predicament.

He expected to be rescued by help from without. For example, he hoped a fire brigade would put a ladder up to him or an outside elevator would come and fetch him; that workers would finish putting a railing on the balcony or make a door at the back of the room permitting him to leave by the staircase, or that his wife would suddenly decide to come over to him and would succeed in her undertaking, etc. just as he expected that it would be the analyst who would do all the work necessary for his cure. He hopefully thought of all kinds of ways out and in spite of some cautious hints on my part, he could not, because of his resistance, see that the key to the solution would not come from the outside but lay within himself. Nevertheless, after having done my best to discuss with him the defense mechanism he had developed concerning certain aspects of the dream, I dropped the thread which the dream pointed out so explicitly. I relied on my knowledge gained from experience that in such cases help sometimes comes unexpectedly from the unconscious when the dream and the analytical work have implanted in the dreamer's psyche the germs of understanding and these grow and unfold. In order to give the spontaneous work of the unconscious its due, I dismissed my secret doubts concerning a successful way out of Carl's situation and decided to wait and see.

In fact, the dream and the confession with which it was accompanied had an astonishing effect, and from this time on there was a rapid improvement in Carl's state.

By the middle of November, only a month later, Carl was totally rid of his writer's cramp and said again and again that he could not understand how this could have happened. I, too, was impressed favorably, for I knew that in analytical work every step forward toward healing is a kind of "miracle." The best techniques, intuitions, skill, and so forth have no certainty of success. Every analyst works *deo concedente* and—in Jung's words —"each new case that requires thorough treatment is pioneer work and every trace of routine then proves to be a blind alley."

"Not theories, but your own creative individuality alone, must decide," he says to the analyst whose personality, therefore, is a decisive factor in the analytic process and not merely a target for all sorts of projections (as in the well-known couch situation in psychoanalysis). Psychotherapy is, in the first place, according to Jung, a dialectical relationship between doctor and patient, a discussion between two psychic entities in which all knowledge is only a tool. For in the dialectical relationship Analyst and Analysand sit face to face and to an extent the Analyst too is subject to the psychic process his patient is undergoing. He has again and again to bring his own personality into question, and only insofar as he himself is "in order" can he contribute to the "reordering" of the psyche of the individual who has entrusted himself to him. Moreover, he has to have, in addition to a thorough training in his own analytical field, a wide knowledge in the most different disciplines, and must be able to add to the subjective associations of the patient objective ones especially when archetypal material (material of the collective unconscious) is involved. For in this case further amplifications from the domain of symbolism, of mythology, of history of religions, and of fairy tales, and of other areas are essential.

Jung's view of the role of the Analyst in the psychotherapeutic process is highly characteristic of his own teaching and like many other points in his interpretation of psychic material, it differs markedly from that of any other psychotherapeutic method. The aim is a transformation which is not predetermined and to a great extent indeterminable. "No effort made by the doctor can provoke the experience. The doctor can at best only smooth the way toward achieving an attitude which will oppose the minimum of resistance to the decisive experience." Thus the Analyst in the Jungian school, compared with other analytical schools, plays a relatively active role in the current of the analysis; but he has also to be exceedingly cautious, always aware of his limitations, attentive, if necessary passive, and illimitably ready "to let happen." It is obvious that problems of transference and counter-transference in such a relationship are of an exceptional importance, and to deal with them subtly and correctly is one of the main demands of the "art of psychotherapy."

The Wife

Shortly after our discussion of the dream, Carl spontaneously brought me a new piece of painting: a picture of a brown horse (Figure 8). He

FIGURE 8. *Brown Horse.*

wanted to show me, as he said, the kind he would like to own. One had to admit that as a representation it was a rather poor picture, but it nevertheless indicated some of Carl's essential problems and was thus very useful for our purposes. In spite of a certain stiffness in the legs, the horse here seems to be a quite vigorous, dynamic animal, just the opposite of Carl's usual passivity. In the picture the tail is in full swing, and the long drooping neck denotes even in its curved, hanging state—perhaps expressing Carl's fear of failing to have an erection—a considerable strength. Although it revealed something of Carl's very infantile state, one could not deny that it suggested a much stronger "animal side" containing much more energy than Carl ever suspected.

The painting helped Carl to objectify his secret longing for the companionship of a horse, and I suggested that he meditate on it and talk to it about all his doubts, worries, and needs as if it were a living friend. He carried on the monologue with the horse and got from it some satisfaction for which his transference on me might deserve credit. Both this monologue and the discussion we resumed concerning the roots and meaning of his disease—and the possible advantages he could have derived from it —added effectively to the disappearance of the writer's cramp. They also increased his confidence that he would finally be healed for good.

We agreed that the cramp symbolized his unconscious wish to withhold the erection, to keep back his penis (i.e., his masculine activity) and thus visibly expressed his hostility toward the world of the feminine. And on the whole it was a symptom also of his fear of committing himself completely, perhaps thus also of his fear of life in general with its insistence upon independence, daring, and procreativity. At this time I had no suspicion whatsoever that in addition to his problems of infantility (i.e., masculinity) which went far back into his early life history, there could have been quite recent and dramatic reasons for his developing such a painful cramp in having to keep the books of his firm in order.

I thus tried, as far as possible, to help him to the insight that he should not look upon the successful cessation of his writing troubles as the end of his psychological need for a better adjustment. I told him that our real work would begin only now that we had detected the sources of his illness; I said that the goal of our strivings should be to confront him, a man of thirty-five years and on the verge of the second part of life, with his repressed and totally undeveloped sides and to put them at his disposal in a matured form. I explained to him that he would have to face his incapacity to distinguish his ego from the different, still unconscious parts of his psyche, and above all, from his own femininity by which he was still possessed; that he would have to try to leave what is called in Faust "the world of the Mothers" and learn to discriminate in an adult way and to grow up in the sense of becoming more active, independent, self-conscious, and self-committing.

I had already suggested in August that he take up some kind of physical activity aside from painting; and when I returned to Bern in October, in the session after the one in which he brought me the painting of the horse, he showed me a canvas on which he had begun to knot wool to form a square carpet representing a beautifully colored dragon on green leaves. He intended to make a cushion of it for the couch on which he took his agreeable naps after lunch. This work, which is not uncommon among Eastern women, now filled his evenings with pleasure, while his wife played "solitaire"—a wonderful image of what Jung calls the "psychic transposition of the sexes." However, he seemed happy to be at least making something nice quite by himself, and he did not notice how humorous it was that he had, surely unconsciously, chosen for his first piece of handiwork the dragon, symbol of the "swallowing mother." Maybe it was a sound intuition which led him to try to banish her infectious influence on his ego by knotting her into a soft cushion on which he could rest, and to separate himself from her by concretizing in the pillow the image of his "inner dragon," his dreaded unconscious depth.

We also discussed ways for him to establish a more satisfactory relationship with the outer world of masculinity, and upon my suggestion he renewed his contact with his brother, whom he had not seen for about ten years. He found him very handsome and was proud of this new friendship. His brother was a Freemason and offered to bring him into his group. I decided this suggestion might be of help since it promised to give Carl the experience of a male society from which women are excluded and the opportunity of acquiring some men friends—a need he had felt for many years.

At this period of our work Carl talked several times of his marriage with much emotion and bitterness and wondered if and how it might be brought into better shape. He urged me to see his wife and try to persuade her to participate in sexual intercourse with more interest and with a greater readiness to conform to his personal wishes.

I was hesitant at first, wondering if compliance with his request might not give him too much opportunity to ignore his share of the marital problems and push them on to his wife and to me, thus relieving him of a burden which he should carry himself. However, since his disease-symptom was cured, his interest in our sessions seemed to diminish noticeably, and I felt some justice in his repeated statements that a marriage problem always had to be approached from both sides; that husband and wife each had to contribute equally if they were to reach a satisfactory solution. And I thought it might be helpful to call for the wife's cooperation and thus try to stimulate anew Carl's readiness for a further psychic development.

I explained to him, of course, that nothing would be solved in itself by obtaining his wife's agreement to his special desires, but that there were much deeper problems involved in their difficulties. The wife's incapacity for and resistance to feminine surrender was, of course, also a symptom of a probably neurotic attitude; surely she, too, was suffering from disturbances in her feeling-domain, and to win her understanding meant making her more conscious—like him—of the underlying problems.

Carl had never known anything of the dignity of the human being and of sexuality in the larger sense, and his psychic difficulties made him meet woman and sexuality too much in their negative aspect without any indication of the beautiful, the uniting, and the soul-satisfying qualities they can also have. To lead the wife to deeper insights about all that sexuality represents and can offer was only one of the goals; the other, even more essential goal, was to bring her to recognize her part and responsibility in the maturation of her partner, for the accomplishment of this task could have had a decisive effect on the lives of both. With the determination of keeping myself from becoming too personally involved in Carl's marriage-situation, I decided to see his wife, silently hoping, like Carl, that our meeting might convince her to take up an analysis, too.

Carl was immensely happy about my agreeing to talk to his wife and looked forward to my meeting her as he would to a possible turning point in his life. And in fact this meeting had a decisive importance, but, unfortunately, not in the direction Carl and I hoped.

About a week later the wife came to see me, a stout woman with a bitter, self-righteous expression around her mouth, a sharp nose, and inhibited manners. It was difficult to induce her to talk, but after the first contact was established, she threw out a huge heap of resentments and could not stop accusing her husband of neglecting her, of rejecting her, of having ruined her life, and so forth. She did not show any insight, any understanding of the state of Carl; she did not even venture to feel her way into the possible causes of his troubles. Like most women, especially primitive ones, she had an exact and unalterable picture in her mind of how a man ought to be, to feel, and to behave, and she was not ready to accept the slightest correction of this picture in order to adjust it more closely to the reality of her husband.

It was obvious that corresponding to her whole attitude toward what she thought to be the marital duty of man and woman, she emphatically refused to do anything that might further a more successful relationship and said: "I am all right. I do everything that a moral person should; it is up to him to change." Well, she may have been honest and moral, but there was no doubt that she was also deeply neurotic. She seemed to be rather narcissistic and unbending and was unable to see the reason why her way of having sexual contact had been accepted by Carl before marriage and ceased to be satisfactory to him later. In her eyes the potency of a man depended on his "good will," and, like a great number of women, she could not believe that a man had almost anything else in the world more in his power than his capacity to have an erection. She was reluctant to take up a new attitude toward sex as such simply because he wished her to; and she, of course, had no idea of her husband's orgasm-escapades with the horse, which he conscientiously kept secret.

She could not admit her share in the failure of their sex relationship, for she was convinced—or tried to believe—that nothing was wrong with her and that only her husband was inadequate. Therefore, she also could not see that she, too, might gain from a better sexual contact. Maybe I made a mistake myself in stressing the state of anxiety into which Carl so easily fell in her presence and upon the benefit he would get from being able to perform in the way of an average male. Perhaps I confronted her too quickly with her own problem: her frightening effect on Carl because of her self-sure, rigid, and criticizing attitude, a consequence of her frustrated femininity. It would probably have been better to let her come by herself to the insight that she too had a big emotional problem to solve; but I stood under the pressure of time, with only an hour at our disposal.

I decided from the beginning to decline to become her analyst, if she ever agreed—as Carl and I hoped—to try to engage in psychological therapy herself. I did not want her as my patient because I had too often had the experience that it proves to be a mistake for the husband's and wife's work to parallel one another with the same analyst. For in such cases the analyst cannot avoid involvement in false reports, competition, jealousy, and so forth, and being called to judge between the two. I also thought that it might be more advantageous for her to go to a male analyst and learn in the transference situation something more about the right ways of feminine reaction. I suggested therefore that she go to one of my male colleagues for psychological help and advice. I thought she should hear from an objective and experienced person how she could stimulate the love of her husband and diminish his fear of criticism, which would as well be the precondition of any further possibility of a better-feeling relationship.

At first she was indecisive and seemed resistant to the suggestion of going to such a male doctor. Later she agreed, but only on the condition that she would not have to undress there, because, as she confessed in embarrassment, she could not allow any man to see her legs, which were hairy and thus a source of "great shame." I vainly argued that hairy legs are frequently seen and that I never met a man who rejected a woman for such a reason. I also assured her that doctors usually have no interest in such details because they are accustomed to seeing all kinds of physical features; and I pointed out that it is expected of psychotherapists that they restrict themselves to the psychic sphere and not go beyond that domain. She looked askance at my attempts to soften her attitude and win her confidence. Finally she left, promising to see the psychotherapist whose address I gave her; but it remained a promise, for she never went.

Her visit left a very mixed reaction in me. I had the distinct feeling that I had lost the deal. Was it a mistake to send her to another person for the analysis? Did she expect to work with me like Carl? And did she feel rejected and resentful when I suggested that she go to somebody else, to a male doctor? What might have been my effect on such a puritanical person in whose views I must have seemed, in spite of my scientific reputation, a very worldly, modern woman and, therefore, a personality with whom she had nothing in common? Was it right to speak so frankly of sexual matters with such a morally self-righteous woman? Nevertheless, she had shown much confidence in me when she so overtly and at great length told me about her feelings concerning Carl and her marriage; she even gave me exceptional credit when she revealed her anxiety in respect to her hairy legs. Might she have expected in reward to be accepted and approved by me? At that moment, it did not occur to me that there might have been other solutions. I could, for example, have stopped working with Carl and taken his wife in analysis. Maybe I was too rigid in my principles of never treating a husband and wife at the same time and should have made at least an attempt to work with both. I knew how difficult it was for Carl to persuade his wife to come to see me, and I was probably too doubtful of winning her for a second consultation and thus felt forced to deal with her in this first and only session. Thus, my whole attitude might have been too calculated and could not be expected to bring the solution which a more detached and passive way of dealing with the situation might have attained.

Maybe I overestimated the possibilities of changing the mind of such a relatively primitive woman from a peasant family and overlooked the gap which separated her from my own differentiated approach. My hope that she would feel rather flattered to get some advice from a woman who could bring her to a more skillful and loving use of her feminine values was unrealistic; and possibly I should have failed under any circumstances, even if a series of sessions had permitted me to proceed more slowly and cautiously. However, to a man of Carl's structure a woman of his wife's kind was appropriate. In her pattern of behavior he met again the puritanical narrow-mindedness of his mother; he found a partner helpful in the nourishing of his masochism and a chance to remain in his ambivalence. There was no doubt, however, that in becoming conscious of the roots and the meaning of his troubles, he gained a considerable degree of insight and thus a more conscious and active attitude.

She never gave any open explanation of her reaction; she did not even admit that she did not want to go to my colleague; she simply postponed going from one week to the next. After her interview with me she did not say much to Carl about our conversation; however, he sensed that she was rather suspicious about what she had heard. She made just a few remarks, indicating her mistrust of psychotherapists in general and me in particular. Her comments were to the effect that I, like the rest of them, seemed interested only in making money and that this is why I had him continue his work with me and tried to induce her to enter it also.

Carl was furious and disappointed by this response. He had hoped so strongly that everything would change for the best after she had seen me. All his attempts to find out what was going on in her inner world were in vain. She remained as unchanged and inflexible as if she never had talked to me. Carl finally became more and more angry at her passive resistance and he lost his pleasure in our work. Since he was cured of the writer's cramp he did not find it worthwhile to make further efforts toward the maturation of his psychic state and persisted in his opinion that there was no possibility of his developing further unless his wife agreed to follow him in analysis. His transference had lost much of its intensity since he recognized that I had had no success with his wife, and one day he declared that he would stop his work with me if it became evident that his wife did not want to cooperate—at least until she showed more willingness. His passivity, his lack of interest in a true enlarging of his mind, his anxiety about running risks and making efforts won the battle and proved stronger than the attachment to me. He did not listen to my words and I tried in vain to explain to him that his development should be considered and furthered without regard to what his wife was doing.

However, for his sake—and maybe as a symptom of my counter-transference—I made a last attempt to change the direction of the events and on November 29th wrote a letter to his wife prompting her to act. I hoped, in appealing to her feelings of responsibility, to play upon her moral prestige and to create a path to another analyst in case she preferred herself to choose one in whom she would have more confidence. The letter said:

> Dear Madam: I learn that you have not yet got in touch with Dr. X., as I suggested. This astonishes me, and I deeply regret your unwillingness to help decrease the difficulties in your marriage. I tried to explain to you that the troubles between you and your husband can only be faced successfully from *both* sides. The attitude and behavior of the woman plays an important role in such cases; and only when you fully understand what is behind the failure of your relationship to your husband will an atmosphere be created which will give the security necessary for a man of his psychic structure.
>
> I am writing you this because I think you should be more aware of the responsibility you bear in this case. Your husband is doing his utmost to become capable of the sexual and other activities needed for a good marriage. If he does not succeed he will at least be able to say he did his part and that the rest was up to fate. If you do not help him you will not be able to say the same.
>
> I advised you to go to Dr. X. because I felt that you should see someone with whom I can cooperate on the basis of our knowing one another. But it is not essential that it be Dr. X. If you would find it difficult for financial or personal reasons to work with him, you could, if you wished, look for someone else. Unfortunately, I cannot suggest that you too make your analysis with me, for I consider it much better for your own personal purpose that you do it with someone other than the person from whom your husband is receiving help.
>
> With kind regards, Sincerely yours,. . . . .

Carl was most anxious about the reaction of his wife to my letter. He had decided to wait only two more weeks and, if my letter did not have the desired effect, he would terminate his analysis with me. In his words there was a note of vengeance, as if he wanted to punish his wife by demonstrating where her attitude would lead him—to becoming "stuck" himself. But he also expressed secret fear, for he was in the bottom of his heart frightened that she would leave him if he continued to want to become more independent of her. Deep within himself he was afraid that she would go back to her parents who were wealthy people; she had threatened him with divorce several times during the last few months. Obviously, he was not mature enough to face the prospects of a separation and the life of an adult. His parents had died two or three years before and he needed his wife as a child needs his mother—if for nothing more, just to be saved from being alone.

Of course, she did not answer my letter. And since she also did not seek psychological help, Carl became more and more bitter and stubborn. He had it in mind to try with other women and hoped that this would stimulate his sexuality and release him from the anxiety he felt in confronting his wife—and thus finally bring him back to her. For in his heart of hearts he was a *petit bourgeois* and was not equipped for the heroic quest leading to a mature individuality.

There was another reason, too, for him to feel uncomfortable: in the eyes of his boss, Carl's continuing to come to see me, now that he was rid of his writer's cramp, was unjustifiable. And it was an odd coincidence that on the same day that I got a telephone call from the boss asking if it were still necessary for Carl to continue analysis—meaning that he did not intend to contribute toward the fees any longer—Carl, without knowing about the inquiry of his boss, declared that he had come for the last time, at least for awhile, and that he wanted to wait and see what happened with his wife.

If Carl had not stopped his work, I should have been in the difficult position of either keeping him on at half my usual fee, or of raising that which he was paying, at least to some extent. To change the original fee in the course of an analysis is always problematical, and it was an open question whether or not it would be disadvantageous for the transference. In the case of Carl this was mixed up with a second problem, namely with whether or not one should let another person pay part of the fees at all, and particularly behind the patient's back. This complicated and subtle matter should, indeed, receive thorough consideration.

Termination of Treatment

The last session took place on December 16th, just six months after the first. We parted in mutual friendliness, but both of us felt that our good-byes were for a very long time, if not forever.

Since that time I have never heard from either Carl or his wife. Not long ago I tried to trace him down, but without success. They left their flat and I could not even determine whether or not they were still living in the vicinity. Maybe they moved to the farm of her parents and preferred that their whereabouts be unknown. They certainly had good reasons.

About one and a half years after Carl stopped his work with me, the firm in which he was employed collapsed. There was a rather scandalous bankruptcy in which many people lost all their money. The police and the court had to intervene and Carl's boss committed suicide. I was never able to learn if Carl himself was involved, or even arrested. The newspapers did not mention his name and aside from his boss I knew nobody who could have given me any reliable information. Nor could I ever find out whether he knew what was going on in the firm, whether he had any idea about the impostures of his boss, or whether he too had a finger in the pie. He had been for nearly ten years the most highly trusted book-keeper in his office, and it would not lead us too far astray to suspect a deeper connection between his writer's cramp and the facts he had to note in his bookkeeping.

It was the forefinger of the right hand which had the painful symptoms, and we know that a symptom is often a symbol for a hidden content. If it is true that sometimes the right hand does not know what the left hand does, we may just as well vary the phrase and think that in Carl's case it may have been the left hand which did not know what the right hand did, as was so impressively demonstrated by his painting his "innocent" left hand. The conversion of a repressed psychic guilt-factor into a physical symptom is a well-known neurotic mechanism; and it does not at all diminish the importance of the material which was elaborated and interpreted during analysis, a labor which had such a healing effect, if we add to the probable causes of the affliction a hidden moral deficiency.

In the course of the analysis Carl never mentioned anything of his boss or the firm he worked for, aside from quite superficial remarks. He seemed so deeply committed to his pains in the finger and his difficulties with his wife that he almost never talked to me about anything else. My questions about his daily schedule, his colleagues, the sort of work he did, were answered, but always only cursorily, and I tried to accept the notion that his job did not offer any material which would stimulate him to talk about it. Thus I was absolutely unprepared, surprised, and alarmed to hear in what a drama the firm was engaged. I did not dare call Carl at that moment to try to get more information from him; I feared drawing attention to him if I inquired where he was, and I was also afraid of hurting his feelings by showing that I knew about the tragedy which had stricken him. Thus the truth was never unveiled; who will ever know it?

* * * * *

Now that about twelve years have passed since I saw Carl for the last time, I still wonder if it would be legitimate to call his psychological endeavor with me successful. There is no doubt that the writer's cramp which led him to ask for my help was healed and did not reappear during the eighteen months he was still working for the firm, otherwise he or his boss probably would have consulted me again. And the cure of his cramp seemed to him absolutely sufficient, at least for the demands of his job. Most people, certainly, do not strive for more than the disappearance of their pains—they are totally satisfied when the problems which made them seek psychotherapy are gone. The healing of a symptom is also regarded as a desired goal from the point of view of therapy.

However, the problems which came to light and the material which was uncovered in the course of the analysis demonstrated unquestionably that the writer's cramp was only a symptom of more deep-seated conflicts, maybe one manifestation out of many, of a frustrated personality growth and a belatedly infantile psychic state or even unconscious immoral tendencies. And as long as all the basic trouble-causing factors are not worked up, there is always the danger that new symptoms and pains will unconsciously develop to replace those already cured. Carl had, indeed, progressed—quite apart from the full healing of his cramp—in many ways, for he had become somewhat more self-aware and displayed more initiative than before; he had acquired insight into himself and his conflicts and into some general human problems. But in his basic difficulty, in his incapacity of performing in his marriage like an average male, no improvement could be observed, as he feared and avoided every sexual contact with his wife, at least as long as my relationship with him lasted. He remained on the whole a relatively immature, inhibited, and egocentric individual, and the prospects of his later improvement did not seem very bright.

Taking all this into consideration I should—following E. Jones' formulation—call Carl's case "therapeutically" successful, but "analytically" unsuccessful—it proved successful from the patient's point of view and unsuccessful from the analyst's. For I must admit that I found the result of the analysis unsatisfactory in the sense that it did not accomplish a conclusive transformation of the patient. But the psychological endeavor was too short, the unconscious material too slight, and Carl's whole personality too narrow for us to achieve more than we did. According to E. Blickensdorfer, many patients have to undergo a kind of preparatory strengthening of their egos to grow out of what one might call their "embryonic psychic condition" before the analysis proper can begin. For they are incapable of taking what analysis has to offer as long as their egos are too weak to face the material of the unconscious and the dangers involved in every encounter with the depths of the psyche. Carl's psyche, too, was in an embryonic state when we began, and he had, as far as I could see, just arrived at a point where an effective confrontation with his inner world and the world around him would have been possible, when he stopped.

So it seems fitting for me to close this report with a quotation from Jung's book, *Psychology and Alchemy:*

> As a doctor it is my task to help the patient to cope with life. I cannot presume to pass judgment on his final decisions, because I know from experience that all coercion—be it suggestion, insinuation, or any other method of persuasion—ultimately proves to be nothing but an obstacle to the highest and most decisive experience of all, which is to be alone with his own self, or whatever else one chooses to call the objectivity of the Psyche. The patient must be alone if he is to find out what it is that supports him when he can no longer support himself. Only this experience can give him an indestructible foundation.

Maybe—and it is my earnest hope—the shakening effect of the loss of his long-accustomed job and the collapse of the firm to which he so faithfully belonged brought the "loneliness" which Carl still needed to find the "indestructible foundation" of which Jung speaks.

ADDENDUM

1. *Optimally, what criteria do you use for accepting or rejecting patients for psychotherapy?*

   Since I am a lay analyst (non-medical), I don't take patients who are obviously psychotic and thus should be treated by a psychiatrist. On the other hand, I accept every person who asks for my help insofar as my schedule allows it, but with the reservation that a trial—six weeks to two months— will determine whether or not we should go ahead. In my opinion, no analyst can work with every kind of patient; but there exists a certain affinity which promises greater success with the one than with others.

2. *Do you make a diagnosis before psychotherapy begins?*

   I never venture a diagnosis before working with the patient for a certain time. Even if the patient brings with him a diagnosis formulated by another analyst, I question it and wait until it is proven correct by the passage of time. If a case reveals characteristic symptoms, it can of course happen that I cannot avoid a diagnosis; but I always look upon it as a hypothesis as long as I am not completely certain.

3. *Do you attempt to persuade the patient or significant relative to change his (the patient's) environment?*

   If it proves unsuitable for the patient to remain in his usual environment, I discuss with him how he would feel about changing the place where he lives or his profession. However, I *never* persuade him to do anything. My conviction is that only a decision which the patient makes by himself, with all the responsibility it entails, can be of help to him.

4. *How did you conceptualize the therapist's role in this case?*

   I do not understand exactly what is meant by this question. I can say that in the present case I took on the role of an understanding and helpful "mother" who never judges or criticizes in contrast to the patient's moralizing and strict mother-image.

5. *What aspects of your theory of psychotherapy were particularly apparent or useful in the case presented here?*

   Using Jung's theories, I found his stress on the stimulation of the unconscious layers by some kind of fantasy production (painting, handiwork, etc.) as particularly useful, as well as his way of dealing with dream material.

6. *Do you feel that this case developed significant insight? If not, can improvement be maintained?*

   I had the feeling that the patient showed a growing insight into his problems which will surely be of value to him in the future. Whether the improvement manifested by the abolition of his symptom (writer's cramp) can be maintained is unpredictable. The analytical work was too short to be able to deal with the deeper roots of the disturbances, as I pointed out in the last paragraph of my case study.

7. *What aspects of your own cultural orientation facilitated or impeded the treatment of your case?*

My training in the different theories and techniques of psychotherapy (the Freudian and Adlerian, as well as the Jungian), added to my wide knowledge of the different fields of psychology, philosophy, mythology, and symbolism, has been of great help to me in the understanding of the different aspects of this case.

8. *If we consider that a continuum exists from superficial to deep psychotherapy, where would you place your own case?*

As I pointed out at different places in my presentation, I would not consider this case an example of "deep psychotherapy." It had to remain, unfortunately, because of the structure of the personality and the lack of necessary time, a rather superficial one.

9. *What did you think about the outcome of this case, and what criteria did you use for evaluating such outcome?*

In consideration of the factors mentioned directly above, I was not dissatisfied with the results. However, I would like to have had the opportunity for a treatment of longer duration and in this way have attained even better results.

10. *How do you terminate psychotherapy?*

I terminate psychotherapy in one of three ways: (a) If the disturbances which brought the patient into analysis have terminated and a satisfactory development of the whole personality has been reached. Such a statement will, of course, always be more or less subjective, but possibly valid if both patient and analyst agree concerning it. (b) If I see no chance of further development in the continuation of analysis and have the feeling that maybe another psychotherapist could give better help to this patient. A negative transference, or any kind of resistance, however, would not represent such a reason, since this has to be worked out during analysis. (c) If dreams or other kind of material suggest the termination or show that one has reached a phase in which the patient must find his own salvation without the help of the analyst. (d) If it proves to be dangerous to continue the analysis because of a possible outbreak of psychotic symptoms precipitated by digging too deeply into the unconscious.

11. *Other.*

I have by chance heard of an unpublished manuscript describing seventy cases of writer's cramp collected in Germany in which it could be shown that the majority had hidden criminal propensities. I never suspected this in my patient and news of the collapse of his firm reached me only much later. Of course, this unpublished material was not available at the time.

I still have a certain resistance to preparing this questionnaire for I would not want my responses to be construed as "rules" of Jungian psychology or of my own in the treatment of neuroses. I therefore want to stress my conviction that *every case is different and there exists in Jungian psychotherapy no general recipes for the ways and means of analytical treatment.*

CHAPTER 6

The Analysis of a Case
of Declining Vision

—R. SCHINDLER[1]

Irvin O. was sent to me by a specialist in internal medicine. He was 21
years old and came together with his mother. She made a nervous and
helpless impression while the patient himself appeared to be quiet and
correct in behavior. He had been treated by the specialist who had sent
him to see me and this is why he came. His manner of always letting his
mother come first, standing aside while she was talking, and only turning
toward me when being addressed showed that by behaving correctly he
wished to keep aloof from his mother. While letting these impressions
deepen, I perused with leisure the rather irrelevant letter of my colleague.
Then I asked the patient's mother to return to the waiting room and to
leave me alone with the patient. Up until now I had asked only three
questions: Who had referred them to me; which of the two was the
patient; and—finally—how old he was. The mother, obviously prepared
to tell a long story of complaints and grievances, was not satisfied with the

[1] Born in Vienna; studied medicine there; M.D. Employment with Psychiatric Clinic
of the Univ. of Vienna; now Chief of the Dept. of Psychotherapy. Teachers in
psychiatry: O. Pötzl, H. Hoff, O. Kauders, and M. Bleuler in Zürich, where he stayed
some time on an exchange basis. Training in depth-psychology in orthodox style by the
Psychoanalytic Association in Vienna. Member of the Wiener Arbeitskreis für Tiefen-
psychologie. Main subjects: New developments and methods of treatment in psychotherapy, especially with regard to the theories of modern Ego-psychology and Anthro-
pology; psychotherapeutic methods of treating schizophrenics. In this field developed
a new technique called "bifocal group psychotherapy" which was adopted by the
Viennese clinic and is now a standard method there. In connection with this work has
made studies of socio-dynamic relations of small groups.

unexpected turn things had taken. Still, she did not make any objections, but complied with my wishes.

We sat down. I just looked at him, waited, and he described to me the course of his life: He was the only child. His parents—both teachers—were very fond of him. He himself, however, could not feel anything toward anybody; there was only an "icy coldness" in him. He had passed his university matriculation examinations with honors, had started to study philosophy, but after the first term his eyes had begun to fail him. He then went to see several oculists and had been to an ophthalmic hospital for several weeks. Only once had they detected high bulbar pressure, but it had not recurred. He had undergone some kind of treatment. Sometimes the condition was a little better; but soon it went from bad to worse until he had to give up studying, although he kept enrolling at the university. He felt unable to do anything. One day it was discovered that he had a high blood pressure. After that he was thoroughly examined and treated in different wards. In the hospital he felt quite well and helped the doctors. He had always left the hospital with great hopes, but after a few months outside his condition had become worse than before. During the last term he had not once been to a lecture, for which he reproached himself since his living near the university in Innsbruck was a great expense to his parents. Yet he felt unable to do anything about it because of his eyes. In order to save them he was observing a strict routine in his daily life which he observed in ritual fashion. It included living on a vegetarian diet, avoiding all contacts, reading a half page of a book on philosophy daily, and avoiding illustrated papers or periodicals printed in gaudy colors. The love and care of his parents were only making him nervous and he preferred to be away from them. With the exception of the holidays this was the case anyhow, since they lived in a provincial town. In Innsbruck he was staying with an aunt of his whom he had trained to comply with his ritual (she was not allowed to ask him how he was, what he was doing, etc.). When she had visitors, he avoided them; when she opened the door for him, he did not glance at her because he wanted "to save his eyes."

He had an intelligent way of talking, using correctly medical terms which he had picked up during his repeated stays at the hospital. He was sitting in his chair in a queer, cramped way, glancing at me only from time to time and avoiding my eyes immediately when they caught his. His gestures were curiously out of harmony, as if he dared not change the posture he had taken. Only once his hands moved a ruler lying on my desk to a position parallel to the edge of the writing desk. He had a thick-set, well-proportioned figure, but his posture was bent or rather crouched and his features were stiff. He obviously wished to appear like "iron," a pose which was, however, marred by his big spectacles framed in the old-fashioned style. This assumed attitude of being a scholar and a man of action contrasted with the impression he gave of being merely a typically well-behaved but helpless swotter.

Diagnosis and Therapy Plan

Some current psychotherapists believe they can do without an exact clinical diagnosis. I do not belong to these. Each psychic breakdown has its aspects with regard to both content and form. There is no specific conflict which necessarily leads to illness and no thought-contents which can be classified as being morbid in themselves, taken apart from the way they show up. On the other hand, I cannot see any reason for discarding the conception of "sickness" and talking only of a specific form of *Dasein*. The uniformity of sick life can be described and defined diagnostically and justifies the conception "sickness."

Besides, the problem has an important aspect which concerns us, doctors and psychotherapists: it determines our attitude toward the patient. Believing in "sickness" makes it easier for us to keep aloof from the patient and to consider him an object which we can move around according to our better insight. If we believed him to be merely another kind of person (*andersartiges Dasein*) he becomes a partner with obviously equal rights.

A discussion of these conceptions only shows up the problem without leading to its source. The hybrid hostility of the doctor toward the patient, turning him into an object of the therapist, cannot have its origin in an abstract speculation only. The slightly depreciatory tinge of the conception "sickness" merely expresses our own attitude which may be defined as a kind of fear of the sick.

I would like to state that—regardless of the diagnosis—everyone sick in mind frightens the therapist at first. Because the sick person turns against any helpmate, he therefore repels the therapist. The problem of helping thus turns into my own problem and I, the doctor, wish to help and to meet the sick person but I feel pushed away. I feel an urge rising in me to go away and not to obtrude upon him. Yet if I want to help him I must conquer these feelings emotionally and not merely intellectually. I have to find my own way to be able to stand the sick person with all his repelling fears. That may be the reason why all theories of depth-psychology hand you a weapon to conquer this crisis. The password is, in short, that his fear is based on a specific error which will be put right in the course of the therapy. Believing in this formula gives me the strength to stand the patient and not to side-step him. Any success of my therapy strengthens my belief in the formula. This element of belief is a part of the system.

Different schools have explained the error differently. The fact that some of these explanations have at times turned out to be based on illusions was apparently not harmful to the psychotherapeutic attitude. For many reasons the total passivity of the classical psychoanalyst seems to be ideal and desirable. But it creates the soothing illusion that one is not dragged into human contact with the patient, an illusion which was disproved convincingly by anthropologic depth-psychology. The patient is not wrong in believing that he is forced into contact with another person; he is only wrong in introducing an element of fear into what is happening. This certainly is not too comforting a thought to the therapist, it being taken for granted that the therapist does not feel himself to be dangerous.[2] It may appear to be moralizing, but I would like to stress that training analysis and high human integrity are both important. By the way, this leads us back to the example Freud set by his ways of living.

When with Irvin O. I observed the effect that he had on me and took stock of my own reactions, I felt an urge rising in me to remove his eye symptom, to interpret it, or at least to point out the clumsy way in which he covered up by being afraid of doing, avoiding doing, or doing with discomfiture. He himself seemed not to notice his helplessness and misery, his bent posture, and obvious poses. He pretended that he did not want anything of me but had just come out of regard for the specialist in internal medicine. He did not really talk to me personally but recounted a standard story about his sickness cooked up for "any doctor." Yet I wanted him to talk to me, to have confidence, to tell me his real troubles. I interpreted my feelings as being just impatient because he had not let me help him. Yet Irvin O. was frightened. He covered up his fear by withdrawing from any contact by expanding on his eye symptoms. If I doubted these he surely would have withdrawn even more because of his growing fear. If I accepted them for the time being, our coming into closer contact would not be obstructed by his growing fear.

Therefore, I told him that I thought his eye trouble was severe and real but that his physical trouble was caused and influenced by mental constraint and discord—that for the time being I could not heal his eyes, and that somatic therapy would not be successful. I would, however, be prepared to help to harmonize his mental life and to free him of what he himself had called "icy coldness." In the long run this would also improve his eyes. Then I asked him whether he believed in the negative reports of the first specialist and the eye specialist. He agreed to the first one but hesitated to do so with the second, which I interpreted to be an ambivalent consent to what I had said. I therefore immediately fell in with his doubts and asked him to have another check on his eyes, knowing this would bring him back to me with feelings of goodwill.

Not before our second meeting did I tell him the terms of the therapy: he was to come regularly; he was obliged to tell me his first thoughts spontaneously; and for at least a half year he had to postpone asking about results of the therapy. I refused to have his consent straightaway. I wanted

---

[2] If he is really honest and self-critical he must admit that this is anything but easy.

his mother whom I had excluded entirely up until now to feel she was helping him with the decision. Every patient has relatives whose behavior may be of great importance in the course of the therapy later. One should, therefore, always give the patient the opportunity of discussing the treatment with them before consenting to the therapy. There is no need to worry about whether the patient will win through. In doing so, he may taste success for the first time and thereby strengthen his own confidence in his helpmate.

So far we have been discussing the unspecific part of psychotherapy. It may be that the therapeutic effect of the treatment may lie in this unspecific way of establishing contact. Human warmth and contact accepted without fear mean a lot to the sick in mind. I personally tend to value this part of psychotherapy rather highly for its effectiveness. I am calling it unspecific, because it is applicable to any form of sickness in mind and can, most probably, be established according to nearly all theories and techniques of depth-psychology. Every psychotherapeutic method agrees to its being effective. The therapist uses the theory to keep up his belief in his therapeutic attitude and in the specific "error" of the patient which has to be rectified. The success of the therapist thus depends on the firmness and inflexibility of his "creed," which gets its quality from the explanatory power of the theory. Seen from that angle, the value of each theory does not seem to be connected with any specific form of sickness, or with the personality of the patient, but depends solely on the personality of the therapist. In short, that theory is the best which offers to the therapist the best model of what happens in the mind in a way which is best understood by and most comprehensive to him specifically. The foregoing may be taken as an interpretation of psychotherapy in a modern sense in which one tends to believe more and more that it does not really matter whether the psychotherapeutic treatment given is of one school or another.

I do not agree with this opinion because it takes into consideration only one part of the truth and generalizes it in a non-permissible way. The patient is not only in need of a friend who can put up with him, but also of a guide to a depth where he feels he can hardly bear himself. Each break in a personality can only be closed where it has opened up.

Let us turn now to the specific problems of psychotherapy and its risks. Any stress constitutes a danger because it can be born for a certain period only. It is not sufficient to stand the ambivalence of the patient, one also has to take into consideration the economy of his mental setup. An exact clinical diagnosis and therapy is therefore essential.

I would recommend a diagnostic classification along the following lines:

A. Reaction-formation of reaction and inhibition of the ego (character neurosis)
B. Disturbances of the ego-defense

(1) Overloaded ego-defense mechanism
  (a) anxiety neurosis (anergic defense)
  (b) neurastheny and actual neurosis (hyperegic defense)
(2) Neuroses-forming symptoms
  (a) on Oedipus level (conversional hysteria)
  (b) on anal level (compulsive neurosis and phobias)
  (c) on oral level (aggression neurosis)
  (d) so-called psychosomatic diseases
C. Disturbances of the ego-nucleus (psychoses). These lie outside the scope of this essay and will therefore not be classified here.

I would like to recommend furthermore that we differentiate between real neurosis and neurotic reactions although their outward signs are practically the same. The crisis touching off a real neurosis comes upon a personality already hampered in the development by a primary trauma. Before the outbreak of a neurosis, reactions and inhibitions have set in which are characteristic and rooted in the primary trauma. The environment ignited the fuse but the consequent outbreak revealed a long lasting latent conflict of development. Seen from this angle, the environment loses its dynamic importance. It is the personality whose desire for development forces it into conflicts again and again. A symptom typical for a neurosis is thus apparent: the compulsive repetition compulsion. In the other case a fully developed and mature personality is hit by the crisis and a neurotic reaction is caused. There are no traces of character disorders having set in before. The conflict simply has its origin in the setup of the environment. In daily life all of us are familiar with neurotic reactions which are quickly brought under control again. But there are permanent constellations, too, which are not taken sufficiently into account and show tendencies toward becoming chronic. That need not be a handicap for a favorable prognosis because changing the environment may have a decisive influence on the situation. This is handy material for sudden and miraculous healing. They strike us like the ingenious "brain wave" of the psychotherapist while the idea was, in fact, in the air all the time.

Irvin O. was suffering from a real neurosis. Massive ego-reaction-formations (poses of "icy coldness") had been present for a long time and they still are. At the university conversion symptoms took place (weak eyes and pains) which are his main complaints at the moment. It certainly takes place on an Oedipus level. The behavior of the mother also points to a deep-reaching Oedipus problem. In the background compulsive tendencies appear (movements, posture, pedantry). It was only recently that he also told me of substantial symptoms of an incipient compulsive neurosis which I had suspected him to have (compulsive thought and movements, ritualizing trivial actions, sado-masochistic fantasies of intrusive impressiveness). Free anxiety did not show plainly. The neurosis had formed symptoms instead and established them well. The man, of course, was put out of action as much by his inability to find contacts as by his lack of fitness for his studies or for a profession. He was indeed absolutely and totally sick.

The following considerations were decisive for my therapy plan:

(1) The build-up of symptoms enabled my patient to be sufficiently free of fear so as not to be too eager to undergo therapy. Yet I believed that the conflict was suppressing his impulses and anxiety had been created; otherwise he would not have renounced living to such an extent. The change from the compensating symptoms to feeling full of fear has to come suddenly since he insists strongly on each detail with regard to his symptoms. He forced them to be acknowledged even when it was not plausible. Furthermore he was reacting in a touchy way. The meaning of the symptoms could be easily interpreted by the whole situation. At the same time he continually and strongly resisted any interpretation. We often find very intelligent patients as well as slightly less gifted than the average patients taking this attitude. It is a great handicap to any therapy since the therapist soon knows how to interpret and set right although he cannot succeed. That is the reason why I chose this case for the book: This is not a problem of difficult interpretation—quite a number of publications have dealt with that sort—but mainly a problem of difficult therapy in spite of easy interpretations.

(2) The therapy has to offer the patient more than his symptoms, otherwise he will soon drop it. In its first phase it must eliminate his fear in even a better way than the symptoms do. This can most easily be done by acknowledging his symptoms at first. When the relationship is growing, a preponderance of confidence may be gained. This would mean practically: (a) I should not allow myself to express an opinion regarding his symptoms; (b) I should not become an exponent of his parents, especially not of his mother, which would make him afraid. I know that the care of his parents aggravates him and creates fear. Consequently, I talk to him alone and ignore his mother who has come to Innsbruck especially to put her son in the hands of the therapist. I do it right from the beginning and intentionally.

(3) The intelligence of the patient helps him to comprehend but also to resist in the sense of a prejudiced apperception (Adler). I shall have to be careful: I must not take any association as plausible nor any position as safe. The value of a truth depends on the fear which it creates. Only when a symptom has been discarded shall I find out that it was not needed any longer. Any sign of impatience before or any attempt to press upon him a knowledge—obvious as it may be—will only create fear and provoke opposition. I have to reckon with a long-term therapy.

(4) The total withdrawal from all contacts looks like a panic. Probably, for the time being, another solution could be found—compromises, whereby the inner core of the symptoms need not be touched. The therapy

will therefore have to develop in at least two phases: first, a social adaptation can be brought about; he may even be made fit to take up a profession. After this the efforts will have to go on. While satisfaction about the success of social adaptation is growing, I have to press harder on essential problems and drive the analysis toward the center of fear.

(5) The problems which produced his fear were first warded off by the poses of "icy coldness," to which belong too the one of the "lonely philosopher." Studying philosophy was a result of this pose. The present conversional symptoms seemed only to protect him from being overworked by his studies; they really are dynamically opposed. It may well be that under cover of the eye symptoms an analysis of this pose could be made. It will come to an end immediately when reaching the point involving both mechanisms of resistance. When analyzing the symptoms of conversion, the tendency toward one of these poses or toward a new one of a similar meaning would arise which will have to be tolerated. Only the third onslaught would be able to deal with the common root where these attempts at resistance come from. It will arouse the greatest resistance and lead to the emotional level of the original conflict which has taken place during the period of ego-maturing at the time of a late-anal or early-Oedipus development (during the second and the fourth year).

The Formal Order of the Therapy

The external order of the therapy runs along the lines of the classical analysis: The patient is lying on the couch and I am sitting behind him so that he cannot see me. Each week we work five hours, and the sitting lasts fifty minutes. In the first sitting I acquaint him with the fundamental rule of psychoanalysis: to verbalize immediately all thoughts and impressions and to pursue without constraint what comes into the mind spontaneously and not to restrain it by any purpose, direction, valuation, or censorship. Should he notice any such unwillful tendency on his part, he is to report it immediately. Furthermore, I would remain passive and taciturn.

I was going to interrupt my silence on the following occasions only: (1) . . . to remind the patient of the fundamental rule when he had just violated it. If he accepted my hint the question would follow as to why this unwanted diversion had taken place. In this form I would do my so-called interpretation work.

(2) . . . to repeat a train of thoughts and to ask him whether he could detect a common direction in them. If he could not detect it himself, I would not exert pressure on him by continuing to ask but, instead, reveal to him my observations. This I would do without being authoritative. I would do it rather as if it just occurred to me in the form of free associations. If he would not accept it, I would not stress the point. In any case, I would permit myself this rather active form of interpretation only during

periods of positive transfer and not with regard to dynamically important problems. It should serve only to take undefended positions quickly.

(3) . . . to add to the chain of associations something I learned from former phases of therapy. I do this ordinarily with the following words: ". . . You know, this reminds me of . . ." This, too, is an interpretation in the form of free associations of the therapist.

(4) . . . to query anything not clear or ambiguous. Sometimes I would repeat what the patient had said, asking whether I had got it right. This strengthens the contact if it is done not only where a double meaning has to be set right but when necessary for the interpretive work. It then points up the therapist in his incapacity, and serves to remove the magic taint of knowing everything. The way in which things are expressed also shows the attitude of the speaker. Thus a repetition with my own words may contain an interpretation of the fear and pathos of the tale of the patient. It may also neutralize and counteract anxiety.

(5) . . . to assist in phases of resistance which have apparently clogged his thoughts. Also, whenever I would have the impression that by my quietly waiting the fear of the patient would grow to a panic. I would then try to help by asking a few questions about things which he can observe easily (how he felt physically or mentally), or I would tell him something about my own frame of mind by free flight of association: ". . . the atmosphere reminds me of. . . ."

These five techniques are listed in a special order. If one applies the first more often, one can reach better results in the build-up of transference and analysis. On the other hand fear will be pressing hard on the patient. I believe that anyone can be disturbed when technique number one is applied consistently. The further down on the list, the more every interference is at the expense of building up the transference and of the analysis. On the other hand, it reduces fear.

The classical technique of analysis does not fight shy of fear. I myself am rather in awe of it, possibly because I work a great deal with psychotics. Immoderate fear can lead to reactions similar to panic, suicide, or stupor. It can make the patient break off the therapy or develop similar attitudes of distrust. It is true that the neurotic can stand far more than the psychotic. But these cases, where an abrupt change from the security of forming symptoms to a full and total insight charged with fear takes place, are quite dangerous, too. I do not believe that the high pressure of fear for a considerable time would be useful to the analysis, but neither is the total absence of fear. I prefer the medium development of fear with a tendency to let waves of fear come upon the patient gradually.

More or less subconsciously the interpretation work of the patient is led in a certain direction since it may happen that one misses the opportunity to intervene. This happens at times simply because one has not grasped these opportunities at all or only too late. The intervening acts thus are selected and the therapist can only keep track of them to some extent by analyzing himself silently and constantly all the time. If this is not done, it is easy to become one-sided in many ways. A discussion about it would prove interesting, but I would like to mention only one point here. It frequently happened to my younger fellow-doctors who worked under my supervision and therefore I think it has a certain bearing in practice. It is the tendency to use the contents of the analysis to force the interpretation of the symptoms. To the therapist it is most interesting and thrilling to observe the dynamic workings of the symptoms. For the patient, however, this is only of secondary importance. To him the symptom is something he needs; he discards it as soon as its presumptions have been cleared up. By doing so, he may quite often understand and talk about its structure. But it may not happen and is of little importance in the long run. On the other hand it is a sign of alert fear when the patient too often relates the contents of the analysis to the symptoms. It should be analyzed by the therapist but not encouraged. All the time the therapist should remain conscious that he is not up against the symptoms but against the conflict. Covered by the symptoms, analysis can progress best. If his interpretation work is directed against the symptoms, it is only a sign of the therapist's own uncertainty.

Irvin O. accepted the above described formal order of the therapy without arguing. He soon asked me if he could accelerate the course of the therapy by working at it outside the normal sittings, since he had nothing else to do. I suggested he write a record from memory about each sitting and bring it back to me next time. He took full advantage of this suggestion. It resulted in my keeping a detailed and most revealing autobiography of his development during the analysis. His notes showed an interesting change in handwriting as well as in style. At the beginning of the analysis his handwriting was straight, disharmonic, hard, juvenile, flowed unevenly, and looked oddly like calligraphy. Toward the end of the therapy it showed a slight inclination to the right, flowed easily, had more rounded forms, and the pressure of the script had changed from being noticeably heavy to normal and unobtrusive. While at the beginning the style was one of an industrious swotter, later it became independent, for a while intentionally uninhibited, then fluent and easy, and seemed to indicate a certain pleasure on the part of the patient in theoretic speculations.

First Phase of Therapy: Repression and Day-dreaming

From the beginning of treatment my patient took a positive attitude and it was obvious that he took great pains in observing strictly all the rules of the therapy. He came punctually and obeyed all my instructions. There were not many. Yet as soon as he had to tell me his thoughts he could not do it. He noticed it and tried to repeat his complaints, waited, then re-

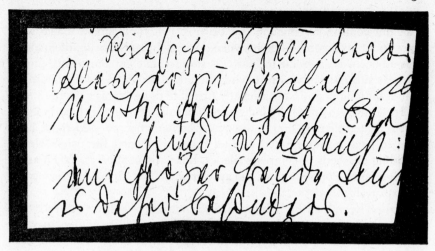

Patient's Handwriting at Beginning of Treatment.

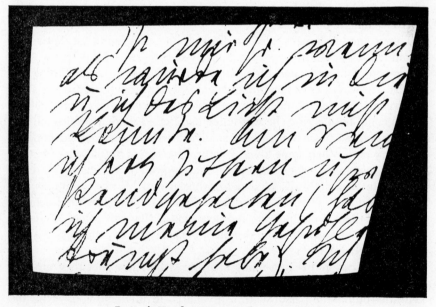

Patient's Handwriting at End of Treatment.

peated what he had just said. He waited again and became upset. But he did not reproach me. He assured me that his mind was quite blank and would stay blank. Why? He said he did not know. He was not even able to think about anything and the thoughts just would not come. He felt unable to grasp them. Maybe they flowed too quickly. He tried again with the symptoms, but broke off because of the "same old story."

The same thing happened at the next sitting. He slept badly and dreamt a lot but could not remember his dreams. I advised him to make short notes about his dreams when he woke up at night and to bring them along. This advice was given far too early. It resulted in complete silence during the next sittings. He was just lying there and struggling with himself. I waited for long periods; occasionally I tried to describe his gestures and to interpret them to myself by imagining him talking to me without words. I later repeated them to him to discover whether I had guessed right. But I seem to have misinterpreted him all the time. I tried the usual stimuli, including one hour of complete silence, but without success. When asked whether he was opposing me, the answer was "No." He said he just could not express his thoughts.

At the fifteenth sitting I happened to interpret a gesture correctly and by then he had grown to know me so well that he fell in with what I had asked: "What thought have you tried to shove away now?" The thought of a girl. "Why does it worry you?" His aunt with whom he was living had said that it was only a girl he needed. For once I discarded my passive role and told him I did not agree with her; he was not mature enough to have anything to do with a girl.

This seemed to have a calming effect on him, and from that time on he began talking about his fantasies. Step by step he enlarged on them and I accompanied him through the neutralizing repetition in an impartial way at first. He was always imagining naked girls and they appeared in all of his dreams. He was afraid this would be misinterpreted as sexual desire, which could not be, since he was unfeeling, "icy." I made no objection and let this defense pass, but asked casually where his feelings had gone to, for every person had some kind of natural feelings. I got nowhere but his sickness somehow took on another aspect. Up until now he had considered himself an absolutely disabled person because of his eye symptoms, but now he suddenly felt sick in a different way. He had lost his feelings— "repressed them" I chipped in—and he accepted this expression. Maybe he was "only sick" and not quite disabled. Perhaps it was even possible that he could be helped.

I have discovered this in many neurotics who stress that they are sick but in reality do not believe it. It is therefore wrong to think that the neurotic—unlike the person with a psychosis—is fully conscious of his being sick. The neurotic's knowledge of his illness is only a relative one. Actually he thinks of himself as a swindler who just pretends in order to disguise the fact that he is incapable and unfit for life. That is the reason for his being so touchy. As soon as he notices that his fellow men see him in the same light, he protests in an aggressive way or he is hurt and runs off like a confidence trickster who has been caught red-handed. The first step in psychotherapy therefore is to convince him of the thing of which he had been at pains to convince the others: that he is really sick.

Our first real contact, the *Begegnung* (significant encounter), occurred on the occasion of his realizing that he was really sick. It was true he did not experience any feelings. Perhaps they were appearing in the sexual fantasies and dreams that he found most unpleasant. But they too were never accompanied by any feelings.

During the first phase of the therapy these fantasies and day-dreams were taking on more and more orgiastic traits. The analysis was only bringing forth details, some of which he had omitted because they were "too wild." They completed the picture without bringing forth any feelings or any connections with the life history of the patient. The association to dreams progressed in the form of a continuation of the dreams; he enlarged on them and everything became more and more obscene. I let him carry on for as long as I noticed any omissions. It went on for about half a year.

Second Phase: Homosexuality and Phallic Conceptions of the Female

When the flow of orgiastic day-dreaming did not intensify any longer but appeared to flow on evenly, I interrupted him one day. I told him that he was day-dreaming during the sitting without really thinking about himself and that he was enjoying talking in front of me about obscene things. Irvin O. was very alarmed. He immediately tried to make me responsible for the way the analysis had developed: I had told him to tell me immediately what was flashing through his mind and that was what he had thought of. All right, but why was he just thinking along these lines? He retaliated with a counterattack: I had told him to word his thoughts freely and now I was reproaching him for it. Why did he take my impartial statement for a reproach? All right, if it had not been a reproach he would go on.

I did not say anything and he continued. But the even flow was interrupted. Again and again there were flashes of thought dealing with my objection. What else should he do? What else could flit through his mind? A lot, really. I challenged him with the observation that I had noticed that he never really remembered anything about his life. He immediately warded me off: those memories he had already told me about at the very beginning. More he could not produce. If more were essential for the success of the analysis, then it would fail. It was said very pointedly.

I did not say anything. After three sittings he came back to the point. He tried to produce memories but could only talk about nondescript scenery. I applauded: there was something else there, "would he please stick to the rule and not select his thoughts?" I got no results, just the reverse: analysis became more and more difficult. After a short interval he stopped his day-dreaming, tried to talk of something else, but failed. I interpreted this search as being in opposition to the first rule of uttering his first thought freely. He said I was right about the opposition but he did not know against what it was directed.

The sittings dragged. Suddenly he used a comparison to describe the situation: he felt like sitting in a car and driving. I was merely another passenger. But the car was smelling badly when driven. Maybe the gases of the exhaust pipes had penetrated to the inside. The only thing to do was to stop and then the car would stop smelling. I replied that it would still be a car with a bad smell, only one at a standstill. I would advise him to have it repaired even if it went on smelling during the test run. This comparison seemed to please him and always turned up in his associations; during later phases of opposition it always served him as a kind of encouragement.

Yet the next thoughts did not mention anything "smelling badly." He only told me how cramped he had felt in grammar school during his last term and during the first year of university. This was the tale in short: when he was ten years old his father had been drafted. He had been alone with his mother for one year and then was boarded out in the country at a home for students. After some difficulties in adapting himself at first, he wanted to stay there, particularly since he had made friends with two boys. But after one year the home was closed because of the war and the patient went back to his mother who had taken refuge with a distant relative who owned a farm in a very remote part of Austria. When his father came back from the war he stayed there, too. About half a year later both parents got jobs as teachers in a small provincial town in the same county. They were still living there. When he went to school there, he did not make any contacts but remained a lone wolf and took refuge in his studies. He became the best in his form and derived only pleasure and pride from being examined. At that time the ideal on which he tried to model himself was strictly a puritan one. Duty was the key word, and to do something for pleasure he thought childish. His paragon was "Moltke" whom he thought of as having been hard and without feelings. Then this ideal changed to a solitary philosopher whose only aim in life was pure and stern knowledge. With this ambition he went to the university. But now he was not modeling himself any longer on these ideals. His breakdown he explained by his overwork. He had been reading so much that his eyes had failed. His thoughts about "Moltke" and the philosopher pointed clearly to a very strict and imposing father-figure, but he could find no connection between both conceptions, especially since he was very critical of his father at the time and did not want to think of him as a model at all.

So much for the first year of therapy. During the summer holidays he stayed with his parents. I felt rather discontented, thinking that I had not been able to clear up some points for my patient. While under treatment he felt justified in doing nothing, and therefore he needed no further symptoms to explain this passivity. This seemed to indicate a certain success. I was therefore rather surprised when the patient returned in the autumn and declared he wanted to work. He said he felt much better and, if he did not strain his eyes too much, they did not hurt. He said he realized that he could not pursue his studies at the university but he would try something easy which would not strain his eyes too much.

I thought this attitude insincere and inspired by his parents. I was therefore rather reserved but did not raise any objections. I soon found out, however, that he really meant it—he took all the necessary steps and within a short time got a temporary job as a handyman. He twice changed his job for a better one and finally got a temporary job unloading parcels at the post office. At the beginning of each job he was very excited and at the same time concerned as to whether his eyes would stand the strain. In his work he proved to be very diligent and exacting and soon became a favorite with his superiors. He reveled in it. He was proud in a child-like way about the money he earned and thought it rather a prank which he was playing on his parents who thought that one could only earn money as a white-collar worker. He regarded me as a conspirator in this prank.

The parents, by the way, behaved sensibly. During the holidays his father had come to see me. Of course he was eager for his son to make progress but he also could see that he was very ill; that it was not a crisis of puberty which one could overcome by procuring a girl for him. And he was glad that there were very good prospects for his son to become well again. Up until now the patient had gone from bad to worse and his father was therefore pleased with any new evidence of progress. What he told me anamnestically was new to me only in respect to one point: he was fearful that his son might have inherited the disease. His mother—the grandmother of the boy—had developed a "jealousy paranoia" against his wife, the mother of the boy, soon after the wedding. That was the reason why they had had a lot of dissension during the first year of their marriage. At a certain period they had stayed together only for the sake of the child. Now their marriage was very happy; both of them were doing their best for their boy and would be prepared to make any sacrifice.

I hardly ever use such information passed on to me beforehand in the analysis itself. It is rather a handicap. The patient is not in need of my previous knowledge but of my helping him to find out for himself. And I am more interested in doing so when I don't know more than he does.

What he was doing outside was now occupying his mind to a significant extent during the sittings. Day-dreaming began again. But not only abstract persons figured in his imagination; real people from his sphere of life were involved. The content was rather massive. He dreamt about his father in the form of a gorilla who whipped him. The gorilla had an enormous penis, and behind him stood a naked woman who was singing. Black snakes were tumbling out of her mouth and jumping toward the patient's eyes. This reminded him that during the last year in Innsbruck he had been repelled when his mother had been humming a tune and making a few dance steps. He had felt it to be "whorelike."

Very seldom can one find such open symbolism in dream fantasies. They occur when the dreamer feels ready to face the problem and therefore almost renounces repressing them. Or when he is so far from recognizing the primary content of the dream that he is not even able to recognize it in such a flimsy disguise. In the latter case one has to be doubly careful in the interpretation work, otherwise the patient will suddenly be confronted with insight for which he is in no way prepared. I therefore let the opportunity of interpretation pass and tried to direct the activity of association towards memories of concrete occurrences or situations.

During this phase swear-words or vulgar expressions were strewn into the course of associations without any connection. The patient usually followed them up with the word "nonsense." Later these expressions did not turn up again but the word "nonsense" continued to be mentioned for a long time. The peak was reached when several of these swear-words were linked together in rows which he spat out like a cannonade. He built a superstructure of such words by merely using their initials which, linked together, gave a new, quite innocent word. From this procedure he gained in two ways: it shortened the time of turning out vulgar cannonades, and it hid the character of the content.

I felt rather helpless against this development and just waited to see what would happen now. It initiated a sudden change of mood. I became the object of several aggressive fantasies and interpolations. I was all bad, shabby, dirty, and lecherous. He thrust into my face intricate schemes for harming me; he was in every respect in opposition, resistive, did not want to tell his thoughts, abused analysis, and called it a means I used to satisfy my lascivious desires.

I remained passive. My questioning him to discover against whom he really felt these sentiments was thwarted with the disdainful reproach that I was only trying to direct attention away from myself. The sittings were less difficult than before, for I was certain now that the patient was wrestling with a transference partner who would come forward more and more. The only critical moments were his comings and goings at which times he averted his eyes while I was friendly as usual. I was secretly wondering whether his work would suffer from all his excitement. I would not have hesitated for one minute to make him give it up. This attitude possibly prevented him from making good his threat to develop worse eye symptoms and to be "thrown out with disgrace."

The peak of this outburst was reached during the seventy-second sitting of the analysis in which I discovered he suspected me of telling everything about him to my wife. The associations suddenly jumped to his grandmother. He saw her as a "lascivious witch and whore who covered herself up with her prayer book while she looked at naked men; she was having sexual intercourse with his father in a scarlet bed." After that he felt like vomiting and exclaimed "Throw me out! I am shuddering to look at myself!" I did not fall in with his dramatic pathos but repeated the association leading from my wife to his grandmother. He was no longer in opposition but tried to take up the train of thought. This time his mother appeared and threw his grandmother into the "snake pit" (the title of a much discussed film which showed scenes in a badly run lunatic asylum). [His mother had indeed arranged for his grandmother to be taken to an asylum for aged people where she had died five years later at a time when the patient was in his thirteenth year.] Then he remembered a time when he was three years old and sitting between his parents who intended to divorce. They had asked him to choose with whom he wanted to stay.

During the next sittings he did not fall back on these thoughts. His excitement calmed down and the phenomenon of an intercipient tic disappeared completely in the course of a few weeks. His attitude became noticeably friendly toward me and he felt well. He discovered that a boyhood friend of his lived in Innsbruck and he tried to contact her through his aunt. He wrote her a few post-cards and took great pains in wording them. He excitedly asked her to the theatre and to a dance. He pretended not to be in love but wrote her a love letter in almost maniacal euphory, which he did not mail afterward. He called it an "eruption" of feelings. At night he dreamt of an old car which suddenly started with a bang.

Again girls turned up in his day-dreaming. His interest turned more and more toward the genitals. I noticed that all the time he made mistakes in the sense of Freudian slips. He was confusing the genitals of the two sexes. I drew his attention to the fact. The word "homosexuality" was mentioned. Yet nothing changed except that he became conscious of the words he was using while speaking. We now noticed another symptom which had turned up occasionally before: he expelled air through his nose noisily and called it "snuffling." It suddenly occurred to him that the same symptom had turned up during the last year in Innsbruck at the time when his father was in the army. He remembered a game that he had played at that time: he had pretended he was a submarine and had crept under his mother's coverlets. He did not continue to do so but remembered that his mother had always tried to distract him from being curious about sex; for example, she had not allowed him to read Boccaccio. The next day he recorded a dream: he had looked at his mother under the coverlet and had not averted his eyes, although she had noticed it. During the next sittings he labored under great strain. After having talked about an anatomical diagram of the female genitals which he had seen once in a medical book, he discussed in a monologue the size of the female clitoris. In this monologue he thought it as big as the genitals of a ten-year-old boy.

He was quite relieved when I put him right from the anatomical angle. It seemed to be very important to him that females possessed an equivalent to the male penis, however insignificant and rudimentary.

When the summer holidays came we both had the impression that we had made great progress. He felt well and optimistic, had discovered different feelings growing, and was bent on developing them. Yet, as if to justify further therapy, he remarked that the eye symptom was still there although it did not trouble him much. His relations to the girl had slowly petered out, but she was not to remain the only girl he knew. In his job he had progressed extremely well before the summer. With the help and encouragement of one of his superiors who appreciated him very much, he had gotten permanent employment with the postal service—a job that for the first time matched his education. He was paid accordingly and derived much encouragement from being successful in his work and popular with his colleagues and superiors.

Third Phase: Significant Encounter with Parents

The summer, however, turned out to be a great strain on my patient. He was nearly always depressed, felt cramped and stiff when with his parents, and was afraid that the improvement would not last. He believed that his new feelings had not come spontaneously but were somehow connected with me. The thought that he might be a homosexual frightened him and he tried to cut loose from me. He felt that it was necessary to be transferred for a period of time to a post office in the provinces if he wanted to get on with his job. Yet, whenever he thought about it, his eyes got worse and then he comforted himself with the knowledge that I would not desert him if he was still having trouble with his eyes. He felt that the whole therapy had been useless. [Probably he had to give up his job anyhow as he had lost all contacts with his colleagues.] He felt again the well known "icy coldness" rising in him and felt he would never be able to get a girl friend, etc. His mother had come to stay with him in Innsbruck for some time since his vacation had been so short. At the same time he made a blunder in his office by which he lost the amount of 700 schillings—which was rather a lot for him. When with his mother, he was very taciturn and ungracious. He did not let her kiss him and felt clumsy and ill at ease with other people too. His behavior could be traced back to the time of puberty, but now he noticed it himself and he suffered. His whole manner had become even harsher. Though he had allowed his mother to kiss him before now even though he had felt it to be repulsive, he now rejected her completely. She was suffering, too, and came to see me about it with his consent.

At the beginning of our conversation she was very inhibited. She obviously felt aggressive toward me but did not dare to express it openly because my reputation with the patient as well as with the family was a very good one. This was true because we had reached such good results in general. I therefore formulated her thoughts by pointing out the lack of affection in the patient. I said I presumed she was cross with me because she felt I was responsible for that attitude. She dissented politely, but then agreed that the great affection of the patient for me had worried her. I tried to quiet her by considering her feelings, but did not offer any explanations because I was sure that she would immediately tell her son everything. Nor did I want to say anything about a possible end of the therapy because any such remark would be taken by the patient to mean that I wanted to turn him out. Yet she seemed content to have told me her worries and left quite at ease. On the following day she left Innsbruck and returned to the small town.

After this a complete change of mood took place in Irvin O. He suddenly felt fine and recognized many psychodynamic connections with regard to his behavior: he interpreted the changing poses of "icy coldness," from the ascetic-puritan pupil with excellent school reports per "Moltke" to the "unworldly philosopher," as misunderstood father poses. In these poses he had tried to imitate his father whom he consciously had wanted to thwart in everything. He remembered also the immediate cause of his breakdown: a remote love affair with a girl who had also studied at the university and often had tried sitting next to him during the lectures. He clearly saw now that it was he himself who had resisted everybody who had tried to contact him because he had been frightened for no reason at all. Suddenly he did not think himself ugly any longer. He bought clothes from his savings, a modern frame for his spectacles, a suit, and a tie. Then he declared that he really was quite popular at the office; that he could radiate charm; and that he even might become a "Don Juan" if he only could overcome his inhibitions. The records of these sittings became longer and longer and took on the aspect of hypomanic humor.

A few weeks later his mood changed to a depressive and plaintive one which he interpreted later as "whining for his mother's love." Manic and depressive phases changed nearly automatically in periods during the first half year. There were often some phases which seemed to correlate with his success or failure with the girls he was acquainted with, but I doubt whether they were directly connected with the change. He was always conscientious in his work, but whether or not he was happy in it varied according to the phase he was in. Looking back, I got the impression that I myself had little influence on the way his phases continued. In them a psychical development was going on which showed thematical duality.

In listing the symbols the patient used for his attitude toward life during the manic phases, the following order is apparent: he first saw himself as a powerful "Don Juan." In the next phase he discarded this ideal which he called a "teddy boy" ideal and saw himself as "Totila" (glamorous and generally popular figure of a king in *Battle of Rome* by Felix Dahn); later as "Schelling," whom he believed to have been a cheerful philosopher; still later as an ingenious writer; and finally he discovered in himself the features of his father. During his manic phases, when his thoughts were not occupied with his actual experiences, they were always circulating around actual experiences of his father. For the most part he saw his father in disgraceful situations: working as a handyman on the farm of a relative upon returning to his family after the war, or having a love affair with a teacher younger than himself. The latter event had broken up because his mother had intervened but not without his threatening to commit suicide. The then seventeen-year-old thought his father a "ladykiller, who was only restricted by his own inhibitions." Also, he did not think much of his father's taste in literature. He judged it from the books contained in his father's large library, which were good literature but of a certain sexy type, such as the *Decameron*. My patient then relinquished his interest in literature and turned more toward another ideal: "the philosopher." All these thoughts came forward during his "Schelling" phase, the emotional peak of his development. In the next phase he returned to his interest in literature and it turned out that he had never quite relinquished it. It had always been there in his fantasies in the form of short stories and in the way he wrote the record of our sittings. The *Begegnung* (significant encounter) with the father within himself took place without exaggerating euphoria but in a still optimistic attitude toward life. I therefore thought I must classify it as belonging to the closing hypomanic phase.

On the other hand all thoughts during the depressive phase were about his mother. The memories were always rooted in the last depressive phase which preceded the euphoric one. I would like to deliberately leave open the question of whether the emergence of these latter memories of the patient had anything to do with his change of mood or whether the approaching change favored their appearance. I do not know. The beginning of that phase was always marked by a resistance against the therapy which took on the form of a provocation. Then suddenly he felt sorry for me "having to sit still while he whipped my face" (comparable to the whip lashes which his gorilla-father gave him). He felt the atmosphere to be full of tension and "on a razor's edge." His eyes smarted as if he wanted to hold back feelings which wanted to flow out through them. He was afraid of sexual feelings toward his mother. He saw his mother standing before him and threatening him. He remembered that during the ominous first year in Innsbruck, when he was alone with his mother, he was often afraid that he would handle his shotgun so clumsily that he would shoot out his eyes. When his father came back from the war he was afraid that his mother would die. I was waiting for him to mention something important but he did not.

I instigated the next change without wanting to. My patient had again reached a state of provocative opposition and did not want to continue with therapy "just to oppose." He wanted to get worse, to commit suicide, etc. I had been on duty the whole night before and it happened that I just dozed off during the sitting. He noticed it and stopped talking, which woke me up immediately. Of course I was very embarrassed about my own weakness. He asked inquiringly whether I had gone to sleep. I replied only "Yes." In that moment his mood changed completely to a tender and affectionate ecstasy. He indulged in eulogies about my "tender frailty." After having been taken by surprise for a moment I understood that his feelings toward his grandmother were now turned toward me.

The next day he was strained again, ambivalent yet without being provocative. Overnight the words "experience with a suitcase" had turned up. He associated "chest" with it. "Grandmother has it and mother wants it." I was thinking of an object of strife between the two women and repeated "chest?!" he associated "coffin—American duel where both duelists have to lie down in coffins. Whoever gets the black ball has to commit suicide." I repeated "a duel in coffins between mother and grandmother." He now remembered a quarrel between his parents which he had overheard on waking up once when three years old. At the time his parents were quarreling a lot. His grandmother did not think there was "any redeeming feature" about his mother while his father had tried to defend his wife. Generally these disputes were kept from the child. On that day it appeared that his mother had come back very excited from a visit to his grandmother who had imagined she was being poisoned. His mother had returned terribly angry about this suspicion and had asked his father to send his grandmother into an asylum. He refused to do so. A quarrel ensued which frightened the listening child terribly. The boy somehow got the impression that his mother wanted a chest for going away. This chest he imagined as an oblong "sleeping box" and he was frightened by the notion that the lid might be shut. At the time he had felt that his mother's love was not sincere and that she only desired his love as a pledge for his father.

In fact neither of the two quarreling women died then but the patient nearly did because he got seriously ill. He said he had had diphtheria. He remembered only that the room was kept quite dark and that everybody was very nice to him. His mother added the missing link by telling me that after this illness, which had been a highly dramatic incident for the whole family, the patient began to run a temperature when he visited his grandmother. These visits were therefore reduced.

These memories helped the patient to understand an important fact. He suddenly understood that he had always been more fond of his father than of his mother, a fact which before this he had never realized. He also saw that he was quite prepared to love his mother, too, but that he was disconcerted by her impulsive quarrel with his grandmother to whom he was very much attached and by whom he felt he was loved. At that time he lost his love for both women. He chose a friend, a boy who was four years older than himself. The characteristic thing was that the mother of this boy was suffering from schizophrenia (she was "mad," as his mother used to call his grandmother).

A short time later the patient had the following dream: a church in baroque style ("church" as well as "baroque" were mother symbols which I knew from previous dreams) was bursting asunder because it was filled to overflowing with babies. Smoke curled up (patient associated "sex bomb"). His father was watching and ridiculing it, which annoyed him so much that he wanted to attack him. The church then was to be rebuilt but with a thin plate of metal before the door. He now recalled his twelfth year, the year his grandmother had died. His mother had often asked him then whether he wanted any brothers or sisters and had emphasized that she had always wanted to have more children. But at the time she had been against having them. Oddly enough, she reasoned that she was afraid the children might inherit the heart complaint which his father had developed that year, a heart complaint which did not save his father from being drafted a short time later. The patient felt these talks to be ambivalent—"very near but somehow indecent." He had then felt himself as "protector, adviser, and gentleman" with regard to his mother and had imposed upon himself several hard tasks as "proofs of courage"—jumping from a high and dangerous branch, for example. For hours he used to think about whether or not he should do it. The notion of shooting himself in the eye with his shotgun was one of them. He was afraid when thinking about it, but not of being blinded. This led to imagining the atmosphere of the dark room during his illness when he was three years old.

By the way, I do not know when he lost his eye symptom. The patient gradually stopped mentioning it. Only in critical moments (before dating girls) did he mention being afraid that it would come back. Later on, talking about a course to which he was sent by his office, he merely said he was afraid of the examination but not that his eyes would fail him. And there it rested.

The changes in his phase-like moods gradually disappeared and his attitude was influenced only by actual occurrences, especially by his successes and failures in making social contacts. He went to great pains to make them and went about it like one not very sure of himself and not very experienced. Toward summer he told me that he was no longer sick but just in love. I said that I thought so too. The sudden shock he felt at this moment was the password for us both to state again that I had taken on the part of his grandmother. We then ended the therapy. It had consisted of 462 sittings.

Discussion

I would like to leave it to the reader to draw his own conclusions from this psychotherapeutic experience. I have tried to relate the particular situations and steps in the therapeutic course, though many details have had to be omitted because of the scope of this paper. I selected these episodes because they seemed to leave a remarkable trace in the patient. The general and total connection of these episodes has become quite clear to me in writing my account, although I had always "believed" the connection to be there. As a biographer one can enjoy a better perspective than a therapist, since the latter stands beside his patient in time.

In retrospect I note that during the circular course of the therapy the depths of regression were reached at least twice. In the second phase of the therapy the same depth of regression was reached as in the third phase, although the aspect of the fantasies—the way they were seen—was quite different. In the second phase of the therapy day-dreaming and illusions created general aspects and figures. The shapes had no names and were impersonal. When the patient spoke of "father" and "mother," these terms were meant to refer to any father or any mother and not specifically his own. Only in the third phase of the therapy was a personal aspect won and formed. The regression toward the same depth of feeling as in the preceding phase consisted in personal involvement with his own mother, father, and grandmother. The act of encountering the "personality" of another person (that which is unique in us and not common to us all), we call *Begegnung* (significant encounter). We can understand now that only this repetition of the regressive process of analysis in the third phase of the therapy made it possible to *begegnen* (encounter) father, mother, and grandmother in different problematic periods of life. Does analysis mean the resumption of and return to that period of development where fear and aggression have torn the direct bond from personality to personality, the *Begegnung* with the principal figures to which we are bound in love— father and mother? The case of Irvin O. seems to confirm it.

TABLE 1. BIOGRAPHIC TIME TABLE

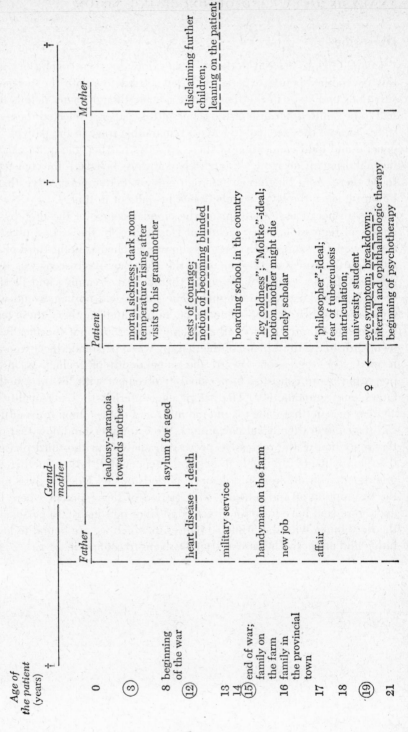

Age of the patient (years)	Father	Grand-mother	Patient	Mother
✝				✝
0		jealousy-paranoia towards mother	mortal sickness; dark room temperature rising after visits to his grandmother	
③				
8 beginning of the war		asylum for aged	tests of courage; notion of becoming blinded	
⑫	heart disease ✝ death			
13	military service		boarding school in the country	
14				
⑮ end of war; family on the farm			"icy coldness"; "Moltke"-ideal; notion mother might die lonely scholar	
16 family in the provincial town	handyman on the farm new job			
17	affair		"philosopher"-ideal; fear of tuberculosis matriculation; university student	disclaiming further children; leaning on the patient
18				
⑲			eye symptom; breakdown; internal and ophthalmologic therapy beginning of psychotherapy	
21			♀	

164

TABLE 2. THE COURSE OF THERAPY

Therapist's activity and interpretations	Rising thought contents of patient	Following change of behavior and insight
He must not have a girl; he is really ill. He exhibits	Obscene sexual scenes	Inhibited. Day-dreaming. Resistance
	Symbol of the bad-smelling car	
Encouragement: This car must be repaired! Standing still it remains bad-smelling. Summer holidays	His "poses" since the 12th year	Starts analytical work. Retrospective memories going back to the 12th year. He wants to work. Renounces his studies
Defend his giving up studies against parents	Oedipal fantasies	Takes up employment and succeeds in it. Maladit tic. Aggressive and provocative transfer affects
	Fantasy: Mother throws grandmother into "snake pit". Memory (of the 3rd year): He has to choose between father and mother	Calming down. Maladit tic disappears. Shy relationship to an old girl friend. Sniffing
	Dream: He looks at his mother under the coverlet. Fantasy: Clitoris = female penis	
Anatomical explanations. Summer holidays		Relief. Feels restraint with the parents and repulses them. Fear of homosexuality
Conversation with his troubled mother; her departure	Hypomanic phases: Remembrance and interpretation of the "poses" as father-identifications. Depressive phases: "Whining for his mother's love"	Acting out his transferences
I doze off	Eye-aches: Fear of sexual wishes concerning mother. "Duel in coffins" between mother and grandmother. Uncertainty about love of mother and grandmother. His serious illness and the dark room. Dream: Of rebuilding of the burst baroque church	Changing from mother- to grandmother-transfer
		Begegnung with mother and grandmother of the 3rd year. Changing of mood ceases. Begegnung with mother and grandmother of the 12th year. Begegnung with himself in this age of "proofs of courage". Insight into the grandmother transfer
Agree with ending the therapy		Begegnung with the therapist's personality

ADDENDUM

1. *Optimally what criteria do you use for accepting or rejecting patients for psychotherapy?*

   The first requirement for an analytical psychotherapy is the wish of the patient to undergo such treatment. The I.Q. should not lie below 90. Cerebral infirmities and heavy hormone troubles (including puberty), I consider to be contraindications. When the patient is more than approximately thirty years of age, the probability of improvement diminishes. Modifications of analytical therapy can be carried out even when the patient has no full insight into the necessity of the therapy. In schizophrenia bifocal group therapy is indicated, and so is psychodrama in cases of moderate debiles and even those involving organic troubles. Suggestive psychotherapy methods have other indications which are outside the scope of this paper.

2. *Do you make a diagnosis before psychotherapy begins?*

   Yes, as accurately as possible. (See text.)

3. *Do you attempt to persuade the patient or significant relative to change his (patient's) environment?*

   There are cases when I ask for this change to be effected even before I undertake the therapy. In the course of an analytical psychotherapy, however, I avoid all attempts at persuasion.

4. *How did you conceptualize the therapist's role in this case?*

   During most phases, at the beginning and at the end, I was sure of having the transference of his grandmother; during other phases of therapy I had that of his mother or father. It is essential to differentiate between the conception of an early and unproblematic mother and grandmother and the changed conception of the later sexually conceived and changed figures of the two women who were fighting each other. The same marked change takes place from the imposing father-figure (type "Moltke") to the despicable conception of his Oedipal and puberty periods. I trust that the change of transference was made clear in the text.

5. *What aspects of your theory of psychotherapy were particularly apparent or useful in the case presented here?*

   You see, what really helps the patient is not only the "insight" into the structure of his symptoms or his conflict, and the deep regression in the course of the analyzing process, but a significant encounter (*Begegnung*) with the personalities of his parents which must be reached. This can be realized only on the regression level where the trauma has torn the natural bond from personality to personality.

6. *Do you feel that this case developed significant insight? If not, can improvement be maintained?*

   The patient is clinically, subjectively, and socially well again. Whether the success will last will have to be seen after a catamnesis period of ten years. I have no reasons to doubt it.

7. *What aspects of your own cultural orientation facilitated or impeded the treatment of your case?*

I attempt in psychotherapy not to influence the patient by my own cultural orientation. Anyhow, I assume that the upper-middle-class scholarly appearance of my therapy room, the background of which is formed by an impressive library, facilitated the contact. The same is true for the personal bearing which had to be in tune with these surroundings.

8. *If we consider that a continuum exists from superficial to deep psychotherapy, where would you place your own case?*

I would class this case as belonging to deep psychotherapy. Anyway, I do not believe in such a continuum. Perhaps one could differentiate better between analytical psychotherapy and manipulation measures on the basis of a depth-psychological theoretical insight.

9. *What did you think about the outcome of this case, and what criteria did you use for evaluating such outcome?*

I consider freedom from symptoms of sickness to be a criterion of a clinical recovery. I think the case is a subjective success because the patient is content with himself and his situation. I think it is a social success because he functions well in a job the level of which is commensurate with his education. He is content with his job and is popular with his colleagues and friends.

10. *How do you terminate psychotherapy?*

A conclusive analysis of the situation of transference seems to be necessary and not too difficult when the therapy is successful. Lastly, the whole course of the therapy is transfer-analysis on the way to the *Begegnung* with the therapist's own personality.

CHAPTER 7

The Managing of Acting Out
in a Borderline Personality

—DON D. JACKSON[1]

Introduction

This is the description of the intensive psychotherapy of a thirty-one-year-old housewife and mother who was pressured into seeing a psychiatrist after years of visiting physicians and trying various medications. Her chief complaints were periods of severe depression and lack of appetite with consequent weight loss (she was 5′ 2″ and weighed 82 pounds). However, questioning during the four preliminary, exploratory interviews revealed that she also suffered from severe headaches, insomnia, nearly total amenorrhea, cancerophobia, and frigidity. She was afraid to be alone day or night, and had made two serious suicide attempts—the last one a few weeks before therapy started.

The patient was a cute, immature-looking person who was cooperative, yet curiously taciturn. As her superficial charm dropped away my diagnosis plummeted from anxiety hysteria to borderline psychosis. Actually, several weeks after therapy started she "recalled" a psychotic period in which she had been hospitalized.

---

[1] M.D., Stanford U., 1943; Interne in Med., Stanford U. Hosp., '44; Asst. Resident, Stanford U. Hosp., '44-'45; Captain, M.C., A.U.S., '45-'47; Resident, Chestnut Lodge San., '47-'49, Staff, '49-'51; Cand., Wash.-Balt. Psychoanal. Inst., '47-'51. Cand. and Memb., San Francisco Psychoanal. Inst., '51- ; Head, Dept. of Psychiat., Palo Alto Med. Clin., '51- ; Consult., V. A. Hosp., Palo Alto, '51- ; Dept. of Psychol., Stanford Univ., '57- ; Asst. Clin. Prof. Psychiat., Stanford U. School of Med., '54- ; Instr., Langley Porter Neuropsych. Inst., '51-'54. Member: Amer. Bd. Neurol. and Psychiat., Acad. of Psychoanal., S. F. Psychiat. Soc., Amer. Psychiat. Assoc., Amer. Med. Assoc.

Her somewhat stormy therapy lasted nearly five years and there were occasional meetings during the next year. The frequency of visits varied from five per week to once a week close to the time of termination.

During the psychotherapy she recovered completely from all her symptoms and they have not returned. However, as will be discussed later, she still has character problems in some areas of her living.

History of the Patient

She was the second of two daughters (five years younger than her sister) in an upper-middle-class family. The parents were of Irish and English stock and had been born in Montana where their families had had somewhat similar backgrounds in small business and farming. Later in therapy, because of the patient's insistence that her parents answer her questions, she discovered that the father had had two brothers who had committed suicide and that he himself was markedly accident prone. He had broken his leg on three separate occasions and had risked his life rather needlessly on several other occasions.

The patient spent the first five years of her life in Montana where her father was mayor of a small town and the owner of a general store. He became dissatisfied and moved to Washington where for a six-month period the mother and the two children lived in a rather large house while he was in the East on business. Upon his return they moved again and he entered business in Los Angeles. One of the most significant aspects of the Washington stay was the fact that this was the first and only time the patient can remember her mother crying, and there is evidence to indicate that at this time the mother was undergoing a moderately severe depression. The patient was exposed to extreme loneliness in a large, unfamiliar house and remembers little of contacts with other people until she started school in the last few months of the Washington stay.

When the family moved to the Los Angeles area, the mother's mother joined them and lived with them most of the time until her death when the patient was thirteen. She became an extremely significant person in the patient's life and one of her only sources of tenderness. The grandmother in the home fostered a cleavage which had become apparent even before her arrival; namely, the mother took care of the older daughter and the father openly preferred the patient. The patient became the grandmother's child and can recall such episodes as asking to have her hands washed before dinner and being told by her mother to get Nanny to do it. It was also interesting, in this respect, that the patient's sister looked more like the mother whereas the patient was always referred to as a "G"—the father's family name.

The father was away from home a good deal traveling as far as New York and Europe. He was so involved with his business that when he came home in the evening he rarely participated in family activities more than to acknowledge the presence of the children, read the paper, and retire early. On Friday evenings he usually took the patient and her sister to the movies, and on Sunday afternoons he took the entire family for a ride. He played bridge regularly with the men in his club and played golf Saturday afternoons and Sunday mornings. He made rather frequent hunting and fishing trips into Wyoming, Idaho, and Canada, and it was on these trips that he managed to break his leg on three occasions.

The mother was inordinately proud of her possessions and her garden, and she devoted a great deal of time to both.

As a pre-teen child, the patient recalled a good deal of loneliness and much lonely play particularly revolving around dolls and animals. There were occasional periods of tomboyishness which, despite mother's displeasure, had their reward and recognition from father. He took her fishing and hiking on several occasions. Her relationship to her grandmother was a pleasant and rewarding one; however, the grandmother was easily intimidated by the mother and father and would limit her contacts with the child if for any reason they had met with displeasure from the parents.

When she was eight, the patient found a girl friend to whom she continued to be rather close until this girl moved to the East when the patient was in high school. One of the most significant things about this friendship was the fact that the girl's parents were extremely nice to the patient, and she recalled having the fantasy that they were her real parents and would some day discover this and adopt her as their own. The contact with this family also introduced numerous questions about what was going on in her own home.

From the time she was nine until the onset of her menses, the patient took occasional two- or three-day business trips with her father to outlying towns. On one of these trips some sexual play occurred and the patient recalls her father becoming markedly upset and sending her to her adjoining room where she cried herself to sleep.

The onset of her menses in her thirteenth year was followed by a rather marked change in her behavior and in her relationship to her father. She menstruated regularly the first three or four times following the onset of the menarche, and then was extremely irregular so that until her marriage, when she was twenty-one, she had numerous periods of amenorrhea lasting six months or longer. Naturally, during this period she had innumerable gynecological examinations, hormone shots, recommendations, and the like. All were to no avail in influencing the persistent amenorrhea. Following an interpretation relating to pregnancy and castration during an interview toward the end of her first year, she began menstruating the same afternoon and has continued to be completely regular ever since. The only exceptions were several periods when she was up to ten days late because of pregnancy fantasies in relation to the therapist.

In high school she was popular, a "go-getter," and wildly active. She participated in girls' activities, was a notable success in sports, and had numerous dates. Her school activities occupied so much of her time that she was rarely home except to sleep. There were no objections on the part of her parents, except a rather consistent questioning on the part of her mother regarding what went on in her dates with boys, and a persistent disapproval of dates at all by her father. Neither of these attitudes was marked to the extent that it interfered with her dating activities. On one occasion during high school she was forbidden because of disobedience to go to a dance. She climbed out of the window of her bedroom, went to the dance, climbed back in and was markedly disappointed the next morning when the parents had not noticed her absence. Probably the most important aspect of her high school days was her relationship to Dick. This was a young man she met when she was a junior in high school and with whom she continued an impetuous off-and-on relationship until after her leaving college during the latter part of her freshman year for supposed "appendicitis." Dick was athletic, tall, dark, and handsome, and considered "wild" by his peers. In physical appearance he was much like her father. He was preoccupied with motorcycles and hot rods, and joined the Merchant Marine as a cadet following his graduation from high school. His membership in the Merchant Marine recapitulated for the patient the turbulent response to father's innumerable trips. When she was seventeen and had been going with Dick for six months, she realized that her attachment to him was great and that sexual relations were inevitable. Following a dance during which she had become convinced of her attachment to him, she returned home and swallowed a bottle of iodine. She went to her sister's room, awakened her, and announced what she had done. The family was, naturally, distressed and during her several days in the hospital and several weeks recuperation were solicitous. This was the first of five suicidal gestures and attempts. When the patient's abdominal pain, diagnosed as appendicitis but not operated upon, subsided following her dropping out of college, she obtained a job in an office much like that which her father headed. She was successful in this work until the time she left work to be married.

Her marriage was to a young man who in most respects was the antithesis of the qualities that she had been attracted to in her father. He was a Catholic, and this met with extreme parental disapproval. He was a rather quiet, sincere, hardworking boy who impressed her with his reliability. She seemed to act out for him the qualities that he himself could not manifest. For example, he was much taken with her talkativeness and her "baby doll" characteristics. In the two weeks preceding her marriage she lost ten pounds. On several occasions she wanted to back out, and the night preceding the wedding she announced to her husband-to-be that she could not go through with it. Her mother seemed pleased that she was getting married, but several days before the wedding the patient was sewing with her mother and grabbed a pair of scissors and made a harmless cut on her wrist. She described her father's attitude during this period as being extremely distant. On the wedding day he absented himself from the house in the early morning and appeared at the church at the last minute. During that morning she felt that she should find him, and on several occasions was tempted to go to him. When she thought of doing this, she would be blocked by the thought: "But what could I say?"

Her first year of marriage was an extremely stormy one. There were frequent arguments, particularly involving her lack of housekeeping and her reckless abandon with money. I may have neglected to mention that her father was very free in giving her money. At one point during the first year she recalled feeling quite at peace with her husband and contemplating him with approval at the dinner table. She then found herself telling him that Dick (she had confessed all) had telephoned her and had come to see her that day. The husband got on the telephone, could not reach Dick, but told Dick's parents that they had better keep him from bothering his wife. When it was made clear that Dick was at sea and could not possibly have been visiting the patient, the game came to its expected denouement. The "game" was played in varying forms throughout the marriage and increasingly resulted in physical punishment from the husband—especially spanking.

Following her discovery that she was pregnant, the patient underwent one of the most creative and peaceful periods of her life. She had no distasteful symptoms as the result of pregnancy and recalls no pain during labor despite her being a primipara. Her first child was a daughter, which was in keeping with her wishes.

She was eager to become pregnant again but did not succeed in doing so until three years later. There was one miscarriage intervening.

The course of her life and marriage prior to her entrance into therapy was one of chaotic, episodic change. She would have periods of managing her children well and of feeling relatively competent, and on the other hand, inexplicable periods of insomnia, anorexia, and depression. As these periods were traced during the course of her therapy it became obvious that in every instance the "bad" periods were ushered in by a fantasied or real involvement in a triangular situation. The most important of these situations involved her best friend and this girl's husband. The four young people would go camping together and on several of these occasions the patient became upset and had to return home. She at no time had any conscious notion of what the trouble was. The summer preceding therapy was the final straw. The two couples had gone to a summer resort and had their children with them. The patient was already feeling somewhat depressed and the solicitous attention of her husband and his ability to handle the children made her feel useless and unwanted. However, the most crucial factor seemed to be that her girl friend had just had a baby and the patient was extremely envious and covetous of the infant. After several days in this situation she threw herself off a porch overlooking a cliff. It seems probable, as the attending physician reported, that she would have been killed on the rocks below if her fall had not been broken by the branch of a tree. She had no serious injuries as the result of the fall but was hospitalized for several days for cuts and bruises. However, following the fall she developed increasingly severe headaches that were attributed to the fall and had to be hospitalized for several weeks. She communicated very little during this time and states that she could have told the doctors that they were on the wrong track about the headaches but did not do so. She finally felt they were mistreating her and one night left the hospital against advice. When she returned home, her husband impressed her with the desperateness of her situation and she agreed to visit a psychiatrist. However, she made another suicidal gesture and was hospitalized in a psychiatric sanitarium where she was diagnosed as schizophrenic, catatonic type. After two weeks, and just before she was to receive her first electroshock treatment, she ran away. Her husband agreed that if she would see a psychiatrist locally she would not have to return to the sanitarium.

The Therapy Proper

For convenience of exposition, therapy in this case may be divided into the following stages:
1. Initial period
2. The talking phase
3. The phase of sexual fears
4. Acting out without insight and the fear of physical harm
5. Acting out with insight
6. Aggressive and murderous feelings and fear of abandonment
7. Working through and anticipation of termination

Initial Period

The patient began treatment with reluctance and on several occasions announced that she would not continue. She had had unfortunate experiences with several psychiatrists at the sanitarium and had a marked fear that she would be locked up again. However, one insight seemed to facilitate my overcoming this early resistance: my discovery that the idea of being different (in any way) was entirely repugnant to her.

The Talking Phase

The initial reluctance to discuss her thoughts was followed by a period lasting several months in which for the first time she tasted the elixir of conversing freely. Much of the material obtained during this period was historical and pre-conscious but the easing of defenses was obvious, especially since dreams were more frequently reported. The dreams began to assume an almost repetitive character and dealt almost exclusively with masochistic sexual themes, involving initially an unknown, tall, dark man (father) and finally the therapist himself though in a disguised fashion.

The Phase of Sexual Fears

The patient's behavior in the sessions underwent a change that included an increase in the frequency and duration of silences, a marked edginess, and finally increased questioning of the therapist's intent toward her.

One morning about four and half months after treatment had started the patient was silent and obviously fearful for a whole session despite active encouragement. She called late that afternoon from the city some miles away asking "what had happened to her?" It seemed that she had blanked out after the session and had revived while driving around in the neighborhood of her childhood home. This incident was the commencement of months of such behavior, taking place during day or night, during which she probably traveled several thousand miles and for the most part circled her childhood home, the therapist's home, or a certain park where it turned out later she had had her initial experience in sexual intercourse with Dick.

Acting Out Without Insight

I have puzzled at length about the morning session that heralded the "go-away-closer" period of circling about in her car. It was apparent that something was disturbing her greatly, yet no obvious clues seemed at hand. If I had it to do over again, I think that with such a fearful patient it would have been appropriate to ask her to sit up to discuss the situation from the standpoint of feelings toward me. At any rate, the difficulty that morning was finally revealed weeks later to have been the experience of seeing the shadow of a penis on the wall. Because of the position of the therapist and the lighting arrangements in the room, it was apparent from whom she thought the shadow emanated, and hence the frozen response which signaled fascination and fear.

Just as the patient's acting out behavior consisted of running away, but running away with a circular motion, so her response to the therapist could be said to consist of diminishing concentric circles. She would be frightened, run away in some form (miss a session, be late, leave the city, or be silent or evasive), gradually inch back into the room, and then make a slight forward step in her understanding of herself. During this time her dreams were strikingly repetitious and consisted of situations in which the therapist became angry at her and spanked her or shut her up in a room and left her. The fear of physical harm particularly was evident in her relationship to her husband. She would at times call in the middle of the night to beg for protection from him. She correctly assessed his hostility toward her but exaggerated its extent. During this phase the therapist concentrated especially on helping her clarify her sexual fears. These were taken up particularly from the aspect of her tie to her father, her dependence on men, and her fear of them. Hostile aspects of her relationships were left virtually untouched. The sessions had the effect, generally, of relieving her temporarily and allowing her to see a tiny piece of the present in terms of the past. There was discouragement on both sides with our inability to make conclusive interventions or interpretations. Thus, she could have a point fairly clearly in mind during the morning session and by afternoon telephone in panic with a misinterpretation. Again, I feel this was not merely because she was a difficult patient but was a reflection of inadequacies in the therapy. The changes I would currently institute are discussed in two papers.[2]

During this period of "acting out without insight and with the fear of physical harm" there were, nevertheless, many gains. For example, the bulk of the psychosomatic symptoms dropped out of sight. The patient began gaining weight, was rarely troubled with insomnia, started menstruating regularly, rarely complained of her chronic fatigue, and began to engage in activities that required creative thinking. Only the occasional severe headaches remained as a persistent original symptom. The other gain during this period was the calling to the therapist's attention of repetitive themes which gradually became clear. These came to be known to the patient and therapist by various appellations such as: "the period of mother's illness," etc. Each theme referred specifically to very traumatic experiences of the patient that had largely remained outside of awareness prior to psychotherapy.

Acting Out With Insight

As repetitive themes began to make their appearance consistently through dreams or associations, the patient began to manifest more in-

---

[2] D. Jackson, "Some Aspects of the Oedipal Situation," *Psychoanal. Quart.*, 23 (1954), 566-80, and "Symptoms, Behavior, Family Dynamics and Some Aspects of Therapy," *Behavioral Science* (in print).

sight. Her acting out did not cease but could be more quickly interfered with. The patient began to regard her therapy as the most important event that had ever happened to her. She began to think of herself as a person with some abilities and some hope for the future. She began participating in activities with her contemporaries as an equal and on occasion would upbraid her husband for treating her like a baby doll. This period, though encouraging, led into one of the most disturbing aspects of her therapy.

Aggressive and Murderous Feelings and the Fear of Abandonment

As the fears became less marked, aggressiveness took their place, and this aggressiveness could only manifest itself out of awareness in acting out behavior. Thus evidences of aggressiveness would be followed by fugues, selective inattention, and amnesia. The particular form that this behavior took toward the therapist was in a "hell hath no fury like a woman scorned" fashion. Her possessiveness toward the therapist would alternate with rage at being excluded, made to feel unimportant, denied a baby, etc. There were occasional overt aggressive acts toward the therapist which would be followed by guilt, self-punishment, and usually a flood of memories from the past. The most important aspects of this period, during which strong dependent feelings on the one hand and aggressive and murderous feelings on the other were being dealt with, lay in the working through. Rather than any particular striking insight or miraculous interpretation that paved a highway to the unconscious, it was the minute, pedestrian repetitiousness of the working through of thoughts and fantasies that made her fear being killed or being abandoned. The reassurance lay in the diluted testing of these fears during each session. Initially, the feeling of being killed was related to father just as the beatings in the dreams had been. The therapist and the husband were included as father figures. The fear of abandonment and the expectation of strong disapproval was attributed to the mother and, to a lesser extent, to the sister. The therapist's wife and secretary were recipients of displaced feelings of this kind. However, what I had expected all along began to come true—that the extreme hostile feelings and extreme fear of retaliation were really primarily related to mother. There were some important recollections that substantiated this change. She recalled, for example, an episode in which the mother lost her usual controls and beat the sister almost into unconsciousness. This she substantiated by discussing the recollection with the sister. It appeared that her mother, usually stoical and quiet, would have occasional outbursts against the children. It was further substantiated that the mother and father used to have violent quarrels before the patient's birth but that *after her birth they were not known to even argue.* It is of further interest that since the patient had begun to undergo a marked improvement as the result of therapy, her parents had begun to quarrel—sometimes in her presence. Her mother upbraided her for causing trouble in the family, although she could not account for the way in which the patient brought it about. In addition, the mother confessed that she had hoped for years that the father would drop dead and that his retirement (which meant an end to his traveling) had been an extreme trial for her. The patient recalled that in actuality her father never laid a hand on her but that she had been spanked on a number of occasions by her mother. These punishments usually took place before the mother "gave her up" to her grandmother when she was still quite young. The patient recalled only one episode of being struck when she was older and that occurred shortly before her suicide attempt when she was seventeen. She and her mother argued about a dress that the patient wished for a dance and the mother slapped her in the face. The patient ran away and took the train to father's office, but was put in a cab and returned home by him. The father spoke to her severely when he returned home that evening and told her that her behavior *"was killing her mother."* This episode evidently took place on a Friday; the dance that the patient attended with Dick was on a Saturday; she spent Sunday in bed withdrawn and silent, and the suicide attempt was made on Monday.

Working Through and Anticipation of Termination

The realistic interaction with her mother, and to some extent with her father and sister, provided a dimension to the therapy that was previously missing. Unfortunately, I did not realize at the time (knowledge painfully acquired since then) that her husband should have been brought into the therapy since her dealings with her family were preliminary bouts to the main contest with him. She became able to speak rather freely of her transference feelings, and the tendency to act them out diminished. The acting out that occurs is mostly restricted to the sessions rather than to her outside life. She was managing her children with ease and was completely free of psychosomatic symptoms of any kind. Her husband had recently been on a three-week trip away from home and the patient managed well during his absence. She had a realistically oriented relationship with her parents and had been assiduously developing her talent for painting.

In order to give a further feeling of what went on during her therapy I would like to report on some specific aspects of it. This includes the notes on her first two sessions, an outline of the sequence of sessions immediately before and after the re-establishment of her menstrual cycle, and several dreams that occurred in the latter part of therapy and that have all the elements of her difficulties incorporated in them.

The First Two Sessions

The patient was seen for four one-hour exploratory sessions during which a history was taken and the practical aspects of psychotherapy were discussed. She agreed to undertake treatment starting four times weekly and during her first psychotherapeutic session was obviously quite apprehensive. She lay down on the couch and after some reassurance reported a dream in which there was a psychiatrist and a swimming pool that was deeper than any she had swum in. She remarked, "I've never actually been afraid of water and yet in the dream I seemed to need encouragement. The psychiatrist kept saying: 'Go on, you can make it if you try.' I felt some confidence then. I don't know why it is I think there are so many things I can't do. That's the way I feel about my little girl, yet she isn't that way at all. Toward the end of the dream the psychiatrist was making love to me and yet I know that I actually hated him. I always feel like I've done something and yet I don't know what it is, something wrong." In her associations she also mentioned the psychiatrist was the one that had suggested she be hospitalized and had frightened her. He had never appeared in her dreams before that she knew of. She felt he did her a lot of harm. She suddenly recalled that she had forgotten a birthday present for her mother.

> I must explain to my mother that I just forgot it. There is some other part of the dream I can't seem to remember. It seems to me that I never dream about any of my family. For example, my husband is never in my dreams. The person I dream about most is a little girl that used to live across the street. One that I felt very sorry for. Her family had so much trouble and her brother turned out to be a crook. She is married and has two darling children. We used to play imaginary games. She was two years younger than me and she didn't learn how to take care of herself somehow. She had so much trouble with her mother and brother that she didn't care just the way I don't sometimes—but really I do. She spent the night with me one night after my suicide attempt. She never mentioned it once. Somehow I think of Dick now. I hated him so much and yet loved him. In some ways he was so much like me. Mother said we were both selfish and egotistical. I wonder what's really happened to him—not that I really care. He caused me so much grief in my life and he had a fascinating power over me. He was so jealous and kept track of me. He felt that what we did was a part of living and yet I really didn't. I must have reacted to the trips that he took. I always wanted to give him up and when I did I wanted him back. I don't know why I'm telling you all this because I'm over it now. I wouldn't marry him and yet even at one time I thought that if I could only have his child. When I told mother about it, she said that father would have killed him if he had known.

She then spoke about the psychiatrist she had seen when she was seventeen after her suicide attempt. He told her that she had always gotten her own way and was spoiled. "I wonder why he said that. Is it so? Then of course they told me not to worry, that there was nothing wrong. But then if there is nothing wrong, why have I felt the way I do?"

In retrospect, it is obvious that the patient touched on many of the main themes of her difficulties in this first session. I was unable to understand the extent of her difficulties and the lucidity with which she first presented them. The fact that she had said a great deal is illustrated by the second hour in which she was already in the process of "taking back."

In the second analytic session she came in and sat in the chair rather than use the couch. She explained that she had not planned on coming back. She had the feeling that there were things that she didn't want anybody to know about and yet it was as if a lot of people did know about them. She recalled dreaming something the night before about soup but couldn't remember it any more. She had thought a thousand times of quitting on the last day as though she felt forced into it and yet knew realistically that she wasn't. She talked about the financial aspect of it. The therapist asked if she had been aware of anything frightening in the first session and the patient agreed that the whole idea of speaking her mind was frightening to her but she didn't know why. She felt that she was under a terrible pressure of time, that it had something to do with the kids getting ready to go to school, that she had to have them ready by September and it did not seem like much time. She was asked if it could have meaning in terms of her own childhood and she brightened noticeably and agreed. She tried to describe her childhood, which she called peculiar and a time of too much fantasy. "I always wanted to be someone else like in a play. I didn't know which way to turn. There is always the feeling of being dissatisfied with anything I do. I'd like to curl up in a shell." She turned to the therapist and asked very seriously, "Do you think I'm capable of taking care of two children? I neglect them and I don't feel that I really can take care of them. It isn't that I don't love them. I'm so preoccupied with myself. I don't watch them well enough." We discussed her realistic care of them and it turned out that she really didn't neglect them, but merely felt as though she did.

It should have been obvious to me after the second session that the patient was too scared to be left alone on the couch surrounded by her emerging thoughts. She was trying to act grown up and to be a good patient when actually she was a hateful, suspicious, and terrified little girl. I suspect that her attractiveness and subtle seductiveness were the main factors in keeping me from noticing the little girl more clearly. An example is the occasion when she asked if I felt she could manage her own children. I failed to question whether she was doubting my capacity to take care of her. Instead, I responded only to the adult and again failed her.

The Re-establishment of the Menstrual Cycle

About four and one-half months after therapy started, the patient began the first twenty-eight-day menstrual cycle she had ever had. She has continued to be regular ever since with the exception of two episodes of delayed periods with pregnancy fantasies that occurred during the height of the analysis of the transference. Since she had had eighteen years of very infrequent and very irregular menstruation, it is pertinent to review the psychotherapeutic sessions of the month that preceded her development of the normal cycle.

December 18th

Dream of being beaten by the psychiatrist who had put her in sanitarium. Called and came in for an extra session during which she acted confused and behaved histrionically. From the associations it was obvious that it was the first dream dealing with my beating her.

December 27th

Dreamed of arriving at the office for a session in a sheer nightgown. In the dream I tell her that "this has gone too far" and spank her. In the afternoon came in for an extra session because of strong suicidal feelings. She was feeling extremely guilty wondering how she could have sexual feelings toward me—concerned about disloyalty to husband and my disapproval.

December 28th

Indicates that I am not entirely catching on to her sexual feelings toward me. Recalls one of the very few occasions in which she held her father's hand. It happened at a fair and she lost him in the crowd and took hold of the hand of a strange man who with his wife kidded her about becoming their little girl and taking her home. She then caught up with her father and discovered that he had not missed her. Recalls wondering if she should have gone off with the other couple. "They didn't have a little girl like her sister."

December 29th

Very concerned about the therapist leaving for a few days. Feels it is because she has been bad. At his first absence she was relieved and felt better; now it is different.

January 2nd

Relates an incident of her father comforting her when she was home with menstrual cramps during her teens. Talks about the extreme discomfort that both of them felt during this episode and at their difficulty in feeling intimate. Said with some feeling that father was never around when anything important was going on and that he couldn't stand to see anybody ill.

January 3rd

Concerned with a sudden upsurge of fear toward her husband because of the "looks he gives her." This look is an indication that he is interested in sexual intercourse. Instead of being flattered she gets terrified.

January 5th

Obvious testing of the therapist begins. Had seen the shadow of a penis on the wall on January 3rd, but hadn't mentioned it. Missed her next appointment. The running-away episodes started following the January 3rd appointment. She saw her father the next day and thought "what have you done to me, you have to get out." After he left she was afraid he would never come back.

January 8th

Indicates vaguely that something happened on the 3rd involving a sexual response on my part and she felt she had to kill herself. She then decided that I still wanted to help her and that she should continue with the treatment. Had run away the previous evening after getting herself prettied up for her husband but then becoming fearful he would take her to bed. Saw the therapist's automobile and felt there was a blacksnake whip in the back of it. Recalls an incident when she was a little girl of a band of gypsies giving a dance in a tent. She had sneaked in and saw a male gypsy wielding a blacksnake whip. Her father had found her and was extremely angry that she had gone into the tent.

January 11th

Dream of intercourse with the therapist in a nearby football stadium. This is close to one of the spots where she and Dick used to park. Decided that this was what she had been running away from. Many other items touching on exhibitionism.

January 16th

Discussing the fact that she could get along with her father better than her mother could. This excited and pleased her but made her feel guilty. Is vaguely aware that she achieved some satisfaction out of showing the mother up.

January 17th

Discusses a suicidal gesture she made the night before her wedding. Connects it in part with the fact that she had been petting with her husband-to-be and he had had an orgasm and that was the first time she had become aware of the ejaculation of seminal fluid. She was horrified and disgusted. Thought something was wrong with him and that he must have some disease. She was unable to explain how she had overlooked this fact when she had had sexual relations with Dick.

January 18th

Talking of the two main boyfriends during her teens, Don and Dick. Discusses how she played them off against one another to mother's immense displeasure and father's amusement. Recalls being fearful that she would lose out with both and yet excited about it. (Therapist's name is "Don" and he was the nice guy in contrast to Dick.)

January 21st

Ran away from home in the evening but finally returned and ended up in bed with her husband. Recalls a girl friend in high school who had to quit school to have a baby. The rumor was that it was her father's. Very visibly disturbed by recalling this incident. Confessed that she felt that in the previous session I had called her a dirty name, someone that walks the streets and takes money from men. Was unable to recall the proper appellation.

January 22nd

Describes an incident of going to a birthday party with her sister when she was a child. Felt left out and went home without giving the other child her present. The mother sent her back and made her leave the present. When father was told the incident he said that he wouldn't want her to be an Indian giver. After she had left the present at the party she left again and went to a butcher shop. Mentions that she loves weiners and bologna. On this occasion she bought several weiners. The mother was still angry with her and said that she was tricky and deceitful. Said that mother's attitude was similar toward her for going out with Dick. Thinks she loved him because of the danger involved. Felt she was pregnant when she made her first suicide attempt (although intercourse had not taken place at this time). Felt that the iodine she swallowed may have caused a spontaneous abortion because she menstruated in the hospital during her recovery. Following this session she took a train and dropped into her father's office. She could not ask to see him but turned around and went to the bank and took out several hundred dollars. Called on the phone that afternoon to say that she was more aware of her fear and her attraction to her father. Mentioned that for the first time in her life *she had started menstruating that afternoon* and that it was just twenty-eight days after the last menstrual period.

Without attempting to venture specific guesses as to why the menstrual cycle became regular at this point, it is apparent that, in general, the patient was now more able to discuss her fear of men, her incestuous wishes now revived by the transference, and her pregnancy fantasies. She dropped some of the amnesias and the mysterious aura that she felt surrounded sex and was more open about her past and present attachments. She voiced her mother's disapproval of her and of sex and put this into a kind of perspective. In effect, can we say that she had had enough fortunate experience at this point to dare to begin to be a woman?

The Final Phase

After nearly three years of psychotherapy the patient had shown sustained gains that can be demonstrated by reporting several dreams. The first dream was unique because it was the first time the patient could ever recall that she had had a dream in which the effect was pleasant throughout the dream.

> She was living in a house that actually belonged to her mother, but that *she and her husband were occupying as if it were theirs.* They were going on a skiing trip and there were lots of people, especially girls, that she had known in the past. In packing she forgot to put her own things into the family's suitcase and started to dig out some old sweaters—quite a stack of them—and as she did she thought to herself, "Some of these will have to go." (Parenthetically, the patient's gain in weight back to one suitable for her stature had resulted in quite a change in her bust.) She was going to clean out the drawers when she got back from the skiing trip. The night before they were to leave on the trip she was going to give a party with a number of people present. She remembered that she

had invited Dick (an outstanding football player and a distant relative of hers on her father's side who had recently married) for her daughter. She remarked to the therapist that her sister-in-law had given her a box of Kleenex like the ones tuberculosis patients carry with them all the time— she had recently had TB. Susan told her to take the Kleenex, that they were going on ahead, and said, "Incidentally, Happy Birthday!" Patient suddenly realized it was her thirty-fifth birthday—"and now I'm really grown up." (The reference to "35" occurs because her next birthday and the tentatively set date of termination coincide.) She kissed her husband and said, "It's been a long time but better late than never." She then noticed that her mother had left a paper over the cold-air return of the furnace and scolded her saying, "Aren't you concerned about the fire hazard?" Mother said, "Not particularly, I wouldn't care if the place burned down." Patient remonstrated that she would, that she wanted to continue living there. She turned to her father and said she didn't know whom she was having to dinner. The next scene was on a skiing trip going up and down the hills with her husband. (The turning to her husband is demonstrated in reality as well.) They were then in a cabin where she was dying. A doctor was called, who said it was due to poison. Her husband asked her if she had taken poison and she said that she wouldn't do such a thing, that she did not want to die, and that she would do her best to fight it and to get it out of her. (Her sexual response was followed by being poisoned by the introjected bad mother. The other side of the coin to her pregnancy fantasies was a fear of cancer.) In the dream she died but then came back to life because it turned out to be a *spider bite* and she had only apparently died. She remarked parenthetically that the doctor had not made the correct diagnosis, and that she had the feeling in the dream that she and her husband would live happily ever after.

In associating to the dream she talked about the previous afternoon which she had spent crying in her room. It was somehow connected with: "giving you up." She also had been thinking of Dick off and on, and the long period of giving him up and going back to him during her teens. She recalled that after her crying session she had gotten up and started to turn on the sprinkler system on the lawn but was balked by a number of small happenings and became quite furious. She realized she was enjoying feeling angry. Interestingly, she was able to right the situation without calling any of the neighbors' husbands as was her usual practice. Then, after she had the sprinkler system going, she deliberately watered the lawn with a hose. She laughed uproariously when I pointed out the symbolic meaning of this act. She discussed, additionally, thinking about Dick the previous evening as though she had finally worked something out: that he was bad for her and yet she could not give him up; that it had something to do with boys and sex. Suddenly she started wondering if she had forgotten anything in the planning of a party. When the relationship to being competent and being a man was pointed out, she agreed and felt that she was angry the previous day because the difficulties that balked her would not have rendered a man helpless. She felt the cold air intake in the dream was related to her mother's coldness, and her own hostility toward the mother was shown in the fear of the house burning down.

The length and completeness of these dreams, as well as the reference to the future which they carry, were unusual for this patient. Her interest in associating to them and pleasure at "catching on" to her own symbol formation was also a new phase.

Termination and Post-Termination

The patient reacted to the idea of termination as a challenge and managed it with less difficulty than I had imagined. The money and the time involved were important levers in the separation process.

Some months later the patient returned and reported that she and her husband had been having a series of fights and she could feel herself resorting to the old passivity. I decided to see her with her husband for a few interviews since previous efforts to get him into therapy for himself had failed. During the joint interviews it was possible to demonstrate to him that he had married a "baby doll" and now resented her autonomy even though it presaged a better relationship. It was also possible to demonstrate to the patient that she did not stand up for herself because she was fearful and also because she was a great believer in the "meek inheriting the earth."

It is my impression that she will return from time to time for moral support, if not for further insight. Therapy could have been more effective if I had not failed to get the husband involved early in the game.

Some Aspects of the Psychodynamics

In the genesis of habitual acting out, Fenichel[3] mentions oral fixation with its high narcissistic need and intolerance of frustrations, the heightened constitutional mobility, and the presence of severe early traumata (producing a repetitive abreactive acting out similar to the traumatic neuroses) as the factors producing tendencies to action and therefore contributing to acting out. Phyllis Greenacre[4] adds to these factors two more: a special emphasis on visual sensitization producing a bent for dramatization (a derivative of exhibitionism and scoptophilia) and a largely unconscious belief in the magic of action. She points out that

---

[3] O. Fenichel, The Psychoanalytic Theory of Neurosis (New York: W. W. Norton & Co.), 1945.

[4] P. Greenacre, "General Problems of Acting Out," Psychoanal. Quart., 19 (1950), 455-68.

in the patients who tend chronically to act out she has found that there was not only increased oral fixation and a heightened narcissism but that typically speech was inhibited, delayed, or otherwise disturbed during development. This was relatively more pronounced than the motor discharge which might progress well into walking. It would appear that the lack of communication in this patient's family, the mother's relative indifference to her, and the father's emphasis on action are factors that would support Fenichel's and Greenacre's conclusions. An additional factor is that the patient's dramatic ability was irritating to the mother, but encouraged by the father, so that it was a relatively potent weapon. There were many factors in this patient's family situation and in some of her life experiences (as, for example, the sexual experience when she was seven) that would aid the displacement from breast to penis. It appears that one of her most abiding wishes from the age of five or six was to be a mother rather than a little girl who needed a mother. There was ample clinical evidence to support the theory that the patient's oral deprivation was carried over to her sexual experiences and led to marked fears of being penetrated, cannibalistic ideas, poison, etc. Material relating to pregnancy was virtually the central theme of the analysis. It is demonstrated, for example, by a dream in which the patient was having intercourse with another woman who had a thermometer for a penis. Among the associations were: pregnancy (thermometer determining time of ovulation), her obstetrician, rectal temperatures and enemas associated with childbirth and hospitals, enemas from mother, and the fear of the analyst suddenly doing something to her. She recalled wishing she had a baby so that she would not be lonely when the analyst went on vacation. She associated to the dream thoughts of playing with dolls and of extreme loneliness. She mentioned having a chick for a pet when she was quite young and killing it by holding it too tightly. The penis-child aspect of her pregnancy fantasies occupied the center of the stage for some time and were gradually replaced by their oral meaning and their connection with her mother.

There was a regularly occurring cycle of sexual wishes, guilt and fear, expectation of punishment, masochistic fantasies, castration wishes, oral deprivation (such as feeling hopeless and lonely in relation to mother), and pregnancy wishes. The latter heightened her fear of abandonment and of being killed and would be renounced by some form of symbolic castration or other self-destructive activity. The meaning of the form and content of these cycles was at first obscured by their being expressed in relation to father, husband, or other males. It was not until the shadow of mother was discernible behind the male object that order was rendered out of chaos.

ADDENDUM

1. *Optimally, what criteria do you use for accepting or rejecting patients for psychotherapy?*

My criteria are far more loose than those of many clinicians; but I have been surprised so many times by the unexpected response of a "poor risk" that I know of no better criteria for accepting or rejecting a patient than my willingness and the patient's willingness to undergo a trial of some weeks of interviewing. If in an interview or two I sense that there is something about the patient that irritates or frightens me, I am very apt to have him see another therapist. Although this only occasionally happens, it is an important point, since one will develop counter transference feelings in relation to any patient and these must be worked through. When they begin early in therapy (on either the first or second visit), then probably there is little hope of the therapist working them through. Life is difficult enough without the therapist expecting himself to handle every patient that comes along.

2. *Do you make a diagnosis before psychotherapy begins?*

My diagnosis is a "working" one and is so automatic that it is impossible not to make it. It consists roughly of three parts: (a) classification of the patient into terms that would be suitable for standard nomenclature. This is done because of previous training, not because of great faith in our present system of nosology; (b) an appraisal and estimation of the patient's assets and liabilities. This is as simple as his next door neighbor might make and consists of determining whether he or she is apparently making the grade; (c) an estimation of my feeling response toward the patient. It is not too farfetched to imagine that some day a nosology of psychiatric types may be based on the response of the therapist to the patient.

3. *Do you attempt to persuade the patient or significant relative to change his (the patient's) environment?*

I urge changes even very early in therapy that are related to making therapy possible. I try not to make other recommendations, believing that it is fatuous for me to tell the patient what to do when he can, in time, tell himself. If the patient seems to be pre-psychotic, or psychotic, and is living with his parents, then I insist that the parents enter therapy themselves or that the patient and parents be seen in family therapy. This I consider to be altering the patient's environment, but it is done for the benefit of those close to the patient because unfortunate reactions can occur in them as the patient changes during his psychotherapy.[5]

4. *How did you conceptualize the therapist's role in this case?*

The ideal role of the therapist in this case, and which I only approached from time to time, was gaining insight while lending the patient support and yet not inviting manipulation. She had never dealt with any significant figure (parent or husband) who was firm, honest, empathetic, and kindly. As long as I maintained this role, despite her being a borderline psychotic, she did very well. When circumstances within the therapy, or in my own personal life, caused me to stray and to become seductive or punishing, then therapy would go very badly.

[5] See Don D. Jackson, "The Question of Family Homeostasis," *Psych. Quart.* (Oct. 1957).

5. *What aspects of your theory of psychotherapy were particularly apparent or useful in the case presented here?*

I honestly believe there is a single outstanding answer to this question—namely, my belief that her complaints, somatizations, and delusions were based on real experiences with real people. This is not to say that she was simply the victim of mistreatment which she in no way invited. It is obvious that she was a provocative and inhibited person who was ensnared in a vicious cycle she helped to perpetuate. However, it was important to find the grain of truth in her charges before she could feel understood and accepted.

6. *Do you feel that this case developed significant insight? If not, can improvement be maintained?*

This patient developed significant insight in many areas, but did not work completely through the transference. For this reason, as previously mentioned, she was sent to another therapist for seven interviews. Following this, there seemed to be a marked improvement in her insight regarding the nature of the transference. There are certain character traits about which she does not have good insight; however, they are of such nature that their social acceptance and even social value make them rather difficult for her to examine, let alone change.

7. *What aspects of your own cultural orientation facilitated or impeded the treatment of your case?*

Perhaps the most significant single item which impeded the psychotherapy of this case was the psychotherapist's tendency to see the patient as a "poor victim." She had had so much mishandling by other physicians, as well as by her family, that it was easy for him to slip into the rescuer role. In general, I have a bias toward saving the mentally ill from the ravages of society. This attitude has obvious unrealistic implications.

8. *If we consider that a continuum exists from superficial to deep psychotherapy, where would you place your own case?*

This patient received deep psychotherapy as defined by frequency of visits, duration of treatment, and kind of interpretation made.

9. *What did you think about the outcome of this case and what criteria did you use for evaluating such outcome?*

Even taking into account my difficulties in managing this case, I would consider the result very successful. The patient recovered from a host of somatic symptoms, some of which were nearly crippling, and has been free of them for several years. Her relationship to her husband seems to have improved markedly and this includes their sexual adjustment. She is active in the community and seems to have some real friends. Rather than continue to be the "sick one," she has attempted to be of use to others in difficulty. There is a marked change in appearance. She is currently an attractive woman, where previously she resembled a somewhat malnourished, submissive, little girl. Perhaps most significant of all, in terms of results, is that her daughter appears to be successfully negotiating the difficult years of adolescence.

10. *How do you terminate psychotherapy?*

Ideally, I hope the patient will take the lead in terminating psychotherapy. If he or she is apparently making a good adjustment and has not considered stopping treatment, then I will bring it up. In addition, termination is always placed at least two months ahead of when the issue is raised so that the reactions to it may be discussed in subsequent interviews. Actually, there are very few cases that I feel could be called "terminated." Mostly it is a matter of stopping with the expectation that the patient may visit me sometime in the future if only for one or two sessions. I think it is unrealistic that the patient continue until he has "worked through" every problem with complete insight. I would prefer that he try his wings and then return if necessary for a further repair job. Psychiatrists do not provide all the answers to living and, additionally, some experiences have to be lived in order to know how well one will do. I am constantly surprised by how well some of my ex-patients seem to get along without me.

CHAPTER 8

Sexual Aggression
and the Need for Tenderness[1]

—BRUNO KLOPFER,[2] JAMES W. PARKER,[3] AND
M. L. VON FRANZ[4]

Introduction

Eva S., an attractive twenty-five-year-old woman of Protestant background, the wife of an Army officer, came for treatment because she was concerned about her hostile feelings toward her four-year-old son. She stated that she had disliked him from the time she intuitively felt she would give birth to a boy, and that she feared she might at some time

---

[1] J. W. Parker, who served as therapist in this case, received his basic therapeutic training in a predominantly Freudian setting; he started his personal Jungian analysis about two years prior to the opening of this case. Bruno Klopfer, who served as supervising therapist, is a Jungian analyst. M. L. von Franz, who served as consultant, has been a staff member of the C. G. Jung-Institute in Zurich from its inception in 1948, and has worked closely with Dr. Jung for more than twenty years.

[2] Ph.D., Univ. of Munich, 1922; Asst., Instit. of Soc. Welf., Univ. of Frankfurt, '22-'25; Assoc., Cent. Instit. of Educ. and Teach., Berlin, '25-'31; Exec. Sec., German Soc. for Orphans, Berlin, and Assoc. for Parent Guid., Berlin, '31-'33; Resident Assoc., Dept. of Anthrop., Columbia U., '34-'37; Lect. ('37-'39), Inst. and Super. in Guid. ('40-'47), Teachers Coll., Columbia U.; Assoc. Prof., Dept. of Psychol., C.C.N.Y., '45-'47; Assoc. Clin. Prof., '46-'53, Clin. Prof., '53- , Dept. of Psychol., U.C.L.A.; Visit. Prof., Claremont Coll., '49- ; Visit. Prof., Univ. of Zurich, '57; Lect., C. G. Jung-Instit., Zurich, '54, '56, '57. Consult. in Clin. Psychol., Vet. Admin., '46- ; Consult., Reiss-Davis Clin. and Child. Hosp., Los Angeles, '53- ; Ed., "Rorsch. Res. Ex. and J. of Proj. Tech.," '36- ; Pres., Soc. for Proj. Tech., '56-'57; Member, Soc. of Jungian Anal., L.A.; Fellow: APA, SCPA, CSPA; Dipl. in Clin. Psychol., ABEPP, '48- .

[3] B.B.A., Univ. of Texas, 1949; M.A., Univ. of Houston, '49; Ph.D., Univ. of Texas, '53; Psychol. Asst., U.S. Army, '51-'53; Psychol. Intern, Walter Reed Army Hosp., '51-'52; Clin. Psychol., Brook Army Hosp., '53-'55; Chief, Clin. Psychol., Ment. Hyg. Consult. Serv., Fort Ord., Calif., '55- ; Member, Amer. Psychol. Assoc.

[4] Current affiliation: Staff Member, C. G. Jung-Instit., Zurich, Switzerland.

physically assault and even kill him. Her other children were girls, aged three and six, toward whom her feelings were normal.

From the beginning the patient related quite readily, talked and associated freely, and produced a great deal of material, manifesting remarkable intuition and ability to grasp psychological phenomena.

It was decided to see the patient for two one-hour sessions per week. A form of analytically-oriented psychotherapy was employed wherein emphasis was on both unconscious and conscious aspects of personality, with dream interpretation and analysis of transference being major avenues for bringing unconscious material to awareness. In order to have more control over depth of transference, the therapist played a more or less active role and, within limits, focused interviews on significant material. Face-to-face interviewing was used throughout.

The following background material was elicited over a period of several weeks. It includes material believed essential for understanding development of the case, and did not necessarily come out in the order it is presented. Whenever significant material emerged, an attempt was made to get the patient to relate it to her present life situation. Sometimes one or more entire sessions were devoted to discussing a particular dream or other event which seemed pertinent, so that by the time the patient's background was brought up to date, there had been considerable therapeutic progress.

Background Information

Eva was born in 1931 on an East Coast farm. She lived there with her parents and maternal grandparents until her father was killed in an automobile accident when she was ten months old. Then her mother took a job in the city, leaving Eva with the grandparents on the farm.

She lived on the farm until she was four. She recalls these years as the happiest of her life. Her grandfather was quite devoted to her, giving her a great deal of attention and affection. She remembers that her grandfather was "crazy about little girls," but did not care much for boys. She slept in the same bed with her grandfather while her grandmother, who was not well and devoted her time to household chores rather than to Eva, slept in a separate bed in the same room.

When Eva was four years old her mother remarried and took her away from the farm to live in a nearby city. This was a particularly frustrating time for Eva; her removal from the farm and the one person who had made her feel loved and wanted left a serious emotional void in her life. She often recalls the farm as being "the one place I felt there was love for me."

Life in the city seemed quite barren to Eva. (She described her mother to me as a cold, rejecting, domineering person who resented the responsibility of caring for her daughter.) Eva was required to address her by her given name, even though she always wanted to call her "mother." Eva consciously felt quite bitter toward her mother for depriving her of "love and understanding" and vividly remembers how her mother used to ridicule and embarrass her, never failing to compare her unfavorably with other children. She also remembers a great deal of contention with her new stepfather at first. She was resentful and spiteful toward him and proved quite defiant to any disciplinary efforts. However, she soon found him to be "kind and considerate, much more affectionate and understanding than my mother." The picture of the stepfather emerged as a rather passive-compliant, dependent individual who was dominated by his wife. Eva and her stepfather found a common bond in their suffering extreme affectional deprivation from the patient's mother. As Eva became aware of his frustration, she felt very sympathetic, and in later years she often thought she would have been a more suitable wife to him, and sometimes consciously fantasied marrying her stepfather after her mother's death.

During these early years Eva saw little of her parents, for they worked, and she was usually left with an aunt. Later, when Eva attended school, she was usually at home alone in the evenings until well after dark when her parents returned from work. She vividly recalls that when she was about seven she often anxiously awaited her parents, "sitting in the dark house petrified with fear" that someone would emerge from the shadows and attack her. Eva continued to think back on her life on the farm—"but my mother would always say that they wouldn't want to take care of me there, full time."

The situation did not improve as Eva grew older. When she was twelve her mother became pregnant, and Eva was convinced that she would be unable to compete with the sibling, especially if the child were a boy. For this reason she felt that her prayers had been answered when this child was born a girl. But now, in addition to having to devote much of her time to caring for her new baby sister, she was required to work after school in her parents' hotel. This made her feel more resentment than ever, for she was becoming more aware of the restrictions placed upon her by the family, particularly by her mother. She had few opportunities to form close attachments to others and she began to feel inferior and self-conscious.

Eva's sexual interests and experiences, meanwhile, dated back to the farm while she was staying with her grandparents. During these years, her mother would visit on certain weekends and she vividly recalled that during one of these visits she was hiding in the bathtub playing with her cousin's penis when her mother called. Although she does not think her mother actually witnessed this, Eva had the feeling that she knew what had occurred. This made her feel quite guilty.

After relating this incident the patient had a vague recollection that this same cousin somehow killed her pet dog, at which point she added that when she was very young she liked dogs but that this attitude later changed into marked dislike. She said that for her dogs were masculine creatures, while cats were feminine.

In the later years, while Eva was living with her parents in the city, she made several visits to her grandparents' and another farm owned by an aunt. She recalls during these visits having sex play again. She told of frequently handling the penises of two of her younger cousins, stating that she "got quite a thrill from this," although she always felt guilty and ashamed afterward. She denied their ever having reciprocated, and states that she was always the instigator.

At twelve Eva had her first menstrual period. She described this as a "very frightening" experience, stating that "no one had ever mentioned such a thing to me." She recalled her mother saying, "Oh, I was afraid this would happen," and felt that she had "displeased and was out of mother's good graces again." It was only with great effort that she was able to tell the therapist of having overheard her mother tell her stepfather, "Eva has such a bad odor during her periods." Eva was haunted by shame and embarrassment following this and, although her stepfather's sympathetic and accepting attitude allayed these feelings somewhat, she has remained over-concerned and meticulous regarding bodily cleanliness. She maintained that she had always "suffered terribly during my periods," and that she used to think to herself, "Why does this have to happen to me? I must be getting punished for something but I don't know why." She then added, "I realized that if I had been born a boy this would not have happened."

With the advent of puberty Eva's mother began continually to implore her to "be a nice girl," warning her of the dangers of sex, and constantly referring to her own prudish background. This seemed to set the stage for her adolescent rebellion, and Eva went to the opposite extreme, refusing to associate with girls of whom her mother approved, and surreptitiously dating boys against her mother's will. She stated:

> If only Mother had shown me more understanding I don't think I would
> have gone overboard in the opposite direction so much. I didn't go with
> girls Mother approved of, and when I was fifteen the nice, good girls
> bored me and I broke away from them. However, I envied them because
> they knew the right things to say and do, and had mothers at home who
> cared.

From the time she was thirteen Eva experienced several sexual advances from various adults. First there was a maternal aunt's husband who would "chase me around the house, grab me and kiss me in a very adult fashion. Although I fought back I really enjoyed it." Later she experienced what proved to be a significant and emotionally traumatic event. At fifteen her step-father, clad only in his undershorts, approached her from behind and sexually embraced her by holding her breasts. When she resisted and broke away from him, he implored her not to tell her mother. Eva was so visibly upset by this that her mother decided something was wrong, and suspecting that she might be pregnant, took her to a doctor. The incident finally got back to Eva's mother who refused to believe it and accused Eva of fabricating the whole thing.

A few months later, when she was still fifteen, Eva's real father's brother made sexual advances by kissing her and fondling her breasts. Eva admits that she might have succumbed had he not been "of my own flesh and blood."

About three months prior to her stepfather's advances Eva had sexual intercourse with a boy about two years her senior. She continued to have such affairs with various adolescent boys and remained sexually quite promiscuous until, at eighteen, she married her present husband who is six years older than she. By the time Eva was twenty-one she had given birth to all of her three children. In describing the details surrounding her son's birth she very reluctantly admitted that when he was first brought home and was in her bed, "I felt an impulse to hug him close and love him intently. This feeling was too strong to be normal for a mother toward her child." (The patient was then reminded of the earlier bathtub incident involving sex play with her cousin.) She stated that this feeling soon disappeared and was replaced with a feeling of repulsion, and emphasized that she had never felt lovable feelings for him since that time.

In describing her relationships with men Eva made it clear, and was aware herself, that whereas she was typically the more assertive one, she greatly preferred men who would not let her dominate but who would tend to subdue her.

Diagnostic and Prognostic Considerations

Within the technical limits of the clinical setting where the psychotherapy took place, a Rorschach record was first obtained immediately preceding therapy. Another record was obtained at the very end of therapy. This offers the opportunity to evaluate, first, the help obtained for the procedure of treatment planning, and second, the clues for changes in the personality organization as a probable result of the therapy.

Within the given space, the two Rorschach records can be reproduced only in abbreviated form and without scoring and other technical procedures. The information elicited during the inquiry period (*Inq.*) is given following each response.

Table 1. Time-Place Chart of Family Situation

Year	1931	32	33	34	35	36	37	38	39	40	41	42	43	44	45	46	47	48	49	50	51	52	53	54	55	56	57	58
Age	1	2	3	4	5	6	7	8	9	10	11	12	13	14	15	16	17	18	19	20	21	22	23	24	25	26	27
Residence	Farm in East				Town in East														Various Military Installations									
School																												
Father																												
Mother																												
Stepfather																												
Grandfather																												
Grandmother																												
Half-sister																												
Husband																												
Daughter																												
Son																												
Daughter																												

The composition of the patient's household is indicated by the lines opposite each family member, beginning at the point the member entered the patient's life and ending—in the case of the grandparents—with their death. The solid lines indicate periods in which the member was living in the same household as the patient; the dotted lines indicate periods in which the member was still alive but not living in the same household as the patient.

195

Consequently, most of the routine information and impressions obtained from diagnostic psychological testing has to be neglected in these considerations in favor of those clues—supplied by the first Rorschach record—which actually pointed the way for the therapist toward the kind of therapy chosen in this particular case—and of the relevant clues in the second Rorschach record, which tend to reinforce the interpretative meaning of the first clues.

FIRST RORSCHACH

Card I
    3 seconds
1. At first it kinda looks like an eagle.
    Inq. (*large side detail*) The wing and the way the head is back. Foot here. A side view.
2. In a way—the Army—on hats.
    Can't see anything. Doesn't remind me of people or anything.
    Inq. The whole thing. Officer's insignia.
90 seconds
3. In fact, these remind me of baby birds with mouths open. Sounds silly to me.
    Inq. (*upper small details*) You see pictures of mother birds feeding baby birds. Looks like they are waiting for mother bird to come feed 'em.

Card II
    5 seconds
1. Gosh! Ever have people who don't see anything? Nothing hit my mind at first.
    Don't know why, but the two black things look like bears.
40 seconds
    Inq. Head, and has one paw up here. Looks like one putting hands together. Looks like they have three legs. One is kinda up. That's funny. Looks real furry in a way. Big and, uh . . .
2. But red things don't—they remind me of a foot—or a hand.
    Inq. Now I'm sure a foot. Has a sock. The red looks like it stops at the ankle. It's stuck up in the air. [*male or female?*] I think a woman's. It's small. In a sense it still looks like a hand. The red stocking kinda looks

SECOND RORSCHACH

Card I
    20 seconds
1. I can remember that I saw these as eagles. I'd like to see different things.
    Inq. (*large side detail*) Side view. One wing here.
2. This looks like the torso of a woman, in a way.
    Inq. Very strong impression. This is the rear. She has no clothes on. Sure has short legs. This could be the outside bust-line. Is she heavy! I don't find a head.
3. Those look like birds still, but the feeling isn't as strong. Don't see anything else.
    Inq. (*upper center details*) They have their mouths open.

Card II
    10 seconds
1. Here again I remember two bears.
    Inq. One paw up against the other.
2. And I said these remind me of feet.
    Inq. That kinda turns my stomach—reminds me of blood in a way.
3. That reminds me of a penis in a way. And yet also of a snake.
    Inq. (*projection from upper red detail*) The way it's shaped.
4. And now this looks like blood.
    Inq. (*lower red detail*) It isn't real red, but as if it were spilled or spattered, as if ink.

Card II (Cont.)
     like Christmas stockings that hang.
     It's funny—me and these animals.
     I'm not animal-crazy.
95 seconds

Card III
6 seconds

1. Those two look like skeletons.
     Inq. The way they are separated and
     look like hanging in a sense. Kinda
     dangling.
2. But looking again, they look like two
     women with almost a bowling ball or
     something like that.
     Inq. Although the balls aren't round.
     As if they are beginning to bowl.
     Though on this side it's in the right
     hand, and on this side in the left.
     Funny looking women. [Why look
     like women?] Figure of a woman.
     Don't look like men. A man with
     his derrière out like that would look
     a little silly.
3. And these look like two chickens that
     have been plucked; but they have aw-
     fully long necks.
     Inq. (outer red details) Up in the air
     being chased. Neck is plucked, but
     feathers here. Feet in air. Feathers
     flying off each one.
4. This looks like a butterfly. But it isn't
     as pretty. It's more on the crude side.
     Or a bow—a red bow with a big
     knot. [butterfly?] It's flying, and it's
     red—though not solid red.

Card III
10 seconds

1. Chickens again with long, long necks.
     Inq. (outer red details) Way they are
     shaped.
2. Those two figures just have to be
     skeletons. Look like women, and yet
     don't look like women.
     Inq. Say the skeleton of a man or a
     woman.
3. Center looks like a butterfly or shoe
     decoration—a bow.
     Inq. More like a bow. Big knot in
     middle. Clamp in middle. [What
     kind?] Don't know, not felt. It's silk
     or something.
4. [Laughs.] Those two things (tiny de-
     tails above "breast") would look like
     hairs if it weren't for those breasts.
     Inq. Just thought of it.

Card IV
15 seconds

1. Well, almost looks like two dogs. Ex-
     cept I've never seen dogs with horns,
     and that's what they look like.
     Nothing else . . .
     Inq. (large side detail) If you leave off
     the horn, it could be a real fuzzy
     cat standing up on two legs lean-
     ing against this. As if against a
     table trying to get something to eat.
     Funny nose.
2. Except here looks like an animal skin
     rug stretched out.
     Inq. (entire center detail) Kinda has a
     lot of tails and feet. Like the kind
     of fur pieces people wear. Has these
     furry lines in it.
75 seconds

Card IV
13 seconds

1. Still reminds me of horns in a way.
     Could be some kind of animal horns.
     Inq. (upper side extensions) Just the
     shape.
2. That reminds me of a rug—skin.
     [Rubs the blot.]
     Inq. It's definitely furry looking.
3. Don't see much. Can remember what
     I said before. Gee! I see something
     new, but—I'm surprised at my crude-
     ness—in a way—this looks like the
     lower extremities of a female. You
     know what I mean—the front part.
     Inq. (upper center detail) Just looks
     like it; the shape and all.

Card V
10 seconds

1. Gee! I tell you! I can't see much of anything . . . except that reminds me of a leg, and that a leg; and that (*top projecting contour of side detail*) reminds me of an arm. But can't say it reminds me of a person or an animal or anything—I didn't tell you much on that, but couldn't see much. Is that all right?
105 seconds
   Inq. Before it reminded me of skins like cavemen wore. Looks like a fur of an animal. Why, I don't know.
1A. That leg almost looks like a bone, like a chicken leg.
   Now this looks like a head, eyelashes, chin, nose—a person; a man leaning against something.
2A. In a sense the whole thing looks like a butterfly. It's distorted—not a good one. Never seen one with two legs.

Card VI
15 seconds

1. There again I can't seem to see anything. Except it might be a skin rug; except there's no head to it.
   Inq. (*cut-off W*) Again it looks like a fur—way it's flattened out. Lines in here. Two feet or something. And now looks like it has two heads (*two bottom projections*).
2. Right there in a way looks like—two snakes. But the rest of it doesn't go together.
   Inq. (*upper black portion of center column*) Don't know why they are stretched out, two right against each other. It's got spots or blotches on it.
   This (*side "wing" extensions of upper detail*) looks like a fur too, with lots of tails. Like women wear.

Card VII

1. Oh, that part kinda looks like a duck or chicken. Doesn't really; but does in a sense—some kind of a bird.
   Inq. (*upper third of blot with extension*) It's been plucked. Long neck. It's looking up. Down here on the

Card V
10 seconds

1. Well, I still see two funny-looking cavemen in a way.
   Inq. (*large side detail*) Lying on backs, relaxing. Yet I'm not happy with the leg part. Too fatty. More like a chicken leg.
   That (*tiny side extension*) could be a penis, but that's stretching it.
2. That leg—it's not a man's. More like a chicken leg—a drumstick.
3. These could be tails or feet (*lower center extensions*).
4. This kinda looks like a snake.
   Inq. (*half of usual center "rabbit" detail*) Again I have the feeling of a female—this is the opening here (*center line*).

Card VI
5 seconds

1. I see a difference already. Before I saw a snake—frightening. But now I see the vaginal area of a female.
   Inq. (*small tip of upper extended detail*) Just an impression—way it's formed.
2. This could be a rug.
   Inq. Furry feeling.
3. And this (*entire upper detail*), made me think of something Indians use (*totem pole*).

Card VII
8 seconds

Well, these could—I think I said birds or chickens—but don't look as much like it now.
1. In a way you think of something fluffy like clouds (*large lower details*).

Card VII (Cont.)
    body it looks like it has plenty of feathers.

2. I thought of two pillows when I first saw it.
3. Well, this—grotesque! Could be a penis. Yet it looks like it's about ready to strike—spring—like a snake.
    Inq. (small side projection)
4. And this—I've seen diagrams of female organs—birth canal and everything *(center bottom detail).*

Card VIII
2 seconds

1. Oh, these very definitely look like two animals. Don't know what kind. Some kind of prowling animal. Wouldn't be a lion. It's not a cat either. I don't know animals that well. Perhaps something like a tiger.
Inq. Way their feet look like they are climbing up. Or quietly walking. Can't see anything else in it.
All of these have this business in the center—like an emblem. Don't know what. Seems to stand for something.
Inq. (entire center detail) All of 'em are shaped like an emblem on an Army hat.

Card VIII
5 seconds

1. Gee, pretty! This reminds me of a polar bear.
Inq. Except a polar bear is white, and this is pink. It's climbing up. Don't honestly see much else.
2. These look kinda like two pillows.
Inq. (blue center detail) Way it's shaped. Looks fluffy and silky.

Card IX

1. These two kinda remind me of witches on Halloween. Peaked caps, funny look, long claws.
Inq. Shape. Claws here. [*Why Halloween?*] They are orange. Nose here. They might be flying in air. Looks like they are suspended. Looks like hands are over a crystal ball or something.
2. These kinda remind me of a bunny or something. Little stubby tail.
Inq. (green detail) Shaped like a bunny. Don't look like they are sitting. Might be climbing. Here is the paw, head, and tail.
That *(bottom detail)* looks like clouds—pink, though.

Card IX

1. Well, still think of two witches weaving a magic spell over their crystal ball.
2. Green looks kinda like a bunny. Bushy tail. Yet, except for that reason only, it doesn't.
Inq. He looks like he's climbing up.

Card X
6 seconds

1. Blue things remind me of scorpions, or maybe an octopus. Something with long legs.

Card X
15 seconds

Before it was kinda scary. Now not as menacing.
1. Blue still looks like a spider.

Inq. Lot of long legs—very danger-ous. Quite big.
2. And those two brown things—first a mouse or a rat—now a deer.
   Inq. A deer. Has horns—looks kinda graceful. Head held up, going this way, listening.
3. And these two green things look like two worms.
   Inq. They are crawling. Caterpillars—little green worms—not dangerous.
4. These two look like something—not an ant. A roach maybe. My, this sounds awful to me!
   Inq. (upper center details) Too big for ants. Now look like rats. I don't think I've ever seen a rat. I think this is the front, because those look like tails and legs; but I don't see a head.
   The red looks like parts of insides of a human body. Don't know why. Don't know if it's intestines or what.

2. This looks like green worms. *(lower center details)*.
3. These look like deer.
   Inq. Horns here. Facing that direction.
4. A wishbone.
5. Everything looks femalish to me. Everything—on all the cards the line down the middle and all.—I don't know.
6. Here *(upper grey figures)* before I saw something frightening. Now I can't make heads or tails of it.
7. Blue looks like some kind of organs in a person's body.
   Inq. (center blue detail) Don't know what.

I. Color and Shading Dynamics

Eva shows clear indications of a fairly intense struggle with the red spots in Cards II and III (initial remark in II, content of II-2, and III-3 and -3A). The color is first disregarded on Card VIII; it may be implied on IX-1, and finally seems definitely used in X-2 and -3, and possibly -4. The first record closes with another uncomfortable reaction to the red portion of X.

In contrast to this intense subjectively-felt discomfort in handling the red color, Eva is definitely more at home with the green, blue, and possibly grey-brown hues, and also shows relatively little discomfort in handling the shading: starting with Card II, the animal "looks real furry," and in the inquiry to IV-1, it is "real fuzzy"; she gives the obvious rug response in IV-2, and VI-1, and uses shading also in V-1A and VII-1. She might even use the shading in responses to the red areas in II-2, and III-3A.

This constellation seems to indicate that her emotional disturbance should be overt and intense rather than deep-seated and compensated by an impenetrable character armor.

In the second record, the aggressive indications of the red spots in II and III come out into the open with a blood response (in II-4, somewhat ameliorated by the inquiry remark). The increased facility to deal with disturbing emotions is also experienced in the whitewashing of the polar bear in VIII-1, and in the skilful combination of color and shading in

VIII-2. The somewhat confused and questioning final remark is now shifted from the red area to the center blue one, just as in the therapy Eva's aggressiveness becomes less of a problem and her need for tenderness is more clearly faced as the central issue.

II. Recoverability

Beyond the indications of Eva's ability to recover from disturbing situations and to learn fairly quickly to handle such situations constructively, as implied in color and shading dynamics, we find throughout the two records that she invariably makes spontaneous efforts to improve the specificity of her responses in the inquiry. The few new responses given in the inquiry show generally a higher form level than the preceding ones. The same is true about most changes from the first to the second record. The next section, on content symbolism, will show her high capacity to recover through her ability to face up to her problems and express them symbolically.

III. Authority-Dependence Symbols Combined with Symbolic Expressions of Sexual Role Problems

Immediately in Card I, the two authority symbols "eagle" and "Army insignia" are contrasted with "baby birds with mouths open," which "sounds silly to me." In Card III, this conflict is transferred to the role which men and women should play, according to her cultural stereotypes. The "skeletons" change into women with bowling balls—"a man with his derrière out like that would look a little silly." The chickens being chased "have been plucked, but they have awfully long necks." Both butterflies in the first record (III-3A and V-2A) are "not pretty." Overt sexual symbols are mostly conspicuous by their absence in the first record, which may be mostly due to the fact that Eva does not yet feel at home with the examiner; but she does use the most obvious phallic area in VI-1, while she avoids all the obvious vaginal areas, especially in the bottom center areas of Cards II and VII.

In this area, the second record shows the most marked change from the first. In Card I, the torso of a woman is seen, and makes a "very strong impression." In Card II, the first penis answer appears, revealing itself as an alternative to the snake seen previously. Another snake appears in V-4, but here this discovery is followed by a vaginal response, and the same sequence is repeated in VI-1. Finally, in VI-3, the previous two snakes fuse into the symbol of the Indian totem pole.

In Card III, her conflict finds the most telling and humorous expression: the two women have, in spite of their big breasts, "hairs" on their chests. At the same time, her positive feminine qualities are coming more clearly to the fore; the loving devotion with which she describes the "silk" in the inquiry to III-3, and VIII-2. Even the two witches in IX-1, are made more acceptable by the help of a crystal ball. Finally, in X-5, "everything looks femalish to me."

These content symbolisms reflect with uncanny accuracy her ambivalent attitude toward sexual aggression, wavering between phallus worship and penis envy, reconciled with a strong natural capacity for feminine sexual arousal, expressed in the search for female sex organs directly following the phallic symbols. In the actual therapy, the dream expressing the first positive reaction toward the female sex organ most likely constitutes the turning point in the therapeutic process.

In spite of the somewhat peculiar flavor of the main referral symptom—namely, her over-concern with incestuous love (the strongly ambivalent relationship to her son, and the flesh-and-blood remark about the uncle and the stepfather)—the combination of these three clues seemed to indicate a fairly intensive insight-therapy, and the results certainly justified this indication.

Therapy Process (First 40 Hours)

Early in the therapy it was apparent that positive transference was quite pronounced, and that unresolved sexual conflicts were thereby being stimulated. At the end of the eighth hour the patient reported: "This morning I dreamt of an old boyfriend, my husband, and my step-father. This boy and I used to carry on in the car. In this dream I felt he and my husband were one and the same, and that I was taking him away from his wife. I felt that my stepfather was somehow present."

Two sessions later, after having asked the therapist where he was from, the patient reported the following two dreams: "In the first dream I was taking a boyfriend away from his present wife as if to say, 'I can offer you more and treat you better.' In the second dream I was feeling sorry for a neighbor's husband and told him I could offer him more than his wife." When asked if these people reminded her of anyone, she replied that the relationship between this neighbor and her husband was very similar to that between her mother and step-father and that the wife is dominant and "is not kind and generous with her husband." At this point the patient suddenly became aware that the dream was a reflection of her own attitude toward her step-father and mother. Suddenly she recalled a dream she once had in adolescence. "I dreamt I was in love with my step-father. That's funny, I keep my distance with him as I do with my boy. I'm afraid of getting too close. In the dream we were rather intimate and I wanted to marry my stepfather. I think I told him in the dream that I would treat him better than mother did."

Following this hour Eva dreamt that a man was behind her "about to do something sexual, and I was receptive." Then she added, "You know, it just occurred to me that I may have been unconsciously receptive that time my stepfather approached me when I was fifteen. I wonder if I used to have a crush on my stepfather and didn't know it?"

The therapist said that this was quite probable, and asked if she believed this could have any effect on her current life situation. To this she replied, "My husband is in a sense my stepfather, I guess; that's why I had to marry an older man."

At this point in her therapy it became apparent that some of her early impulses were being stimulated by, and cathected onto, the therapist. This was indicated by a dream reported in the thirteenth hour. In this dream a man who was both her stepfather and husband watched her sexually arouse her uncle. When the patient was asked if this uncle reminded her of anyone else, she appeared surprised to suddenly discover that "he does look like you." She became embarrassed and added that patients always get crushes on their doctors merely because the doctors are so understanding. Eva was reassured that such feelings are quite natural, that there was nothing to be embarrassed about, and that these attitudes should be discussed whenever they are felt.

> COMMENT:[5] The initial dreams always point out that she should rescue a weak masculine man from his domineering wife, i.e., should free her objective mind-side from the negative mother-complex. Also to learn to distinguish between what her real husband is and what she projects on him (*i.e.*, her own weakness).

By now it appeared that Eva's sexual conflicts—particularly incestuous urges—had not been resolved partly because her sexual impulses were so persistently stimulated by father figures—especially by her stepfather, who manifested overt sexual desires for her. Moreover, as therapy progressed, it became more apparent that she had been unable to identify with her mother and, thus, had failed to achieve an adequate, stable, feminine identification. From anamnestic data it is evident that the patient's background was not conducive to such identification, and from the material brought out in her fourteenth and fifteenth hours it is evident that she had begun to cope consciously and unconsciously with sexual role conflicts. During the fourteenth hour Eva stated that her mother "seems to push me away. She gives me material things rather than love and understanding which she can't give. I think she's wonderful and I love her, and wish I could break down the barrier. I wonder how she feels about me; I sometimes wonder if it's disgust." Later in the hour she stated:

> I didn't breast feed any of my babies. The idea was repulsive to me, and so is being pregnant. Maybe I feel that being a woman is shameful. Maybe mother wanted to be a man and brought me up to feel not proud of my sex. Mother wanted a boy when my sister was born; I wonder if she wanted a boy when I was born? You know, when I was pregnant

---

[5] Interpretations of dreams by the consultant, Dr. von Franz, are given in this form.

with my son I felt like I did when mother was pregnant with sister. I felt she just had to have a girl. I've always felt like my son kind of takes my place and gets affection I should have.

At another point in the hour Eva said of her son, "Maybe in my distorted mind I think of him not as a child." Throughout this hour the therapist was notably inactive, merely lending an attentive, sympathetic ear, and occasionally reflecting her feelings.

Following this hour she had a dream which she felt was highly significant because after the dream "was the first time I felt good and happy. I must tell you, I've lost a lot of my bad feelings for my boy. I put my arms around him and had a good feeling." (It should be noted that her son had just returned from having a tonsillectomy.) In the dream Eva was looking at a nude man and woman in bed, and "suddenly got the impression that this girl was not a girl but was a boy. I saw what looked like testicles on her, and then it seemed I was that person, and I put my hand there and found her to be a girl after all. Then I got a feeling of great sexual warmth —a feeling of anticipation for intercourse." The therapist and patient then discussed the feeling of warmth upon discovering a vagina, and how this probably reflected a changing trend in her basic attitudes.

Eva's dreams began to get more involved with her unconscious attitudes toward sex, revealing that she unconsciously feared her sexual impulses because they were incestuous and, thus, destructive. She apparently identified a part of herself—a side that may have been deprived of mature psychosexual development—with her six-year-old daughter. One of the earliest of a series of similar dreams was as follows:

> I dreamt that my daughter fell in the bathtub and was killed. I blamed myself and felt horrible. Later I dreamt of a dirty, sneaky, sexy guy. He always killed girls, and he was chasing me. I felt that stepfather was somehow in the dream. This man grabbed me by a ponytail hairdo, held my hands behind my back and with the other hand was going to fondle my genitals. I had a smile on my face and seemed receptive. Yet I was scared to death because I knew he was going to murder me. The girl in the bathtub reminded me of my sister, and yet it wasn't. I sometimes wonder if stepfather would ever harm my sister. I'm sure he wouldn't; she is his own flesh and blood.

Because many of the implications of this dream were not apparent and were not discussed at the time, variations of it persisted over several sessions.

> COMMENT: Girl in bathtub: her "drowning" femininity, which is still childlike. The murderer: her negative opinions and her aggressiveness against her own feminine side = negative animus.

Many of the patient's conflicts and anxieties were exacerbated and brought into sharper focus by an extended visit from her husband's parents. Her husband, an only child, has a prominently dependent relationship with his domineering mother who openly dislikes and has always resented the patient for marrying her son. Eva was very distraught throughout their visit, and even prior to their arrival dreamt that she was "looking for my in-laws but couldn't find them because they lived high on a hill. I was with a boy who represented my husband, when they came by in a car and picked him up and took him away. The homes on this hill were not very expensive, but were a lot like those where my parents live." Eva interpreted this dream to mean that she reacts to her in-laws as she does to her own parents, making it clear that she was afraid her own need for affection would be completely frustrated, and that her husband and mother-in-law would psychologically abandon her. After tolerating this situation for about two weeks Eva and her husband got in a heated argument during which he told her, "If you keep this up, you won't have me either." A little later Eva told him, "If only I were a man, I'd knock you down." Following this argument when Eva was feeling more than ever "as if no one cared for me and that I was completely incompetent and un-wanted," she made a suicidal gesture by swallowing seventeen APC tab-lets. She immediately told her husband what she had done, and he con-sulted a physician and had her empty her stomach by vomiting. When Eva next saw the therapist she was feeling quite ashamed, stating that she had acted as a little child seeking attention from her parents. She then said that following the suicide gesture she dreamt that she gave birth to a baby, and that, in marked contrast to her earlier attitude, she felt good and proud in the dream. About this dream she said, "Perhaps it means I am accepting my femininity more; I see similarities with the earlier dream where I was glad and felt good to find I was feminine."

During the twenty-sixth hour Eva reported three dreams of a previous night following an argument with her husband regarding her harsh treat-ment of their son. Of her first dream she said, "I touched my son's throat and he was suffocating. I was terrified, and then relieved when he got all right." This was interpreted as a guilt dream since one time the patient had actually choked her son briefly.

In the second dream Eva "was in a restaurant when a blonde waitress sat on my husband's lap. I was angry and got up and pushed her off. My husband just sat there and did nothing. The blonde woman and I were both jealous and I said, 'She's got B.O.' " This reminded Eva of her mother once telling her stepfather of Eva's unpleasant odor during menstruation. She then thought of her mother-in-law "who makes a lot of fuss over her own blonde hair," and who implicitly ridicules the patient's red hair. She was also reminded of her husband "who does just sit there." The therapist pointed out that this dream expressed the problem Eva was having with her mother-in-law, and it was suggested that the last part of the dream may have been offering a possible solution when the patient pushed the blonde waitress from her husband's lap.

COMMENT: The blonde waitress: her own unconscious promiscuous side which weighs on her husband. She behaves to her own femininity exactly as her mother did accusing her of B.O.!

In the third dream the patient

was visiting a girl friend and her husband—a big masculine man who in real life is a heel. He was lying on a couch and was in an oxygen tent. He had a bad heart, and had all kinds of lunch meat around him. I said, "Don't eat so much because it's bad on your heart and might get you too heavy and kill you." I had entered the room in a nightgown which was given me by my husband. I had on panties but no bra. The gown was thin and I held my arms over my chest out of modesty. This man's wife was in the room and I was surprised she wasn't angry with me. She asked me to tell him not to eat so much, because she had already warned him. She also said that there was nothing really wrong with him, if only he would get up and go to work.

In associating to this dream Eva said that in real life, "Although he is a promiscuous heel, there is something about that man that always attracted me." She then added that this man's wife had said he probably was guilty of an incestuous relationship with his mother.

COMMENT: Her own "heartless" attitude towards life. Eating too much: greed for other thrills in order to replace feeling the emptiness of her family life. End of dream: it would be good for Eva to do a bit of real work to satisfy her father-complex.

Eva then said that since she had no more associations she would relate another recent dream she had put off telling

because it was so unimportant and silly. In this dream a woman friend of ours came to visit. Both in the dream and in reality this woman reminds me of my grandfather; in the dream she had big feet like my grandfather. She was going to spend the night with us, and I put her to bed but had some difficulty covering her bare feet which persisted in sticking out from beneath the covers at the foot of the bed.

Eva was immediately reminded of how her grandfather's feet used to stick out from the cover at night, and how she used to see him walking around in his nightgown with just his feet sticking out. She then recalled that her grandfather was obese, and that he would not listen to her grandmother who frequently told him not to eat so much because it was bad for his heart. Eva readily saw that this dream was related to the dream of the man in the oxygen tent on the couch. She apparently accepted the therapist's interpretation that these latter two dreams implied that her own sexual impulses were aroused when she used to sleep with her grandfather, and that she herself may have been sexually provocative then just as she was in the dream. Eva pointed out that these two dreams clearly showed a parallel in many ways to how she used to sleep in grandfather's bed while grandmother slept in the same room in another bed.

Subsequent Therapy Process and Closure

Again the material brought up in her therapy hours began to deal predominantly with fears of sexuality and sexual role conflicts. She frequently mentioned that since an early age she had had "a terrible fear of a man coming in at night and murdering me—usually with a knife, or by choking me." During her fortieth hour she related the following dream:

> I went to the apartment of a man to give him a little black kitten. He was a man to be feared in that he would kill me. I left there by a glass-enclosed stairway, and when I got to the street I met his wife—a woman who in real life is married to a leg amputee. However, I felt I was his wife.

Later that night she dreamt that a certain obstetrician was making sexual advances toward her, and he had both legs amputated.

In her associations to these dreams Eva stated that her cat recently had four kittens, and that as soon as her husband remarked that the black one was "a runt and the puny one of the litter" she began to hate this kitten, and to think of it as a male, although she had previously thought of all of them as females. Later when she picked this one up and it cried she had a strong impulse to choke it to death.

> COMMENT: Man murderer: negative animus. Amputee: she cannot move mentally. The black kitten: she always delivers her own femininity to her lame negative opinions.

Although neither the patient nor the therapist understood all of the implications of the above material, they both felt that it had to do with distorted attitudes and fears regarding her sex role and her sex impulses. Her conscious attitudes again were explored, and she emphasized how distasteful weakness in males was for her. She added that she had a need to see men as being far superior to women and that she needed to look up to them, and had an "irrational feeling" that males "see through" her and knew of her inner feelings and impulses. The therapist pointed out that the puny cat seemed to be unconsciously equated with a castrated male, and that this somehow precipitated her destructive impulses. Later when talking about her role in the family she stated that she felt more secure when she felt needed, as when her husband was helplessly intoxicated, or when her son was ill and required her. She said that at such times she felt affection for him and actually wanted to "mother and love" him. However, she emphasized that nothing caused her to feel more destructive than when her son whined and whimpered.

During the next hour Eva said that she no longer had the destructive feelings toward the black kitten. This reminded her of a dream she had the night immediately following the last hour.

I was driving down a road in a car with my children when the police picked me up for speeding, but it turned out that it wasn't for speeding, and they took me to a house in the woods. I have a feeling it was the cabin in which I sometimes carried on with boys when I was younger. In this house was a woman and a doctor. They were evil people who killed, cut up and buried cats, dogs, and humans. I was afraid for my child and for myself, though I feel it wasn't my son I was afraid for. I felt that if I would give the little black kitten—the puny one—to the woman, this would suffice, and we could get away. It seems I did this, and we ran away, and instead of going through the gate we went over a wall. Next I was at a grocery store and it was the next day. I then went to that doctor's office, and it seems I was attempting to stall him off while awaiting the police. I stalled him by offering myself as a victim, and it seems I was saved by the arrival of the police.

It became apparent that this was the first dream in which a destructive, murderous person had been a female, and that here the patient established a contact with the destructive force, and offered a sacrifice. The patient felt that the woman was one aspect of herself, and was uncertain as to whether or not the doctor represented the therapist. Both therapist and patient believed that the kitten symbolized something in herself that she was trying to eliminate.

COMMENT: The "Hansel and Gretel" fairy tale: witch house in wood, archetype of the negative mother, and Bluebeard motive. Sacrificing the kitten to get away: she should give up her childish claims for tenderness and for being nursed (= kitten) and grow up in order to escape the native mother-complex. She projects the latter again into the analytical treatment: she should be killed as a victim—give up her present ego situation.

The following night Eva had a dream the content of which she could not recall—"only the feeling—a good feeling regarding my new role with my mother-in-law and children. I feel rather confidently that progress is being made—that I feel better toward my boy since the last session."

However, a few sessions later she told how she and her husband had been having arguments, the most violent of which "was probably precipitated by my husband spending a lot of time telling our son good night, and I got jealous and fussed about it. It's as if my son were my brother. It's so childish of me. He and my husband are a team, and they seem to team up against me." Here the therapist reflected her feelings about being completely at a loss to compete for attention in this situation.

Eva then said that she resented any show of authority from her husband, and added, "Then I wonder if authority is what I want. On the other hand, I'm sure fighting to get that upper hand."

Following this hour Eva had several dreams dealing with her underlying resentment about being a woman. Then during the fifty-fourth hour she stated that her husband had pointed out that she was more upset following her therapy sessions, citing how well they had gotten along during a recent bout of illness when she was bedridden. She added, "At that time I was flat on my back and he had to take care of me; but then when I recovered and got out of bed, the discord started again."

When the therapist merely repeated this, Eva replied:

> I know what you're driving at. It's like when we were first married; I was in a sense flat on my back with him being the protector and boss, and at that time things went very smoothly, but then when he went to Europe things changed; I had to have a different role—had to be more independent and adult-like. Later when I rejoined him, I found this role caused trouble.
>
> *Therapist:* "When first married you were a passive child, and your husband was like a father to you."
>
> Yes, I was afraid to do anything—even to entertain. By the time I joined him in Europe I had to stand on my own two feet.
>
> *Therapist:* "Recently you were more like a child when you were bedridden."
>
> Yes, and my husband said he enjoyed taking care of me. I know that if I can be like a little child and always be good he would be happy. He wants me to be like his mother's treatment made him. He won't admit he wanted someone who was insufficient. I was completely a child when first married, but gradually I relaxed and to some extent grew up.

A few sentences later Eva said that her husband identified with her son, adding that "Sometimes I've felt like hitting my husband, but knew I couldn't so I would take it out on my son." Here the therapist pointed out that in addition to her husband identifying with their son, she seemed to identify the two of them as one in her mind.

During the fifty-fifth hour Eva reported a dream suggesting that a crucial turning point had been reached. She began by telling how afraid she was at night, especially when her husband was away, stating:

> It's always a man I'm frightened of—never a woman—a ferocious, scary man. It seems I'm afraid he will choke me. He would probably rape me and harm my children. I had a dream that I was on the porch of the house I lived in as a child. A bug was after me, and it seemed to be jumping like a jumping bean and squirming like a snake. This bug was coming from within the house. On the other side of me there was a dog with a face like a wolf, and it was going to kill me; but then it turned into a man and it didn't kill me. The man wasn't ferocious looking, and it seemed that he talked to me. In the last part of the dream I was sitting between two colored women and I thought, "I don't like the body odor that colored people give off."
>
> COMMENT: The bug: an autonomous nervous impulse like autonomous sexiness or involuntary ideas about it, etc. Dogwolf: see fairy tale of "Little Red Riding Hood"; it is the archetype of the negative mother: greed, resentment, cold rage, murder. Colored woman = the still rejected primitive, true femininity of herself!

In associating to this dream Eva said, "The dog turning into a man might mean that this fear turns out to be something not to be afraid of. The dog might have been my own savage side. When I meet it, it isn't going to kill me. That seems far-fetched." Further associations led to an earlier dream wherein she was chasing a Negro man who changed into an ant. This in turn reminded her of ants in a cabin in which she, her husband, and her son vacationed when her son was only six weeks old.

> I remember I was especially mean to him; I seemed to be feeding a need —a savage need, especially when I was bathing my son and we were alone. Actually I didn't bathe him well because I didn't want to touch him there. With girls it's different, although actually it's easier to keep boys clean. The other day I saw a neighbor bathing her son and I felt this was something dirty, as if I needed to wash my hands to get the filth off. I feel that to look at a little boy, or to feel him there, is unclean. In the past year or so I have been somewhat reluctant even to touch my husband there. I felt that you were thinking that when I was alone in the cabin with my son I was fondling him; I wouldn't stoop so low.

When it was pointed out that this was her association, she was reminded of her very early "abnormally strong desire to hold" her son, and she stated that perhaps her later feelings of revulsion were "some kind of a defense."

Associating to the bug that jumped and squirmed, the first thing that came into Eva's mind was a penis. She then stated with conviction that this must have symbolized her own sexual impulses which were stimulated when she actually lived in this house when she was seven.

> *Therapist:* Now we see a fear on one side, and on the other side is a dog which changes into a man.

> Yes, I used to like dogs, then I changed.

> *Therapist:* Dogs can see through you.

> Yes.

> *Therapist:* We can see a parallel to your feelings toward your son, which you have pointed out before. You feel that he too can see these sexual urges within you.

The patient readily saw the parallel here and went on to tell about how men—especially masculine types—can see the sexual urges within her. She pointed out that the men in her dreams were always chasing her, and added that while it was these masculine men she consciously desired, in her dreams it was these men who were brutes and of whom she was "afraid they were going to do something sexual and kill me."

The therapist pointed out that her feelings for dogs paralleled her sex play with boys when she was young. She readily saw this and added that her attitudes toward dogs and boys and men are similar in that she feels that when dogs look at her they have impulses such as men have when they look at her.

Therapist: In this dream with the sex urge being symbolized by a bug and frightening you, a change occurs and you see a dog with a wolf face.

Wolf face reminds me of the [vernacular] term wolf. Then I just now realized for certain that this creature turned into a man with glasses and it was definitely you—imagine, you a wolf.

COMMENT: As the therapist takes the side of her instinct (dog), she is in danger of identifying him with the instinct and rejects him together with the mother-complex and with her own femininity. The therapist sees through her like dogs do!

Here we discussed how our relationship was teaching the patient that a person can have a close, affectionate relationship with understanding and affection, and even with some sexual feelings as her dreams have clearly portrayed, without there being any danger as always occurred in her dreams regarding masculinity, sex, and affection. It was pointed out that this dream clearly tells her that she no longer has to be afraid; that getting emotionally close to the opposite sex means a sexual relationship— that men equal sex and nothing else. She no longer had to believe that affection must be involved with sexuality. In associating to the colored people in the dream, the patient was reminded of the time her mother told her stepfather about her body odor during menstrual periods: "I dream of colored men and savages who represent my own savage feelings; it's a part of me which is repressed, and this dream regarding these colored women might also be related to that. Maybe I feel that sex is in some ways unpleasant."

At the beginning of the next hour Eva stated that her relationship with her son had improved so noticeably that her husband had commented she was too lenient with him. She then reported the following strikingly lucid dream:

> I had a dream which occurred during a nap yesterday afternoon. It was a horrible dream, and I know it must have a lot of significance. I was crying when I awakened. In the first part of the dream I saw my youngest girl on a farm; she was lonely and lost; she was waving to me; she had no father, and it seemed she had no mother. It seemed I was there but that I was going away, as if I were dead. The farm was clearly the one near my grandfather's farm which was owned by an aunt and uncle. This uncle was big and fat and his son was the one involved in the bathtub incidents. This part of the dream tells me that I am my youngest daughter. I wonder if at her age I realized the sadness of my predicament. How could I have known?
>
> In the next part of the dream I am working in a hotel, which I did when I was twelve years old, which suggests that this was the little girl part of me in the dream. This hotel is laid out just like my grandfather's farm was, but it had sliding doors like my present house does. The room in the dream was just like the room I slept in when I used to visit my grandfather's farm when I was about seven, and when I slept with my four-year-old cousin—a cousin with whose genitalia I once played. Some

movie stars came to this farm, the most pronounced in my memory being
H. L., a quiet, gentle, masculine, not too aggressive man—gentle but sexy.
He was staying in the room in which I used to sleep with grandfather, and
which also had the bathtub located nearby. H. L. seems to have written a
book about gangsters which seemed to have some secret information in
it, and I wanted to seduce him; but he told me to stay away from him for
my own sake. He said I really had it bad. There was a dark-haired girl
there—pretty—who wanted him also. This girl was very ladylike, and I
wanted to be like that; but in the dream she pulled her dress down in
front and showed her bra, and I knew she had the same feelings that I
have—sex urges. Only I was the kind who didn't cover mine up, and
she did.

I had been planning to go to his room, but instead I took my oldest
daughter and ran from the house in my uncle Ben's car—long, black
Lincoln. I saw another dark-haired girl walking across the street, and I
wished I looked like her. I drove up the street and turned around; daughter was in the back seat. Then I saw three men who were the Killers, and
I knew I had no chance; they were going to kill me. They were the ones
in the book written by H. L. He had known of these men and that's why
he didn't want me to come to his room lest I get killed. These men were in
a car and I came up close behind them, and one of them told me to move
over and let someone else drive. While he had two other men, it seemed
that there was to be an older woman who was to drive my car. I told
daughter to stay on the floor, that someone was going to shoot me, and I
felt sad because she didn't have a father, and wouldn't have a mother for
long, and she was going to be so alone. The man in the back seat of the
other car reached out, and I stepped on the gas, real brave-like, and went
around him. I looked back and he had a gun in his hand, and I knew I'd be
shot in the back, and I told daughter to stay down. Seems I had two of the
men in front of me and I hoped they might get hit if I ducked. But my car
was stopped and I begged the man not to kill me and thereby leave daughter alone in the world. I talked so much of my daughter that he killed her—
stabbed her, and I knew she was going through pain and torture. He
stabbed her several times. Next, my daughter and I were in an ambulance
and I held her hand and told her not to move. I thought "Why did I have to
be brave and try to get away; maybe if I'd been a coward I could have
saved both of us—if I had let this older woman get in and drive." I woke up
crying, and I was very upset but at the same time I was pleased because
this dream seemed to show me something. Definitely my daughter, my
older daughter, in the latter part of the dream was playing the same role
as my younger daughter in the early part of the dream. They were the little
girl in me. In the end of the dream my daughter was not killed—just the
little girl part of me. This is the first dream where a real killing took place.

COMMENT: The lonely lost girl is the dreamer herself! She has no feeling
for this side of herself that makes her so split! Hotel with movie star: her
untrue side playing a role and having sex urges underneath. Gangsters and
killers: her destructive impulses (negative animus).

Last night I dreamed I had shot someone. I thought it was a girl I once
knew and didn't like; she was a smelly, unfeminine girl in real life. I
don't know if I killed her in the dream. I was in a fight with her and in

the end I wanted to kill her, and then she turned into an ape. At the end of the dream I felt I had killed someone.

(Therapist questioned her regarding any change in her own self-concept.)

I could have said that this changed before the dream. I have felt better with my husband, and I seem to have let the barriers down some.

COMMENT: She should kill the untrue femininity but not the ape, but she cannot yet disentangle these two aspects of herself. This has probably to do with the transference situation.

In discussing last hour's dream the patient clearly sees that the ladylike brunette represented the therapist's wife, and that H. L. undoubtedly represented the therapist. She verbalized that if H. L. (the therapist) had ever in reality allowed her to seduce him, the "applecart really would have been upset." To the part of the dream regarding her getting shot at from behind she associated: "a dirty meaning, and it reminds me of my stepfather standing behind me. In the dream I begged him not to kill me, and instead my daughter was stabbed. The question in the dream about why did I have to be so brave means why did I talk about what my stepfather did; why didn't I keep my mouth shut." The patient readily sees the sexual symbolism in the stabbing incident, and sees the parallel to her behavior toward H. L. and her stepfather's behavior toward her, and she understands that if either incident had led to seduction, her "applecart would have been upset."

At this point the patient happily stated, "You know, I don't have the destructive feelings toward my son. I definitely do not. I am no harsher on him, and it hurts me to discipline him now. Also in drying him after his bath I don't feel funny regarding certain parts of his body."

Monday I dreamt "of a diaper box with a lot of bugs flying out of it. The bugs surely equal sex urges, and I know it was a good dream. My son was somehow in this dream."

COMMENT: The sexual urges move out of her fantasying on the boy and probably go over onto the analyst. In the former dream the analyst is identified with a movie star—the true feeling situation of the analysis is falsified, probably because she doesn't confess her transference feelings and her "ape-reactions."

This proved to be a crucial turning point in the therapy process. Her outlook was generally positive and optimistic now, as she marked in one of her later hours, "Well, I don't have anything to tell you. Things are going very well. If everything goes as smoothly as lately, I won't have any trouble to complain about."

Her pressing symptoms had largely disappeared. She no longer had destructive feelings for her son. Her mother-in-law, once so threatening, no longer worried her. She and her husband both thought their sex life had improved because she was less inhibited.

When Eva first mentioned termination, she expressed regret about "eventually having to break off therapy," and went on to say that she wished she could know the therapist and his wife better, adding that she had never known anyone like the therapist. Her husband was reassigned while these feelings were being dealt with, and therapy was terminated.

Notes of the Supervising Therapist and the Consultant[6]

Before the supervising therapist left for a teaching assignment at the University of Zurich, there were several supervisory contacts which covered the first twenty-six hours—or approximately one-third—of the therapy. The impressions gained during these contacts were the subject matter for the first consultations between the supervising therapist and the consultant.

In these consultations, the following picture emerged of Eva's personality development and her initial reactions to the therapy: During her first four years, when she desperately needed tender parental affection, her grandfather—the most significant parent figure in her life at that time—provided her largely with attentions which stimulated her sexual reactions. His fantasies and his corresponding actual behavior were so seductive sexually as to result in a sexualization of Eva's own affective needs. Her resulting behavior was clearly rewarding, since it succeeded in monopolizing her grandfather's favors which were so essential, despite their sexual nature, because there was no other source to gratify her affectional cravings. Neither her mother nor grandmother seemed to have any time for her. As a consequence, Eva's needs for tenderness came to be largely replaced by and fused with sexual aggressiveness. On the other hand, her experiences with maternal behavior were greatly impoverished, to the extent that such behavior became actually suspect to her and was regarded merely as a screen for hostile and destructive impulses.

> COMMENT: That is why she got frightened of her own feelings when she first embraced her boy. The whole area of the "heart" is neglected (that's why she dreams of a man with a heart disease!) and replaced by sex. Also the "dog" is rejected—i.e., attachment, tenderness, loyalty, faithfulness—all reactions which belong to the animal instinct side of our nature, including sex. If these reactions are rejected sex becomes their only "replacement," and through this it becomes too dominant and autonomous.

During the subsequent phase of her development, covering childhood and early adolescence, her experiences with the grandfather were reinforced through the behavior of the uncle and the stepfather. There is hardly any question that this behavior, just as the later overt sexual activities with boys of her own age, was mainly provoked by Eva herself. (During the last phases of therapy, she actually approached some insight into her own contribution to all these experiences.) However, these successes of her sexual aggressiveness were accompanied by an increasing resentment against the sexualization of her life, which led more and more to her feeling of being dirty and worthless (atti-

---

[6] The interpretation of the case history and the therapy process was jointly worked out by the supervising therapist and the consultant. The comments inserted into the "Notes of the Supervising Therapist" and the comments containing samples of Jungian dream interpretations were contributed by the consultant.

tudes usually described as "castration anxiety" in Freudian terms). Her mother greatly reinforced this intensely negative attitude toward the feminine functions both by her own example and by her remark, overheard by Eva, about the "bad odor." Conversely, the male penis became to Eva simultaneously the object of great curiosity and envy and the hated symbol of her inferiority and sexual enslavement.

One possible way out of her dilemma might have been for Eva to have developed into a real tomboy, but the tendency in this direction was cut off by the mother.

> COMMENT: She could have at least developed normally in her "masculine" side —*i.e.*, in her spirit of enterprise, mental interests, perhaps creative impulses, because such impulses normally go with a positive father- and a negative mother-complex. Later she could have from that basis also normalized her feminine side—by a detour over the masculine side, so to speak.

Thus, Eva came to conceive of the sexual role of the female as that of a helpless child, while the ideal male role was that of a forceful, decisive protector.

> COMMENT: This conception created in Eva a further problem because she was forced to play a pseudo-feminine role, *i.e.*, to be an actress, as one of her later dreams put it very clearly. So her lack of femininity was covered up but not really cured.

In reality, none of the men or women who were significant in her life approached these ideals. Both her mother and mother-in-law were exceptionally domineering women, while their male partners were weak and dependent individuals—as was Eva's own choice of a husband. The two most hateful personages in her system of values became the misformed, castrated, but dominating woman and her male complement—the man who is passive, ineffectual, and dependent. (Significantly, the only periods when Eva was really happy with her husband were when she was sick and he had to take care of her.)

> COMMENT: If we interpret this on a subjective level, *i.e.*, as representation of an inner fact in herself, it would mean that Eva herself is in the unconscious part of her personality a domineering, harsh woman and that her mental, creative and spiritual side (the man in her) is weak. This shows in the banality and suggestibility of her thinking.

It is understandable, then, why Eva was so afraid that the child resulting from the mother's second marriage might be a boy, and why the birth of her own son became such a threat to her.

> COMMENT: The boy appealed to her maternal feelings and therefore brought into the open the fact that she had none. One cannot "act" to be a mother—so she had to be "real," and this revealed that she had only effusive, exaggerated, childish feeling impulses (like a girl with her doll), but no grown up femininity. On the other side, the boy symbolizes also the beginning of a new creative life which she wants to strangle in herself too.

The emergence of a new male being (the birth of the sibling and her own children, and even the birth of kittens) possessed Eva with fear lest this be the "ideal" male which would deprive her of any remaining value. This extended even to the masculine side of her own personality, experienced as a ruthless, aggressive, and sexually destructive element in her which had to be exterminated before she could be reborn as a worthy female being. Eva's destructive feelings for her son could not be alleviated until she experienced her own early needs for tenderness as something acceptable and separate from sexual aggression. Through the transference relationship, which permitted her to give and receive affection without sexual aggression, this was made possible.

The therapist's notes for the twenty-seventh to the forty-first therapy hours were forwarded to Switzerland and became the subject for further consultations. During the last phase of the therapy, some direct supervisory contacts were again possible. The Jungian interpretation as outlined in these notes proved to be quite helpful for the course of the therapy, and found a practical validation in the positive outcome as described in the "Addendum."

ADDENDUM[7]

1. *Optimally, what criteria do you use for accepting or rejecting patients for psychotherapy?*

    Personally, I prefer analytic cases with the goal of self-realization or self-actualization to psychotherapeutic cases which aim primarily at the relief of disturbing symptoms and the overcoming of inadequate adjustment mechanisms. Disturbing symptoms and faulty adjustments should not be too much in the foreground, and the motivation for the unfolding of internal potentialities for a richer and more meaningful life is the primary prerequisite for analytic cases. The case on hand falls distinctly into the category of psychotherapy.

2. *Do you make a diagnosis before psychotherapy begins?*

    Not necessarily a clinical diagnosis with a clinical label, but definitely a careful survey of the ego organization with its strengths and weaknesses, and with special emphasis on indications of potentially unused ego strength.

3. *Do you attempt to persuade the patient or significant relative to change his (the patient's) environment?*

    Manipulation to better the environmental situation is certainly to be included in the goals of psychotherapy, but it should be a result of growing ego strength and not of persuasion.

4. *How did you conceptualize the therapist's role in this case?*

    The most important function of the therapist in this case was to help the patient to differentiate her affectional and sexual needs, with the help of the transference reactions and their interpretation.

5. *What aspects of your theory of psychotherapy were particularly apparent or useful in the case presented here?*

    The hypothesis that emotional relatedness is as basic a need as sexual gratification seems to have been indispensable for the understanding of the symptoms in this case. Furthermore, the assumption that sexual impulses might serve as the screen for other needs was a corollary hypothesis.

6. *Do you feel that this case developed significant insight? If not, can improvement be maintained?*

    The amount of insight developed in this case exceeds the usual amount to be gained in therapy cases. There are indications of self-realization which

---

[7] The answers to this questionnaire reflect the opinions of the supervising therapist in this case, as far as they refer to general principles. Factual evaluations of the role of the therapist in this case refer to the military psychologist who actually conducted the therapy, as seen by the supervising therapist.

promise that improvement during therapy will not only be maintained, but will continue to grow.

7. *What aspects of your own cultural orientation facilitated or impeded the treatment of your case?*

    The role of the therapist as a military officer—having even the same rank as the husband of the patient—definitely facilitated the development of the transference reaction.

8. *If we consider that a continuum exists from superficial to deep psychotherapy, where would you place your own case?*

    As pointed out under (6), this case developed beyond the midpoint between superficial and deep therapy.

9. *What did you think about the outcome of this case and what criteria did you use for evaluating such outcome?*

    The primary criteria for the positive outcome are to be found in the symptom relief and the subjective evaluation by the patient of the change in her life situation. On a more objective basis, I would mention the fact that the husband was able, for the first time, to take a stand in support of his wife against his mother, along with other improvements in his own adjustments (*e.g.*, drinking). In the therapy with a marital partner, the positive outcome should always result in "getting two therapies for the price of one."

10. *How do you terminate psychotherapy?*

    Fortunately, termination was in this case a coincidence between the internal development of the therapy toward a good closure point and the external termination of the military service of the patient's husband. Internally, the patient had firmly established the experience that strong affective ties were possible without sexual gratification.

CHAPTER 9

The Involvement of the
Professional Therapist

—CARL A. WHITAKER,[1] JOHN WARKENTIN,[2] AND
THOMAS P. MALONE[3]

Introduction

The Setting

The patient (Hilda) was a thirty-year-old, married female with the chief complaints of repeated severe depressions, psychotic behavior, and suicide attempts. The onset of the present episode was associated with sexual infidelity, followed by paranoid delusions that her lover would kill her. Four months after the onset the illness developed into a catatonic muteness. Psychotherapeutic efforts at this time were unsuccessful. Seven months after the onset she attempted suicide by wrecking her automobile and was hospitalized for serious physical injuries. She was transferred to a

---

[1] M.D., Syracuse U., 1936; Syracuse U., Psychiatry, '38-40; Univ. of Louisville, Coll. of Med., '40-44; Dir., Dept. of Psychiat., Oakridge Hosp., '44-'46; Prof. & Chairman, Dept. of Psychiat., Emory U., '46-'55 (full time); Priv. pract., Atlanta Psychiatric Clin., '55- ; Author of *The Roots of Psychotherapy* (with Thomas P. Malone) and other works.

[2] Univ. of Rochester, Ph.D., 1938; Northwestern U. Med. School, M.D., '42; Army of the U.S., '43-'46, Psychiatric sections of Walter Reed, Welch Conval. and Oakridge Gen. Hospitals; Chief, Psychiat. Sec., Lawson V. A. Hosp., '47-'49; Asst. Prof. of Psychiat., Emory U., '49-'55; Private pract., Atlanta Psychiatric Clin., '55- ; Editor, *Physician's Handbook* (fiirst edition, 1941; current (8th) edition, 1954) and other works.

[3] Duke U., Ph.D., '42; Emory U., M.D., 1952; A.U.S., Neuropsych. Sec. of Robinson Gen. Hosp., '42-'45; Assoc. Prof. of Clin. Psychol., Duke U., '45-'48; Asst. Prof. of Psychiat., Emory U., '48-'55; Priv. pract., Atlanta Psychiatric Clin., '55- . Author of *The Roots of Psychotherapy* (with C. A. Whitaker) and other works.

psychiatric hospital and treated with insulin shock. One month later she attempted suicide by cutting her wrists and her inguinal ligaments. A week later she had improved to the extent that she was discharged from the hospital. On the day of discharge she turned on the gas in her room in a large hotel and the subsequent explosion destroyed a large part of the building. The patient was not seriously injured and was returned to the hospital for insulin and electric shock. Shortly thereafter her attempt to commit suicide by leaping out a window was frustrated and she was transferred to another hospital as too severe a suicidal risk. There she was diagnosed as schizophrenic, progressive, and the family was told that no matter what was done she would probably kill herself. Three weeks later she was referred to the authors for treatment.

Past History

Since adolescence the patient had been having recurrent depressions with preoccupations about suicidal acts, specifically the amputation of her left breast and disembowelling herself through the vagina. The patient was a nail-biter and thumb-sucker as a child and was broken of the latter with steel mitts when she was six-years-old. From the age of six she was cared for in private schools. As a child she was timid, self-conscious, nervous, cried a great deal, particularly about her obesity. She had been preoccupied with guilt about masturbation and this eventuated in a clitorectomy at the age of eleven. This operation was instigated by her father "to cure her of her self-consciousness." Despite this her masturbation continued until the date of referral. Her parents were divorced when she was twelve because of the father's infidelity. After this the patient was provided for by the maternal grandmother. Menarche began when she was fourteen. After puberty she was withdrawn and isolated, afraid of groups, and comfortable only with one person. She was known to hate her body, especially her hands and her breasts, and avoided all physical contact with other persons. She had several affairs with older men and was finally married at the age of nineteen, but was frigid in her sexual relationship with her husband. She began to doubt her love for her husband and became involved in a series of flirtations. When she was twenty-three she had her first child, and this birth was followed by a serious postpartum depression. A second child was born one year later. Her husband was a very practical but masochistic and rather passive, ineffectual male. The patient described him as "dull."

Her father was a schoolteacher. He was a dependent person who compensated with over-assertiveness and developed a gastric ulcer. He was excessively prudish and obsessive in his treatment of the children. The mother was a dominating, frigid, but socially adept person who had a psychiatric history of depression at the age of thirty-eight. The patient had one older sister who also suffered from depressions.

Definition of the Therapeutic Task

The authors saw four therapeutic problems. The first was the satisfaction of the patient's *dependent oral need,* as indicated by her thumb-sucking, obesity, sexual promiscuity, and preoccupation with oral sexual behavior. The second objective was helping the patient to find a better way to *express her hostility,* previously expressed by her acting-out, her repeated suicidal attempts, and her severe depressions. The third need was the resolution of her *infantile sexual anxieties.* The authors saw the Oedipal problem as an inability to relate to both parents simultaneously. Her sexual anxieties had been previously indicated by her frigidity, excessive shame, her fear of men, a preference for impotent or older men, her hatred of her body, and impulses to destroy her breasts and her sexual organs. The fourth problem was the *resolution of the flatness* of her psychosis by an attempt to induce some experience of positive affect in her through her participation in a relationship where others were expressing positive affect. The need for this was indicated by her cynical indifference, emotional withdrawal, fear of being touched or of any positive affect, and the precipitation of suicidal impulses by positive emotional experiences. She had never at any time requested psychiatric help.

Administrative Task

The patient had been told in two previous psychiatric hospitals that she could be neither contained nor kept from suicide. She was told by the referring doctor that treatment by the authors was the final effort, and would be an "explosive experience" that would be "different from anything she had seen before." Her mother was to be the custodian and to pay for the treatment.

In her initial contact with one of the authors he explained that he knew she could kill herself at any time. Thus she was told that she was able to defeat the two therapists at any time. During the initial family conference the mother brought out the financial limitations which made three months the maximum time available for treatment. She was to be seen in six 45-minute appointments per week by two therapists. She was to live with a couple in a private home where the wife was a trained psychiatric attendant. This couple was responsible for the patient's constant custody and for her transfer to and from appointments. The mother was seen daily in some orientation interviews for two weeks by the author who was not part of the multiple therapy team. This contact with the mother was planned to neutralize some of her guilt and to isolate her from the treatment situation.

Any further contact the mother might want with the doctors doing the actual treatment was to be made through a fourth doctor who was introduced to her as the "administrator" in this case.

Follow-up

One month after the discontinuation of therapy the referring physician reported by letter that the affair previously mentioned had not been reactivated and the patient "seemed to be getting along all right." *One year* after treatment the patient sent a note to the psychiatric attendant expressing appreciation for her help, and the conviction that the attendant was an integral part of her recovery. She expressed some fantasy about returning to the city of treatment for a "quick visit." She spoke of her satisfaction in her housekeeping chores, and said, "The home front is the same but I am fine." "Things are the same but they look differently to me or I am different. Anyway, I feel so unruffled that I can hardly believe it."

Two and a half years after therapy the authors had a letter from the patient saying that she had gone abroad for the summer and that she was "getting along beautifully." At the same time she sent a card to the attendant saying that she was "still going strong" and that she was "living and loving it."

Five years after treatment a note from the patient to the attendant said, "All is fine with me and bless the doctors."

During the past three and a half years no further word has been received regarding the patient and it is assumed by the authors that this means she is making a satisfactory adjustment.

Process Notes of Treatment

First Interview. The two therapists, Dr. White and Dr. Brown, sat down in absolute silence, saying nothing in response to Hilda's coy, hesitant efforts to establish a conversation. Dr. White went to sleep, awoke for a brief moment, and went back to sleep a total of five times. He awoke with "a series of dreams." He forgot the first two. In the third dream, a girl had her arm cut off and the therapist had hit it from below. The fourth dream was of a conical rock pile; Hilda threw three rocks up onto this pile and they rolled back down at her; there was no danger involved for Hilda. In the fifth dream, Hilda came with her parents as a poor little rich girl to the big orphanage to find a little brother; she went through a devastating search for the little brother but could not find one. The rest of the forty-five-minute interview was entirely silent. Finally, Dr. Brown said, "The time is now up." He walked to the door and opened it so that it was clear that Hilda was expected to walk out to her mother, who was waiting.

DYNAMICS:[4] The approach to the patient in the first interview here was obviously intense and rather abrupt. It represented a significant change from the rather social and affable contact of the therapists with the patient and family during the history-taking and administrative interviews which preceded the onset of psychotherapy. The non-social approach began the isolation of the therapeutic experience from the rest of the patient's world. Silence in the first interview increased the resistance of the patient. At the same time it raised problems to be faced in psychotherapy and emphasized the personal relationship between her and the people treating her.

This interview is, in some ways, atypical of the usual first interview in psychotherapy. Because of the extensive therapeutic treatment of this patient by other psychiatrists, and because of the time limit of three months, both therapists had the conviction that ordinary approaches to the patient's problems would be of little value and that what was needed was something more in the nature of an emergency approach.

The patient's response was basically a sexual defense against any type of really personal involvement with the therapists. The therapeutic onslaught seemed to increase her psychotic response. The therapist's inability to respond to the intense needs in the patient (because of the lack of any relationship) made him sleep. Sleeping, with dreams which basically involved the therapist's concept of the patient and her resistances, replaced the ordinary communication with the patient by the therapist's *communication with his own feelings*. The dream of the therapist hitting the cut arm of the patient appears to have been a reaction of hostility on the part of the therapist to the patient's extreme defensiveness.

Second and Third Interviews. These interviews were spent in absolute silence. Hilda maintained a cynical reserve. The therapists offered no respite. During these silences, Hilda spent a good bit of her time sitting on her hands, or pulling at her clothes and assuming odd postures with her body. She never looked directly at either therapist. In each instance the interview was terminated by the therapists. Hilda left with studied indifference.

DYNAMICS: In retrospect, the two therapists were not really comfortable working with each other with this specific patient. In this sense the preceding two interviews represented an impasse.

Fourth Interview. Dr. Brown failed to arrive. The interview was almost entirely silent. Dr. White was not comfortable in this silence and verbalized some hostility toward Dr. Brown for not appearing. Hilda became more anxious and left abruptly when the time was up.

DYNAMICS: The impasse reflected an absence of togetherness on the part of the two therapists. Dr. White was ambivalent about the absence

---

[4] In some interviews, further information regarding the subjective experience of the therapists is given under "Dynamics." Interview notes are all summary in character. Where interviews are labeled "not remarkable" this indicates limited overt content. Where the interviews are labeled "continuation," this connotes that though there may be reportable material it does not significantly differ from that which is described in the previous interview.

of Dr. Brown, feeling on the one hand that he perhaps could take care of the patient by himself, and on the other hand feeling some hostility toward Dr. Brown for leaving him with the responsibility for a very sick patient. Dr. Brown's absence reflected his ambivalence about his participation in this therapeutic experience, and an unconscious effort to involve Dr. White more personally. The relationship between the two therapists became the paramount concern of each at this point.

Fifth Interview. Dr. Brown was angry because Dr. White had seen the patient alone the day before, and said to Dr. White, "What do you mean by seeing her alone yesterday?" Dr. Brown continued to storm at Dr. White for several more sentences to the effect that he had no business trying to treat the patient alone when they had agreed to treat her together. In the middle of this discussion Hilda tried to say something and Dr. Brown said to her, "Shut up, there are more important people talking and you just listen." Dr. White finally exploded, "You were the one who didn't show up! This is a new patient, somebody had to see her. Not only that, but you were the one that dragged this patient in here and then forced me to get in on it when I wasn't interested in seeing her at all." The therapists talked back and forth with gradually diminishing affect and became increasingly more at ease with each other. Hilda interrupted with remarks that she was quite satisfied and didn't much care which one of the therapists saw her. She was told that she had no rights in this situation, that it had nothing to do with her, and that it was more important at this point for the two therapists to straighten out their feelings about each other than to do anything for or with her. Dr. White slept for the last twenty minutes and dreamed that Hilda was approaching a huge old house, that she wanted to get into it but the front door was locked, also the back door and the windows, but she found a loose board in the bathroom wall and wriggled through into the house by this means. No interpretation was made of this dream. It was agreed that Hilda would be seen by whichever therapist was present.

DYNAMICS: The impasse between the two therapists began to resolve here.[5] Dr. White was forced to treat the patient in spite of his already over-crowded schedule and consequently he resented Dr. Brown who had already elicited some transference. The dream expressed Dr. White's involvement. It was also an expression of his sense that the patient had broken through this impasse. The patient had gotten to Dr. White (had wriggled through the bathroom wall) through her relationship with Dr. Brown who was relatively compulsive in his relationship to patients.

Sixth Interview. Dr. White forgot the interview. Dr. Brown gradually became more satisfied to see Hilda alone and talked with her, in contrast to the silent interviews. Hilda was also glad to talk sociably. She said, "My trouble is that I don't know how to suck." Dr. Brown was pleased but the interview seemed empty.

---

[5] The absence of one therapist is discussed after Interview Thirty-one.

DYNAMICS: Dr. White's absence reflects some continued ambivalence. The patient was testing the relationship between the therapists by wedging herself between them. Dr. Brown accepted his need for the presence and participation of Dr. White. In multiple therapy, when one therapist is absent the interviews are often more verbal, with more intellectual insights. They are less threatening, and usually relatively superficial affectively. However, such individual interviews help to structure the relationship. It appears as if in some way the single therapist "instructs" the patient in how to gain access to the absent therapist when he returns.

Seventh Interview. After fifteen minutes of silence the therapists began to fall asleep alternately, but unwilling to go to sleep at the same time. Dr. Brown related a dream in which he saw a circus shooting-gallery where the manager was very busy shuffling back and forth between the targets and the contestants, carrying the bullets back to them to shoot over and over; the situation seemed very strange to him but not frightening. (Long silence.) Toward the end of the hour Hilda exploded at Dr. White, "Supposing I can't find the back door?" (See dream of interview No. 5.) Hilda said "Thank you" when she was ready to leave. The therapists paraphrased this as, "You are both feeble and there's nothing I have gotten out of this interview except what I can pay you back for with a ceremonial 'thank you.'" By this time Hilda was perspiring very profusely and left apparently confused.

DYNAMICS: This was the first interview in which the therapists participated together in a deep affective relationship to the patient. With this togetherness there emerged a fairly typical dynamic of multiple therapy— *i.e.*, the alternating participation of the two therapists. Dr. Brown slept first and reported his dream to the patient, followed by Dr. White's exchange with the patient about a previous dream. Dr. Brown's dream expresses his awareness of the patient's effort to wedge herself between the two therapists (her aggression), and its ineffectiveness (using the bullets over and over again). For the first time the patient accepted consciously her relationship with the therapists by her response to Dr. White's dream. It now became clear that the apparently unplanned, non-technical behavior of the therapists conveyed to the patient an understanding of the strength which they had between them. In short, she was now involved in "sweating it out."

Eighth Interview. Dr. Brown explained that extraneous circumstances limited the time to twenty minutes today. Early in this interview he had a strong feeling of wanting to feed Hilda, and fantasied himself as having no sexual organs, only breasts; he immediately felt more at ease with the patient and relapsed into silence. Dr. White went to sleep and when he woke up reported a pleasant dream in which he was going down the aisle of the church with Hilda who was dressed in a white bridal costume; they went past the large group of guests and past the chancel; Hilda took off her right arm and laid it on the altar; at this, the groom fainted and Hilda's mother dashed cold water on him, apparently with the intent of killing him; he and Hilda then got out behind the church and mother followed them but never quite got there. To this dream, Hilda made no response as usual, as if she had not heard. (Long silence.) At the end of the interview Hilda went to the door and said her usual "Thank you." By this time Dr. White was so angry that he pushed her with the side of his foot in a rather inadequate, guilty manner. Both therapists felt uneasy about this initial breach of accepted professional conduct.

> DYNAMICS: Dr. Brown's fantasies about his own castration as a prerequisite to mothering the patient expressed not only insight on his part that the patient needed mothering but his sexual counter-transference as well. His fantasy was both constructive and defensive. Dr. White's dream expressed acceptance of Dr. Brown's sexual counter-transference. In so doing he accepted the femininity of the patient. Their aggression toward the patient at the termination of the interview was probably an expression of their anger and frustration at the patient's refusal to consciously and verbally participate in their fantasy experience with her.

Ninth Interview. (Silence for 10 minutes.) Hilda said, without evident provocation, "I don't like to be touched." Dr. White put his feet in her lap. When she acted as if this offended her, Dr. White wiped his shoes on her dress and then put his feet back in her lap. (Silence.) Dr. Brown sat up closer to her chair, picked up her chin in his hands, and turned her face directly to him. Her response was a deeply hostile glaring and searching look. Dr. Brown then moved away again and there was a further silence. Near the end of the interview Dr. Brown picked up her hand to kiss it and she violently objected and tried to pull her hand away.

Tenth Interview. (Silence for 45 minutes.) During this period, Dr. Brown for the first time felt the helplessness and dependency of Hilda. He saw her as a baby. Dr. White was disinterested during the first half of the interview, then suddenly had a fantasy of Hilda going into the corner of the room, defecating, and then sitting down in her feces; however, neither therapist spoke. At the end of the interview Hilda said, "Can't you say anything to me?" Dr. Brown responded, "Our time is up now." After the interview the therapists said to each other that they had both assumed that what she meant was that they should not say anything.

Eleventh Interview. Not remarkable. Both therapists were present.

> DYNAMICS: These three interviews had in common the effort of the therapists to decathect content and previous history as an important aspect of psychotherapy. Experience rather than intellectual insight was emphasized. Two techniques emerged which are commonly used in multiple therapy with psychotic patients. In the ninth interview the patient flatly stated that being touched made her anxious. The therapeutic response in these situations is the production of further anxiety by precipitating the patient into the very kind of relationship which she insists she is unable to tolerate. In the ninth and tenth interviews she continued to deny feelings and needs which she so obviously experienced. The therapists denied the defensive distortion and accepted the unconscious need implied by the

patient's behavior. This technique frequently brings the relationship to a more honestly unconscious-to-unconscious level than any effort to verbally work through the patient's distortions. The eleventh interview was an effort to force regression of the patient. This involved the acting-through of a relationship with the patient which was similar to the relationships which the patient had earlier in life and which gave rise to the patient's problems in the first instance: The therapists displaced their own hostility toward each other onto the patient. Dr. Brown was angry with Dr. White and expressed his hostility toward the patient. Such reactivation of early traumatic experiences is of no value unless there is some different resolution to the experience than that which the patient had experienced in early life. This was provided by Dr. White's final statement to the patient in which he pointed out to her that hostility is expressed only toward people we love.

Twelfth Interview. Dr. Brown opened the interview by saying that the night before he had a dream at home of naked love-making in bed with a woman. He didn't recognize the woman, but on the previous day Hilda had reminded him of his sister. Today she reminded him of his mother. Hilda did not respond. Dr. White slept and reported a dream that all cars had license plates and could thereby take off into the air and fly. At the end of the interview Dr. Brown became aware that he had been rubbing his right index finger.

DYNAMICS: This interview now revealed the occurrence of what we regard as a *sine qua non* for adequate treatment of psychotic patients. Dr. Brown had become counter-identified with the patient. Dr. Brown's dream in which the patient was identified with both his sister and his mother communicated to the patient the depth of his unconscious involvement with her. Dr. White's dream expressed a comfortable control of Dr. Brown's sexual counter-transference. This control enabled Dr. Brown to precipitate therapeutic movement with his counter-transference. At the same time it precluded serious distortions or acting-out by the therapist at the patient's expense.

Thirteenth Interview. (Silence.) Dr. Brown said he could visualize her as about two and a half years old. Unexpectedly, Hilda said, "I was probably lying on my back." Dr. White saw her as one year of age, and then fantasied her as being intra-uterine, and was trying to determine whether she was head up or head down. He then loosened his belt and asked, "Do most deliveries take place with the head down? Is that the heaviest part of the baby?" The two therapists related the fantasy to the fact that Hilda always sat with head bowed and this annoyed them. Dr. White became personally concerned about Dr. Brown's emotional absence from the interview and accused him of just sitting.[6]

DYNAMICS: Dr. White here became maternal. This amounts to more than his passively recognizing the patient's projections. It is an emotional

---

[6] The night following this interview the patient escaped from the home in which she was living, was gone for fifteen minutes, and returned of her own volition.

acceptance on his part of his own maternal feelings toward the patient (birth fantasy). This inaugurated a very personal relationship between Dr. White and the patient, which developed into one of the major therapeutic experiences operating in the patient's treatment. Embarrassment and guilt developed, coincidentally. These were expressed in his inappropriate attack on Dr. Brown for the latter's withdrawal. The patient's A.W.O.L. from custody was probably related to this new development. Her voluntary return may have been an unconscious acceptance of this new and more meaningful relationship to her therapists.

Fourteenth Interview. (Silence, as usual.) Hilda said, "I'm sure glad to be here today." After a while she repeated the same statement. In response to this Dr. Brown felt some genital sensations and finally said, "For the first time in our interviews, I feel like masturbating here." Dr. White had a fantasy of being a pigeon and trying to get into the French windows of Hilda's home from a ledge out in front. (Silence.) Dr. White said with some sharpness, "I feel as though I'm the only patient in the room." (Silence.)

DYNAMICS: For the first time the therapists felt that she became "the patient." They struggled with the changes brought about by Dr. White's developing maternal function. A mutual acceptance by each therapist of the other's involvement with the patient is a crucial dynamic in this therapy.

Fifteenth Interview. Dr. White opened with a complaint that Dr. Brown was stealing the patient. Dr. Brown felt less responsibility as a result, and began to talk in clinical terms about the necessity for her getting well. Hilda started to leave the office. Dr. Brown stopped her. She turned back into the room and then began to scream at Dr. White as though he were responsible for Dr. Brown's holding her in the room. She then began an active physical struggle with Dr. Brown, who maintained his dominance of the situation. She fought bitterly and fiercely, with enough strength so that she precipitated them both to the floor. After about ten minutes of this, with no direct aggression against Dr. Brown but merely an effort to get out of the room, she began clinging to Dr. Brown as though exhausted and in need of protection. Dr. White became increasingly involved and threatened to stay all night and for breakfast if she remained aloof in the next interview.

DYNAMICS: The patient had been hopeless about getting better. The therapists here expressed their involvement in her recovery, but the patient questioned their motives. This interview revealed Dr. Brown's active acceptance of the father-role in the treatment experience, and in a sense defined the therapeutic group. The three roles were now accepted by each therapist, and in a sense designated by the patient. A "role" here is not a psycho-drama technique, nor simply the acceptance of the patient's transference projections by the therapists. "Role" refers to an acceptance by each therapist of his deepest responses emotionally to this patient as a person. The patient's response was openly that of a child revealed in a "temper tantrum." In multiple therapy the progressive involvement of both therapists usually develops simultaneously.

Sixteenth Interview. Hilda arrived silent and tense, her left fist digging into her *mons veneris* and her right hand grasping her left wrist. Dr. Brown watched this for a while, then turned away and lit a cigarette. Hilda looked at him with deep feeling and tears began to run out of her eyes. Dr. White began to cry also. Hilda then moved her lips as if to talk to Dr. Brown, who stopped her silent struggling with her mouth and said, "We won't let you do anything wrong." She was still unable to express any words. Dr. White saw her as tender and soft, and became very pained at Dr. Brown's coldness. Dr. Brown offered a cigarette to Dr. White, who said, "To hell with your cigarette, give me your hand." Dr. Brown reached over and took Dr. White's hand. After ten minutes of this hand-holding, Dr. White offered Hilda his hand. She ignored it at first, and then suddenly broke her hands apart and used her right hand to force her left hand way out to Dr. White. Then she extended her right hand suddenly to Dr. Brown and said, "What can I give you?" as though she were assuming that she could get something but did not see how she dared take it unless she could pay for it. Dr. White said, "A bigger breast, the more you suck the bigger it gets." She then pulled both therapists over toward her as though she were trying to pull her left hand over to meet the right hand, but with tremendous ambivalence and tremendous muscular exertion. When she had accomplished this the two therapists brought their other hands together also. As soon as the therapists had brought their four hands together she threw them apart, took her hand away, and put them behind her head as if she were helpless against attack. The therapists waited for her to put her hands back and then, as though uniting without her, united their four hands. At this she became excited, aggressive, and in panic struck aimlessly and violently at Dr. Brown's left arm. She then broke the therapist's hands apart and reinserted herself into the family group, and immediately put her head in Dr. White's lap with dry sobs. After a few seconds, she jerked herself upright, saying, "I don't know what I'm doing." She released the two therapists and said, "You hold each other." Hilda then said over and over, "It can't be done, it can't be done!" The therapists felt exhausted, relaxed, and the interview ended comfortably.

DYNAMICS: This interview was the first total therapeutic experience for the patient. Previous interviews made this possible. The outcome of this was the patient's acceptance of her role as a child in her relationship with the two therapists. The expression of such a dependent relationship through physical behavior is seen occasionally in therapy with psychotic patients. Two further dynamics are interesting. In the early part of the interview the patient faced the problem of having to know what satisfactions the therapists got out of this experience. The clearer definition of both maternal and paternal roles allows the patient to express more of her ambivalent feelings. In the latter part of the interview, the patient responded to the therapists holding each other while excluding her; this shows her that their relationship to each other is paramount and more intimate than either of their relationships to her. She at first panics, but then accepts her role as a child more fully and is able to take from the therapists more deeply, by putting her head in Dr. White's lap. The patient's statement that she did not know what she was doing probably referred to her attempt to separate them since it is immediately followed by her statement, "Now you hold each other." This in turn is followed by the patient's psychotic expression, "It can't be done." The togetherness of the therapists is not unlike the significance of the togetherness of the parents in developing a feeling of security in the child. The ending process in which the therapists suddenly sat back, let go of each other's hands, and felt tensionless, is in many ways characteristic of the ending feeling in all significant interviews. Such a complete ending is an important factor in precluding the patient from acting-out her psychotic feelings outside of the interview situation.

Seventeenth Interview. The entire forty-five minutes were spent in absolute silence. At the end the two therapists simply stood up, and Hilda left the room silently. Both therapists felt flat and uninterested. Dr. White had a dream of a child coming to him to ask a question; the child felt unsure whether she dared ask, and that she might be rejected, and he actually felt like having nothing to do with the child. Dr. Brown slept and had five dreams. In the first dream a mother was chasing after her child outdoors. In the second dream he was in a room with several hassocks of different colors—he was supposed to sit down, finally chose to sit on two shades of red, and then got up in horror. In the third dream he and Hilda were having an argument in which he insisted, "You live with your mother." Hilda kept answering, "No, I live with my grandmother." Both of them continued this argument, shouting louder and louder. In the fourth dream he saw himself as being a mother who had a child who was really a girl but who looked like a boy in the dream; the mother had a struggle inside herself over rejecting her child, which she resolved finally by killing the child. Dr. Brown forgot the fifth dream. After the interview, Dr. Brown felt that they had rejected Hilda by being silent about their dreams.

DYNAMICS: After the depth of the exchange in the preceding interview, communication had apparently broken down. This typifies "the second interview reaction," and may have been due to guilt, embarrassment, and some hostility in both the therapists and the patient about the experience of the previous interview. The complete silence at this point was in itself a technical as well as a personal failure. Some of the guilt which motivated the withdrawal from the therapeutic interaction arose out of the therapists' awareness of the acultural experience of the preceding day. Despite this rejection the depth of the participation was revealed in Dr. Brown's dreams. His first dream suggested a real concern on his part about the patient (child) backing away from the therapeutic experience and in consequence being hurt. His second dream reflected against his uneasiness at sitting on (repressing) his deep feeling and his reaction of horror when he recognizes this. His third dream reflected his recognition of the patient's denial of the therapeutic relationship and his insistence that he, as a therapist, would continue to be deeply involved with the patient in spite of her overt denial. His fourth dream reflects his perception of the patient's resistance. Hilda brought her masculinity as a defense against her dependence of the previous day.

Eighteenth Interview. Hilda entered with a new self-assurance, a more erect posture in place of her previous hovering stance, a direct tone of voice, and a more feminine manner. She seemed less artificial and her pseudo-smile seemed gone. She said, "I'm well. You're finished." She repeated this three times somewhat facetiously and added, "You better let me go before I start; I promise I'll not despair and dispose of myself again." She crossed her heart in the manner of a little girl. She was physically shaking and seemed to be becoming more dependent. She said, "I don't know how long you plan to keep me here." The therapists said nothing. She whispered to herself, which she had done earlier in therapy, but this time with less anxiety. Finally she said, "Why don't you say something?" Dr. White was in favor of agreeing that she was well enough to be on her own. Dr. Brown was literally gritting his teeth and said, "Hilda is not well and should not be permitted to leave the therapeutic relationship." Hilda said, "I'm not going to have an emotional experience like my referring doctor said I should; I'm not going to fight my way out of here." (Long silence.) Dr. White went to sleep, awoke, and reported a dream that Hilda was living on a ferryboat anchored to the edge of the river. Twelve pirates who turned out to be chorus girls were on the ferry fighting with the patient, while Dr. White looked on with the director of the production. He then awoke within his dream and saw a chair with Hilda sitting in it and with a five-year-old child on her knees. Dr. Brown said to her, "You are really a five-year-old child trying to leave home." Dr. White added, "You are trying to leave without your hat and coat; you're in shirt sleeves." Actually, although he did not report this to Hilda, he was having a fantasy that she was a small boy, not properly dressed to leave home. (Long silence with Hilda staring at the floor.) Finally Dr. White said, "Now you are ready for a bigger fight." Hilda immediately pushed her hands against each other and folded and unfolded her feet. Dr. Brown was anxious at the end of the interview because he felt uncertain as to how he and Dr. White would work further together with Hilda.

DYNAMICS: The patient's attempt at ending treatment appears, in retrospect, to have been a flight into health. The therapists denied this premature ending. With this denial, the patient then became dependent and hostile. Her hostility was expressed in another effort to wedge between the two therapists. Her success was indicated by the terminal anxiety of

Dr. Brown when he felt specifically and consciously his separation from Dr. White in the therapeutic task. Dr. White's dream resolved this, since he saw the patient both as an adult and as a child who obviously was not ready to leave home. This was expressed at the end of the interview when Dr. White asked the patient whether she was ready for a bigger fight— i.e., dealing with her psychosis. There were two other incidental techniques illustrated in this interview. The first was the absence of verbal response on the part of the therapists when the patient asked a question based primarily on their fantasy rather than on reality. The therapists did not respond to the patient's twice-asked question, "How long do you plan to keep me here?" The patient's remark that she was determined not to have an emotional experience like her previous psychiatrist said she would have in this treatment process illustrates a second problem. Patients repeatedly act-out in response to the commands and comments which referring physicians rather innocently make to them, but which the patients take very seriously.

Nineteenth Interview: Hilda came wearing a mixture of clothes denying her feminine role. Dr. Brown asked, "Where's the brutality to go with your tender smile? You remind me of two arms, two legs, and an ass hole." She responded with a whisper like a criminal, "I have nothing to say." Dr. White said, "Now you're going to sit on your hands and your voice." Hilda answered, "Haven't we been looking at the inside of me for two weeks?" (Silence.) Dr. Brown went to sleep and dreamed that he was twisting someone's arm behind his back; the dream then changed so that Dr. Brown was driving in the park behind a pick-up truck which was moving very slowly and laboriously with a canvas over its rear end but nothing inside the truck. Dr. White made this dream into a joint fantasy and asked, "Was the truck without gas?" Hilda repeated: "Yes, without gas." Dr. Brown: "What happened then?" Hilda: "The car goes around and on." Dr. White: "If we could push that truck over the hill it could coast to a gas station." Hilda: "I'll never be ready to go home." Dr White: "If we could get some gas we could go anywhere." (Long silence.) Dr. Brown fell asleep and dreamed of a house filled with rats, and overrun by them, and awoke in a very anxious state. He expressed a new conviction that Hilda was paranoid. After some further silence, Dr. White said, "I feel we are giving chunks of our heart to you, and what do we get back?" This was free association. He added, "I'm afraid that I might have a hole in my heart and could bleed to death." He went to sleep and dreamed of a kitchen in which the floor consisted of four-inch rings of bright, shiny metal, hooked together so that the floor could be walked on. Dr. Brown exclaimed, "That's wonderful; now we can shit and piss right into the basement!"

DYNAMICS: Dr. Brown expressed resentment that he could not proceed without Dr. White and felt compelled to follow his lead in therapy. Dr. White converted the dream into a joint fantasy in which the patient then participated. This use of the joint fantasy to resolve impasses in therapy and to facilitate communication on an affect level is an important technique in the process of multiple therapy. The togetherness of the therapists promotes an expression on the part of the patient of her deep affect hunger and her belief that it is insatiable. The depth of the therapists' response to this was revealed in Dr. White's panic with the free association about a hole in his heart and bleeding to death. This is typical in the treatment of very sick patients. Dr. Brown's final dream subjectively defined the patient's paranoid feelings. This diagnostic perception was based on his feeling response to the way the patient participated in this particular relationship. The patient's remark that they had been looking inside of her for two weeks coincided with the fact that two weeks prior to this interview Dr. White had made first physical contact with the patient.

Twentieth Interview. No movement. Both therapists were present.

Twenty-first Interview. Continuation of the twentieth, except for Dr. Brown's desperation as expressed in a dream that all three were heading for an electric-shock treatment room and someone had yelled.

Twenty-second Interview. All three walked in emotionally flat and in silence. Hilda walked between the therapists, looked out the window with her back to them, and said, "I can't stand your eyes on me." All three became extremely tense. Dr. Brown feel asleep. With some hesitancy he reported his dream: that he had seen a disembodied penis, flaccid, up in the air, with ejaculate drooling out of it. He added, "Hilda, I wonder if you'll ever be able to give me a 'hard on'?" After some silence Dr. White said to her, "I've had my 'heart' in my eyes many times." He added, "I wonder if you realize that we have our own craziness to fight as well as yours?" Hilda answered, "I never thought of that." All this time she was standing with her back to the therapists and Dr. Brown became very sternly administrative as he said to Dr. White, "I think we've let her go to hell long enough." With that Dr. Brown stood up to lead her back to her chair. She immediately started fighting his physical contact with her arm. Dr. White got up and helped Dr. Brown to put her back in her chair. She was strong enough physically so that all three fell on the floor. She then stopped fighting and lay on the floor awhile, resting. Then she got up, walked over to Dr. White, who was again sitting in his chair, and hit him hard on the side of his face. Dr. White put her on the floor and both therapists spanked her. After lying on the floor awhile she again started fighting and bit Dr. White on the leg. In the process of this fight she got some bruises. Finally, completely exhausted, Hilda crawled over to Dr. Brown, who was again sitting in his chair, got halfway up between his knees, and said, "I'd hit you if I had enough strength," tapped him lightly on the face, and then simply laid her head in his lap. When the time was up, Hilda made a special effort to walk out in a dignified manner, and Dr. White said, "You're wonderful."

Twenty-third Interview. Continuation of dynamics of the twenty-second interview.

DYNAMICS (*twentieth to twenty-third interviews*): A typical impasse has developed. The patient actively intervened in the relationship between the two therapists in order to resolve this impasse. As is true of delinquency in adolescents, the effect of her asocial behavior was an augmentation of the togetherness of the parents in response to her need. The physical response to the patient was precipitated by the patient's acting-out, which informed the therapists that their response to the problem up to this point had been ineffectual. Dr. White tried to verbally communicate his hostility to the patient, and Dr. Brown attempted to administratively control the patient's acting-out. Both failed. The relationship had developed a sense of desperation in both therapists. They had committed themselves affectively beyond the point where verbal administrative or social interchange would adequately answer the patient's implicit question. With their physical fighting they indicated to the patient a willingness to go beyond the cultural limitations (which limited all three people in the interview) in order to get the patient well. The warmth with which the interview terminated is rather characteristic of interviews where such a primitive physical interchange occurs.

This constitutes a "therapeutic feeding experience" for the patient. The result of such a deep, positive response was strikingly indicated in the twenty-third interview when she wiped the tears off Dr. Brown's face and then felt his face as if she were a blind person who was trying to perceive its real shape. This revealed a breaking through by the patient of her projections onto the therapists of feelings and attitudes which were typical of her original schizophrenogenic parents. It was the first obvious instance of a non-transference (or pre-transference) affective relationship between the patient and therapists. This we feel is crucial in therapeutic movement.

Twenty-fourth Interview. Not remarkable.

Twenty-fifth Interview. Not remarkable.

DYNAMICS: Both these interviews were with both therapists present, and reveal a continuation of the feeding experience begun in the preceding interviews. In the twenty-fourth interview the patient resolved some of her ambivalent feelings through the simultaneous experience of aggression and warmth. In the twenty-fifth interview the patient asked whether her positive dependent feelings would hurt or kill. The therapist's answer, "You have to face us, you need not leave us, and you cannot kill us." With this the patient regressed into relatively primitive, dependent, infantile behavior, expressed largely in silence.

Twenty-sixth Interview. Not remarkable.

Twenty-seventh Interview. Hilda came half an hour late. She showed the usual body ambivalence, tension, awkwardness, difficulty in getting out of her coat, and profuse perspiration. Dr. White said, "My left arm tingles to the elbow and seems paralyzed." Dr. Brown rubbed his eyebrows and said, "Are you going to help him with it?" Hilda didn't answer. Dr.

White's left eye began tearing and he spoke of a pain behind it. Then he had a free association of being a resident in obstetrics and gynecology, wearing a long podalic version glove on the left hand (obviously for the right hand). (Silence.) Hilda asked, "Do you have to love me to help me?" Dr. White replied, "I can't help it, I love you in the same way I love myself, I see your arms as my arms, fighting with each other." (Silence.) Then Hilda said, "I don't want to be like Mummy—mother had treatment with doctors for a long time and stayed the same; she never changed on the inside." After some further silence she said, "The first time I saw Dr. Brown and talked about coming here for treatment, he didn't look at me, paid no attention at all to the stuff I'd been saying, and I thought, 'This is different; I'll change from the inside.' " At the end of the interview, as she tried to get her coat back on, she had a fight with it, tore the lining in both sleeves, and left in a very agitated state, saying at the door, "I'm still trying a little bit."

DYNAMICS: The anxiety which Hilda presented was resolved by a primitive form of therapeutic communication involving body-image language. The therapists expressed their counter-identification with Hilda. Dr. Brown did so in the spontaneous gesture of rubbing his eyebrows after he perceived sweat on one of Hilda's eyebrows. Dr. White, in response to her question, "Do you have to love me to help me?" identified himself with the patient. In both instances the identification was specifically in terms of body. The patient's statement concerning therapy, that "this is different; I'll change from the inside," illustrates the depth of the therapeutic affect present.

Twenty-eighth Interview. Not remarkable. Both therapists were present.

Twenty-ninth Interview. Dr. White was absent. Dr. Brown closed the windows even though it was a hot day. Hilda was wearing a heavy coat, a black sweater, pale blue slacks, white sweat-socks and tennis shoes, and smiled in an embarrassed, coy way. She asked, "Why did you close the windows?" Dr. Brown: "Because we always do. I'd rather have them open." Hilda: "That's like I do, I underestimated you." She was seductive and Dr. Brown said, "I'm bothered by the adult-date quality." Hilda: "I feel differently too; that's why I wore slacks, and I wiped off my lipstick before coming in." Then she continued, "I wish you were home with your family. I thought it before I came in but didn't say it because it would sound too sociable." Dr. Brown: "You are my family." Hilda then pulled up her knees in a typical fetal position. She said, "The other night I wanted Dr. White, I wanted to throw my arms around his neck and to tell him I wanted to go with him." She added, "I feel as though you are my mother today." Dr. Brown suddenly felt less tense, took out his handkerchief, and wiped her perspiring face and neck. Hilda said, "I sweat like a pig and I fight like a man. The other psychiatrist said I wanted to be a man and I never believed him. Thank you." She moved her chair up to Dr. Brown's, grabbed him around the neck in a bear hug, then relaxed and became more loving, like a three-year-old child. Dr. Brown gently put his arms around her for two or three minutes. Then she put her head in his lap briefly, straightened up, and held both his hands with both of hers so that all four hands were together. Dr. Brown said, "You get me all excited." She said, smiling, "I can't fool a psychiatrist; I can just fool the lay public."

DYNAMICS (*twenty-eighth and twenty-ninth interviews*): Dr. Brown's sexualization of the therapeutic relationship is very clear. Despite this, he was able to relate to the patient in a meaningful way. In regular, individual treatment, Dr. Brown's response would have been a rigidly structured defensive denial of this spontaneous interchange with the patient. He probably would have "acted like" a psychiatrist instead of functioning as a person who is a psychiatrist. Dr. Brown rejected the fantasy presence of Dr. White when he replied that she, the patient, was his family. At this point, if he had responded in terms of his family being Dr. White, who was present in fantasy, the parental loving of the frightened child which occurred later in the interview might not have been as contaminated with counter-transference problems as it was.

Thirtieth Interview. No movement.

Thirty-first Interview. Not remarkable.

DYNAMICS: These two interviews were with Dr. Brown alone, as explained to the patient in the twenty-eighth interview. The question arose of whether in multiple therapy it is wise for one therapist to see the patient in the absence of the other therapist. In some instances in this case report the absence of a therapist created real problems in the therapeutic process. In the beginning of multiple therapy with a patient, when the parental roles and the togetherness as a primary group has not developed, it is usually unwise to see the patient without the co-therapist. When, however, the presence of both therapists is felt, even though one is absent physically, treatment of the patient by one therapist alone can proceed with an expectation of success. This is similar to the experience of a child who constructively relates to one parent in the absence of the other. This in turn becomes a working part of the tripartite relationship when the other therapist returns. Even though with the co-therapist absent there are more disruptive interchanges and the seeds of what in individual therapy might turn out to be serious impasses, these experiences enhance the therapeutic movement when the co-therapist returns.

Thirty-second Interview. Dr. White failed to arrive. The interview was not remarkable except for the patient's remark: "I'm not innocent enough to be a child." After a pause, she continued—"The day we fought I could have killed somebody."

Thirty-third Interview. Not remarkable. Both therapists were present.

Thirty-fourth Interview. Dr. White was forty minutes late. Dr. Brown (aggressively to Dr. White): "You've been late every time." Dr. White:

"You've invited me in to administrate this situation after another co-therapist had refused. I came in and tried to steal her and more and more became convinced that the two of you had a better relationship than I could ever establish." Dr. Brown: "You've hit on something. Hysterics do have fun together." Dr. White: "To me this is a schizophrenic problem and I can't get with it. I do and can bring my soma and I think that's the real contribution I can make. I am haunted by Hilda's body ambivalence and I identify very closely with it. I respond with my own body ambivalence. To me the struggle between her two arms is a very painful thing. If I didn't hold myself so much out of this situation I'd be more of a person. I somehow feel as though it's too late to get you two to help me with that problem in myself." Dr. White (to Hilda): "I'm more crazy with you than with anybody else." Dr. Brown was shocked by this statement and said, "Hilda, sometimes I wish you'd dribble, you always seem to be waiting for the big shit." Hilda asked, "What do you want me to do?" Dr. Brown answered, "Eat shit."

> DYNAMICS: Again the therapists, when rejoined, ignored the patient in order to work out their personal relationship in this particular therapeutic experience.[7]

Thirty-fifth Interview. Not remarkable. Both therapists were present.

> DYNAMICS: Dr. White aggressively demanded that the patient become more immediately and intensively involved in the treatment process.

Thirty-sixth Interview. The interview lasted ninety minutes. Both doctors expected physical aggression; Dr. Brown took his glasses off; Dr. White put his pipe on the shelf. Hilda: "It's no use, I can't get better." Dr. Brown: "I don't know if I'll let you go home." Hilda: "Do you have a reason for committing me?" Dr. White answered: "If you move to get out, I'll be between you and the door. The trouble with you is you just can't stand it when mother and father love each other." Hilda stood up and both the therapists stood up. Hilda seemed very disturbed by this and said, "I'll sit through today but I won't come back tomorrow." Dr. White's free association was that his face was dead on the left side, and Dr. Brown simultaneously fantasied that his left arm and hand were paralyzed. Hilda: "What time is it?" Dr. White: "It's 6:16, almost daybreak, time for breakfast." Hilda responded: "I'll stay all night." Dr. White: "It's after breakfast, time to go to work again." Dr. Brown: "I feel rested up and ready to eat again." Dr. Brown fell asleep and had two dreams, one in which he was eating a cream puff and his nose dripped into it, and a second one in which he went with the patient to see her room for the first time and she changed and became an old man needing a word for a cross-word puzzle that she was working. When

---

[7] Compare interviews five, thirteen, fifteen, and sixteen, also interview sixty-five.

Dr. Brown had described these dreams, Dr. White suggested, "You added our two ages together and you ended up with an old man." The two therapists felt relaxed with each other and Hilda seemed much more tense. Dr. White: "Can't you stand it to have mother and father feel close to each other?" At the end of the interview, Dr. White said, "I'm through for the day," and Dr. Brown said to Hilda, "Go on home." She said, "Who are you speaking to?" and he answered, "You," and threw his cigarette butt in her lap. She took it, got up very slowly, fumbled at the door, and walked out saying her usual "Thanks." Hilda returned to the interview room almost immediately, the first time she had ever done this. She was very anxious and agitated, and said, "Are you writing a letter?" Dr. White was a bit taken aback and said, "What are you asking?" and Hilda said, "May I come back?" Dr. Brown responded, "If you're not here tomorrow I'll come and find you." Dr. White said, "We'll see you tomorrow."

> DYNAMICS: What occurs here is a kind of emotional cross-ruffling interchange between the therapists. The central problem in the interview is obviously the patient's developing initiative for her own growth. The responses of the therapists are basically non-reassuring. This apparently is effective, judging by the patient's return after the interview situation and her expression verbally of her desire to come back for the next interview. Perhaps the one technical error is in Dr. Brown's response to this, "If you're not here tomorrow I'll come and find you." Despite the obvious warmth of this remark it to some extent takes the initiative away from the patient again.

Thirty-seventh Interview. Dr. White opened by saying, "I just had a fantasy that Hilda walked over to us with her arm around each one, pulling us together and hugging us." Hilda: "My fantasy was to come in alone first, put your chairs together, have you sit in them, then knock your heads together hard." The entire interview had a much more adult quality. Hilda: "I made a thousand speeches since yesterday, and I read *The Snake Pit* where it says about knowing I am well because now I know I used to love you." The therapists and Hilda joked with each other, made explanations to each other, and spoke of comparing notes regarding the interviews. She said that her diary was in German. She wanted it understood that she loved both therapists, not just one. Dr. White spoke of a fantasy of asking his wife for an individual photograph of herself for Christmas. Dr. Brown responded with telling Hilda that she was not through with treatment even though she was now "well," that she was still very immature, and that they were not releasing her. She replied to Dr. Brown, "You are all the things I say and don't say, and do and don't do, and I've been worrying about you." To Dr. White she said, "You are all the things I do to myself." At the end she asked Dr. Brown, "May I take your handkerchief?" Dr. Brown gave it to her. She wiped the perspiration off her face and neck with it and was going to leave with it. Dr. Brown insisted that she return it.

DYNAMICS: This interview beautifully illustrates the process of therapy in which the question of terminating therapy becomes, for the first time, a part of the therapeutic give-and-take. This is the first time that the patient seriously introduced the notion of her leaving therapy. This was not a defensive reaction but a real one. The relationship thus became less intrapersonal and more interpersonal and social, *i.e.*, more real. The patient specifically took up with the therapists her perception of their own pathology. She was saying, in essence, "I am going to leave you, I have loved both of you, but I know both of you are sick." Her perception of this was revealed in her comment first to Dr. Brown, that he was "all of the things I say and don't say, and do and don't do." (Dr. Brown had some tendency toward obsessiveness and compulsiveness.) The patient then turned to Dr. White and said, "You are all the things I do to myself." (Dr. White had some tendency toward dependency and depressiveness.) The resolution occurred when at the end she wanted to take Dr. Brown's handkerchief with her. Dr. Brown rightly insisted on keeping it. In doing this he was saying, in essence, "My controls, my reality, my life is my own. You have to find your own, my dirt (handkerchief) I will keep and deal with myself. You are free to go and live your own life without any concern for what sickness is left in me as a parent." It was interesting too that the ending process began when the patient was able to express to both therapists her love for each of them simultaneously. To some degree the triangular relationship, which had been so much a part of the genesis of her problems, had been resolved. What in these last two or three interviews accounted for the shift in the patient's relationship to the point where she functioned rationally, realistically, and with a good bit of flexible adultness? The important change occurred in the preceding interview (thirty-six) where, in the face of the therapists' joint firmness, non-reassurance, and even aggression toward the patient, her psychotic evasion of a dependent relationship broke and she openly and totally accepted her childish dependence on the therapists. With this honest acceptance the patient was in a position to decide freely whether she wanted to be a child or an adult. She chose to be an adult, and in the present interview she functioned on the basis of a free choice and in consequence began the process of ending. It was not the therapists' expectation at this point that the adultness and the ending process would proceed without regression or without interruption, but the patient had made the first experiential step toward her own independent functioning and this, paradoxically, was made possible by forcing the patient to accept her dependence.

Thirty-eighth Interview. Hilda came with a new, attractive coat, looked more alive and yet anxious, was perspiring, and kept her hands in her pockets. She asked, "Why was I panicked last night after such a good interview?" When the therapists did not answer, she said, "If you don't close those wide-open windows, I'll jump out and kill myself." Then she added, "Maybe we've graduated to open windows." She then leaned over confidentially to Dr. Brown, and whispered, "I'll yell if you leave them open." Dr. Brown closed them, partly as a gesture, and said, "You're still a virgin." After a few minutes of thought, Hilda said, "I never did love my husband. I found a boy friend to see if I could get over being a virgin, but here I'm still a virgin. I'm sort of worried about my daughter's mouth, the shape of it worries me." Dr. Brown answered, "You worry about your *mouths.*" Hilda asked, "What do you mean?" Dr. White answered, "The mouth of your heart." Dr. Brown disagreed by saying, "I meant your vagina and your mouth, and for you thus far they both go to your stomach." Dr. White said, "You're a virgin because you can't have intercourse with yourself; you stand back to back with yourself, and I can just see you in my fantasy. That's why your hands are in your pockets." Hilda said, "I don't like my hands."

> DYNAMICS: This interview represented an attempt on the part of the patient to integrate her previous affective experiences and to consolidate some of her growth in the form of insights.

Thirty-ninth Interview. Dr. Brown said that he had been having nightmares for several days now with a feeling that he had lost Hilda. He fell asleep and had an involved dream about being a cadaver, whom the medical students called Mr. Smith, but he didn't remember the details of what happened to the cadaver. Hilda: "Something." Dr. White: "What?" Hilda: "I thought if I said 'something' I'd get started talking." Both Dr. White and Dr. Brown were so taken aback by this dry humor that they didn't catch on in time to do any laughing. After a prolonged silence, Hilda became very tense and wanted to leave but Dr. White woke up from his boredom and prepared to stop her, physically if necessary. Dr. Brown went back to sleep. When Hilda left the room she seemed very tense, and she slammed the door for the first time since the beginning of treatment.

> DYNAMICS: This interview illustrates graphically a dilemma in the treatment of psychotic patients which is encountered rather frequently. With the growing insight of the patient begun in the previous interview and to some extent continued in this interview, the patient demanded a reality relationship to the therapists which was denied her. This was a failure on the part of both therapists to accept the patient's growth and a refusal to give up the psychosis of the patient. Her reaction to the interview at its termination was quite understandable.

Fortieth Interview. Hilda took her overcoat off for the first time, explaining that she had never done this with her previous psychiatrist. Both the therapists felt very kindly, gentle, and close to Hilda as "their child," and somehow felt more legitimate about the whole relationship than ever before. Hilda said she was "hard" and reported a dream: "I lay down after the last interview and felt disturbed or something, in armor plate, and my boy friend came in and touched me, and my heart beat, and I couldn't feel anything, I was metallic all over." Dr. White said, rather "out of the blue," to Dr. Brown, "You certainly took quite a risk when you brought her here for treatment." Hilda: "Yes, Dr. Brown said that nobody had risked enough for me." This seemed to irritate Dr. White and he said to Dr. Brown, "Be more honest, what you really meant was that you wanted to take the risk." Hilda: "I responded sweetly to Dr. Brown to get back at my previous psychiatrist." (Silence.) Hilda: "Would you ever think of marrying me?" Both therapists answered, "Yes," simultaneously and with much feeling. The tone of the interview was that of parents who were explaining things to a rather small child.

> DYNAMICS: The patient presented a hysterical dream at the beginning of the interview. She then precipitated some struggle between the two therapists. In the beginning of the interview, Dr. Brown, by his acceptance and deep identification with the patient, apparently risked his relationship with Dr. White. Dr. White immediately expressed his comfort with this, being secure in his love of Dr. Brown. The child grows psychologically in this way. The parent-to-parent relationship is characterized by an ebb and flow in which the child is a significant factor. A psychological catastrophe could occur if the child successfully stopped that ebb and flow between the parents so that the relationship of the parents to the child became compulsive, guilt-laden, and repressed.

Forty-first Interview. Dr. Brown was late and Dr. White was annoyed by something before the interview. Hilda was inaccessible and sarcastic; "Have you eaten?" Dr. Brown: "I've eaten well." Dr. White: "I'm not sure, maybe my dessert was bad and I have indigestion." Dr. Brown suggested that maybe she was holding back her words because she didn't have guts enough to spit them out; he taunted her by saying that he was glad he didn't have to see her every day and that he was planning to be away other days, including a period of two weeks in the next month. Dr. White reinforced this by taunting her about the fact that she was taking no responsibility for the interview and asked why she didn't walk out. After Dr. White had done this repeatedly, Dr. Brown told Hilda that he wasn't ready for her to leave. Hilda asked with great bitterness, "Do you have anything else to say?" Dr. Brown said, "No, but you have," and when she opened the door to leave Dr. Brown got up and slammed the door so that she couldn't get out. She immediately froze in panic and Dr. Brown said, "OK, I give up," and let her leave.

> DYNAMICS: Both therapists participated in a demand that the patient accept the initiative in therapy. After a period of defensive sarcasm and negativistic testing, the patient finally did so at the termination of the interview. At this point she took over the control of the interview and Dr. Brown effectively resisted this when he sarcastically said, "I give up." Thus he again made the patient dependent.

Forty-second Interview. Dr. Brown: "So you came with slacks and sneakers today." Hilda: "I plan to have a fight." Dr. White: "Shall I put my pipe up?" Hilda: "No, I had Dr. Brown in mind. I wish I hadn't said that, I never can start at the right time." Dr. Brown thought about this for a minute, noticed her hands deep in her pants pockets, and said, "Maybe I can knock the chip off your shoulder." He started pulling her hand out of her coat pocket. After a brief tussle over who would hold whose hands, in which both Dr. Brown and Hilda fell to the floor, she said, "I'll fight you if you'll let me take my coat off." She and Dr. Brown stood up formally, took off her coat very politely, draped it over her chair, and as soon as this was done she hit Dr. Brown. The fight did not consist of an effort to hurt each other, but of Hilda trying to prove that she was stronger than Dr. Brown. He kept taunting her with, "You're no man," and similar comments. She stopped fighting and, when he taunted her with not even being a woman, since she wouldn't bite his arm when she had her teeth on it, she started again. When she stopped, Dr. Brown asked, "Well, Hilda, are you ready to be (a woman) now?" At this she exploded with anger and fought until she was exhausted, then said to Dr. Brown, "Now you help me up like a lady." Dr. Brown refused and added, "You have such nice soft breasts, and I like breasts." At this she screamed with hatred and fought some more. Finally Dr. Brown was exhausted and asked, "Aren't you tired? I'm ready to quit." Hilda said, "I am too." Dr. Brown asked, "Anything else you want?" Hilda: "No." Dr. Brown stood up and sat down in his regular chair again, and she continued groveling on the floor and crawled under the desk where the therapists could not see her. At this point Dr. Brown said, "She took out half my hair." Hilda answered from under the desk, "You leave the office first today, I'll come out." Dr. White said, "We're going to stay for breakfast." (Ten-minute silence.) Dr. Brown commented, "Did you notice that every time she hit me hard she was the one who said 'ouch'?" Hilda then crawled out from under the desk holding a piece of curly hair in her fingers, offering it to Dr. Brown, saying, "This is hair from my scalp where it's curly." During the entire struggle today Dr. White felt somewhat left out but not irritated, just bored, and made notes. At the end of the interview, Hilda sat back down on the floor, obviously waiting for Dr. Brown to help her up politely. Dr. Brown did.

DYNAMICS: The patient took over the initiative which she had refused in the previous interview. Her immediate response was aggressive. Her physical aggression in this interview was non-psychotic. It was warm, realistic, and non-compulsive. Some resolution of her ambivalence was coincidental with a kind of physical aggression which occurred in the context of a fusion of her aggression with her sexuality. This fusion was also associated with a clear delineation of her own femininity and the acceptance on the part of the therapists of her feminine role in the physical fight. Her behavior was less dependent. For the first time the patient accepted a "castrative" experience as being constructive in nature. In terms of her previous clitorectomy her warmly handing Dr. Brown a piece of curly hair represents a therapeutic undoing of a significant trauma in early life. Dr. Brown's terminal acceptance of her as an adult woman as he helped her from the floor integrated the therapeutic experience into her whole person.

Forty-third Interview. Dr. White was absent. Not remarkable except for patient's comment, "I'm tired of being a pygmy among giants." And later, "I've been getting to pink, but never red. I can't get to red, just a little pink. When I was pulling your hair it almost came." At the end, she said, "I haven't been able to eat, my guts are growling so loud you can't hear me."

DYNAMICS: Dr. Brown controlled the spontaneity of the patient not only by talking but by repeated intellectualization in situations where, with the co-therapist present, he would have responded more spontaneously. He did accept the previous growth of the patient and related it to the patient's total life. He also successfully conveyed to the patient the knowledge that all of her needs weren't going to be answered in psychotherapy. He pointed out that every person, regardless of therapy, will have persistent residual needs, just as he has. ("My guts are growling too, I could not hear yours.) The outcome of the interview was the patient's ending in a rather clear-cut, adult way and leaving with a great deal of self-assurance and a dramatic loss of her dependent stoop.

Forty-fourth Interview. Not remarkable. Both therapists were present.

DYNAMICS: The transition into this interview was very good. Dr. White began this interview by bringing up to the patient an "incidental" feeling when he raised the question of why he had not told her that he would not be present in the interview of the preceding day. It is very important to bring to the patient relationship even the most inconsequential dishonesty subjectively experienced in relationship to the patient. Dr. White accepted the patient's therapeutic capacity and identified her as an introject within himself. This provided the basis for a constructive dependent experience for the patient.

Forty-fifth Interview. Continuation. Both therapists were present.

DYNAMICS: The therapists firmly refused to accept the infantile sexual relationship offered by the patient in her panic over the dependent regression in the preceding interview. The patient's reaction to this was an activation of her homosexual feeling, which was responded to by Dr. Brown's dream of an elderly masculine woman who came to a church, followed by his verbal expression of this non-sexual response when he said, "I feel my penis shrinking." Once the therapists have counter-identified with the patient, the hysterical sexualization of the therapeutic relationship by the patient is ineffective and does not provoke any deterrent countertransference problems. His counter-identification enables the therapist to deny the infantile sexuality as a meaningful substitute for oral needs. It is also significant that once a counter-identification has occurred with the patient, the emotional insights of the therapists in the therapeutic relationship become more accurate and, when communicated to the patient, are a constructive factor in her therapeutic growth.

Forty-sixth Interview. Not remarkable. Both therapists were present.

Forty-seventh Interview. Not remarkable. Both therapists were present.

Forty-eighth Interview. Dr. White alone. He had been depressed before the appointment. He sat in Dr. Brown's chair to have a greater sense of Dr. Brown's presence. Hilda started at once to remove her coat, revealing a gold silk blouse. Then, "I can't do it." Dr. White fantasied that she had come without any brassière and that this was why she could not take her coat off. She added, "But I'm here anyway," as though this in itself had been quite an accomplishment. (Long silence.) Dr. White slept and reported a dream of a gold core with lightning arrows coming out of it. (Five minute silence.) Hilda was very tense, her right hand holding her left hand so it could not get free. Both were tearful. Hilda: "I've had a twitch in my face since yesterday evening," and then, "I don't know how to help you." Dr. White answered, "I don't know how to help you either." Dr. White had a fantasy of two rivers which were flowing together but couldn't become one. After a long period it seemed as though whatever was wrong in the togetherness of the two rivers was righting itself. Above the two rivers was a large sign with the words "Ting" and "Tang." (Twenty-minute silence.) Hilda: "Close your eyes." Dr. White did so, soon became afraid of Hilda, and opened them.

> DYNAMICS: A recurrent theme in the interview was the subjective dissatisfaction of both persons at their inability to communicate all of what was felt. It was as if when words failed the tendency was to become physical in the effort to communicate the deep responses felt toward the other person.

Forty-ninth Interview. Dr. Brown alone. Hilda: "You should have taken a vacation today." Dr. Brown: "I just took two days." She: "You seemed so glad to miss one day. And you'd had a drink before you came another day; I could have knocked your head in." (Dr. Brown had not had a drink.) Dr. Brown: "I don't remember." She: "Do you think I should stay another month?" (Pause.) "I'm serious, I want to get well for you and Dr. White but I don't think I'll love any more a month from now. (Pause.) There's a small chance I'll ever die a natural death. I'm ready to go home now; I don't mean home, but to leave. A month ago I wasn't." Dr. Brown: "I'm not ready to say good-bye to you." Hilda: "I won't be whole when I leave here and that's the only way you'll ever let me go." He: "The three-month limit worries me, but I also am glad for it. I want you to get well, but you let me worry about my motivation." She: "That's what Dr. White said yesterday." (Silence.) Hilda: "I always talk about enjoying things, never people." Dr. Brown: "Wish you could but you have to learn to masturbate before trying to get married." She: "You mean literally or figuratively?" Dr. Brown: "Both." She: "I do masturbate literally and I hate it." Dr. Brown: "I wish you could enjoy it for all there is in it." She: "You're not supposed to after you're married; then it's a substitute. Do you think I should be committed? I wish you'd answer me." Dr. Brown: "I have." Hilda stood up and walked behind his chair and Dr. Brown was embarrassed because he felt she was about to be overtly sexual.

> DYNAMICS: Dr. Brown at points seemed to be somewhat embarrassed by his affect. However, he supported the patient in her ending attempts, primarily through a process of non-reassurance (*e.g.*, his repeated refusal to answer the patient's direct question of whether she should be "committed"). His failure to respond directly to a question which the patient repeatedly asked was a technique of some importance to the authors. It is important that the therapist not put an obvious feeling into words, even though the patient repeatedly demands it. Dr. Brown responded in feeling sexual but remained passive when the patient made an overt sexual approach. His passivity precluded the patient's acting-out and the patient promptly returned to her chair. In effect, the sexual problem was reduced to a dependent problem and the patient was then free to return to the fundamental question which she was asking in this interview: "Do I need to be committed?" *i.e.*, should the patient commit herself further to this developing dependent relationship with the therapist?

Fiftieth Interview. The interview opened with a general discussion about talking initiated by Hilda: "It doesn't help to know about psychosexual development and about fixation. I talked all last year and it didn't do me any good. I couldn't understand the crazy things they said." Dr. White suggested that maybe she was learning now to talk with her eyes as well as with words. Dr. Brown: "Words are boats to ride and pictures to draw together, soft hands to love each other with or fists to fight with." (Twenty-minute silence.) Dr. Brown: "I like your smell." Hilda: "Those brown books, I've seen them for years." (Silence.) Hilda seemed "strange" to the therapists, as if requiring a new type of relationship. They talked to each other because the patient was a "big girl." She no longer seemed to need tender loving care. The therapists felt some impulse to clip or "castrate" the patient as if she were getting "too big for her britches."

> DYNAMICS: The patient tried to make talking a part of her total experience (ego therapy?) and not simply a dissociated intellectual interchange which promotes avoidance rather than togetherness.

Fifty-first Interview. Hilda: "Do you think talking will teach me anything? Dr. White: "It may help you to talk to yourself." Dr. Brown: "I'm more concerned that you're ashamed to be seen naked. For several times you've looked as though you had no clothes on and were afraid of what you'd see in our eyes." (Dr. Brown was consciously concerned with his own voyeurism.) Hilda: "In college I was silly. We even took a long barefoot walk in the snow, six of us girls, and we argued about the war and about the secret of the universe. I was the only one really hunting for it.

I couldn't find it and despaired. It seems like I was the only one who could not find the secret, so I crawled under my bed and stayed there for a week, real depressed." (Pause.) "As a child I used to write about fat souls and lean souls and I liked the lean souls; they do the worrying and are depressed about everything, but they are always hungry." Dr. White: "And the lean cows ate up the fat cows. What do you suppose happened to the fat cows? (Pause.) You know, Hilda, you ate Dr. Brown and now he is eating you." After a silence she said, "I had a dream in which I saw a little dictionary and a big one. Dr. Brown was saying that what Mrs. X needed was not education but conjugation, so I looked in the little dictionary and it said 'to carry a verb into all its tenses and variations.' Then I looked in the big dictionary and it did not seem so good so I went back to the little dictionary; it was very nice." The therapists laughed heartily. (Silence.) Dr. Brown said, "Thank you for coming today." Hilda: "I want to thank you for letting me come next month, I want very much to come."

> DYNAMICS: The patient seemed determined to discover what the therapists got out of this relationship. A failure to answer this question produces impasses.
>
> The patient said that she needed not education (simple insight) but conjugation (togetherness). She looked in her little dictionary (regression to childhood) and it said "to be carried in all ways" (to be dependent in every way). She then looked into her big dictionary (her conscious intellectual adultness) and what she found was not so good, so she went back to her little dictionary. This was then "nice" (satisfying) to all three participants. The response of the therapists to this was, paradoxically, a therapeutic recognition of her growth and her adultness manifest in their responses to her in the latter part of the interview and in Dr. Brown's final social and almost ceremonial thanking her sincerely for coming that day.

Fifty-second Interview. Not remarkable. Dr. White was absent.

Fifty-third Interview. Not remarkable. Both therapists were present.

> DYNAMICS: These interviews involved primarily a working through of some aspects of the patient's sadistic impulses. When she found that her aggression did not threaten the therapists, it became less threatening to her.

Fifty-fourth Interview. Dr. Brown alone. He moved a piece of paper on the desk and Hilda said, "Don't make me draw the figure of a man." Dr. Brown: "I think you'd prefer to draw the figure of a woman," and they continued to talk rather superficially. Hilda: "That time you had an erection worries me; I don't think I meant to do that; I had a prolapse on you and put my head down." Dr. Brown: "Maybe you'd like to try again and give me an erection intentionally. I sure get them with little girls." Hilda: "You mean actual little girls?" Dr. Brown: "Yes, ages four, five, and six, like you are emotionally." (Silence.) Hilda: "This is the part that was supposed to take three years, talking this out." Dr. Brown: "That's right, but I'm not ready to let you go yet." Hilda: "Why was it we planned for three months, because of money or because of me?" Dr. Brown: "Because the amount of money the family could afford would only finance three months." Hilda: "I had a dream—there were a group of soldiers jumping across a deep ravine, some fell in and we three, you and Dr. White and I, were watching, and one of the soldiers looked up with his mouth open although he was already unconscious and he looked right at me." And then, "Dr. White said that I would never know what death felt like until I was dead and you just said, 'Bitch. Do you think people only commit suicide because they're sadistic?' " Dr. Brown: "Sure, for no other reason than to hurt somebody." Hilda: "I suppose I wanted to pay Mommy back, I don't know what for but I knew she wouldn't survive it." (Silence.) Hilda: "I had a dream about Dr. White. I came up here with another man; he was nothing to me but I wanted to introduce him to Dr. White; I put my head on Dr. White's shoulder and saw that he was going to kiss me on the mouth, so I closed my eyes and when I opened them the other man had kissed me and Dr. White was at the other end of the hall and he was furious." (Silence.) Hilda: "In my dream I'm honest, other times I never know when I'm lying." (Silence.) Hilda: "I had a dream of having intercourse with you [Dr. Brown] and you were reading a funny paper all the time and I blamed you because the sexual relationship was no good. That's the first time in all my life I've ever dreamed of having intercourse." Dr. Brown: "It worries me about the funny paper." Hilda: "Oh, that's all me." Dr. Brown: "It certainly isn't. It's our relationship and you've just got delusions of grandeur." Hilda: "I've always blamed the man for its being unsatisfactory." Dr. Brown was feeling upset and said, "Our time is up," and Hilda got up to leave saying "Sorry."

DYNAMICS: The patient's first dream revealed insight into her sado-masochistic feelings, the subject of the preceding interview. Her second dream clarified her transference to Dr. White as a maternal-feeding person. She said that he set up a situation in which the patient (the child) was ready for a personal, warm relationship and then found herself in a specifically sexual relationship with the father. Although the mother (Dr. White) had set up this situation, he was furious at the child (patient). Dr. White repeatedly fostered a warm relationship with the patient, then abruptly was absent, leaving the patient to struggle with her sexual relationship with Dr. Brown. Her second dream of intercourse with Dr. Brown defined Dr. Brown's sexual response to her as being that of a father to a child rather than that of a man to a woman. The beginning resolution of the Oedipal problem, despite any specific working through of the problem in the preceding interviews, was interesting. It was as if, when the dependent problem was resolved to some extent and a personal togetherness was possible, many of the patient's hysterical problems began to resolve themselves. It was significant that for the first time in her life the patient had a dream of intercourse.

Fifty-fifth Interview. Not remarkable. Dr. Brown alone.

DYNAMICS: In multiple therapy, after the core phase of therapy is established and as the ending phase of therapy begins, one therapist functions as if it were multiple therapy even when the other therapist is physically absent. Dr. Brown's initial concern was with his femininity, *i.e.*, his maternal response to the patient's dependent needs. The emotional interaction was quite reciprocal and the patient was given status emotionally. In cases where the therapist communicates some of his physical sensations as well as his subjective fantasies, these contribute to the accuracy of the affective communication. Patients have done this for years with all therapists, and it is startling in retrospect to realize the failure of therapists to communicate their own physical sensations and discomforts to the patient.

Fifty-sixth Interview. First of a series of nine interviews to be held with Dr. White alone; the patient had been forewarned.

Fifty-seventh Interview. Not remarkable. Dr. White alone.

Fifty-eighth Interview. Not remarkable. Dr. White alone.

DYNAMICS: Therapeutic interactions were limited here. These interviews revealed the impact of the personality of the therapist on therapy. Dr. White's personality channelled the interview into problems dealing primarily with dependent feelings and ambivalent aggression. (Dr. Brown had been using the sexualization of the interview as a transition into problems which specifically relate to the anal phase of development.)

Fifty-ninth Interview. Hilda: "I'm sorry about last night." Dr. White: "What about tonight?" Hilda: "Did mommy hate me because I was like her?" Dr. White: "I always hate in *you* what I don't like in me." Hilda: "I get you and mommy mixed up." (Silence.) Dr. White slept. Hilda: "I had two dreams; in the first one you were on the other side of a door and there was no knob on my side; in the second one I was sitting on your lap, you had a watch charm I thought was like the one my father wore, then I noticed it was a Phi Beta Kappa key. [Pause.] My daughter had fallen into a sewer but I didn't want to disturb you; after a while in my dream I did get up and went over to look, but she had gone and I knew she had gone down the sewer." Dr. White: "Can we go after your daughter?" Hilda: "Can I sit on the floor?" Dr. White: "Sure," and the patient sat down between Dr. White's knees and said, "I wish I could be tiny." Dr. White: "You are." (Twenty-minute silence.) Hilda's right fist was very tight for the first few minutes, then she put her arms around Dr. White and began to nuzzle at the buttons on his shirt. Finally she relaxed and said, "I won't go back to my crib until you carry me." Dr. White said, "You can sleep here all night and if you wake you can have some more to eat, and if I wake I'll wake you so that you can eat." During the initial report of the patient's dreams, Dr. White felt sexual impulses; thereafter he felt maternal.

DYNAMICS: The patient began by projecting her own mother image onto Dr. White. She suggested in her first dream that she was unable to reach Dr. White, apparently because of her femininity (she had no knob on her side of the door). In her second dream she expressed the conviction that feeding leads to psychosis. Again, her feelings were hysterical and their presence in the interview was projective. At this point Dr. White brought about an emotional transition in the relationship which successfully converted a transference recapitulation into a significant therapeutic experience. He did this specifically by accepting the dream presented as part of the current relationship between himself and the patient. He interjected himself into the dream material and began to use the present tense. The patient followed this lead, and what had been transference material presented in a dream now became a significant emotional experience in which the therapist actively participated in the current relationship. This technique we have referred to in the literature as the *joint fantasy*. It successfully leads to the interchange which is described in the terminal part of the interview, where the patient's response was that of the regressed child. The feeding by the therapist was not simply a role but the warm, real response of an involved person.

Sixtieth Interview. Dr. White alone. Patient was more relaxed. Silence. Hilda: "I think I'm a vampire, I'll suck you two doctors all out and then you'll die." Dr. White: "If you would really suck it would increase the size of our breasts." (Silence.) Hilda: "Do I have to eat you?" Dr. White: "Not 'til you're ready, say about the time you are weaning." (Silence.) Hilda said, "I just had a funny fantasy about you; there was nothing left of your breast except skin and it was hanging down way to the middle of your belly."

DYNAMICS: Her concept of herself as a vampire: "to feed is to kill," is fairly typical of the schizophrenic patient in treatment. The therapist in this interview reassured the patient not by expressing his counter-identification but by saying in essence that feeding *gives* to the mother.

Sixty-first Interview. Dr. White alone. Hilda: "I thought after I went home yesterday that this was the first time anybody had ever loved me in all my life. I used to wonder if anybody ever would." Hilda and Dr. White looked at each other and then she said in a fairly objective manner, "I had a dream last night; a room was visible and I knew that you were there but I kept calling and you didn't answer. I kept wanting you to take off those big red gloves you were wearing." Dr. White went to sleep and dreamed that he was spread-eagled on the wall with ropes pulling at each arm and each leg and feeling there ought to be two more ropes and then he'd come apart at the belt line. He reported this to Hilda. She said, "Then I could crawl inside and stay there for a long time and get born again." Dr. White converted this joint fantasy into the present tense and said, "You feel good inside of me but you keep kicking. I guess I should have eaten more for breakfast so that you wouldn't be hungry." Hilda: "No, I'm just sleepy." Then she started to leave. Dr. White: "Why are you leaving?" Hilda answered, "It's only five minutes before the end of my time." Dr. White: "Are you going to cheat yourself again?" Hilda sat back down. After two minutes of silence she precipitated herself onto the floor again with her head in Dr. White's lap, making nuzzling motions as though she were breast feeding, and then said, "I wish I were tiny so that I could sit on your lap. It seems as though I've always been big."

> DYNAMICS: Therapy moved through shared fantasies. In response to the patient's fantasy-wish that Dr. White take off his red gloves, Dr. White responded with a dream in which he separated the sexual from the maternal feelings (came apart at the belt line). Immediately after this the patient became comfortably dependent with less ambivalence.
>
> The patient precipitously attempted to leave before the interview time had elapsed. The therapist fortunately maintained the administrative structure and during the remainder of the interview the patient had a very meaningful dependent experience.

Sixty-second Interview. Silence. Dr. White went to sleep, saw in his dream a line of floor tile, the first half of which line was dark and the second half white. Dr. White reported the dream to Hilda and later added, "I feel you don't trust me, you think I couldn't control you." Hilda: "Why do you go to sleep?" Dr. White: "When I can't stand your turning your back on me I go inside of myself to get to you; you can't turn your back on me there." (Silence.) Hilda: "I just want to lean against you." Dr. White: "Why don't you?" Hilda: "It seems silly when I think of it outside this office. I guess I trust you less during the last ten days. You didn't push me." Dr. White: "I can't; I feel you must fight for what you want. It hurts me when you don't do that but I just will not force you." Hilda (pleading): "It's such a short time before I have to walk [leave this treatment situation]." Then Hilda put her head on Dr. White's knee and sat this way for three or four minutes. Dr. White said, "I guess this is why you don't trust me; it's three minutes past the time for the end of the interview." Hilda got up and left.

> DYNAMICS: Ending emerged as a problem in this interview. The patient was concerned with her inability to resolve her dependence on the therapists. She "just wants to lean against," *i.e.,* she doesn't want to be swallowed up. She did not trust them since they did not push her. The therapists, by their refusal to put certain reality pressures on the patient, seduced the patient into a continuing dependency. At the termination of the interview Dr. White forced dependent relationship on the patient after the designated time for the ending of the interview had passed. In so doing, he in essence had made her dependency a reality, not a fantasy experience. Fortunately, he was honest enough to verbalize what he subjectively felt was an error. Another interesting sidelight is the use of the expression, "I trust you less," by the patient. If this had been said in the

beginning or middle phases of therapy it probably would have indicated an impasse. In the ending phases of therapy the same words and phrases of the patient frequently had an entirely different meaning. "I trust you less" may in this case have meant "I need you less."

Sixty-third Interview. Dr. White forced himself to be completely passive. Hilda: "Uncross your legs, will you?" Dr. White did, and Hilda, as she had done twice before, crawled up between them on her knees and nuzzled at his shirt with intense sweating. From time to time she would hug his neck, then lean back, and look up into his eyes. She did this for approximately thirty minutes, seemed very reluctant to get up and go back to her chair, and finally kissed him on the cheek and left the office without further comment.

> DYNAMICS: Here we have an ending within an ending. The patient had a relatively long series of interviews with one therapist. The experience had been mostly on the basis of a dependent relationship. In this interview the patient continued her feeding experience but ended as an adult by kissing the therapist on the cheek. During the entire interview she was paradoxically adult, while at the same time relating to the therapist as a hungry child. The feeding behavior here was less compulsive than previously, rather as if she were feeding for fun and not out of hunger.

Sixty-fourth Interview. Hilda welcomed Dr. Brown back by saying, "I had planned to give you my hands—ah, this is the worst day you could have come back." Dr. Brown: "Hilda, any day would be the worst." She said, "No." (Twenty-minute silence.) Dr. White fell asleep and dreamed of urging a little boy to keep his coat on because of fear of Dr. Brown. Dr. Brown: "I resent the idea of Hilda needing protection. I would prefer this without contraceptives." (Silence.) Dr. Brown: "This morning when I woke up I had been dreaming a bad nightmare from which I awoke screaming. I dreamed that I was trying to work with two other men to whom I could not feel close, and I was trying to back my car up to Dr. White's and then it all changed into two rows of chairs facing each other, and this made me feel scared. One man, who looked like Hilda, brought a table so that we would sit around it, and this anchored me, but I didn't throw the table out, I just told the others to go to hell and walked out." (Silence.) Dr. White: "I feel that now we are over our separation. It surprised me that we could feel so distant." Dr. Brown: "I expected the separation, but expect to live through it." Then he said to Hilda, "But you don't." Dr. White (to Hilda): "I hope you can get some more from us." She (to Dr. White): "I didn't think you were Mommy, but you are."

> DYNAMICS: It would have been technically wise if the two therapists had met with one another prior to the interview to re-establish their relationship and to talk briefly of what had ensued in the therapeutic situation in the interim period.
>
> The variation in the interpretive approach of the two therapists to the responses of the patient reflects the highly tenuous and subjectively vari-

ant quality of interpretations. Each therapist interprets on the basis of his own inner subjective response. In a sense, both are right. The importance of the interpretation in each instance is not its correctness but the fact that in each case the interpretation communicates accurately to the patient the deepest feeling-responses of the individual therapist.

Sixty-fifth Interview. Hilda: "I feel fine today, better than yesterday." Dr. Brown: "I am still uneasy about our relationship." Dr. White: "That's between you and me, and not Hilda's problem." Dr. Brown: "I think it is a problem to all three of us." Dr. White: "At first I thought I was separating us." Dr. Brown: "Maybe I'm just embarrassed about the breast feeding that's been going on here." Hilda: "I really wanted to tear his shirt and bite him. What about getting pregnant with anybody?" Dr. Brown: "I think you can get close enough to any man that you want to." Hilda: "You are saying that I simply want to get pregnant." She had tears in her eyes, and both therapists got a new sense of how deeply significant this experience was to her. After a few minutes Dr. Brown said, "I now feel some genuine concern about how many more days we have for this therapy."

> DYNAMICS: For the second time the patient came to the interview stating that she felt better and the therapists denied her ego growth by silence. It would have been helpful had they accepted the reality basis for the interview and supported the patient in working through the interview of the preceding day. Dr. White attempted a resolution when he directly confronted the other therapist with his feeling of being "distant." The patient finally helped in this impasse by reaffirming the deep significance of her experiences with the therapists and with her tearful and intense emotional outbreak at the termination of the interview, in essence asking the therapists not to deny their importance to her.

Sixty-sixth Interview. The interview seemed social. Hilda (to Dr. Brown): "I like your tie; it reminds me of the two woodpeckers I saw many years ago against the sky; they were so upsetting to me that I spent many days very upset, crying and laughing, and laughing because they both had white breasts." (Silence.) Dr. White began talking about where Hilda was in treatment. Then she said, "It bothers me for you two to be talking to each other." Dr. Brown: "It's about time you took an interest in what was going on; this is not an island that you're living on all by yourself." Hilda: "Yesterday I came in feeling good and after I left the interview I felt upset. I hadn't written in my diary for several days; last night I wrote again and suddenly realized that the whole diary was a pack of lies, lies, lies." Hilda, trying to light a cigarette, set the entire book of matches on fire. She exclaimed with horror, "Oh God, excuse me." Dr. White: "It sure scared me." Hilda: "I knew it would." Dr. Brown: "I liked it." Everyone then laughed at the way each of them had identified himself. Then Hilda began talking about a building, how the roof blew up, the door came off, and that she thought Dr. Brown was saying that she was mean (reference to an incident in which she had blown up a hotel). Hilda asked Dr. Brown if he thought she lit the match book on purpose. The two therapists then became involved with Hilda in a joint fantasy about all three of them committing suicide together. Finally Hilda said, "It's my overwhelming vanity; I'd forgotten about it for a while and last night remembered it again." This developed into a three-cornered fantasy of each of them being God, at which point the patient became visibly more straight in her chair and thrust her breasts out. Dr. Brown: "This is the second time in our therapy that I've had acute hunger pains here in the interview. It must mean you are no longer in acute need."

> DYNAMICS: In the beginning the patient related in a very social and reality-bound way and so brings up the problem of ending. The patient presented her own fantasy of ending and symbolically burned her written record of the interview experiences. (The patient actually burned her diary a few days later.) This attempt at ending was reinforced by the therapists who for the first time emotionally affirmed her ending attempt by sharing the fantasy. The final joint fantasy of the suicide (ending) of all three participants was followed by the emergence in each of a sense of being God (with separation comes independence and power). In multiple therapy the authors have found it of paramount importance that the ending cues presented by the patient be emotionally reinforced and developed in this phase of treatment. When they fail in this, ending becomes quite extensive. The impasse which develops is sometimes insurmountable.[8]

Sixty-seventh Interview. Hilda came in with a broad smile. She asked Dr. Brown, "Have you always worn loud ties like that?" And to Dr. White, "Have you always gone without ties like this?" Dr. Brown: "That's all right, you never see the little sins. Even a discourtesy against the Crown is punishable by death." The conversation got around to the Ten Commandments and Dr. White said, "They ought to be like any other examination; answer any five. For instance, 'Thou shalt not covet' could even mean thou shalt not fantasy." Dr. Brown remarked casually, "We just can't remain superficial, can we?" Hilda: "I never went to church 'til I came here. But I don't like what the Confessional says there, about there being no health in us." Dr. White: "That's just because some author of the Confessional thought we were made in the image of the devil and should spend our life beating the devil out." Hilda then described a fantasy in which she had seen a circle and Dr. Brown kept interrupting using the word "shit," and the patient would respond to this by saying "ouch." Dr. White: "The trouble with you, Hilda, is you're eating your own fantasy."

> DYNAMICS: The patient again tested the therapists' need of her dependence. The therapists tried repeatedly to involve the patient in a continuing fantasy relationship despite her efforts at ending. Toward the end of

---

[8] Note responses to ending cues earlier, *e.g.*, interviews eighteen, thirty-seven, forty, and forty-nine.

the interview the patient stated how deeply significant the therapeutic experience had been when she said, "I never went to church 'til I got here." It would have been wise at this point if the therapists had responded to the real adult feeling expressed in this metaphor; instead they erroneously developed the shared feeling as a fantasy transference experience. Having worked hard at developing the patient's potential, they felt a very real need for experiencing the actuality of their person in a way that would be satisfying. The rather poignant outcome of this in therapy was revealed in Dr. White's final statement in which he said (reflecting his own feeling), "The trouble is you're eating your own fantasy."

Sixty-eighth Interview. Hilda came in sloppy old slacks, and seemed to be disturbed all through the interview. Dr. White: "You certainly had that hair-do done so that it leaves the right side of your face open." Dr. Brown: "Your husband called last night [this was the first contact the family had made with the therapists since the onset of treatment]. He asked about you and I said you were better but still needed help; that you would be finished here within approximately one week." Dr. White: "I disagree; I don't think you'll need help after you leave here; I think you may want it and it may be rough without it, but maybe that's the way you'll get the most strength." (Silence.) Hilda: "I've nothing to talk about." Dr. Brown: "You look crazy but what bothers me is you seem socially insecure with it." Hilda said reassuringly, "I don't think I'll go to another doctor."

Sixty-ninth Interview. Dr. White was unexpectedly absent. Hilda had come without her attendant for the first time and was very proud of it. This was done without the knowledge of the therapists. She said, "I wish Dr. White were here." Dr. Brown: "I do too, I miss him today." Hilda: "I'm going home. What will I say when they ask me to tell what happened down here? I don't want to tell them anything." Dr. Brown: "You're a bright girl." (Silence.) Hilda: "I think I'm well, I've been hiding behind my patient status and I hate like hell to give it up." Dr. Brown, irritably, "That's probably no harder for you than it is for us to give you up as a patient. You know, you will always suffer and life is worth it." Hilda: "I sculptured a statue once and it made a hit; it was of a man praying with great big hands and I called it 'Despair.' But somebody told me, 'Why hell, that's not prayer, he's getting ready to knock the devil out of God.' Then I looked at his hands and face and sure enough, he looked angry." Dr. Brown: "Sounds like a real prayer to me." She: "You certainly are amiable today, now I'll go home and say, 'he's my friend after all.' "

Seventieth Interview. Dr. White was absent. Hilda's manner was casual and friendly; she spoke with some insight on the generations of emotional illness that she knew of in her family. (Silence.) She became discouraged and put her head in Dr. Brown's lap, but it was a social gesture without much meaning. Hilda said that she was now afraid of meeting her relatives again.

Seventy-first Interview. Both therapists were present. This was the last interview. Hilda came with a red shirt, her new overcoat, and good slacks. She said to the therapists, "I wore this coat because I felt so good." Then she seemed like a shy girl, coy, sexy like a small child, and at her prettiest, with superficially entertaining talk. She discussed the fact that her husband was coming the following day and that they would see the administrative psychiatrist they had seen three months before; that she was glad nothing was being done behind her back in terms of these arrangements. After a very relaxed and comfortable interview, she got ready to leave and say good-bye. All three people stood up. Dr. Brown put out his hand and said, "I want to shake hands." Hilda answered aggressively, "I won't." She walked out comfortably without any special farewells being said.

> DYNAMICS: These four interviews constituted the terminal segment of the ending phase of therapy. Typically, they were characterized by reality talk, verbalization, social interchanges, and emphasis on interpersonal rather than intrapersonal facets. They were characterized by an absence of fantasy, an absence of silence, and a readiness on the part of the therapists to accept the words and behavior of the patient on a conscious social level without any effort to develop the unconscious component. The whole ending effort involved an attempt by the patient to decathect the therapeutic experience. This the therapists reinforced and supported. At points the therapists tried to decathect the experience for themselves. The closing interviews involved a fusion of therapeutic material and real-life administrative problems. The isolation of the therapeutic experience was violated repeatedly. This assisted the patient in making the transition from the fantasy experience to her real-life situation. In order to end, she had to be able to take with her comfortably the introjects of the therapists; this needed to be balanced in some way with a certain amount of freedom and independence from the therapists, so that she could work comfortably with the introject without the actual physical presence of the therapists.
>
> At the end of the last interview, Dr. Brown said he wanted to shake hands. The patient, with a good deal of feeling, exclaimed, "I won't." His effort to make the relationship that real and that social was a tactical error. If the patient had accepted such a relationship it would have disturbed the post-interview ending process. This small incident illustrates well the need on the part of the therapists to gauge with sensitive accuracy the point at which a decathexis is too rapid and disturbing to the patient. The patient needs a period of time subsequent to the actual interviews to complete the ending process.

ADDENDUM

1. *Optimally, what criteria do you use for accepting or rejecting patients for psychotherapy?*

The primary criterion for accepting or rejecting a patient is the subjective certainty of the therapists that the patient is consciously or unconsciously "out to grow." However, if the administrative structure for the care of the patient is insecure, for example, if there is no family to control the patient's acting-out, then the final decision must be evaluated with this in mind. Patients are not accepted for psychotherapy if there seems to be no shadow of hope in the patient, as perceived by the subjective responses of the therapists, or if there is an overpowering drive in a close member of the family to keep the patient sick.

2. *Do you make a diagnosis before psychotherapy begins?*

No administrative or nosological diagnosis is made as such, but the therapeutic and administrative problems are defined and counter-transference problems of the therapists are evaluated in the consultation before therapy begins. This process is aided by a consultation appointment between the patient, the therapist, and a second psychiatrist, in addition to the initial individual consultation. All available case information is then presented to the clinical staff conference, and the recommendations given to the patient later that are representative of staff opinion.

3. *Do you attempt to persuade the patient or significant relative to change his (the patient's) environment?*

No. The therapeutic problem is conceived to be purely an intrapsychic one. On rare occasions and for administrative purposes the environmental situation may be structured for suicidal protection or for the control of the patient's acting-out, so that the therapist will not be in trouble with his community.

4. *How did you conceptualize the therapist's role in this case?*

See "therapeutic task" as outlined in the text. The therapist is not simply a projective screen but an active participant in a person-to-person relationship in which he participates with as few technical maneuvers as possible. He introduces as much spontaneity as he has available within the limitations of the total setting. The therapist's effort is to communicate as fully as possible his feeling responses to the presence of the patient, and his experiences in this relationship. In addition, he is committed to gain as much personal growth from the relationship as is possible without harm to the patient. Finally, all of the therapist's functioning is contained within the administrative, medical and social setting defined beforehand.

5. *What aspects of your theory of psychotherapy were particularly apparent or useful in the case presented here?*

(1) Multiple therapy is presented as a method of preference for *the seriously ill patient.* It affords a means to free each therapist for the necessary personal involvement with the patient, and provides the patient with an opportunity for relating to two parental images simultaneously.
(2) Non-verbal communication is of primary importance. The therapist must avoid intellectual verbiage, lest it be a barrier to the unconscious-to-unconscious affective relationship between therapist and patient.
(3) Non-reassurance and even aggression by the therapist promotes the growth of the patient.
(4) Counter-transference and counter-identification can be useful to stimulate therapeutic movement.
(5) Silence as such can be a valuable medium for the conduct of the communication between therapist and patient.
(6) The patient has value as a therapist to the therapist.

(7) It is an error for the therapist to delay artificially the development of transference and counter-transference. In other words, therapeutic failures are more often sins of omission than sins of commission.

6. *Do you feel that this case developed significant insight? If not, can improvement be maintained?*

If by insight is meant conscious insight, then the answer is "no." If by insight is meant unconscious or felt insight, then the answer is "yes." In either case, the patient has maintained her improvement for a period of five years. (*Conscious* insight has the quality of intricate fact-finding, or even of simple memory of related details. Through hindsight, the patient forms such details into a significant *gestalt*. *Unconscious* insight has a quality of experiencing in the present a previously not activated capacity. The patient may never become aware of what has occurred in him to change his behavior.)

7. *What aspects of your own cultural orientation facilitated or impeded the treatment of your case?*

Psychotherapy is a method for establishing a special, small sub-culture where the patterns of relating are redefined according to the individual needs of the particular patient. In developing this sub-culture, the therapist must cross his own customary social barriers to relating. With a seriously ill patient, the necessary deviation of this sub-culture from the culture is so great that the integration of the individual therapist is severely strained. Multiple therapy makes this strain tolerable.

8. *If we consider that a continuum exists from superficial to deep psychotherapy, where would you place your own case?*

The depth of the therapy is a function of the depth (maturity) of the therapists as this is evoked by the varying depths of the patient's need. To the two therapists this treatment was an unusually meaningful personal experience.

9. *What did you think about the outcome of this case and what criteria did you use for evaluating such outcome?*

At the end of therapy there was some doubt by the therapists of the outcome, but the follow-up for five years indicates that the outcome should be rated as successful. Criteria include: (1) Social adjustment. (2) Absence of symptoms. (3) Continued growth. (4) The resolution of transference dependence. (5) The subjective satisfaction of the therapist.

10. *How do you terminate psychotherapy?*

In this case the duration of therapy was set by the administrative situation and the termination was forced. Usually, with the authors, termination is a function of the patient's establishing those relationships outside the therapeutic situation which yield greater satisfaction than the therapeutic relationship itself. This is supplemented by the decreasing affective involvement of the therapist.

11. *Other.*

Psychotherapy must maintain a relationship to the cultural situation of patient and therapist. The therapeutic process in this case is unique in that it was more free of social and psychological safeguards than is present in the usual psychotherapy as done by the authors.

CHAPTER 10

Paradox and Choice
in Schizophrenia

—ARTHUR BURTON[1]

Introduction[2]

While the treatment of schizophrenia can be considered to be merely in its formative stages, we are somewhat more advanced in the phenomenology of the illness as a result of a century of scientific observation of cases. Since the behavior of a psychotherapist with any individual case implicitly and explicitly depends upon his theoretical conceptions and formulations, it is contingent upon me to clarify this before discussing the therapeutic interaction proper of the patient we call Tess.

My theoretical formulation is subsumed under five descriptive vectors

---

[1] A.B., 1936; M.A., '38, U. of Calif. at L.A.; Ph.D., U. of Calif., Berkeley, '40; Dir., Voc. Coun. Bu., L.A. Serv. Lea., '40-'42; Assoc. Personn. Exam., Calif. State Personnel Bd., '42-'45; Clin. Psychol., Calif. Youth Auth., '45-'46; Assoc. Prof. Psychol., Idaho State Coll., '46-'47; Assoc. Prof. Psychol., Willamette U., '47-'48; Clin. Psychol., V.A. Hosp., Vancouver, Wash., '47-'48; Chief Clin. Psychol., '48-'57, Agnews State Hosp.; Chief Clin. Psychol., Neuropsych. Inst., U. of Calif. School of Med., L.A., '57. Chief Clin. Psychol., Agnews State Hosp., '58- . Priv. Prac., '48- ; Certified Psychologist, State of Calif., '59- ; Visit. Lect., C. G. Jung-Institute, Zurich (Summer, '58). Fellow: A.P.A., Soc. Proj. Tech., Amer. Acad. of Psychother., Inter. Amer. Soc. for Psychol., Calif. State Psychol. Assoc., and others. Editor (with R. E. Harris) of *Clinical Studies of Personality* (1955) and *Case Studies in Clinical and Abnormal Psychology* (1947). *Psychotherapy of the Psychoses* (ed.), Basic Books, Inc. (to be published).

[2] The introductory part of this paper was read at the University of Basle, Institute for Psychotherapy and Mental Health, in the spring of 1958. I am indebted to Professor Gaetano Benedetti and his colleagues for their suggestions. Walter Rapaport, M.D., Medical Director and Superintendent, Agnews State Hospital, made the study of this patient possible.

which interact dynamically to offer conceptual meaning to the unique and puzzling behavior known as schizophrenia. These five vectors do not constitute a closed system in the sense that they are definitive. There may be more than five such vectors; but the principle of parsimony applies here to the extent that my own observations and experiences with schizophrenia have led me to isolate these five as most suitable for my own theory of schizophrenia.

(1) *Omnipotence*

Every act for the schizophrenic is an omnipotent one. He has in his power the capacity to destroy his therapist or anyone else with whom he interacts. But this is an antithesis, for every act is at the same time a demeaning one in which his nonhuman properties or worthlessness are verified in existence. This is why in psychotherapy the patient seems unable to make the smallest personal commitment and the slightest offer of love is assumed as a most momentous burden. By the same token, rejection is implied in everything the therapist does in the interaction.[3] In contrast, the nonschizophrenic can take a position at any one point on the omnipotence continuum and maintain it by sufficiently ordered ego-forces. We may say on the level of the schizophrenic that the latter gives birth to the therapist but also destroys him by doing so. It is symbolically the role of Christ and anti-Christ in Christianity, and is one basis for the very frequent religious delusions seen in schizophrenia. The pan-sexuality and the birth fantasies in these patients involve just such conditions of giving and taking—of giving birth, but at the same time of not giving birth. The correlation between the incidence of schizophrenia breakdown at puberty and the physical ability to conceive at this period is another case in point. The universal omnipotence-fantasies of schizophrenic patients in therapy confirm the presence of what may be archetypal remnants of racial and individual attempts to survive in the past.

(2) *Bi-sexual Balance*

It has seemed to me that the bi-sexuality ratio in schizophrenics is disturbed. By this I mean that the identity confusion of the schizophrenic extends to the male and female principle. Both masculinity and femininity are in ascendance in the schizophrenic or both are primitive and undeveloped. There is no major masculinity or femininity that the patient can seize upon; all is either latency or conflict. One may say that the schizophrenic fertilizes himself and so requires his sexual complement in equal ascendancy. There may be a biological or endocrine

---

[3] This is well illustrated by the cases of Hafner and Whitaker, *et al.*, in this volume.

basis for this factor, for one is constantly struck by the frequency of hirsutism in schizophrenic women. There may also be some analogy possible here to more primitive organisms and their sexual organization. Psychotherapy of schizophrenia must recognize this M-F confusion and restore a potency or polarity. Heterosexuality or homosexuality rather than bi-sexuality is the desideratum.

(3) Communication

It has by now been well documented that the formal language and imaginal structure of schizophrenics is impaired. In fact, this impairment is often employed diagnostically as the hallmark of the condition. To some extent this is the resultant of vectors 1, 2, 3, and 4, but is principally related to an economic principle. Communication in any system or organism is evolved to meet the biological and social needs of the organism and is never elaborated beyond the point of function. The schizophrenic has no need of more than paleological communication development in terms of his personality. This is probably also true of societies which we call primitive but which are self-contained and at equilibrium on their own level. Let us face the fact that schizophrenics do not want psychotherapy—it is the therapist who has the need to communicate with them and to cure them.[4] It is the therapist who seeks them out and plagues them to be cured by vague promise of love, of undoing and redoing, of newer and better things to come. This is why getting the schizophrenic into psychotherapy at all is probably the major achievement of the therapy, as Hafner so well points up.[5] This seduction on the part of the therapist is revealed by the "touchiness" of psychotherapists about their schizophrenic patients as compared to other patients. They are weighted down by promises they must keep—but they are not sure! Let us say, for the time being, that the schizophrenic speaks and thinks a language foreign to the therapist, is puzzled by ours, and, as in a foreign country, must have a need to learn the new language. Left to himself, his communication system is adequate.

(4) Ethical Sense

The term, ethical sense, is a poor one for this vector but provides an image for a number of points to be drawn together. Culture embodies a system of ethics which defines interactional relationships in terms of

---

[4] Our experience has been that psychotherapists who treat schizophrenics are a most unique and dedicated group and are probably unlike their colleagues who treat only neurotics. This would make a fascinating study in its own right. I am reminded of C. G. Jung's statement, when I saw him on May 9, 1958, that schizophrenics make greater demands than any one therapist can bear.

[5] See this volume.

their humanitarian, hedonistic, and aesthetic qualities. Love, for example, characterizes a set of values and behavior having an ethical quality. Culture promotes and proscribes love, and is at any rate constantly preoccupied with it (witness popular songs and literature in the United States). It provides both subtle and overt rewards for people who can love and rejection for those who cannot. Now love is an entirely unsatisfactory word—somewhat analogous to the confusion Freud discovered in his use of the word *sex*. But there is a long tradition for it in poetry, religion, the arts, and human relations in general, and we can think of nothing better to convey the special transfer of feeling taking place between people. Schizophrenics lack an ethical sense because they cannot love. In the inability to love there is lost the basis of ethics—for ethics assumes a giving and receiving in a reciprocal humanitarian relationship. This is not the place to discuss the reasons for the schizophrenic's inability to love because this has been well done elsewhere.[6] Put more aptly we may say that these patients are not unethical but aethical, and this becomes the touchstone of their existence. Any psychotherapy of a schizophrenic must contend with this interpersonal problem in an acute and poignant way. We set out in a stormy sea to offer communion to a person who has no ethical basis for relatedness and must re-experience his infancy (and the love in infancy) to find it. This brings with it special therapeutic problems we will discuss later in connection with Tess's treatment.

(5) *Body Image*

If you were to ask a series of average individuals what parts of their bodies they would sacrifice if this were absolutely necessary to continue existence, we would probably find some commonality in their sacrifices. In fact, a sacrificial gradient could be established for the significant parts of the body. This gradient would not have a significant deviation from individual to individual, and general organizational principles or order would govern each set of sacrifices. We may thus say that there is consistency in body image for all people but this is apparently not so for the schizophrenic. With him there is no basis for ordering the parts of his body and there is no gradient. He will sacrifice his head as easily as his genitalia—or, moreover, he will confuse his head with his genitalia. Consider for a moment this dream from Hafner's patient Gisella.[7]

> Regarding the feeling of my body it has become much worse. It is a kind of paralysis. When I am bending down and then stretch back everything threatens to dissolve and to become invisible. I have never sensed my

---

[6] See, for example, Lewis B. Hill, *Psychotherapeutic Intervention in Schizophrenia* (Chicago: University of Chicago Press, 1955).

[7] Heinz Hafner in this volume.

body in a matter-of-fact way. I remember how the girls laughed at me during the gymnastic hour when I was nine years old. "There are already hairs growing under your arms," they said, laughing horribly. This meant to me treason and at the same time a hint to my looks. I allowed the mind to awake but I repressed the body.

Hafner implies that the body image changes with successful treatment—that the body structure becomes organized into some proper hierarchy so that there is order in the body image. It must be clear that this confusion is introjectional and that these people as children must have had difficulty in knowing where to suck. Because of the inconsistency of the source of nourishment—the breast—provided by a poorly organized mother herself, they can now neither offer their own breasts for nourishment or receive it because they simply do not have the body-image hierarchy for it. Since the primary erotigenic zones cannot be found, the organism is driven to settle for the secondary or tertiary, or even more primitive areas, or to make the entire body erotigenic. But adulthood requires primary pleasurable zones and a valuative hierarchy if body-image language is to function.

In the treatment of a chronic schizophrenic[8] all the above vectors must be contended with in some fashion. This highlights the problem of getting the schizophrenic into treatment. He does not speak our language, his body organization is not like ours, his masculinity-femininity is confused, he lacks an ethical sense, and he is so omnipotent or so valueless as to not need us at all. Certainly there is little basis here for the introjection of a therapist.

It is obvious that the problem cannot be attacked as though it were a neurotic one. The neurotic needs us—the schizophrenic does not. The customary "gambits" conducive to the classical transference will not operate specifically because of our five vectors. While some of these vectors are also found in neurotic patients, the peculiar intensity and constellation of them is uniquely schizophrenic. We are not yet ready to quantify the vectors, or to relate one to the other or to a common source, but there is much clinical data which supports them.[9] These vectors seem also to be specific to schizophrenia and not to all the psychoses.

A better approach to the schizophrenic is to meet him on his own level. This is not easily come by since the therapist is not after all a schizophrenic[10] and it is deeply disturbing to even act as one.

---

[8] I include under this term the treatment of the ambulatory and pseudo-neurotic schizophrenic of long duration.

[9] A first experiment on the body-image, sacrificial heirarchy in schizophrenia is now in the experimental stage.

[10] The success of treated schizophrenics in assisting in the treatment of still other schizophrenics is well known. This may be due to vector residuals. (See, for example, Rosen's work.)

It is my observation that those psychotherapists who treat schizophrenics successfully are just those people who are not intrinsically fearful of schizophrenia and who can make a fundamental commitment to such patients without anxiety or guilt. Can we say that such therapists have a form of schizophrenic identification—an introjection of the patient and a feeling for his suffering? Karl Barth feels that suffering is the distinguishing mark of humanity.[11] I would paraphrase this to say that suffering is the distinguishing mark of schizophrenia. It is the most heroic, and at the same time the most senseless act, for the schizophrenic suffers for an eternity without at the same time being bound by time and space. But his suffering is not ethical; that is, it is unique rather than socially binding or creative. To make it a form of communion with fellow men is the task of the therapist.

So the psychotherapist must be capable of, and interested in, a unique human commitment—a dedication, as it were—on a number of levels of personality development. This we call the "Begegnung" or encounter.[12] The *Begegnung* has been the subject of considerable philosophical thought, *e.g.*, Kierkegaard and Buber, but here we interpret it as a fundamental "thou-I" encounter similar to what occurs between mother and child, man and woman, and in the tenderest moments wherever love transfigures the relationship and gives it that very special quality of transcendance. Thus we see a *Begegnung* as necessary on the oral level of development, at the anal stage, and on the Oedipal and genital levels, if the character basis of interpersonal relatedness is to be established. Failure at any of these levels results in fixation at that level with consequent regression to an earlier level a possibility. The searching quality so evident in the psychically troubled is just such an attempt to re-experience the *Begegnung* where it fell short or was absent in a particular developmental period. In schizophrenia the *Begegnung* is of the earliest and most fundamental kind, for here the mother-child encounter was lacking or was devoid of all essence. All levels of *Begegnung* must be recapitulated in the treatment of a schizophrenic. The patient, so to speak, must "undo" and "redo" within the new framework of the encounter with the therapist.

Psychotherapeutic technique is of secondary importance with schizophrenics, and no facile technique will succeed if the therapist cannot promote the successive *Begegnungen*. Technique, of course, is the tactic of psychotherapy, and there is room for tactics. But here we get into difficulty when we attempt to teach students how to proceed in psycho-

---

[11] Personal visit, April 27, 1958.

[12] For my first acquaintance with the concept of "Begegnung," I am indebted to Dr. Raoul Schindler in both his paper in this volume and in personal discussions. I understand that this concept stems from Hans Trüb's *Heiling Durch Begegnung*, circa 1935.

therapy with schizophrenics. We can teach technique but we cannot teach how to communicate our being. When we teach tactics and strategy we may miss the point of the *Begegnung,* but we feel more comfortable as teachers since we take refuge in mechanics.[13] The challenge of the schizophrenic, however, soon places the student in the position of an encounter with which he must cope.

The typescripts of the psychotherapeutic interviews with Tess are to be measured in pounds rather than in single protocols, and the task of bringing some order into this vast quantity of material is a rather formidable one. Our past experience with schizophrenics has been that no current reporting medium reproduces the essence of the interaction and that one has to be reconciled to a somewhat abstracted if not distorted picture. Thus we will make no attempt to reproduce the course of the psychotherapy but will rather discuss certain phases of the treatment as they bear upon our vector and *Begegnung* formulations.

The patient was first seen for thirty hours of group therapy, and then had eighty-six hours of individual therapy as a resident patient and then as an out-patient—over the period between April 15, 1956, and July 1, 1958. She was twenty-eight years old on admission. Just prior to July 1, 1958, and following my departure from the area, she was followed by a psychiatric social worker in connection with post-hospital adjustment.[14] No report is given of the latter work here or of the group therapy. Before we discuss the treatment proper, a synopsis of the life history will be offered.

Life History

As far as is known, Tess first came to the attention of a psychoanalyst in September, 1948. She was unkempt, confused, and somewhat depressed. There was a philosophical tone to her mental content, but she was also preoccupied with sexual fantasies about her father. Death, rape, and sex were recurrent themes. After a brief period of treatment she became paranoid, believing that the FBI was following her. She wanted complete gratification or extinction. She then remitted her symptoms in a few months, but suffered a second psychotic episode late in 1949.

Again she improved rapidly and was in good enough condition to marry in 1951. She moved to another part of the United States—3,000 miles away—with her husband and suffered further breakdowns necessitating out-patient psychiatric treatment. She returned to the original city in 1955, having separated from her husband, and resumed treatment with

---

[13] Helm Stierlin describes the historical attempts to keep the schizophrenic divorced from the therapist and considers this as related to Aristotelian modes of thought current at the time. The shift to the Galilean concept of understanding is best seen in Sullivan's conception of "participant-observer" relationship. My own philosophical approach is to go even beyond Sullivan. H. Stierlin; "Contrasting Attitudes Toward the Psychoses in Europe and in the United States," *Psychiatry, 21* (1958), 141-47.

[14] I am indebted to Miss Joan Bathrick for her contribution in this area.

the original psychoanalyst. At this time her defenses were severely decompensated, which she complicated by drinking to reduce tensions. It became necessary to hospitalize her in a private sanitarium in November and December, 1955, where she improved rapidly. She was not, however, capable of handling her environment and was referred to the state hospital where I saw her.

Upon admission Tess told the psychiatrist that her emotional difficulties were chronologically related to the time her father fell ill. (He subsequently died of this illness.) She had fantasies that her parents were not her real ones. She bordered on the delusion that she was the daughter of a famous art figure—Picasso—but at the same time was able to be critical of this delusion. She said that she was unstable and uncertain about her future—that she couldn't control the impulse to escape conflict by drinking. The psychiatrist described her as "oriented, relevant, mildly depressed, but revealing a great deal of anxiety and instability if left unprotected." She adjusted well to ward routine.

Because of her talent in art she was assigned to this section in the occupational therapy department. There her designs were quite creative but she tended to be intense, and worked slowly and cautiously.

About two months after admission she surreptitiously obtained some form of stimulant—possibly alcohol—and appeared to throw herself in front of an oncoming car, but without damage to herself. It was not clear whether the intent here was self-destruction. Again she improved, and asked to leave. Since she was a voluntary patient, and the improvement seemed general, this was granted in May, 1956. Her diagnosis was schizophrenic reaction, chronic undifferentiated type, although a neurosis and character disorder had been considered.

However, Tess returned in just six days and told a strange story. She said that she had started to drink again, that she was raped in a bar, that she wanted to drown herself but could not. She was depressed and vague, but oriented and without delusions. Her ward psychiatrist at this time mentioned pseudo-neurotic schizophrenia with acting out. At this time we agreed that she would discontinue group therapy with me and that I would see her individually. This was done. After fifteen hours of individual therapy she became so increasingly tense, tearful, and depressed that she was considered actively psychotic and transferred to a ward where maximum supervision was afforded. She also lost considerable weight. Reserpine (2 mg. a day) was administered by the ward psychiatrist and, when this was ineffective, electric-convulsive therapy was started. The patient was now actively delusional, withdrawn, confused, and depressed.

She showed marked improvement with six ECT and was no longer delusional or depressed. Tess returned to an open ward. Psychotherapy was continuous, varying from the initial two hours a week to four hours as the circumstances dictated.

A month later she had two extended visits to her mother and then became delusional again. This was a brief psychotic period which the patient gave up by working through basic conflicts in the psychotherapy to be described below. In February, 1957, she obtained employment in the book department of a large department store and left the hospital. She continued to come in for psychotherapy as an out-patient until I left for another part of the state.

Tess is the younger of two siblings—both girls. She is a little more than twenty months the junior of her sister who is now happily married to a professor and has several children. The sister had been in analysis and had been helped by it.

Tess's father was born in Puerto Rico and was the export manager for a large United States company. He was full of energy and ambition but suffered from stomach trouble over the years. Early in the marriage the father and mother were reportedly happy. Later he was attracted to other women and many years of discord followed. The father was apparently a seductive person in his relationship to his daughters, if not with all women.

The mother—whom I never met—is reported as a nongiving person, but on short acquaintance has been described as pleasant, intelligent, and charming. She was born in the Middle West and has been troubled with a chronic duodenal ulcer and a heart complaint. Her father was an alcoholic and her mother committed suicide.

The patient was educated in Cuba at a private school and came to the United States at age eleven. She was a very bright girl and graduated from high school at sixteen. Her achievement was reduced, however, because of persistent headaches and an illness of undescribed origin. She obtained a scholarship to an art school and attended for a time.

In 1951 she married the son of an artist of considerable renown. The husband, a Ph.D., was a scientist who later came into some stature in his own right. The patient considers him cold, unresponsive, and perfectionistic; but he seemed genuinely interested in her welfare. Tess said that he was a good provider, and that their sexual adjustment was good but deteriorated.

"I just drank too much starting after a miscarriage in 1952. I was extremely depressed. . . . We agreed intellectually and philosophically. But he was overly critical of me in order to boost himself up. He needed to show me off rather than to have me for himself. He had a compulsion to go skiing and tried to make a skier of me, but I was afraid."

There was no issue from the marriage. They were divorced after four and a half years of marriage, but they were together for only a part of this time.

The mother described Tess as a "delightful person, charming, sweet, like a balm. She is gentle and soft-spoken. She is easy to make friends with and everyone appears to like her."

The patient had difficulty in learning to read and complained frequently of headaches. Glasses were obtained for her. She would have frequent "acidosis" and stay home from school. Her sister was exemplary in school and attained some prominence at the university she attended. A considerable rivalry was soon established and Tess always felt that her mother favored her sister under the pretext of her sister's nervousness.

Tess was very idealistic, according to her mother, and had difficulty choosing a husband, although she was admired by many. The patient was encouraged in her art ability but wanted to start at the top. She could not work consistently.

At twenty-one, Tess, when her father died, showed the first flowering of her psychopathology. She was depressed for three months and completely inactivated in bed. She seemed to recover but became psychotic in Europe where her mother took her for a change.

Both girls were largely raised by a nursemaid—one who was faithful to the family, a Cuban, and who stayed with them until her death. Tess was her favorite. She is described by Tess as "having a lot of common sense, a lot of warmth, very religious, and a fine person."

The Dynamics of Psychotherapy

Tess first became the focus of my attention as one of seven women who participated with me twice weekly in group therapy on the hospital admission ward. She was small in structure—almost petite—with brown hair not distinguished in any way and certainly not for its abundance. Her complexion was on the pale side, but her features were classic— I often thought like a cameo. She spoke quietly but with distinction. There was a tendency to measure her words, but it was not the clipped speech of the frightened who hold back. She was obviously quite bright and her factual information on aesthetics, travel, history, and other matters distinguished her from the other members of the group. (I remember thinking then that she was somewhat misplaced.) There was an intensity about her difficult to describe. This is probably better reported as "sincerity," for she radiated a quality of purpose which brooked no compromise. She wanted to get well, knew the costs, and was there to settle them.

Every psychotherapist of schizophrenia is challenged by the suffering and struggles of such patients. Each of us unconsciously introjects certain of these patients and attempts to bring them to treatment—the relationship. After a number of hours of group therapy I offered Tess the opportunity of seeing me individually. She was reluctant and made references in which she deprecated me in comparison with her former analyst. This continued even after she was in treatment with me and is important dynamically in its own right. At any rate, in terms of the selection of patients for psychotherapy, I was ready to make a fundamental commitment to her for her treatment.[15] She came one to four hours a week—the frequency was consistent from week to week but varied with the needs of the patient. Thus, when she became overtly delusional, I saw her four hours a week; when her delusions passed over, we returned to two or three hours. In this way I manipulated our presence together for support and independent action, honored special requests to see me, and often went to her ward to see her when she was disturbed. This was particularly true in the earlier stages of treatment. Acting-out and suicidal attempts—mock or otherwise—were taken as a matter of course and made the focus of examination, subject of course to the proper timing. She was very much afraid of her drinking propensities but would have wished to pass as an alcoholic. I did not accept this and considered her drinking as just another event, which fortunately

---

[15] See *Addendum* to this chapter, in which the selection of patients for psychotherapy is discussed.

later turned out to be correct. Her drinking was a screen which could have left us "high and dry" in therapy—if I may be allowed a pun! The viccisitudes of the therapy were always buttressed by our encounter—by the knowledge, conscious and unconscious, that we were together in this great struggle of hers. This of course she tested in many ways—silence, aggression, absence, psychosis, over-determined affection, suicidal attempt, returning to her earlier analyst, and so on. The basic commitment never varied although the therapist was sorely tried. As a rule I handle the patient's aggressions much better than I do their love. I now found that not only was more love required than I was prepared to give, but later that I gave it and then became anxious and guilty about my feelings. This limited our therapy to a plateau until I successfully resolved them.

Conventionally the progression of the psychotherapy involved the development of the transference, counter-transference, and their resolution. This is an elementary fact of treatment which masks more basic and dynamic factors. These involve our five vectors and the concept of *Begegnung*. The vectors in relationship to treatment are discussed below. I want only to comment further on the *Begegnung*.

Sechehaye[16] sees the problem of schizophrenia as an oral one—the therapy as a compensatory one on this level. I would say that the treatment of schizophrenia involves this level but is not limited to it. One is also impressed with the anal and Oedipal trauma encountered. This was certainly true in Tess's case. Psychotherapy, then, according to our formulation, involves the "undoing" and "redoing" of all these levels by encounters or *Begegnungen*. This is, in essence, the process of growth which psychotherapy makes possible.

The question arises naturally as to how the *Begegnung* operates on the various levels. The literature on the oral phases is now well documented and one can be referred to Sechehaye,[17] among others. About the Oedipal period we also have some facts, but less is known of the anal and genital levels.

Unfortunately, there is as yet too little objective information about what happens at a significant *Begegnung*, say, in a child's life. We know it occurs and can see its effects—that just as it is the source of behavioral pathology, so it is the source of behavioral therapy. The difficulty in being specific is that much of it occurs symbolically and we know too little about symbolism in general. *The schizophrenic redoes and reintegrates through the meaning of symbols and the acting out of symbols.*

---

[16] Personal visit with Madame Sechehaye, May 7, 1958.

[17] M. A. Sechehaye, "La Realisation symbolique, un catalipeur de la structuration du Moi Schizophrenique," Bale: S. Karger, 1957. *A New Psychotherapy in Schizophrenia: Relief of Frustration by Symbolic Realization.* New York: Grune & Stratton, 1956, "The Transference in Symbolic Realization," *Int. J. Psycho-anal.*, 37, 1956, 270-277; and others.

This is not a distinguished statement in any sense, for how else could the archaic, paleologic, and primitive psyche of the schizophrenic be expressed? This was patently true for Tess. The symbolic value of black-white, the Virgin Mary, father, and rape are discussed below. The *Begegnung* is the highest point of symbolization in the patient's treatment.

At some variable point in the psychotherapy the schizophrenic has the choice of giving up his own inner reality for the reality of the "here-now"—his other being for the being he really is. I may call this the process of *becoming*. The following fragment from an interview fairly late in the psychotherapy illustrates this. The patient had again become psychotic and had to be returned to a closed ward. More tranquilizers and electric-convulsive treatment were being considered by her ward psychiatrist. The situation seemed such that all of our work might be undone. It was therefore necessary to confront her with her "choice"—to evade the *Begegnung* by being psychotic or to accept its meaning. Of course our work had been a prelude to this point and, while there was considerable danger in such a confrontation, I believed she had the necessary ego-strength.

(*T is the patient; B is the therapist.*)

B.: You were starting to say I—I did something?

T.: I—sort of have a feeling that you forced some of it.

B.: Oh. By what I did or what I am as a person?

T.: By, in a sense, . . . uh . . . you're telling me "Listen you're just going around and about, now let's get to the point." And then I felt (*pause*) this—if I went on going around I'd never get to the point and I'd never get well. Or—and that you would not continue therapy.

B.: The fear of losing me?

T.: That—that was pretty strong.

B.: But I never threatened you.

T.: No, I know. I don't know what it was. But I know I had that feeling.

B.: Maybe you had another feeling too. (*pause*) A feeling of a relationship with me.

T.: Yes, I did—very strongly I remember until . . . uh . . . at one point when—remember when I felt that you were accusing me of terrible crimes and ___?___ .

B.: Hm—m.

T.: At this point . . . uh . . . it sort of went around and I (*buzzer*) you became in a sense the opposite—an enemy, not as a friend.

B.: At that time I was an enemy.

T.: Yes, I felt very strongly that you didn't—you didn't like me and you were somehow . . . uh . . . it was like a trap that . . . uh . . . well that you were going to hand me over to the authorities and so on if I told you anything about my ___ associations and all these other crimes. But in a way I think that maybe you're saying well, you're—there was something about—I don't know if it was the tone of your voice or what and maybe I . . . uh . . . associated it with my father. Uh . . . it was a little bit like—as though if I had told him a lie and he was aware of it and he was forcing me to say that I had and that if I didn't say that there would be punishment or even if I did say that there would be punishment anyway. I don't know, it's something (*pause*) I guess a little as though you had become authoritarian and . . . uh . . . (*pause*) and a little as though you were treating me like a child. I . . . uh . . . now stop wandering around and come to the point (*laugh*).

B.: Hm-m.

T.: And—(*pause*).

B.: But you wanted to be a child then. (*pause*) Your psychosis represented that. (*pause*) And remember I put it to you either you take your psychosis or you take reality. It was up to you, remember?

T.: Un-huh. (*pause*) Yes. Well, it was that. It was sort of (*pause*) putting it like that and the . . . uh . . . (*pause*) (*long pause*) (*sigh*) I can't—well, I'll try. It was as though you were . . . uh . . . you could have suddenly become my parents and they were saying you have to grow up and be responsible or you have to go away and find your way somehow. (*long, long, long pause*) And maybe I wanted to be a child, yet I have the feeling that I resented this treatment. Uh . . . (*pause*) __?__ way for treating children. (*mutual laughter*)

B.: Was it after this that you felt I was against you? Going to punish you for being a criminal?

T.: Un-huh.

B.: After that, huh?

T.: Uh-huh. It began I think around then—well around that time, maybe a little earlier. I had this feeling . . .

B.: You were __?__.

T.: Sort of getting discouraged with me now and . . . uh, uh, . . . that this was sort of like a last resort and if I didn't respond then that was it. And . . .

B.: I remember being discouraged at that time.

T.: Well, I could feel it. (*pause*)

B.: But discouraged not at you. At both of us that we hadn't been able to work it out. You were again psychotic.

T.: (*pause*) I think this is a little bit when I began to feel and feel a little more clearly that this—psychosis; though that prior to it that we had begun to establish good relations and to be working fairly well until it became a little more difficult and then that the psychosis is like a way of getting away. Almost as though I could hardly live without psychosis to carry me through.

B.: Hm-m.

Vector Dynamics

In the *Introduction* to this paper the vector of *omnipotence* was introduced. It was stated that every schizophrenic is preoccupied with life and death—and *their* power over life and death. In their relationship to the psychotherapist they skirt a narrow path between destroying him and finding rebirth through him. In some way they feel that their suffering permits another to live—if they were to give it up, someone else must die. In a primitive way this was the potentiality with one or another parent, and so it is now with the psychotherapist. They either refuse the therapeutic encounter or they take refuge in ever deeper regression. With Tess this was present in three different aspects. In the first she told about a feeling of omnipotence in childhood in relationship to ants and a fantasy about her control of the world.

> T.: It was like . . . uh . . . flat I suppose, second story flat, and in the back was the porch. (*pause*) It wasn't covered over and the sun beat down on it and I used to go out there and play. And . . . uh . . . (*sigh*) playing was lying on my stomach and—and having a—a tray of water and collecting ants and killing them or maiming them and dumping them in the water to see how long it would take them to come back to life and how . . . uh . . . , torture. And thinking during that time, oh, about God and why we're here and also feeling sort of supernatural as though I was in contact with some sort of supernatural cosmic mind or something. (*pause*) But I guess I—I'd feel very powerful because I could do this to those little ants—kill them, torture them. (*long pause*) And I guess maybe I was thinking of these—I was probably (*pause*) saying this ant is so and so and this other ant is so and so. I'm going to do this and that to it.
>
> B.: You mean you identified them?
>
> T.: I don't remember actually doing it too clear, a little hazy feeling that I did. Maybe it's too horrible for me to think that I could do such a thing. (*long pause*) And I remember another time I was—it was in the afternoon and I was lying on my bed and I was having a fantasy. And the fantasy was where I—as if I was like God and I was going to—this was my world. I had a whole world that belonged—and I was going to tell everybody what to do and control them. Like little dolls in miniature and all these people were little miniatures and I was enormous and could force them to do whatever I wanted. And the fantasy of what I wanted them to do was that they were all going to have a room of their own and there was going to be a man and a woman in each room and they were all going to have sexual intercourse. And I was going to force them.
>
> B.: You would manipulate them 'til they would?
>
> T.: In some magical way. Sort of like those ants had grown into more distinctive creatures. (*pause*) I felt really that I was omnipotent or (*pause*) I remember thinking so strongly that if I weren't living, if I—almost if I died or I wasn't there, the world wouldn't exist which is true in a way it wouldn't for me. And this (*pause*) so from there I went to thinking well the world then and everything exists only because I'm here to perceive it. Which has some truth in it too. For any of us it does, if we're not living or here. . . .
>
> B.: We perceive the world through our own senses.

T.: Otherwise— Yes, if we are dead, then we don't . . . uh . . . (*pause*).
But I had it so much more involved in the way that (*pause*) I had the
feeling that I was almost like in contact with God. I was special, special
messenger or sometimes (*pause*)

In the second fragment the patient brings up the association of the
Virgin Mary in her discussion about the social worker she is seeing.

T.: And not as someone always to criticize and tell what to do. . . . uh
. . . (*long pause*) And in a sense who I feel is older and more mature,
someone that I sort of look up to and sort of like an ideal. I well, like
a mother figure, I guess—supposed to be. The Virgin Mary (*laugh*).

B.: The Virgin Mary?

T.: I do a lot of thinking about the ideal woman and how the Virgin
Mary is the ideal woman to a lot of women.

B.: To you?

T.: No.

B.: Well, you mentioned her.

T.: Maybe deeply, unconsciously she is. I—

B.: You see Miss ——— as . . .

T.: No, I . . .

B.: As an analogy there?

T.: No, not as—I don't see her as the Virgin Mary.

B.: No, but as an analogy.

T.: As an ideal. Yes, somehow.

B.: Hm-m.

T.: Or (*pause*) well, she—I would like to be more like her, say, than I
would like to be like my mother. I don't want to be like my mother.
(*pause*) And I don't want to be exactly like Miss ——— either but . . .
uh . . . there's more in her that I would like to be like. (*long, long
pause*)

B.: It is rather interesting that of all the women in history you might
have picked, you picked the Virgin Mary.

T.: Well, I think she was—she would be the one that Caridad[18] always
selected. It was her ideal woman and I think she had her all confused
with her mother. She feels that the Virgin Mary is her mother in
heaven. She lost her mother when she was two or three days old or
something. And she always—she had pictures of the Virgin Mary all
over her room and she would always point her out to me as the mother
and maybe I associated her with my own mother . . . as far as actual
close motherly feelings I always felt Caridad supplied this. My mother
was distant. Uh . . . (*pause*) I used to see her once in awhile. Well, she
never fed me or clothed me or did anything like this. It was always
Caridad. And Caridad always told me that I should in a sense have
sort of reverence for my mother that one has for the Virgin Mary.
(*long, long, long pause*) (*sigh*) There's a lot going through my mind
and I can't seem to get it out.

---

18 A servant who took care of Tess in her infancy and youth.

Not only is Tess omnipotent but she controls through procreation and death. This is why sexuality in her own psyche had not only overtones of creation but of death. The Virgin Mary represents first her mother, and thus her own, that is, Tess's immaculate conception and her Christ-like qualities. But since she is also her mother,[19] she is at once the Virgin Mary. It is similarly significant that Tess first became overtly psychotic when her father died. Her incestuous and thus omnipotent wishes were in fantasy construed as causing his death and she needed to give him rebirth. In therapy these fantasies and wishes were worked through so that the need for *all power* was no longer necessary.

The second vector, *masculinity-femininity*, is perhaps best portrayed by a series of drawings she did. Because the communication vector is so intimately involved in the treatment, I asked Tess at the beginning of each hour to "draw-a-person" and at the end of the hour to "draw the therapist." I left the room when she did this to allow her fantasies some play and to avoid portrayal effects. It soon appeared that the "draw-a-persons" represented Tess herself and the second series me. Figures 1 to 4 represent successive drawings in the treatment but separated from one week to several months in time. Figure 1 is most interesting for it appears to be a male. At first I confused it with a "therapist drawing," not accepting it as a female; but the patient confirmed it as a "draw-a-person." This is the way she saw herself at the time! Obviously it is somewhere *between* a male and a female, or a male *and* a female. In Figure 2 we have a definite female, sexually at any rate, but unclothed, lifeless, with no intellectual, emotional, or social possibilities. Figure 3 shows warmth—an object, but with relatedness to the world. In Figure 4 we see the flowering of latent capacities—a woman, feminine and receptive, eyeing the world for its possibilities. Can we say that the therapy has permitted polarization of her bi-sexuality? Not long after this she consummated and maintained a relationship with a man, married him, and begot a child by him.

At the same time she was making the series of drawings of me (Figures 5 to 8). I cannot discuss the significance of these drawings in terms of the transference at this point for lack of space. In brief, they show a progression from a cold, inanimate, intellectual projection to an virile, athletic male in motion.

Under the M-F vector we can subsume also the Virgin Mary fantasies, the rape fantasies, and the Oedipal-incestuous relationship to the father discussed elsewhere in this paper. All of these were altered with therapy.

The *ethical sense* vector is related to the basis of all interpersonal relationships—to that process of identification and introjection which makes human society possible rather than a race of hermits. I have said

---

[19] A social worker who interviewed the mother at length was struck by the physical and psychological identity of the two.

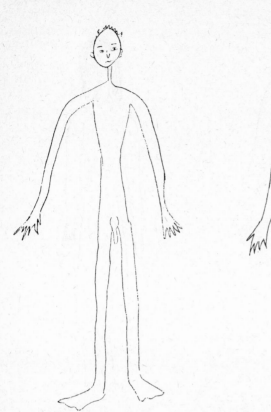

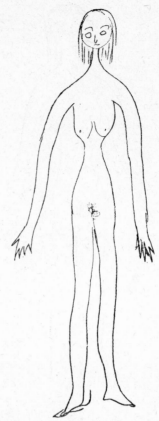

FIGURE 1. *Drawing of a Person.*   FIGURE 2. *Later Drawing of a Person.*

that conceptually love—that most limited but most embracing of terms
—is the foundation of the ethical sense and without it there is no basis
or motive for human relationships. In the light of five decades of psychoanalysis, it is of course axiomatic today that the earliest years are crucial
in the development of the ability to give love and receive it. The pattern
set by those adults, who having conceived and produced, love is expected,
is determinative. But in order to make love possible the parents must be
capable of it in a very intrinsic way. It is questionable whether this
was true with Tess's parents. They seemed everlastingly engaged in a
process of denying to each other significant parts of their own being
with the conscious (and unconscious) justification of their enduring
sacrifices. Tess was soon left to a maid who rather ironically was called
(in Spanish) "love." This allowed the existing relationship between father

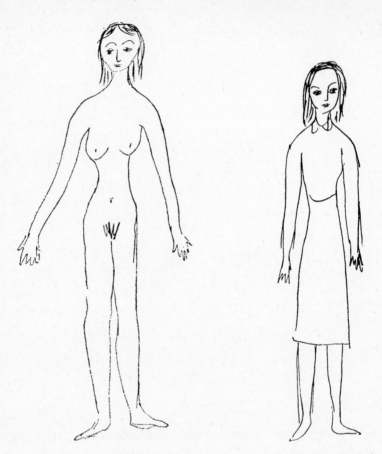

FIGURE 3. *Still Later Drawing of a Person.*   FIGURE 4. *Final Drawing of a Person.*

and mother to continue undisturbed—but only for the time being. Tess's identification with her mother symbolically allowed her to be both mother and daughter. Thus unique feelings developed in Tess toward her father, her mother, and herself. Her mother denied Tess nurturance because she rejected in herself that part which Tess represented and because, at a later date, her intuition revealed that she had a rival in Tess. The father, needing his own reflection constantly mirrored in the sexuality of women, pulled Tess close. Later, however, he became frightened at his own incestuous needs, but not before a host of sexual fantasies were stimulated in Tess. In the psychotherapy dreams and fantasies of "black and white" were prominent and recurring at certain stages in the treatment. Fantasies and dreams with this content are not unusual in schizophrenics and involved archaic images of purity and filth—of self-worth

FIGURE 5. *Drawing of the Therapist.*

and abnegation—of creation and death, and similar theses and antitheses. Tess symbolically recapitulated the encounter with her father in her relationship with me through the "black and white" medium. In this way the basis for the ethical sense, diverted and distorted, was restored.

The *communication* vector is dependent upon a number of variables and has been the subject of considerable research. As discussed in our *Introduction,* communication exists for the service of the ego and takes many forms. The economy of the schizophrenic is such that he has no communication structure beyond what he needs in terms of current functioning. There exists only a potentiality in terms of the archaic and unconscious. The therapist's problem is first to be able to communicate with the schizophrenic on his own level rather than to change his communication system to conform to the therapist's. The beginning psychotherapist is amazed and confused by the symbolic language of the patient. He may even be frightened by it for it reaches into his own archaic self. He has difficulty also with the non-verbal, *i.e.,* postural, physical, and other body language of the patient. In fact, he is entirely unaccustomed

FIGURE 6. *Later Drawing
of the Therapist.*

FIGURE 7. *Still Later Drawing
of the Therapist.*

to thinking in these terms. Therapeutic communication involves silence, fantasy, symbolism, body language, creative expression (as painting, drawing, etc.) and verbalization. Conventionally, psychotherapists have stressed the latter for this is our form of communication and it is the simplest to document.

While Tess had a highly developed verbal sense, a fine intellect, and variegated factual information to balance both, her communication was schizophrenic in its autistic and isolationistic qualities. Schizophrenic communication is not a constant but fluctuates from moment to moment, and so it did with her. As our encounter became more meaningful, she would advance toward my communication system and I would obversely retreat from hers. Later, she could experience her being directly rather than through symbols, body language, and similar methods.

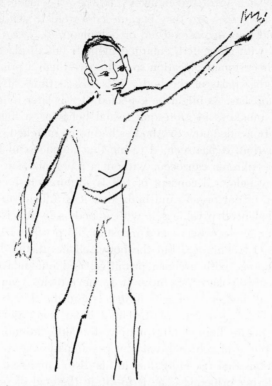

FIGURE 8. *Final Drawing of the Therapist.*

Parenthetically, it has appeared to me that our current conceptions of schizophrenic thinking, in terms of the abstract-concrete dichotomy, grossly oversimplify the question of schizophrenic thinking and that the diagnosis cannot be made on this alone, as is so often done. In doing so we act as though thinking has been abstracted from the thinker. Modern communication theory needs to be brought to bear on this problem.[20] However, it must be recognized that such advances await a more perspicacious understanding of schizophrenia itself and of the recent developments in communication theory.

The *body image* vector is the least developed of our five vectors. Not much is known about the body image and this is particularly true where schizophrenia is concerned. The drawings which Tess made of a woman (Figures 1 to 4) show no gross deviations in body hierarchy but rather a primitivization and sexual confusion. These drawings represent rather late stages in the treatment and are not conclusive because of this. Of

---

[20] A beginning is being made in this direction by J. Ruesch, *Communication* (New York: W. W. Norton and Co., 1951); and J. Ruesch and G. Bateson, *Disturbed Communication* (New York: W. W. Norton and Co., 1957).

greater significance were the monkey fantasies. To make self-fantasies acceptable to her super-ego they became converted to conscious images of monkeys and thus depersonalized or dehumanized. Tess fantasied not only monkeys with elongated, enlarged genitals but displaced the genitalia from their customary location so as to give them a primacy usually reserved for other parts of the body. This was at times also done with the head and breasts. As might be expected, it was later followed by the pairing up of monkeys in grotesque sexual behavior—a higher form of body organization since now two bodies had to be matched organizationally and in rhythm. It has seemed to me that no sucessful treatment of a chronic schizophrenic can occur without a reorganization of the body image. The psychological concept of self is so minutely bound up with our conception of our organs and body that it is difficult to conceive of a holistic or balanced psychic self with a body-self that is incomplete. It is much simpler to observe and measure the psychic self as, for example, by the Q technique,[21] but the body self lies in the deeper layers of the unconscious, with archaic, primitive, and imaginal components, and is not easily evoked for study. It is, nevertheless, very much the foundation of all higher level self-constructs and the therapist gradually but certainly becomes aware of it. There is an isomorphism principle which must operate here. Unfortunately, too little attention has been given to this phase of schizophrenia by psychopathology.

Jung[22] mentions that the individual in his dissociated state needs a directing or ordering principle if he is to attain the goal of *synthesis*. The latter we may consider as permitting the harmony of the opposed or dialectical parts of the psyche—the conscious and the unconscious—but also with the soma as the substrate of the ego.

Each vector contributes to *synthesis* in the personality and is related to the other vectors in a dynamic balance. When these become united through integration, which therapy provides, then the symptoms or defenses known as schizophrenia are no longer needed and the patient can cast them off. This comes about, as we have said before, through the encounter of two beings in the therapeutic situation. Each *witnesses*, as it were, the existence of the other in a new and, hopefully, more promising cosmos.

So it was that Tess, after many fruitless years of psychoanalysis and other psychiatric treatment, came to find her true being and could live with less discomfort than before. The history of a schizophrenic is never written until the final day of human interaction and this was simply a milestone in her human journey.

---

[21] W. Stevenson, *The Study of Behavior; Q Technique and its Methodology* (Chicago: University of Chicago Press, 1953).

[22] C. G. Jung, *The Undiscovered Self* (Boston: Little, Brown and Co., 1957).

1. *Optimally, what criteria do you use for accepting or rejecting patients for psychotherapy?*

   Since I work with both neurotic and schizophrenic patients, and in residential and out-patient settings, the criteria for acceptance of patients vary somewhat from one situation to another. The basic rationale of therapeutic possibility, however, is unaffected by these circumstances. With schizophrenics it is necessary to ask oneself whether a fundamental commitment approaching an infinite relationship is possible from the point of view of the therapist's feelings. We must be drawn together to make this possible, and it is not always easy to verbalize the basis for this togetherness even after many months of therapy. Sometimes I know about the commitment after two or three hours of seeing the patient—if I do not, then longer periods are usually valueless. I look for something from the patient as a possible reward for my efforts and do not fool myself in this regard—a challenging intellect with the capacity to introspect and verbalize, the presence of deep suffering with a willingness to share it, and the basic need for an encounter or *Begegnung* at the earliest developmental levels. I seriously weigh the patient's projection of the situation in relationship to my own feelings and expectations. I realize that some may consider this a nebulous way of selecting patients for treatment, but I do not think we have progressed sufficiently to measure this with any great objectivity. As a psychologist I like to see a Rorschach or other tests on the patient but not at the expense of disrupting something sensitive in the first few hours. In the past I think we have shifted the responsibility of suitability for therapy to the patient—to qualities in him which offered a favorable prognosis. I now think that the responsibility more properly belongs with the therapist—with his own conscious and unconscious needs.

2. *Do you make a diagnosis before psychotherapy begins?*

   I do not give much credence to formal diagnosis before psychotherapy begins. This does not mean that I do not consider the diagnosis at all. I believe every psychotherapist mulls this over in the course of psychotherapy and revises his formulations as he goes along. Formal diagnosis, as, for example, psychiatric hospital diagnosis, catches the patient at a cross-sectional period which may be not at all representative of his psyche and his functioning. These formulations then tend to become solidified and interfere with psychotherapy because of implications of a poor prognosis. The history of a long-term psychoanalysis or psychotherapy is that the patient may experience phobic, schizoid, obsessive, depressed, paranoid, manic, compulsive, and similar manifestations at one or another stage in the course of treatment, and of course has alternating neurotic and psychotic phases, however mild. I tend to agree with Whitaker and his school that, in treating schizophrenics at any rate, we more properly speak of a transference psychosis rather than transference neurosis. Formal diagnosis seems at times to be somewhat a function of the training, psychiatric milieu, and unconscious needs of the one making the diagnosis rather than something indigenous to the life history of the patient. In the case presented here a diagnosis of psychoneurosis, character disorder, and schizophrenia could have been made at several cross-sectional points in her illness career. All of these were correct and all were incorrect if interpreted as intellectual abstractions of some hypothetically median patient.

3. *Do you attempt to persuade the patient or significant relative to change his (the patient's) environment?*

   My experience with relatives has been that they have a tremendous stake in the patient's illness in a reciprocal and symbiotic way. With schizophrenics they can very well defeat the psychotherapy, and often do. Since manipulating the environment means essentially manipulating the significant relatives, I refrain from doing it. I can, however, understand the need for environmental changes. Whatever success may be ascribed to this case was certainly due to keeping the patient in focus rather than the mother who attempted to insinuate herself into the treatment. Even in the hospital proper no changes in ward milieu, request for leave of absence, etc. were applied for by the therapist.

4. *How did you conceptualize the therapist's role in this case?*

   This is discussed in greater detail in the *Introduction* to this paper. In essence, our *Begegnung* at the various developmental levels, within a framework of love, made it possible for the patient to reintegrate the five vector forces so as to find meaning and value in interpersonal relationships. I was a participant with her in her fantasies and suffering, and became individuated with her in the process.

5. *What aspects of your theory of psychotherapy were particularly apparent or useful in the case presented here?*

   In the case of Tess, I was able to clinically validate the hypothesis that schizophrenia is related to the absence of significant emotional encounters in earliest childhood which give meaning and substance to social existence. In the psychotherapy we were able to substitute our encounter or *Begegnung* for the crucial developmental ones so that the patient could give up her schizophrenic existence. Her encounter with me, within the therapeutic framework, helped her integrate the ethical, body image, omnipotent, communication, and M-F vectors so that she could accept herself in relation to her culture.

6. *Do you feel that this case developed significant insight? If not, can improvement be maintained?*

   Intellectual insight is no longer a *sine qua non* of improvement in psychotherapy. It may be epiphenomenal but not necessarily causal. While we know very little about emotional insight, some such experience may take place. However, this is a function of the *Begegnung* and the change in the vector forces which come about through it. Such process is largely symbolic. (I have since regretted formulating this question for the *Addendum* except that heuristically it does reveal the present state of insight in modern-day psychotherapy.)

7. *What aspects of your own cultural orientation facilitated or impeded the treatment of your case?*

   The fact that the patient and I both represented the middle-class, American culture with all of its implications gave us an initial foundation in our relationship. A common interest in aesthetics, literature, art, and Hispanic-American culture were further buttressing devices. The latter also gave me some basis for understanding her Cuban father and her upbringing in that culture.

8. *If we consider that a continuum exists from superficial to deep psychotherapy, where would you place your own case?*

The patient became psychotic twice during psychotherapy and as a direct consequence of the transference. This and the fact that the *Begegnung* took place on the oral as well as higher levels indicates a deep or regressive form of psychotherapy.

9. *What did you think about the outcome of this case and what criteria did you use for evaluating such outcome?*

The outcome of the psychotherapy of a case of schizophrenia is not easily established. The usual criteria are most often faulty and the length of follow-up too brief. Many times the patient needs to return briefly at critical points in his life, so that one wonders whether this is not actually a life-time sort of thing. For these reasons I am loath to claim any form of "cure" or even improvement for Tess. However, we must consider the following data in any such determination.

(a) The patient thinks that she is improved, as does her mother.
(b) The therapist considers the patient improved.
(c) The patient has given up her psychosis and has been out of the hospital for over sixteen months. (She returned briefly for two weeks when I resumed my old post at the hospital.)
(d) She has married, is having a child, and for the first time has demonstrated a sustained love for a man.

10. *How do you terminate psychotherapy?*

With schizophrenics I do not, initially, think of the duration of the psychotherapy or when termination may take place. If I take the patient on, it is with the deeper personal feeling that I will see the patient for as long as he or she needs me or until it is manifestly demonstrated that I can no longer help. It is easy, however, to fall into the trap of a life-time arrangement and this has to be avoided. Usually this comes about through the growing strength of the patient and the strength of the therapist in encouraging greater independence. A number of technical devices are possible in promoting this but they can only be used within the solid framework of love, which is the relationship.

CHAPTER 11

A Case of Pseudo-
Neurotic Schizophrenia[1]

—HEINZ HÄFNER[2]

Introduction

Presenting the essential events occuring during the psychotherapy of schizophrenics appears to be much more difficult than describing the treatment of neurotics. The reason for this is the fact that, in contrast to the experiences of Freud and his followers, two important things have changed or at least have been questioned: the psychoanalytic technique, and the usual transference formation. Freud himself had thrown light on the psychodynamics of the various schizophrenias. He doubted, however, that these "narcissistic defense neuropsychoses" (*narzisstische Abwehrneuropsychosen*) could be influenced therapeutically, for he did not think schizophrenics were able to establish a sufficient transference.

During the past decades this assumption of Freud has been refuted by the therapeutic trials and successes of a growing number of analysts (Federn, Bak, Eissler, Fromm-Reichmann, Knight, Rosen, Sechehaye, Benedetti, and others). And the experiences gained in the meantime made it apparent that in the case of many schizophrenics there could not develop a workable communication between the analyst and the patient in the framework of the frustrating ritual of a normal analytical situation.

---

[1] Translated from the German by Helm Stierlin, M.D., Ph.D.

[2] Studies in medic., philos., psychol., and psychother. in Münich (M.D., Ph.D.); Resident at the Univ. Hosp. for Nerv. and Ment. Disease in Münich (Professor Sterz), 1949; Scientific assist. and head of a psychotherapeutic dept. at the Univ. Hosp. for Nerv. and Ment. Diseases in Tübingen (Professor Kretschmer), '51; Scientific Assist. and Head of the Psychodiagnostic Laboratorium at the Univ. Hosp. for Ment. and Nerv. Diseases in Münich, '54-'58; Prof., Psychiatric Clinic, U. of Heidelberg, '58– .

The patients were for the most part not able to associate freely, so that the analyst himself was forced to intervene. He would either act by approaching the patient spontaneously and fulfilling certain of his needs (Federn, Knight, Sechehaye, and others) or by intruding into the delusional world of the patient with attempts at interpretation (Rosen, Benedetti, and others).

The change in analytic technique in the treatment of schizophrenics—and in this Freud was basically right—was solely necessitated by the inability of the transference to operate. To understand this we may look, for instance, at a completely autistic schizophrenic patient. He has lost verbal contact with the world around him and refuses, let us say, to be dressed and fed and smears his feces. It is obvious that an expectative analytic attitude cannot find access to the delusional world of such a patient. The schizophrenic patient who has undergone a deep narcissistic regression often has no notion at all of the therapist around him unless the latter actively takes steps to reach him. In other cases he defends himself by delusional maneuvers (Knight, Sechehaye, and Benedetti). A genuine willingness to cooperate that we take for granted in most neurotic patients does not exist at all in the majority of schizophrenics; on the contrary, anxiety and defensive attitudes often win out over the still existing need for contact. The essential difficulty for the therapist lies, therefore, in the task of establishing a relationship at all and to win the patient into a meaningful cooperation. For this eventually will determine the success of any analysis (Sullivan, Knight, Bak).

However, it would certainly be a mistake to overdo the loving acceptance of the patient by uncritically fulfilling all of his wishes, whether of a delusional or realistic nature. Recently H. Segal and F. Fromm-Reichmann have pointed out the dangers which might result from the analyst's uncritical closeness. It cannot be overlooked that the infantile needs which the schizophrenic may still be able to express out of the depth of his regression sometimes show pathological traits themselves. Fulfilling them would further threaten the schizophrenic's relation to reality which, in itself, is already so very precarious.

In critically reviewing the stand that has been taken by F. Fromm-Reichmann, emphasis has been put by Vangaard on the fact that the difficulties resulting from the analyst's spontaneous emotional approach must be faced. However, according to him, it would be self-deception to believe that they could be totally avoided. For him the important thing is to find the right balance between spontaneity on the one hand and a controlled investment of emotions on the other. Only a therapist lacking this art or offering the schizophrenic patient too little genuine warmth might stumble over these difficulties or even fail in his therapy. If, however, it is necessary to walk on this narrow precarious path between spontaneous acceptance and dangerous excess, between controlled analysis and daring interpretations or interventions, then we can improve our orientation only by deepening our insights and experiences.

It appears that the neurotic patient can re-enact early experiences in the transference of the analytical situation since he hopes thereby to find at least a partial fulfillment of his needs. There is therefore still a limited "contact with the world" (*Welthaftigkeit*) which, in spite of the limitations drawn by the neurotic's concept of reality, still reflects a fundamental trust. It is the trust in the possibility of finding meaningful ways of life by accepting help from a human partner or by facing reality. This trust of finding a helpful responsiveness in the world is lacking or hardly exists in the schizophrenic patient. Especially Sullivan and his followers have pointed out the fact that his retreat from the threatening, anxiety-loaded world has an important basis in the lack of acceptance by the mother during early childhood. It is the frustration of interpersonal needs that results for the schizophrenic in the destruction of his communication with the human world. When the fear of being frustrated and rejected by the world becomes too great, the flight into the autistic world of one's own fantasies is the only way left. Then all needs that press for a new contact with the world have to be fought by delusional maneuvers.[3]

The schizophrenic's loss of the world and, going with it, his delusional defense against a transference, are thus his reaction to the frustrations he suffered originally from the world around him. An analyst facing such a schizophrenic patient can hardly expect to build up a relationship out of a distant analytic attitude. There will be denial of him as a person, since the schizophrenic views him as part of a hostile human environment. Or he will provoke delusional defenses as his presence throws the patient into a painful ambivalence between his excessive need for contact on the one hand and his unsurmountable fear of it on the other.

We learn from these insights the fundamental fact that a therapeutically constructive relationship with the schizophrenic cannot be based on new experiences of frustrations in the sphere of human relatedness, but can only be hoped for by the therapist's active and accepting approach.

Thus the doctor working with the schizophrenic has to take the first steps in building the relationship. He must give the patient a feeling of being accepted beyond all possible conflict. Only as soon as there arises the possibility of a completely new experience of the world that promises satisfaction and contrasts with the early experience of a frustrating hostile environment can the world again become something worthwhile at

---

[3] Lewis B. Hill says: "Since reality for these children is so unsatisfactory, they cannot develop those ego functions which should relate them intimately with reality. . . . One sees the schizophrenic devoting himself, of necessity, to his inner fantastic reality and at best trying to maintain it side by side with reality or to superimpose it upon reality, but never replacing it with reality. The reality is too hopeless."

all. The regaining of an access to the world, as it becomes possible by the loving and helpful approach of the therapist, creates the basis on which the patient may now become able to project infantile needs and expectations on this therapist. Dealing with this context M. Sechehaye has recommended that we distinguish between *Pretransfert* and *Transfert greffe*. Only when faith in the fulfillment of the patient's contact needs has been established by means of a pretransference, can a transference in the proper meaning of the word be grafted thereon.

The manner in which the analyst provides the schizophrenic with a basic experience of acceptance varies fundamentally with the clinical picture and structure of the psychosis. In the case of a completely autistic and regressed schizophrenic patient who is operating on a very infantile level, refusing to eat and defying verbal communication, it will probably be necessary at first to take over the maternal care for the vital well-being and the oral needs of the patient. M. Sechehaye gave an example for this. The situation is different with the reflective paranoid schizophrenic. The schizophrenic's "loss of world" and, along with this, his relative inability to establish a transference are not of the same intensity in all patients. Especially in the case of pseudo-neurotic (Hoch and Polantin) and ambulatory (Zilboorg) schizophrenics we find often a certain rest or anchorage in the world. There exists, side by side, reality-adjusted behavior and reality-estranged delusions, a fact for which E. Bleuler has proposed the instructive term "double bookkeeping."

Even in the case where the pseudo-neurotic schizophrenic is still precariously getting along in his social environment, and is still having access to a limited sphere of real satisfactions, we find that frustrations and disappointments have destroyed the faith in the possible fulfillment of essential interpersonal needs. The still-existing capacity for transference in these cases thus brings the therapeutic approach close to that used in the analysis of neurotics. At the same time, however, it is faced with the specific difficulties encountered in the therapy of schizophrenics. Pseudo-neurotic schizophrenics may sometimes quickly cling to their therapists, but just as fast retreat into an autistic unverbal state upon the slightest stress (Zilboorg). For it is just during contacts that their deepest anxieties are mobilized, since it is here where they make a new start in accepting a piece of the so much feared reality. Therefore, every schizophrenic tends to destroy a relationship as soon as he has established it and tends to deny and, in delusional ways, to reject the reality of that person whom he actually wants to love. An analyst who in this situation would remain impersonal and distant, would not only—as has been pointed out by Racamier—be playing a role in the game of the psychosis, but he would have no chance to counteract the schizophrenic defense mechanisms. The emotional approach, however, that the therapist must choose under these circumstances, has to be controlled and balanced.

This accepting approach must not, consciously or unconsciously, promise anything to the most critical and suspicious patient that cannot be fulfilled in reality. Any dishonesty would throw the patient into new disappointments which might be unsurmountable. Furthermore, the therapist cannot address himself only to the infantile ego of the patient by giving maternal care. In any case, he must also take into account the social reality which sometimes represents the last hold the patient has (F. Fromm-Reichmann).

It appears that in any case the schizophrenic will need definite proof of the interest the analyst has in him. It seems that a constructive way, especially in the analysis of pseudo-neurotic schizophrenics, has been delineated by Racamier, who emphasizes an attitude characterized by an ever-reliable presence and goodness of the therapist that gives security and warmth. This had to be presented first in order to provide a key to the understanding of the following case.

The First Encounter

Gisela Keller, twenty-year-old art student, was admitted to the Psychiatric Hospital in August with the diagnosis of "schizophrenia." One year prior to this, she had gone to an analyst because of pressure from her family physician. The analysis which then started failed, however, because of the patient's autism. After the ninth hour Gisela dropped out without informing her therapist. Following this, she saw several psychiatrists for consultation but had no medical treatment until immediately prior to her hospitalization. The admitting physician's report showed that the patient had a most unfavorable background. The father was an alcoholic; the mother was described as an unhappy woman filled with resentments. The admitting physician who had witnessed the patient's gradual slipping from a neurotic into a schizophrenic state asked us to make a psychotherapeutic attempt with her.

When Gisela entered my office on the first day, having not yet been formally admitted, she barely greeted me and then stood still in the center of the room. Also when she, following a friendly request from me, had taken a seat, she remained in a rigid position and answered all my questions in a monotonous, poorly modulated tone of voice. She followed all requests like an automaton but made no spontaneous comments. To any questions regarding her personal life, she would either not answer at all or become evasive. In doing this, she seemed to look at some faraway spot and had a peculiarly rigid expression on her face.

As it became obvious that I could not get into contact with her or even make myself understood by means of a simple conversation, I gave up any further exploration for the time being. Instead I tried to understand her situation intuitively and to communicate my sympathetic interest in her. I told her I would not expect her to tell of her suffering to a strange man during the first encounter. But I ventured my guess that she had lost the ground under her feet completely and that she was in a rather desperate mood. Therefore, I told her, I would like to help her and do whatever was necessary, although I had no idea as to what could be the matter with her. When I said this she listened carefully for the first time. The fact that no demands were made, that there were no expectations to live up to, and that there was simply some real human interest in her, seemed to have made possible a degree of trust in her human environment. But she retreated quickly afterwards. For only a few moments later Gisela stated that she had already consulted a good many doctors and that she had lost faith that she could still be helped. Nevertheless I got the impression that I had established some contact when Gisela left the office and went to her ward.

Half an hour later she knocked at my door and rushed into my room, restless, almost panicky, her eyes anxiously looking around. She stated in a hasty manner that she wanted to be discharged at once. For in the dormitory of the open psychiatric ward she would perish. Without any inhibition she bubbled out that she was frightened by the other patients and that she felt herself persecuted and hypnotized by their stare. By talking with her I succeeded in calming her, probably by my assurance that I would protect her and that I would not permit anything harmful to be done to her. But she continued to insist on her discharge, stating that she could not exist in one room with other people. Since I thought it better to show her some trust than to make demands, I suggested that she should come to see me every day as an ambulatory patient. She agreed immediately. Before leaving me she said in a somewhat shy tone that she felt I was different from all the other doctors who had treated her so far.

However, this unexpected confession of her sympathy was followed by a retreat that came just as promptly. For eight days Gisela stayed away and kept silent, although she had promised to come back to my office on the following day. She appeared eventually on the ninth day but acted then in the same autistic manner she had shown during our first conversation. However, from now on and for some time to come she appeared regularly every day.

Life History

In order to facilitate the understanding of the following steps in treatment, it appears necessary to say a few words about the patient's history, although the pertinent data became apparent only during the further course of the analysis: The mother of the patient had married her husband upon the insistence of her own father. Neither before nor after her marriage did she have friendly relations with another man. On the contrary, she had always hated men—as she confessed once to her daughter. Also, she never had any genuine feeling of love or respect for her own husband. There was some romantic idealization of a friend, a girl with whom she had fallen in love during her youth. Otherwise she was known as a hard, unhappy, and constantly nagging woman who, however, always showed a front of a somewhat artificial warmth to strangers. When guests were present she would also meet both her children with a marked friendliness. She put great emphasis on the fact that her daughter always made an excellent impression in public.

Gisela's father never did get along with his wife. He was a low-ranking civil servant, a man of rather soft character who had resorted to drinking. When he came home drunk at night—which happened once or twice a week during the childhood and adolescence of our patient—he would occasionally beat his arms about aimlessly and damage the furniture. Sometimes there were also fights and beatings between the parents, in the course of which the father would also hit Gisela when the latter supported the mother. Gisela was always immensely afraid of the staring look her father had when he was drunk.

The mother treated her husband with contempt and never missed an opportunity to depict him to her daughter as a despicable example of men in general. In front of strangers, however, the parents presented an appearance of complete agreement and friendliness.

Several times the mother had predicted that the father would drink himself to death. When Gisela was thirteen years old he once ran into a car at night and suffered serious injuries. One leg had to be amputated. After this experience he stopped drinking but soon thereafter became ill with tuberculosis of the lungs. This made it possible for him to retreat from that time on into a sanatorium which he left only for short intermissions.

Gisela was born about one year after the wedding. The mother had not particularly looked forward to her birth. Nevertheless, the baby was sufficiently breast-fed for six months and developed well physically. The mother felt, however, that her daughter was always a serious child who laughed little. Otherwise, there was nothing remarkable about Gisela's emotional development until a brother was born who was three and a half years her junior. Though Gisela did not seem to be hostile to her little brother while her parents were present, she became, from this time on, still more withdrawn and melancholic than ever. She had very little contact with other children and usually withdrew to a lonely spot when she wanted to play.

At the early age of five Gisela began to have genital play, first with a neighbor's girl somewhat older than herself and later with her little brother. It appears that Gisela experienced these infantile sexual contacts as a way of escaping from her oppressing isolation, for later this genital play increased to a considerable extent. During the first grade she used to stimulate her classmates, boys and girls, to commit exhibitionistic acts in which eventually the whole class participated. In doing so she often placed herself on the teacher's desk and let the boys see her genitals, but would not allow them to touch her. At this time she felt not quite as unhappy as before or later; she had apparently succeeded in finding some human acceptance by carrying out these impulsive exhibitionistic activities which placed her at the center of interest of her classmates.

Finally, however, these sexual activities were discovered by the teacher and Gisela's mother was informed. Merely stating that Gisela was a swine, she gave her daughter a severe beating.

A way of communication with her human environment, poor as it was, was thereby destroyed for Gisela. This silent and sharp condemnation by mother resulted in a cutting off of the future expression of her sexual drive. Her instinctual needs toward her human environment were repressed; Gisela became stiffer, more isolated from her contemporaries, and subsequently still more dependent on her mother.

In connection with this, there arose around this time a vehement jealousy directed against her brother. During mother's absence there was much quarreling between the two siblings and not infrequently Gisela would hit her brother because she felt he was preferred by her mother. While doing so she was caught several times by mother and, at times, was cruelly punished. Following this, Gisela's hate for her brother became enormous. When Gisela was about eight years old, she moved the carriage containing her brother to the top of a mountain road and let the carriage roll downward. She had actually hoped her brother could thus be killed. The carriage ran into an ox cart and no serious injury was done to the little boy.

The mother, pale at the shock, took her son home and treated him with special kindness during the period which followed. For some time she hardly spoke a word to Gisela. The incident, itself, was never talked about. For a long time Gisela was in an inner turmoil, longing for a punishment that would, she felt, relieve her. More than by any corporal punishment she was upset by the complete stoppage of communication, which was the price she had earned by her hostility toward the brother undertaken with the aim of possessing mother alone. Thus she had also experienced aggression as something that would destroy communication. From now on she repressed almost all aggressive impulses.

Gisela became still more anxious, and more helpless and withdrawn than before. She found no happiness and tried to avoid both her parents as much as possible. Only in a very narrow sphere did she stay in contact with her mother—but this will have to be dealt with later.

It is difficult to determine when the psychosis actually started. Her relatedness to reality as well as her human contacts were shrinking more and more in the course of her development. The older Gisela became, the less she could deal with people. From the threatening, anxiety-provoking reality she escaped increasingly into a private fantasy world. It is probably also for this reason that she chose the career of an artist and started studying painting on her own initiative. In her first semesters she was able to show some good results along with failures. Later she achieved less and less.

During the last semester preceding her admission to the hospital she had no longer studied, but had spent most of her time, alone and lonely, in the room she occupied in the university town. At this time she had occasionally fallen into a state of stupor-like passivity which each time lasted up to a week. She would then rest in her bed, eat nothing, and indulge in a superficially euphoric mood while experiencing a complete emptiness of thoughts. According to her report, Gisela had to terminate each of these phases by an active endeavor on her part. Each time afterward she was in a state of deep anxiety and desperation which sometimes had the mark of an experience of world collapse (*Weltuntergangserlebnis*).

When Gisela went out on the street she suffered considerable insecurity. She had a feeling that the earth under her feet would vanish or of being drawn to the left into an awesome abyss. At times she believed she was not in control of her movements. Instead she felt she was moved like an apparatus by strange forces. She felt herself influenced and hypnotized by numerous men and women. She felt that men pulled her in different directions on the street. Everywhere she thought herself being stared at and therefore waged a desperate battle with her own eyes in order to break the spell of the strange stares.

Psychoanalysis Begins

The therapy which started on the ninth day after the first interview could at first elicit hardly any cooperation from the patient. When asked by me whether she preferred to lie on the couch or sit in front of me in a chair, she answered she could not lie down while I was in the room. So she sat down in an armchair where, at first, she appeared to be rigidly fixed. She answered my questions in short, abbreviated sentences that were bare of meaning and interrupted by long silences. I, therefore, decided to make another emotional step toward the patient and to remove as much as possible the social demands usually required by the analysis. It was my intent to thereby loosen the frustrating side which Gisela experienced in the social order. By taking away this oppressing burden I hoped to open the way for new experiences of interpersonal relatedness. I thus told Gisela once more that I would help her and stay with her as long as she needed me. I didn't even request that she stick to the basic analytic rule. I further assured her that she could reach me out of therapy hours in case she was in need. I knew perfectly well that by doing so I had given promises with which I surrendered myself to a certain degree to the patient. For I knew I had to fulfill my promise in any case.

My active steps toward Gisela resulted at least in a loosening of her defenses so that she was able in the next hours to describe a dream. However, she did not dare tell it to me but gave it to me in written form:

> I was sitting beside a vaguely existing woman on a garden bench. The woman had a child. I, myself, was present only down to my breast. Below that my body appeared to dissolve. It was very dark and gruesome. I had a feeling that I was standing on a high, steep peak on the left side of an awesome castle. In front of me there was a big cat willing to rush on me. It caused me pain in an undescribable manner. In the air there was road traffic. All of a sudden there was a male corpse in front of me, which, however, had still some life in it. I realized immediately that I knew the man. Suddenly there was an explosion and the man was torn apart. I saw him burning in front of me, but it looked as if there were burning two pieces of wood. The head did immediately disappear. I was

deeply shocked. I turned away since I had been sitting in front of him on the ground. Then a catastrophe began to spread. Then I was in a vast space where a lot of celestial bodies were turning themselves. In between it looked like an abyss stretching into eternity. An older woman who was looking like my mother took my hand and jumped with me from star to star. Finally I got afraid she could lead me a dangerous way. I fled to the other side; the woman called behind me. There was a glowing gas pipe that looked like a cross. I had a feeling that everything would explode in a moment like an atom bomb.

The uncanny, awesome feeling of a catastrophe which is expressed in this dream, had been felt by Gisela for some time. She was afraid something horrible and unthinkable might happen. In the dream Gisela was surrounded by ominous, threatening dangers. Her jumping from one celestial body to another symbolizes her state of being lost in the world. Only in the celestial space of her fantasy world, distant as it is from the world, could she find the stars to provide her with some precarious ground under her feet. Her hand was held by her mother while she danced around the abyss until she finally realized that her mother also could not be trusted and was even leading her astray. But when she was about to leave the mother she was threatened by a total catastrophe. The last hold, the last human relationship she had, was thereby lost. The fact that the impending atomic explosion took its origin from a simple gas pipe which looked like a cross is evidence that the danger arose from the sphere of the familiar which really should have given her protection. For the parental home represented for Gisela not only a last resort but also a world of uncanny dangers to which she was exposed.

For a long time Gisela was not able to freely associate to this dream and several later ones. I, therefore, carefully started talking about the various contents of the dream, in which, however, I was the main participant for a long time to come. Gisela always used to say only a few words and then fell back into her autistic silence. I, myself, said relatively little. When she arrived I greeted her with joy and in other ways showed a friendly attitude toward her. I emphasized the fact that our silence was not fruitless but brought us a little closer to each other. Finally it would make it easier for her to talk. Above all I stated repeatedly that there was no hurry—that I would never press her to talk but could even wait a whole year if she wanted me to. Only after the first twenty-five hours of therapy had passed without any real conversation having been established could Gisela be moved to express an opinion of her own or to state ideas she might have regarding the dream. Eventually she reported with great reluctance that the torn corpse, which had burned in her initial dream like two pieces of wood in front of her eyes, resembled her father. When saying this she remembered the father's serious accident which resulted in the amputation of one upper leg. But she was as yet unable to gain insight into the deeper meaning of the dream. She told of her mother's hate for her father and her own unrelatedness in regard to the two parents. She emphasized that she never did find reassurance or help from her father or her mother.

Gisela became a bit active in our conversation when her own body image, as it had shown itself in the dream, was dealt with. This body image consisted only of her head and neck while her body from the breast downward had been experienced as unreal. In a cautious interpretation I tried at first to offer her the idea that she had retreated to an existence of the head only, for example, the world of thinking and fantasy. But in doing so she had left out the body, the sphere of instinctual, full-blooded life. Yet she could not get rid of her vitality completely so that she would now encounter her instinctual side in the form of the cat now rushing on her from the outside. And if this was so and she, within her own limited concept, was threatened by her own instinctual needs, it would be likely that she also was afraid of being loved and of again feeling in a simple feminine way.

This careful partial interpretation of her dream as it had been initiated by the therapist did precipitate Gisela's first consistent report. It became apparent that it was in the sphere of sex and drive that Gisela would establish a relationship more quickly than in any other way. By sensing in the words of her therapist an open and positive attitude toward her vitality, it apparently became possible for her to at least tell a few things to her partner and thereby give way to the strong pressure of this inner dynamic. She said that she felt a deep, insurmountable fear of anything connected with sex and that she was particularly afraid of men. At this time she also gave her first report about her sexual play during childhood. She said that she could never feel guilty about what she did then, although she was so rigorously condemned and punished by her mother.

After a long period of silence during which her need to communicate became more apparent, she went on to say that a year ago she was lying in bed sick with influenza. A fellow student, who at first appeared to her quite likable, visited her. Sitting on her bedside he reached beneath the blanket and touched and caressed her whole body. Inwardly and outwardly she became stiff as a rock and was unable to defend herself.

At first Gisela expressed a violent dislike for this student. I made a careful attempt to defend the friend, stated that his action was not particularly indicative of any deep feeling for her and suggested the possibility that his overture toward her masked a longing for real love. To this Gisela carefully listened. I also ventured the idea that she might be prone to sexual sensations like the rest of mankind and thereupon asked her whether she might not have desired the young man whom she seemed to have liked originally. It was then, only out of fear, that she turned stiff. To this she answered with a shy "Yes," reluctantly admitting her own repressed needs for the first time. During the same hour Gisela told of a similar occurrence in which, at the moment of the other's approach, she had become stiff and had passively endured everything.

On the following day Gisela made the point that she did not want to talk any further about things that touched her so deeply. Instead, she asked me to deal with her current everyday problems. Though this would block a further investigation of the deeper context of her illness, I abstained at this early date from an active analysis of her resistances. I told Gisela that we would come back to this theme at a later date when she would have gained more inner security. For the present, I asked her to tell me about her current difficulties. Gisela began, in fact, to talk relatively consistently so that there could gradually develop a fluent conversation. She gave me a good many reports about her previous achievements in the art academy, about her male and female fellow students, about the tensions she had with her landlady, and about numerous other things which were more or less meaningful. In doing so, she probably avoided establishing a deeper contact that would have touched her inner fears and conflicts. But this mutual exchange of thoughts, limited as it was to the thin surface of her social reality, resulted in an improvement of the therapeutic relationship.

When about twenty hours had passed in talking about such peripheral themes, Gisela again brought up her fear of being observed, persecuted, and molested by men on the street. After a considerable discussion of this subject Gisela confided that she had been fascinated by her two experiences with fellow students who had made sexual advances toward her. But, at the same time, she said, her anxiety was so great that not only had she remained passive but had actually become stiff. I hinted then at the possibility that her feeling of being stared at by all men on the street might have a similar basis, namely, her need, unadmitted to herself, to be desired by men. To this, she reacted for the first time with vehement denial—without retreating into her schizophrenic defenses. But she refused to continue with the same subject. Only when I said goodbye to her at the end of the hour did she say, quite unexpectedly, that I was, after all, right: her insecurity on the street might have something to do with her fear of sex.

Although this insight had not yet sunk deep, Gisela reported in the next hour that her feeling of being oppressed on the street had somewhat decreased. This first little success of the treatment was, of course, not only a result of her having gained insight into inner connections which up to then had been unconscious. Rather it was so that Gisela's statement and our conversation, the prerequisite of her gaining this insight, had only become possible after some genuine trust had been established in her relationship to the therapist.

Again there was no progress in therapy for some time to come. Gisela was afraid of talking about a subject which touched her so deeply. She became evasive and tried to find neutral topics of conversation. However in her relationship with me she had already developed a certain loyalty. Finally, when I carefully described her evasiveness as a means of covering up that which troubled her most, she answered: "I can only reject and defend, yet I cannot give in and retreat like other people. Behind me there is nothing. If I would recede only one step I would fall into the abyss."

This desperate statement has its basis in the fact that Gisela had found no ground or stability with her parents. Only when she did fulfill the strict demands of the mother was she accepted at all. When, however, she did not comply with the parental orders, or when she tried to bring out her own needs, she was severely punished and rejected. There was no trust but only the knowledge that she was basically a rejected outcast. Thus she anxiously kept up with the orders of the parents in order to be able to live, at least, in this limited frame of existence. She had never experienced absolution or forgiveness; every fight, every punishment at home had only deepened the cleavage between the child and her parents. Therefore her violation of the parental orders had caused guilt which amounted to a life-destroying burden. After having passed the boundaries of the forbidden, there was no way back to the experience of love; guilt for her was a catastrophe that could not be remedied. It had to be dissociated in order that she would not die of it. Since, however, almost all of her needs had been condemned, basically she had to carry a hidden guilt that encompassed practically her whole being. This guilt was the eerie abyss that threatened immediately as soon as Gisela attempted to admit even some of her repressed wishes or to make a little confession of guilt.

Thus Gisela escaped from the hate-ridden human world into the isolation of a pseudo-world of her fantasies. She covered the awe-inspiring abyss of her inner reality with her schizophrenic façade. It was a repetition of the example of her parents whose pretense of warmth in front of other people actually covered up a hopelessly damaged marriage. They had taught her the value of keeping up a front as the only possibility of human relatedness and as a means of protecting herself from hate-ridden reality.

In this phase of the treatment Gisela brought up a dream which illustrates what has just been discussed.

> I am alone in a beautiful paradise-like garden where I am admiring the gorgeous plants and flowers. But suddenly I realize that it is a high mountain on which I am standing. Beside me there are standing my mother and my brother. It appears as if the mountain were descending in an immeasurable depth. Then the mountain suddenly breaks apart and I call to the various sides in order to make sure my mother and my brother are safe. Finally I am sailing on a giant truck, formerly having been the mountain, into the air. I have a feeling that also my mother and my

brother are on the car. It is a long journey away from home into the uncertain. In travelling I am looking back and have a feeling of trust that the morning will be all right.

This dream makes apparent the flight into paradise before the dawn of sin, into an existence free of any guilt. This form of schizophrenic avoidance of guilt has been called *ego-mystification* by W. T. Winkler, since it often leads to an identification with the models of mythology. The catastrophe, however, also came up here as in the initial dream, but had already lost its character of an absolutely threatening event. Gisela had not yet landed on earth. She was still flying above the world loaded with the burdens of the past. But she was moving. She was moving away from the world of her parental home, filled with the first trust that the future would turn out all right. And this trust made it possible for her to look back into her threatening past.

Meanwhile sixty hours of treatment had been reached. At this time Gisela reported the severe punishment she had received from her mother through her mother's condemnation of sex and men in general. In the dreams more and more sexual symbols provoking anxiety appeared, and Gisela became increasingly troubled by the gradual pressure of her sexuality to show itself in conscious manifestations. In connection with this, she again temporarily used schizophrenic defense mechanisms which correspond to the changed experience of her body as shown in the initial dream. This may best be shown by Gisela's own words:

> Regarding the feeling of my body, it has become much worse. It is a kind of paralysis. When I am bending down and then stretch back everything threatens to dissolve and to become invisible. I have never sensed my body in a matter-of-fact way. I remember how the girls laughed at me during the gymnastic hour when I was nine years old. 'There are already hairs growing under your arms,' they said, laughing horribly. This meant to me treason and at the same time a hint to my looks. I allowed the mind to awake but I repressed the body.

This situation of resistance at first did not really endanger the therapeutic relationship. Again, however, Gisela became very evasive. She was talking beside the point and as soon as I tried to go deeper into the subject she attempted to change the line of talking and to push the discussion in the direction of some trivial matter. At this time I dared to analyze her resistance. I showed Gisela how she had only slightly touched on everything that was of real concern to her; how she did not want to dwell on this, and how she, by becoming hasty and evasive, only avoided her actual inner misery. This was her answer: "You always stick so long to one thing. You tie me down. I have fear of being tied down. With other people it is much easier. I can get away from them when something forbidding comes up." I tried to show her that by her evasiveness she was avoiding a deeper relationship with those people who were sympathetic with her and who tried to give her support. To this she replied: "Must I waken up the whole past again?—it is all hurting so much—I cannot have any other feelings than I have."

In the following weeks Gisela remained in a state of inner freeze. She did not dream any more, talked very little, and spent a good deal of her time at home lying in bed. Again she ate very little and I was afraid that she would fall into a stupor. She came much too late to her hours, though she was still seeing me regularly. Any emotional contact seemed to have died. I continued to be as friendly with her as ever and for the time being abstained from actively analyzing her. Soon Gisela complained that she found herself in an unbearable inner tension. She reported that her face was "completely stiff" and that her arms and legs were "so peculiarly rigid." When it became apparent that she again was gradually slipping into a schizophrenic autism, I carefully tried to talk with her about this. I would ask her, for example, whether her inner tension might result from the fact that she was strongly longing to be accepted and to be loved by some human being. This longing, I suggested, might have become very intense by my readiness to help her and by our joint dealings with her difficulties. But it was quite logical that now her deep fear of disappointment and frustration would also become more intense. Thus her rigidity might well serve as a defense against her growing longing for a relationship. In this connection I reminded her of the reaction she had at the sexual advances of those two fellow students. Gisela did not answer but complained only about headaches that became increasingly more intense.

In the next hour she complained again that her headaches were becoming more and more unbearable. She blamed me for this since I, looking only at the emotional side of things, had refused to give her some medication for this. I gave her some headache pills but stated at the same time that her headache probably was expressing her great inner tension that existed between her great longing for love, on the one hand, and her fear of it, on the other. This, I told her, could be alleviated but could not be cured by the pills. Then she became thoughtful. After a while she said: "I have no idea where I belong. I am not at home with my parents. I have no center in the world. One is only at home when one is loved. I do not know at all who I am."

Sullivan and F. Fromm-Reichmann have shown that the schizophrenic is without a center of belonging. By this they mean a constellation of interpersonal relatedness which not only provides protection and security but also permits him to meaningfully express his needs, to satisfy them, and to mature by experiencing human love. Such a background of a relatively reliable human relatedness is necessary in order that he may not be overwhelmed and confused by his own ambivalent needs and by human encounters.

This fact was of central importance in Gisela's treatment. Beyond the therapeutic hour there was nothing she could resort to. She was always helplessly exposed to numerous stimuli but, at the same time, was supposed to stand up reasonably well in a world viewed by her as hostile, while she was further undergoing critical periods provoked by the analysis. Thus I decided to give her one more support. She was to have a firm place of protection while she was waging her battle with the world and with her own ambivalent experiences: I took her into my family, as if she were someone who had always belonged to it. She could, without any conventionality, come and go when she wished. From then on she came at irregular intervals, each time only for a few hours, and otherwise maintained an independent pattern of life.

Out of this new helping approach of the therapist there now developed relatively quickly a transference that revealed a complete acceptance of the situation. Gisela drew pictures showing herself as an infant in the crib, with the therapist and his wife bending down to her. To this she commented: "I thought I would like to be right in the middle between you and your wife. I would like to be your child, for then I would know where I do belong."

At this time Gisela's attitude again became child-like and she saw the therapist in the role of a good father. She asked the therapist for advice at any little step she was considering. She brought numerous, sometimes quite simple, questions to which she wanted an answer. In her dreams she often saw herself as a little girl sitting in a room asking a man—the therapist—for the names of all visible objects. When doing this, however, she knew at the same time that she was there in the capacity of an adult person.

Protected by this positive relationship to a father, Gisela gradually and reluctantly became able to expose herself to reality. Like a little child she was discovering the objects around her and was asking "father" for their names. Thus there developed out of this new relationship, laden with dependency as it was, a new access to the world.

After some tentative endeavors during this phase of the treatment, Gisela had started to study again. It was the social reality itself which gradually brought her to question her infantile transference relationship. There were also dreams that indicated a re-awakening of her instinctual needs. At first there were mainly snakes that were threatening Gisela when she was alone with somebody. Then again there were cats who would tear her flesh. Eventually the dreams became increasingly weird. There appeared horrible toads or alligators that would devour men. Behind all this there was often the presence of Gisela's mother, threatening and unreal.

When Gisela played her child-like role in transference, I saw this positively as a new beginning of her relationship to the world and did

not analyze it further. Gradually, however, this situation with its implication of child-like protection began to disappear. In accordance with
her own childhood development there appeared, in the beginning, her
need for relatedness on an infantile-sexual level, which, at the same time,
did provoke guilt and anxiety. A dream from this phase, no more carrying the marks of a psychotic dissolution of reality, initiated a new phase
of treatment. Of this dream she said: "I am a five-year-old child and I
am sticking in the mud up to my nipples. At the same time, however,
I am Princess Margaret of England."

Again there is escape from humiliating reality into a fantastic self-
aggrandizement. But Margaret of England is not only a much-admired
Princess, she was—at the time this dream is occurring—also the center of
a great romance. However, Gisela was not yet able to raise herself up
to the ideal image of the beloved Princess because the lower part of her
body was still sticking in the mud and morass. The age Gisela revealed
in this dream corresponded to the time when she had her first sexual
play.

There was, however, the surprising fact that Gisela, herself, could say
hardly anything about this dream. But I, on my part, considered this
dream important, viewing it as a transference dream and keeping in
mind the fact that other dreams which expressed instinctual needs had
had a very threatening aspect. Therefore, I carefully tried an active
interpretation. Above all I asked Gisela whether her inability to take
on fully any female role might not be understandable on the basis of her
mother's extreme condemnation of sex. It is likely, I suggested, that she
felt dirty and like an outcast whenever she experienced something in
the area of her drives. While this conversation was going on, I had the
impression that Gisela was retreating more and more into herself. My
endeavors at an analytic interpretation of the dream were experienced
by her as a frustration of the needs for contact she had expressed therein.

In the next hour she reported that she had seen me while I talked
as if I had been becoming narrower and narrower until I was only a
line that hardly existed. She brought out the following dream:

> I was with you and complained that again I was faced with an emptiness.
> You examined me with an iron hammer and, subsequent to this, you
> wanted to clean my toenails. I was a little ashamed and looked down to
> see whether it was really so bad. You said "This shows again what a primi-
> tive human being you are."

Essentially I could have found some basis for considering my attitude,
as it was apparently criticized in the dream, to have been completely
normal. In this case I would have had to analyze Gisela's fear of being
humiliated and condemned because of her instinctual nature which she
experienced as dirty and guilt-laden. However, it occurred to me that
in a certain sense I had acted toward Gisela as her mother did in an

area where Gisela considered herself an outcast, and where she tried to escape into self-aggrandizement I had pointed out her "world of dirtyness." I had treated Gisela with an iron hammer—that is, crudely and without understanding. She felt I had sent her back to where she had been cast by her mother, for her immeasurable feeling of guilt accompanying any instinctual need was still insurmountable. Once more I had frustrated her hope of being loved by me and of thereby being taken out of the dirt and being promoted to the rank of Princess. Thus Gisela again slipped back into her psychotic defense by trying to extinguish the one who had disappointed her.

When I realized this consequence of my attitude, I was shocked myself. My first reaction was to ask Gisela to pardon me, a method employed in similar situations with surprising success by Benedetti and Ch. Muller. I explained to Gisela that this time I had had too little understanding of her. Then I tried to explain how it had come about that again I had rejected her trust. While this conversation was going on, Gisela appeared to mellow and stated finally: "I realize you are a person quite unlike my parents." She then continued to state that up to now her parents had relegated all guilt to her and had never taken any guilt upon themselves.

The little confession of guilt on the part of the therapist had, indeed, made a deep impression on her, and somewhat alleviated her fear of being condemned and humiliated. Thus it became possible for the first time to uncover a part of the areas of repressed instinctual needs as a phase of the positive transference that had now been established. There followed a good many dreams with obvious exhibitionistic content, for example: "I was walking on a high plateau, a country full with the sun of spring. Here I discovered a man, about forty years old, standing behind a few trees and admiring me. I let him look at my body without letting him come close. I was in my bathing suit."

Already this dream characterizes the new transference situation. I had not destroyed the exhibitionistic tendencies by applying a strict analytic interpretation but, instead, had taken them to be a first positive step toward the acceptance of a feminine reality and toward a degree of contact. At this time Gisela came to the hour dressed quite seductively and in her dreams placed her therapist more and more in the role of an admiring onlooker. I then told her that she was pretty and attractive and that she should have the courage to feel like a girl among her fellow students and among men in general. There was no great risk, I added, in being admired.

In fact, Gisela succeeded in finding a much freer way of contacting people. Her morbid ideas of reference and her experiences of being influenced and hypnotized had suddenly vanished. Instead, Gisela experienced real pleasure when men looked at her. By succeeding in identifying herself with her need of being looked at and wanted, there developed out of an oppressing unintegrated need a positive way of relating herself to reality.

After Gisela had experienced a first positive relatedness of her fellow human beings to herself, she became able again to adjust socially. Without fear she could walk in the street and enter restaurants. She even found a friend with whom she attended dancing parties.

Even at the beginning of this phase of therapy, I had noticed that Gisela made daily visits to a swimming pool. Then a series of dreams appeared in which Gisela sat in a bath tub while her mother washed her. To this, she reported that her mother had bathed her until she was fourteen or fifteen years old. Her mother, otherwise always hateful and nagging, at these bathing scenes appeared to be—apparently out of her latent homosexuality—completely changed. Then Gisela experienced her mother's face as friendly. She played and joked with her daughter, who, however, remained passive and inhibited, though she always longed to be bathed. Above all, her mother admired Gisela's naked body and told the latter again and again that she had grown big and beautiful and that one time she would be admired and desired.

This explained why Gisela's exhibitionistic tendencies were so strong from the beginning. While all other ways of relatedness to her human environment had been cut off, in this sphere she was greatly spoiled by her mother. Thus it was rubbed into her that her only hope for a human relationship in the future rested in the possibility of being admired and desired. It was for this reason that Gisela's exhibitionistic needs broke through with such intensity when she had refound a little trust in her human environment.

The dreams of the following hours were connected with the sexual play during her childhood. More and more, however, her longing for admiration and aggrandizement, and her need to be the center of attention became more marked while her longing for sexual contacts receded into the background. She dreamed of herself standing on a pedestal, raised above the ground like a monument and being venerated by many people. She dreamed of being a noble lady and princess, thus again repeating the theme which had already appeared in the dream of the little girl sticking in the mud who at the same time was Princess Margaret.

When these dreams were talked about, Gisela complained that she always had been humiliated by her parents. She also expressed her fear of being quite frank with the therapist, since such candor would make her feel still more inferior and humiliated. She asked me whether I was willing to change chairs with her, for as long as I sat in the therapist's armchair she would experience me as being in a high position and as being able to condemn her. This change of chairs I willingly conceded.

After this had been effected, I cautiously tried to analyze whether even now she was fearful of being punished and humiliated by me just as she had been punished by her mother when she had carried on her sexual play. Gisela gave no answer to this but asked me, instead, to take off my white overcoat and to do away with my title. This too was willingly conceded to her.

In spite of this and quite understandably, she was not satisfied with what she had achieved. She brought up a dream in which she was again excessively aggrandized but in which, at the same time, she got the feeling of only performing a play. At this moment she awoke. When she fell asleep again she dreamed that she had grown older.

In the following conversation she appeared to be depressed. She stated that she had the feeling of never talking to a human being. It was, she said, as if she were carrying a mask about an inch in front of her face and as if she were murmuring words while she herself was feeling quite unconcerned. The other people were forcing her into a stereotype; she had to adjust to everybody and then to talk about whatever they wanted to hear. As soon as she felt that the someone was becoming pensive, that he was retreating only a little bit, or even becoming critical, she inwardly would become like ice and would be unable to talk any more.

Thus Gisela, without any further analysis, had realized how superficial a relationship her exhibitionism created. Apparently, there was a longing for a more genuine and deeper human contact that had made her realize the façade-like nature of these exhibitionistic strivings. Gisela's hysterical structure, as it lay hidden behind the schizophrenic defense mechanisms, had characterized her attitude toward her human environment for about four months of therapy, but it had been overcome by her need for a more personal relationship.

The next phase of therapy dealt mainly with her aggressiveness. Gisela brought out dreams in which aggressive impulses made themselves apparent. I tried to encourage her, but Gisela said that she could not fight except to defend herself. Never when there was fighting in her home was it followed by reconciliation. Instead, quite frequently, an unabated tension between the two parents poisoned the air for days. She went on to reveal that once she had had a fight with her brother and on this occasion slapped his face. The brother fell down just when mother came home. Seeing this, the mother became wild. Without asking who the guilty one was, she started hitting Gisela. Mother's face was then so distorted by hate that Gisela felt she had to fight for her life. Mother then grasped a fire hook and, in a blind fury, hit Gisela with it until the latter collapsed, her body smeared with blood. For almost fourteen days after this incident mother did not speak one word to her.

We both were greatly moved by this story. Gisela wept for a long while. When she left the room she told me that at home she never had been allowed to cry. Mother would not have tolerated her children crying.

It seemed, however, that this strong emotional reaction on the part of both of us had peculiar consequences. When Gisela came to the next hour she was again as stiff and silent as she had been at the beginning of therapy. Her only words were complaints about headaches. Thus more than thirty hours went by without any palpable results. Gisela brought no dreams. She remained silent or she complained about headaches.

At first I had no clear idea as to what had brought about this new serious form of resistance. I thought first that her awakening aggressiveness had caused a negative transference but my cautious questioning got no answer. I then attempted to learn whether I again had made a mistake, but Gisela stayed silent. Finally, for long periods we silently sat in front of each other, since I was afraid of committing mistakes by further attempts at blind interpretation.

In this phase of treatment my counter-transference for the first time became a serious problem. After several, apparently fruitless hours, I felt considerable unrest creeping up in me since I was increasingly groping in the dark in front of my silent patient. I felt pressed to do some active analyzing, but I had to concede to myself that in this situation activity on my part might well have endangered everything that had been achieved so far. Gradually, I felt a certain resignation. I feared my treatment could fail after all. Thus I recognized aggressive impulses within myself coming up against Gisela as I anticipated the frustration of my own wish for a successful completion of her treatment. I experienced these hours that apparently had passed uselessly as a waste of time.

Under these circumstances I found it difficult to carry through the treatment with a persistently friendly attitude. But it seems, after all, that I succeeded in it. At the end of the thirty-third hour of this phase of resistance, Gisela stated when saying good-bye to me:

"You are kind to me." When I asked her what she meant by this, she answered: "When you are acting so friendly, in such a natural way, it is horribly painful to me. I am longing so much for someone to be kind and warm with me, but at the same time I am afraid you could not mean it. In front of strangers mother was always kind to me, but otherwise she was mean. I hated her because of her insincerity and never could tolerate the tenderness which she produced for me in front of other people. Later I could not even tolerate being touched by her. From the beginning it caused pain to me when you were kind to me since I was afraid it was insincere."

It thus became apparent that in this phase of resistance Gisela had tested me. It had not been easy for me to stand the test. But now that the ice had been broken another longer phase of positive transference had been started. Gisela could now explain why she had again been overcome by stiffness. For the first time, she felt that she had exposed her feelings without any inhibition to another human being and this had been followed by deep anxiety. She said:

> When I was talking with feeling, I could say nothing more. This is so uncanny. I was afraid you would throw yourself upon me. I have to defend myself. At home there was no room for feeling. When I was frank as a child, mother would reject me. I have completely encapsulated myself.

Protected by the therapeutic relationship which meanwhile permitted much freer emotional expression, there began now an outbreak of all her sexual guilt feelings. Gisela was experiencing the therapist as a seducer and, at the same time, as a priest bringing the message of God's all-encompassing forgiveness. She brought out a great number of dreams full of sexual content, no longer of an exhibitionistic, façade-like character, which offered incest motives that became increasingly clear. In these experiences there was an infantile pan-sexualism clearly apparent. Gisela was dreaming not only of having sexual relations with numerous people, male and female, who at some time or another had aroused her interest, but in her dreams was also experiencing incest with father, mother, and brother. This obvious early infantile sexuality is, for instance, expressed in the following dream sample: "My mother, my brother and I were all one big bundle of flesh with sexual feelings." Concomitant with this, there was a strong outbreak of oral needs. Gisela began to eat excessively and for a few months gained considerable weight. Her original need for uninhibited saturation, for an infantile-carnal communication with the world, had finally broken through and was now dominating her life for several months.

Toward the end of this phase of treatment, I began to notice that Gisela was discontinuing her visits to my home. Increasingly, she was dreaming once more of a beast-like, cruel mother who had murdered father. Mother always had rubbed into her how bad father was, so that, as a consequence, father remained strange and fear-inspiring. At the same time, she had a feeling that father was really much more human than mother. Until now she had been terribly afraid of all men since mother had always told her what horrible creatures they were.

This dream and the shift in transference which had been coming for some time were forewarnings of a new crisis. This crisis was precipitated mainly by her fear of her own mature sexuality and the guilt feelings that were still connected with it. Again for several weeks Gisela was silent or complained about headaches. At this time I was able to profit from the training period I had had with her and could stand her silence in a friendly way, though I still had to fight some doubts. Gradually she began to talk again, but she said that she felt I could not demand that she exhibit her weak spots. Instead, she wanted me to criticize her so that she could either concede or deny my assumptions. This I refused to do by cautiously pointing out she would have succeeded in placing me in the role of mother. At this moment a need to be punished became increasingly apparent. Gisela demanded that I be strict and cynical with her—that I punish and humiliate her. Now I began to tackle her guilt feelings for the second time, suggesting the possibility that she was longing for punishment out of intense guilt feelings. I added that probably all of us had at least just as much guilt heaped upon us as she had but that in contrast to her we also had experienced forgiveness. Thus we had learned that we would be loved in spite of our guilt. After this talk Gisela again wept for a long time. But in the next hour she remained just as silent as she had been before. Again my patience was put to the test, for another forty hours of treatment passed by without any palpable result. For the most part Gisela escaped into trivial talk about trivial affairs of everyday life.

Finally she produced a letter in which she confessed to me that for several months, during therapy and other conversations, she had been constantly thinking of the male genitals. When she realized how happy I was about this information that had broken the long spell, she appeared to be very relieved. She confessed to me that she had always been afraid that I would leave her as soon as I got to know this. Following this hour, she again fell into a depression caused by guilt. Gisela suddenly felt a deep guilt and sadness for once having seduced so many children into sexual activities. She experienced guilt toward her brother which so far she had never realized consciously but only dimly sensed. However, the therapeutic relationship could no more be questioned by this depression.

In the further course of therapy nothing extraordinary happened. It proceeded now like the treatment of a neurotic patient. Gisela overcame her depression relatively quickly. Thereafter she entered a relatively fruitful phase. Her diligence and her achievements at the academy became considerably better. She won several awards and prizes. There followed another phase during which she became quite aggressive toward the therapist. She expressed very serious and well-aimed complaints which had their basis in succinct observations she had made during two years of treatment. Yet the personal relationship already had become so strenghtened that a very frank exchange of opinions had become possible between us.

At about this time, there grew also a friendship which Gisela had started some time ago. She began to have frequent walks with her friend and also talked over with him their mutual and personal problems and difficulties. A dream she had during this final phase of treatment showed how Gisela was able to disentangle her life from her mother's influence by using the help of friends of whose love she could feel sure:

I was taking a walk with my friend. There was the problem of outwitting an old woman who had a precious book. A spirit was to come and tear away from her this book of life. I stood in a room and was talking quite innocently with her about my new knowledge. In this moment the spirit rushed into the room—he looked like the therapist—and fetched the book of life. Once more I felt fear, for the old woman was very tough and had succeeded in getting a hold of the book again. But finally the spirit won out and got away with the book. Thereupon the woman was quite exhausted and collapsed.

After about three hundred hours and a treatment period of two and a quarter years, Gisela's therapy was terminated. Since then she has been doing well. In her studies she continued to do better than average and her friendship, started during therapy, appears to be lasting.

Addendum

1. *Optimally, what criteria do you use for accepting or rejecting patients for psychotherapy?*

The criteria for accepting a schizophrenic patient for treatment are essentially different from those which apply to neurotic patients. In the case of psychotic patients, one can hardly expect an active readiness for therapy and a corresponding desire for health. It is only with the therapist's spontaneous acceptance that the patient's willingness may be aroused in therapy, for along with this comes new hope that his deeply frustrated contact-needs may be gratified. Since the schizophrenic's active cooperation is thus something which only gradually develops out of the deepening doctor-patient relationship, it is not a criterion which can be given at the beginning. Instead, it already represents a significant initial success of therapy.

The criteria for accepting a schizophrenic patient for therapy are to be sought less in the patient himself than in his environment and his therapist. In each case one must seriously consider whether there is enough time and personal willingness to go through with therapy until either definite success or failure is reached. A premature discontinuation of therapy or a change of therapists is a much more serious matter with the schizophrenic than with the neurotic patient since it will be experienced by the schizophrenic as the break up of a trusting relationship which he has dared to establish for the first time.

The patient's environment should be free of unfavorable influences. The schizophrenic's immediate dependence on one parent who, consciously or unconsciously, uses his influence against the therapy must be considered a contraindication against ambulatory treatment.

2. *Do you make a diagnosis before psychotherapy begins?*

With schizophrenics the diagnosis is important for determining the nature of the therapeutic approach. Furthermore, one should try as much as possible to get an impression of the depth of the psychotic regression and of the still existing possibilities for communication.

3. *Do you attempt to persuade the patient or significant relatives to change his (the patient's) environment?*

It is the patient himself who is in the center of the intensive psychotherapy of schizophrenics. His treatment can be made easier by the elimination of pathogenic factors in his home or his social environment. In some cases the additional treatment of the marital partner or of one parent is mandatory.

4. *How did you conceptualize the therapist's role in this case?*
5. *What aspects of your theory of psychotherapy were particularly apparent or useful in the case presented here?*

The primary task the therapist has with the schizophrenic consists in finding a relationship at all. If this has been achieved it becomes possible to deal with the patient's conflicts at a later date. Due to acute pressures, there was, in the case of our patient, insufficient time to obtain enough information about the specific structure of the psychosis and the available possibilities of contact. Since patient was trying hard to leave the hospital, a quick decision had to be reached. Thus the attempt was made to approach Gisela in a general way as the need presented itself in her situation by making use of the still existing verbal communication. Our first encounters were very definitely marked by the therapist's active engagement, which promised help and reliability for a long time to come.

Gisela appeared to be caught in a network of innumerable needs which she could not express due to deep fears of new disappointment and bitter experiences in a frustrating world. The therapist's warm and at first completely undemanding approach, as well as his always reliable presence, made possible a new experience of trust in human reality, though still small and precarious. It is the hope of finding the satisfaction of one's needs through others, of finding a basic security in the "eternal homeland of love" (*der ewigen Heimat der Liebe*—L. Binswanger) that we consider, figuratively speaking, the hook by which one can gradually succeed in pulling the schizophrenic out of an unresponsive world of his own to the solid ground of reality.

For the schizophrenic the therapist is the representative of reality. But he would be completely wrong in imposing his own concept of reality upon the patient, seeing it as an apodictic system of demands in no further need of discussion. Too often the schizophrenic's need for love has been frustrated by his parents in the form of moral righteousness. Most frequently the parents of schizophrenics have forced upon their children a rigid and questionable system of morals in order to hide their own helplessness and their own inability to cope with their childrens' needs. For this reason alone it would be incorrect to make demands on the schizophrenic and to expect his submission to rigid, frustrating principles. Benedetti has very convincingly demonstrated that the schizophrenic may only fit himself into the framework of human living when he is not met in an authoritarian fashion but with personal understanding. Only when the therapist is willing to have his own concept of reality questioned while meeting the patient and permitting the limits of togetherness to develop in the course of a loving struggle, can the frustrating and destructive power of the unloving parental authority be overcome.

Particularly with ambulatory schizophrenics one must give special attention to the social problems of the patient. One must not forget that most social conventions and demands carry a frustrating and hostile meaning for the patient. By putting pressure on the patient—e.g., by too active therapy

—to accept an apparently better concept of reality, one may perhaps effect a change of symptoms. But the patient continues to live under the compulsion of a set of rules not geared to his personality and remains basically incapable of finding gratification of his needs in dealing with reality or a partner.

The life history of our patient serves to illustrate the fact that the schizophrenic even during childhood is forced to live in a narrow, impoverished world which defies life. With extreme harshness, Gisela's parents demanded of her the adoption of a most onesided and narrow ideal. All other demands of the child were stigmatized as bad and, in case they returned, cruelly suppressed. Only within a very limited scope of existence was Gisela allowed to have new experiences. She was restricted to the few areas of life which her parents provided and delineated for her. Anything beyond this—her own unrealized needs and also the full reality of the world—not only remained strange and unfamiliar to her, but were experienced as an awesome abyss of threat and uncomprehensible guilt. Her total condemnation by mother and the fact that she never experienced absolution, made it appear to Gisela that there was an insurmountable barrier separating her from that kind of guilt which could be worked through in reality.

Fixed in the absolute dilemma of either being guiltless and angel-like or of being completely condemned, Gisela could only stick to the basically hostile world design of her parents. Any step made beyond it was threatened by the breaking through of the strange, uncanny, inner world leading to the destruction of the still available remainder of the real interpersonal communication.

In view of all this, it would probably be a mistake for the therapist to maintain an attitude of aloof distance, for in this way he would be experienced by the schizophrenic as the pharisaical idol that his parents were. Instead, the patient in therapy must have human experiences which may help him in crossing the border to the part of reality which is guilt-laden and unaccepted. In order for this to happen it is necessary, first, that the therapist himself remain human with all possible openness to the human side of problems. Thus the patient should be able to have the immediate experience that one can be loved in spite of one's guilt and, also, that this guilt can be overcome.

Furthermore, it is of importance to note that the therapist in the earlier phases of treatment must not destroy any need by directly analyzing it, no matter how pathological it may appear. Any opening up to the world should primarily be valued as a step toward communication. Only when this step has actually been taken and has met with acceptance and gratification in the world does it become possible to further analyze the defense mechanisms connected with it. One always has to keep in mind the fact that, as a rule, the schizophrenic is unable to shift to another mode of communication when encountering frustration. Instead, he will completely withdraw from the frustrating reality and thus seriously endanger the therapeutic relationship.

6. *Do you feel that this case developed significant insight? If not, can improvement be maintained?*

The patient developed practically complete insight into her illness.

7. *What aspects of your own cultural orientation facilitated or impeded the treatment of your case?*

[Not answered.]

8. *If we consider that a continuum exists from superficial to deep psychotherapy, where would you place your own case?*

I think one can consider it to be a case of deep psychotherapy.

9. *What did you think about the outcome of this case and what criteria did you use for evaluating such outcome?*

The psychotherapeutic cure of a schizophrenic has not been reached when the patient does not show any more schizophrenic symptoms. Instead, the goal should be to effect a restructuring of the personality, which means, in effect, that the latent psychosis must also be overcome. It is not easy to find relatively reliable criteria for this. First, it is essential that the patient has gained openness and the capacity to trust other human beings. Also, he must have gained a good deal of insight into the deeper connections and into the origin of his psychosis. Of decisive importance, however, is the fact that the patient not only has learned to face reality but also has learned to gratify his essential needs in an open interchange with the world.

This will be mainly proven by his ability to bear frustrations without resorting to deeply ingrained defense mechanisms. It will be further manifested in the way he is able to deal openly with his own anxiety and guilt.

10. *How do you terminate psychotherapy?*

When the above described goal has been reached termination of therapy should present no major difficulties. The patient then will have reached considerable inner independence in regard to his therapist.

CHAPTER 12

Time-Limited, Client-Centered Psychotherapy: Two Cases[1]

—MADGE K. LEWIS, CARL R. ROGERS, JOHN M. SHLIEN

Introductory Comments
by
Carl R. Rogers[2]

It is a privilege to be invited to introduce these two cases, each representative of client-centered therapy, and each dealt with by an experienced therapist. I will make some comments about the process of change in these clients, and some comments about the therapists, which may give more meaning to the case material which follows.

[1] The authors are indebted to the Wieboldt Foundation for generous support of this research in its early phase. Further analysis is made possible by the grant of the Ford Foundation (Psychotherapy Research Program) to the Counseling Center, University of Chicago.

[2] A.B., U. of Wis., 1924; M.A. and Ph.D., Teachers Coll., Columbia U., '28, '31; Fellow, Inst. for Ch. Guid., N.Y.C., '27-'28; Psychol., Child Study Dept., SPCC, Rochester, N.Y., '28-'30, Dir., '30-'38; Dir., Roch. Guid. Center, Rochester, N.Y., '30; Prof. of Psychol., Ohio State U., '40-'45; Prof. of Psychol., Depts. of Psychol. and Psychiat., U. of Wis., '57— . Part-time positions: Lect., U. of Rochester, '35-'40, Teachers Coll., Columbia, '35, UCLA, '47, Harvard, '48, Occidental, '50, U. of Calif. (Berkeley), '53-'54. Vice Pres., Amer. Orthopsychiatric Assn., '41-'42; Pres., Amer. Assoc. for Appl. Psychol., '44-'45; Pres., Amer. Psychol. Assoc., '46-'47; Pres., Amer. Acad. Psychotherapists, '56-'57. Author: *Counseling and Psychotherapy*, '42, *Client-centered Therapy*, '51, *Psychotherapy and Personality Change* (Ed.), '54.

The Process in the Clients

In one sense I approached this material in exactly the same manner as the reader of this chapter. I knew nothing of the clients here described —Mrs. Teral and Mr. Tapa (pseudonyms, of course)—or of their therapy. Yet as I read the accounts of the course of their interviews I found all of the phenomena which have gradually come to stand out in my experience as evidences of therapeutic movement. In each of these clients certain characteristic trends occur. Let me list a number of them.

The client moves from guessing what his feelings are, to remembering them in the past, to experiencing them fully in the immediacy of the therapeutic moment.

He moves from fearing and defending himself against his feelings, to letting these feelings *be* and exist, acceptedly, in him.

He moves from a role relationship (a "client" in relation to a "therapist") to a real relationship (person to person).

He moves from living by values introjected from others to values which are experienced in himself in the present.

From existing only to satisfy the expectations of others, and living only in their eyes and in their opinions, he moves toward being a person in his own right, with feelings, aims, ideas of his own.

From being driven and compelled, he moves toward the making of responsible choices.

From poor communication within himself—being out of touch with some aspects of his experience—he moves toward free inner communication, a greater awareness of what is going on from moment to moment within.

Likewise he moves from poor communication with others to freer, more real, and direct communication.

He moves from a distrust of the spontaneous and unconscious aspects of himself to a basic trust of his experiencing, of his organism as a sound instrument for encountering life.

He moves from rigidity and defensiveness to an inner flow of experiencing in the moment.

From behavior which is at odds with what he consciously desires, he moves toward behavior which is an integrated expression of a more integrated self.

Each of these clients, in my estimation, illustrates in specific fashion each of these trends. Mr. Tapa is especially articulate about the process going on in himself, and Miss Lewis has let him speak for himself at length. This material will repay very careful study.

It is of interest to me that though each of these clients was limited in the hours he could spend in therapy, as is explained by Dr. Shlien, the process in each seems very similar to that in unlimited therapy, except that certain aspects become intensified.

The Attitudes of the Therapists

In reading the client material, I am, as I stated, in the same position as any reader. In regard to the therapist responses I am in a very different position, since I have known each of these therapists for a number of years. I believe that a few comments about each of them—which they cannot very well make about themselves—may give more meaning to the recorded client-therapist interchanges.

These are most assuredly not therapists who are using the *techniques* of client-centered therapy. They are therapists whose own attitudes are such that a client-centered orientation is a natural and congenial expression of their own genuine attitudes. Let me be more specific.

Dr. Shlien, in his relationship to his client, seems to me to feel a deep interest, and a thorough-going confidence in the client that rarely wavers even when the going is roughest. He accepts the client as he is. He feels a tenderness or even compassion (in its literal sense of feeling with) toward the client in his struggle to meet life.

Miss Lewis, as I have known her in her work with clients, is sensitively empathic to an outstanding degree. She is a most understanding companion to her clients. She is modestly in the background in the relationship (as in her portion of this chapter) but is quietly and unobtrusively present to the client. She is deeply concerned with being her own self in the relationship.

Both of these therapists are very warm individuals in their therapeutic relationships, Dr. Shlien perhaps more openly so, but both with a genuine human concern for the other person.

As individuals, aside from therapy, each has his own difficulties, tensions, achievements, and failures, his own satisfactions, fulfillments, and disappointments. In short, they are very human, but in therapy their humanity exhibits itself much as I have tried to describe.

I have given this personal sketch because I believe it will enable the reader to gain a much more accurate picture of the relationships. When Miss Lewis says, in one response to the client, "You are a fraud," this could be grossly misunderstood unless it is realized that she is speaking warmly, empathically from within the client's frame of reference, expressing his feelings in a way thoroughly acceptable to him. It occurs quite frequently in each of these cases, that the counselor is so deeply involved in the relationship that he speaks from *within* the client's world, not as an outsider.

All this description, however, is but a poor substitute for the raw material of therapy. Let us permit the therapists and their clients to speak for themselves.

CASE I

MRS. TERAL: A CASE OF BRIEF,
TIME-LIMITED, CLIENT-CENTERED THERAPY

— JOHN M. SHLIEN[3]

There is no special "strategy" in typical client-centered therapy. There is only the general effort to provide a steady empathic understanding of the feelings and perceptions of the client (and this is no small thing if it can be achieved). The specific elements of this therapeutic behavior have recently been given a specific statement by Rogers.[4]

This is not quite a typical case. There is no special strategy, but there is a special structure, one which is a radical departure from customary procedure. Usually, the client determines the general course of therapy, the pace, and the point at which he wishes to terminate. This has been an effective policy, one in keeping with our over-all philosophy. In the present case, the termination is set in advance. The client was offered a maximum of twenty interviews, at the suggested rate of two per week, to terminate at the end of ten weeks. She was told, truly, that this limit was imposed because of the practical necessity to meet our long waiting list. This client was the first of many who were offered therapy under one of three conditions: (a) a maximum of twenty interviews; (b) a maximum of forty interviews, with a ten week "vacation" after the first twenty sessions, (c) without limits, to terminate voluntarily. A case from the second group is included in this volume. A case, "Mrs. Oak," from the third group is described in another volume.[5] The over-all design of this research, and its purposes, are described elsewhere.[6] It is enough to say here that the basic aim is to evaluate and compare time-limited cases, longer and shorter, with unlimited cases, longer and shorter. Mrs. Teral,

---

[3] Ph.D., Univ. of Chicago, 1957; Psychological Asst., USSAF, '42-'45; Lect. in Soc. Anth., Univ. College, U. of Chicago, '48-'50; Chief Examiner, Chicago Civil Serv. Comm., '49-'50; Serv. Coordinator, Counselor, Counseling Center, Inst. Comm. on Human Development, '51-'57; Res. Assoc., and Asst. Prof., U. of Chicago, '57—   . Consult. in Psychother., Manteno State Hosp., '57— .

[4] C. R. Rogers, "The Necessary and Sufficient Conditions of Therapy," *J. of Consult. Psychol.*, 21 (1957), 95-103.

[5] C. R. Rogers, "The Case of Mrs. Oak: A Research Analysis," in C. R. Rogers and R. F. Dymond (eds.), *Psychotherapy and Personality Change* (Chicago: University of Chicago Press, 1954).

[6] J. M. Shlien, "An Experimental Investigation of Time-Limited Therapy: Practical Value and Theoretical Limitations," *J. of Counseling Psychol.*, in press.

though she did not know it, was the first person offered therapy under the first research condition.

Some Theoretical Considerations

There is more to the background of this research than the need to provide service for more people. A long and controversial history of opinion on termination contains some profound theoretical problems. Can the "end" of therapy be advanced in time? What is the end? When is the end? Is there ever an end? Can termination be more than an accidental point in time coinciding with the decision to stop?

Otto Rank was the first exponent of end-setting. He chose to limit time mainly because it was so opportune and unavoidable an issue with which to mobilize the patient's will. Students and interpreters of Rank have stated that the practice of end-setting has connections with Rank's theory of birth trauma and separation anxiety, though Rank himself seems less interested in time than in limits, and would have challenged the will by "forbidding the patient certain foods, smoking, or sexual activity," had not time seemed a more generally applicable category.[7]

Freud wrote of his experiment in setting an advance termination and called it "a blackmailing device." He believed it would be effective in overcoming certain resistance, but would at the same time drive important material underground, where it would be "lost to our therapeutic efforts."[8]

Rogers has taken the position that time limits are valuable for two reasons: (1) They furnish an aspect of reality to which the client must adjust. (2) They enable the counselor to function in a more open and responsive way, such as he could not do if he were bound to the therapeutic session for an unlimited period.[9] Rogers has spoken in favor of time limits only for the period of the appointment, not the duration of therapy, however. That, he believed, should be left to the client.[10]

More than anyone else, Rank's student and translator, Jessie Taft, has developed the theoretical significance of time-limits, which she calls "one of the most valuable tools ever introduced into therapy." She argues that time is supremely representative of all limitations in living. Her emphasis on the *quality* of therapy, as contrasted with the quantity, led to her famous statement on the "single contact," in which she points out

---

[7] O. Rank, *Will Therapy* (New York: Alfred A. Knopf, Inc., 1936).

[8] S. Freud, "Analysis Terminable and Interminable," in *Collected Papers, Vol. V* (London: Hogarth Press, 1950), 316-57.

[9] C. R. Rogers, *Counseling and Psychotherapy* (New York: Houghton Mifflin Company, 1942).

[10] The opinions given are now fifteen years old. It is worth noting that Rogers, while still holding that all limits are a function of the counselor's needs, was active and helpful in planning and carrying out this experiment.

that unless the therapeutic quality is present, no amount of therapy will help; it cannot be time that heals, but a process taking place in time. Perhaps, then, to eliminate the reliance on time will heighten the quality of the process.

That process is more than a means to an end. *The process is a criterion in itself,* for it means that the individual is learning to come to terms with time, his lifetime, and his limitations. Insofar as he can use the given hour, from beginning to end, knowing that it cannot last forever, yet has all the value he can put into it, to that extent he has "learned to live, to accept this fragment of time in and for itself, and strange as it may seem, if he can live this hour he has in his grasp the secret of all hours, he has conquered life and time for the moment and in principle."[11] The writer, and many colleagues on the staff, were deeply influenced by the writings of Taft. It is in this context that Mrs. Teral's case is presented.

The Client

Mrs. Teral came to the Counseling Center after months of hesitation. In a preliminary interview, she agreed to participate in the research. She was twenty-three years of age, married to a young lawyer, and was herself employed as a grade school teacher. Why did she come for help? At first, she could not express herself. With trembling fingers, she tried several times to light a cigarette. The counselor said, "Feeling awfully scared?" She nodded, looked determined, and said (as do many clients), "What do you want to know about me?" When the counselor said he was ready to hear whatever she wanted to talk about, she began with information about her age, her job and its location, her education, and so forth. Then she began to talk about her "problem." They began simply and built up to a poignant crescendo.

First: I want to give up smoking. (It makes me nervous, I feel a slave to it, etc.)

Second: I can't read. Need to read, need to learn, want to know things, be a knowing person, but look at the same page for an hour. I don't know *what* makes me that way.

Third: I sleep all the time. I hate to wake up, and whenever I dare, I crawl into bed and sleep.

Fourth: I can't work. Can't clean the house, never finish anything, hate to start anything.

Fifth: I feel *so* worthless. Why should I even bathe? What difference does it make? If other people didn't insist, I wouldn't bother to keep myself clean.

---

11 J. Taft, *Dynamics of Therapy in a Controlled Relationship* (New York: Macmillan Company, 1933).

Sixth: [*crying*] I don't know who I am, or what I am—I don't know if I'm beautiful or ugly. I just don't *know*. I have no idea.

In this initial interview, she ran the gamut from the usual "presenting problems" (how can I stop smoking, lose weight, recover my wife, learn to study, choose a profession, etc.) to the basic, ultimate questions every human being in trouble asks of himself: Who am I? What am I? What am I to think of myself?

Early Interviews

In the second interview, the client looked back at her early life, considered her family and school experiences, and *guessed* at how she must have felt—"I must have been afraid, I guess I was shy."

In the third interview, the client still looked back, specifically at her relation to her parents and sisters during childhood, this time *remembering* her feelings. After the interview, she took the appointment slip offered her and looked at it silently for a minute. She said, "I still can't believe that you are willing to see me again. How can I be worth your time?"

In the fourth interview, she began to report recent events, and intense feelings *experienced* in connection with them. Her sister blamed her for spoiling an occasion they had shared and the parents sided with her sister.

C 3: Oh! And when . . . that's all I needed. They kept repeating this about two or three times. And we took my folks home and I blew. I haven't spoken to my parents the way I did since . . . for a long time. But I said . . . I really blew up then and I said, 'If you're going to,' . . . I said, 'you can blame me for what I do, but don't blame me for what someone else does. She's old enough to make up her own mind. . . .' Well, I was really . . . it hit me down deep. And afterwards I told [*husband*] that if I was searching for a way to find out about the past, that did it, cause that just . . . that knocked right down into me. Because to me it wasn't just a little insignificant thing, but it typified *every* thing that had been done in my lifetime in my parents' attitudes toward my sister and me. It really got down in there.

T 3: That really struck so deeply it just brought out all the things you've been feeling now. You really *blew*.

C 4: Oh boy! And to me it . . . I mean my parents just going right along with her . . . I mean, she's old enough to make up her mind what she wants to do. And to come down and say a thing like that—that really annoyed me. But for that I could pass it off as ignorance. I said, 'Don't blame me; you did what you wanted to do.' And to her . . . I told her that. Then my parents started with this business of, see? If you would have gone up there [*sister*] would have done it. And this is it; my sister's word was always it.

T 4: That's . . . that's how its been—that's the end, huh?

C 5: I mean, my sister's word—whatever she did—went. And this feeling that came into me was just the feeling that I remember as a kid. That sometimes I remember feeling, 'I'm right, I *know* I'm right.' And yet they would just . . . they would always see her.

T 5: And this is exactly what I've been through so many times before.

C 6: Absolutely. I just . . . 'cause the feeling just welled inside of me. I hadn't felt this because the occasion hasn't . . . has never come up before since I've, you know, been at home . . . since I was at home and since I was . . . and this was the first time something like that happened. And it brought back all those feelings—that constant feeling that was within me. I just . . . I said to [*husband*] afterwards, I said, 'I'm glad it happened because it gave me a really . . . a good chance to see.' I mean, I was saying it before, but this time I really felt it. And is it any wonder that I felt so darn lousy when this was the way it was, that they would . . . they would give me . . . they did me a dirty deal plenty of times. And conversely, I was no angel about it; I realize that. But. . . .

T 6: And this is it. This is just what I've been talking about, and no wonder I've been feeling so lousy because look how they treated me. And I've . . . I'm no wonderful person in reaction to that kind of treatment.

C 7: That's right.

Mrs. Teral had begun to be aware of her emotions, to express them, and to understand her experience—even to take responsibility for her part in it. Next she declared that she had been denied the chance to think independently.

C 16: There was no need for me to make decisions. All my decisions were automatically made for me. My parents made them in the home. . . . My mother made them in the home, my sister made them outside. There never . . . there was no room for my own opinions, there was no room for me to learn to think. There was no room for me to experiment and . . .

T 16: So you're saying, of *course*, I never learned to have my own opinions. There just wasn't any chance.

She described a choice now facing her as a test.

C 33: Um-hm. So I don't know what I'll do. [*Slight pause.*] I usually do wait till the last possible moment and then make a quick decision. [*Laughs.*] One way or the other.

T 33: You're kind of saying you won't handle it very well.

C 34: No, I won't; that's right. I'll do it the way I usually do it. Slip-shod. [*Pause; sighs.*] Could I use a cigarette now, oh! [*Trembling.*]

T 34: Right this minute, that is just what you would want.

C 35: [*Sighs; tears; pause.*] I guess I'm upset now. [*Sighs; pause.*] Having state visitors come and visit our school tomorrow and they put up such a big show. And everyone gets very excited and . . . big fuss. [*Pained, stricken look.*]

T 35: What . . . what's hitting you now?

C 36: I don't know.

T 36: Something upsetting, something that makes you feel like crying?

C 37: [*Pause; crying softly; words lost.*] I could use a little more self control, too.

T 37: You don't like to have to cry.

C 38: No, I don't. [*Pause.*] And I don't know why, either. I just got very upset [*still crying.*]

T 38: Um-hm. Something just came over you and you really don't know what started it.

C 39: [*Long pause; still crying.*] I must have been getting a little too close to something—I didn't want to talk about, or something.

T 39: You really don't know what made this happen. [*Client looks for clock.*] You've still got about fifteen minutes.

C 40: [*Pause; still crying.*] Something hit me [*laughs*].

T 40: Hm?

C 41: Something hit me.

T 41: Something hurts.

C 42: [*Long pause.*] Here I go again. [*Pause.*] I don't know what it was. I just . . . I'm completely gone now. My knees are shaking all over me.

T 42: Um-hm. [*Pause.*] You don't know what started this but it's really taken hold of you. [*Pause; client crying.*] Your whole . . . your whole body is in a turmoil.

C 43: I really can't concentrate on what I'm doing. All I can concentrate on is the feeling that I'm not going to smoke, I'm not going to smoke [*laughs*].

T 43: I don't know exactly what you mean there.

C 44: I can't even try to think what it is because I want a cigarette so bad I just have [*laughs*] to keep myself going. I'm not going to smoke, I'm not going to smoke [*laughs*].

T 44: All your energy is just bent toward that one thing, just . . . to keep yourself from having a cigarette, huh?

C 45: Yes. [*Long pause.*] I'm not very . . . I'm upset cause I said something about being dependent on [*husband*]. Maybe I just didn't want to start talking about that. That could be it.

T 45: Maybe that's kind of a tender spot.

C 46: [*Pause.*] And that's something that's closest to me—right now. It's these other things that I've been trying to get at, but things that happen today are really very important to me. [*Words lost; cries hard.*] It scares me more than. . . .

T 46: That's really the touchiest thing, the most frightening thing, your relation to [*husband*].

C 47: No, the idea of bringing it up, that's most touchy because it's the most immediate thing. My parents I have . . . I mean. . . .

T 47: They're things you can look back at [*both together*]. . . .

C 48: Back at, yeah.

T 48: But [*husband's*] right with you, that's. . . .

C 49: That's something right now.

T 49: . . . closer and somehow more immediate and more risky.

Now the present had come into focus. History was left behind for the current and more upsetting relations. The relation with the therapist was touched upon, in connection with time.

C 52: [*Laughs.*] I mean, it didn't seem so to me, but now it . . . I guess now it [*words lost; long pause*]. Maybe I'd better not waste your time just sitting here and I could come back and maybe next Saturday I'll be able to be calmed down about it. I'm all upset now.

T 52: Maybe you shouldn't just take my time being upset and . . .

C 53: And just sitting here.

T 53: Well, I'll tell you how I feel about that.

C 54: Okay.

T 54: I feel that this time is your time and you can do whatever you want to. You don't have to stay, but if you just want to sit there and do nothing, that's your privilege.

C 55: [*Pause.*] It won't come out [*sighs*].

T 55: Um-hm. I don't . . . maybe one reason you felt you shouldn't stay is that you feel as if you know what the next thing is but it won't come out, so, maybe you just better creep away and come back next time. Is that. . . ?

C 56: [*Laughs.*] Yes. I . . . I guess so, yeah. To me, I myself don't want to deal with these other problems. Excuse me [*cries*].

Then she declared that the past was relatively useless though the present was most difficult to face.

C 58: I mean I got uncomfortable there; I guess that's the thing. I've been talking about my past, and I gotta talk about the present. I am what I am. No matter what it is that I . . . why the reason is that I am the way I am now, or how I will be in the future is . . . that doesn't . . . now I am this way. And certain things that I . . . that have taken place and they exist right now and they will have to come out too and that's the biggest threat to me.

Finally, she makes the first mention of her awareness of the limits.

T 60: Well, now our time is about up.

C 61: Okay. Thank you.

T 61: Shall we make it [*date and time*]? [*Pause.*]

C 62: I was thinking—only twenty sessions—you gotta make use of all of them. But, sometimes it can't be helped.

T 62: You feel sort of that it doesn't seem like an awful lot of time or . . . ?

C 63: No, I mean that, seems that since there is a time limit, that you don't wanta dawdle about, and let yourself waste the time. I mean I guess it . . .

T 63: I see. You mean that there's a little sense of pressure, and that's part of what's upsetting to you.

C 64: I don't know if that's upsetting me. I mean I just said that as an after-thought, that it shouldn't be wasted. But then maybe it's not wasted, so . . .

T 64: Um-hm. Well, I'll see you [*day*].
C 65: Okay. My eyes all red?
T 65: They feel all red?[12]
C 66: Yeah, very much.
T 66: See you. [*Client waves.*]

Excerpts from the fourth interview give some flavor of the client's mode of expression and examples of the interaction between client and counselor. Henceforth, the material is compressed into summary statements.

Fifth Interview

The client expressed much interest in the counselor and in herself in relation to him. She was surprised at his casual dress, showed much concern about whether he was above her or was an equal. She was surprised at her own daring to ask such questions.

Sixth Interview

She was deeply depressed and despaired of accomplishing any change. She felt inadequate in her job, and guilty about mishandling the children. She felt that there were things it would be impossible to tell the counselor, but that it was hopeless to expect help without revealing them. After a long pause, she mentioned, almost inaudibly, an itching sensation in the area of the rectum, for which a physician could find no cause.

Seventh Interview

She felt much encouraged and considerably changed. She expressed surprise and satisfaction that the counselor had not tried to reassure her in her most despairing moments. She felt that she had lived through that, and continued to relate very deep fears of utter inadequacy, possibly mental deficiency, sterility, and ultimate disaster. At the end, she asked, "What interview was this?" And she said, as if to herself, "I think I'm going to make it."

Tenth Interview

The time between the seventh and tenth interview was a very full and complex period of development for Mrs. Teral. "I've never had so many

---

[12] Some more "directive" therapists have asked, in connection with C 65, "My God, can't you even answer yes or no to *that?*" One could, but there is no point in so doing. The counselor is not needed for such information, but is much needed for understanding of the feelings about herself.

feelings in my life," was her first statement. She wandered in a stupor downtown until she bought a dress she felt uncertain about. Her husband didn't like it, and she spent a sleepless night. For the first time, she became hostile toward husband, and wished she could hurt him, make him miserable—but claimed, "he doesn't react to me. I don't matter enough, I guess." She had stopped smoking. The itching had now moved to her fingers. She sighed, expressed the wish she could talk about sex, and asked, "What interview is this?" Fearfully, with great embarrassment, she whispered, "I'm bad," and described undressing games, and playing with the genitals of a little boy and later with another girl during childhood, and the scorn her sisters had directed at her ("You're dirty, no good") for these acts of masturbation. She added angrily, "They didn't tell me that they did it too!" She dreamed of being a prostitute. Emotionally, she couldn't accept sex, couldn't read about it, and was even ashamed to buy sanitary napkins, "because I'm just bad, dirty, that's all." After minutes of sobbing, she expressed confusion and uncertainty—"I want to be desired, and feel it's okay, but I'm so ashamed—am I lovable? —or desirable? Is it bad and dirty? I think I'm oversexed inside and not sexy enough outside to attract the response I want. Oh, I don't know, outside, what I am—plain or what?" Later, "Inside, at least, I know, I'm bad or at least sexy. I don't know what I want to be outside, or don't want to be, *I'd like to be the same inside and out*." Beyond her yearning for sexual comfort and satisfaction, and her confusion about it, she expressed the basic drive for congruence and integration.

Twelfth Interview

She remarked that she was no longer sleeping to escape. Now when she went home in the afternoons, she took a bath, and said she "enjoyed it." She had found much relief in talking about sex, and decided she wasn't just *born* to be promiscuous. She mentioned that the therapist didn't seemed shocked, but wondered if he disliked her for what she had revealed. Now the itching had returned, and she wondered if it was connected with guilt about childhood masturbation. After a period of discussing affection in her family, she said she wondered if the counselor liked her, and admitted she had been afraid to come in today. She wondered if the counselor was married, and felt that if she knew more about him, he would be less threatening. "You're a man, a good-looking man, and my whole problem is men like you. It would be easier if you were 'elderly'—easier, but not better, in the long run." She was very upset and embarrassed after she said this, and wondered how long it took before a client could fully trust a counselor. "It's like being naked—I'm so revealed to you, and you're so unknown to me." Mrs. Teral had now confronted the therapist with her feelings about him in a very honest and direct way. It made her uncomfortable, but also brought relief and intimacy.

Fifteenth Interview

She began by talking about time. "It always seemed so fleeting to me. Now a minute seems like an amount in which I can get something done." She remembered always getting up late for school, and then said: "I feel more that I want to use time as I have it rather than waiting until I'm sure there is plenty of it. Somehow, a minute has body to it. It was a second to me. It was a 'one.' Not big enough to use. And an hour was too much. I could never do enough to use up a whole hour." Mrs. Teral turned again to an exploration of attitudes toward sex, and "her concept of men." She had never seen her father naked, but once she saw a man urinating on the street; another man displayed himself on a streetcar. "I was so shocked, and scared, I stayed home all summer." She feared being raped, also felt suspicious of herself and her desires. It seemed that all men were bad, "out to get you," except Dad, who almost doesn't have a penis. Later, "I wanted to hurt myself, so I started going with men who would hurt me—with their penis. I enjoyed it, and was being hurt, so I had the satisfaction of being punished for my enjoyment at the same time." She felt very much ashamed of her enjoyment of sex. Her two sisters, the neat, respected daughters, could not have orgasms, "So *again* I was the bad one." Suddenly she asked, "Or am I really lucky?" Beauty has always been equated with goodness for her. She felt bad and saw herself as ugly. She still thought herself plain, but possibly attractive. She believed she might be likeable, but not lovable, and thought she might become promiscuous had she been more attractive. She felt that her husband did not consider her pretty and that he was holding out for the same ideal of beauty she held, which made her lot all the harder.

Eighteenth Interview

The stress of impending termination was apparent. Mrs. Teral said, truculently, that she still had tremendous problems, but didn't want to talk anymore. She had gone far, she said, but not far enough. She asked for a drink of water; then asserted that she would now go home. Sarcastically she asked if that would be "all right for the damned research." When the counselor reflected her feeling of anger and resentment, she said she was not being honest, and wouldn't dare to be, for fear of his disapproval. "I don't want to talk about it, I'm just running away from it. I feel like number 20349." The counselor said, "You feel that I don't care anything about you as a person." Mrs. Teral replied that a teacher should never get emotionally involved with a child, since the two must separate as soon as the child graduates. "That's what is wrong with this," she said.

The counselor replied: "You mean it's like giving you something, then taking it away—having to say good-bye before you are ready makes you feel unwanted?" "Exactly," she said. Having been understood, Mrs. Teral asked herself, "Do I really want more time, or do I just resent not having the choice? I know I wouldn't stop now if I didn't have to. I feel awful." She watched the clock for a while, said our time was up, and left after saying good-bye.

Nineteenth Interview

Mrs. Teral postponed her regular appointment, delaying the termination. Some important themes in the next-to-last interview are summarized:

It upset me to miss the appointment; showed me how meaningful therapy is, how dependent I feel.
Last interview, I was hurt, indignant, self-pitying. I wish I could have told you then and there.
I'd like to go on, on my own. I feel that you'd take me back if I needed more help. I know not all my problems are solved, though.
I have, and need to have, faith in myself.
I have felt I was making headway only because I was able to talk to you. I need to know that I can make it on my own.
I brought a friend in today to see about the possibility of therapy for her.
I talked with my husband about things I've wanted to discuss for a long time.
It might take a lot longer to work through my sexual problems completely. At first, I was so afraid I couldn't finish, I didn't dare to start.
I would almost like for this to be the last interview, for I have nearly closed off things. I'm afraid to have that "unfinished feeling."

Mrs. Teral had been preparing herself for the separation—by talking to her husband, by considering the value of independence, by recognizing the incompleteness of her therapy, and by making plans to continue personal growth. At the same time, she hesitated to open any new areas. She showed some confidence in therapy by bringing a friend, and in the therapist by expressing the belief that he would not refuse to see her if she returned for help at a later time.

Twentieth Interview

Important themes in the last interview are summarized:

[Enters laughing.] I did want to come, after all.
It has always been my way to say that if I can't finish something, I'll just give up. Any gains I did make, I'd just lose—felt I hadn't done any-

thing, not even what I'd *done*. Now I've done a lot, and I have hopes that I'll be able to move forward.

I think I've hit the basic things—not everything but the substance, and I feel good enough about myself that I can go on thinking *for* myself.

I see myself now as a good, worthwhile person, but still *react* sometimes with old feelings of a no-good person. Those feelings still influence me.

I'm changing more slowly than I want, but I know I'll go on changing.

Last week, I was so disgusted with myself, my self-pity and sulking that I just decided to stop it. I got down and scrubbed the floors. For the first time, I'm ready in advance for company coming tonight.

I feel so delighted to have come to know myself. Will I go on learning more, alone?

I didn't force myself to come back and say I'm happy—usually I can't bear to say good-bye, I really feel this way.

I'm not subservient to you any more. If I need to come back, I have the right to ask for more time. You might not have it, but I can ask.

I'm a person, with the right to disagree with you or anyone else, and to have my own opinions.

I've been reading, and enjoying it so. Now that I have the right to make decisions, I love to read; it's worthwhile to read. The time I used to spend sleeping I now spend reading.

"Well, that's it. Time to go?" Asked Mrs. Teral at the end of the interview. "Yes," replied the counselor, "and I want to say that you can call me or communicate anytime, and that the door isn't being slammed behind you." Mrs. Teral's last words were: "If something comes up and I have to see you, I'll call." They said good-bye.

A Review

In twenty interviews Mrs. Teral had accomplished much. Early in therapy the focus moved from past to present, and soon thereafter to immediate relations with significant people, including the therapist. Even later, when she returned to recollections of sexual episodes, the main value of the hours seemed to be direct confrontation of the painful embarrassment and shame, rather than the relating of any specific experience.

The emphasis changed quickly from others and their doings to self-explorations, and also from remembered feelings to directly experienced ones. These are changes to be expected in therapy; they seemed to be accelerated in this time-limited course.

Some Measures of Change

Considering the presenting problems, much movement may be observed. Mrs. Teral stopped smoking midway through therapy, as a test of her will. She no longer slept to escape life. Instead, she spent the time reading (with great enjoyment), which she had been unable to do, or taking a bath, which she had formerly felt too unworthy to do. She worked more effectively than before, particularly in her home. She felt that she knew herself fairly well, with prospects of knowing still better the person she had come to be, and found that person no longer ugly, certainly not unknown, but moderately attractive, and likeable.

A follow-up interview two years after termination found all these gains maintained. Mrs. Teral said she would like to have continued therapy, but that she felt at worst interrupted rather than deprived, and at best, given a great momentum toward continued growth. Now she was so pre-occupied and happy with her family (a daughter was born, ending her fears of barrenness) that she could not take time away from it, though she had a great respect for therapy as a helpful experience. Relations with her husband had been both better and worse, and certainly more intense. Indifference was no longer a problem.

Did Mrs. Teral profit according to the criterion described by Taft, learning to live in the allotted time, and using it in such a way that she may be said to have grasped the principle of living? There is evidence that to some extent she did. Her awareness of time and the limits of the treatment showed as early as the fourth interview, and again in the seventh. There, and in the tenth interview, she seemed to feel the limits as pressure. In interview fifteen, her attitudes toward time were those of one who could use what was available without greed or despair about the amount. In the eighteenth interview, she struggled with the problem of limitations in the relationship (separation) rather than with time. In her final interview, she seemed to be ready to say good-bye, satisfied that her experience, though incomplete, had for her the full value it deserved. To a large degree, Mrs. Teral may be said to have come to terms, by meeting the limits, with time, and with some basic problems of time and limits in life.

Of the many research instruments, one outcome measure can be reported here. That is the self-ideal correlation. The method has been described and validated in previous research.[13] Stated simply, the correlation measures the degree to which one feels himself to be a person he desires to be. The higher the correlation, the greater the degree of congruence and comfort. To illustrate the change in Mrs. Teral, her scores are compared with those of a previously mentioned case, that of Mrs. Oak, who voluntarily terminated after forty interviews. (Both clients were rated "8" by their counselors on a nine-point scale of success.) The self-

---

[13] J. M. Butler and G. V. Haigh, "Changes in the Relation Between Self-concepts and Ideal Concepts Consequent upon Client-centered Counseling," in C. R. Rogers and R. Dymond (eds.), *Psychotherapy and Personality Change* (Chicago: University of Chicago Press, 1954).

ideal correlation is administered at pretherapy, after seven interviews, at the end of therapy, and six to twelve months after termination. The clients are plotted in Figure 1 against a scale showing the range of self-idea correlations, so that the extent of change is easily seen and compared. Mrs. Teral began therapy with a "score" of —.26, a considerable

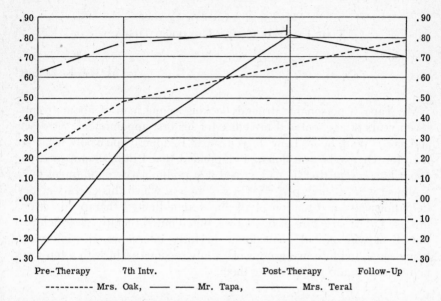

FIGURE 1. *Self-Ideal Correlations Through Therapy. For Mrs. Oak (40 interviews), Mrs. Teral (20 interviews), and Mr. Tapa (38 interviews).*

disparity between her perceived self and desired self. After seven interviews, she moved to +.26, and at the end of therapy, to .82, a very high degree of congruence. Her follow-up level dropped to .70, which is not a significant decrease. Mrs. Oak started with a .21, a low level of congruence, though not so disparate as Mrs. Teral's, and moved after seven interviews to .47, and at post-therapy to .70. Her follow-up level increased to .79. Both cases were highly successful, according to this measure. Mrs. Teral achieved as much or more measured gain in half the time.

A Caution

The presentation of the successful case does not intend a recommendation for arbitrarily terminated therapy. Like most innovations in therapy, this one must be thoughtfully explored for both values and flaws. Particularly, the therapist must be prepared emotionally to use this tool, for if it is imposed simply as a mechanical salvation for the overworked clinician, it may be useless, or even destructive. Used with a real acceptance of limitations on the part of the therapist, and with intelligence and good will, it may be, as it seems to have been for Mrs. Teral and her counselor, an experience to grow on.

CASE II

MR. TAPA: A CASE OF LONGER TIME-LIMITED, CLIENT-CENTERED THERAPY

— MADGE K. LEWIS[14]

Mr. Tapa, a personable, friendly-looking young man of about twenty-seven years of age, entered my office for his first appointment, sat down, and said, "Well, hello. How do you start? I suppose you know what I'm here for. Or maybe you don't." I responded that I didn't know anything about him except that he had agreed in a preliminary appointment to be a subject in a research project. The research in which this client was participating was an extension of the brief time-limited therapy described in Case I. The structure of this longer time-limited therapy was such that the client was offered a maximum of forty interviews, the interviews being separated into two groups of twenty sessions each, with a ten-week non-therapy interval separating them.

Presenting Problems

Mr. Tapa felt that there was a lack of continuity about his life, a "drifting along with the tide" that left him with the feeling that he didn't have life well in hand. Things just *happened* to him. He had a vague sense of dissatisfaction, but he didn't know with what. "Disorganization keeps cropping up in my life," he said. He felt that he should be leading a different kind of life, or looking at life differently, with more command or thoughtfulness of what he was doing.

His first marriage had gone badly, and had ended in divorce when his wife had left him for another man. Now, he was eager to marry another girl; but problems that had been present in his first marriage were beginning to crop up again. He felt a painful dependency on his new girl friend, a fluctuation in himself caused by her moods, which upset him very much. He wished he could drain his feelings out somewhere else and not impose them on her.

---

[14] A.B. and M.A., U. of Southern Calif., 1938, '40; Instr., Long Beach, Calif., Publ. Schls., '40-'42; Instr., Corona, Calif. Publ. Schls., '42-'44; USNR (WR), '45-'46; Counselor and Instr., Long Beach, Calif. Publ. Schls., '46-'54; Staff Research Counselor, U. of Chicago, '57– ; Ph.D., U. of Chicago, '59.

T: You can't let her know.

C: In a way, you're right. Very good. Yes—I can't tell her how this makes me feel without doing exactly what I'm trying to avoid doing [*i.e.*, imposing his problems on her].

This led him to realize that perhaps he was not giving her credit enough for being understanding. Then he went on to a consideration of the quality of his relationship with her.

C: I try hard to be perfect with her—cheerful, friendly, intelligent, talkative —because I want her to love me. It's as simple as that.

T: This is the way you feel you must be in order to be loved by her.

This interchange led to his feelings of not knowing what she liked about him nor of knowing what he really was.

C: I'm not being me; I'm being directed by what I think she expects of me— which is probably completely wrong. I don't know what I look like from her position. I probably never will know, but it's as if all of this I *have* to know. I must make sure I won't be rejected.

This was the beginning of many expressions on his part of not feeling genuine and of playing roles he felt were expected of him and which he thought would please pople, but which induced in him feelings of being "totally artificial."

C: I can feel myself smiling sweetly the way my mother does, or being gruff and important the way my father does sometimes—slipping into everyone else's personalities but mine. . . . I've been aware of things about myself I dislike, but I've never known what to do with them.

When he was young, he had problems about honesty, and had lied and stolen things. He was lazy at school and at home. This caused his father to tell him to sit down and think about himself, and to do something about himself. This had brought about a complete blank.

C: How do you *do* something about yourself—a hopeless feeling. How *can* you—this is the way I *am*. So *many* things I couldn't tell people—nasty things I did. . . . felt so sneaky and bad."

He had felt that he had to have someone to talk to before he'd be able to do anything about it; yet he couldn't talk to his parents because he knew they wouldn't understand, and he couldn't talk to a stranger because he was so afraid.

T: You felt like a bad boy—not knowing what to do about it all by yourself and needing help.

He explored some of the ways in which he experienced people during his childhood and youth. He had a poor opinion of people then; they all had an idea of how he should behave and no one thought he was being the way he ought to be. He felt that they were stupid because they couldn't understand how much information he needed about "how the world works" and about sex. They weren't answering his questions, or they wouldn't give answers *he* could understand. This made him feel stupid, so he withdrew from them, and got his revenge by lying awake at night fantasying tearing limb from limb his father, mother, other relatives, or any stupid-looking person he happened to think of. He fought doing this, but couldn't control it until he was fourteen years of age.

Second Interview

Mr. Tapa reported that he had been able to tell his girl friend that he hadn't trusted her enough to tell her some of his feelings about their relationship, and that in so telling her had "felt more like me." During this interview he revealed more problems that bothered him in his daily life. Relationships with his colleagues were unsatisfactory; he felt unhappy and dissatisfied with his job and couldn't make a decision as to whether or not he should continue college work on the graduate level, partly because he doubted his ability and partly because he didn't want to. This led to the uncovering of his own lack of confidence in himself.

C: I feel I can't ever do anything right—can't ever finish it.

He expressed it as a feeling that the world was too complicated for him and that if he *did* succeed, this would only call forth more and more effort in a way to which he would eventually not be able to respond. He felt very much squeezed by external pressure. Part of the pressure was a sense of being compelled to do something great, something important; yet at the same time the idea of succeeding was frightening to him. Further explorations revealed that he had very little notion of what was realistic as far as his own ability was concerned. He set up high goals which he could not reach and found himself incapable of thinking up projects which were simpler. In the past he had enjoyed some success in a creative effort, but his creativity now was turned off. He analyzed part of his difficulty to be that of having a lot of ideas without the ability to develop any of them. But on the other hand he was not willing to settle for this picture of himself because he felt that there were times when he *did* feel competent and inventive. In his seachings on this point, he indicated the difficulty of the process.

C: You see, I don't even *really* know what the right question is to ask myself about this. I seem to be missing a point somewhere. There's some subtlety about this that will put a different light on it.
T: As if there's some hidden answer you can't find.
C: Yeah, guess that may be an illusion too. Maybe that's the way I hide it from myself. Well, *maybe—maybe*—what the hell! That's a good way of avoiding something. A good way of glossing over the right answer—put a "maybe" in front of it.

T: To put a maybe in front of a "hidden answer" is a way of glossing over the fact that it may not be hidden.

C: Well, that's obviously important because my mind has slowed down and stopped. [*Laughs.*] The ultimate defense—you grind to a halt. The hidden answer—dredge it out of my subconscious—*maybe—maybe.* [*Laughs.*]

T: You want to laugh at this "maybe."

C: Yes, I find myself sticking it in front of anything significant; it amuses me. Why? Oh, because it's a little stupid of me—and I feel a little tense about it, or a little embarrassed—and a little helpless. [His voice softens and his face looks sad.] Humor has been my bulwark all my life; maybe it's a little out of place in trying to really look at myself. A curtain to pull down.

T: Something to hide behind.

C: I feel a little naked and unprotected from you without it. Here I am sticking out all over.

T: Sort of embarrassing—and almost hating to show without this curtain of safety.

C: It's easy to give an impression of confidence when you don't feel it—almost as easy as when you do feel it.

T: It's easy to pretend.

C: The way I'd like this to go would be to sit down and think soberly about my problems, clearly and accurately—put my finger on them and let one thing lead to another; and there are some things where that works just fine. With others it doesn't work at all.

T: You'd like it to go honestly, simply, and logically.

C: I wish I were as honest as I can sound. . . . I feel sort of at a loss right now. Where was I? What was I saying? I lost my grip on something—that I've been holding myself up with.

Mr. Tapa was surprised to uncover extremes in himself. On the one hand he had expectations of doing something great; yet on the other he felt he might very easily end up a "bum."

C: What I actually do goes on in an even keel between. . . . Maybe I'm waving my arms to keep my balance.

Further exploration led to the insight that whether he kept his balance or not was up to him.

C: No one can really decide what I am to do and what I am to like and what my standards are going to be—no one can decide that. . . . I *have* to make a living—or *do* I? I don't *have* to. . . . Who's going to tell me?

T: You *do* have choices.

Then he saw that he might be exaggerating the pressure; that while people did expect something, they didn't expect very much, and that the pressure he felt was something he had internalized and was using on himself. During this interview, his self-concept emerged a little more clearly. He saw himself as fearful of the future, not quite believing he could ever do what he professed to be able to do. In his work, he could see the logical way to proceed, but also the difficulties and the time in-

330 CLIENT-CENTERED PSYCHOTHERAPY

volved; and he became bored before he ever got started. He said, in disgust at himself:

C: Gosh! As long as I keep doing that, I'll be crippled in my work.

Then he became aware of another feeling—that he really wasn't able to *do* the work.

C: . . . not knowing enough—learning—something about learning. That if I don't already know it, then I can't learn it. That it's too late—or beyond me.
T: You *should* have learned it by now.
C: *Should have*—another sign of my guilt. There are guilt feelings involved here that I hadn't realized. I feel as if I'm bamboozling people I work for because I don't know these things. I feel they expect me to.
T: You're a fraud.
C: I'm a fake. Then I start *really* being a fake.

Third and Fourth Interview

Mr. Tapa explored again his feelings about his girl friend. He had talked to her about getting married and had found her to be very uncertain of her own mind in regard to him. He felt "clutchy and possessive" when he was with her and was afraid of her being so overwhelmed that she might run away from him altogether. In this way he saw his resemblance to his mother who grasped and possessed, and tried hard not to, and failed utterly. This in his mother he recognized as dependence on others, even on him. This led to a consideration of his own dependency in his adolescence and in his first marriage.

Fifth Interview

Mr. Tapa was concerned with his increasing feelings of hostility. He had had a big blow-up with his girl friend, which had revealed to him a depth of anger within himself of which he had been unaware. Anger with his wife and his mother had elicited a cold, brooding hostility that went on for days. My reflection that he had been punished effectively when he expressed anger at them caused him to realize that his girl friend did not seem to punish him in this way. This brought echoes from his childhood. They were memories of

C: . . . being a small boy, and being spanked, and getting madder than hell, and getting punished for *that* but good!

He was taught that the honorable thing to do was to accept punishment if it was deserved without complaining about it. It was wrong to object to it.

C: . . . and I felt guilty for so much of my young life that I expect I felt I deserved to be punished most of the time anyway. If I didn't feel I deserved it for one thing, I felt I deserved it for another.

He felt that guilt had been the foundation-stone of his personality. This is what made him "so nice to everyone."

Seventh Interview

This interview added to his self-concept the experiencing of having patterned himself after both his father and mother. He felt that when he got angry his father's pattern in him would emerge in a compulsive feeling of the necessity of *"doing* something—just *anything"* with a sort of inexorableness. His mother's role, however, had been that of pacifier.

C: I have some of that, too—putting on a pretty face for people—too careful of what others are thinking and feeling. Putting myself out for them—and feeling hostile about doing it. *She* felt hostile about doing it, too; and this came out in painful little ways. I have that in me, too.

The combination of his parents' patterns in himself felt like "going back and forth between mother and father and not being myself." Going still another step in his consideration of his parents' influence, tied in with eventual response to authority of all kinds.

C: I'd feel so damn helpless about it [parents' punishment]. I felt they had complete power over me. . . . Whatever they decided, *that* was going to happen to me—no matter what—even if they decided to send me away.
T: You felt completely in their hands, and this was pretty frightening.
C: My father said he didn't ask much of me—just that I'd obey him. To me, this was the *most* he could ask, not the *least*. I wanted to do what *I* wanted, not what *he* did. . . . Or if I did what he wanted, I wanted it to be because I *wanted* to, not from duty. . . . I responded to authority in the worst possible way. . . . Still do. I was a rebel.

His mother's influence had made him ambivalent about growing up. When she would say, "No matter how big you grow up, you'll always be my little boy," half of him would squirm and say to himself, "How can I tell her I'm *not* going to be," and half would relax comfortably and say, "How nice! I'll never have to grow up." So his mother became a protection that stood between him and growing up; but to keep her protection, he had to keep her pleased, and she was hard to please.

Eighth Interview

Mr. Tapa's relationship with his girl friend improved gradually and they were able to talk freely with each other more and more often about their feelings. He continued to search for more insight into his work problems. He spoke of his tremendous feeling of lassitude when confronted by something that looked like hard work; yet he felt that he wasn't trying to handle more than he could, but rather more than he felt organized to handle. He became aware that "it consumes a whole lot of energy to fulfill the expectations of others."

Ninth Interview

In the ninth interview the client related a dream that had a great deal of significance for him because it brought back "an old dark emotion" from his youth when he liked to do things that were against the law, but felt completely isolated from the rest of society in consequence. The therapist did not interpret the dream for the client, but allowed him to express his own thoughts about it and make his own interpretation. Mr. Tapa felt the dream showed the dark sort of pleasure he had experienced from expressing hostility to people through infractions of the law. There was one figure in the dream that puzzled him—an interested bystander who could have been dangerous because of having seen his "crimes." He decided that *I* was this person. Before this, his relationship with me had been one of easy friendliness and apparent trust; but at this point, he laughed and said, "Oh, all right, I *don't* trust you."

Another part of his dream that puzzled him was the fact that in his attempt to evade "the cops," he ended up "back home only to find that they were there."

C: Oh, sure, the cops were there! Naturally they were!
T: Where else would they be!
C: That's where they came from. Thank goodness, that ties *that* up. That's why I went home, and why they were there. Well, I guess my underground was telling me that *I'm* still afraid of these rules and am trying to get protected from the consequences of living in a society by somehow relying on my parents. . . . As an adult I know differently. . . . The cops aren't very interested in people like me and neither is society.
T: You are more fearful than you need be.
C: Yes. I instilled these fears in myself a long time ago with my hyperactive imagination.

Eleventh Interview

From the eleventh interview on, it became evident that he saw good communication with his girl friend as a crucial means of working out their problems together. Then he began trying to put into words from time to time his experiencing of the therapeutic process. He used to feel that therapy called for action. Experientially, however, it meant talking about ways he felt he *was,* and finding that the feelings, one by one, lost their intensity and dissolved away.

Twelfth Interview

Mr. Tapa said he had a vague feeling that he was sitting on something, but didn't know what. He felt that a lot of his childhood was vague to him now.

C: It was mostly being afraid—angry—feeling as if I wanted to bust loose from something. I'm not living up to what I am. I really should be doing more than I am. How many hours I spent on the john in this position with Mother saying, "Don't come out 'til you've done something." Produce!

T: And your freedom was curtailed until you *did* produce.

C: That happened with lots of things. "You sit there until you've finished that plate." I don't care if you sleep or not, but you're going to lie there for an hour.

T: Forcing you to go through the *outer* signs of producing even when you didn't produce.

His father's attitude was even more forceful.

C: In high school it was, "I don't care whether you study or not, but you're going to sit in front of that desk with a book in front of you; maybe some of it will sink in."

T: A feeling of "You're under my power whether you do anything or not."

C: So I'd sit there and have fantasies of murdering everyone in the whole family—in horrible ways.

T: You had your revenge.

C: But the next day, everything was as usual.

T: It wasn't *real* revenge.

C: I sure wanted revenge. . . . There were so many restrictions. I hated them. . . . felt every one of them was a direct invasion of me. . . . There were injunctions to love and respect—whatever that meant—my parents—to obey them. Every time they said something like that—meant I was their property. . . . I hated them for it.

T: Hated to feel you belonged to anybody.

C: Yeah. I didn't feel I belonged to *them.* I was *mine!* Every time they treated me like property, I *became* like property.

Then he would fantasy finding a long lost friend who would beat up his parents and say, "There! Don't you ever mistreat your child again." His parents would issue an order such as, "Don't go downhill on your scooter."

C: So I did. So I got my scooter taken away from me. So I said, "I don't want my scooter any more. Keep it!"

T: You were trying to tell them, "You can't buy me!"

C: 'Course, I'd always relent because actually I wanted my scooter back.

T: You let them buy you.

C: Yeah. I gave in. Childhood was one long process of giving in.

T: They beat you all the time.

C: And so often the reason they won was that they were *bigger*—not that they *knew* more. . . . It was their size.

T: You felt overwhelmed by their size.

C: Yeah. I was thrust into a world of giants—with no rights. I had to learn how to please them—fool them. I learned how to make them think I loved them.

T: You learned to fool them and to pretend.

C: Yeah, and it carried over into school where they wanted me to do things I didn't know how to do and was afraid to do. . . . I gave the impression of knowing how to do it: paid attention out of the corner of one ear, read the book quick, passed the exam, and got a good grade.

T: That's why and where you learned to bluff.

C: Yeah. I learned to bluff because I reflected the values they were thrusting on me, not because of the values, but because of the methods they used. . . . The people I learned to respect and like were those who never threatened me with anything. I didn't feel they were trying to gain control of me. . . . Rebellion means: keep away from me—don't touch me— I don't want to have anything to do with you. It's not selective at all. It's thrusting away everything indiscriminately.

T: A desperation measure.

C: A last resort. I'll build my wall now—and that's that!

Thirteenth Interview

Mr. Tapa wondered if improving himself was really the goal of therapy.

C: Maybe that isn't the point of therapy at all. I feel sort of discouraged and flat now.

T: You thought you had a reason, and now you haven't. . . .

C: I think that when I find what I need to do, it's going to hurt. I feel stopped right now. Why is my mind blank right now? I feel as if I'm hanging onto something, and I've been letting go of other things; and something in me is saying, "What more do I have to give up? You've taken so much from me already." This is *me* talking to *me*—the *me* way back in there who talks to *me* who runs the show. It's complaining now—saying, "You're getting too close—go away!"

T: How much more is going to be demanded? How much more am I going to hurt?

C: Yeah. I'm afraid of being ordinary. Yet I'm afraid this is what is asked of me.

T: You want to be different and you want to—

C: [*Breaking in*] I want to live a life I can enjoy. . . . And the kind of life that seems to be offered to the average man is not to me enjoyable. Sitting and watching television five nights a week. Alternating television with movies.

T: You're not contented with the lot that most people have.

C: No! I hate it!

T: Something better, and something more exciting—

C: That's right! But I don't know how to *get* it. That's the trouble. I feel bound—by something or other—it must be *me!* [*Laughs.*] There's nothing else that seems to be doing it. I can't blame it on anything else. But there's this *knot*—somewhere inside of me.

T: Feel tied up by something in you that's kind of a mystery to you.

C: Yeah! Makes me want to get mad—and cry—and run away.

T: Lots of mixed-up feelings about it.

C: Yeah. Also feel I never can get at it the way I've been trying to get at it. . . . It's as if I can't put my attention on it.

T: Like a blind spot.

C: Yeah. I can see effects in my life I don't like; yet I can't see their cause. I must be deliberately blinding myself because it would be painful to know. But what could it be?

T: What could it be that might cause me so much hurt?

C: Yeah. Do I think I'm a failure—a ruined human being—or something of the sort? It must be something like that. That I don't feel worthy—of anything.

T: Am I a flop—completely unworthy of *any* kind of good life?

C: Yeah. I mean, is this what the feeling is? I've got too much of a conscious mind now; it makes too much noise. My conscious mind tells me I'm worthy . . . but some place inside I don't believe it. I think I'm a rat—a no-good. I've no faith in my ability to do anything. . . . Usually this is quiet; I'm able to do things anyhow, but it's like slogging through mud. I have enough energy to do something, but it's like a broken shoe-lace—always on your mind until you get it fixed.

T: On one level you're able to go ahead and get things done and pretend you're okay, but that underneath—

C: Yeah. Put it this way. I can work extremely well on a mediocre level—at mediocre things.

T: But underneath is the feeling you can't do anything better than mediocrity and—

C: Yeah. There's two possibilities. One is that this feeling is true—and that somewhere inside is a pretty good evaluation of myself and my abilities; and it says—"Don't push too hard; don't try to go too far, settle for less; don't try for all these things you're trying to do!" . . . I don't know if that's the voice of wisdom or defeatism.

T: M-hm. That's *one* voice you're hearing.

C: Yeah. And that this is the urge. It seems that there's so much fear in it—it *can't* be right.

T: You don't want to listen to *that* voice!

C: I don't want it to be right. Damn! Damn! Damn! [*Strongly*] I *know* it can't be right!—because I've never worked hard in my life at anything, and this is the voice that keeps me from working hard at anything. . . . It takes very little effort to do anything on a mediocre level. The problem is tackling it. . . . I seem to be afraid of working hard. What is keeping me from working hard? . . .

T: I guess you feel the voice *isn't* right about you because things have been pretty easy for you without you're half trying—

C: That's right—as long as I don't try to—to go—too high—fly too high. . . . Somewhere inside there's a voice that says "You can't do it." I'm tired of that voice; it's been around all my life. I've got to do something about it. . . .

T: M-hm. Good and sick of having it around—

C: Yeah. I don't know what to do about it, but I've *got* to do *something* about it. Well, that's a good place to stop! Have a wrestling match with myself the rest of the week. [Collects cigarettes and matches.]

Fourteenth and Fifteenth Interviews

Mr. Tapa fitted together some more pieces into the picture of himself that was emerging in therapy. He felt that he wasn't a changing, moving, developing person, but the little boy he used to be. This little boy had felt that above all else he was bad; yet, in a way, he had been almost crying out to be caught.

C: Please catch me—and let me pour out all the things I've done; let me get rid of them.
T: Won't someone listen to all my guilt and make me feel better?
C: I wanted someone to catch me doing the most terrible things, so that then I could confess the others, and they wouldn't seem so bad. Boy, I felt bad in those days! [*With a deep sigh*] Just a bad boy. So dishonest and deceitful and so caught in it, as though once I started I couldn't stop.
T: Nothing to do but keep on being bad.
C: And there was the fear of admitting things because of punishment. . . . And there was a terrible amount of resentment . . . that society demanded its revenge—in a cold way. That was my father—justice and revenge. . . . I seem to be jumping around, but it's all connected. Me not changing—with this picture of myself as a child—which is still very much with me.

He felt increasingly free in having and showing emotions. He was rather tentative in saying this, and went on to explore this area a little.

C: I also see that . . . I must be alert as to what's inside me.
T: It's important for you to be clear about your feelings. To *really* feel them.
C: Yeah. And not to distrust them all the time. You see, I've been going on the basis of what's "right" and what I felt I *had* to do; and what I *felt* like doing was irrelevant . . . I got to be an expert at ignoring my emotions.
T: Saying "no" to a part of yourself you had learned to feel was wrong.
C: Yeah. Got to be good at it. Now that the intensity of the emotions is toned down to a point where I no longer feel violently angry at somebody . . . that what's left is not so intensely hostile towards everybody and everything, I feel I can start integrating with them.
T: Less explosive and more safe now.
C: Less explosive because I'm not holding them back so hard.

Then he saw a conflict within himself: wanting to be certain of outcomes and often being successful in taking chances.

C: Failing at something is too damned important to me. I need to learn to take in stride a few whopping failures. When I do fail, it's a blow; but fundamentally, I don't really mind. There's a surface feeling of humiliation and "am I really worth anything?", but this belongs to an old habit pattern; and fundamentally I don't really mind—and bounce back—no matter how bad I felt. And that's *really* me—that's what I'm *really* like.

T: I can *count* on bouncing back.
C: But the surface is active enough to interfere with these deeper feelings.
T: It really is upsetting to fail. . . .
C: I've been over-generalizing about failure. I've been over-extending the con- clusion—taking generalities from one incident and applying it to the whole me—the rest of my life. . . .
T: One little failure has such a significant meaning for you.
C: And the thing is, it doesn't *really;* in some ways it almost seems as if I *ought* to be very concerned about failure—so I go ahead and get disturbed about it.
T: You feel an obligation to be disturbed.
C: Yeah. It's expected of me. . . .
T: You were expected to feel something very different from what you *were* feeling.
C: Yeah. It's going to take some living with, but I think I can get this straightened out.

In a movie, he had seen two characters who had impressed him greatly because he felt they had real integrity and were doing what they wanted to do.

C: That's the sort of thing I'm after—just me—not what other people think of me. I'll be the way I choose to be. By God, I have a right to. Well, I'm getting onto that now. That's one of the feelings that led me into therapy —the feeling that you have to be a very good person—you have to be the right kind of person in order to create a good impression in other people— in order to be a successful human being—and sort of gradually realizing that whatever kind of person I am is pretty much up to me. . . . If I'm really myself, I suppose there'll be somebody that will like me [*uncertain laugh*].
T: If I'm really myself, that *should* be good enough.
C: If I can say what I feel and what I think [*excitedly*], then maybe I can feel and think better. . . .

Approaching the First Termination

A large part of the sixteenth interview was devoted by Mr. Tapa to a summary of his therapeutic experience and his feelings of greater comfort. After a while, however, he began to be a little suspicious of what he was doing. He felt that remaining problems might be very difficult to reach and that his behavior at this point was a way of "talking away from them" by conveying an impression to himself and to me that he wasn't greatly troubled any longer.

The ten-week interval in therapy demanded by the research design occurred after the nineteenth interview. It seemed as if the client was gradually preparing for this period by a sort of weaning process. He talked of material that he had brought up before, always a little differently, but with, perhaps, a lack of the freedom and openness that had characterized his therapy up to this point. Almost his only reference

to the coming separation was one about wondering how it would feel
not to be coming in to see me twice a week. He did know, however, that
if he needed to see me, he could.

Twentieth Interview

During the ten-week non-therapy interval, Mr. Tapa and his girl friend
were married. In the interview following the first termination, he described a way he had developed as a child of "changing subjects" in his
mind. It began as a voluntary experience. For example, if he were
criticized in a way he felt he deserved to be, he pushed back the sense
of realization and turned off the whole subject.

C: The result was that I sort of wanted things blindly, without self-awareness
   that was a *critical* self-awareness. I think I still do that—very hard to find it
   because there are hidden things.
T: You consciously pushed things you didn't like away from you, and then
   approached the problem with all of that missing.
C: That's right—forgot all about it. . . . If I hadn't turned it off, I would
   have felt very uncomfortable and extremely guilty; but I avoided feeling
   guilty simply by avoiding feeling at all. I can almost recapture it.
T: The same feeling now.
C: Yes—how it felt to turn those things off, in a sense a definite little effort—
   I can almost feel how it felt to make that effort—a sense of pressure of the
   thing pushing back—and a sort of hot sensation—something in here [*hand
   on chest*]—you know—tightening. It was accompanied, too, by a sort of
   desperate feeling that "I can't deal with this—I have to forget it—I have to
   get it out of my mind or it will bother me and go on bothering me—I'll
   have to do something I don't want to do."
T: Consciously and deliberately pushing this away—turning it off so that you
   wouldn't feel it inside and wouldn't have to deal with your feelings.

Twenty-second Interview

During the twenty-second interview he expressed some hostility toward
me for not giving him more active help. This led to an exploration of his
feelings of dependency.

C: Vague thoughts in back of my head are about relying on other people.
   I've gotten the idea that I can't rely on anyone other than myself.
T: You can't *really* trust anybody.

He told with increasing anger in his voice of once having been in obvious
trouble without receiving any help from people.

T: Makes you furious—people see—but won't help. . . .
C: Every now and then the thought crosses my mind—maybe some day you'll
   make a comment on my case—very helpful—break the tie—I'll feel helped—
   sort of active help.

T: You're feeling angry with me for not giving you more active help.

C: *If* you were to see something about my case—and wouldn't give me that interpretation.

T: That I might have this secret knowledge—that I wouldn't be willing to share with you so that you would be helped by it.

C: Yeah. Every time I felt therapy is dragging—I was not getting at things I want to get at. Every time it's happened, I felt it dragged on purpose. Felt that I was waiting for something to happen—probably for you to push the magic button. Part of what I'm feeling now is that I'm so very much on my own—and so inadequate to do it. . . . It would be nice to have some positive goals to aim for in therapy.

T: Feeling alone in this and wishing somebody could give you a push forward.

Later in this interview, he returned to this material.

C: . . . intellectually, I'm not really resenting you, though I feel dependent partially because I feel I got in over my head and "help, help," you know. . . . It discourages me to feel dependent because it means I'm kind of hopeless about myself. . . . Maybe I'm still being dependent—waiting for someone to guide me—show me what's right . . . see me through—this would make for discouragement and hopelessness.

T: Your very *wanting* to be independent, and sort of going all out to *be* independent may be a kind of reversal of what you're *really* feeling—sort of hopelessly dependent and unable to find your way.

C: Yeah. That's right! It's a circle . . . being dependent—and feeling the dangers of being so dependent—I try not to be—which doesn't work. You can't do it that way. You can't just oppose it. You have to go on the other side, so to speak, and undo it—which is a different matter. Very hard to keep straight what you're doing, and which side of the fence you're really on—opposing it, or undoing it.

He felt that he had not unraveled his dependency needs, but that he was trying to be independent forcefully instead of trying to understand his real feelings about them.

Twenty-fourth Interview

In terms of explorations and insights, interview twenty-four seemed to be a very significant one. During the week, Mr. Tapa had been aware of little thoughts that went flitting by. To hold onto these thoughts was like trying to "catch butterflies," he said. "You catch a quick flutter— but if you look, it's more than just a flutter. You have to be pretty alert." He felt that these thoughts went on all the time and that he was becoming more sensitive to them.

C: I think I'm feeling a little threatened by this concept, having put my finger on it.

T: There's something significant about the idea of these tiny thoughts being so important.

He felt he was looking at the source of a lot of secret thoughts about himself, thoughts he had sat on and pushed away.

C: I'm just sitting here staring right at it—a pretty deep well—with my eyes out of focus.

He had a frightened feeling of not wanting to see these things.

C: The butterflies are the thoughts closest to the surface. Underneath there's a deeper flow. I feel very removed from it all. The deeper flow is like a great school of fish moving under the surface. I see the ones that break through the surface of the water—sitting with my fishing line in one hand, with a bent pin on the end of it—trying to find a better tackle—or better yet a way of diving in. That's the scary thing. The image I get is that I want to be one of the fish myself.

T: You want to be down there flowing along, too.

Shortly after this interchange, he said that the longer he talked, the more he felt as if he were play-acting.

C: I'm kind of uncomfortable—acutely conscious of the inflections of my voice —the way it sounds—the way I'm constructing my sentences—ugh!

T: Something you very much dislike about what you're saying and the way you're saying it.

C: Yeah. It's all so stilted and artificial—striving for effect. Very uncomfortable to try to talk when you're feeling this way—about what you're saying.

T: Nothing can stop you faster than that.

C: Yeah. I have a feeling that what I have to do is leave the vantage points that I have now—from which I look myself over. In a way, being *less* conscious of what I do—*more* spontaneous. Less conscious *in advance*—of what I do. Take more the position of passenger rather than driver. See how things go when they're left alone. It's awful kind of scary—feeling that nobody's at the wheel.

T: Instead of looking on—you sort of participate. Feels like a dangerous trip ahead, nobody in control of it.

C: Yeah. I'm realizing now that I don't know how to let go—nor what I'm trying to let go of, even. That's the trouble. I've gotten sort of advance notice that something is going to happen—might happen. Maybe I just can't do it all of a sudden—just like that—just aimlessly. I don't know what I have hold of—that's why I can't let go. Don't know what I'm holding on to.

T: You've caught a glimpse of something that lies ahead, and it feels uncomfortable and sort of frightening, and you're not sure.

C: Of course, tremendously challenging feeling, too; I mean, I wasn't talking about *that* part of it. But *that's* there, too. Perhaps, this is what I've been— looking for—perhaps *this* is the key to that old freedom.

T: Maybe it's something tremendously important. [*Silence.*]

C: Well, I'm blanking out completely on it now.

T: Having gotten that far, something closes up.

C: I've a feeling I don't know how to get from here to there right now. There's a distance from where I am now to there. It isn't as near as I thought [*softly and sadly*]. There are steps to go through on the way, I guess. . . . This is the trouble—you just can't be spontaneous on purpose. It's something you have to fall into backwards, so to speak.

T: You can't just *will* yourself to be what you want to be.

C: No. That's exactly the opposite of what I'm trying to be in the first place. . . . I have a pretty rigid concept of what's expected of me at work. I'm beginning to think I have a pretty rigid concept of how the whole society

works. That it's a lot looser and more fluid and permissive than I thought.
. . . So far I've been keeping myself on this slope headed upwards by pushing myself along—by inching myself along—by effort. But here come a
certain point where this becomes self-regeneration, and I'm almost there.
I can—I can—gives me a very funny feeling—almost like grief to think of it.
That perhaps this long struggle is finally getting to the point where it's
going to pay off, you know.

T: Almost the feeling of the poignancy of grief, accompanying this—

C: The idea of not having to support my activities by an effort of will all the
time. It's damn tiring.

T: For it to be something that *is*—would be so wonderful.

He noticed that in his relationships with people he found it very hard
to allow himself to express irritation, although he thought he probably
communicated it anyway. He was afraid to "really let go" because he
felt he could be "pretty damn nasty."

C: Maybe getting irrationally irritated is best.

T: Guess you're considering the possibility of *being* the way you feel—and
letting the chips fall where they may.

C: Yeah. . . . The real truth of the matter is that I'm not the sweet, forbearing guy that I try to make out that I am. I get irritated at things. I feel
like snapping at people, and I feel like being selfish sometimes; and I don't
know why I should pretend I'm *not* that way. Perhaps it's because I feel
that so much depends upon not being that way. In a way I feel I can get
things by being nice that I can't get any other way. And if I were to react
just as an ordinary, irritable-type person, that I'd have a lot harder time
making my way through life.

T: Things will be easier for you if you're nice, kind, quiet.

C: Yeah. Uh-huh. "I'm popular," you know. "Everyone likes me!" A disgust-
ing goal—to have everybody like you!

T: You don't like the sound of that.

C: It does smooth the path for a lot of things, but I don't think it's worthwhile. It probably didn't impress people as much as I think it does, in the
first place. Maybe I've been giving myself too much credit for knowing
how to be forbearing and understanding.

T: Wondering if you're putting too much of a value on "niceness."

As therapy proceeded, he felt his adjustment increasing, then slipping
away again.

C: Some discouraging days—here I am getting depressed again—doing the
same old things. But the depressions don't last as long—ten minutes, thirty
minutes.

T: Actually—a pendulum swinging a little less intensely. . . .

C: Yeah. Pendulum is a very good way of describing it. . . . I guess what
I'm doing is giving a confused progress report. I'm saying that I've made
progress, but it's intermittent. Little confusing because it isn't always there.
It goes away and comes back again. It's hard to say I have changed in such
and such ways, because I've changed different ways on different days. It
isn't progress—because that's going from here to there. . . . But this is like
going from one shape into another—neither shape has any particular value—

except that one doesn't seem to work very well. . . . And I can't stop at any one point and say, "Well, this shape represents progress." . . . The most I can say about it is, "Well, it's different in these ways: a little more intense—longer in between depressions, and shorter in between happiness. And I like it! I like the way it's going, but I couldn't give you an objective analysis." . . . Also another thing about the change in shape—that I'm not changing from *me* into something else over there, which is the way I have been thinking of it. I'm changing from *me* to *me*. More like being an amoeba than a caterpillar-butterfly. The amoeba changes shape, but it's still an amoeba—made of the same stuff.

T: It's still very much and uniquely *you*.

C: In a way, that's sort of a relief you know. . . .

T: It's sort of a relief to know you're not going to have to get acquainted with a stranger.

C: Yeah. I'm not going to have to abandon me. I've spent a good portion of my life defending me. . . . I've felt vaguely guilty about this. But in therapy, my ego isn't being attacked at all by you. . . . Although it's a little frightening to have the full responsibility for *me* thrust into my lap. Also, I can go ahead and defend my ego by tripping over my own defenses —when there's no opposing force. I can find out whether they are really necessary.

T: You can be more aware of them since you don't have to protect them.

C: Yeah. And I can keep the part of me I really like. I don't have to chuck the whole thing—and start all over again.

Thirtieth Interview

In the thirtieth interview he puzzled over the process of his therapy and went in the direction of concluding that there were richer possibilities available to him if he could trust his unconscious processes.

C: In therapy here—what has counted is sitting down and saying, "This is what's bothering me" . . . and play around with it for a while until something gets squeezed out through some emotional crescendo, and the thing is over with—looks different. Even then, I can't tell just exactly what's happened. It's just that I exposed something and shook it up and turned it around; and when I put it back, it felt better. It's a little frustrating because I'd like to know exactly what's going on.

T: That even to you who have experienced it, it's a kind of mystery.

C: . . . All I can really say is that it does work that way.

T: The reasons are not obvious.

C: No. That's right. This is a funny thing because it feels as if I'm not doing anything at all about it . . . the only *active* part I take is to—to be alert and grab a thought as it's going by. . . .

T: Just being aware of what's in your own mind and feelings.

C: That's right! Simply bringing it to the point where it's talkable about. But once I've done that, I've always had the feeling I should *do* something with it. You know—here it is—both hands full.

T: That there must be some kind of action to follow the experiencing of the feeling.

C: Yeah. Well, here's—I've discovered an attitude of mind that bothers me—a feeling that bothers me—that I don't like. I've managed to state it very clearly—at least, in my own terms—clear to me. And there's a sort of a feeling—well, now—what will I do with it—now that I've seen it—right? There's no—there's no handles on it you can adjust—or anything. Just talk about it awhile, and let it go. And apparently that's all there is to it. Leaves me with a somewhat unsatisfied feeling, though—a feeling that I haven't accomplished anything. It's been accomplished without my knowledge or consent or anything.

T: It's been easier than you expected it to be, and that's disappointing to you.

C: I don't play as much a conscious part in it as I felt that I should.

T: You expected to be *doing* something.

C: That's right. I think part of the trouble is that I don't quite trust my unconscious workings yet.

T: If it happens this easily and without as much of my *conscious* self functioning as I expected, then I'd better watch out—because I can't trust my *unconscious*.

C: Well, no! The point is, I'm not sure of the quality of the readjustment because I didn't get to see it—to check on it. I don't know what happened inside me; so I don't know exactly what the results will be. All I can do is observe the facts—that I look at things a little differently and am less anxious—by a long shot, a lot more active. Things are looking up in general. I'm very happy with the way things have gone. But I feel sort of like a spectator. [*Laughs.*] It is as if there are things going on inside my mind that are important and may affect the way I do things, but over which I don't have any control. Feel a little bit cheated that I don't. Maybe it's this old business of my ego again. I can see how I've spent a lot of effort in trying to make myself a more definite character in other people's eyes—different, stronger, and so forth. And I can see how this has led me into a lot of traps.

T: It sounds as if you're saying, "When I *do* try to change for certain people in a conscious kind of way, then it doesn't always feel too good."

C: Well, yeah. It feels false in the first place. Anything I try to be—and the fact that I can feel myself trying, automatically makes it feel false. I know that it's false. It isn't spontaneous. . . .

He expressed the feeling that his conscious and unconscious selves were rivals; he knew that he depended on his unconscious mind all the time.

C: It's where I get all my ideas from. Things come popping into my head. Something in me has been working on them and thinking about them—putting pieces together and arriving at answers, and I have had very little to do with it. On that creative level I get along pretty well. But when it comes to manipulating myself, then there's this little war on inside that says, "Who's in charge here?"

T: You're a battleground for your conscious and unconscious rivalry. . . .

C: I seem to work best when my conscious mind is only concerned with facts and letting the analysis go on by itself without paying any attention to it.

T: If you go by your experience you really can rely very much upon the workings of your unconscious mind for being ready to supply what you need when you need it. . . . Maybe you can trust your unconscious.

C: Yeah. But—I don't know. Am I cut out for this intuitive type work—or not? I feel as if I am—in some ways.

Approaching the Final Interview

In the thirty-fifth interview he explored some of the reasons for his lack of confidence in himself. He felt that much of it was induced by his father who told him in all sorts of ways that he was neither as smart nor as capable as himself. With the present as a vantage point, however, Mr. Tapa felt that what his father was *really* saying was "Don't get too big for your boots—and don't be over expectant." While his father and others were undermining his self-confidence, they were also telling him what great things were expected of him.

C: I had to change into something else—acceptable. Yeah. They all thought they were doing me a favor *encouraging me*—telling me how smart I was.
T: Guess you're saying, "Little did they know what they were doing to me!"
C: Yeah. It's taken me a hell of a lot of pain and a lot of years even to get to the point of *starting* to explore the way I am.

At the beginning of interview thirty-six Mr. Tapa said,

C: I'm getting a little bored with therapy. I'm getting to the point where I have to dig and snatch to find something to talk about. I'm feeling generally in pretty good shape.

He felt that in between the thirty-fifth and thirty-sixth interviews something had changed.

C: I don't know what—but I definitely feel different about looking back at my childhood, and some of my hostility about my mother and father has evaporated. I substituted for a feeling of resentment about them a sort of acceptance of the fact that they did a number of things that were undesirable with me. But I substituted a sort of feeling of interested excitement that—gee—now—now—that I'm finding out what was wrong, *I* can do something about it. Correct their mistakes.
T: That it wasn't inevitable damage that was done to you by them.

He continued in this vein for a while, reached a stopping place, and said:

C: It's all very interesting! [*Laughs.*] It doesn't sound very interesting! Ho hum! The dead past!
T: As though it's lost its sting and the power to hurt you.
C: M-hm. At least, that part of it has.

Although Mr. Tapa could have had two more interviews according to the research design, he terminated after the thirty-eighth.

C: I really think it'll be a good thing for me to get out of therapy for a while. I found myself thinking—Friday—as I was staring glumly at a project in front of me—not wanting to do what I had to do, "Oh, gee, I wish I could go and talk to Madge—and get this off my chest." When it gets to a point that the therapy hour is a pill I take twice a week—that gathers me up and carries me on to the next therapy hour; it's time I quit for a while. See if I can make it on my own.

T: Oh, dear! Am I getting dependent on the therapy hour?

C: That's right. It's a feeling of "I shouldn't have to wait for the therapy hour to do this."

T: I should be able to do it another way.

C: Therapy hour is very convenient for this—pleasant—sort of talk—and feel concentrated into one package in thinking about myself. I can't be in therapy all my life.

T: There must be some other way of accomplishing the same thing—something I ought to be doing myself.

C: There's a time—for me, at least—when therapy largely turns from a helping hand to a crutch. . . . I feel I've settled to my own satisfaction what I want to do with myself. I have a feeling that I'm capable of doing more. . . . I'm getting a clearer picture of things I *don't* want to do, and things I *can* do. . . . I'm not really as afraid of being told "no." If someone doesn't care for an idea, I'm not going to tear my self-concept to pieces.

T: You'll be able to stand hearing "no" and remain intact.

C: Yeah. Maybe even argue a little bit!

Follow-up Interview

About eight months later, a follow-up interview was scheduled. Mr. Tapa was full of enthusiasm over a creative venture that had engaged much of his time since the termination of therapy. He said, "Lots of things have been happening to me," and it seemed to me he was saying that this was because of his increased creative ability and productivity. He was also enjoying the rewards of creativity in terms of the interest and respect not only of his colleagues, but of well-known men in his field. He expressed the feeling that the reason he couldn't create to his satisfaction before therapy was that he got "worked out somewhere along the way."

C: I've no idea when or how, but it did—you know the way these things happen—something changes and a few months later you find out it did by seeing the effect.

Something of the quality of his improved functioning seems to be caught in these snatches of expression:

C: . . . But now I *want* to. . . . It's *fun* to exercise my mind this way. . . . When I do that sort of thing, it's *easy*. . . . No blocks—no nothing. . . . I'm communicating to people something that I *really* want to say.

He felt that his creative activity was not only his expression of *himself*, but also a symbol of his new social consciousness, because it was for *others*, too.

He felt that during and following therapy he had become acquainted with the way in which his mind functioned. Before this, he had tried to think in an organized way according to a model, or according to his conception of what orderly thinking was, "You begin at the beginning and you progress regularly through to the end." Now he realized that his mind just didn't work that way.

C: When I'm working on an idea, the whole idea develops like the latent image coming out when you develop a photograph. It doesn't start at one edge and fill in over to the other. It comes in *all over*. At first all you see is the hazy outline, and you wonder what it's going to be; and then gradually something fits here and something fits there, and pretty soon it all comes clear—all at once.

T: The whole is there instead of one piece at a time.

C: Yeah. That's the way *I* think. Now afterwards—after working out something like that, it's easy to go back over it and say: "Well, now, the first thing to understand is this—and the next is that—and so forth.". . . The business of learning how my mind works . . . has made a great difference to me.

He expressed his experiencing of therapy in much the same way.

C: I have a feeling this is what I was doing in therapy, too. I'd go from one thing to another—to another—to another. I talked about *so* many different things, and none of them seemed to lead anywhere in particular; though every now and then—as a matter of fact, quite often—I'd see a new viewpoint—that I'd been looking for but just had never taken the trouble to find. . . . But actually what I was doing in therapy was developing this negative—developing a *positive*—is more like it. All the different things I talked about added up to something, and I can look back over therapy—and the way I see it now is that I was doing very much the same thing toward the end as I was in the beginning—and all the way through, but it was sort of a cumulative effect of all these different little viewpoints—insights—that sort of let things settle into a more coherent framework.

By realizing that his own demands on himself were heavier than the demands of other people, he had been able to rid himself of the external ones. In addition, his interests and enthusiasms were centered in the present—in the moment he was experiencing.

C: I'd say that a lot of the emphasis in my life has changed from a contemplation of the rosy future to a more solid interest in what's happening *now*, and wanting to get things straightened out *now*. There's still a lot of work for me to do—and reorganization inside of myself, but it's different—it's just the sort of thing one would ordinarily expect. . . .

His problems, he felt, had become manageable.

C: I don't feel it's a problem. It's almost as if I don't feel the problems I have left *are* problems any more. I know what it is—I don't feel threatened by the fact that they're not solved. . . . I suppose that's what they call "self-confidence.". . .

When he was considering the changes within himself, he expressed some surprise that these had stemmed from his experience in therapy.

C: . . . I hadn't really thought of any of these things in connection with therapy until tonight. . . .

T: Just sort of strikes you now that it might have something to do with that period.

C: Yeah. Gee! Maybe something *did* happen. 'Cause my life since has been different afterwards—my productivity has gone up. My confidence has gone up. I've become brash in situations I would have avoided before. And, also, I've become much less brash in situations where I would have become very obnoxious before.

Toward the end of the interview he summed it up:

C: . . . The longer I talk about me, the closer we get to *right now*. It's where I am *now* that I'm interested in. . . . It's today, and tomorrow and next week, and not much more than that actually.

The Therapeutic Relationship

Since the reader may sense a lack of more personal exchange between client and therapist in this case, except for rare examples of it, an explanation may seem called for. In comparison with other clients, Mr. Tapa used his relationship with me as a focal point of therapy to a somewhat lesser extent than some do. While many work out their problems in the actual face-to-face relationship—sometimes a demanding one, sometimes an angry one, sometimes a loving one—Mr. Tapa seemed to come to me mostly for understanding. It was only occasionally that he indicated—by a word or two—even that. Yet, there was in our relationship a great deal of warmth and closeness that was implicit if not explicit.

A Review

While Mr. Tapa's presenting problems were vague ones, they emerged during therapy with considerable more definiteness; and towards the end of therapy, he appeared to have changed in many ways. He felt an increasing ability to work and to be more creative. In relating to people he experienced considerably more comfort and freedom. His self-confidence increased, and he achieved a greater sense of independence. Instead of fighting society, he felt a desire to contribute to it. In general, he had a feeling of being in control of his life.

Some Measure of Change

Mr. Tapa's self-ideal correlation scores are plotted in Figure 1 together with those of Mrs. Teral and Mrs. Oak. It will be noticed that Mr. Tapa's pretherapy score was .61, considerably higher than the scores of Mrs.

Teral and Mrs. Oak; his post-seventh interview score .76; and his post-therapy score .84. No follow-up testing was done in this case. This represents a somewhat different pattern from that of Mrs. Oak and Mrs. Teral because the client's starting point was much higher. The trend is the same, however.

Both counselor and client rated their evaluation of the outcome of therapy as "8" on a nine-point rating scale (see Figure 2). To rate the amount of change occuring during the therapy experience, a scale extending from —5 (change for the worse) to +5 (change for the better) was used. The client evaluated his experiencing of the change in himself as +3, while the counselor rated her perception of the change in Mr. Tapa as +4 (see Figure 3). According to all three research instruments, the case was highly successful.

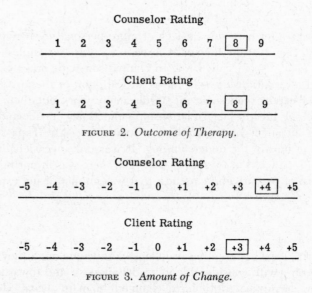

Counselor Rating

1   2   3   4   5   6   7   8   9

Client Rating

1   2   3   4   5   6   7   8   9

FIGURE 2. *Outcome of Therapy.*

Counselor Rating

-5   -4   -3   -2   -1   0   +1   +2   +3   +4   +5

Client Rating

-5   -4   -3   -2   -1   0   +1   +2   +3   +4   +5

FIGURE 3. *Amount of Change.*

ADDENDUM I

John M. Shlien

1. *Optimally, what criteria do you use for accepting or rejecting patients for counseling?*

   Optimally—that is, when the counselor is operating with a very high degree of skill and security—the only criterion would be, "Is this person dead or alive?" If alive, and wanting help of a psychological nature, there is no further consideration, except as scarcity of time might force a policy of "to each according to his need." Optimally, there is no basis for *rejecting* anyone. However, counselors seldom achieve this optimal state. Therefore, they need to ask themselves, "Am I afraid of this person? Can I comprehend him? Do I like him well enough to commit myself to the task when the reward is dim or not forthcoming?" These questions frankly put the main limitations where they are, in the therapist, to be recognized and accepted. It is surely more therapeutic, and I think more professional, to ask these than to ask about the client, "Is he psychotic? Can he respond to therapy?" and other such questions. The client is a candidate for therapy insofar as he wants to grow, and that is not a fixed quality. Though prognostic research is improving, and may produce useful criteria, I think that the mature therapist will always bear a large share of responsibility for the interaction which does or does not help the client.

2. *Do you make a diagnosis before counseling begins?*

No. Diagnostic techniques are not sufficiently valid, for one thing. Also, they do not help: if anything, they have an adverse influence on the relationship, since they tend to categorize the client in the counselor's eyes, and give the counselor an intimidating and unwarranted "expert" status (he should be an expert, in fact, but not on that basis), and in general focus attention on artificial and impersonal issues. Finally, there is no specific treatment to be applied, so of what use would specific diagnosis be if it were accomplished? Psychotherapy is not medicine. Human misery is not an organic disease.[15]

To clarify, diagnosis as discussed here does not mean the *judgment* exercised by the counselor at almost every step. Neither is it *prognosis*, which assesses the constructive resources and estimates the probability of achieving health. Diagnosis is the classical psychiatric classification and description which is static, and focused wholly on pathology. Therapy, in contradistinction, has a fluid tone and anticipates change. It will encounter the pathology ("what is wrong") but can rely only on "what is right" with the organism.

We do indeed use measures of change in therapy, but these are for research to discover the facts about change in groups of clients, and these measures are not yet so keen as to be satisfactory for even that purpose, much less for individual diagnosis.

3. *Do you attempt to persuade the patient or significant relative to change his (the patient's) environment?*

No. Conceivably this might be wise and necessary, but usually the client knows it before the counselor, and would change it if he were psychologically or physically ready and able. More often, clients begin by asserting that they *must* change their environment, or have changed it many times. But it is the *internal* environment that matters most, though there are indeed life situations more strenuous than they are worth, and to tolerate such is only mock-heroism. When the external environment is clearly perceived, the client will make the best move in relation to it. The task of the therapist is to aid that perception.

4. *How did you conceptualize the counselor's role in this case?*

I did not. This is a question upon which I no longer dwell, certainly not as I enter into the therapeutic relation. Then my role is of no concern to me. It is almost habitual. However I may be seen: friend, enemy, mirror, doctor, judge, teacher, surgeon, authority, or fool. I have only one objec-

---

[15] No one has stated the case so well as C. E. Jung, "The Practice of Psychotherapy," *Collected Works, Vol. XVI* (New York: Pantheon Press, 1954).

tive—from which it is easy to be distracted—to listen and to understand, without any prejudice whatever, the thoughts and feelings of another person. Sometimes, looking back at therapeutic experience, I feel that my role is like that of a gardener, who labors to provide the conditions for growth because it is his satisfaction to see the growing—but he knows, no matter how sophisticated a botanist or chemist, he cannot *make* the growth take place. That is up to the plant. I would also sometimes conceptualize my role as that of a child—innocent of preconceptions, trusting, and accepting even absurd distortions. Out of this grow mature adults. This last conceptualization will never become widespread. It offers none of the customary status satisfactions, and is quite opposite to the "father figure" so often used to characterize the authority of the therapist. Yet I would assert that at his best a good therapist is much like a good child; a good child *is* a good therapist, and that in general children are by far the most therapeutic element in our culture.

5. *What aspects of your theory of counseling were particularly apparent or useful in the case presented here?*
   In *general,* the introductory statement by Rogers answers this question very well. In *particular,* this case bears on the theory produced when Taft's question, "If one cannot live forever, is it worth while to live at all?" is translated into terms of therapy. If one cannot continue indefinitely, is brief therapy of any use?

6. *Do you feel that this case developed significant insight? If not, can improvement be maintained?*
   Yes, there is much evidence of that. But insight alone (understanding motives and patterns of one's behavior) does not assure improvement, much less maintenance of it. Achievement of "insight" can become a dry and evasive exercise, or it can be a crushingly painful experience. With insight there must be an emotional acceptance of self to free one of self-conscious introspection, and allow for thought and action unhampered by preoccupation with self-analysis.

7. *What aspects of your own cultural orientation facilitated or impeded the counseling of your case?*
   In general, I believe that therapy can transcend the powerful channels and constraints of cultural orientation, social class, sex, status, and even, to some extent, language. This is possible because, in therapy, a unique effort is made to *communicate, in one frame of reference,* without sham or defense. These communications, when achieved, constitute the most significant collaborative moments of therapy. Elsewhere in life, communication has somewhat the purpose of defending, maintaining differences, jockeying for position, sending subtle messages, etc. Were this not so, there would be no need for the specially designed and institutionalized communication of psychotherapy. While I believe this, I also recognize the existence of many aspects of cultural orientation which do operate and did influence both parties in the case, but are too complex for brief analysis.

8. *If we consider that a continuum exists from superficial to deep counseling, where would you place your own case?*
   Moderately deep, with occasional profound moments, but not the huge and spectacular reorganization sometimes seen. At the same time, there was relatively little really superficial behavior.

9. *What did you think about the outcome of this case and what criteria did you use for evaluating such outcome?*

Outcome very satisfactory. The client accomplished a large part, but not all, of her goals and developed enough momentum to carry on productively beyond therapy. Main criteria used were the Q-sort, the Thematic Apperception Test, and ratings by counselor and client, plus a clinical interview two years after therapy ended. The tests were administered immediately before and after therapy, and at two follow-up periods, three and six months beyond posttherapy. It is interesting to note that Mrs. Teral refused to take her second (six months) follow-up test. She politely but firmly told the psychometrist that she had taken many tests for us, appreciated her therapy, but was unwilling to submit to continued examination. As a researcher one regrets the loss of data, but as a therapist one can only revel in the new-found self-assertion of a girl who was once so submissive and self-depreciating that she would not even take a bath for her own sake!

10. *How do you terminate counseling?*

Ordinarily, in the same way we begin—by the client's expressed wish to do so. In this case, of course, the very plan of the research called for termination set in advance. In the light of our further experience, it would seem that, ideally, the client should always have some considerable say in the matter, and that if termination is set in advance, it should be by mutual plan and agreement rather than arbitrary and unilateral decision. The question of termination is truly a giant one; it involves decisions concerning the whole of therapy, from a theoretical definition of ends and goals to a development of means.

ADDENDUM II

Madge K. Lewis

In general, the statements by Rogers in the Introduction and Shlien in the Addendum represent my point of view so well as to make separate statements unnecessary in most instances. Except for a few additional comments in No. 1, most of my responses will apply therefore only to those items which call for an answer specific to the case of Mr. Tapa.

1. *Optimally, what criteria do you use for accepting or rejecting patients for counseling?*

Optimally, there is no criterion of particular importance to consider. Problems that may arise within the therapeutic relationship are ones that may often and ideally be dealt with there. When this, for some reason or other, seems impossible, the therapist can take responsibility by other means for trying to understand his feelings about some aspect of the client and the relationship that is troublesome to him. At the Counseling Center small groups of counselors organize into "Training Teams." These provide the psychological climate where problems can be freely discussed, and where acceptance by other therapists can help the one who is experiencing some difficulty in understanding his own reactions to the client or to material the client is considering.

❖   ❖   ❖

6. *Do you feel that this case developed significant insight? If not, can im-provement be maintained?*

Mr. Tapa developed considerable insight during therapy, and the follow-up interview indicated that this process continued after therapy was ter-minated. Equally as important, perhaps, was (1) his tendency to move from experiencing rigidly in some area to experiencing fluidly in that same area; (2) the loosening of structure to permit greater spontaneity of be-havior; and (3) the experiencing of the therapeutic relationship itself—one he could count on for understanding. The whole area opened up by the sixth question is one in which we have many unanswered questions. What *is* the essence of therapy? What *are* the most important factors in the process that cause a personality to change toward maturity and self-actu-alization? More and more research is now being done on the *process* of therapy and will undoubtedly add to our knowledge and consequently sharpen our skill as therapists.

8. *If we consider that a continuum exists from superficial to deep counseling, where would you place your own case?*

There was relatively little superficial material in this case. The continuum of the case itself was chiefly from moderately deep to deep. The twenty-fourth interview, for example, contains material illustrative of depth in therapy. The client approaches what he calls "butterflies" of thoughts and feels frightened of them, wanting—yet not wanting—to experience them. Later, in the thirtieth interview, he begins to realize that perhaps he *can* trust his unconscious processes.

9. *What did you think about the outcome of this case and what criteria did you use for evaluating such outcome?*

The outcome was very satisfactory. Criteria used were the Q-sort, the Thematic Apperception Test, ratings by counselor and client, and a fol-low-up interview eight months later. Tests were administered immediately before, several times during, and immediately after therapy was termi-nated. Mr. Tapa changed from "drifting along with the tide" to feeling in control of his life. He became increasingly creative and productive. Com-munication with others and with his own self improved, and he felt wish-ful of contributing to society rather than being at odds with it. His self-confidence and feelings of independence increased.

CHAPTER 13

Psychotherapy Based on the Principle of Reciprocal Inhibition

—JOSEPH WOLPE[1]

Introduction

The approach to psychotherapy exemplified by the case presented in this chapter is still unfamiliar to many. Its logic may be summarized as follows. The three kinds of processes that can bring about lasting changes in behavior are growth, lesions, and learning. Neurotic behavior has its origin in learning, and its elimination is therefore a matter of "unlearning." On this premise, known laws of learning have been applied to the special problems of neurosis, and highly effective new techniques have emerged.

In various papers[2,3,4] I have presented evidence in support of the view that neurotic behavior, whether induced experimentally or observed in the clinic, is persistent, unadaptive, learned behavior in which anxiety is almost always prominent and which is acquired in anxiety-generating situations. By "anxiety" is meant the autonomic response pattern or

---

[1] M.B., B.ch., U. of Witwatersrand, 1939; Resident, Johannesburg Gen. Hosp., '39-'40; General practice, '40-'42; Med. Offic., South African Med. Corps., '42-'46; Experimental psychiat. research, '46-'48 leading to M.D. in psychiat., '48. Private psychotherap., '48- ; Part-time lecturer, Dept., of Psychiat., U. of the Witwatersrand, '49. Fellow, Center for Advanced Study in the Behavioral Sciences, Stanford, Calif., '56-'57.

A good deal of the general expository material in this chapter was previously published in my paper, "Reciprocal Inhibition as the Main Basis of Psychotherapeutic Effects,"

patterns that are characteristically part of the given organism's response to noxious stimulation. The term is applied irrespective of the duration of the autonomic responses or of what has led to them. An anxiety response is unadaptive when it is evoked in circumstances in which there is objectively no threat. I have discussed in some detail[5] the conditioning mechanisms that determine the variants and secondary behavioral effects of neurosis such as obsessional behavior or hysteria, and the "aberrations" that may be found in the character of the anxiety response itself. These "aberrations" consist of unusual elements among the autonomic reactions that constitute the anxiety response and they may lead to physiological changes that account for some of the psychosomatic manifestations of neurosis. This will be seen to be true of the dermatitis in the case presented here.

Therapy of the neuroses *by any therapist,* insofar as it is successful in more than a merely palliative way, seems in the great majority of cases to depend upon obtaining reciprocal inhibition of neurotic anxiety responses, *i.e.,* the complete or partial suppression of these responses as the result of the simultaneous evocation of other responses physiologically antagonistic to anxiety.

The argument on which this statement is based is as follows. In most reports on the treatment of neurosis[6,7] the percentage of cases either apparently cured or much improved has been between fifty and sixty, no matter what the theory upon which therapy has proceeded. This strongly suggests that what is effective is some nonspecific factor in the interview situation that operates with about the same frequency and in about the same measure whatever the particular operations that the therapist may *think* important. Now, in three series of neurotic patients[8,9,10] (more than 200 in all) whose treatment included measures designed

---

Arch. Neurol. Psychiat., 72 (1954), 205-26. It is reprinted here by permission of the editor. This chapter was written during a Fellowship at the Center for Advanced Study in the Behavioral Sciences, Stanford, California, 1956-57.

[2] J. Wolpe, "Experimental Neurosis as Learned Behavior," *Brit. J. Psychol., (General Section),* 43 (1952), 243-68.

[3] J. Wolpe, "Reciprocal Inhibition as the Main Basis of Psychotherapeutic Effects," *Arch. Neurol. Psychiat.,* 72 (1954), 205-26.

[4] J. Wolpe, *Psychotherapy by Reciprocal Inhibition.* (Palo Alto: Stanford University Press) (1958).

[5] *Ibid.*

[6] C. Landis, "A Statistical Evaluation of Psychotherapeutic Methods," in L. E. Hinsey (ed.), *Concepts and Problems of Psychotherapy* (New York: Columbia University Press, 1937).

[7] J. Wilder, "Facts and Figures on Psychotherapy," *J. Clin. Psychopath.,* 7 (1945), 311-47.

[8] J. Wolpe, "Objective Psychotherapy of the Neuroses," *S. Afr. Med. J., 26* (1952), 825-29.

[9] *Op. cit.*

[10] *Op. cit.*

to procure reciprocal inhibition of neurotic responses, the proportion of highly favorable results has consistently been in the region of 90% after a mean of about thirty interviews. The addition of 30% or so of favorable results over and above the 60% customarily found with psychotherapy would seem to be attributable to the use of these measures. If special measures toward reciprocal inhibition are therapeutically effective, there is some presumption that the non-specific factor that seems to operate in *all* psychotherapies *also* works through reciprocal inhibition. I have found some indirect support for this in the observation that those of my patients who have improved *before* I have applied special measures have had considerable emotion of a nonanxious kind evoked in them by the interviews.

Apparently, these emotions reciprocally inhibit the anxieties that are aroused during the interview by verbal stimuli, and *it makes little difference whether the context of the words is in the present or in the past;* or, if in the past, whether the context is well-known to the patient or long-forgotten. Sometimes, the recounting of past events brings forth a particularly powerful emotional discharge (abreaction); and this, *in the conditions of a therapeutic situation* and not outside it,[11] is often markedly therapeutic provided that unrelieved terror is not the only component of the discharge.[12] It also does not seem to matter whether the memories recalled were previously remembered or not.[13]

Experimental Background

In the course of experiments during the years 1947 to 1948,[14] I found that cats could be made neurotic merely by placing them in a small cage and then, immediately after presenting an auditory stimulus, subjecting them to a small number of high-voltage, low-amperage shocks from an induction coil. (It was not necessary for the reaction to the shock to conflict with a previously conditioned food-approach response.) The animals all reacted violently to the shock, showing various combinations of rushing to and fro; clawing at the roof, floor, and sides of the experimental cage; crouching, trembling, howling, and spitting; and evidencing mydriasis, tachypnea, piloerection and, in some cases, urination or defecation. After a variable number of shocks, these reactions would become stabilized, and it would then be found that if the animal was

---

11 R. R. Grinker and J. P. Spiegel, *Men under Stress* (London: Churchill, 1945), p. 392.
12 R. R. Grinker and J. P. Spiegel, *War Neuroses* (Philadelphia: Blakiston Company, 1945), p. 81.
13 *Ibid.*, pp. 83-84.
14 *Op. cit.*

replaced in the experimental cage on a later occasion, it would manifest a
reaction pattern similar to that observed at the time of the shock. Con-
finement in the cage for several hours did not diminish the reactions,
nor did they show remission when the animals were put in the cage day
after day without ever again being shocked. The disturbance was such
that an animal starved for twenty-four to seventy-two hours would not
eat meat dropped in front of him in the cage. Months of absence from the
experimental cage did not weaken the reactions evocable there.

It was thus clear that the usual means by which ineffectual responses
are eliminated—experimental extinction, which depends upon a process
associated with fatigue of the response[15]—was ineffective as far as the
anxiety responses were concerned. It seemed for a time as though these
responses would have to be regarded as permanent and irreversible; but
in considering possible methods by which they might be eliminated, it
seemed reasonable to try causing some other response to occur in the
experimental situation that might be expected to be incompatible with
the anxiety responses. The obvious response to try was feeding. Neurotic
animals were placed inside the experimental cage after having been
starved for forty-eight or seventy-two hours, and pellets of meat were
tossed in front of them. As usual, no eating occurred. Now since in their
living cages the animals were accustomed to having food conveyed to
them by the human hand, it was presumed that the hand had become
a conditioned food-approach stimulus, and it was hoped that, added to
the food-approach tendencies aroused by the sight and smell of the
meat, the presentation of the human hand might lead to the overcoming
of the inhibition of the feeding response. Accordingly, meat pellets were
offered to the animals on an ebony rod held in the hand. Some of the
animals ate the food after various periods of hesitation and then took
subsequent offerings with increasing readiness.

In those animals that were not induced to eat by the above technique,
a method was tried that proved to be very instructive. In addition to their
reactions in the experimental cage, the animals also reacted with anxiety
anywhere in the experimental laboratory and also in each of a series of
rooms that had varying degrees of resemblance to the experimental
laboratory. They were offered meat pellets in each of these places,
starting with the rooms that more closely resembled the laboratory. In
the case of each cat, a place was eventually found where the evocation of
anxiety responses was not great enough to inhibit the feeding response.
The animal would be fed about twenty pellets in this place and on the
next experimental day would usually be found to accept food in the
room next closest in resemblance to the laboratory—which it would not

---

[15] C. L. Hull, *Principles of Behavior* (New York: Appleton-Century-Crofts, Inc.,
1943), pp. 277-302.

have done previously. From day to day further advances were made until the animal would eat in the laboratory and eventually, through several stages, in the experimental cage itself. There it would be given numerous pellets of meat on successive days and at last would move about in the cage freely without any signs of anxiety.

But at this stage the anxiety responses could again be evoked by presenting the auditory stimulus that had preceded the neurosis-producing shocks. The effects of this stimulus could be eliminated in a manner parallel to that applied to the visual stimuli—by feeding the animal first at a considerable distance from the continuously sounding stimulus and then gradually coming nearer day by day. Meanwhile, the auditory stimulus would incidentally have become linked to a food-seeking response; but extinction of this by repeated nonreward did not lead to a recurrence of anxiety in any animal.

These experiments seemed clearly to confirm the expectation of a reciprocal antagonism between the anxiety responses and the feeding responses. As long as, in a given situation, the anxiety was strong enough to inhibit feeding, anxiety would continue to be dominant, and would even increase or spread, as certain supplementary experiments[16] showed. But if conditions were so changed that the feeding tendency was relatively stronger and feeding could occur in the face of some measure of anxiety, the strength of the tendency to respond by anxiety to the stimuli concerned was gradually weakened.

The above findings led to the framing of the general hypothesis that *if a response incompatible with anxiety can be made to occur in the presence of anxiety-evoking stimuli it will weaken the bond between these stimuli and the anxiety.* A considerable number of responses are incompatible with anxiety. It is not surprising that this should be so, for although Sherringtonian reciprocal inhibition associated with spinal reflex activity is apparently rather specific, at higher levels of organization reciprocal inhibition is clearly often diffuse within the functional "modality" concerned—for example, accompanying the articulation of any word there is ordinarily an automatic inhibition of all simultaneous tendencies to pronounce other words.

Procedure in Reciprocal Inhibition Psychotherapy

The patient faces the therapist across a desk. The first step is to take a history of each symptom and each difficulty of which complaint is made. This is followed by an account of the life history, encompassing early home background and relationships, behavior and experiences in educa-

---

[16] J. Wolpe, "The Genesis of Neurosis: An Objective Account," *S. Afr. Med. J.,* *24* (1950), 613-16.

tional institutions, work life, sex life from first awareness of sexual impulses, and social life. Then the patient is questioned about early nervous reactions and asked to recount any distressful experiences he can recall. The order of procedure is varied if the natural flow of the story demands it. Nothing that the patient says is criticized nor is his credibility questioned. When the history appears to be complete, he is given the self-sufficiency questions from Bernreuter's questionnaire to do as "homework."[17] At the next interview the Willoughby schedule is administered to him.[18] This gives a measure of neuroticism, mainly in relation to social situations. About 80 per cent of patients have an initial score of thirty or more, and this drops when therapy is successful.[19]

After disposing of the Willoughby schedule, I tell the patient that his symptoms are all manifestations of fear, even the bizarre ones and those that seem distinctly somatic. If situations of real danger alone aroused these fear reactions, they would be so infrequent that he would not consider treatment necessary. But various situations that are not dangerous have acquired the power to produce fear in him. I explain this by saying that when an experience or series of experiences produces a great deal of fear or tension in an individual, anything that has some aspect of resemblance to things closely associated with these experiences may subsequently evoke fear even though no objective threat is present. I illustrate this by two or three examples, and then try to show the patient how experiences of his own have led to his present sensitivities. However, it is not necessary to establish the causal relations, for the patient's neurotic reactions are to stimuli, internal or external, that are present here and now. I therefore do not permit the expenditure of a great deal of time on probing into the past.

I now tell the patient about the measures that will be used to break down his anxious habits, pointing out that regardless of where a measure is used, its aim is always to oppose the anxiety with other emotional states incompatible with it.

Apart from the anxiety-inhibiting emotions already referred to that seem to be induced in many patients by the interview situation itself, I have made use of the following kinds of responses for inhibiting neurotic reactions:

1. Assertive responses
2. Sexual responses
3. Relaxation responses

[17] R. G. Bernreuter, "The Measurement of Self-Sufficiency," *J. Abn. Soc. Psychol.*, 28 (1933), 291-300.
[18] R. R. Willoughby, "Some Properties of the Thurstone Personality Schedule and a Suggested Revision," *J. Soc. Psychol.*, 5 (1934), 91-96.
[19] *Op. cit.*

4. Respiratory responses (carbon-dioxide-oxygen mixtures by La-Verne's method)[20]
5. Conditioned motor responses
6. "Anxiety-relief" responses (conditioning to a "neutral" stimulus of the effects of cessation of a punishing electric current)
7. Conditioned avoidance responses to obsessions

The first three of the above response categories are by far the most commonly used, and will be briefly described below. The reader is referred elsewhere[21] for an account of the use of the other methods, as well as for a fuller account of those described.

Assertive Responses:

The essence of assertive behavior is most often anger and aggression, but it may also take other forms, such as the expression of friendly or affectionate feelings. Some evidence of an antagonism between anger and anxiety has been presented by Arnold.[22]

Assertive responses are of therapeutic value only in the case of neurotic anxieties arising out of interpersonal relationships. Examples are being afraid to express one's opinions to one's friends lest they disagree, or being afraid to make protest when there is something wrong with the food one has ordered in a restaurant. Some such fears may be revealed in the history or in the responses to the Willoughby questionnaire. Others are often elicited by asking how he behaves when, for example, (1) he notices after leaving a shop that he has been short changed; (2) he discovers that a garment bought two days before is faulty; or (3) someone pushes in front of him in a queue. The patient is told that such fears may be overcome through asserting his legitimate rights in the various situations and he is given a few examples from the histories of previous patients.

Inadequacies in the patient's own handling of interpersonal relations are now discussed and he is given detailed instructions for assertive behavior in individual situations. Everything possible is done to motivate him to actual performance of this behavior. He is told that he will feel better if he acts according to instructions. His attention is focussed on the enormity of any injustices being perpetrated on him and, in addition, he is shown how undignified and unattractive to others it is for him to behave in his accustomed spineless way. These pressures lead to the desired behavior in most cases, though not always immediately. In subsequent interviews he will be asked to recount his experiences in situa-

---

[20] A. A. LaVerne, "Rapid Coma Technique of Carbon Dioxide Inhalation Therapy," *Dis. Nerv. Syst., 14* (1953), 141.

[21] *Op. cit.*

[22] M. B. Arnold, "Physiological Differentiation of Emotional States," *Psychol. Rev., 52* (1945), 35-48.

tions of the kind described above, and his handling of them will be discussed and corrected. In those who do not begin to perform as required within a reasonable time, I employ a kind of "psychodrama" in which I take the role of various persons with whom the patient cannot cope, while the patient "plays himself" according to instructions. More often than not, this proves to be a stepping-stone to a successful relationship with the real person.

Sexual Responses

As would be expected, sexual responses have their application in overcoming anxiety reactions that have been conditioned to stimuli involved in sexual situations. Although complete or partial impotence or frigidity is practically invariable in the patients concerned, the ability to be aroused sexually in suitable circumstances usually persists. The manner of use of the sexual response varies, the most important determinant being the identity of the anxiety-evoking stimuli. When these are closely associated with coitus itself, a typical procedure employed that is very effective is the following:

The patient is instructed to tell his sexual partner that his impotence is due to certain automatic fears that the sexual situation arouses in him, but they are fears that he can easily overcome with her cooperation. All she has to do is to agree to lie with him on a few occasions in a more or less nude state without expecting intercourse and without suggesting it. The patient is instructed to be as relaxed as possible on these occasions and to do just as much as his sexual impulse dictates without arousing anxiety. He is on no account to attempt intercourse unless he has an unequivocal positive desire to do so. As the occasions are repeated, it is found that sexual excitation increases and anxiety decreases, erections become increasingly strong, and usually within a surprisingly short time (between two and four weeks) normal coitus becomes possible and then progressively improves.

Such favorable consequences occur, it seems, because each time a positive sexual feeling occurs and is intensified by a sexual approach, there is reciprocal inhibition of whatever anxieties are also being evoked by the situation, and the strength of the anxiety-evocation tendency is each time slightly weakened. There is no apparent basic difference at all between this process and that which occurred in our cats, in which anxieties were overcome through appropriate manipulations with feeding reactions.

Relaxation Responses

(a) *Relaxation responses in life situations:* Jacobson's work has shown that deep muscle relaxation is accompanied by autonomic effects that are antagonistic to the characteristic effects of anxiety.[23] I have repeatedly found clinical confirmation of this in the rapid drop of a pulse rate from 120 to 80 or in the equally rapid drying of profusely sweating palms in a patient who is practiced in relaxation. Jacobson himself obtained impressive results by training patients in "progressive relaxation" and then urging them to be as relaxed as possible all the time. It would appear that the improvement in a patient who follows this kind of program may be explained as follows: Persistent relaxation implies some measure of reciprocal inhibition of the effects of any anxiety-producing stimuli that happen to appear, and the occurrence of repeated temporary inhibitions of this kind enables gradual development of conditioned inhibition of the anxiety responses.

I have sometimes obtained highly gratifying results in patients placed on Jacobson's regime, but more often than not its value is limited, seemingly because the patient is unable to relax at short notice deeply enough to counter the high degree of anxiety produced by the relevant stimulus situations. In a few patients this difficulty has been overcome when the subject has learned how to anticipate such situations and to relax deeply in preparation for them. The following technique, in which the therapist has a good deal of detailed control, has proved to have far wider application. This technique played a leading part in the treatment of the case presented below.

(b) *Systematic Desensitization Based on Relaxation:* This method of systematic desensitization to anxiety-producing stimuli is carried out in the consulting room.

The patient is given training in progressive relaxation in the course of several interviews. Preliminary experiments on his responses to hypnotic techniques are meanwhile conducted, and during the same interviews steps are taken toward the construction of what is called an "anxiety hierarchy." This is a list of stimuli to which the patient reacts with un-adaptive anxiety. The items are obtained from his history, from his answers to the Willoughby schedule, and from a list of everything he can think of that can in any way disturb or embarrass him. The items are then ranked so that the most disturbing items are placed at the top and the least disturbing at the bottom. The arrangement is usually derived solely from the patient's answers to questioning. Multiple hierarchies are very often obtained, sometimes interrelated, sometimes not.

In the session after the preliminaries have been completed, the patient is hypnotized and given powerful relaxation suggestions. (A good relaxer can do almost as well without hypnosis just by closing his eyes.) He is then asked to imagine a scene consisting of the feeblest member of the

---

[23] E. Jacobson, *Progressive Relaxation* (Chicago: University of Chicago Press), 1938.

anxiety hierarchy. Sometimes it is advisable to start even more gently by causing the name of the feared object to be visualized. The patient is instructed to signal if any time he feels more than the slightest disturbance. Usually, two to four items from the hierarchy are presented at each session, the speed of progression depending on how much disturbance is shown or afterward reported. (It is always preferable to advance too slowly rather than too fast. During early experiments with the method I produced serious setbacks in two patients by the premature presentation of stimuli with a high anxiety-evoking potential.) It usually takes between ten and thirty desensitization sessions before the highest items in the hierarchy can be accepted by the patient without disturbance.

It is natural to ask: Does it follow that because a patient can imagine a scene calmly, he will also be calm when he comes upon a similar scene in reality? Experience shows the aswer to be in the affirmative. Sometimes there is a tendency for the real-life improvement to lag behind somewhat, but even then it eventually catches up. The one proviso for success, given the ability to relax, is that the imagined stimulus must at the outset be able to evoke anxiety. A small minority of patients experience no anxiety when they imagine situations which in actuality are anxiety-producing, and in them desensitization is not accomplished by the above procedure. Sometimes a patient who has failed to respond emotionally to images aroused by verbal cues from the therapist has shown considerable disturbance on verbalizing the same situations himself.

The above procedure, originally confined to "simple" phobias, has in the past few years been applied to a wide variety of disturbing situations, often of a social nature. The case presented below includes examples of both kinds.

Treatment of a Case

The case that follows is a representative one as far as the application of the above methods is concerned. It was selected in part because the patient had a dermatitis whose dramatic response to direct hypnotic suggestion showed that its presence was related to emotional disturbance. This meant that the state of the affected areas of the skin provided an index of the patient's emotional state in addition to her verbal report. The dermatitis was regarded as an offshoot of her anxiety reactions—the result of vascular disturbance due to a "preferential" sympathetic outflow such as Wolff[24] has pointed out.

The objective of therapy was as usual to overcome unadaptive anxious reactivity. The reciprocal inhibition technique that had the largest role in this case was systematic desensitization under hypnosis which em-

---

[24] H. G. Wolff, "Life Stress and Cardiovascular Disorders," *Circulation, 1* (1950), 187-204.

ployed relaxation as the anxiety-inhibiting response; but, as will be seen, some use was also made of assertive behavior in the life situation.

First Session (September 1, 1954)

Verna Blue, a forty-year-old elementary school teacher of pleasant bearing, was sent to me by her physician because of an atopic dermatitis. The present attack, which was the ninth or tenth in a period of five years, was the longest-lived and the most severe. Its first manifestation, an itching eczematous eruption of the face and neck, had appeared fourteen months previously and had persisted in the face of a large variety of therapeutic methods. Eight months after its onset a similar eruption had broken out in both of her elbow flexures and armpits and on the opposed surfaces of her thighs. In all these parts there was a very distressing degree of itching, especially in the armpits. Marked amelioration of the rash in all areas for about three days at a time was regularly obtainable with injections of ACTH.

The cervico-facial eruption had alone been present during earlier attacks. On the first occasion five years previously, its appearance was related to the end of a school vacation when Verna had been unhappy about the prospect of starting to work full days instead of half days. Intradermal injections of tuberculin had cleared up the eruptions within a few days. The second attack, exactly like the first, had occurred eighteen months later, when she found training a new staff member in addition to her regular work more than she could cope with. Again, injections (of an unstated nature) had cleared up the eruption; and at each of its subsequent reappearances, it had lasted for a few months and terminated after the doctors had "found out something," and applied some previously untried method of treatment.

Both Verna Blue and her physician had strong expectations that I would cure her dermatitis by the use of hypnotic suggestion; and certainly the multiplicity of measures that had in the past terminated attacks made it likely that temporary improvement would be obtained. Accordingly, I decided to devote the second half of the first interview to hypnotizing her and trying out the use of direct suggestion. If it was effective it would confirm the existence of a nervous foundation for the dermatitis, and at the same time establish in the patient a buoyant feeling about the therapeutic situation—a "nonspecific" emotional effect with therapeutic possibilities, as mentioned above.

I used the levitation method. Her hands rose to her face and her eyes closed. The suggestion was repeatedly given that she would have a feeling of smoothness and coolness of her face and neck, which would persist after she left the consulting room and would be followed by a clearing of the rash. A post-hypnotic suggestion was also given that the rash in the *left* elbow flexure would also clear. After arousal from her trance, she said that she felt much less nervous after having been extremely nervous before the trance.

At the end of the interview I asked her whether she had any persistent emotional difficulties, and she said that she was very sensitive to any failure or defect in her children and was easily hurt if misunderstood by members of her own family.

Second Session (September 7, 1954)

The moment the patient entered the consulting room, it was plain that she was pleased. She reported that the rash had cleared away from her face even though it had been in an itchy phase which in the past had invariably been followed by worsening. The day after hypnotic trance, it was already obviously better and since then had improved further every day until now there was nothing but a slight roughness around the neck. No medication had been used. Her last ACTH injection had been on August 21. There was noticeable improvement in the rash in both elbow flexures, the left (which had been worse at the first session) being better than the right. No change was evident in the armpits.

Verna gave her history as follows: Her father having been a member of the Diplomatic Corps, she had been born in the Orient, the eldest of a family of three. Her parents were both still living. She described her mother as very energetic, determined, and intelligent, a woman who treated her children firmly but lovingly. Rules were very rigidly maintained by her, but punishments were moderate. She often greatly irritated Verna by her nagging. Verna's father was also firm about discipline, but she was much more fond of him than of her mother. He punished only with words, adopting a severe voice, but always justly in Verna's view. She had always got on well with the younger of her two brothers, but had a great deal of friction with the elder, whom she hated not only because of direct acts of hostility toward her, but also for his impertinence toward their parents. Verna would then try to make amends to them by being especially affectionate or helpful. She had always hated anybody who made those dear to her miserable.

She recalled two exceedingly terrifying experiences. The first was at the age of six when she came round a corner to see a Japanese adult masturbating with "an insane expression on his face." She had run away in terror and never mentioned the incident to her parents. Then, when she was eleven, the family had spent a period on a volcanic island. She was in a continuous state of terror during a tremor that went on for two weeks. (The possible connection between these experiences and the items of Hierarchy A on page 369 should be noted.)

As a scholar she had done well until she was fourteen and after that only moderately so. Being very conscientious about her homework, she had little time for sport. She felt some slight awe of the sterner of her teachers, but was confident in relation to everybody else. She made friends easily. When she was sixteen, her father was transferred to South Africa and she took a four-year-course of child care and education with a distinguished record. She taught for a year, spent two years at home as a lady of leisure, and then, at twenty-three, married. She did not work again until she was thirty-two years old, when compelled by financial difficulties to do so for eighteen months. Since 1950, she had again been working continuously because of the heavy expenses occasioned by her growing family of five.

Verna's first sexual feelings had arisen at thirteen when she was infatuated from a distance by a young man's bodily strength, merry laugh, and open face. At fourteen, she had a year-long association with a boy rather similar to the first, with a good deal of mild petting. At sixteen, a very intelligent boy had fallen in love with her and wooed her earnestly. After some months of indifference, she had begun to feel very fond of him, but one evening after dark when she was very receptive to lovemaking and showed it, he became scared and backed out.

I interrupted her at this point of her story to hypnotize her again. I gave suggestions of coolness of the face and of a complete clearing of the rash there, and similar suggestions about the elbow flexures and axillae. On wakening, Verna stated that itching in her armpits had disappeared and that she felt very relaxed.

Third Session (September 9, 1954)

Verna reported that her face had become entirely clear and that the flexures of her elbows were continuing to improve. Her armpits were no better since they were hard to keep dry. This was the first time that the elbow condition had not been an index of the armpit condition.

Resuming her story, Verna said that when she was eighteen years old she had become engaged to Roger, a childhood acquaintance who was regarded as "a good match." She wasn't in love with him and didn't like him to kiss her on the mouth. After trying unsuccessfully for three years to cultivate more positive feelings for him, she broke off the relationship.

On the rebound, she fell in love with a "film star type," made frequent, violent love without intercourse, but in a few months grew tired of him and gave him up. She then resolved to remain unattached for a while, went out with many men, and enjoyed herself. At twenty-two, she met Arnold, an accountant—tall, well-built and handsome—and there and then felt she wanted to marry him, which she did eighteen months later.

The eighteen years of her married life had been quite satisfactory on the whole, but recently there had been some deterioration. From the beginning Verna had felt that her interests were far wider than Arnold's, but had hoped that he would cultivate interests as the years went on. He had not done so, and, in any event, he had even ceased to tell her anything of the day's events, picking up the newspaper when he came home and becoming engrossed in it. Verna would feel much put out when, on returning from church service, Arnold would say that he hadn't understood a word of the sermon. For years her sex life had been entirely normal with almost invariable orgasms; but in the past year she had had very little sexual desire and no orgasms at all.

Fourth Session (September 10, 1954)

During the early part of this interview, discussion was directed to Verna's children. She said that she got on well with all of them and was happy about them except for the third, a boy of ten, who was rather nervous and had had more than his share of illnesses.

We then turned our attention to the Willoughby questionnaire. In administering this test for neuroticism, it is my practice to discuss each question with the patient so that its meaning and purpose are clearly understood by him before he answers it. Take, for example, Question 3: "Are you afraid of falling when you are on a high place?" Since a positive answer is of significance only insofar as it indicates unadaptive anxiety, I explain that the answer can be positive only if the patient is afraid in situations where there is *no actual danger of falling.* Similarly regarding Question 20: "Are you self-conscious about your appearance?"—the patient is told that this refers to being self-conscious about his appearance even though he knows himself to be clean and suitably dressed for the given occasion. The highest possible score on the Willoughby schedule is 100 (twenty-five questions with 0 negative and 1-4 positive in increasing degrees). Answering it for the first time, about 80% of neurotic patients have scores of 30 or above. While a high score is positive evidence of excessive neurotic reactivity, a low score does not prove the converse, since a patient's anxieties may lie in areas not covered by the questionnaire. Though Verna's score of 29 was on the low side, perusal of her individual answers revealed a marked sensitivity to situations involving blood and injuries. An average degree of self-sufficiency was shown by her score of 48 per cent on the Bernreuter self-sufficiency questions.

Fifth Session (September 11, 1954)

Verna's dermatological state continued to improve. Her armpits had scarcely itched and were now less red. She was much less aware of the flexures of the elbows which previously irritated her. The patches on her thighs were clearing and her face had remained clear.

The time was now ripe to discuss with Verna the emotional factors in her skin condition. I spoke to her as follows:

> It is obvious from the fact that such measures as hypnotic suggestion are able to improve the condition of your skin that there is an emotional factor playing a most important part. We know from experience that the kind of emotion which is responsible is basically fear or tension. Of course, fear is sometimes useful—in situations of real danger. You are not exposed to situations of real danger sufficiently frequently to produce the kind of chronic emotional state that could form a basis for your chronic skin condition. Clearly then, various day-to-day situations, not in themselves dangerous, have acquired the power to produce fear in you. If, in the past you have had a highly fearful experience, the subsequent encountering of anything closely associated with it may subsequently evoke fear though no real threat is present. Apparently, there are persistent, or frequently recurrent, features of your life situation that, because of a fear-connected history, are capable of arousing fear in you. It would not be surprising if your experiences with the masturbating Japanese or the earthquake have something to do with your present condition.

I now gave Verna some examples from the history of other patients to illustrate how unadaptive fears originate in objectively fearful experiences. She interrupted at one stage to say that she had just recalled a great feeling of fear she had had at the age of five when required to go aboard a ship.

I told her that various measures would be taken to break down her habit of reacting with fear and that some of these would be applied in her life situation and others in the consulting room. The essence of all of them was to oppose the state of fear with other emotional states incompatible with it. I described the case of a young man who had overcome many of his fears by means of expressing his resentment against people whom he feared. On each occasion he inhibited the fear thus and so gradually diminished its habit strength. Verna said that her husband often hurt her feelings; for example, by criticizing her for offering to help somebody. I told her on future occasions to counterattack instead of defending herself when unjustly criticized.

Sixth Session (September 15, 1954)

Verna reported that the lesions in her armpits were much better. Oozing had stopped and there appeared to be less thickening. Her elbow flexures showed further improvement, but not yet complete healing. There was no sign of facial eruption. Since the previous session, Arnold had been inexplicably more interested and affectionate than for some time and had talked much more easily. Besides responding to his affection she had had no occasion for assertive behavior either with him or anybody else. The anxiety-countering effects of relaxation were described

to her during this interview. She was made cognizant of the difference
between muscle tension and other sensations in her arms and forearms,
and then shown how to procure deep relaxation of the arm, forearms,
and forehead by Jacobson's method.[25] The rest of the period was spent
in her practicing what I had shown her.

Seventh Session (September 19, 1954)

Verna was clearly in low spirits. She said that her axillae had become
noticeably worse again. She was very annoyed and upset because Arnold
had told her that the previous week he had ceded to his mother a very
considerable sum of money inherited from his grandmother and had not
mentioned this to her beforehand.

She was very eager to speak about Arnold. This was not the first
occasion on which he had taken important steps without consulting her.
Four months previously she had been upset to hear that he had made
application for a new job. He had tried to excuse himself by the argument that it was important for him to do something all by himself. A new
job had not been forthcoming but as a result of his threat to leave his
present job he had secured promotion. He had very considerable feelings
of inferiority. He was the only member of his family who had not had a
university education and, when he was on the point of marrying Verna,
he was much teased by his family with such remarks as "So you are going
to go before the professor." Having failed an important professional
examination in 1946, he had not had the courage to try again.

Verna said that she had practiced relaxation of the arms, forearms, and
face, and felt that she was achieving increasing success. I spent the latter
part of the session teaching her how to relax the muscles of her face,
jaws, and tongue.

Eighth Session (September 22, 1954)

The axillae were much better and the skin otherwise unchanged. There
had been no further friction at home and Verna had felt quite calm. She
said that part of the trouble with Arnold was that he was insufficiently
articulate. Sometimes he was unjust to the children.

Her skill at relaxation had improved further. I gave her instructions
in relaxing the muscles of her neck and shoulders. I asked her to make a
list at home of everything she could think of that could possibly make
her fearful, anxious, tense, or distressed, and to bring it to me at the
next session. I said, "Obviously I don't want you to include items that
would be disturbing to anybody, such as being confronted with a
poisonous snake."

---

[25] *Op. cit.*

Ninth Session (September 25, 1954)

Verna reported slight exacerbation of the elbow and axillary eruptions since the previous day. This had followed the news that her son had not done as well as expected at an examination.

She presented me with her list of possible disturbing situations. After studying it, I came to the conclusion that the items were divisible into three thematically separate groups: (1) situations suggesting danger and misery, (2) being devalued, and (3) failing to come up to expectation. The items were separated into these groups, and she was asked to re-arrange each group in a graduated order with the most disturbing items at the top and the least disturbing at the bottom.

The list below was largely constructed during this interview, but in-cludes a few items that arose later inserted in their appropriate places.

ANXIETY HIERARCHIES

A. 1. Reading accounts of sexual mutilation
   2. Reading books describing tortures or miseries, *e.g.*,
      (a) The Apostle, (b) The Golden Fleece
   3. Howling or moaning wind
   4. Hearing a quarrel
   5. Driving a car alone on an isolated country road
   6. Being driven on a mountain road, especially in rain
   7. Being driven in a car on a flat country road
   8. Certain music of Chopin suggesting childhood
   9. At home at night without a protecting male
   10. Traveling in a train, especially if it moves swiftly
   11. Walking alone at night, even in a populated area
   12. Continued weeping of a strange child
   13. Visiting a doctor or dentist

B. 1. The thought of not being trusted, *e.g.*, if husband or
      children withhold confidences from her
   2. Somebody shows a dislike for a child of hers
   3. Reference made to her skin condition by
      (a) stranger, (b) friend
   4. She criticizes (a) an equal, (b) a servant
   5. Being criticized by people she likes
   6. Being snapped at
   7. Performing before people, *e.g.*, acting
   8. Addressing a meeting
   9. Being "left out" at a gathering

C. 1. The achievement of one of her children falls below
      expectation
   2. Organizing a function (anticipates possible lack of success)

In the last fifteen minutes of the session, I showed her how to relax the muscles of her back and abdomen and how to use the normal relaxa-tion of the respiratory muscles that occurs with expiration as a coordinating point for rhythmic decrements in the tension of other muscles. This simply means that in coordination with expiration the patient tries to add "a quantum of relaxation" to that already achieved in her other muscles.

Tenth Session (September 29, 1954)

The itch in Verna's axillae and elbow flexures had decreased markedly in the past few days. She had slept the previous night without the itch waking her—for the first time for months. Examination showed that there was no longer any congestion at all in the elbow flexures and the papules were much less prominent.

Life had passed pleasantly, free from upset. When Arnold had made a fuss about Verna buying clothes, she had listened calmly and coolly and had not given vent to her usual bitter retort that he unhesitatingly spent considerable money on his collection of tropical fish. Such a calm response implies inhibition of the tendency to respond in the old disturbed way and a weakening of the habit strength of that tendency.

I said:

> At your first two visits to me I used hypnosis to improve your symptoms by means of direct suggestion. In doing so I was in a sense undoing some damage. The damage, in the form of your skin disease, was in the first place set off by emotional disturbance. The things that can disturb you are on the list we worked on last time. From now on I am going to use hypnosis in such a way as to remove from these things, one by one, the power to disturb you, so that eventually it will not be possible for your emotions to produce harmful effects on your skin. During the trance that I am now about to induce, I shall present to your imagination a number of scenes. There will be one or two with no special significance to you, and one or two mild items from your list.

I now hypnotized her as previously by the levitation method, and then gave her suggestions for deep relaxation, going through the muscle groups systematically.

I then said, "I am now going to ask you to imagine a number of scenes, and you will do so clearly and calmly. If by any chance any scene disturbs you you will at once indicate this to me by raising your left hand three or four inches."

I then presented in succession the following scenes:[26]

(1) Standing at a busy street corner

(2) Sitting in a dentist's waiting room

(3) One of her children comes home and says that he only got 45% for history.

---

[26] It should be noted that the numbering of the scenes presented does not correspond to that in the hierarchy list. This is because the hierarchy in many instances only indicates the general character of a scene, and the details have to be improvised.

Each scene was terminated after it lasted about four seconds, and between the scenes relaxation was intensified by further suggestions. She did not raise her left hand to any scene. After being left to enjoy her "pleasant calm state" for a few more moments, she was roused from the trance. She reported that the scenes had been clear and the only disturbance she had felt was a very slight one in the third scene at the words "child comes home." This means that the relaxation entirely inhibited the anxiety that would ordinarily have been evoked by scenes (1) and (2), and largely inhibited that which would have been evoked by scene (3).

Eleventh Session (October 2, 1954)

Verna had been aware of itching recently only during warm weather in her axillae and occasionally very slightly in the elbow flexures. Examination revealed papules and slight redness in the axillae and no discernible active process in the elbow flexures but some post-lesion pigmentation. Verna stated that when her daughter had arrived home two days previously with a bad report, *she had not minded at all* and had not reprimanded the girl, but had merely told her that she would be rewarded if she did well next time. She was pleased at this unprecedented calm reaction of hers. On the other hand, after her last interview she had felt slightly upset when Arnold had failed to ask her how she fared at the interview.

She said that she was practicing relaxation regularly. At this session training in relaxation was concluded with the muscles of the inferior extremity.

Verna was hypnotized thereafter and made to relax as at the previous session, this being the routine procedure. The scenes presented to her were:

(3) same as for tenth session;
(4) undertaking to organize a community function;
(5) hearing the weeping of a strange child; and
(6) being at a party and finding herself unattended.

At (5) she appeared to breathe more rapidly. On waking she said that the scenes had been clear and none of them had evoked any disturbance in her at all. Of the scenes given at the tenth session only (3) was repeated, because it had evoked some disturbance.

Twelfth Session (October 16, 1954)

There had been some deterioration of the condition of Verna's armpits and elbow flexures since October 6. This had gradually developed over two days, after she had had a scare regarding the possible serious illness of one of her children, and thereafter had remained stationary. (This scare has obvious connections with Heirarchy A.) Examination showed slight redness and some papule formation in the elbow flexures and some congestion of the axillae. Her face was, as before, completely clear.

The school term had begun on the twelfth and as usual she had found it unpleasant to resume work. There were no stresses at home. She was practicing relaxing fairly conscientiously.

A hypnotic trance was induced in the usual manner. She was made to relax, and the following scenes were presented: (5) (see above); (7) riding in a suburban train; (8) addressing the women she is directing in preparation for a community function. The suggestion was given that the affected areas of the skin would become cooler and cooler and would gradually heal. On waking she said that the scenes had been clear and that there had been some disturbance to scene 7, but not to the others. Her elbows and axillae had felt distinctly cool.

Thirteenth Session (October 23, 1954)

The eruption was clearly better. Verna was finding work rather tiring. Her home situation had been pleasant except for mild affrays with one of her daughters and with a servant. She had been to a sad film that she had expected would make her very tense but had relaxed beforehand and had been far less disturbed than at similar films in the past. She had become increasingly conscious of her ability to reduce her tensions actively by the use of relaxation. She had also noticed that if she felt any itching it could be relieved by relaxing for a few minutes.

Under hypnosis the following scenes were presented. (7) (see above); (8) being snapped at by a dissatisfied parent of one of her pupils; (9) hearing a piece of music by Chopin redolent of childhood; and (10) being driven by Arnold along a flat country road. On waking, she reported that the scenes had all been clear and none of them had disturbed her in the least.

Fourteenth Session (October 30, 1954)

The eruption in Verna's armpits and elbow flexures had practically disappeared but she still complained of itching at times. She had noticed that itching appeared immediately whenever she told anybody (including me) about the status of her skin condition. Mere thinking about her skin did not have this effect. One morning itching was brought on when a woman whom Verna thought knew nothing about her condition suddenly said, "How are you? Mrs. X told me about your trouble." The itch was also continuously present during the evenings when she went out with strangers, especially if she was not quite correctly dressed.

Verna had been brought to her appointment this morning in a car driven by her brother and though they had gone through country roads in heavy rain she had been *quite undisturbed.*

In the hypnotic trance the following scenes were presented: (10) being criticized by a friend regarding her behavior toward a child; (11) being driven in hilly country in the rain by Arnold; (12) eldest daughter asks her how her rash is; and (13) hearing a man and woman quarreling in a house outside of which she has parked her car. The scenes were clear and there was slight disturbance in (11) only.

Fifteenth Session *(November 7, 1954)*

Verna still complained of occasional itching in relation to tensions of which, however, there had been very few in the past week. She had had much less reaction to talk about her rash. On examination there was still very slight redness on the posterior margin of the right axilla whereas the left looked greyish-white. Hair was beginning to grow on both sides.

The atmosphere at home had become increasingly pleasant, especially since Arnold had been promoted at work and was now working under a particularly pleasant superior. Verna was pleased that he had recently shown some interest in art.

Though feeling much calmer, she was also feeling unusually fatiguable. (This is a phenomenon I have frequently observed. It is as if the once overtaxed nervous system is now taking a rest. I told her this.) She was no longer plagued by the constant feeling of "I have to. . . ."

Verna was hypnotized and the following scenes presented: (14) criticizing a servant for omitting to do a task as ordered; (12a) a friend asks about her rash; (13a) two teachers quarrel; and (11). There was a very slight disturbance in scene (11) only. (As usual, the reason for the re-introduction of (11) was the fact that it produced some disturbance last time.)

Sixteenth Session *(November 21, 1954)*

Verna's skin was slowly continuing to improve. She no longer had any reaction when speaking about it to anybody, evidently as the result of the inhibition of the anxiety-evoking tendencies of scenes (12) and (12a) by relaxation during hypnotic sessions.

She reported having felt pleasure in remonstrating with a shopkeeper who had been unfair to her assistant—an act that in the past she would have dreaded. (In the very act of remonstrating she would, of course, have reciprocally inhibited any vestiges of anxiety that might have been evoked. She stated that this morning it had seemed likely that she would have to drive alone between two large cities, and she had felt itchiness in her armpits at the prospect. However, she had managed to persuade a relative to give her a lift and by the time she was picked up was completely free of itching and remained so. At this session hypnosis was induced by direct verbal suggestion. The scenes presented were: (11a) (see above); (11b) driving alone between two cities through an un-inhabited area; and (15) at home with her children while the wind howls outside. The scenes were all clear and none of them disturbed her. The re-introduction of (11a) was merely as a stepping stone to (11b).

Seventeenth Session (November 28, 1954)

Although there was now only the slightest evidence of active eruption, Verna continued to suffer from a certain amount of itching. With the warmer days that marked the onset of summer, she perspired more on exertion and some of the itching was associated with this.

Verna said that if she had a sudden fright while driving—for example, having to avoid a dog on the road—she was aware of a disturbed feeling much like that which she used to feel previously when people talked about her eruption. Such a feeling was always accompanied by itch, and if the disturbance was very mild, the itch tended to be its most prominent manifestation.

On November 27 she had had a mild altercation with Arnold—the first for weeks—when he criticized her for having reversed the car so that she scratched it against a pole. He said he *knew* she was going to do that. Verna replied very quietly and deliberately, "If you *knew*, why didn't you warn me?" This silenced him. Nevertheless, she felt a slight itching which lasted for about five minutes.

From the seventeenth session onward, all hypnotic trances were induced by direct verbal suggestion. The scenes presented at this session were: (16) reading a story about a man who had the lobe of his ear shot off; and (17) one of her children refuses to disclose to her the details of an interesting activity that he is doing with a friend of his. I gave post-hypnotic suggestions that there would be coolness of the elbow flexures and axillae and numbness there (to remove the itching and the consequent need to scratch). She reported that the scenes did not disturb her.

Eighteenth Session (December 4, 1954)

The skin condition was better than at any time since its onset. Verna reported that after leaving the consulting room last week, while on the way home, she was witness to an accident in which a car, whose driver had fallen asleep, hit two cyclists, killing one. Verna got out to help and (in marked contrast to past scenes of trauma) was absolutely calm though she spent one and one-half hours at the scene. However, six hours later, she felt tremulous and had some itching in both arms. Bursts of itching recurred during the whole of the following day.

She recounted an argument with Arnold a few days previously which brought on the itch, although she was not really badly agitated. (In the past in such a situation, she would have had a fit of uncontrollable crying.) In telling me of this argument, she again felt a mild itch.

Under hypnosis, the scenes presented were: (18) Arnold failing to understand why she has to spend a sum of money and (16a) reading a story of a man's finger having been amputated because it had been bitten by a snake. (16a) was markedly disturbing, (18) not at all. She stated that (16a) was a particularly abhorrent idea. Nevertheless, it owed something to the previous week's experience with the motor accident, since she had continued to feel a slight general unsteadiness for some days after.

Nineteenth Session (December 11, 1954)

The last vestiges of Verna's rash were now disappearing and she had slept without being waked by itch the whole week although she hadn't used any medication. She had had a little tension—in the form of mild "normal" anxieties, such as when she had to phone a lady to withdraw the help she had previously offered a certain committee. Itching had not accompanied this. There were certain meetings at which she had to speak Afrikaans, and since she was not fluent in this language this produced a good deal of tension in her. This provided the substance for one of the items introduced into the hypnotic trance at this session. The items were: (16b) seeing a child at her school bleeding from his wrist; and (19) speaking at a meeting clearly though not in the best possible Afrikaans. The scenes did not disturb her.

Twentieth Session (December 18, 1954)

At this session it was seen that Verna's elbows were absolutely smooth and retained only slight pigmentation. Her axillae were smooth too and showed no evidence whatever of congestion. She had had to give a statement to the police about the accident she had witnessed. She had felt nervous and had been aware of some tightness of the jaws but no itch, and had felt relieved when they had gone. She noticed that a slight itch lasting for about a minute could be produced in her by a brief startled reaction such as produced by a sudden noise. The scenes presented under hypnosis were: (16c) a child with a half-inch bleeding cut on his scalp, and (16d) a child with a fractured wrist. Neither disturbed her.

Twenty-First Session (December 24, 1954)

During this week, Verna had felt emotionally very much at ease. There had been no itch at all even when she had expected it, for example,

when driving her car without brakes and then seeing another car suddenly emerge from a side street. After talk on some indifferent topics, she
was hypnotized and given scenes: (16e) seeing a child with bleeding
hand, and (20) sound of caning from inside the principal's office. Neither
of these disturbed her.

Twenty-Second Session (January 2, 1955)

Verna stated that she felt slight itching when talking on the telephone.
She had always disliked phoning and this was now the only thing that
could bring on itching. It made no difference whether she called or was
called. Although she had felt slightly anxious watching her daughter
participate in a debate, this had caused no itch.

Under hypnosis the scenes presented were: (16a) child on playing
field lying pale and weeping with fractured leg; (21) reading the story
of parched men walking across the desert; and (22) speaking on the
telephone. No disturbances were produced.

Twenty-Third Session (January 9, 1955)

Verna had had a clash of arms with Arnold because he had reproached
her with not having saved enough for the children to go to the university.
She felt that to some extent this was really an expression of Arnold's resentment at her superiority in the more "cultural" aspects of life. I suggested to Verna to be very positively appreciative of anything Arnold
does well but not to desist from being honestly critical where this is
required.

Under hypnosis the following scenes were presented: (21s) reading
a news item to the effect that the Sahara Desert will be closed to cars at
its western end since Mr. and Mrs. Jones died of thirst there last week;
and (23) reading the story of Captain Scott and his comrades dying of
hunger and cold in the icy wastes. She reported visualizing the scenes
clearly and without disturbance. These scenes, it will be noted, are variations of item 2 in Hierarchy A.

Twenty-Fourth Session (January 16, 1955)

Verna's skin was giving no trouble at all except for a very slight itch
in the armpit after knitting for a period as long as two hours. Examination
showed no signs of any active skin lesion at any of the original sites. In the
axillae hair was growing normally.

Verna had had a completely trouble-free week. She had adopted a very
positive appreciative attitude toward Arnold which had very noticeably
improved the atmosphere. Whereas in the past she had resisted going
on trips because of the anxieties that arose in her during car journeys,

she was now able to pander to Arnold's eagerness to see new places and as a consequence they had arranged a holiday in another state. She said, "As a result, it has been heaven at home." She had deliberately left it to Arnold to make all the detailed arrangements.

Verna's reaction to stories of injuries, bloodshed, and mutilation had been very much better recently. In a book she was reading, war episodes which always in the past would have left her disturbed for days had had scarcely any effect at all. It is no coincidence that this followed the presentation of relevant scenes during hypnotic sessions.

Twenty-Fifth Session (January 25, 1955)

Verna had been away alone with Arnold on a five-day trip. She had actually *enjoyed* being driven by him through mountainous country. She had, however, felt some resistance toward going before leaving on the trip, and a few uneven elevations had appeared in her armpits. What mainly disturbed her was the idea of leaving the children to themselves because she felt that they needed her, especially one of her boys, who was having emotional difficulties. While away, although she had a great deal of pleasure, the desire to return was often in her mind. She felt in a diffuse way that there were hazards in such journeys and that in endangering herself she was threatening the children's welfare.

She stated that she still felt some anxiety at the prospect of coming into the city where the therapist had his office. The anxiety had originally been great.

The scenes presented under hypnosis were: (20) on the road between the two cities, and (21) on a week's holiday alone with Arnold. Neither scene produced any disturbance.

Twenty-Sixth Session (January 30, 1955)

The mild relapse of the axillary dermatitis precipitated the previous week had improved a great deal but there was still some unevenness. Verna was especially pleased at the improvement that had occurred because school was starting on February 1. In the past, at the very thought of a new term she had gone into a state of depression in correlation with which any skin lesion had become worse. This time she felt only a slight apprehension, and it was quite remarkable to her to have her dermatitis improve in association with the commencement of a new term. At a film show she had seen an episode of a Fu Manchu serial. It was a horrifying sequence in which Fu Manchu says to the hero, "I'll take your soul away from you," and then shows him the transfigured faces of previous victims. Verna felt disgust but no disturbance. Although she couldn't get the faces out of her mind for a little while, her companions were similarly affected and she thought her response "very normal!" The scenes under hypnosis were: (21a) two weeks out of town alone with Arnold; (22) reading a story of a man wasting away in a dungeon; and (16a) reading about a man's finger having to be amputated after a snake bite. There were no disturbances. In the case of (16a) this was in contrast with the session of December 4, 1954.

Twenty-Seventh Session (February 12, 1955)

Verna said she felt well except for some itching in the axillae in hot weather and also one day after she had eaten some cream—a usual response. (Milk could also aggravate the dermatitis apparently not in small amounts such as taken in tea.) She had not been aware of any anxiety or tension.

I initiated a discussion about her sex life in which, it will be recalled from her history, she had lost interest about a year previously. She said that she liked caresses and other outward demonstrations of affection and missed them when she did not receive them, but that Arnold would engage in caresses exclusively as an entré to intercourse. Even then the period of preliminary love play was far too short for her liking. Her completely negative attitude toward lovemaking had actually had a long development over four years, beginning when Arnold had on two occasions forced intercourse upon her against her will. She had felt tremendously humiliated. I instructed her to discuss the whole topic of sexual approaches with Arnold.

Twenty-Eighth Session (March 16, 1955)

The eating of ice cream had been followed by some renewal of itching in Verna's axillae, but this had cleared up after three weeks of abstinence from milk products. Once, after two days in the open air, exposed to a hot dry wind, she had noticed a slight recurrence of her facial rash but this had entirely subsided after about a day.

She had raised with Arnold the topic of his sexual approaches one evening about a month previously when he had made amorous advances. For the next fortnight he had made no approaches of any kind to her and thereafter had been very pleasant to her generally and at times affectionate even outside the sexual context.

Verna said that she had been deliberately reading books describing cruelty and mutilations (for example, Sakim) and had not been in the slightest degree upset by any of them. The howling of the wind no longer affected her.

She wished to cease therapy for financial reasons. She felt that she had derived great benefit from it and was now emotionally stable enough to cope on her own.

Follow-up Information

In December, 1955, Verna's physician informed me that although she still complained of a little itching at times, her skin had virtually ceased to be a problem. He saw her only occasionally and at each encounter she referred to her greatly improved emotional well-being.

In June, 1957, Verna replied to a progress questionnaire. She had had a moderately marked recrudescence of itching in her face and armpits in December, 1955, associated with her son having to leave home while in an emotionally disturbed state. But she adjusted herself to this in a few days and the itching stopped. Subsequent similar unhappy situations had scarcely affected her at all. Itching had reappeared occasionally when she was "abnormally tired and compelled by circumstances to do too much," but even then was usually "negligible." Her reactions to all stresses were much milder than they used to be. Her relationship with Arnold had improved greatly in all its aspects.

Clinical Summary

The case of Verna Blue illustrates the deliberate use of (a) assertive and (b) relaxation responses for inhibiting anxiety and thereby progressively weakening neurotic (persistent unadaptive) habits of responding with anxiety to a variety of stimulus situations. Systematic desensitization based on relaxation was much the most important procedure used in this case.

Although financial considerations prevented the treatment from being finalized, there was a marked and lasting amelioration of the patient's sensitivities and, correspondingly, the elimination, apart from very minor and transient recrudescences, of a severe atopic dermatitis.

ADDENDUM

1. *Optimally, what criteria do you use for accepting or rejecting patients for psythotherapy?*

   I accept for psychotherapy all cases of neurosis whether or not there are psychosomatic accompaniments. I do not accept psychoses or psychopathic states. My rejection of psychoses is based on the presumption that they are caused by cell damage or metabolic derangement. All changes achieved by my therapy are through the learning process. Thus, even though some of the undesirable habits of reaction acquired within a psychotic framework are probably learned and therefore capable of unlearning, such unlearning would not affect the organic basis of the psychosis. I do not treat psychopaths because, although learning is probably the origin of their condition, unadaptive anxiety, which in particular my methods are designed to overcome, appears to have little or no part in it.

2. *Do you make a diagnosis before psychotherapy begins?*

Yes. In the first place, as indicated above, I do not begin therapy unless I have made a diagnosis of *neurosis*. Then application of specific methods depends upon identifying stimulus sources of neurotic reactions. At least some of these sources must be identified before active therapy can begin.

3. *Do you attempt to persuade the patient or significant relative to change his (the patient's) environment?*

Not often. Sometimes I encourage the termination of a relationship that is incompatible and disturbed, *e.g.*, a marriage. Sometimes I advise temporary absence from a stressful environment because the tension it arouses is unfavorable to psychotherapy. For example, a sensitive young woman developed a severe anxiety state because of her husband's impatience and his caustic remarks, toward which she was utterly helpless. I persuaded her to move to another town. In the course of two months, she learned the principles of assertive behavior and was desensitized to some relevant situations. She was able then to cope with her husband and an extremely successful marriage was the sequel.

4. *How did you conceptualize the therapist's role in this case?*

In this case, as in all others, I conceived my role to be that of a person in a position of authority who does not moralize to the patient or reproach him either directly or by implication but uses his authority to elicit specific behavior, *e.g.*, assertion, relaxation, in contexts in which inhibition of anxiety may result. I was aware that the psychotherapeutic situation itself could also have anxiety-inhibiting effects.

5. *What aspects of your theory of psychotherapy were particularly apparent or useful in the case presented here?*

This case illustrated in the first place a very close relationship between certain emotional upsets and the state of the patient's skin. Then, it provided an illustration of therapeutic effects due to reciprocal inhibition. When various stimuli that ordinarily aroused anxiety in the patient were presented to her while she was in a very relaxed state, the anxiety response was inhibited and this had the effect of weakening the anxiety response habit to the stimuli concerned—as shown by the fact that similar stimuli encountered in life no longer disturbed the patient.

6. *Do you feel that this case developed significant insight? If not, can improvement be maintained?*

This patient developed helpful insight in two directions: (1) she realized that emotional disturbance could aggravate her skin condition; (2) she understood that her fears were unobjective and undesirable. She also had some insight into part of the ontogeny of her sensitivities. This last insight was probably of no use to her at all. Insight concerning the origins of a neurosis is probably never of value unless either (1) abreaction occurs at the same time of its emergence, or (2) it leads to changed behavior such as assertive behavior that is therapeutic.

7. *What aspects of your own cultural orientation facilitated or impeded the treatment of your case?*

I believe that my completely non-moralistic biological orientation facilitated my treatment in this case and most of the others I treat.

8. *If we consider that a continuum exists from superficial to deep psycho-therapy, where would you place your own case?*

From my standpoint the adjectives "superficial" and "deep" are misleading when applied to psychotherapy. Psychotherapy is either palliative or funda-mental. It is fundamental when it permanently deprives stimuli of their power to evoke anxiety or other neurotic responses. In this sense I classify the therapy of my case presented here as fundamental.

9. *What did you think about the outcome of this case and what criteria did you use for evaluating such outcome?*

I regard this case as very greatly improved. The main criterion is the fact that most stimuli that used to be disturbing now evoke no disturbance. The disturbance produced by a few remaining stimuli is very slight indeed. The state of diminished emotional reactivity is reflected by the persistent derma-tological improvement. Lasting diminution or freedom from symptoms *in the situations which would previously have evoked them* must always be the most essential criterion of fundamental psychotherapeutic success.

10. *How do you terminate psychotherapy?*

I terminate therapy theoretically when the patient has no symptoms and no unadaptive neurotic reactions in any circumstances that I know. In practice I do not insist on this absolute criterion. Minor unadaptive anxieties are almost universal and probably do not matter. Take, for example, an answer of "slightly, sometimes" to the Willoughby questionnaire item, "Are you afraid of falling when you are on a high place?" Since the understanding is that a place without obvious risk is meant, strictly speaking any anxiety is unadaptive. But I do not prolong therapy in order to overcome anxieties of this order. Frequently patients terminate therapy when much improved, though I would prefer more desensitization than has been accomplished.

CHAPTER 14

Intellectualizing Techniques
in Psychotherapy

—RUTH L. MUNROE[1]

Introduction

This contribution focuses on what I call "intellectualizing techniques." I mean here the use of "intellectualization" *by the therapist* as a conscious tool. He falls in with the patient's way of thinking, but is not the dupe of the patient's intellectualizing defenses. He uses the capacity of the patient to "think" and his wish to "understand" constructively within the therapeutic situation as a means of (a) building up the transference on a *broad* ego-syntonic level, (b) using this transference as the stabilizing background for the ups-and-downs of therapy, and (c) as security for relatively bold active interpretations, guarded by their "intellectualized" format.

To make sure that the emphasis of this paper falls on the word *technique*, I must say at the outset that in my opinion therapy is essentially a deep emotional experience for the patient mediated by the transference. Far from wishing to associate myself with sundry "objective" approaches in psychotherapy, I believe that their reported successes are more understandable in terms of an easily deducible transference relationship than in terms of the "objectivity" presented. While there is often some affinity with what I am presenting as a *technique*, the basic dynamics are fundamentally different.

---

[1] A.B., Vassar Coll., 1924; M.A., Columbia U., '26; Ph.D., Columbia, '45; Teaching, guidance, and research at Sarah Lawrence Coll., '32-'49; Prof., Grad. Dept. of Psychol., City Coll. of N.Y., '47– ; Private practice and writing; Consult. for several social agencies; Pres., Soc. for Proj. Techniques, '44-'46; Fellow, APA, Div. 12; Author of *Schools of Psychoanalytic Thought* (New York: Dryden Press), and other works.

It must be admitted, however, that this general definition of therapy includes "faith-healings" in variety. The major omission is the factor of insight. Let me quickly distinguish between the insight of the *therapist* and the insight of the *patient* that we consider essential to a more profound "cure." The insight of the therapist has a familiar label: *diagnosis*. Every patient is indeed a child of God and we love the sinner while repudiating the sin. But the therapist who handles schizophrenic, hysterical, obsessive, and overtly delinquent children of God in exactly the same way is no more a professional therapist than the parish priest, and is often less successful. Our diagnostic skill helps us tailor our approach to the special requirements of a *kind* of person, however modified by adaptation to his individual needs and resources.

The role of insight *for the patient* is stated well by Fromm-Reichmann. "The aim of psychoanalytic therapy is to bring . . . rejected drives and wishes, together with the patient's individual and environmental moral standards, which are the instruments for his rejections, into consciousness and in this way place them at his free disposal."[2] It is this self-understanding which frees the patient not only from the limitations imposed by his own unconscious needs but also from the purely emotional power of the transference.

Freud remarks that the therapist enters into an alliance with the ego of the patient for the purpose of helping it confront more directly the demands of the id and superego. In early years Freud saw the process as a release from repression, but by the 1920's he was breaking down his initial overgeneralizations about the ego and preparing the way for the current strong development of a highly-differentiated ego psychology.

My impression is that most contemporary schools of psychotherapy are in a phase of undue reaction against "intellectualization" in any form. If the patient risks an intelligent broadening of his experience by reference to theories, literature, art, and music, we deplore his "intellectualizing defenses." Though I suspect that many of my colleagues do in fact talk intelligently to intelligent patients, we do not readily admit the fact in print. It has come to seem incidental to the emotional or attitudinal relationship, if not a positive error in technique. Until recently I have myself been vaguely ashamed of a tendency to accept and use the intellectual orientation of the patient. I thought of it as an unfortunate hangover from my days as a teacher when I often had to "sneak in" a spot of psychotherapy. Finally it occurred to me that this tendency is not necessarily a technical error but may be a technical asset which I could formulate and use consciously; which I could recommend as a *technique* for other therapists if

---

[2] F. Fromm-Reichmann, "Recent Advances in Psychoanalytic Therapy," in P. Mullahy (ed.), *A Study of Interpersonal Relations*, (New York: Hermitage Press, 1949), p. 122.

they could see it in the manner I have suggested in the opening paragraph.

The illustrative case is chosen because the therapeutic story is so short (three sessions) as to allow a very detailed description of the to-and-fro between patient and therapist. The quick "success" was mediated mainly by an accidental event in the patient's life, and I consider the patient essentially "normal." Her "normality" was not a foregone conclusion, however, in view of a fairly dramatic presenting symptom, and I am vain enough to agree with the patient that she could not have handled the accidental crisis so well without the image of the therapist established in the first two sessions.

In presenting the case I shall intersperse a detailed account of our sessions with comments on therapeutic technique—usually in small type. Following the case presentation, I shall discuss the intellectualizing technique briefly in relation to other types of patients for whom it is contra-indicated, or must be so modified that only the very general principle of somehow allying one's therapeutic self to constructive aspects of the patient's ego remains.

The Case of Mrs. S.

Mrs. S. was an attractive, intelligent woman of 35. She worked full time in a small advertising agency and engaged in creative artistic work on the side. She had two boys, one by her first husband who was killed in the war; the second, by her present husband—a businessman who, on the whole, was successful, although there had been times when her steady, relatively slender earnings were necessary to tide them over temporary difficulties (two official bankruptcies and other "tight" periods). Both marriages had been "ideally happy" in different ways. As will be explained later in some detail, the therapist had the impression that the patient handled a complex work-family-social life very well—in fact with marked "ego strength."

The presenting problem was that two months ago her husband had told her about his affair with another woman which had taken place last summer, i.e., several months previous to the patient's knowledge of it. The confession had been made in the aftermath of an emotional scene with his brother, who was also a business partner. After a few episodes, the husband had abruptly terminated the affair, realizing that he did not love the woman and that his behavior could cause only pain to all concerned. At least this was his story.

The presenting symptom was that the patient could not get the problem out of her mind. She had immediately forgiven Fred, amid tears and embraces, but had quizzed him every night about the details of the affair until he finally said, "I can't take any more. Divorce me if you must." So she had stopped talking. Thinking about it, however, had become an obsession which she herself described as ruinous to her work, to her children, and to her relationship with Fred. She was preoccupied by day and frigid by night. She felt that she was living a lie.

First Session

Preliminaries. This patient selected her therapist from a book she had found meaningful—*The Happy Family*—which I wrote with my first husband.[3] The initial phone conversation was unsatisfactory. The patient refused to state the nature of her problem. I leaned over backward to explain that I was not a psychiatrist and that I could give her the names of psychiatrists whose point of view was similar to that of the book.[4] She insisted upon seeing *me*, however, at least for an evaluative talk.

It became apparent later that she had more than her share of the layman's anxiety about psychiatry or indeed any formal psychotherapy. The doctor's wife was less threatening than the doctor. Moreover, as a professional woman happily married for the second time, she felt that I might have a direct understanding of her problem. In this she was probably correct. I did spontaneously *like* her, and found it relatively easy to build up the transference in the direction of friendly, appreciative neutrality.

An example. She began the session by talking in very general terms with no concrete mention of any problem except that she knew what she should do and what she should feel, but she couldn't feel it. She kept thinking and thinking, and felt miserable. Could I understand? I said, "Do you know Millay's lines, something like 'The heart is slow to learn what the swift mind perceives at every turn'?" The patient changed the seating arrangement to come much closer, and talked "freely"—as "freely" as she could. The therapist had passed the grade.

> *Comment.* The symbol value of our words is often more important than their content. Quoting Millay dates the therapist unwisely for many young moderns. A slang phrase is as good as a quote for *symbolizing* one's general understanding—but it is even more "datable." Whereas I present my quote as very useful in the present instance, the essential moral is the patient's sense of an aura of understanding. When this aura is genuinely absent, when the therapist cannot really carry through at the symbolized level of social understanding, he should use words strictly for their communicative value or else deliberately to impress, or to not-impress, as the nature and course of the transference may dictate. The erudition of the therapist should sit lightly on his shoulders, whether poetry, science, or slang. "Intellectualizing" in therapy means calling upon the intellectualizing processes of the patient at whatever level is helpful to the transference.

---

[3] J. Levy and R. L. Munroe, *The Happy Family*, (New York: Alfred A. Knopf, Inc., 1938).

[4] This excess of caution on my part is the result of a fairly extensive experience with impecunious cranks who have found this book "meaningful." One is often saddled with the chronic misfit not even a clinic will take on who makes one feel an utter heel for not "doing something" about human misery.

The first session with this patient was allowed to continue for two hours. Perhaps this was a mistake. Certainly it would not be necessary if the therapist worked on a tight schedule. I thought it desirable not to rush her initial outpouring and to use it (a) for transference building, and (b) for diagnosis. As to her relationship with me (the transference), it was quickly obvious that she was a suitable patient for me, and that her expectation of a friendly talk with the doctor's wife would have to be converted into "therapy." The conversion was prepared by a slight emphasis on my therapeutic status when she wanted a too directly personal exchange of confidences, sympathy, advice, etc., and was definitely confirmed before she left. I said clearly that I now thought I could help her, but the usual session was one hour. I mentioned my standard fee. Could she afford it? Would she prefer a referral? She should think it over and let me know whether she wanted to return the following Friday. I further remarked that she might not want to. She might find herself even more upset and it would be natural if she blamed me.

The patient called back promptly to confirm the appointment. She remarked early in the next session that she *was* upset, but I had known she would be, so I was even more to be trusted. She realized that this was "therapy," not just a friendly talk. In fact she realized that she could talk to me more freely as therapist than as friend. I smilingly agreed that while we might easily be friends, she was right in thinking of me differently.

> *Comment.* Friendly trust is an excellent initial basis for transference, but I think it *must* be transformed into a more neutral therapeutic trust for continued treatment. My major assignment here was the shift from my status as the understanding doctor's wife to that of trusted therapist. Direct verbalization of the professional relationship, direct statement of fees with consideration of ability to pay, the possibility of referral, friendly warning about negative reactions, leaving decision to the patient—these are formal devices of considerable usefulness in most cases.[5] The real transformation depends, of course, on the attitude of the therapist throughout the session, and on the quality of his small comments or encouraging, questioning silences. No formal devices can substitute for the *feeling* of being understood and accepted. Most patients, however, and especially intelligent verbalizers like this one, benefit from having their reactions, including their anxieties and resentments, put into words. Although I would have been surprised if Mrs. S. had elected not to continue treatment, I felt that her own decision away from the warmth of our "friendly talk" was important in establishing a relationship different from her initial intention. Too often the therapist underestimates the residual fear of treatment in such patients after a successful first session. He mistakes *his* feeling of acceptance of the familiar therapeutic enterprise for acceptance by a patient to whom it is a new and possibly dangerous game.

Content and diagnostic evaluation. I have little to add to the facts about

---

[5] Occasionally the patient is so panicky or so anxiously indecisive that this "intellectualizing" is inappropriate.

the patient presented in the opening paragraphs. They were produced gradually, and in an "obsessional" manner. After an initial burst of crucial information—her husband's infidelity—she described scene after scene in meticulous detail as she had thought them over for the past two months. Mainly the therapist listened. My interruptions were mostly matter-of-fact questions, asked partly for necessary information and partly to maintain the *feeling of interchange* when my real reaction was "no comment."

The obsessiveness stated as a presenting symptom was fully exhibited. However, the patient showed a high degree of sensitivity to any comment or even gesture on my part, and her account of actual episodes often included some emotional outburst on her part. I found it easy to believe her description of herself as an emotional person. It seemed to me, indeed, that the basic personality structure was hysterical with the typical affective lability and tendency to feeling-dictated distortion, and that the strong obsessive reaction was essentially a secondary defense, although of long standing.

Apart from their function in handling the transference, my matter-of-fact questions had the aim of diagnosing "ego strength." Partly this was a sort of direct experimentation in interpersonal relations and her appreciation of reality. Could she interrupt the flow of her talk to orient a stranger to the major facts of her life? Some patients assume that if you don't know all about Uncle George you don't know about anything, and the unhappy therapist tries to guess the identity of the people talked about without further direct questioning. This patient became apologetic about the use of any proper name the therapist could not be expected to know. I kept really important life-history questions to a minimum and tried to interject them at neutral points in the session because the answers tended to become overly detailed and distant from the small events important to her. I did, however, ask about maids, acquaintances, restaurants—other trivia. As of the transference this was often a way of saying nothing in a cooperative way, but the information was valuable. One can often learn more about the general ego adjustment of a new patient from these unconsidered details than from the most effective questionnaire. If I say that Mrs. S. leads a moderately active social life in a community where friends easily take over care of a child for a while, that she has little maid trouble, takes the PTA seriously, and seems generally adjusted to her culture, it is not because of formal questions on such matters. I merely asked, "What did you do about the kids?" after her description of a crisis involving the husband. Or, "Who is this Mrs. Brown?" Or just listened to the detail that Mrs. Jones had driven her home from the PTA meeting when . . . From this overly meticulous type of reporting, very slightly directed by questions, the therapist can learn a great deal about the patient's way of life without what may seem to the patient irrelevant probing.

Comment. I have gone into some detail about how the small question may serve both in handling the transference and in establishing a diagnosis. At the end of this session I knew the essential facts about the patient's life and had a pretty sound impression of what she was like in her daily living. I knew almost nothing of her childhood, and that nothing was, I suspected, incorrect. A slight hesitation after the statement that her parents were wonderful awakens the latent suspicion of every therapist, but apart from respecting the pause, I made no comment, and deliberately avoided any provocative questions.

This policy does not mean that I consider the early history unimportant. Indeed, if I am interviewing a patient for advice on type of treatment and choice of analyst,[6] I try hard to obtain a clear picture of the "facts" and so far as possible the patient's feeling about them—albeit with careful superficiality. (It requires about as much clinical tact to *avoid* becoming involved with a definitely temporary patient as to develop a continuing therapeutic relationship.) The very great importance of this patient's early experience in determining the nature of her problem will be indicated in the account of her third and last session. I think she should not have been dismissed without some insight into its operation.

But the initial session of a continuing therapy should, I think, be confined rather strictly to what the patient considers important at the moment. Otherwise the early material comes out in such a fashion as to be meaningless and distant, often with some immunization against really feeling its importance when the time is ripe. Or it may be *so* meaningful as to upset further the already precarious balance of the person so distressed as to seek therapy. The latter eventuality seems likely in this case, as will be seen.

Although there are periods in almost every treatment when emotional shock—or at least vigorous direct feeling—seems productive, even essential to real progress, I feel that in general we should make haste slowly. In more technical language, the ego controls of the patient should be respected, especially at the beginning. The transference may be used to extend and correct them whatever the underlying problem.

Interpretation. Thus far I have presented only such remarks and questions as served (a) to build up a sense of sympathetic understanding, and (b) to clarify the diagnostic picture in its most general outlines—good ego-strength, probably an almost hysterical lability beneath the presenting "obsessional" syndrome. This picture seems to me fundamental to observing and handling more specific manifestations.

However, I did offer two relatively deep interpretations aimed at specific dynamic problems which were strikingly in evidence: excessive idealization (her manifestation of the obsessive-compulsive trend), and the soul-searching tendency to blame herself for her husband's dereliction as well as her inability to accept it emotionally. Both interpretations were stated clearly in memorable form, each at a time when she paused in her story in expecta-

---

[6] Both as specialist in diagnostic testing and as author of *Schools of Psychoanalytic Thought* (New York: Dryden Press, 1955), I am frequently consulted about treatment possibilities with no expectation that I would undertake it myself.

tion of the therapist's judgment. Both were highly "intellectualized" and immediately dropped. In fact, I unobtrusively changed the subject myself. Reacted to at once, given with the flavor of authority or argumentativeness, they might easily have provoked an emotional or intellectualized resistance from the patient, if not acute disturbance and/or flight from therapy. As neutral possibilities I thought they might pave the way for a deeper insight when the patient was ready for it.

(1) "Have you ever heard of Horney's concept of the idealized image?" (No) "Well, her idea is mainly that if one has *too* idealized an image, one misses out on the real thing."[7] This impersonal interpretation was followed immediately by a reminder of very good experiences with Fred she had described occurring since the affair but before she knew about it. "Were those unreal?" (No!)

(2) "A woman is not only hurt but angry under such circumstances. I don't know you well enough to say this *is* why you're stuck in so much thinking about how you were to blame, but one *theory* would be that you don't want to blame Fred, so you blame yourself instead. What's so wrong with anger when someone hurts you?"

One further item from this interview is worth reporting. The patient wanted, indeed insisted upon, advice on one point. Should she tell her husband about her feelings? She felt she was living a lie with him. After some discussion of the fact that advice was not my province, I finally did say I thought it would probably be wiser if she waited at least a week or so until she knew better what her feelings were, but no calamity would occur if she had a strong urge to talk. It did not seem to me very important.

Second Session

On arrival the patient wondered whether I would want to continue with such a weak person. She had insisted on advice—about talking to her husband—and then had not taken it. She *had* talked to him; she couldn't help it; and the results were poor. I asked her to repeat exactly what I had said, which, after a little prodding, she did quite correctly. I pointed out the exaggerated tendency to blame herself, and probably it was at that juncture that I described the therapist as a "stick figure" reflecting the attitudes of the patient to which she referred in the letter quoted below. To continue with technique instead of the patient, I asked her several times during this session to repeat what I had *really* said—whenever I could pick out a clear instance of self-critical distortion, without interrupting a flowing account

---

[7] This is, of course, an unduly superficial definition. Unless the patient is especially well-informed and pedantic, I often use the big words of psychology for their suggestive value as *words* with the flavor of scientific authority, adding whatever semi-accurate definition aids the purpose of interpretation. One must not be *too* inaccurate, however.

of her troubles. Very soon we smiled together when she made a self-deprecatory statement. About three energetic transference-laden brief comments, plus the joint smiles, made her aware of this trend with relatively little sense of shame, and some sense of how it affected her behavior. It was not interpreted, as it should be eventually in continued therapy.

Deliberately at random—*i.e.*, after a pretty factual account of a difficult situation—I made the remark, "You're a pretty wonderful person." Tears came to her eyes, although she grimaced a negative, shrugged her shoulders, and went on with her story. A "random" remark of this nature builds up the ego and the transference for a while. (In continued therapy compliments must become more subtle.) I was very careful *not* to offer an evaluative judgment on actual events reported, since although the attitude of self-blame predominated, her account contained a high proportion of rational embellishment. A specific compliment, wrongly placed, awakens either guilt or mistrust of the therapist's insight.

During this session she reviewed in wider perspective the background of her marriage—back to the death of her first husband. She analyzed her relationship to her work and her employer in relation to her marriage. Her employer had been deeply in love with her, very generous and paternal; perhaps it was wrong of her to feel she could not let him down work-wise in order to cater to her husband's wishes. Although I suspected that she partly cherished the romantic aspect of this relationship as ego-consolation for the hurt of her husband's infidelity, my comments were strictly on the work problem, and merely echoed her own judgments. She said, "I know you've worked all your life too." I grinned and said I thought I could quote the chapter my husband wrote in *The Happy Family* to the effect that women who work feel guilty and women who don't feel frustrated. She grinned back, and said actually the work aspect of her life went very well on the whole for her children and husband, and was satisfying to her. She felt she was just picking off leaves instead of getting at the root of the problem. (Her account had sounded to me rehearsed and remote. For some women the work problem *is* important.)

She then went into her husband's relations with his son by his first marriage. After a bitter divorce, the mother had taken the child, aged four, to the West Coast. Too poor and too busy and too preoccupied with his new marriage to travel so far, Fred had soon lost touch with the boy entirely. He did know that the mother continued her former shenanigans. Eventually she married a man of means who wanted to adopt the boy. This Fred finally agreed to. At the age of sixteen (last spring) the boy ran away from home and telephoned his real father to ask for shelter. The call was reinforced by one from the mother to the effect that she concurred entirely—he was *so* difficult they were glad to be rid of him. Fred said, "Come." My patient, however, argued with Fred that this break was too precipitous; that the boy should finish out his school year (less than a month); that the thing seemed more an adolescent crisis than a mature decision; that a lad accustomed to Cadillacs and swimming pools would not easily be content with their relatively humble home—and above all, what would it do to their own family? Better wait a month and have a vacation visit first. So Fred called back postponing the trip, and shunting the onus of the decision to my patient. Although the boy did come east for the following Christmas vacation (a happy time all round), and although he made out well enough at home and school, he was temporarily sour toward the father who promised and withdrew. My patient thought that Fred had resented her intervention, however sensible. This episode very shortly ante-dated the beginning of his affair.

I echoed her painfully defensive conviction that her action had been sensible, even necessary, but also might have been upsetting to Fred. Brief interpretation to the effect that she was prepared to grant *Fred* the com-plexities of human nature, but allowed none to herself or to his relationship with her. I also said at various points, "He must have felt very mixed up and guilty." . . . "Ever hear of ambivalence?" . . . "Maybe he's the kind of person who projects and you mainly introject." Through brief and slightly inaccurate explanations of these terms I hoped to deliver home truths that (a) were so generalized that she could reject them as mere theorizing, and (b) emphasized the therapist's attitude that neither she nor Fred should be condemned. Any direct taking-sides with her against Fred would, I think, have been fatal.

As she was leaving "we" remarked that the head-heart problem had not been solved. She was thinking too much and should allow more direct feeling—but that was easier said than done. That was a Friday. She would return the next Friday. It would take time.

Intercurrent Semi-Contact

On Tuesday night I found a note from my secretary to the effect that Mrs. S. had called at 5:50 and had sounded very upset. She had been told I was teaching a class, could not be reached, but would be home about 8:15. She did not call again. I decided that since I had been fairly reach-able and was engaged in an activity unlikely to involve transference prob-lems, further initiative should come from the patient, no matter how "upset" she was. I could not possibly have imagined what had actually happened. When Mrs. S. asked me in the next session what I would have done if she had reached me, I laughed and said it was lucky that I was out. I couldn't have told her anything she wasn't telling herself. It had been better for her to work it out alone. Actually I suspect I would have had less trust in Fred than she had. While I *hope* I could have maintained an atti-tude of noncommittal support, this is not easy in handling a real-life crisis by phone.

Third Session

The patient arrived promptly on the scheduled Friday—smiling, and looking less tense and drawn than previously. She explained that just as she was leaving the office on Tuesday—*i.e.*, no one around but the office-boy whom she dismissed—she had received a phone call from a man who thought she ought to know how her husband was two-timing her. Not the infidelity she knew about, but another with a woman she had never heard of. I gather that the man went into considerable detail about his own relationship with the woman for whom he had left his wife. Mrs. S. half thought he was "nuts," but he gave details about Fred's absences on business which coincided uncomfortably well with her own knowledge. Although the evidence was not conclusive, it was very impressive to a woman already sensitized to this problem. After insistence by Mrs. S., the man gave his name and that of the woman.

The patient's first reaction, she says, was one of stunned belief, and her decision was to leave Fred at once. She called me, and I wasn't there. She was entirely alone in the office. Finally it occurred to her that she must at least see to the children's going-to-bed and try to protect them—(basic "ego-strength"). And she had to drive home—another hour of solitude. She described her thoughts on the way: "But I love him. I can't have been *so* wrong about him all these years; I'm disloyal to believe this for a minute. . . . I was really coming apart at the seams. I don't know what I would have done if it hadn't been for you. The things you said kept flashing through my mind. *You* would understand how I could hate him so much and love him so much. I was really *angry* about the thing with W. [the first woman] for the first time. Remember you said once I should be? Well, I was. But then I could see him with the children—such a wonderful guy. I began to think maybe—just maybe—I could take even this if it were true. What you said about the idealized image and all."

How she would really have made out is happily an academic question. Fred was clearly bewildered by the accusation about an acquaintance he had taken out to lunch a few times for business purposes. He at once phoned the man who had introduced them—who knew nothing but suggested calling a friend of the woman. Mrs. S. listened in on an extension. This was a pathologically jealous man who had called the wives of handsome male acquaintances twice before. The patient fully accepted this explanation—correctly, so far as I could judge.

"We were wonderfully close that night, closer than ever before. I did ask him some things about W., but not many. It didn't really seem important any more."

Therapeutic comments during this typically over-detailed account were essentially sympathetic *Oh*'s and appreciative *Ah*'s. Then the patient said,

"I've been thinking about why I got so terribly upset about W. I didn't really tell you about my parents. Didn't seem important, but I guess it was. Should I tell you?" (Of course.) Abbreviated here, her story was one of an essentially devoted couple, both "temperamental." They quarreled loudly and made up equally loudly. She thought that probably both actually had had affairs; certainly this was a frequent topic of accusation during the quarrels and of amicable teasing in the good periods between quarrels. Nevertheless, they stuck together in tight spots, were miserable apart, and were deeply concerned about each other and the children. "In a way I wasn't wrong in telling you they were wonderful people." They died within a few months of each other when Mrs. S. was in her early twenties. She went home for a while when she had a baby and a husband in the service (latter he was killed), but apparently there was no great problem about leaving home when she could re-establish independence and renew life with her second husband. The death of her parents did not seem to have been traumatic for her, but to have given her a deeper insight into the love of the parents for each other. Her father had said, "Life really isn't very interesting without your mother."

As a little girl, the patient had been terrified when her father went away on business trips, which he did rather often. She didn't remember whether her mother actually said he was off with a woman, or whether she imagined it, but this was a typical thought, with the childish anxiety that he would never come back.

With no more than occasional small, neutral questions from me, the patient said, "I guess I've been too idealistic about my marriage, because I wanted it to be different. I couldn't stand *any* quarrels. I knew, but I didn't realize how fine their marriage was."

Therapist: "Do you really realize it now?" Patient (*after a pause*): "I see what you mean. It can't have been *that* good. I'm still idealizing or whatever you called it, but I really think I'm on the right track." Therapist: "I think so too. Just remember that people don't usually change over night, neither you nor Fred."

I was slightly more energetic about the childhood reaction to the father's trips because the patient had mentioned it casually and did not return to the topic. With no immediate lead from her, I said, "Let's go back a little to how you felt when your father went away." This was almost the only point at which the therapist took some initiative about the choice of topic discussed. She described her "foolish terror" more concretely, but again as something far away and long ago—mere childishness. So finally I asked whether this terror could have anything to do with the way she had felt about Fred's affair. "After all you've said yourself that you took it a bit too hard."

This "interpretation" did not ring a bell at once like the others; in fact, even after a longer discussion I felt that there was only a faint tinkle of genuine response, if any. Her answer to my question was a puzzled "no" with some intellectual effort to understand what I could mean and to debate it. Her point was that as a child she couldn't understand what was happening and couldn't do anything to help. Now, of course, she could. I remarked that maybe she still worked too hard at trying to understand, with a back reference to Millay's "swift mind." There was a tinkle of real response. So I went on to the effect that feelings of helplessness in childhood often made people feel they had to control everything intelligently, especially when anything happened to make them feel helpless, especially in the old childhood way. I did not insist.

This very brief disquisition rounded off the treatment nicely as a sort of return to the intellectualization of *The Happy Family*. It was not *therapeutic* intellectualization and was indeed deliberately cautious and terminal. The patient felt fine and saw no reason for continued therapy. Although she had shown vulnerability to a certain kind of crisis, she had surmounted others well and in general handled a complicated life admirably. Deliberate—or careless—*meaningful* intellectualization about the childhood material could easily have reopened the problem. "Feeling abandoned" is an appropriate term which I would certainly have used like the "idealized image" if I had wanted to open up this chapter. The term is not very threatening and would offer an easy introduction to gradual discussion of how she handled it—*i.e.*, the dynamics of excessive intellectual control beyond the over-idealization she had recognized, the aggressive aspects of her behavior, direct and compensatory, and eventually the deep infantile components, however defined.

My diagnostic feeling was that Mrs. S. could probably resume function at about the level she had established previous to the acute, obsessive reaction to an event peculiarly threatening to her. This level was high, if not ideal. It seemed to me undesirable to open any new chapters beyond the intellectualized hint that they were there to read if she needed to.

She asked if she could come back if she got in a jam again, and if I would see Fred—adding promptly, "If *he* wants to come. I know he shouldn't come just to please me. I guess he is kinduv mixed up." Knowing Fred only through her, I privately agreed with her diagnosis. A presumably psychogenic heart attack, a couple of bankruptcies, a very bad first marriage with problems about his son, not to mention the affair itself, suggest some difficulties—not, however, so obviously and necessarily severe that I felt a social responsibility about getting a respectable businessman into treatment. About *her* possible return I merely said, "Of course," with the cheerful predictions that she probably *would* get into jams again like most of us and to call whenever she liked. I was also cordial about seeing

---

[8] Fred did call during the summer, but left no message when he was told that I was in Europe for two months.

Fred, but underlined her statement that it should be on his own initiative. "It's almost impossible to help people unless they feel the need of help."[8]

Patient's Summary

Two weeks later on the occasion of paying her bill the patient wrote with typical detail of the continued happy solution of her problem and added, "I seem suddenly to have grown up. . . . I'm married to a *real* wonderful guy. . . . The chemical is thanking the catalyst. For it seems to me you were more than the 'stick figure' you referred to. What you didn't say in words I felt implied in your smile and the way you phrased simple questions."

Therapist's Summary

I have tried to explain how I arrived at the opinion that the rather severe presenting symptom and obsessive manner in therapy seemed essentially a secondary defense against a strong hysterical lability; that ego-strength was good; finally that the particular symptomatic break could be related to a specific childhood problem.

The patient was not "cured" in the sense of a fundamental change in personality structure. The symptomatic cure was dramatic, and perhaps one is entitled to hope she will become more "grown up" at least in one aspect of her marital life, and that she will be less compulsively idealistic and less vulnerable.

She was assured that she could call on the therapist in any future jam— indeed was told that jams are likely. One may hope that the vivid and potentially real *image* of the therapist—words and understanding smile—will continue the treatment for a while until her new insights are confirmed. These are inevitably very shaky in contrast to the rigid idealizing defenses she has lived by for years. Presumably the defenses cover quite strong dependency needs which were deliberately not interpreted. The image of the therapist remains "supportive" in this case. The aim was not to undermine a generally serviceable line of defense, but to modify it in the direction of a more flexible understanding of herself and a less exigent "understanding" of Fred.

Insofar as she was able to grasp and incorporate the therapeutic attitude, she may have been helped beyond the symptomatic level. I like to think that the therapist supported her independence rather than her regressive needs.

> *Comment.* The role of the real-life crisis is an interesting point of speculation. In this case, certainly, there would have been no such quick, apparently meaningful development of insight without it. The carefully intel-

lectualized interpretations suddenly achieved an emotional immediacy which I would never have ventured to provoke even as transference reactions so early in treatment. They had been offered as preparation for insight, not insight itself. However, there they were when she needed them, along with the aura of the therapist's understanding support.

What would have happened that Tuesday night if in the two previous sessions I had (a) been more cautious in offering interpretations, (b) encouraged more direct emergence of feeling even in the transference relationship along whatever lines the patient "chose," and/or (c) opened up in any way the childhood story? I suspect that Mrs. S. would have been *less* able to handle the situation on her own, and that if she had continued therapy at all its course would have been more agitated and more demanding. It would probably have been necessary to see her more frequently for a while, the problem of concrete advice would probably have become acute, the therapist would have been forced into a more directly supportive role, and the level of therapy would have deepened. I suspect that I would have been presenting the accidental crisis provoked by the phone call as a complication of a much longer treatment rather than as a resolution.

Should the level of therapy have been deepened anyhow? I suggested above that I felt such deepening to be easily within my powers on a sound basis, and that I put out a few gentle feelers in this direction to which barbs could have been added. I hope I have already explained why the feelers were withdrawn instead. The patient seemed to me essentially "normal" and well able to handle her life with a bit of help over a rather specific problem. Return was made easy in case I was wrong, and as a tempering of her own over-confidence.

It seems to me that many therapists today are overly idealistic for their patients and are unwilling to accept basic problems such as insecurity, which are endemic in our culture. At the other extreme, a few therapists seem so impressed by a cure of the presenting symptom that they do not even try to evaluate the general personality picture in its social setting. My justification for allowing Mrs. S. to terminate treatment because she felt fine rests upon the diagnostic evaluation described in detail above. With another diagnostic picture, or even a less secure diagnostic picture, it is, I think, the active responsibility of the therapist to bring the patient back into therapy after a symptomatic "cure." There are no general rules as to how and when, because so much depends upon the nature of the individual case. The general *danger* is that a premature, essentially accidental "success" may become a focus of resistance and of the irrational demand: "You did it once, now do it again."

But I think the diagnosis "essentially normal" should be one of the categories the therapist considers in early contact. We might have more quick successes of enduring value if our best therapies were not so specifically tailored to neurosis, with such leisurely expectations of the therapeutic process.

The Intellectualizing Technique

The technique, as I remarked at the outset, has three aspects. The first is building rapport. Most patients come to therapy wanting to be understood and wanting to understand themselves, however great their misery or anxiety. This ego attitude is one of our best resources for constructive effort, a natural potential of independence and control of his destiny by the patient himself. Too often, nowadays, this initial attitude is dissipated by our fear of the conscious mind as a distorting, concealing agent. We deliberately try to bring the patient into a feeling rather than a thinking relationship. Theoretical analysis of the transference is usually made in terms of underlying emotional attitudes, almost in contrast to "superficial" thinking.

I have tried to illustrate in this case how the therapist may fall in with the patient's *way of thinking*, although not with specific ideas. The quote from Millay *said* nothing more than simple repetition of the patient's words with an accepting nod, or any direct statement that her problems were not unique. But it cut the ice of the initial interview and put me in the category of an understanding person. The romantic quote is not suitable for all patients, indeed contra-indicated for many, and I warned against attempting a promise of broad ego rapport on a basis one cannot really sustain. The major generalization is alertness to the quality of the patient's ego experience, and the effort to *indicate* capacity for understanding on this basis. I am tempted to call it "intellectualizing" at whatever level the patient's conscious mind suggests—e.g., teen-age slang or the lingo of a religious sect.[9]

The aura of understanding needs occasional conscious reinforcement during therapy. During meaningful stretches of therapy, both patient and therapist tend to forget about ways of thinking. In the doldrum periods

---

[9] An extreme example of nonintellectual "intellectualizing" occurred when an hysterical, near psychotic patient of my psychiatrist husband phoned in his absence—screaming, crying, and assaultive toward the husband who helped her phone—and explained the immediate cause of the outburst. My contribution here was to ask with friendly firmness, "Can you *listen* to me, Jessica?," then to make clear that the doctor would return in an hour, and after obtaining some quiet to suggest that she *do* something meanwhile, which we jointly agreed should be fixing her hair. This brilliant meeting of minds was followed the next day by her request to the doctor that she talk with me because I could "understand." Needless to say, she was not given the opportunity for disillusionment.

Mainly this patient liked the firm definiteness of my remarks—so easy when the issue is to wait an hour for the trusted doctor! I think, however, that her sense of "understanding" did not come from the hortatory quality of the remarks, but from their relation to her temporarily overwhelmed ego. A sharp *Listen* is the main thing, but "Can you *listen?*" adds an appeal to her total ego that brings it back into the picture. (Of course she can listen, she's not crazy, is she?) She pulled up and said, "Yes, I can." The gradual, simplified restitution of ego-control was confirmed by the active discussion of what she was going to do. Although this was in fact only fixing her hair, the experience had *for her* the quality of a genuine "ego" rapport which she generalized to "understanding" on a very broad level.

To call this brief handling of a near-psychotic episode an "intellectualizing technique," would denature the purpose of my paper, but it illustrates well the principle of a call on the ego resources of the patient *at the level of the patient*, temporary or general. Fuller recognition of this basic resource of the transference is to me more important than the more restricted "technique" here presented.

they may again become of crucial importance. Ego resistance can often be overcome by a subtly vivid reminder of ego rapport distant from the immediate problem. The reason is clear. The therapist easily becomes ego-alien as the ego entrenches itself against incursions from disturbing impulses released in therapy. Renewed wooing of the ego along lines generally characteristic for the patient may facilitate renewal of the alliance between ego and therapist so important for cure. Far from encouraging a giving in to impulse or more rigid repression, such renewal of a sense of understanding on a *broad* ego level may allow further ego-syntonic release. I think we have not sufficiently realized how the primitivization of emotional (impulse) expression in therapy typically involves a narrowing of ego control almost in proportion. I think the *therapist* often becomes hostile to a narrowed ego defense or anxious about it. We expect the patient to behave decently during treatment, at least outside of the office. On the one hand we attack his last-ditch defenses, and on the other expect him miraculously to continue ego business as usual the moment the session is over.

This schizoid interruption of the normal unity of a person's life is doubtless possible and uniquely fruitful for many patients on the couch. In psychotherapy it is often confusing. In practice, probably every therapist does adapt his interpretations to the on-going ego-defenses of the patient as a matter of "tact." I suggest that is *our business* to discern and utilize the major ego orientation of the patient. This is more than tact. It is a therapeutic assignment of at least equal importance with discerning the underlying emotional constellations in the transference.

My second point is almost a corollary of the first, namely, a positive effort to bring the patient to a shared understanding of the therapeutic attitude. This is not, to my mind, a wishy-washy tolerance of any behavior on the part of the patient and his associates. Fundamental *values* must be respected. Although I would not be able to draw up a formal list of such values, and although patients are often caught in situations where conflicting values are a quite real issue (*e.g.*, the independence of an adolescent vs. the hurt to a parent who somehow needs support), I have never found it very hard to reach common ground with patients. This means preliminary acceptance of whatever specific code the patient holds, and at times his continuation of specific beliefs I may consider deplorable (*e.g.*, race prejudice). Direct discussion of such points on an intellectual basis is usually fatal to therapy. The common ground becomes the effort to understand *why* a person behaves "badly," whether he's a "dirty nigger" or the patient's mother or the patient himself. The concrete definition of "bad" often shifts. What does not shift is the attitude of understanding.

The primary aim is, of course, the patient's understanding of his own problems, enormously facilitated by the acceptance of the therapist. With many patients, at least in some phases of the treatment, discussion of other people's problems subserves this aim. I did not, for instance, apply the concept of ambivalence directly to Mrs. S. The term was used only in connection with Fred's possible attitudes toward her following the episode with his son. Yet when she herself for the first time consciously "hated" Fred, she promptly made the personal application. The therapist's accepting attitude was more truly vivid toward herself because she had shared actively in working it out for Fred.

This example can also serve as illustration of the third point, namely earlier and bolder interpretations than could be risked either as authoritative statements by the therapist or as the guided self-discovery of the patient. There is often—indeed there must be—the shocking and painful realization, "*Thou* art the man." If it does not come spontaneously, the therapist must shove the patient into the deep water of direct insight. After prior intellectualization, however, the patient usually finds himself wearing water-wings. Being that man is not so utterly devastating! The therapist understands; the patient more easily finds that he himself has an unsuspected potential of understanding and self-forgiveness beyond immediate terror and guilt.

"Intellectualizing" with the patient is a technique to be used carefully. Its use as mere padding dulls the instrument, like using fine sewing shears to cut paper for the shelves and to snip off flower stalks. The patient is not helped and may thicken his skin against any interpretive comment. At the other extreme, we often do not realize the sharpness of this tool. Any teacher knows how a discussion, an exciting lecture, or a field trip may be generally stimulating to the class—and may occasionally prove seriously disturbing to one student. I wish I did not have to add that the same thing often happens in therapy. It has happened to me both as therapist and as patient. Also, I have fairly often had to cope with people acutely upset by what their therapist said. On checking with the therapist I often find that he had spoken precisely as quoted, but is surprised at the reaction. "It was just a passing remark," or, "The patient seemed to know all about this sort of thing."

It is impossible to know exactly how a patient will take our "intellectualizations," deliberate or not. A very common error is to support the patient "intellectually" in recognizing and rebelling against the sanctimonious domination of a parent or spouse. The condemning words spoken in this connection often remain to plague us when we wish eventually to bring the patient to recognition of similar trends in himself. We have in effect reinforced and broadened the patient's resistance. Supportive silence is no great help, since the patient generalizes our judgment from his own "ideas." It seems to me, therefore, that *all* our remarks should be given a benign *slant*.

Dulling the instrument is avoided if we try to keep our remarks within the orbit of what we feel *this* patient must eventually see. Our comments may be distant from the immediate problem as seen by the patient, but they should be essentially preparatory. In illustration, consider the way Mrs. S.'s work problems were dismissed with a cursory laugh—although a wry and understanding one. ("Women who work feel guilty and women who don't feel frustrated.") Directly meaningful intellectualizations on this point were deliberately not used because *clinically* the work area seemed unimportant at the moment. I am not a Horneyite in general. Choice of the *term* "idealized image" was dictated by what I thought might reach *this* patient.

Contra-indications

Patients in a state of panic, whether as presenting symptom or as a temporary phase of therapy, usually need *directness*. One does not discuss principles of fire control in the midst of a blaze, however fruitful such discussion may be before and after the crisis.

Patients of very limited intelligence or education also require a more direct approach. The use of simple words and homely examples may counteract this difficulty if the problem is only lack of education. The therapeutic attitude suggested is, however, intrinsically complex. It may be literally impossible for some *minds* to grasp the idea of condemning actions while trying to understand motives. The therapist is necessarily seen as for or against. Even a light word in extenuation of a person toward whom he feels hostile often means to the patient a total going over to the enemy, and should be risked only when the therapist considers the patient emotionally ready for a change in attitude.

This warning applies also to some types of psychotics, sometimes rather generally,[10] sometimes only in restricted areas of paranoid involvement.

What we might call an extreme authoritarian attitude may have its roots in the character of the patient, rather than in his poor intelligence. In such cases the intellectualizing technique is not entirely excluded, but it must be greatly modified. Sometimes one's very refusal to give a black-or-white judgment must be couched in an authoritative manner. Such patients are typically hypersensitive to a mere *show* of authority, but quiet confidence is essential.

The dyed-in-the-wool "intellectualizers" present a special problem to which there is no single answer. Some of them are essentially authoritarian characters who by virtue of intelligence and training make special use of intellectuality as a defense and a weapon. With them one must be extra

---

[10] The intelligent "borderline" psychotic may not be sensitive to the for or against problem, but often needs a general simplification of his rampant intellectual processes— a sort of *tuition* in common sense and ordinary values, supported by the therapeutic aura of understanding.

careful to allow *no* arguments to develop, and no feeling that the therapist is afraid to face their arguments. One may say in effect, "That's an interesting point. I wish we could discuss it further, but our job here is *you*. Why is it so important to you?" This question often leads to revealing material with no further "argument." Not always. At times there must be direct interpretive discussion of the intellectualizing defense and/or weapon as such.

Saving the *patient's* face should, however, be as important to the therapist as saving his own. Such patients are often inconsistent. They should never be accused of illogical thinking except as a *deliberate* hurt. One does not lightly undermine a major defense system. Inconsistencies are best left alone or slightly modified, in my opinion, until confrontation serves a therapeutic purpose. A general challenge to logic and memory is, for these patients, tantamount to keeping a cat in the office when the presenting symptom is allergy to cats.

"Intellectualizers" of this order should be distinguished from the true obsessives, of whom Mrs. S. is a pallid example. Some of them are not intellectuals in the common sense of the word, but specific thoughts are emotionally determined and/or their "thinking has an emotionalized quality. Freud called it "isolation" and "erotization." In intellectualizing with these patients one is dealing pretty directly with the very stuff of their emotional life. To fall in entirely with their thoughts merely perpetuates the pathology. It is, however, comparatively easy to disentangle the process of thinking from particular ideas and from the defensive reliance of "logic" described above. These patients *know* that they are "thinking too much" and come quite easily to joint recognition with the therapist of how their thinking obscures their feeling. It is all too easy to "intellectualize with" them, and become lost in a common fog. Direct *feeling* in the transference is nowhere more important, and must be actively provoked if not supplied by external incidents. But if we fail to relate the direct feeling to our previous "intellectualizing with," the patients may experience a sense of *personal rejection* out of all proportion to the pain of the insights achieved.

In brief summary, I have suggested "intellectualization" as a tool of therapy, and have illustrated its use in one especially suitable case. *In essence* I would define "intellectualization" as a call upon the broad ego stance of the patient in building and utilizing the transference relationship for therapeutic ends. In its narrower clinical definition, the technique is unsuitable for panic states, for unintelligent patients, and those with a rigid authoritarian character structure. For dyed-in-the-wool intellectualizers, it is useful mainly in helping the patient understand why one does *not* fall in with his way of thinking.

The novelty of "intellectualizing techniques" lies in the suggestion we do consciously what we are already doing unconsciously. Clinical tact in this area could become more resourceful and less subject to the ups and downs of counter-transference if the therapist were more aware of the "intellectual" aspects of the therapeutic relationship.

ADDENDUM

1. *Optimally, what criteria do you use for accepting or rejecting patients for psychotherapy?*

   The main desideratum for me is the possibility of good "ego" contact. I reject patients from the urban "lower classes" because of my own inability to offer an "aura of social understanding." At our country home I do have enough friendly knowledge of the local scene outside my own "class" to ask intelligent questions in decent rapport. Lack of temperamental affinity is difficult, but less overwhelming for me than inability to speak the "cultural language" of the patient.

   I refer patients able to benefit by and pay for full psychoanalysis.

2. *Do you make a diagnosis before psychotherapy begins?*

   Diagnostic *alertness* seems to me essential, as illustrated in the case here presented. *I* use test devices frequently because they are my specialty. For me they are a safeguard against clinical error; a means of ascertaining deep constellations without hazardous probing, and often offer an "intellectual" wedge into the patient's defenses when selected results are used *with* the patient.

   Most of my "guidance" cases come to me initially for testing, so of course the results are the basis of discussion. I have never used them as systematically and concretely as Harrower's projective counseling technique suggests, partly from lack of imagination and partly from caution. Anything called a test packs a terrific wallop. Few of us entirely laugh off even an examination of our palms in the Gypsy Tea Room. Harrower offers a very valuable and very sharp tool for counseling—so sharp that with her encouragement I would like to reinforce her emphasis on preliminary "diagnosis" and handling in relation to the broad ego stance of the patient.

3. *Do you attempt to persuade the patient or significant relative to change his (the patient's) environment?*

   The answer here is *usually* no, except in quite minor matters. As a rule, the patient's attitude is the pathological factor likely to spoil any new situation. The patient is usually caught by the reality of his total social situation so firmly that changes of school, job, marriage, etc., introduce more problems than they solve.

   The general rule should recognize exceptional cases.

4. *How did you conceptualize the therapist's role in this case?*

   I like the patient's word "catalyst." I tried to set her to thinking and feeling more flexibly and constructively in her own way. I think she did not realize how far my role was also "supportive" in the broadest sense of the term.

5. *What aspects of your theory of psychotherapy were particularly apparent or useful in the case presented here?*

   This patient was especially apt in responding to and assimilating "bits" of intellectualized interpretation. I tried to explain that the "bits" were carefully selected for their appeal to *her* problems, and were consciously used within the transference. The pages on contra-indications for "intellectualizing techniques" suggest their limitations, although I think we should pay more attention to the "broad ego stance" of the patient in all of our therapeutic approaches.

6. *Do you feel that this case developed significant insight? If not, can improvement be maintained?*

I think this patient achieved significant insight in regard to the aspect of her marriage which precipitated the pathological break, and will probably be less compulsively idealistic about her marriage in general. Her basic personality structure was not changed.

7. *What aspects of your own cultural orientation facilitated or impeded the treatment of your case?*

I have enough fringe contacts with suburbia to grasp the main outlines of her life and enough general culture to adapt to a wide variety of patients at some point significant for them—with the very important exception noted above in Question 1.

8. *If we consider that a continuum exists from superficial to deep psychotherapy, where would you place your own case?*

Obviously superficial. I *hope* there was a constructive modification of the patient's defense systems which will continue.

9. *What did you think about the outcome of this case and what criteria did you use for evaluating such outcome?*

See Therapist's Summary and Comment.

10. *How do you terminate psychotherapy?*

Much of my work has been with students whose termination was set by the college year, and with patients for whom my aim was getting them into psychoanalysis with a suitable person. "Guidance cases" come for help on a particular problem, expecting only a few sessions. Termination is automatic unless psychotherapy seems necessary and feasible. Return is suggested "if things don't work out." A fair number do call in later crises. I suppose the sympathetic but firm statement that I am not able to help some of them further may be called termination technique. One often feels more "sensible" than happy in situations where deep problems remain unsolved and seem insoluble. One is careful, however, not to make them worse by undermining what defenses the patient has unless one can arrange for effective treatment.

Formal termination in psychotherapy has thus far followed the pattern described for Mrs. S. When the patient "feels fine" and the currently active or immediately predictable areas of conflict have been well set toward resolution, he is encouraged to stop treatment. I think it very important to temper his over-confidence with smiling cynicism, disregarded at the moment, but easily remembered as a reassurance when he falters; also to leave with him some definite *hint* as to the nature of unresolved problems;

to make return easy.[9] It may be only my limited experience in formal psychotherapy that has given me good results thus far, but I like to think that the technique of calling upon the "broad ego stance" of the patient has prevented slobbery appeals for support later on, along with instances of serious return when the patient has recognized for himself the meaning of an earlier "hint."

---

[9] In this approach I feel allied to Freud's discussion of the responsibility of the psychoanalyst in deliberately provoking the necessary deep response from the patient in areas where no current problem exists. *Freud* is, in general, cautious. ("Analysis Terminable and Interminable," 1937; *Collected Papers,* Hogarth Press, 1950, Vol. V.) I was also impressed by Alexander's discussion of how prepared breaks in therapy may reduce the doldrum periods of analysis. (F. Alexander and T. M. French, *Psychoanalytic Therapy.* New York: Ronald Press Co., 1946) They may affect the transference adversely in full analysis, but seem to me very useful in psychotherapy.

CHAPTER 15

Hypnotherapy in Anxiety and Depression

—JEROME M. SCHNECK[1]

Mr. Brandon Bea sought treatment for anxiety and depression of three-years duration. He was thirty years old, married, and had two children. Six months following the onset of symptoms, psychotherapy had been initiated elsewhere. During the one year of this therapeutic contact, anxiety and depression had fluctuated in intensity; but more lasting and satisfying relief had not been obtained. Mr. Bea also felt that he had not reached an understanding of his basic problem that might account sufficiently for his disturbance and the knowledge of which might help preclude a recurrence. He seemed to believe that such understanding, when meaningful enough, might be essential for future well-being. The patient requested hypnotherapy after having read about it in a popular periodical. He claimed no special interest in the details of such treatment but felt it might offer possibilities for assistance.

[1] A.B., Cornell U., 1939; M.D., Long Island Coll. of Medic., '43; Resident and Senior Resident Psychiat., Menninger Clin., '44-45; Chief, Psychiat. and Sociol. Dept., Fort Missoula, Mont. and Camp Cooke, Calif., '46-'47; Priv. Pract., 47— ; Consult., Audiology Clin., Veterans Admin., '47-'48; Dir., Mt. Vernon Ment. Hyg. Clin., '47-'52; Instr. in Clin. Psychiat., Long Island Coll. of Medic., '47-'50; Assoc. Chief Psychiat., '49-'50 and Consult., '51-'52, Westchester County Dept. of Health; Clin. Assoc., '50-'53 and Clin. Assist. Prof. of Psychiat., '55-'58, Clin. Assoc. Prof., '58— , State Univ. of N.Y., Coll. of Medic., at N.Y.C.; Bd. of Editors, *Personality: Symposia on Topical Issues*, '50-'51; Assoc. Editor, *J. of Clinical and Experimental Hypnosis*, '52— ; Superv. Psychiat., Community Guid. Centers, '55— ; Amer. Acad. of Psychotherapists, V.P., '56— ; Diplomate, Amer. Bd. of Psychiat. and Neurol., '49; Fellow: Amer. Psychiat. Assoc., Amer. Psycholog. Assoc., Amer. Assoc. for the Advancement of Science, The Soc. for Clin. and Exper. Hypnosis (Founder, '49, President, '49-'55); Author of 135 contributions to professional literature.

Initial Impressions and Evaluations

The patient was of medium height and weight. There was nothing unusual about his appearance. His speech, however, reflected some shyness and self-consciousness. He did not verbalize freely. At times he seemed brusque, and this was viewed as an attempt to appear firm in an effort to counteract basic feelings of insecurity. He was not deliberately evasive.

In approaching therapy, Mr. Bea's attitude was somewhat different from that often encountered among patients who have been in treatment previously. They often claim that hypnosis has been decided on as a last resort. Their words or manner imply it must be effective and completely so. Furthermore, they stress time, and hypnotherapy is invariably regarded as a short-term procedure regardless of how long the emotional problems may have been present or the number of years already spent with one or more therapists. This approach places heavy demands on the treatment procedure and the new therapist. It is a serious impediment to effective progress because of the degree of hostility present, mounting feelings of self-depreciation, and difficulty in permitting natural unfolding of a type of doctor-patient relationship that might otherwise have developed in the hypnotherapeutic setting. Impatience precludes opportunities to test adequately the techniques and types of treatment approach suited best to the needs of the patient. Such contacts are, as a result, frequently and unfortunately abortive. None of these issues are intrinsically unusual, but they are generally more intense in hypnotherapeutic settings. Given time, these problems often can be analyzed and worked through effectively. When the patient terminates contact prematurely, he unknowingly prevents the introduction of specific hypnotherapeutic measures through which he originally had in fact hoped to gain.

Mr. Bea was surely interested in as short-term therapy as he could possibly obtain; but he made no special demands, nor did he press for inclusion of certain occasionally dramatic procedures, such as regression and revivification, as is often done by patients who have read much and come to treatment with preconceived ideas as to what should be effective for them.

Hypnotherapeutic Measures

It is desirable to work with the most simple hypnotic techniques a patient can use well. More involved methods need be introduced only when necessary. Hypnotherapeutic devices may be graded generally in terms of lesser or greater difficulty based on experience with large numbers of patients. Each individual, however, must be tested for his own abilities and these cannot be evaluated in advance with certainty.

Hypnosis was induced for Mr. Bea with visual fixation and stress on increasing feelings of relaxation. Initially, he was seated in a chair opposite the therapist. Later, he assumed a reclining position on the couch for greater comfort.

Hypnosis sessions were used during most interviews. Therapeutic interviews lasted forty-five minutes. The portion devoted to use of hypnosis varied from time to time. Treatment sessions were initiated with spontaneous comments by the patient regarding thoughts, feelings, or recent events. He was seen once a week and there were occasional missed appointments owing to illness or unforeseen interferences. Hypnosis was induced when the patient's verbalizations were no longer sufficiently free and when periods of silence could not be utilized in a therapeutically constructive fashion.

During hypnosis Mr. Bea was offered opportunities for free association. In addition there was simple conversational exchange. Visual imagery also was employed within the hypnotic state. The patient would be asked to picture a scene and to describe its content. Depending on the type of issues at hand, such scenes might be structured or unstructured. They might deal with the present, past, or future. "Scene visualizations," the term used when such settings were realistic and consistent with everyday living, would arise spontaneously at times. When this happened, Mr. Bea would on occasion proceed to describe images and issues, or there might be periods of silence and immobility followed only by a sudden change in position. For example, his hands might be folded over his stomach and he would suddenly place them behind his head, conveying an impression of obviously assumed relaxation. Such movements often reflected termination of intense concentration on images with subsequent intent to suppress ideation and affect. At such points he would be encouraged to verbalize.

An interesting motor phenomenon was the tendency to scratch himself after periods of silence. This reaction seemed to reflect itching as a miniature somatic conversion. Apparently unconscious conflict was projected ideationally, followed by attempts to repress the conflict and its representation in imagery. As his pattern of hypnotic behavior developed it seemed clear that this reaction also involved his method of establishing contact with the therapist subsequent to a period of more intense withdrawal into his own fantasies. Many patients experience a large variety of sensory and motor phenomena during hypnosis. They are psychologically meaningful and can often be analyzed and incorporated significantly into the total therapeutic contact. This is accomplished mostly in hypnoanalytic settings in contrast with other forms of hypnotic therapy.

Mr. Bea tended to verbalize more during hypnotic states than otherwise. In part this might be ascribed to general relaxation. On a different level one might see such verbalizing as stemming from an ability to become more aware of his thoughts and feelings, with greater acceptance of them and less need to suppress or repress significant and disturbing issues. The interpersonal relationship in general, and the hypnotic relationship specifically, were rather permissive and non-authoritarian. The hypnotic setting could be construed as combining both authoritarian and non-authoritarian features. On the one hand it was a specially structured setting in which definite attempts to work on problems were expected by implication. There was the expectation to comply. This would be true of the office setting without use of hypnosis; but the former was closer to his everyday living experience, whereas the latter constituted a special, technically structured arrangement. In addition to interpretation of such setting as implying expectation to comply, there was, as mentioned, the aura of permissiveness. He was free to say whatever he wished and to express himself as he saw fit. This poses a new impression of authority, and patients react differently to it. Such reactions may be analyzed according to the needs of the patient and manner in which he develops the hypnotic relationship.

Mr. Bea displayed another ability during hypnosis which is rarely stressed in relation to its actual importance. This is the ability to integrate data meaningfully. Patients often function in this respect to a degree superior to therapeutic settings not employing hypnosis.

Returning to imagery, it was possible for this patient to recall dreams during hypnosis he was unable to recall prior to the hypnotic state. In some instances dreams had been recalled poorly and hypnosis enhanced their completion.

The hypnotic setting permitted use of post-hypnotic suggestions which generally took the following form. Mr. Bea would be told that he would dream between sessions about a particular issue under discussion, and that analysis of such dreams would help him to understand better the underlying problems. He would be told that during the ensuing week he would particularly observe his relationship to specific people at work and in family and social settings, and that he would become more aware of the nature of these relationships than he had heretofore. A variety of such suggestions for increasing self-awareness would be used and proved fruitful during the total therapeutic contact. Another type of suggestion was that he would be working unconsciously on understandings pertaining to his problem in general or to special issues. Gradually, newly discovered ideas, feelings, and understandings would become consciously evident. The rate of such rise to consciousness would keep pace with his growing ability to tolerate insights without undue anxiety, and he would then be able to put such gains to use in everyday living.

During periods of anxiety direct suggestions might be used to decrease its intensity along with suggestions noted above to enhance gradual development of understandings in relation to underlying conflicts. When indicated, and within the assumed level of his ability to cope with his anxiety,

Mr. Bea might be told during hypnosis that he would become aware of thoughts or emotions relating to the anxiety he was experiencing at a particular moment. Utilization of these measures would depend on the therapist's clinical judgment. Timing, wording, and the tone of all suggestions involve subtleties which are difficult to impart in a descriptive account.

As hypnosis sessions came to a close, the patient was permitted a moment or two in the hypnotic state with instructions that he need say nothing at all. The purpose of this procedure was to allow time for psychological elaboration, in a very permissive setting, of issues discussed during the hypnosis. Often, silence would prevail. At times, while at work on crucial issues, Mr. Bea would feel impelled to comment further. When doing so it was clear at times that data previously elicited were being integrated effectively. He was permitted to say whatever he wished. On occasion he would not speak at this point, but would deal further with issues after coming out of the hypnotic state on simple signal, uually a count of one to five. The latter signal was used as a decisive termination point between the hypnotic and his usual waking state, precluding confusion, and allowing enough time in termination to forestall any feelings of drowsiness or dizziness produced in some patients by too rapid change. Mr. Bea occasionally noted a tendency toward depth reversal during termination of the hypnotic state. Such deepening rather than a subjective feeling of lessening depth was usually related to the need to complete mental work in which he had been engaged prior to termination. Other issues may be involved also in this reaction.

Mr. Bea, having sought hypnotherapy and found suited to its use, employed it during early sessions as routine. When his attitudes were tested indirectly later on by offering him the choice of using hypnosis or postponing it to subsequent sessions, he permitted the therapist's judgment to influence the decision. Still later, after significant improvement had been obtained, he showed no particular interest in the use of hypnosis as a point of necessity. Contrary to claims still extant, usually by therapists inexperienced in hypnotherapy, the patient demonstrated no dependence on hypnosis and this is almost invariably the case in hypnotherapeutic and hypnoanalytic practice. Mr. Bea was seen for thirty-eight visits within a period of 10 months.

Therapeutic Issues

Background Data

Significant background information was obtained during treatment. Mr. Bea's mother had died when he was quite young. His father could not, or would not, keep his son with him and had him placed in a foster home.

Mr. Bea's older sister remained with her father. This childhood period was recalled as quite lonely, with a feeling of having been rejected for reasons that were not understandable. Visits were few and not comforting. When nine years old, he was taken to live with his father who meanwhile had remarried. Wanting to be accepted, he found only a chilly atmosphere in this new home. While his stepmother was not especially hostile, she was essentially disinterested. He felt that he received little attention or interest from his father except to be criticized unfavorably. These are some of the pertinent details revealed, among others, by Mr. Bea. His schooling involved completion of high school, after which he continued to work in his father's business as he had done after school during adolescence. His period of military service was uneventful. He increasingly recognized his mechanical skills and found employment with a utility company. During the next few years, he advanced to increasingly responsible positions calling for higher salaries. He continued to work while in treatment.

Symptoms

As mentioned previously, the presenting complaints were feelings of depression and anxiety. In treatment, amplification of Mr. Bea's problems disclosed that he had suicidal thoughts at times, although there had not been any actual attempt. He was plagued particularly with thoughts that he might harm his children and that he might kill them. He was unable to account for these feelings. With the additional unfolding of problems it was learned that Mr. Bea had fears of old age, sickness, and death. He feared authority figures, and had conflicts over his own ambitions and competition with men. These and other issues will be elaborated later.

Relationship With Father

The feeling of rejection by his father, which Mr. Bea was gradually able to see as having been of fundamental importance in his childhood, continued also into adult life. He recalled no encouragement in connection with schooling or work. He was expected to abide by certain regulations when helping his father, but his activities brought no favorable comment or reward. When his father spoke to him it was usually in criticism. The description of this relationship unfolded gradually and hesitantly. It was evident that he was testing the therapist's reactions and, when censure was not elicited, Mr. Bea became freer in his comments. Finally, he was able to state unequivocally that he hated his father. The next phase was for him to describe feelings of guilt about the antagonism he harbored, despite his claims for justification. He grew less emotional in commenting about it and finally appeared capable of accepting his feelings with greater ease and objectivity.

The expression of these feelings coincide with certain changes in the therapeutic relationship. His brusqueness has already been alluded to. It seemed that this related in part to an acting out of his hostility to figures in authority. Gradually his comments incorporated personal references to the therapist's office and personal possessions, and at times with critical connotations. No need was felt to press for interpretations of such behavior. The very acceptance of such comments without verbal response by the therapist was sufficient to show the patient that he could express himself without running the risk of fantasied fears of attack on himself in return. Revival of early memories about his father occurred spontaneously, or with direction during the hypnotic state, and they were offered also by the patient in his ordinary waking state.

Problems With Authority

It was not long before Mr. Bea could reveal his considerable fear of figures in authority. He claimed he would feel flushed, have difficulty in organizing his thoughts, express himself poorly, and experience considerable anxiety. In hypnosis, scene visualization techniques were used. They were structured and unstructured. He would picture himself in conversation with specific persons, such as his superiors at work, and people in executive positions. Such scenes might be duplications of actual experiences, or fantasies of conversations, in order to clarify his feelings and fathom the involvements. These revealed his great concern with making good impressions, his feelings of hostility, and his marked efforts to please. As this area was explored, the patient became aware of the persistent wish since childhood to please his father and gain his love. This was, of course, all to no avail. This failure intensified his hatred which in turn accentuated his guilt.

Competitiveness

The relationship with his father influenced Mr. Bea's contacts with other men. This appeared to be more pronounced at work. Mr. Bea was efficient and promotions were based on his abilities. He moved into supervisory roles only to encounter mixed personal feelings. It was necessary for him to do his tasks properly, and this in turn required the cooperation of his workers. To assume an authority role clashed with his resentment of authority figures and thus increased his discomfort. Furthermore, he wanted to be liked and hesitated placing even reasonable pressures on his workers. This hesitancy was present even when they were lax or refrained from doing work that actually had to be performed. The fine points in these relationships were clarified additionally with the scene visualization techniques mentioned earlier.

It became evident to Mr. Bea that he was entitled to his own rate of development in keeping with his abilities and efforts. His doubts about his work abilities were clearly related to the family setting of his earlier years. His strivings were, on a psychological level, a competitive issue involving his father. And his competition with co-workers, many of whom were older than he, reflected unconsciously his wish to surpass his parent, a drive that involved a heavy burden of guilt.

Masculinity-Femininity Conflict

Some of the issues and relationships described above merged with the patient's problems in sexual identification. Before he could come to grips with this in a way that would ultimately permit more normal functioning, an interview under hypnosis reflected the ingredients of the problem, the degree of anxiety associated with it, and his techniques of defense. Symbolism which emerged offered clues to this issue and could be interpreted strictly in accordance with psychoanalytic principles, or might be evaluated in keeping with other theoretical orientations.

Prior to this hypnosis, the patient had mentioned at the start of the interview that when he looked at his children he developed a peculiar feeling at times. He would wonder whether the older child was actually his. Nothing further could be offered in connection with this. Later, during hypnosis, no direct reference was made to his statement. He was simply told that he would have significant thoughts now in relation to his problems. The suggestion was deliberately general in order to furnish him with a wide range of possibilities. Mr. Bea remained still and silent, following which he clasped his hands behind his head. This had been observed previously to occur as an indication of forced nonchalance and relaxation, apparently to counteract anxiety relating to issues silently worked on, and it amounted to a behavioral attribute peculiar to him in the form of a motor ingredient of the psychological mechanisms of repression and suppression. When asked what he was thinking, he mentioned his wife, and that he seemed to be getting along better with her. When asked to elaborate he claimed that he seemed to be developing more feeling for her. Mr. Bea was then told he would see a scene which would point up for him an important part of his problem. After some silence he scratched his neck. Then he said that he saw a wheel, a pin wheel, and he gestured to demonstrate. Then he saw a roulette wheel. He paused again, was asked what else he saw, scratched once more, and said that he saw a bar with bottles on it. After awhile he added that he saw a cup. When asked what all of this signified, he said he did not know, scratched his nose and armpit, and then reported that the wheel was spinning and then it stopped. With further inquiry, he said it was he who was spinning and that he did not know where to stop. He did not know the implications of the bar setting at first, but then associated to it his previous inclination to drink "a lot." After his marriage he still wished to go out on weekends to visit bars, but his wife refused to accompany him. His next thought was that he should remain at home the following day. He seemed unable to get beyond this point and said he felt "lousy." He did not know why; his mind grew blank; and he spontaneously emerged from the hypnosis. This happens at times, is not unusual, and is often related to a degree of anxiety associated with the hypnotic transference or the emotional content of a particular session which reflects conflict that cannot be tolerated at the moment. Mr. Bea's handling of the situation in this fashion, while indicating response to pressure inherent in the treatment setting and the technique used, did not preclude adequate progress thereafter. It served as a gauge, however, to the patient's anxiety and the amount of pressure he could bear. It furnished an important clue also to this area of conflict.

At a later session the patient revealed an incident reflecting a problem he often experienced. He entered a bar and sat near some men in conversation. One in particular was the center of attention. He was talking to the others and Mr. Bea began to feel a great deal of anxiety for which he was unable to account. He felt like running away. During the hypnosis which followed this description, the setting was again established by Mr. Bea, on instruction, and he viewed this scene in great detail as it unfolded. The purpose was to recapture detail of thought and feeling. The significant additions were that the man central to this theme was large and masculine in appearance. He was expounding authoritatively to the others. The patient felt a surge of antagonism and resentment and had the urge to hurl his drink into the man's face. A summary of the main issues stemming from this material includes the following. Mr. Bea was acutely aware of the man's physical appearance which seemed distinctly masculine. This, in conjunction with his air of authority, stirred up within the patient doubts about his own masculinity. These doubts reverted to his relationship with his father toward whom he experienced strong hostility and at times impotent rage. This rage was invariably suppressed or repressed for fear of reprisal and the concurrent need to be loved and accepted. The seemingly contradictory needs and impulses left the patient with unresolved conflict and a well of emotion which he felt unable to contain and incapable of acting on. His wish to please and to oppose authority figures at the same time was too much to bear. When his hostility reached a point near overflowing, he would experience it forcefully with destructive urges which he then attempted to restrain. The guilt engendered by the conflict gave rise to feelings such as those in the setting outlined above. He believed he was noticed by others and that their attitudes toward him were critical.

This pattern of functioning is of interest from the point of view of the treatment selected by the patient although it does not apply in all cases.

Latent homosexuality, and a personality with considerable conflicting passivity needs and aggressive strivings, may invite a hypnotherapeutic approach when the hypnotic interpersonal relationship is consciously identified as involving an essentially passive role for the patient and an active one for the therapist. Also, it may be desired by some patients who see the hypnosis as a fulfullment of sado-masochistic needs. If conflict about such needs is very great, and resistances strongly incorporate the hypnotic situation from the beginning, there may be difficulty in hypnotization, or easy hypnotization with a need by the patient to deny the very effectiveness of the hypnotic induction procedure.

Marital Discord

Although the patient was attracted to his wife at the time of their marriage, it would have been questionable to describe his feelings as distinctly loving. He believed they got along sufficiently well and it was time for him to settle down. Soon he noticed that his wife simply did not seem greatly interested in him and she began to limit the frequency of sexual relations. She expected him to remain at home more than he preferred and her attention shifted more and more to their children. In some ways Mr. Bea found himself involved in a situation that repeated the experience of his earlier years. After he had been in treatment for some time, he mentioned that his wife had originally been interested in another man. The break in that relationship was followed by this marriage. This could only revive the feelings of being second best and unloved. The situation duplicated the absence of a warm, loving, maternal figure in childhood. The alleged loss of sexual interest was viewed by Mr. Bea as a reflection on his masculinity, and this feeling merged consistently with the sexual conflict mentioned earlier. His own sexual advances were compulsive and stereotyped. His resentment of his wife prevented him from taking her feelings into consideration and allowing for mood variations. When he was able gradually to see her as an individual in her own right and to break through some of the neurotic identifications he tended to established compulsively, the difficult relationship eased and at least some warmth emerged.

Wife and Children

While these feelings and issues were being investigated, a significant interview occurred. The patient was more comfortable in general when he mentioned that for several days he had been experiencing pain in his stomach. He considered it a somatic expression of his anxiety and conflict. During hypnosis he was asked to think about issues that might possibly be connected with his physical complaint. His only reaction was the recurring thought, "Why did you poison the cat?" He was perplexed because it had no meaning and he had no cat. While mulling over this idea, he recalled suddenly that he had been scratched by a cat when he was six years old. His foster mother put the cat into a bag and asked the patient to get rid of it. Mr. Bea vividly recalled taking the cat to an old factory site and throwing it into an enclosure. Since the cat was still in the bag, it might not have been able to escape, and at times thereafter he wondered whether he had in this way killed the cat. He began to scratch himself at this point, commenting that perhaps this accounted for his having occasional difficulty in getting his breath. He proceeded to tell of periodic feelings of suffocation and inability to get enough air. This was quite frightening and he wondered now whether he had been identifying himself unconsciously with the fantasied death of the cat in his guilt-ridden action. On inquiry about any associations to cats, he mentioned promptly the frequently encountered claim that cats cannot be trusted because they might turn on people at any time. This reminded him of his wife. When a comment was made, simply but meaningfully, that he had not however poisoned his wife, he remained silent. Then he said he was thinking about a snapshot of his wife and son. Looking at it gave him a funny feeling.

A reconstruction of the sequence of events showed the following pattern emerging over several interviews: He was puzzled about his wife marrying him because he believed she had had better choices. His wife was critical of him, and the marriage had not been smooth. Even before his children were born he had wondered about terminating the marriage. The arrival of the first child produced in him a sensation of being trapped, although he was not thoroughly aware of this feeling. The appearance of the second child strongly reenforced it. When his general economic status improved and he purchased a home, he felt hopelessly enmeshed in an unsatisfactory marriage with no way out. After this, he became plagued with disturbing thoughts about killing his wife and children without awareness of the underlying reasons.

The originally unconscious wish was evidently converted into an apparently meaningless thought symbol: poisoning. This in turn was linked to a childhood episode through identification of himself and his wife with the animal involved. His aggression was aimed at his wife and at himself. As far as the over-all personality picture was concerned, the aggression was displayed too in his masochistic relationship with his father, an introjected image of whom he was attacking. After he had improved considerably, Mr. Bea was able simply to feel sorry for him. Hostility toward his father and his wife were reflected unconsciously in his self-destructive, suicidal thoughts. His own death he saw as hurting his wife especially. It had self-pitying and punitive connotations.

The "poisoning" theme occurred when the patient was feeling better but circumstances at home had not improved. Unconsciously there appeared to be an equating of poisoning and impregnation as suggested by the picture of his wife and his first child who was very young when it was taken. This picture had come to mind after his comment negated any evident reality aspects of the poisoning. Several possibilities were involved in the symbolic killing since the marriage at that time was worse than it was currently. The patient felt so trapped that he considered himself essentially dead. All of these points emerged during a long series of comments, evaluations, and expressions of feeling supplied by the patient himself.

Considering the subjective personal improvement and generally unsatisfactory situation at home, the guarded prognosis was reflected in happenings during the sessions which followed the recollection of the cat. Mr. Bea was told, shortly after entering hypnosis, that he would see something he wanted very much. He saw a body covered with a white cloth lying on a table, and he could not determine who this was. As he looked carefully he saw men's shoes on the body, and he noticed that the figure had gray hair. The legs were in a position similar to his own as he lay on the couch during the hypnosis. The position of the body and its white covering suggested to him a hospital or morgue. The body was apparently dead. Finally he said it was himself. The thought and scene were disturbing to him, and he commented that he felt badly whenever he thought about sickness, old age, or death.

As Mr. Bea continued in treatment and improved further, he was able to be more considerate toward his wife whose feelings for him softened in turn. She became more attentive also. She knew of his treatment but displayed, according to Mr. Bea, essential disinterest or a doubting attitude toward it. Mr. Bea's anxiety about his children decreased, his frightening thoughts about them diminished and disappeared, and he began to spend more time with them instead of staying away in fear.

Ambition and Escape

Mr. Bea was aware of his basic aptitudes and sensed his potentialities for development and achievement. At the same time he had doubts about himself which dated to the time when censure and criticism appeared to predominate and encouragement was absent. As his confidence in himself increased he became more aware of specific ambitions and was able to discuss them. He was a little uncomfortable about his lack of higher education and realized that this would limit his ultimate goals at work. But he was interested in and willing to take advantage of technical educational opportunities within his work environment. He did well and advanced his over-all status in this way. This very movement, however, was taking place in the midst of conflicting interests. The problems already outlined were reflected in a distinctly escapist tendency. He would have thoughts of wanting to leave his home, family, and work, and just go away. It did not matter where. He could work aboard ship and travel abroad. He might simply move about indefinitely. He had dreams at night—peculiar empty dreams. Somtimes he could not remember them and they were retrieved during hypnosis sessions. At other times hypnotic fantasies essentially duplicated such dreams. In essence they were as follows. He would be on a ship or on a bridge. The setting was dreary. He would apparently be heading for some territory beyond, but it was not clear just where this would be, what it was like, and what it would hold in store for him. He would feel alone, anxious, and unhappy. Evidently this unknown territory could be his future, uncertain despite realistic gains and efforts, based on the unhappiness in his total marital and family life, and some question as to whether his goals were worth striving for. On the other hand, the unknown territory was the land of escape, away from all responsibility, yet dismal and void. There was a basic ingredient involving the concurrent fear of life and death.

Termination

Mr. Bea's movement was toward life and growth. His anxiety disappeared. His fear of experiencing anxiety lessened. His depression lifted. Suicidal thoughts receded and some warmth began to pervade his relationship with his wife. Concerns about harming those close to him faded. He became more accepting of himself and others. Now he felt he must see how he could move on without help and test his ability to mature further. Treatment came to a close.

Favorable, lasting change seemed to depend on two major items. First, there was the question of adequate release from bonds related to early childhood years and associated restraining relationships. Some movement and growth had occurred and spontaneous, healthy alterations thereafter might conceivably develop. His strong, masochistic tendencies darkened the picture, but he might be able to deal with these forces. Second, his marital relationship was still of doubtful substance. His own behavior had evidently produced reactions in his wife suitable for establishment of an improved bond between them, but the nature of any future constructive change in this relationship could not be predicted.

The data outlined in this report touch on several significant general and specific areas of Mr. Bea's functioning. Needless to say there must be limits to the amount of material offered and the extent of discussion. Often an important question is whether any particular patient has had sufficient treatment. It is difficult at times to decide whether termination is premature or whether a patient has been treated too long and too much. Part of this issue consists of certain practical details that frequently remain unmentioned. These pertain to travel time, frequency of visits, financial status, and associated concerns. As mentioned earlier, Mr. Bea was seen once a week. His income, for a family of his size, was adequate yet modest. He traveled from an adjacent state seeking a specialized type of treatment approach which prompted him to consider such travel warranted. Four to five hours were required for the round trip depending on weather and traffic conditions. The cost of travel itself was significant for him, and during the course of treatment the fee was lowered at his request. No discernible effect for better or worse was observed as a result of this change.

Termination involved consideration of the ingredients of total treatment and the attendant pressures and problems. The suggestion came from the patient. He was encouraged to continue if reasonably possible. The travel problems were realistic. Weather and increasingly difficult travel conditions were well known. The basic psychological ingredients of the treatment process indicated the probability that termination might be premature with insufficient understandings and working through of conflicts. Yet continued treatment in the face of general, reality considerations might imply unwarranted pressure on the patient with lack of sufficient confidence in him. This point, along with the absence of another suitable therapist for his purposes, precluded serious consideration of any change in therapists. Termination at this time constituted, therefore, a calculated risk. This risk has apparently been warranted on the basis of the patient's status during the ensuing two-year period. What the future may hold remains to be seen.

Discussion

Data presented here, although brief and limited, indicate possibilities for the incorporation of an hypnotic setting into total therapy for the exploration and treatment of characterological problems and distortions in interpersonal relations. Trends in these directions are reflected in the case of Mr. Bea; but his therapy is not presented as necessarily typical of a large variety of treatment procedures involving the use of hypnosis. The diversity of approaches in hypnotherapy and hypnoanalysis probably precludes designation of any one case as essentially typical, although many cases may possess basic similarities.

The utilization of relatively simple therapeutic devices brings the description of this case closer to many treatment procedures that do not involve hypnosis. This permits use of such material for purposes of instruction of therapists who are not too familiar with hypnotherapy. It can be helpful only if students are not overly expectant of, and insistent on, demonstration of highly complex technical procedures which make the hypnotic approach emerge as basically dramatic and certainly essentially different from nonhypnotic therapies. These procedures, valid when indicated and properly employed, would involve measures such as induced auditory and visual hallucinatory experiences, self-hypnotic dream techniques, regression and revivification, experimental conflicts, and the combinations of various methods with certain psychological testing procedures such as the Rorschach, H-T-P, TAT, Word Association-Scene Visualization, and other projective test administrations.

Hypnotherapeutic and hypnoanalytic methods may focus on delimited problems, symptom difficulties, characterological involvements, and diverse interpersonal difficulties. Decisions about the type of procedures to be used, extent of explorations and goals to be achieved, are based on the needs of the patient, his general and special aptitudes, and his abilities in connection with grasping psychological issues and employing specific hypnotic methods. The manner in which—and the degree to which—resistances are by-passed or analyzed depends on the patient and the unfolding of the total treatment situation. Utilization of transference relationships as leverage, or the analysis of transference reactions, are based also on the needs and aptitudes of the particular patient and clinical judgment of the therapist. Ego-strength and ego-weakness are constantly assessed. Hypnotic alleviation of anxiety may be brought into play directly from time to time in keeping with therapeutic needs while varieties of issues are elucidated and problems worked through. The fine points involved sometimes defy description, as would also be true for treatment which does not involve the use of hypnosis.

Initial and subsequent hypnotic inductions may be helpful diagnostically because the multiplicity of reactions of patients reflect a variety of personality attributes. Some patterns that come to expression directly or indirectly relate to the wish to control or be controlled, reassured, praised, criticized or encouraged. Excessive compliance or resistance may come to the fore and negativistic reactions and tendencies toward detachment may be discovered. Spontaneous psychosomatic reactions peculiar to each patient may be observed frequently. Gross sexual and aggressive features are often pronounced. Awareness of counter-transference reactions as they apply to the hypnotic interpersonal relationship may be available for observation during induction and subsequent hypnotic settings, aside from such reactions that tend to emerge in the same therapist during non-hypnotic psychotherapy. In evaluating the foregoing patterns, induction, trance state, and termination are seen to constitute a behavioral continuum. Separation of these phases may be helpful for purposes of description, discussion, and experimental investigation, but such separation is basically artificial and disrupts the view of holistic functioning.

In addition to stressing the induction and termination setting as obviously significant parts of the total interpersonal relationship, the induction and termination reactions in a series of sessions involve carry-over of the total therapeutic contact developed during previous sessions, hypnotic and nonhypnotic. These reactions are reflected in overt patterns of behavior and in hidden fantasies.

Allowing for individual variations, greatest success with hypnotherapy and hypnoanalysis is experienced probably with hysterical disorders and some character neuroses. Obsessive-compulsive patterns are more difficult to deal with than conversion and phobic reactions. Very severe characterological problems are somewhat refractory. Some borderline and mild psychotic reactions often prove amenable to varying degrees of help. Psychophysiologic reactions respond frequently. Of course, the personality of the therapist in relation to problems with which he works best is an important point to be considered as with any other treatment approach.

The hypnotic settings and techniques may decrease total treatment time if the patient uses them effectively; but broad generalizations often offered on this score are, it would seem, frequently exaggerated. It is most likely to apply to some cases of traumatic neuroses, character disorders, anxiety states, and conversion, phobic and dissociation reactions in patients with fair ego-strength and good adaptive and reorganizational potentialities. If patient and therapist stress treatment time unduly, in contrast for example to opportunities for enhanced self-awareness and possibilities for more effective integration of data made available, both are likely to be disappointed.

It must be stressed that no one therapy eliminates the potential usefulness of another, especially when very many patients respond in general to variety of treatment approaches. Hypnosis is an adjunct to psychotherapy and analysis, not a substitute. Some patients do better than others in treatment involving special hypnotic methods, and any particular method must be assessed in terms of broad, general applicability, and special suitability.

The role of hypnosis in coping with the mechanism of repression is usually stressed in analytic literature. Aside from this alleged primary effectiveness, usually connected with enhanced recall of buried memories, hypnotic techniques have, in more subtle fashion, been helpful in elucidating the operation of a variety of significant dynamisms. These include symbolization, projection, condensation, isolation, identification, introjection, and rationalization.

Summary

Mr. Bea, thirty years old, married, with two children, requested hypnotherapy for anxiety and depression of three years duration. He was seen for thirty-eight sessions, each lasting three-quarters of an hour. Most, but not all of these sessions, involved the use of hypnosis. The over-all treatment approach was hypnoanalytic in orientation. Measures included conversational exchange with the patient in hypnosis, free association, visual imagery (with scene visualizations), evaluation of spontaneous sensory and motor phenomena, recall of nocturnal dreams, completion of dreams not adequately remembered, varieties of post-hypnotic suggestions furthering therapeutic endeavor, and hypnotic suggestions for control of anxiety, among a variety of others. This report stresses use of relatively simple hypnotic methods incorporated into a treatment matrix based largely on psychoanalytic theory, with applications limited to the particular needs and aptitudes of the patient at this time. It was learned during treatment that the patient had suicidal thoughts with obsessive fears of harming his wife and children. He was frightened by old age, sickness, and death. Mr. Bea investigated problems pertaining to his hostility toward his father, fear of figures in authority, competitive feeling toward other men, conflicts between ambition and the need to escape responsibilities, his masculinity-femininity conflict, and various aspects of an unhappy marriage. Several related issues were dealt with during treatment and some of the bare essentials of many involvements were conveyed in this report, with excerpts from specific interviews and explanations of hypnotherapeutic and hypnoanalytic activity. Gradual improvement was outlined and some issues were presented in connection with decision and timing of therapy termination.

The use of hypnoanalytic and hypnotherapeutic devices are dependent on individual attitudes and aptitudes of patients, experience and orientation of therapists, with areas of considerable flexibility in application. Hypnotic therapy is an adjunct to total psychotherapy. Hypnotherapy is not limited to symptom conflicts. Rather, it incorporates characterological issues and may be adapted to investigations and therapeutic efforts involving numerous behavioral patterns and problems of interpersonal relations. Although usually considered with specific reference to coping with the mechanism of repression, numerous dynamisms in personality functioning are actually subtly amenable to hypnoanalytic elucidation.

Addendum

1. *Optimally, what criteria do you use for accepting or rejecting patients for psychotherapy?*

Acceptance of patients for psychotherapy is based on criteria which apply regardless of whether such therapy does or does not incorporate hypnotic technique. I see patients whose problems are in the categories of neuroses, character disorders, psychosomatic reactions, and occasionally some borderline or mild psychotic reactions. All patients must be capable of keeping appointments as scheduled and meeting the designated fee payment.

2. *Do you make a diagnosis before psychotherapy begins?*

A tentative diagnosis is made at the initial consultation and modified if necessary during the course of treatment.

3. *Do you attempt to persuade the patient or significant relative to change his (the patient's) environment?*

Rarely.

4. *How did you conceptualize the therapist's role in this case?*

A basic element was psychological support, the specific ingredients of which would be predicated on transference elements as they unfolded. Gradually, inroads would be made wherever and whenever possible into the enmeshed conflicts in order to reach understandings and move toward more effective solutions. As this happens, the aforementioned support lent by the therapist would decrease in significance and would ultimately be relinquished.

5. *What aspects of your theory of psychotherapy were particularly apparent or useful in the case presented here?*

The primary orientation was psychoanalytic. The complexities of theory were not expected to reach a verbal level during treatment for patient or therapist except insofar as was deemed necessary to further understandings in relation to central themes of immediate importance to the patient. In addition, the belief was inherent that a hypnotic relationship could unfold in a meaningful way to assist the patient with problems involving his total personality and with a view to long-term goals and character alteration.

6. *Do you feel that this case developed significant insight? If not, can improvement be maintained?*

I feel that the patient developed significant insight, but within limits described in this report.

7. *What aspects of your own cultural orientation facilitated or impeded the treatment of your case?*

I was not of the impression that any special issues of cultural orientation were involved in this therapeutic relationship.

8. *If we consider that a continuum exists from superficial to deep psychotherapy, where would you place your own case?*

Probably this case is closer to the designation of deep psychotherapy, although such an evaluation is always a matter of opinion linked to prejudices of theoretical orientation and views of orthodoxy, etc. The terms superficial and deep really have little meaning and certainly have no direct connection with relative degrees of ease or difficulty in treatment management. Patients experiencing deep psychotherapy, within the usual terms of reference, are often easier to treat than others whose therapy would be called superficial.

9. *What did you think about the outcome of this case and what criteria did you use for evaluating such outcome?*

The outcome was good, within the limits outlined in the case study. Criteria consisted of symptom relief, improved interpersonal relations, avoidance of repetition of a variety of neurotic patterns, and confidence in future growth with development of individual aptitudes.

10. *How do you terminate psychotherapy?*

The patient often suggests termination when he feels capable of continuing satisfactorily on the basis of changes already observed. I may suggest this if the patient's uncertainty about making the decision is understandable and reasonable. Termination may be abrupt and complete, or it may be introduced first with more widely spaced appointments followed by cessation. Variations are based on individual needs of patients.

Index

425